Alternatives to Prison

Alternatives to Prison

Options for an insecure society

edited by

Anthony Bottoms,
Sue Rex and
Gwen Robinson

WILLAN
PUBLISHING

Published by

Willan Publishing
Culmcott House
Mill Street, Uffculme
Cullompton, Devon
EX15 3AT, UK
Tel: +44(0)1884 840337
Fax: +44(0)1884 840251
e-mail: info@willanpublishing.co.uk
Website: www.willanpublishing.co.uk

Published simultaneously in the USA and Canada by

Willan Publishing
c/o ISBS, 920 NE 58th Ave, Suite 300,
Portland, Oregon 97213-3786, USA
Tel: +001(0)503 287 3093
Fax: +001(0)503 280 8832
Website: www.isbs.com

First published 2004

ISBN 1-84392-104-9 (paperback)

British Library Cataloguing-in-Publication Data

A catalogue record for this book is available from the British Library

Project management by Deer Park Productions, Tavistock, Devon
Typeset by TW Typesetting, Plymouth, Devon
Printed and bound by T J International Ltd, Trecerus Industrial Estate, Padstow, Cornwall

Contents

List of figures and tables

Figures

Tables

Notes on contributors

Dr Roy Bailey is Research Associate, De Montfort University and formerly Chief Probation Officer for Devon.

Professor Sir Anthony Bottoms is Wolfson Professor of Criminology, University of Cambridge and Professorial Fellow in Criminology, University of Sheffield.

Rob Canton is Lecturer, Community and Criminal Justice Research Division, De Montfort University.

Professor James Dignan is Professor of Criminology and Restorative Justice, University of Sheffield.

Professor Hazel Kemshall is Professor, Community and Criminal Justice Research Division, De Montfort University.

Anna King is a doctoral student, Institute of Criminology, University of Cambridge.

Dr Chris Lewis is Senior Research Fellow in Criminology, University of Portsmouth and formerly Head of the Offender Unit, Home Office Research Development and Statistics Department.

Professor George Mair is E. Rex Makin Chair of Criminal Justice, Liverpool John Moores University.

Dr Shadd Maruna is Lecturer in Criminology, Institute of Criminology, University of Cambridge.

Dr Rob C. Mawby is Research Fellow in Criminology, Keele University.

Professor Gill McIvor is Professor of Social Work and Director of the Social Work Research Centre, University of Stirling.

Dr Mike Nellis is Senior Lecturer in Criminal Justice, University of Birmingham.

Professor Peter Raynor is Professor of Criminology and Criminal Justice, University of Wales, Swansea.

Dr Sue Rex is a Senior Policy Analyst at the Home Office, and formerly Senior Research Associate, Institute of Criminology, University of Cambridge.

Dr Gwen Robinson is Lecturer in Criminology and Criminal Justice, University of Sheffield.

Dr Judith Rumgay is Senior Lecturer in Social Policy, London School of Economics.

Professor Martin Wasik is Professor of Law, University of Keele and Chairman of the Sentencing Advisory Panel for England and Wales.

Dr Andrew Wilson is Research Fellow, Centre for Criminological Research, University of Sheffield.

Professor Anne Worrall is Professor of Criminology, Keele University.

List of abbreviations

ACE	Assessment, Case recording/management and Evaluation
ACMD	Advisory Council on the Misuse of Drugs
ACOP	Association of Chief Officers of Probation
ACPS	Advisory Council on the Penal System
APO	Action Plan Order
ASBO	Anti-Social Behaviour Order
ASRO	Addressing Substance-Related Offending
BCS	British Crime Survey
CCPs	Core Correctional Practices
CDP	Crime and Disorder Partnership
CEP	Conference Européene de la Probation
CJA	Criminal Justice Act
CJCIG	Criminal Justice Chief Inspectors' Group
CJIP	Criminal Justice Interventions Programme
CJSW	Criminal Justice Social Work
CPA	Committee of Public Accounts
CPO	Community Punishment Order
CPO (NI)	Custody Probation Order (Northern Ireland)
CPP	Community Punishment Pathfinders
CPRO	Community and Rehabilitation Order
CPS	Crown Prosecution Service
CRO	Community Rehabilitation Order
CRP	Crime Reduction Programme
CSAP	Correctional Services Accreditation Panel
CSO	Community Service order
CSR	Correctional Services Review
DAO	Drug Abstinence Order
DAR	Drug Abstinence Requirements
DAT	Drug Action Team
DCA	Department of/for* Constitutional Affairs (*both forms used)
DTO	Detention and Training Order
DTTO	Drug Testing and Treatment Order
ECPS	Enhanced Community Punishment Scheme
EM	Electronic Monitoring

GPS	Global Positioning of Systems
HDC	Home Detention Curfew
HMIP	Her Majesty's Inspectorate of Probation
HORU	Home Office Research Unit
ICCJ	Issues in Community and Criminal Justice
ICCP	Intensive Change and Control Programme
ICVS	International Crime Victimisation Survey
IMD	Index of Multiple Deprivation
IMPACT	Intensive Matched Probation and After-Care Treatment
ISM	Intensive Supervision and Monitoring
ISSP	Intensive Assessment and Surveillance Programme
JIR	Joint Inspection Report
JRC	Justice Research Consortium
LCCS	Local Crime: Community Sentence
LPU	Local Policing Unit
LSI-R	Level of Service Inventory – Revised
MAPAM	Multi-Agency Planning and Assessment Meeting
MAPPA	Multi-Agency Public Protection Arrangements
MORI	Market and Opinion Research International
NACRO	National Association for the Care and Resettlement of Offenders
NAO	National Audit Office
NAPO	National Association of Probation Officers
NDPB	Non-Departmental Public Body
NICS	Northern Ireland Crime Survey
NIRC	Northern Ireland Restorative Cautioning
NOMS	National Offender Management Service
NPD	National Probation Directorate
NPP	National Policing Plan
NPS	National Probation Service
NRPP	National Reassurance Policing Policy
NTA	National Treatment Agency
NTORS	National Treatment Outcome Research Study
OASys	Offender Assessment System
OGRS	Offender Group Reconviction Scale
OTA	Offender's Tag Association
PBNI	Probation Board for Northern Ireland
PICA	Public Interest Case Assessment
PNC	Police National Computer
POS	Persistent Offender Scheme
PRISM	Programme for Reducing Individual Substance Misuse
PSR	Pre-Sentence Report
RISE	Re-Integrative Shaming Experiment
RJP	Restorative Justice Programme
RLO	Restriction of Liberty Order

SAO	Supervised Attendance Order
SCI	Street Crime Initiative
SEU	Social Exclusion Unit
SGC	Sentencing Guidelines Council
SOCRU	Scottish Office Central Research Unit
SSR	Specific Sentence Report
STOP	Straight Thinking on Probation
TWOC	Taking Without Consent
WAG	Welsh Assembly Government
WORP	Women's Offending Reduction Plan
YIP	Youth Inclusion Programme
YJB	Youth Justice Board
YOI	Young Offender Institution
YOP	Youth Offender Panel
YOT	Youth Offending Team

Preface

In March 2003 an Independent Inquiry into the adequacy of alternatives to prison in the United Kingdom was announced. Led by Lord Coulsfield, the Inquiry was set up by the Esmée Fairbairn Foundation as part of its *Rethinking Crime and Punishment* initiative. Later in 2003, one of us (AEB) was appointed as Research Director to the Inquiry.

By agreement with the Coulsfield Commission, the research programme that was developed had two distinct strands. First, a series of substantial literature reviews on key topics relevant to the Inquiry was commissioned, with the three of us acting as joint commissioning editors. This work was accomplished under a contract between the Police Foundation (acting on behalf of the Esmée Fairbairn Foundation) and the University of Cambridge, Institute of Criminology. Secondly, the University of Sheffield Centre for Criminological Research was asked to conduct a small piece of original empirical research, to investigate attitudes towards offending and punishment among residents of high-crime communities.

This volume is the final product of the first of these two strands of work. We are most grateful to our team of distinguished contributors, who readily agreed to help with the volume, at rather short notice which often involved some juggling of priorities. Reflecting the scope of the Coulsfield Inquiry, the remit of each of the main chapters is broad: authors were asked to address relevant developments in the three UK jurisdictions of England and Wales, Scotland, and Northern Ireland, as well as provision for both adult and juvenile offenders, although the primary focus throughout is on adult offenders in England and Wales.

The second strand of the Coulsfield research programme is also represented in this volume, in the shape of Chapter 15. While this is not the final report on this strand of work, the results seemed sufficiently interesting, and complementary to some of the themes pursued in the literature review chapters, to warrant inclusion here.

We are most grateful to Lord Coulsfield and his commissioners for entrusting us with the task of preparing this volume. It has been an exciting and demanding opportunity. We also wish to thank the Commission for allowing us relatively free rein in selecting the topics for the chapters, and complete independence in relation to the content of the chapters. We are glad that our endeavours have been found useful to the Commission, as reflected in the frequent references to our work in the Commission's final report, which is being published concurrently with this volume (Coulsfield 2004).

As commissioning editors, during the last year we have been at times acutely conscious that we were dealing with a rapidly changing field. Indeed, we sometimes feared that the pace and quantity of changes in criminal justice might outstrip our ability to analyse and make sense of them or, worse still, render redundant at least some of the work that we had commissioned. Of particular importance in this respect was the publication, some four months after our chapters were commissioned, of Patrick Carter's independent Review of the Correctional Services (Carter 2003). As many readers will be aware, the Carter Report and the Home Office's response to it (Home Office 2004a) heralded a number of potentially very significant changes for the delivery of community penalties – not least the establishment of a National Offender Management Service (NOMS) just three years after the creation of the National Probation Service. The new NOMS, combining prison and probation services, would dissolve the existing 42 local probation boards in favour of a much smaller number of regions. Even more significantly, Carter proposed the introduction of a purchaser–provider split in the delivery of correctional services, with the purchaser (NOMS) committed to a principle of so-called 'contestability' in the commissioning of services – an approach that would eventually lead to a much more significant role for the private sector in the delivery and management of alternatives to prison.

The process of change has, however, pursued us all the way through the production of the volume. Just as we were finalising the text, in July 2004, there were no fewer than three further developments, each relevant to the questions posed and issues discussed in at least some of the chapters. We have, therefore, chosen to comment on these developments in this Preface.

The first, and in many ways the most important, development concerns the implementation of NOMS. On 20 July 2004, following a national consultation exercise on the proposed organisational design of the new service, the Home Office announced a significant rethink. A statement by the Minister for Correctional Services confirmed that, whilst remaining keen to follow Carter's recommendation in respect of, in due course, introducing a greater degree of contestability in the delivery of services to offenders, the option of moving immediately to granting purchasing power to new Regional Offender Managers had been rejected as 'unlikely to deliver better management of offenders and better services' (Goggins 2004). Instead, a decision had been taken to retain for the time being the structures, experience and local links of the existing 42 probation boards. In the context of this 'interim model', the role of the new Regional Managers (whose appointments were confirmed) will be to support the existing probation boards in moving more gradually towards an 'offender management model', to develop contestability, and to pilot commissioning in their area. Meanwhile, the focus will be on the introduction of the concept and practice of 'end to end offender management' – an approach perceived by the Home Office as crucial to the reduction of reoffending, and commanding widespread support (Home Office 2004b). A subsequent statement from NOMS Chief Executive Martin Narey conveyed his own view that the scale and pace of change proposed earlier in the year were essentially too much too soon, and that the approved interim arrangements were likely to be both less disruptive for the current Probation Service, and more effective in the longer term (Home Office 2004b). It is to be hoped, also, that this deceleration of the process of change will allow policymakers and probation managers more time to reflect on the potential relevance of the research results summarised in this book, and in the Coulsfield Report, for the future of 'alternatives to prison'.

Earlier in July 2004, the annual publication *Crime in England & Wales* had brought good news about crime rates, announcing a further five per cent fall in household and personal crime in 2003–4, as measured by the British Crime Survey (BCS), and a 39 per cent reduction since 1995 (Dodd *et al.* 2004). It also announced increased public confidence in most aspects of the criminal justice system, and reductions in worry both about the main categories of crime, and perceived levels of anti-social behaviour, as compared with the previous year. This news was not, however, uniformly treated by all sections of the media. On the day the figures were released (22 July) the *Daily Express* chose to highlight a 12 per cent increase in recorded violent crime (attributed in the Home Office report largely to changes in police recording practices), and carried a headline exclaiming 'we have created a vicious breed of young monsters'. In stark contrast, the *Independent* presented the BCS statistics under the headline 'Crime: the truth', with a strapline adding: 'New figures reveal . . . the biggest sustained fall since the 19th century'. It went on to ponder the question why sections of the British media seemed to be obsessed with painting a picture of 'a rising tide of violence and lawlessness'. This question is an important one, and has particular resonance for this volume, which confronts the problem of how alternatives to prison can be delivered and presented in a society in which the 'facts' about crime are often distorted or hidden, and in which both fear of crime and punitive attitudes are frequently taken for granted as given features of the landscape.

Finally, July 2004 also saw the publication of a number of policy documents by the Home Office. Just a week before the publication of the 2003–4 crime statistics, the Home Office published its five-year strategic plan, *Confident Communities in a Secure Britain* (Home Office 2004c), in parallel with a strategic plan for the Criminal Justice System (Office for Criminal Justice Reform 2004). It also published a national action plan for reducing re-offending, the latter comprising the Home Office's response to the Social Exclusion Unit's influential report on the resettlement of ex-prisoners (Home Office 2004d, Social Exclusion Unit 2001). The Home Office's strategic plan makes particularly interesting reading in that it firmly locates the Government's strategies for crime reduction in the context of wider concerns about security. As the Home Secretary explains in his Foreword, security underpins 'everything in this plan' (2004c: 7). In the context of twenty-first century Britain, the Home Secretary argues, economic prosperity has brought with it new threats to security whilst at the same time undermining traditional community bonds. Post-September 11 2001, trust and security have been further undermined, and fear heightened. In an interesting re-vamping of the Labour Party's 1990s mantra, the Home Office claims that it is now striving to 'tackle insecurity and the causes of insecurity' (Home Office 2004c: 9). A belief that feelings of insecurity among ordinary 'law-abiding citizens', rather than objective crime levels, present the greatest challenge, explains why the Home Office acknowledges falling crime rates, but also insists that that there is 'no room for complacency' (2004c: 5). It also means that much of the content of both this document and the strategic plan for the Criminal Justice System is devoted to pledges to increase community policing and to targeting low-level anti-social behaviour and the 'prolific' offenders who, it is claimed, make the lives of ordinary citizens a misery (Office for Criminal Justice Reform 2004: 37). This is an extremely important perspective from which to view the future of alternatives to prison. The feelings of insecurity which are referred to are undoubtedly very real in many local communities, although (as the data in Chapter 15 show) there is also sometimes significant variation in this respect, even in neighbouring areas. The future of alternatives to prison cannot now be seriously considered without taking this issue into account, which is why we have subtitled this volume 'Options for an Insecure Society'.

In his introduction to the recently published *Reducing Re-offending: An Action Plan*, Goggins states that 'We are at a point in time where there is a real prospect that we can make a difference' (Home Office 2004d: 1). We hope that the contents of this volume can contribute to that process.

Anthony Bottoms
Sue Rex
Gwen Robinson

References

Carter, P. (2003) *Managing Offenders, Changing Lives: A new approach. Report of the Correctional Services Review* (London: Strategy Unit).
Coulsfield (2004) *Crime, Courts and Confidence: Report of an Independent Inquiry into Alternatives to Prison* (London: Stationery Office).

Dodd, T., Nicholas, S., Povey, D. and Walker, A. (2004) *Crime in England & Wales 2003/2004* (London: Home Office).

Goggins, P. (2004) Statement regarding NOMS, 20 July 2004 [www.probation.homeoffice.gov.uk/print/page239.asp].

Home Office (2004a) *Reducing Crime, Changing Lives* (London: Home Office).

Home Office (2004b) *National Offender Management Service Update,* Issue 3, 29 July 2004 www.probation.homeoffice.gov.uk/files/pdf/NOMS%20Update%20Issue%203_29.07.03.pdf.

Home Office (2004c) *Confident Communities in a Secure Britain: The Home Office Strategic Plan 2004-08,* Cmd. 6287 (London: Home Office).

Home Office (2004d) *Reducing Reoffending: National Action Plan* (London: Home Office).

Office for Criminal Justice Reform (2004) *Cutting Crime, Delivering Justice: A strategic plan for criminal justice 2004–08,* Cmd. 6288 (London: OCJS).

Social Exclusion Unit (2001) *Reducing Re-Offending by Ex-Prisoners* (London: Office of the Deputy Prime Minister).

Chapter 1

How did we get here?

The editors

This chapter outlines the policy-related history of 'alternatives to prison', particularly community penalties – by which we mean personally restrictive sanctions structurally located between custody and nominal or financial penalties (see Bottoms *et al.* 2001). Together with Chapter 2, it provides an essential contextual background for the discussions that follow in the remaining chapters in this volume. As in those chapters, there is a special (though not exclusive) focus on England and Wales, the largest of the three UK jurisdictions.

To tell the story properly, it has been necessary to go back to the 1960s, but particular attention has been paid to developments in the last 15 years. We have also included some possible implications of the important provisions in the Criminal Justice Act 2003 for new forms of custody and a customised community sentence, which are likely to have a significant impact when they are implemented in the near future; and we have briefly noted the arrival in 2004 of the National Offender Management Service, which brings together the prison and probation services under a single umbrella. Finally, we have summarised recent developments in the jurisdictions of Scotland and Northern Ireland.

Non-custodial options: the impact of successive 'eras'

It is no overstatement to assert that what we now know as community penalties are the product of a turbulent history during which they have gone through a number of permutations. The wide range of community orders now available to the courts represents a relatively recent innovation. Indeed, until almost 1970, the main 'alternative to prison' for adult courts was the probation order, a welfare-oriented 'alternative to sentencing'.[1] However, since then there has been a proliferation of orders, shaped by the different 'eras' in which they were introduced. Thus, the probation order held sway during the 'penal-welfare' era, which started with the dawn of the twentieth century and also saw the introduction of the juvenile court and borstal training. This was succeeded by the era of 'alternatives to custody', starting in the late 1960s, which gave us the Suspended Sentence and the Community Service Order (CSO), as well as probation with special conditions (e.g. attendance at specified activities or day centres). The late 1980s heralded in 'punishment in the community', with the introduction of the Combination Order and the Curfew Order with electronic monitoring. The punishment theme has since blended with a focus on public protection in what we will argue is a 'new generation' of orders: the Drug Treatment and Testing Order; the Exclusion Order; the Drug Abstinence Order; and for young offenders the Reparation Order and the Action Plan Order. The customised Community Order, introduced by the Criminal Justice Act 2003, is perhaps the culmination of this latest trend.[2]

Below, we look at each of these eras in turn, considering what caused the shifts in thinking, and with what consequences.

The era of 'penal welfarism'

The historical origins of 'penal welfarism' in England in the early twentieth century have been fully analysed by David Garland (1985). Garland has provided persuasive evidence that the birth of measures such as probation and borstal can best be understood against the background of other social changes of the period, such as the development of compulsory school education and the creation of the national insurance system. All these developments were aimed at the 'inclusion' of the working class within the dominant social structures of the time; however, this took place within a normative framework that required educative, re-educative, or corrective measures to provide an appropriate discipline for the individual. In the administration of the probation order, penal welfarism moved during the first half of the twentieth century from a dominantly religious and 'common sense practical' supervisory system to a version of psychoanalytically-based 'social casework'.[3] However, the underlying rationale remained the same: in the case of individuals for whom there was some reasonable hope of reclamation and also some need for individualised treatment, a penal-welfare sanction should be used instead of a tariff 'punishment' to meet their treatment needs, and to help reintegrate them into mainstream society.

The end of the penal welfare era came with the decline of the so-called 'rehabilitative ideal' (Allen 1981), which arose from three related crises. Perhaps the best known is the 'empirical' crisis surrounding the effectiveness of treatment, closely associated with the research review led by

Robert Martinson (1974; see also Lipton *et al.* 1975). However, this was coupled with a 'resources' crisis surrounding the continued rise in the prison population;[4] and an 'ideological' crisis surrounding the wide discretion often granted in the name of treatment, with its scope for misuse and injustice (see Bottoms 1980, Cavadino and Dignan 1992). The dramatic implications for probation work, captured in the infamous phrase 'Nothing Works', have been well-documented (see e.g. Raynor and Vanstone 2002). Of more immediate relevance to the present discussion, the 'resources' and the 'empirical' crises together contributed to the 'alternatives to custody' movement that succeeded penal welfarism. The ideological critique prompted a 'return to justice' (Bottomley 1980, Hudson 1987) originating in the United States but destined to have a major impact on the English jurisdiction, as we shall see below.

The era of 'alternatives to custody'

When rehabilitation seemed to have been thoroughly discredited, the key aim of the diversion from custody movement became to offer judges and magistrates options that might avoid the damage and expense of a custodial sentence. However, the first real manifestation of 'alternatives to custody' actually preceded the full 'collapse of the rehabilitative ideal'. This development occurred in the Criminal Justice Act 1967, which allowed for shorter sentences of imprisonment to be suspended. This was followed soon afterwards by the introduction of a new 'intermediate' sanction, the community service order, in the Criminal Justice Act 1972. A certain amount of confusion was undoubtedly created by the fact that the community service order lacked the explicit status of an 'alternative to custody' that the statutory framework had conferred upon the suspended sentence (see McIvor 1990a).

In the event, however, 'alternatives to custody' clearly failed to have the desired impact on the prison population, which continued an upward trend (see Bottoms 1987). McWilliams (1987) suggests that one reason for this was that, in the absence of the kind of 'transcendent justification' provided by penal-welfarism, diversion carried insufficient conviction to sustain itself as an aim. Empirical research suggested that both suspended sentences and community service orders replaced terms of imprisonment in only about half the cases in which they were imposed (see Bottoms 1981, Pease 1985). It was widely accepted that 'alternatives' sometimes led to 'net widening' and 'mesh thinning' (Cohen 1985) – that is, the bringing of greater numbers of less serious offenders into the penal net than might otherwise have been the case, and the imposition upon them of more severe sanctions.[5] To take one possible scenario, although suspended sentences were intended to be passed only where an offender would otherwise receive an immediate prison sentence, it is clear from research evidence that some offenders were given a suspended sentence where previously they would have received probation. Suppose such a person re-offended in a minor way. At the subsequent court hearing, he might more or less automatically receive imprisonment for the second offence, in view of the apparently 'alternative to custody' nature of the earlier sentence. He would also normally have the suspended sentence activated consecutively with the sentence of imprisonment for the new offence. Thus, on reoffending, he might actually receive two consecutive sentences of imprisonment where, prior to the enactment of 'alternative to custody' legislation, he might credibly have received none. McIvor (1990) found that similar kinds of mechanisms were operating in relation to community service.

Faced with a rising prison population in the late 1980s, the Government realised that it was time for a rethink.[6] For this, it turned to the 'justice model' widely associated with the renaissance of 'human rights' as well as with the ideological doubts mentioned above over the excesses and injustices of 'treatment'. Thus, the late 1980s and early 1990s brought a new era, to which we turn next.

The era of 'punishment in the community'

Essentially, the Government considered that judges and magistrates had to be offered sanctions that were credible in their own right if the judiciary were to be persuaded to make less use of custody (Home Office 1988, 1990). As the 1990 White Paper put it:

> The Government believes that more offenders should be punished in the community . . . a new approach is needed if the use of custody is to be reduced. Punishment in the community should be an effective way of dealing with many offenders, particularly those convicted of property crimes and less serious offences of violence, when financial penalties are insufficient. (para 4.1, 4.3)

In a radical step, it was decided to adopt the justice model as a new rationale for community-based sanctions, applying 'just deserts' principles developed most fully by von Hirsch (1986, 1993) in which *proportionality* plays a key role. Based on the idea that the central purpose of any punishment is to convey blame or *censure*, desert requires punishments to reflect the relative blameworthiness of the offences for which they are imposed. This means that the severity of the sentence should be commensurate with the seriousness of the offence. It will be seen that this rule potentially clashes directly with the approach underlying 'penal-welfarism', in that the emphasis is on the offence rather than on the offender's background and treatment needs.

The Criminal Justice Act 1991 established a desert-based sentencing framework for both custodial and non-custodial sentences. Section 6 of the

Act coined the term 'community sentence' to cover the 'intermediate' band of sentences (between custody on the one hand and fines or discharges on the other) which could be used only for offences that were 'serious enough' to warrant that level of intrusion, but not sufficiently serious to merit a custodial sentence. In imposing a community sentence, the sentencer was required *both* to select the most 'suitable' community order(s) for the offender (a needs-based approach) *and* to ensure that the sentence's restrictions on liberty were commensurate with the seriousness of the offence (a desert approach). This sentencing structure appears to have been modelled on proposals by Wasik and von Hirsch (1988) as modified by Bottoms (1989) (see Rex [1998]). The underlying aim was to convince the courts that certain non-custodial options could appropriately carry restrictions sufficient for the kind of offences that might previously have resulted in a custodial sentence; hence, the introduction of new kinds or combinations of restrictions in the shape of the combination order[7] and the curfew order with electronic tagging. The probation order was also made a sentence of the court to underline its status as a punishment rather than an 'alternative to sentencing' (which proved to be a somewhat uncomfortable transformation for what had been the archetypical 'penal-welfarist' sentence).

The era of the 'new generation' of community penalties

The 1990s brought a new era of community penalties. At the beginning of the decade, it seemed likely that this new era would be dominated by the just deserts model, as the Criminal Justice Act 1991 seemed initially successful in reducing reliance on imprisonment (see Chapter 2). In practice, however, although the proportionality principle remains on the statute book, it seems increasingly to have been sidelined by growing concerns with public safety and the reduction of risk, a point that is highlighted by the greatly increased prominence given to previous convictions in the Criminal Justice Act 2003.[8] Indeed, many key features of community penalties have changed significantly since the passing of the 1991 Act, and they now appear to revolve around a central theme of public protection. Before considering why this theme has recently become prominent, it is worth examining several features of contemporary community penalties in a little detail. It is no coincidence that many of these features reappear in Chapters 6–11 of this volume, which address the current range of non-custodial penalties, as well as in the chapter on sentence management (Chapter 13).

1. Punishment in the community – The emphasis on punishment in the community remains, and has actually intensified. In the 1990s, there has been a tendency deliberately to emphasise the punitive character of community penalties, a rhetorical approach that culminated in the renaming of key community orders to incorporate

the word 'punishment'.[9] There has also been a strong political emphasis on the enforcement of orders to ensure that offenders actually experience the intended restrictions on their liberty, or are punished if they do not.[10] One important reason for this fresh emphasis on 'punishment' in community penalties seems to have been to reassure the general public that significant restrictions are being placed upon offenders receiving community sentences, so ensuring public safety through the use, for example, of curfew restrictions and drug testing.

2. Technology – Perhaps allied to this, there has been a growing reliance on the use of technology to enforce the requirements of community orders, apparent both in electronic monitoring in relation to curfew orders and in the new Drug Treatment and Testing Order. The Criminal Justice and Court Services Act 2000 widened these provisions by enacting new and more general powers relating to electronic monitoring and drug testing in the content and enforcement of community sentences. Electronic monitoring has also enabled provision to be made for the early release of certain prisoners under so-called Home Detention Curfews (HDCs) introduced in the Crime and Disorder Act 1998, the use of which has been gradually extended since their national implementation in 1999.[11] The use of technology in the surveillance of offenders is fully discussed in Chapter 9 by Mike Nellis, whilst Judith Rumgay looks in Chapter 10 at drugs testing as a component in the treatment of drug-dependent offenders. Information technology has also played an important role in the development of risk assessment tools, as discussed in Chapter 13, and more generally in supporting an increasingly managerial approach in the delivery of community penalties.

3. Management – There has been a 'managerial revolution' in the probation service in the last two decades, which can be linked to wider social policy changes beginning during the 1980s, sometimes described as 'New Public Management' (see Pollitt 1993, Pollitt and Bouckaert 2000). Starting in the mid-1980s with the issue of the National Statement of Objectives and Priorities for the Probation Service (Home Office 1984), this development has been largely Home Office-led. Amongst its features are 'National Standards' (see Home Office 2000 for the most recent version) and strategic plans with 'performance indicators' and targets, based on the key managerialist concepts of 'efficiency' and 'effectiveness'.[12] One major development, in April 2001, was the establishment of a new National Probation Service under the Criminal Justice and Court Services Act 2000, replacing over fifty local services. Unsurprisingly, the Director of the new Service quickly rose to the managerialist challenge with the publication of an integrated management strategy (National Probation Service 2001). But the managerial revolution is not simply Home Office-driven; many proba-

tion managers have embraced it enthusiastically because they see it as helping them, for example, to exercise better local control and leadership of 'effective practice' developments (see, for example, Statham and Whitehead 1992). Hence, on the ground, the concepts of 'management', 'technology' and 'effectiveness' are in practice often very closely intertwined (see further below).

One strategy often favoured in the new public management is the contracting-out of some services to the private sector, in the belief that the competition engendered by this process will drive down costs (hence delivering enhanced efficiency) and promote innovatory ways of working (hence delivering enhanced effectiveness). The first major contracting-out development in the English criminal justice system came with the privatisation of some prisons (see James *et al.* 1997). There is a widespread consensus that the threat of privatisation has provoked some individual public sector prisons to enhance their performance (to avoid the threat of market testing and possible loss of staff employment), though it does not follow from this that private prisons are necessarily 'better' than public ones.[13]

In the field of community penalties, electronic monitoring was from the outset contracted-out to the private sector, in part because of the reluctance of the probation service to administer this type of penalty. This of course produced competitiveness between private sector bidders, but not public–private 'contestability' (as it is now called) – unlike in the prison context, where private firms and public sector consortia now frequently bid against one another for the contract to manage a particular contracted-out institution (with the public sector sometimes winning the race). 'Contestability', however, was arguably the dominant concept in the Carter Report (Carter 2003). This report, as well as proposing to bring together the delivery of custodial and non-custodial penalties under the single umbrella of the National Offender Management Service (NOMS), also suggested a radical purchaser–provider split for the delivery of non-custodial services. Ultimately, the Report envisaged, the existing local Probation Boards would be swept away, and nine NOMS Regional Offender Managers would be appointed. They would select specific offender services on the basis of a large number of competitions between public service providers (the probation service), private sector companies, and the voluntary sector. Policy (i.e. the type of services bought) would be settled solely by NOMS, and the probation service would become simply a service provider. This was a logical outworking of managerialist principles, though one that was not fully supported, in terms of efficiency and effectiveness, by empirical evidence (Pollitt and Bouckaert 2000; see also Dobson 2004).[14] Interestingly, as we have noted in the preface, the Government, while initially accepting the full Carter Report's vision of contestability, has now put at least the radical plans for a purchase–provider split on hold for the time being, leaving open, at least temporarily, an interesting space for future policy debate.

4. Partnership – One aspect of the new managerialist approach has been the development of partnerships. This has taken two distinct forms. First, there is the concept of 'inter-agency co-operation', whereby different parts of the public sector – some with a history of ideological conflict – are encouraged or required to work collaboratively, in the interests of enhanced efficiency and effectiveness.[15] This approach has perhaps been taken furthest in relation to young offenders, with the establishment of a nation-wide network of multi-agency Youth Offending Teams (YOTs) under the Crime and Disorder Act 1998.[16] It has also manifested itself in other important ways. For example, the Crime and Disorder Act 1998 set up multi-agency 'Crime and Disorder Partnerships' in all local areas, which now form an important backdrop to the delivery of community penalties (see Liddle 2001). Moreover, the attempt in *The Correctional Policy Framework* (Home Office 1999) to unify the purposes of probation and prisons has been taken a stage further by the Carter Report, which effectively operationalises a 'joined up' approach to the management of offenders in NOMS. A more specialised development of this kind of partnership can be also found in the Multi-Agency Public Protection Arrangements (MAPPAs), according to which probation services work alongside police and prison services, as well as other public sector agencies, to protect the public from various categories of 'high-risk' offenders (see chapters in Matravers 2003).

   The second form of partnership is a partnership between the probation service and another body, on a contracting-out/joint working basis. This type of partnership began in earnest in the late 1980s, largely involving not-for-profit organisations (Nellis 2002, Rumgay 2003); but it has somewhat diminished in prominence since the creation of the National Probation Service. Nevertheless, if the future structures of NOMS will allow it, this kind of arrangement is potentially of some significance, not least in enabling the probation service to work closely with voluntary agencies that are deeply embedded within local communities in particular areas.

5. Effectiveness and risk management – Recent years have seen a complete reversal of the 'Nothing Works' thesis so influential at the end of the 1970s. We are now in the heyday of a 'What Works' movement, firmly committed to the view that some treatments, especially cognitive-behavioural treatments, are indeed more effective than others (e.g. McGuire 1995). This has also led to the development of a core curriculum of accredited programmes and integrated systems, as discussed by Peter Raynor in Chapter 8.

   These changes have coincided with the development of IT-based systems permitting the calculation of 'risk scores' – for example 'risk of reconviction' based on the Offender Group Reconviction Scale (OGRS) and the Offender Assessment System (OASys) diagnostic tools, both of which are discussed in Chapter 13. The aims of maximising effectiveness and minimising risk, in order to secure public protection through the reduction of offending, have increasingly shaped probation service practice as delivered 'on the ground'. This emphasis is reinforced by a strong focus on the monitoring of programmes on a number of dimensions, including programme integrity and the subsequent reconviction of offenders.

This increasing focus on risk is strikingly illustrated in the Carter Report (2003), which mentions the principle of proportionality but places far more emphasis on risk. The Report also appears to envisage that the new provision on previous convictions in the 2003 Act (see above) will lead to a gradient of sentencing severity by previous record, which is seen as congruent with risk principles because more previous convictions predict a higher probability of reconviction. Other illustrations of the pervasive importance of risk in the contemporary criminal justice system can readily be found, for example in the work of MAPPAs (see above).[17]

6. Creative mixing – A threefold concern with punishment, effectiveness and public safety seems to have contributed to a trend towards the 'creative mixing' of different kinds of interventions in offenders' lives (rather than imposing a single type of punishment or treatment). Community penalties have traditionally involved a discrete and special mode of intervention in an offender's life: for example, keeping in touch with the probation officer under the probation order; doing unpaid work under the CSO/CPO; or staying at home under electronic monitoring in the curfew order. In the 1990s, however, we have seen an apparently increasing desire to *mix creatively*, for a given offender, two or more of these discrete kinds of intervention. This trend has been seen in the enactment, and then in the growing popularity, of the combination order (see above). But there have also been other important 'mixing' provisions, including the Criminal Justice and Court Services Act 2000, which allows additional requirements relating to Drug Abstinence, Curfew and Exclusion to be included in a Community Rehabilitation Order. A particular focus for 'creative mixing' initiatives has been the persistent offender – this can be seen, for example, in the introduction of the Intensive Supervising and Surveillance Programmes for juvenile offenders, in the analogous Intensive Control and Change Programme (ICCP) now being piloted for 18–20 year old prolific offenders,[18] and in other programmes for persistent offenders discussed by Anne Worrall and Rob Mawby in Chapter 11. More generally, 'creative mixing' has now been endorsed as a normal feature of community penalties in the customised Community Order of the 2003 Criminal Justice Act, discussed below.

7. Reparation and the rights of the victim – The last half-century has seen a considerable growth in a concern with the rights of victims in a number of countries, leading to the restorative justice movement and having a direct impact on the community supervision of offenders in two ways. First, there has been an increased interest in direct or indirect compensation or reparation as a sentence ordered by courts.[19] Second, we have seen the creation of new restorative justice models for supervised encounters between victims and offenders. As discussed by Gill McIvor in Chapter 7, Australia and New Zealand have been at the forefront of these kinds of initiatives. In England, both developments have been incorporated in provisions relating to young offenders: the reparation order introduced under the Crime and Disorder Act 1998; and reparation as part of the contractual package agreed with a Youth Offender Panel under the so-called 'referral order' introduced in the Youth Justice and Criminal Evidence Act 1999 (Crawford and Newburn 2003).

We would suggest that the above seven dominant features of contemporary community penalties are explicable largely in terms of the apparently increasing development of a form of 'late modern society' (see Loader and Sparks 2002 for a summary of the burgeoning literature in criminology relating to crime and criminal justice in late modernity). While such a society has important continuities with what has gone before (and is hence 'late modern' rather than 'post-modern'), it is a society that is increasingly globalised, and with less reliance on the traditional 'community bonds' of extended families, local communities, schools and voluntary associations. It also increasingly relies on technology and other 'abstract systems' for day-to-day living, as is evident in the rapidly growing reliance on the internet for communication, and on CCTV to provide safety in public places. In short, people decreasingly define their identities as deriving from settled groups (such as families, or a particular town), and increasingly define themselves as individuals with rights. Furthermore, precisely because many of the older community bonds have declined in importance, people often feel a greater sense of insecurity (Giddens 1990).[20] As a consequence, there is a heightened preoccupation with the idea of 'risk', to which the management response has particularly been to develop techniques for the calculation and avoidance of significant risks (see Beck *et al.* 1994).

Such a society seems significantly different from that which produced earlier types of community penalties, particularly those grounded in concepts such as 'penal welfarism', as has been recognised by Garland (2001). Relating the main features of late modern societies to the seven characteristics outlined above of the 'new generation of community penalties', the technology, management, effectiveness/risk, and partnership strands seem easily explicable in a society increasingly dominated by *abstract systems* as sources of trust in day-to-day living. The punishment/

public protection strand can perhaps be seen as deriving from late modernity's preoccupation both with individual rights (translated here into individuals' rights to carry on their daily business in safety) and with an increased sense of insecurity. 'Creative mixing' might be read as a secondary principle, deriving its appeal both from a concern with public protection (restricting the offender more, and keeping the public safer) and from the utilitarian ethics that tend to underpin the managerialist/ effectiveness strands.

The one feature of new generation community penalties that at first sight seems much less compatible with the 'late modernity' thesis is that of reparation. Reparative and restorative models of the criminal process are prominent in pre-modern societies, and it is not uncommon to find leading proponents of restorative justice such as Christie (1977) offering pre-modern examples in their writings. Such village-society scenarios seem far removed from our contemporary globalised, abstract-system-dominated world. But restorative justice approaches can also be seen to have their origins in a very late-modern concern with victims' rights. It has been powerfully argued that they derive much of their appeal from the fact that, in late modern societies, 'criminal law cannot be legitimised any more by the self-evident social [and moral] cohesion of a community, [but] it can at least be understood as the protection against victimisation . . . [so that] in the 'victim' we find a criterion that draws a line on moral relativism' (Boutellier 1996: 15; see also Boutellier 2000). Certainly, Garland (2001) includes a focus on 'victim policy' as one element in the crime control practices that he sees as having supplanted penal-welfarism.[21]

New forms of custodial and community provision

What has also been witnessed over the last decade is an unprecedented rise of around 30,000 in the prison population, which cannot be explained by a more serious mix of offences or offenders coming before the courts (Hough *et al.* 2003; Lewis, in Chapter 2 of this volume). Alongside the rise in the prison population, we have also seen the 'silting up' of the Probation Service's caseload with low-risk offenders (Morgan 2003). The use of community orders has increased from 102,000 in 1992 to 187,000 in 2002, but much of this growth has been in the use of community orders for summary offences, which has increased by nearly 170 per cent (their use for indictable offences has increased by 50 per cent). Equally, the proportions of community orders imposed on offenders with no prior convictions increased dramatically over the decade.[22] According to the most recent figures, nearly half of the offenders who receive a community punishment (previously community service) order are convicted of the least serious type of offences, and over half have been convicted for the first time.[23] These increases have taken place largely at the expense of financial and nominal penalties, and George Mair discusses the dramatic fall in the use of the fine in Chapter 6.

This, then, is the context in which radical provisions have been enacted in the Criminal Justice Act 2003 (the '2003 Act'). The customised Community Order replaces the various kinds of community orders with a single sentence in which courts will be able to combine any of a wide range of requirements (see note 2 to this chapter). But that is only a part of the Act's radical intentions. Above the so-called 'custody threshold', three new short-term sentences are being created, namely 'custody plus', intermittent custody and a new form of suspended sentence with conditions. All will allow a custodial sentence to be combined with requirements served in the community. 'Custody plus' replaces prison sentences below twelve months with a short period of custody (between two weeks and three months for a single offence) followed by community supervision and requirements (for a minimum of six months). Intermittent custody enables a prison sentence to be served at night or at the weekend, with a community programme during the day or through the week. The new suspended sentence allows a short custodial sentence to be suspended on condition that the offender complies with specified community-based requirements; breach will normally result in the activation of the term of imprisonment.[24]

As is well known, many of these provisions of the 2003 Act originated in proposals in the Home Office Consultation Paper widely known as the Halliday Report (Home Office 2001), and they implement policy set out in *Justice For All* (Home Office and Lord Chancellor's Department 2002).[25] The overall aim of the approach embodied in the Act is to introduce a clearer and more flexible sentencing framework based on the five purposes of sentencing as set out in s.142 of the Act, namely punishment, crime reduction, rehabilitation, public protection and reparation (all of which have particular salience for the 'new generation' of community orders discussed above). The generic community sentence is intended to tackle the lack of understanding and the confusion surrounding the purposes, and use, of the multiplicity of community orders introduced over the last three decades. As the National Probation Directorate acknowledged in its response to the Halliday Report, the relevant legislation has become highly complex, and we have already moved some way towards a single sentence through the Criminal Justice and Court Services Act 2000 (National Probation Directorate 2001). According to the Government, the aim of the custodial reforms is to 'ensure [short prison sentences] support for our overall aim of reducing offending' (Home Office and Lord Chancellor's Department 2002: 92). This follows concerns that neither a short custodial nor a suspended sentence does anything to tackle the offending patterns of the offenders made subject to them.[26]

In attempting to rectify the perceived deficiencies of the current arrangements for custodial sentences, the new provisions nevertheless seem likely to blur the boundaries between custody and community penalties. Fine judgements will be required as to when to select an intensive community sentence, when to give an offender a short taste of custody combined with or followed by community requirements, and when to use the threat of custody to reinforce community requirements. In theory, choices between these varying provisions will be governed, first, by the legislative criterion that a custodial sentence can be imposed only when the offence(s) are 'so serious' that only custody can be justified (Criminal Justice Act 2003, s.152(2)); and secondly, by whatever guidance comes from the Sentencing Guidelines Council established under the 2003 Act. In practice, however, it seems likely to be difficult if not impossible to provide sufficiently exhaustive guidance. These questions will be returned to in Chapter 12, in which Martin Wasik considers the influence of legislation and guidance on sentencing decisions; as he points out, the Court of Appeal has found it very difficult to provide clear guidance about the 'custody threshold' in the last decade.

What we know about offering sentencers a wider menu of conditions for community penalties suggests that the effect is to increase the number of requirements imposed (Hedderman *et al.* 1999).[27] If this occurs, it will inevitably increase the likelihood that offenders will fail to comply with some requirements, which will hardly enhance the long-term credibility of the new Community Order.[28] A related danger is that a 'pick 'n' mix' generic order will make it more difficult to sustain a reasonable relationship between the gravity of the offence and the overall severity of the order (Ashworth *et al.* 1995). Alive to these concerns, Halliday offered an outline tariff for the community order with requirements arranged in three tiers, which was 'not intended to be prescriptive in illustrating possible combinations' (Home Office 2001: 41). The Sentencing Guidelines Council will have the opportunity to reduce the risk of the 'condition creep' (gradual extension in the number of requirements or conditions) identified by Halliday, but there remains a real danger that community orders will be used for progressively less serious offenders, as a credible 'punishment' becomes one that contains a custodial element. This makes the recent radical proposal by the Chief Inspector of Probation (HMIP 2003) for the Probation Service to contract out its supervision of low-risk offenders potentially more relevant.

Youth justice

The arrangements for dealing with young offenders in England and Wales underwent something of a revolution in the late 1990s, in an avowed move away from the 'excuse culture' by which the previous youth justice system, according to the Government:

> Excuses itself for its inefficiency, and too often excuses the young offenders before it, implying that they cannot help their behaviour because of their social circumstances. Rarely are they confronted with their behaviour and helped to take more responsibility for their actions. (Home Office 1997: preface)

Such comments echoed the verdict of the Audit Commission (1996) on the 'minimum intervention' principle frequently pursued in English youth justice since the 1980s and early 1990s: according to the Commission, 'little or nothing' was happening to children and young people dealt with by the then English youth justice system. The changes announced in 1997 and implemented over the next few years have introduced a correctionalist agenda into English youth justice and one that stands in contrast to the clear official commitment that remains in Scotland (for offenders under 16) to the paramountcy of the principle of the welfare of the child. To some extent, this distinction arises from the fact that the Scottish children's hearings system retains a single jurisdiction for children who have broken the law and those in need of care and protection, whereas the Children Act 1989 separated the care from the criminal jurisdiction in England (see Bottoms and Dignan 2004 for further discussion and comparison of the two systems). The central aim of the reforms in England is preventive; the principal aim of the English youth justice system, as stated in section 37 of the Crime and Disorder Act 1998, is now to 'prevent offending by children and young persons', and this is pursued principally through early intervention, reparation, and the intensive supervision of persistent offenders.

Many of the new Labour reforms will be familiar to the reader: for example the establishment of the Youth Justice Board under the Crime and Disorder Act 1998; the duty on local authorities to draw up 'youth justice plans' and establish multi agency YOTs. The 1998 Act also replaced the old-style formal cautioning system with the more restrictive regime of 'reprimands' and 'final warnings', so abolishing the pre-1998 practice of repeat cautions in favour of a system whereby an offender can receive just one reprimand followed by a single final warning (usually also involving an intervention, or 'change package'), and then prosecution. The Youth Justice and Criminal Evidence Act 1999 introduced a further major innovation in the form of the Referral Order by which ten to seventeen-year-olds appearing before the youth court for the first time, and who plead guilty, are referred to a local Youth Offender Panel (YOP) comprising one member of the YOT and two laypersons; the offender and the YOP are then encouraged to construct a contract aimed at improving the offender's behaviour (for an evaluation of this measure, see Crawford and Newburn 2003). The range of disposals available to the Youth Court has also been extended under the 1998 Act, with the introduction of the Reparation Order as an 'entry-level' disposal for less serious offences and a new community sentence, the Action Plan Order, designed as a shorter and more focused version of the Supervision Order. In addition, new community-based Intensive Supervision and Surveillance Programmes (ISSPs) have been introduced and can be attached to supervision orders.

The above reforms will be addressed as relevant in a number of chapters. For example, Chapter 6 looks at pretrial diversion, Chapter 7 considers initiatives influenced by restorative approaches, including Referral Orders, and Chapter 11 examines intensive projects for persistent young offenders. In keeping with the Government's commitment to an 'evidence-led approach', most of the new youth justice reforms have been piloted and some research findings are already available on these important changes, although it is difficult to reach definitive conclusions on their success or otherwise at this early stage (for a review of available evidence to 2003, see Bottoms and Dignan 2004).

Non-custodial measures in Scotland

The Scottish jurisdiction has experienced a number of similar trends to England and Wales, albeit with a less dramatic impact. One major difference between the two jurisdictions, however, has been the continued supervision of offenders within the remit of social work following the disbanding of the probation service in Scotland in the Social Work (Scotland) Act 1968. Consequently, criminal justice social work has been a Local Authority responsibility, although funded latterly by the Scottish Executive (see Robinson and McNeill 2004 for a comparison of arrangements and aims in the two jurisdictions). By the late 1970s, commentators were questioning the viability of probation and after care services when subsumed within Social Work Departments,[29] and ring-fenced funding for criminal justice social work with adults was introduced in 1989–91 to deal with this issue.[30] At that time, Scottish criminal justice social work was following the 'alternatives to custody' model discussed above, a policy of penal reductionism being expounded in Scottish penal policy (Rifkind 1989). 'Punishment in the community' did not take hold in Scotland as in England and Wales, but a focus on re-offending emerged in the early 1990s in an attempt to enhance the credibility of community penalties and reduce reliance on custody (see McIvor 1990b). This rapidly evolved into 'public protectionism', as articulated in *The Tough Option* (Scottish Office 1998) and incorporated in the current Scottish statement of *National Priorities* (Justice Department 2001).[31] However, to a greater extent than in England and Wales, this has been tempered by a continuing commitment to anti-custodialism and social inclusion, expressed in both of the above policy documents (McNeill 2004). It is this kind of approach that enabled the Scottish Consortium on Crime and Criminal Justice (2000) to declare that custodial sanctions did not make better citizens and that community sanctions with a rehabilitative orientation were more effective at reducing offending, despite a lack of evidence on the latter. The Consortium concluded that the Scottish Parliament and Executive should take immediate action to increase the use of the most effective community sanctions and reduce the use of custody, especially short custodial sentences.[32]

Most recently Justice 1 Committee of the Scottish Parliament has published a report following its *Inquiry Into Alternatives to Custody* (see Justice Committee 1 2003), which was prompted by concerns about a recent increase in the Scottish prison population. The Committee concluded as follows:

> The Committee has established that Scotland has a wide range of community penalties available, but that the prison population continues to rise. It is also clear that community disposals are at least as effective as short term imprisonment. A range of recommendations has been made by the Committee to promote community disposals as alternatives to custody, including more resources for community disposals to ensure that they are effectively delivered and that breach is dealt with rigorously, more research on the effectiveness of community disposals in order to increase public confidence in them, and effective communication with sentencers about the availability, effectiveness and rigour of community disposals to improve judicial confidence in the sanctions. The Committee believes that it is vital that these recommendations are taken forward in the next Parliament. (Justice Committee 1: para. 37)

Further developments can be expected in Scotland within the near future. What form these will take is, however, at present unclear, not least because possible organisational change has also been mooted. There is, at the time of writing, a formal Consultation in progress on proposals to create a 'single agency' structure, to include prisons and criminal justice social work. Most local authorities (who are responsible for Social Work Departments) oppose these proposals, but the Scottish First Minister has said publicly that 'the status quo is not an option'. (McConnell 2003: 21; see further McNeill 2004)

Northern Ireland

In common with the Scottish experience, the development of community penalties in Northern Ireland has broadly mirrored developments in England and Wales, but at the same time some significant differences stand out. It is worth noting that there is relatively little in the way of literature covering the history of community penalties in this jurisdiction.

Much of what is distinctive about the delivery of community penalties in Northern Ireland stems from the particular social and political context in which criminal justice operates. As Breidge Gadd, then the Chief Probation Officer for Northern Ireland, has explained, in a jurisdiction ghettoised by civil conflict and in which large sections of the population question the authority of government, establishing the Probation Service as a legitimate community organisation and cultivating a culture of community involvement have been difficult, but critical (Gadd 1996; see also Blair 2000: 11). To this end, in 1982 the Probation Board (Northern Ireland) Order inaugurated one province-wide probation service, to be governed by a community-based Board, but with 100 per cent funding from the Northern Ireland Office. Since its inception, the Probation Board for Northern Ireland (PBNI) has placed a particular emphasis on working in partnership with local communities. Not only is the Board itself composed largely of lay members, it also endeavours to fund a large number of community-based projects and to be responsive to local needs, e.g. by providing services seven days a week (Gadd 1996). The Board currently devotes 20 per cent of its annual budget to funding 'community development' projects (Rooney 2004). As Blair (2000) has pointed out, the status of the PBNI as a Non-Departmental Public Body (NDPB) has helped the Probation Service maintain its image as an independent organisation, at one remove from central government. In a further effort to establish its legitimacy with all sections of the population it serves, the Probation Service has rejected a statutory role in respect of those convicted of politically motivated crimes. One outcome of this is that, with the dual exceptions of (i) non-paramilitary released life-sentence prisoners, and (ii) Custody Probation Orders (see below), all work with prisoners in custody and on release is on a voluntary basis. In common with Scotland, and in growing contrast to England and Wales, the professional background of probation practitioners continues to be that of social work.

In respect of objectives, Gadd explains that from the outset the PBNI essentially rejected the 'nothing works' doctrine, opting to adopt an overarching purpose, 'to help prevent reoffending'. Gadd argues that the Board has essentially continued to pursue this singular goal for over two decades through the development of a range of services and programmes for offenders. Indeed, a Quinquennial Review of the work of the PBNI undertaken in 1997 reported that the PBNI is distinguished from equivalent bodies in England, Wales and Scotland by its singular focus (PKFA 1997). Nonetheless, in defining its 'mission' as 'Integrating offenders in the community by effective assessment and supervision thereby reducing re-offending and contributing to public protection',[33] the PBNI has clearly taken on board the emphasis on public safety which has risen to prominence in other parts of the UK.

As in other parts of the UK, Northern Ireland has seen a proliferation of community sentencing options in recent years. Northern Ireland's response to the 1991 Criminal Justice Act involved the publication of *Crime and the Community* (NIO 1993), which proposed an enhanced range of community penalties, including the combination order. Subsequently the Criminal Justice (Northern Ireland) Order 1996 defined the range of available community sentences as: a probation, community service or combination order; a supervision order and an attendance centre order. It also introduced the Custody Probation Order,[34] a 'seamless' sentence intended to compensate for the absence of a parole system and to provide statutory post-custody supervision for appropriate offenders (Blair 2000). The PBNI Annual Report for 2001–2 provides statistics on the courts' utilisation of five community penalties: the probation order; the community service order; the combination order; custody probation orders and juvenile justice centre orders.[35]

In 2000 the Government published the recommendations of a wide-ranging *Review of the Criminal Justice System in Northern Ireland*, which was set up in 1998 under the Good Friday Agreement (Criminal Justice Review Group 2000). A series of research reports relating to different aspects of criminal justice were published alongside the Review, including separate reports relating to prisons and probation (Blair 2000), juvenile crime and justice (O'Mahony and Deazley 2000) and restorative justice (Dignan and Lowey 2000). Paralleling recent developments in England and Wales, the Review made a number of recommendations in respect of promoting 'joined-up' working between Prison and Probation Services, including a shared management structure and the cooperative development of shared programmes of intervention. As Blair (2000: 69) observes, proposals to integrate the two services have to be understood in the context of growing concerns with modernisation, accountability, new technologies, cost-effectiveness and multi-agency working.[36] The Review also recommended that restorative justice should become a central part of the formal criminal justice process for juveniles. It further argued that the courts had too few options in respect of community sentences for juvenile offenders, and recommended the development of a form of community service for those under 16, and the introduction of reparation orders.

The Government published its response to the Review Report in 2001, which comprised an Implementation Plan and draft legislation covering those recommendations requiring statutory provision.[37] The Justice (Northern Ireland) Act 2002 received Royal Assent in July 2002, and an updated Implementation Plan detailing progress to date was published in June 2003.

Conclusion

In this introductory chapter we have outlined a history of 'alternatives to prison', focusing in particular on the changing profile of community penalties over the last two decades or so. As indicated in our introduction, both this and the following chapter (in which Chris Lewis examines trends in crime, victimisation and punishment over the same period) are intended to provide the contextual background for the remaining chapters, each of which addresses a specific area relevant to 'alternatives to prison'. We hope that this introductory chapter has made clear the ways in which the concept of 'alternatives to prison' has been variously interpreted in the last forty years, within a social context that has itself been changing rapidly. 'Alternatives to prison', then, is not a static concept, and there is scope for innovation and creativity as we look towards the future.

Notes

1 The Criminal Justice Act 1948, s3, provided that 'where . . . it is expedient to do so, the court may, *instead of sentencing* [the defendant], make a probation order' (emphasis added). This statutory formulation was not repealed until 1991.
2 The Community Order will, for adult offenders, replace the current range of orders with a single order in which the court can combine any of the following requirements: supervision; compulsory work; activities or prohibited activities; offending behaviour programmes; treatment for substance misuse or mental illness; residence; curfews and exclusions; and attendance centres (for offenders under 25 only). The government is considering a similar single community order for juvenile offenders.
3 See the quartet of articles by McWilliams (1983–1987) on the history of the Probation Service.
4 This had already manifested itself in the 1950s, though at that date it was linked with the penal-welfarist concern that 'in a substantial number of cases a short term of imprisonment does no good and may do some harm' (Home Office 1957: 4).
5 However, empirical evidence for these developments was often overstated or poorly presented in the academic literature – see the incisive critique by McMahon (1990).
6 The 1988 Green Paper containing the Government's initial proposals estimated that the prison population could rise to 70,000 by the year 2000 (Home Office 1988). See generally Windlesham (1993).
7 The Combination Order was created by the Criminal Justice Act 1991; under it, the offender must *both* perform between 40 and 100 hours' community *and* be supervised by the Probation Service for a period between twelve months and three years. In *National Standards for the Supervision of Offenders in the Community* (1992), Home Office advice was that the new order was 'in practice . . . likely to be most appropriate for an offender who has . . . committed an offence which is among the most serious for which a community sentence may be imposed'. (p. 81).
8 s.143(2) of the Criminal Justice Act 2003 provides that the court, in considering the seriousness of the current offence(s) committed by an offender with one or

more previous convictions, '*must* treat each previous conviction as an aggravating factor' (emphasis added) if the court considers it can reasonably be so treated, having regard especially to the recency of the previous conviction(s) and the nature of the previous offence(s) and its/their 'relevance to the current offence'. This replaces the current law, which provides that in considering the seriousness of the current offence(s) 'the court *may* take into account any previous convictions of the offender or any failure of his to respond to previous sentences' (Criminal Justice Act 1991 s.29(1), as amended by the Criminal Justice Act 1993; emphasis added). For the history of this issue in English sentencing law, see Ashworth (2000, Ch. 6). For a strong criticism, from a desert-based perspective, of the approach embodied in the Criminal Justice Act 2003, see von Hirsch (2002).

9 The Criminal Justice and Court Services Act 2000 renamed the probation order as the community rehabilitation order (CRO), the community service order as the community punishment order (CPO); and the combination order as the community punishment and rehabilitation order (CPRO). However, these names will shortly disappear when the new generic Community Order (see above, note 2) is implemented.

10 Under the 2000 version of National Standards governing how offenders are supervised in the community (Home Office 2000), breach proceedings must normally follow a second unacceptable absence rather than, as before, a third. For a discussion of enforcement practice, see Chapter 13.

11 Most prisoners serving sentences of at least three months, but less than four years, can now be released up to 135 days early under HDC – see Prison Service Instruction 31/2003, amending Prison Service Order 6700. According to the latest Prison Population Briefing available at the time of writing (August 2004), over 3,500 prisoners were out on HDC in England and Wales.

12 *Efficiency* is normally defined as the achievement of a given outcome at the lowest unit cost, and *effectiveness* as the degree to which programme outcomes meet the original programme objectives: see Pollitt (1993: 59).

13 There are many complex issues involved in this debate: see for example Liebling (2004), especially Chapters 2 and 10.

14 For example, Pollitt and Bouckaert (2000) report that the devolution of operational decision-making to small independent units – as in the local management of schools – produces operational efficiencies within that unit, but also makes it less likely that the low-level organisational units will work together. If the 'units' in the case of community penalties are individual programmes or activities, there is an obvious potential danger of fragmentation. See further, Chapter 13.

15 See for example the comments by Faulkner (1989: 1), then a senior Home Office civil servant, noting that five different services dealt with crime (police, prosecution service, courts, probation and prisons). Faulkner considered that these five services were, operationally, rightly distinguished, 'but at a more general level the services *all share or ought to share a common purpose and common objectives*, even though their character is very different. Each can frustrate any of the others . . . *so they must understand one another and they must work together. The point is obvious*, but it does not easily happen' (emphasis added). Whilst there is of course an important truth within these observations, the emphasis is – as is common in managerial thinking – entirely on 'common objectives',

with no explicit recognition that some of these services (such as the Crown Prosecution Service (CPS)) were originally created as separate agencies precisely in order to put a brake on the powers of another agency (in the case of the CPS, the police) in the interests of justice.

16 By statute, YOTs must involve co-operation between the local authority (in practice through its social services and education departments), the police, the probation service and the health service (Crime and Disorder Act 1998, s.39).

17 For academic discussions of the risk theme in contemporary penology, see for example Feeley and Simon (1992) and Garland (2001).

18 Billed as an alternative to a short custodial sentence, the ICCP comprises: eighteen hours of intervention, including an offending behaviour programme, education, mentoring and employment and training; up to 100 hours of community punishment; a curfew order with electronic monitoring; and a compensation order (see National Probation Service Briefing Issue 12, April 2003).

19 This has included the compensation order, created in 1972; the reparation order for young offenders, created in 1997; and the indirect reparation provided through the community service order (now the community punishment order).

20 These insecurities have, amongst other things, recently led to the creation of the National Reassurance Policing Programme. Some of the evidence underpinning this initiative is briefly discussed in Chapter 15.

21 For a fuller discussion of the paradox of the growth of restorative justice in late modernity, see Bottoms (2003).

22 See Probation Statistics for England and Wales 2002. The proportion of summary offences among those sentenced to a community order increased from 28 per cent to 41 per cent between 1992 and 2002. Twenty-seven per cent of those sentenced to probation in 2001 had no previous convictions compared with eleven per cent a decade earlier; the corresponding proportions for community service were 51 per cent and fourteen per cent (Probation Statistics 2001; the corresponding figures are not included in the 2002 volume). Fascinatingly, too, in 2001/2, the CRO was being used for more serious offences and riskier offenders than the CPRO (i.e. the renamed combination order), despite the original guidance relating to combination orders (see note 7 above).

23 Contrast this with the early vision of community service as an 'alternative to custody' (see earlier discussion). Pease (1985: 61) for example cites a Home Office source in 1983 that described community service as 'intended to be an alternative disposal for offenders who might otherwise have received a custodial sentence'.

24 This differs radically from the existing suspended sentence, where except in rare cases no supervision or requirement can be linked to the sentence; the offender simply walks free from the court, but with the threat of the suspended term of imprisonment hanging over him/her during the 'operational period' of the sentence. A further important difference from the present law is that the Criminal Justice Act 1991, s.5, restricted the courts' exercise of the power to suspend a sentence to cases in which there were 'exceptional circumstances', but this restriction is abolished by the Criminal Justice Act 2003. The 1991 restriction led to a very large reduction in the use of suspended sentences; the removal of the restriction might well reverse this pattern.

25 The 'custody plus' and Community Order provisions derive directly from the Halliday Report. Halliday discussed, but made no firm recommendations with regard to, intermittent custody and the suspended sentence, and the final form of these initiatives was developed later within the Home Office.
26 This is because at present (i) the suspended sentence normally involves no specific intervention (see above), and (ii) custodial sentences of less than twelve months have no subsequent licence period, and the time in custody is usually too short to permit the delivery of programmes aimed at reducing reoffending. This last point was particularly emphasised in the Halliday Report, as a background to the proposal for the new 'custody plus' sentence.
27 This evidence derives from 'demonstration' projects following earlier proposals for a generic community order that the Government decided not to pursue, apparently persuaded by some respondents to its consultation exercise that the current range of options was already sufficiently wide (Home Office 1995, 1996). In the demonstration projects, the aim of which was to promote judicial and public confidence in community options within the current legal framework, sentencers were more satisfied with the information they received and felt more informed about probation programmes. The most significant impact on sentencing, in both higher and lower courts, was not on the use of custody, but an increase in the use of probation orders with additional requirements, largely at the expense of other community penalties and especially relating to summary cases. Sentencers also expressed an interest in being able to fuse a community sanction with a short spell of custody.
28 Completion rates for CPROs, for example, are lower than those for either the CPO or CRO (see Probation Statistics for England and Wales 2001). Reporting very low completion rates (30 per cent) for DTTOs, Hough *et al.* (2003) pointed to the importance of applying standards of enforcement which maximised the chances of retaining a drug-dependent offender in treatment.
29 This was because local authority Social Work Departments (SWDs) had discretion as to how to prioritise their budgets, and sometimes they decided that the supervision of some kinds of offenders was of lower priority than (say) child protection or assisting the elderly. Hence, notwithstanding that a probation order was an order of the court, it could remain unimplemented by the SWD.
30 However, this does not apply to children brought before the Children's Hearing on offence grounds, within Scotland's integrated child care and youth justice system (see above).
31 This development was partly prompted by adverse publicity following the murder in 1997 of a seven year-old Aberdeen schoolboy, Scott Simpson, by Steven Leisk, who was the subject of a Supervised Release Order at the time.
32 The following community penalties are available in Scotland: probation order, community service order, restriction of liberty order (a curfew), drug treatment and testing order, and supervised attendance order (educational activities in place of a fine).
33 See www.pbni.org.uk/probation1.htm.
34 The Custody Probation Order empowers a court to sentence an offender, with his or her consent, to a minimum of twelve months, to be followed by supervision on probation for one to three years (Blair 2000).
35 In Northern Ireland juvenile offenders have continued to be the responsibility of the Probation Service, and probation and community service orders are

available to both adults and young persons from the age of ten. PBNI statistics indicate that in March 2002 32 per cent and nine per cent of those on probation and community service orders respectively were 10–17 years of age (www.pbni.org.uk/anreport.htm).

36 See Blair (2000: 52–58) for a discussion of some of the practical and ideological problems around integrating prison and probation services in Northern Ireland. As she notes, the desire to 'join up' prison and probation services conflicts with a desire to maintain probation's status of relative independence from government.

37 The PBNI responded positively to the proposal to retain its status as a NDPB pending devolution of criminal justice matters to the Assembly (Probation Board for Northen Ireland 2002).

References

Allen, F. A. (1981). *The Decline of the Rehabilitative Ideal: Penal policy and social purposes* (New Haven, CT: Yale University Press).

Ashworth, A. (2000) *Sentencing and Criminal Justice*, 3rd edition (London: Butterworths).

Ashworth, A., von Hirsch, A., Bottoms, A. E. and Wasik, M. (1995) 'Bespoke tailoring won't suit community penalties', *New Law Journal*, 145, 970–172.

Audit Commission (1996) *Misspent Youth: Young people and crime* (London: Audit Commission).

Beck, U., Giddens, A. and Lash, S. (1994) *Reflective Modernization* (Cambridge: Polity Press).

Blair, C. (2000) *Prisons and Probation*, Research Report 6 (Criminal Justice Review Group, Belfast: HMSO) [http://www.nio.gov.uk/pdf/06.pdf].

Bottomley, A. K. (1980) 'The "justice model" in America and Britain: development and analysis', in A. E. Bottoms and R.H. Preston (eds) *The Coming Penal Crisis: A criminological and theological exploration* (Edinburgh: Scottish Academic Press).

Bottoms, A. E. (1980) 'An introduction to the coming penal crisis', in A. E. Bottoms and R. H. Preston (eds) *The Coming Penal Crisis: A criminological and theological exploration* (Edinburgh: Scottish Academic Press).

Bottoms, A. E. (1981) 'The suspended sentence in England 1967–1987', *British Journal of Criminology*, 21, 1–26.

Bottoms, A. E. (1987) 'Limiting prison use in England and Wales', *Howard Journal of Criminal Justice*, 26, 177–202.

Bottoms, A. E. (1989) 'The concept of intermediate sanctions and its relevance for the probation service', in R. Shaw and K. Haines (eds) *The Criminal Justice System: A central role for the probation service* (Cambridge: Institute of Criminology).

Bottoms, A. E. (2003) 'Some sociological reflections on restorative justice', in A. von Hirsch, J. Roberts, A. E. Bottoms, K. Roach and M. Schiff (eds) *Restorative Justice and Criminal Justice: Competing or reconcilable paradigms?* (Oxford: Hart Publishing).

Bottoms, A. E. and Dignan, J. (2004) 'Youth crime and youth justice: comparative and cross-national perspectives', *Crime and Justice: A Review of Research*, 31, 21–183.

Bottoms, A. E., Gelsthorpe, L. R. and Rex, S. A. (2001) 'Introduction: the contemporary scene for community penalties', in A. E. Bottoms, L. Gelsthorpe and S. Rex (eds) *Community Penalties: Change and challenges* (Cullompton: Willan Publishing).

Boutellier, H. (1996) 'Beyond the criminal justice paradox', *European Journal on Criminal Policy and Research*, 4, 7–20.

Boutellier, H. (2000) *Crime and Morality* (Dordrecht: Kluwer Academic Publishers).

Carter, P. (2003) *Managing Offenders, Reducing Crime: A new approach. Report of the Correctional Services Review* (London: Strategy Unit).

Cavadino, M. and Dignan, J. (1992) *The Penal System: An introduction*, 1st edition (London: Sage).

Christie, N. (1977) 'Conflicts as property', *British Journal of Criminology*, 17, 1–26.

Cohen, S. (1985) *Visions of Social Control* (Cambridge: Polity Press).

Crawford, A. and Newburn, T. (2003) *Youth Offending and Restorative Justice: Implementing reform in youth justice* (Cullompton: Willan).

Criminal Justice Review Group (2000) *Review of the Criminal Justice System in Northern Ireland* (Belfast: HMSO) [www.nio.gov.uk/pdf/mainreport.pdf].

Dignan, J. and Lowey, K. (2000) *Restorative Justice Options for Northern Ireland: A comparative review* (Belfast: HMSO) [www.nio.gov.uk/pdf/10.pdf].

Dobson, G. (2004) 'Get Carter', *Probation Journal*, 51(2), 144–154.

Faulkner, D. (1989) 'The future of the Probation Service: a view from government', in R. Shaw and K. Haines (eds) *The Criminal Justice System: A central role for the Probation Service* (Cambridge: Institute of Criminology).

Feeley, M. and Simon, J. (1992) 'The new penology: notes on the emerging strategy of corrections and its implications', *Criminology*, 30, 449–474.

Gadd, B. (1996) 'Probation in Northern Ireland', in G. McIvor (ed.) *Working With Offenders*, Research Highlights in Social Work 26 (London: Jessica Kingsley Publishers).

Garland, D. (1985) *Punishment and Welfare* (Aldershot: Gower).

Garland, D. (2001) *The Culture of Control: Crime and social order in contemporary society* (Oxford: Oxford University Press).

Giddens, A. (1990) *The Consequences of Modernity* (Cambridge: Polity Press).

Hedderman, C., Ellis, T. and Sugg, D. (1999) *Increasing Confidence in Community Sentences: The results of two demonstration projects*, Home Office Research Study 194 (London: Home Office).

Her Majesty's Inspectorate of Probation (2003) *2002/3 Annual Report* (London: Home Office).

Home Office (1957) *Alternatives to Short Terms of Imprisonment: A report of the Advisory Council on the treatment of offenders* (London: HMSO).

Home Office (1984) *National Statement of Objectives and Priorities* (London: Home Office).

Home Office (1988) *Punishment, Custody and the Community*, Cmd. 424 (London: HMSO).

Home Office (1990), *Crime, Justice and Protecting the Public*, Cmd. 965 (London: HMSO).

Home Office (1995) *Strengthening Punishment in the Community*, Cmd. 2780 (London: HMSO).

Home Office (1996) *Protecting the Public*, Cmd. 3190 (London: HMSO).

Home Office (1997) *No More Excuses: A New Approach to Tackling Youth Crime in England and Wales*, Cmd. 3809 (London: The Stationery Office).

Home Office (1999) *The Correctional Policy Framework* (London: Home Office).

Home Office (2000) *National Standards for the Supervision of Offenders in the Community* (London: Home Office).

Home Office (2001) *Making Punishments Work* (London: HMSO).

Home Office and Lord Chancellor's Department (2002) *Justice for All*, Cmd. 5563 (London: The Stationery Office).

Hough, M., Jacobson J. and Millie, A. (2003) *The Decision to Imprison: Sentencing and the prison population* (London: Prison Reform Trust).

Hough, M., Clancy, A., McSweeney, T. and Turnbull, P.J. (2003) *The Impact of Drug Treatment and Testing Orders on Offending: Two-year reconviction results*, Home Office Research Findings 194 (London: Home Office).

Hudson, B (1987) *Justice Through Punishment: A critique of the 'justice' model of corrections* (London: Macmillan Education).

James, A., Bottonmley, A. K., Liebling, A. and Clare, E. (1997) *Privatizing Prisons: Rhetoric and Reality* (London: Sage).

Justice 1 Committee (2003) *Inquiry Into Alternatives to Custody* [www.scottish.parliament.uk].

Justice Department (2001) *Criminal Justice Social Work Services: National priorities for 2001–2002 and onwards* (Edinburgh: The Scottish Executive).

Liddle, M. (2001) 'Community penalties in the context of contemporary social change', in A. E. Bottoms, L. Gelsthorpe and S. Rex (eds) *Community Penalties: Change and challenges* (Cullompton: Willan).

Liebling, A. (2004) *Prisons and Their Moral Performance* (Oxford: Oxford University Press).

Lipton, D., Martinson, R. and Wilks, J. (1975) *The Effectiveness of Correctional Treatment* (New York: Praeger).

Loader, I. and Sparks, R. (2002) 'Contemporary landscapes of crime, order, and control: governance, risk, and globalization', in M. Maguire, R. Morgan and R. Reiner (eds) *Oxford Handbook of Criminology*, 3rd edition (Oxford: Oxford University Press).

Martinson, R. (1974) 'What works? Questions and answers about prison reform', *The Public Interest*, March, 22–54.

Matravers, A. (ed.) (2003) *Sex Offenders in the Community* (Cullompton: Willan).

McConnell, J. (2003) *Respect, Responsibility and Rehabilitation in Modern Scotland*, Apex Lecture 1, September 2003 (Edinburgh: Scottish Executive).

McGuire, J. (ed.) (1995) *What Works? Reducing reoffending* (Chichester: John Wiley and Sons).

McIvor, G. (1990a) 'Community service and custody in Scotland', *Howard Journal of Criminal Justice*, 29, 101–113.

McIvor, G. (1990b) *Sanctions for Serious and Persistent Offenders: A review of the literature* (Stirling: University of Stirling Social Work Research Centre).

McMahon, M. (1990) '"Netwidening": vagaries in the use of a concept', *British Journal of Criminology*, 30, 121–149.

McNeill, F. (2004) 'Desistance, rehabilitation and correctionalism: developments and prospects in Scotland', *Howard Journal of Criminal Justice*, 43(4), 420–436.

McWilliams, W. (1983) 'The mission to the English police courts 1876–1936', *The Howard Journal of Criminal Justice*, 22, 129–147.

McWilliams, W. (1985) 'The mission transformed: professionalisation of probation between the wars', *The Howard Journal of Criminal Justice*, 24(4), 257–274.

McWilliams, W. (1986) 'The English probation system and the diagnostic ideal', *The Howard Journal of Criminal Justice*, 25(4), 241–260.

McWilliams, W. (1987) 'Probation, pragmatism and policy', *The Howard Journal of Criminal Justice*, 26(2), 97–121.

Morgan, R. (2003) 'Thinking about the demand for probation services', *Probation Journal*, 50(1), 7–19.

National Probation Directorate (2001) Probation Circular 145/2001, *Consultation on Sentencing Reform: National Probation Service Response* (London: Home Office).

National Probation Service (2001) *A New Choreography: An integrated strategy for the National Probation Service* (London: Home Office).

Nellis, M. (2002) 'Probation, partnership and civil society', in D. Ward, J. Scott and M. Lacey (eds), *Probation: Working for justice*, 2nd edition (Oxford: Oxford University Press).

Northern Ireland Office (1993) *Crime and the Community: A discussion paper on criminal justice policy in Northern Ireland* (Belfast: HMSO).

O'Mahony, D. and Deazley, R. (2000) *Youth Crime and Justice* (Belfast: HMSO) [www.nio.gov.uk/pdf/17.pdf].

Pannell Kerr Forster Associates (1997) *Quinquennial Review of the Probation Board for Northern Ireland* (London: Pannell Kerr Forster Associates).

Pease, K. (1985) 'Community service orders', in M. Tonry and N. Morris (eds) *Crime and Justice* (Chicago: University of Chicago Press).

Pollitt, C. (1993) *Managerialism and the Public Services*, 2nd edition (Oxford: Blackwell).

Pollitt, C. and Bouckaert, G. (2000) *Public Management Reform: A comparative analysis* (Oxford: Oxford University Press).

Probation Board for Northern Ireland (2002) *Corporate Plan 2002–2005* [http://www.pbni.org.uk/corporate.htm].

Raynor, P. and Vanstone, M. (2002) *Understanding Community Penalties* (Buckingham: Open University Press).

Rex, S. A. [1998] 'Applying desert principles to community sentences: lessons from two criminal justice acts', *Criminal Law Review*, 381–391.

Rifkind, M. (1989) 'Penal policy: the way ahead', *The Howard Journal of Criminal Justice*, 28(2), 81–90.

Robinson, G. and McNeill, F. (2004) 'Purposes matter: examining the "ends" of probation', in G. Mair (ed.) *What Matters in Probation Work* (Cullompton: Willan Publishing).

Rooney, N. (2004) 'Working in partnership: the Northern Ireland experience', Paper delivered at Hertfordshire Probation Area Partnership Conference, 23 March 2004.

Rumgay, J. (2003) 'Partnerships in the Probation Service', in W.-H. Chui and M. Nellis (eds), *Moving Probation Forward* (London: Pearson Education).

Scottish Consortium on Crime and Criminal Justice (2000) *Rethinking Criminal Justice in Scotland* [www.scccj.org.uk].

Scottish Office (1998) *Community Sentencing: The tough option – Review of criminal justice social work services* (Edinburgh: Scottish Office).

Statham, R. and Whitehead, P. (eds) (1992) *Managing the Probation Service* (Harlow: Longmans).

von Hirsch, A. (1986) *Past or Future Crimes* (Manchester: Manchester University Press).
von Hirsch, A. (1993) *Censure and Sanctions* (Oxford: Clarendon Press).
von Hirsch, A. (2002) 'Record-enhanced sentencing in England and Wales: reflections on the Halliday Report's proposed treatment of prior convictions', *Punishment and Society*, 4, 443–457.
Wasik, M. and von Hirsch, A. [1988] 'Non-custodial penalties and the principles of desert', *Criminal Law Review*, 555–571.
Windlesham, Lord (1993) *Responses to Crime, Volume 2: Penal policy in the making* (Oxford: Clarendon Press).

Chapter 2

Trends in crime, victimisation and punishment

Chris Lewis

This chapter summarises trends in crime, victimisation and punishment in the three United Kingdom jurisdictions (England and Wales, Scotland and Northern Ireland) from 1980 to 2003.[1] Because current influences on crime and techniques for managing crime are common throughout the Western world, the chapter also considers trends in other countries, in particular those in Europe.

The main sources used in the analyses are Home Office statistical and research material, equivalent data from Scotland and Northern Ireland, international data collections and academic commentaries. The statistics used are those available up to March 2004. As some of these are moving quite fast, e.g. those relating to prison populations, for a more recent picture readers should consult the websites quoted.

Behind each set of statistics quoted there are counting rules and technical procedures that vary from time to time and country to country, thus making any statement about trends subject to certain caveats. For example, the main caveats noted here for crime data are:

- changes in counting rules for police-recorded crime data;
- difficulties in comparing police-recorded crime and survey crime;
- difficulties in comparing trends across jurisdictions.

Statistics about crime

Crime figures are needed:

- to see how well policies are working;
- to allocate resources;
- (by the public) to:
  - hold governments accountable;
  - judge whether they, as individuals, need to supplement government spending by crime prevention measures, private security, or increased insurance.

UK government statisticians have been encouraged to improve crime statistics since 1997, and British crime and justice statistics are now very good by international standards.

The level of crime is a difficult concept. To appear in police-recorded crime statistics, a crime must be committed, discovered, reported and recorded. There is potential for incompleteness at any of the last three stages. Thus police crime statistics can give only a partial picture. Recent developments have greatly improved our understanding: e.g. the growth of IT collection/analysis systems; improvements to the consistency of data collection; new techniques for data collection, especially using victimisation surveys to complement police data; and improved presentation of statistics.[2] A detailed description of developments in the measurement of crime data can be found in Maguire (2002).

Police-recorded crime

Police crime statistics are compilations of data derived from police records. They were published for many years in *Criminal Statistics, England and Wales* (see e.g. Home Office 2001) but are now published in a bulletin on crime separately from the sentencing figures (e.g. Simmons *et al.* 2002). These figures are used at local and national levels to allocate resources, set targets, produce crime audits and crime reduction plans, and to justify the success of government initiatives.

Police-recorded crime statistics have several limitations[3] and this chapter allows for these when commenting on trends. It has been estimated, for example, that about 40 per cent of crimes known to victims and reported to the police are not recorded (Kershaw *et al.* 2001).

There have been some important technical changes to recorded crime data, both in England and Wales and in Northern Ireland during the period covered by this chapter. In the mid-1990s pressures to improve police-recorded crime statistics in England and Wales led, in July 2000, to the publication of a wide-ranging and far-reaching discussion document (Simmons 2000).[4] The report stated that the current way of producing crime statistics would be recognisable to the nineteenth-century officials who invented them. It proposed to end a historical continuity that had become a virtue in itself and replace it with a system more appropriate to the demands of the twenty-first century. It recognised that such changes would not come about quickly, especially where changes to IT systems would be needed. Many of the report's recommendations have been put into effect, but it is likely that the full implementation will take ten years. The most important changes were:

- Counting rules were amended from April 1998 and further revised in April 2002 to allow for the National Crime Recording Standard to be introduced, promoting consistency (see Home Office 2004d). These changes mean that comparisons between figures before and after 1998 are complex. Similar changes were made in Northern Ireland.
- For England and Wales and for Northern Ireland statistics are now published on a financial year basis.
- Police statistics and victimisation survey statistics are now published in the same document, and comments on trends in crime in England and Wales and in Scotland are made using both sources.

The counting rules in Scotland have been much more stable. There was a small change in 1995 and all Scottish figures now used have been reworked to allow for this.

Trends in police-recorded crime

Trends in police-recorded crime in England and Wales since 1980 are given in Table 2.1. There is a break in the series at 1 April 1998, due to the new counting rules. The picture is broadly that:

- Recorded violent crime rose quickly between 1980 and 1997, and has continued to rise since then, although much of the increase since 1997 has been due to counting rules changes.
- Recorded property crime rose less quickly than violent crime, to a peak in 1992. It then fell throughout the rest of the 1990s, and has remained broadly stable since 2000.
- Recorded vehicle crime also rose until 1992, but then fell throughout the rest of the 1990s and has remained broadly stable ever since.
- When adjusted for population (see final column) the picture remained broadly the same as the unadjusted figures.

Similar data for Scotland and Northern Ireland are given in Table 2.2.

Figure 2.1 compares changes in recorded crime, for the three jurisdictions, from 1980 to 2000, with the figures for 1980 indexed to 100 for each jurisdiction. The much lower rate of increase in crime in Scotland since 1980 is notable, with total crime in Scotland in the early years of the

Table 2.1 Police-recorded crime in England and Wales, 1980 to 2003 (indexed, 1980 = 100)

Year	Total recorded violent crime	Total recorded property crime	Total recorded vehicle crime	Total recorded offences	Total recorded offences per 100,000 population
Calendar years					
1980 actual	133,000	2,547,000	619,000	2,688,000	5,459
1980 indexed	100	100	100	100	100
1985	128.5	134.4	136.7	134.4	133.0
1990	188.0	167.4	204.7	169.0	164.6
1995	233.8	186.1	213.6	189.7	181.0
1997	260.9	164.5	180.6	171.0	162.0
Financial years					
1997/8	*265.4*	*162.2*	*177.1*	*169.1*	*160.1*
1998/9	*249.6*	*160.5*	*173.2*	*166.7*	*157.2*
1998/9	*455.6*	*169.0*	*174.3*	*190.1*	*179.2*
1999/00	*528.6*	*173.2*	*168.7*	*197.2*	*185.2*
2000/01	*551.1*	*167.3*	*156.4*	*192.4*	*179.8*
2001/02	*611.2*	*177.7*	*158.8*	*205.4*	*191.2*
Year to September 2003 (estimated)	*785.7*	183.1	155.1	219.9	203.2
Year to September 2003 actual (estimated)	**1,045,000**	**4,665,000**	**960,000**	**5,910,000**	**11,090**

Note: There is a break in the series around 1997/8. This is partly due to a move from calendar to financial years, but mainly because of new counting rules introduced at 1 April 1998. Numbers of recorded crimes will be affected by changes in reporting and recording. For further information see Chapter 3 in *Crime in England and Wales 2001/2*. (Home Office 2003b). The national impact of recording changes in 2001/2 was estimated to be a 5 per cent rise for total recorded crime. This impact will vary for different types of offences and for different police forces.

twenty-first century little higher than it was 20 years ago (see also Smith and Young 1999; Bottoms and Dignan 2004).

In contrast, for Northern Ireland, total crime has more than doubled. However, Northern Ireland experiences very low levels of overall crime, despite a high rate of serious crime and high rate of vehicle theft (Lockhart 1994).

Comparisons with non-UK jurisdictions

Comparisons with other countries are made difficult by differences in judicial and statistical processes, although such differences are too numerous

Table 2.2 Police-recorded crime: Scotland and Northern Ireland, 1985 to 2002 (indexed, 1980 = 100)

Year	Total recorded crime in Scotland[1]	Total recorded crime in Northern Ireland
1980 actual	*380,000*	*55,000*
1980 indexed	100	100
1985	113.1	114.5
1990	141.1	104.0
1995	125.3	125.0
2000	111.3	218.2[2]
2001[2]	110.8	254.5
2002[2]	112.4	258.1
2002 actual	**427,000**	**142,000**

[1]In Scotland before 1996, breaching the bail condition that no further offences would be committed while on bail was treated as an offence in its own right. From 1996 breaching this condition ceased to be a separate offence. The recorded crime series has been revised to remove all crimes of 'offending while on bail' for 1983 to 1995 to enable comparisons over time to be made.

[2]Northern Ireland figures for 2000 onwards were recorded using new counting rules (see Police Service of Northern Ireland 2004). Data from 2001 for Northern Ireland are on a financial year basis (e.g. 2001/2 rather than 2001).

to detail here (but see Barclay and Tavares 2003, WODC 2003). It is generally accepted that absolute levels of recorded crime, even when adjusted for population, are not a good basis for comparisons, but changes in crime levels can be more valid. Trends in recorded crime in other countries (Table 2.3) show that, over the period 1997–2001, recorded crime in the EU rose on average by 4 per cent with the largest rises in France, Greece and Portugal (all 16 per cent), followed by the Netherlands and Spain (both 10 per cent). There were falls in Denmark and Italy (both 11 per cent), Finland (3 per cent), England and Wales (2 per cent) and Sweden (1 per cent).

Over the longer period 1991–2001, recorded crime in the EU fell by just 1 per cent, whereas crime in England and Wales and Scotland fell considerably (by 11 per cent and 27 per cent respectively). Because valid international statistics have been collected only since the 1990s, no valid comparisons are available for the whole 20-year period since the early 1980s.

Crime and victimisation surveys

There were few significant crime and victimisation surveys before 1980, but pioneering work in the USA led to local and national victim surveys in the three UK jurisdictions from the 1980s. There have also been

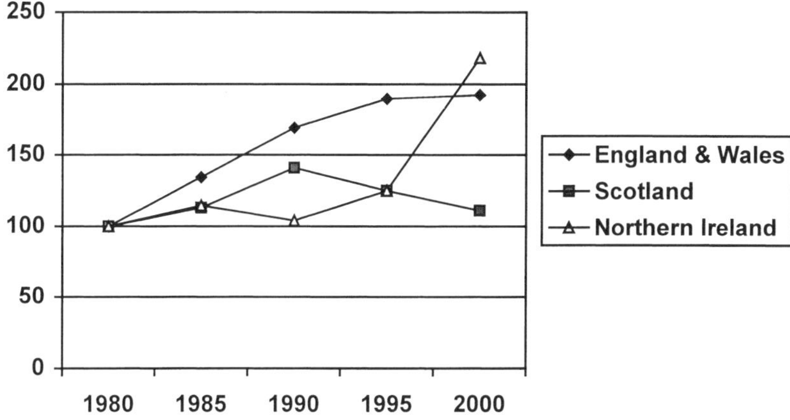

Figure 2.1 Total recorded crime in the three UK jurisdictions 1980–2000 (1980 = 100)

Table 2.3 Percentage charges in police-recorded crime in European and other jurisdictions 1991–2001

Country	1991–2001 (%)	1997–2001 (%)	2000–2001 (%)
EU Average	−1	+4	+3
England and Wales	−11	−2	+7
Northern Ireland	—	—	+17
Scotland	−27	+0	+0
Austria	+11	+9	−7
Belgium	—	+17	+0
Denmark	−9	−11	−6
Finland	−7	−3	−6
France	+8	+16	+8
Germany	—	−3	+2
Greece	+22	+16	+19
Italy	−18	−11	−2
Netherlands	+13	+10	+4
Norway	+28	+5	−2
Portugal	—	+16	+2
Spain	+3	+10	+10
Sweden	−1	−1	−2
Switzerland	−28	−28	+2
Canada	−17	−5	+2
USA	−20	−10	+2

Table 2.4 Estimates of BCS incidents of crime 1981 to 2002

Year for which crime was measured by BCS: calendar years	Estimates of BCS crime (millions)
1981	11.2
1983	12.2
1987	14.2
1991	15.1
1993	17.8
1995	19.4
1997	16.8
1999	15.1
2000	13.3
Year ending June 2002	12.7
Year ending June 2003	12.1

Table extracted from Simmons *et al.* (2002) and Allen and Wood (2003)

international crime surveys of households in different countries in which similar questions are asked in the same year (van Kesteren *et al.* 2002).[5]

The main benefit of crime surveys is that asking households about their experience of crime avoids their reluctance to report crime to the police and for the police to record it. There have, however, been large differences in the frequency of surveys in the three UK jurisdictions. The British Crime Survey applies to England and Wales and has been carried out many times on a relatively consistent basis: it can be used to estimate trends in crime. The Scottish Crime Survey has been carried out five times, only three of which were for the whole of Scotland, and it therefore allows only limited trend estimates. The Northern Ireland survey has been carried out twice, first in 1994/5 and again in 1998.

British Crime Survey

The first sweep of the British Crime Survey (BCS) took place in 1982, asking questions about respondents' victimisation in 1981 (Hough and Mayhew 1983). Further sweeps took place in 1984, 1988 and 1992. It was then two-yearly up to 2000, since when it has been annual. The sample size has now been raised to 40,000 households. Results show broadly the same trends over the period from 1980 as for police-recorded crime (see Table 2.4).

BCS crimes reported by households in England and Wales rose steadily between 1981 and 1991, at an average of three per cent a year, and continued to rise until 1995. Since 1995, BCS crime has reported a fall each time. This parallels, although not exactly, the rise and consequent fall shown by police crime statistics.

Table 2.5 Survey estimates of crimes in Scotland 1981–1999, and comparison of survey results for 1992, 1995 and 1999 with police recorded crime (all data in thousands)

	All Scotland: comparable survey crime[1]	Police-recorded crime	Central and Southern Scotland: comparable survey crime[1]	Central and Southern Scotland total survey crime[2]
Acquisitive crime				
1981	—	—	105	
1987	—	—	157	
1992	186	104	170	
1995	130	81	106	
1999	120	66	101	
Violence				
1981	—	—	146	
1987	—	—	170	
1992	168	50	153	
1995	159	50	140	
1999	211	58	153	
Total crimes				
1981	—	—	478	942
1987	—	—	506	938
1992	566	218	495	924
1995	523	194	447	830
1999	549	180	436	671

Source: Scottish Executive (2002).
[1]Those survey crimes that are comparable with categories of police-recorded crime.
[2]All survey crimes, whether or not they are comparable with categories of police-recorded crime.

Scottish Crime Survey

Although the 2000 Scottish Crime Survey (SCS) was the fifth in a series, only the last three, in 1992, 1995 and 1999, were conducted throughout the country: the first two surveys, in 1981 and 1987, were conducted only in Central and Southern Scotland (see Table 2.5).

In broad terms the SCS results parallel the trend in the police figures, with an increase in total comparable crime throughout the 1980s being succeeded by a fall throughout much of the 1990s, particularly in acquisitive crime, although the trend in violent crime tends to be rising towards the end of the 1990s. No survey has taken place since 2000, so that more recent survey trends cannot be estimated.

Northern Ireland Crime Survey

The Northern Ireland Crime Survey (NICS) was carried out in 1994/5 and repeated in 1998; also, the International Crime Victimisation Survey (ICVS) has been carried out there more often. NICS results show that 23 per cent of households experienced at least one crime in 1997 compared to 34 per cent in England and Wales. Northern Ireland experiences a lower level of property crime, as one would expect in what is essentially a rural environment: for example, 2.5 per cent of households experienced a burglary in 1997 compared to 5.6 per cent in England and Wales. However, the level of violent crime is about the same as in England and Wales.

Surveys of crime in commercial properties

One of the gaps in victimisation surveys is that statistics on crimes against commercial properties are not included in a household survey. The Commercial Victimisation Survey carried out in 1994 filled this gap for England and Wales only (Mirrlees-Black and Ross 1996).

The main estimates of this survey of retail and manufacturing properties were that in 1993:

- there were 8.6 million crimes against retail premises;
- nearly 80 per cent of retail premises had experienced one or more crime incidents;
- a quarter of retailers had been burgled, especially sellers of alcohol or cigarettes;
- nearly 63 per cent of manufacturing premises had suffered crime;
- the total direct cost of stolen and damaged property was around £1.1 billion.

Victimisation levels as a whole (e.g. for burglary) were much higher for retailers and manufacturers than for households.

Public perception of the figures

Unlike health, where the public can see relations and friends living longer and being cured of previously fatal illnesses, the perception of crime trends, fed by 40 years of rising crime statistics up to the mid-1990s, is that things are always getting worse. This has led to the public and the media being very suspicious of any positive trends. Also, despite routine warnings of the limitations of crime statistics, especially police figures, most commentators ignore these caveats.

Any rise in crime figures leads to publicity in the media about criminal justice ineffectiveness, and to calls for tougher justice measures. This tends to be the case whatever the level from which this rise has occurred, and however recently new and tougher justice measures may have been introduced. British politicians tend to be less than robust in responding to such publicity, and many recent changes to criminal justice policy can be argued to have been heavily media-driven.

In addition, there is considerable public scepticism over the reported fall in crime over the last decade of the twentieth century, with the public unable to reconcile the government's claim that crime is falling with the statement that prison populations of England, Wales and Scotland are at record levels and the fact that crime in Britain is still high in an international context. The BCS now asks questions dealing with people's perceptions of crime (see Simmons *et al.* 2002: 79 *et seq.*), with the following main results:

- As far as national crime rates are concerned, where the media is the only source of information, results for 2002 showed that 35 per cent of respondents believed that crime had risen substantially in that year, despite the fact that it had actually fallen.
- As far as local crime rates are concerned, where people have more first-hand knowledge to rely on, respondents are much more positive than they were in the mid-1990s. However, around 24 per cent of respondents in 2002 still believed that local crime had also risen substantially.

It is clear that the more recent message of crime falling is still very new in the political and media environments. It will take a few years to become fixed in the public mind because it is so different from the message put forward in the past.

International comparisons of victimisation

The main source for international crime comparisons is the International Crime Victimisation Survey (ICVS) survey of criminal victimisation (van Kesteren *et al.* 2002). This has been conducted in 1989, 1992, 1996 and 2000. The latest survey covered 17 industrialised countries. The broad picture is given in Table 2.6; this is arranged in descending order of prevalence rates (see note to the table for explanation of this term), so that the relative position of the three British jurisdictions can be noted.

The three British jurisdictions vary greatly from each other. England and Wales shows very high rates, exceeded in prevalence only by Australia. Northern Ireland, as one might expect for what is mainly a rural jurisdiction, is at the bottom in prevalence terms, and Scotland is just

Table 2.6 Overall victimisation in 1999 across 17 jurisdictions: ICVS (% victimised)

	Incidence[1]	Prevalence[2]
Average of 17 countries	**38**	**21**
Australia	56	30
England and Wales	*58*	*26*
Netherlands	51	25
Sweden	46	25
Canada	42	24
Scotland	*43*	*23*
Denmark	37	23
Poland	42	23
Belgium	37	21
France	36	21
USA	43	21
Finland	31	19
Catalonia (Spain)	30	19
Switzerland	24[3]	18
Portugal	27	15
Japan	22	15
Northern Ireland	*24*	*15*

[1]Total number of crimes experienced per 100 people.
[2]Percentage of people victimised once or more in 1999 by any of the 11 crimes covered by the survey.
[3]Estimated figures.

above the average for these 17 jurisdictions. There are only slight variations in these positions when one looks at the incidence rate. The broad picture is that England and Wales shows a high incidence of crime reported to the ICVS, Scotland has a more average position and Northern Ireland is generally below average

The position is different by offence. Table 2.7 shows results for theft of cars, residential burglary with entry and selected contact crimes. For each type of crime, England and Wales is well above average and, for theft of cars, has the highest rate. Northern Ireland has a low rate for burglary, an average rate for contact crime and slightly above average for theft of cars. Scotland has a high rate for contact crime but close to average rates for burglary and theft of cars.

Trends in detection

Police do not clear up (detect) all the offences they know about. In England and Wales, the clear-up rate has fallen considerably from 38 per

Table 2.7 Percentage victimised once or more in 1999: ICVS

	Theft of cars	**Residential burglary with entry**	**Selected contact crimes**[1]
Average	**1.2**	**1.7**	**2.4**
England and Wales	*2.6*	*2.8*	*3.6*
Australia	2.1	3.3	4.1
France	1.9	1.3	2.2
Poland	1.7	1.3	2.8
Sweden	1.6	0.7	2.2
Canada	1.6	2.3	3.4
Northern Ireland	*1.5*	*0.9*	*2.4*
Denmark	1.4	1.5	2.3
Portugal	1.2	1.2	1.4
Scotland	*1.0*	*1.9*	*3.4*
Belgium	0.8	2.8	1.8
Netherlands	0.5	2.7	2.0
Finland	0.5	1.0	3.2
USA	0.5	2.7	1.9
Catalonia (Spain)	0.5	0.6	1.5
Switzerland	0.4	1.8	2.1
Japan	0.1	0.8	0.4

[1]Robbery, sexual assault and assault with force.

cent of offences detected in 1981 to around 23 per cent detected in 2001. However, the position in Scotland has been the reverse, with a rise in the clear-up rate to around 45 per cent in 2001. This is possibly because of the low rise in recorded crime in Scotland since 1980 (see Table 2.2.)

Between 1981 and 2001 the numbers cautioned for indictable offences in England and Wales rose from 104,000 to 144,000 and the numbers found guilty of indictable offences fell from 465,000 to 324,000 (see Home Office 2002a, Table 1.1). However, there have been considerable changes in the numbers of offenders processed by the justice system over the last two decades: e.g. the drop in numbers processed has been much greater for young men and boys than for males over 21. It is clear that recent rises in the prison population do not stem from more people being found guilty: see Table 2.8.

Trends in punishment

We must therefore look to changes in sentencing patterns, not of offenders' numbers coming forward, to see why there are now more people in prison than ever before. This section of the chapter is confined to data on England and Wales, although comparisons of prison

Table 2.8 Males found guilty at all courts or cautioned, England and Wales: 1981–2002

	All ages	10–11 year olds	12–14 year olds	15–17 year olds	18–20 year olds	21 and over
Per 100,000 population						
1981	2,255	—	—	—	—	1,297
1991	1,969	956	3,489	7,416	7,444	1,296
2001	1,666	519	2,388	5,891	6,623	1,184
2002	1,773	435	2,145	5,594	6,834	1,327
Indexed 1991 = 100						
1981	114.5	—	—	—	—	100.1
1991	100	100	100	100	100	100
2001	84.6	54.3	68.4	79.4	89.0	91.4
2002	90.0	45.5	61.4	75.4	91.8	102.4

Source: Home Office (2003b).

Table 2.9 Percentage of offenders sentenced for indictable offences who received various types of sentence, England and Wales: 1980–2002

Year	Discharge	Fine	Community sentence	Fully suspended sentence	Immediate custody	Total number sentenced[1]
1980	11	48	19	7	14	456,000
1985	13	40	23	6	18	385,000
1990	17	39	23	6	14	342,000
1995	19	30	28	1	20	302,000
2000	16	25	30	1	25	325,000
2001	16	24	32	1	25	323,000
2002	15	23	33	1	25	337,000

Source: Home Office (2003b).
[1]Includes otherwise dealt with.

population levels in other jurisdictions (including Scotland and Northern Ireland) are given later.

The two main messages from Table 2.9 that explain why custodial sentencing has increased over this period are:

- The decline in the use of the discharge, the fine and the suspended sentence, especially the fine. Magistrates in particular tended not to use the fine during periods of high unemployment in the 1980s, when offenders were unlikely to be able to pay: however, there was no reversion to using the fine once economic times improved.

Table 2.10 Average length of sentence in months for males aged 21 and over sentenced to immediate imprisonment at the Crown Court, England and Wales: 1980–2001

Year	Total indictable offences	Violence against the person	Burglary	Theft
1980	16.7	16.7	16.6	10.6
1985	17.3	17.4	16.0	10.4
1990	20.5	19.2	16.4	10.3
1995	22.0	23.1	17.7	11.6
2000	24.2	22.4	22.5	11.0
2001	26.0	23.1	23.9	11.8
2002	27.8	24.7	25.0	11.9

Source: Home Office (2003b).

- The fall up to the early 1990s in the number of offenders sentenced, particularly because of increased cautioning, followed by a small rise to 2002.

At the same time, as well as the rate of imprisonment having increased, there have been sharp increases in the average lengths of sentence for those given immediate custody, for most types of offence. This is particularly true for the Crown Court, as is shown in Table 2.10, although there have been similar trends in magistrates' courts.

Thus the average sentence length for burglary in the Crown Court has increased by nine months since 1990 (from just over 16 months to 25 months); the average for violence has increased by five and a half months since 1990 and by eight months since 1980.

Taken as a whole, these trends in sentencing have led to a substantial increase in the numbers imprisoned, as well as a substantial rise in the workload of the National Probation Service (see Table 2.9 on the growth in use of community sentences).

The rise in the total prison population is shown in Table 2.11 and Figures 2.2 and 2.3 for males and females. The latest figures are for 14 May 2004, which reveal that the prison population had further risen to 70,661 males and 4,633 females (Prison Service 2004). All these figures include both sentenced and remand prisoners.

Home Office projections of the prison population, based on the situation at June 2003 (Home Office 2004a), imply further rises over the next decade (see Table 2.12). The two central scenarios lead to a population of over 86,000 males and 5,500 females by the year 2009. This contrasts with the conclusions of the Carter Report (Carter 2003) and the Home Office reply (Home Office 2004b) that imply a target of no more than a 80,000 prison population in the medium term.

Table 2.11 Prison population, England and Wales, by sex of prisoner: 1980 to 2004

	Male prisoners	Female prisoners	Total prisoners	Percentage of females
Average for calendar year				
1980	40,700	1,500	42,300	3.6
1985	44,700	1,500	46,200	3.3
1990	43,400	1,600	45,000	3.4
1993	43,000	1,560	44,700	3.5
1995	49,000	2,000	51,000	3.9
2000	61,300	3,350	64,600	5.2
2001	62,600	3,750	66,300	5.6
2002	66,560	4,300	70,860	6.1
Average for FY 2002/3	67,229	4,350	71,579	6.1
Population at 14 May 2004	70,661	4,633	75,294	6.2

Source: Home Office (2002b).

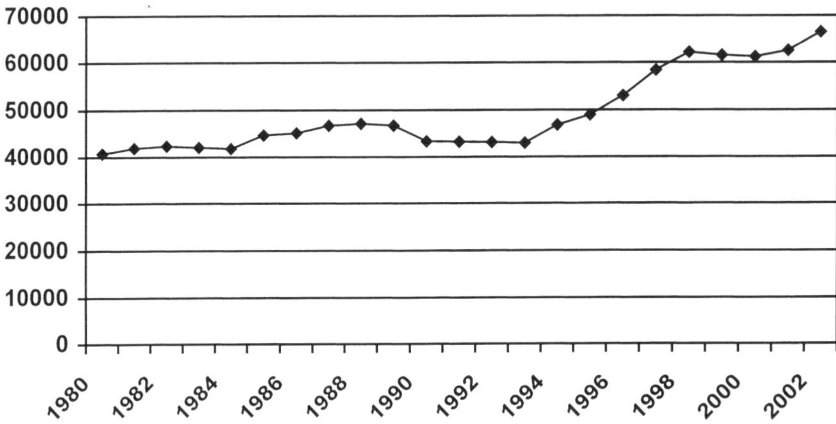

Figure 2.2 Male prison population in England and Wales, 1980 to 2002

Figures 2.2 and 2.3 show the trends in the prison population for males and females; they may be compared with Figure 2.1 on recorded crime. Two main messages stand out from these graphs:

- The rise in the prison population has not been paralleled by a rise in crime: the main rise in the population occurred from 1993 when crime and victimisation were falling or relatively stable, and the rise in crime and victimisation during the 1980s happened at the same time as a relatively stable prison population. The possibility that this is due to a

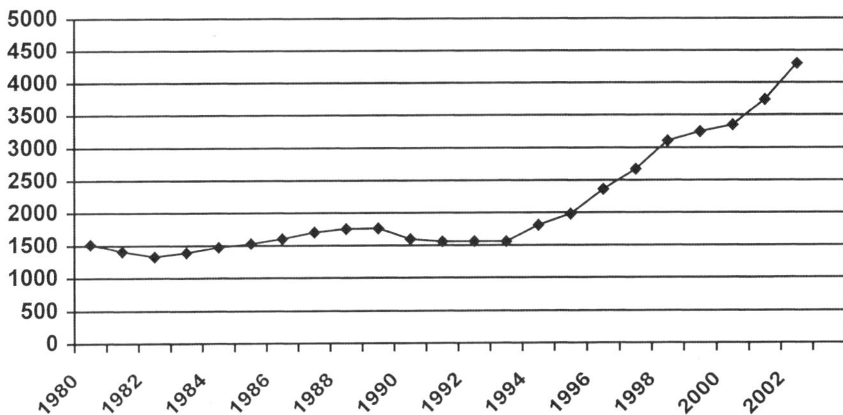

Figure 2.3 Female prison population in England and Wales, 1980 to 2002

Table 2.12 Prison population projections, England and Wales, by sex of prisoner: 2003–2009[1]

	Male prisoners	Female prisoners	Total prisoners	Percentage of females
Average of calendar years				
2003	69,200	4,700	73,900	6.4
2004	72,300	4,700	77,000	6.1
2005	77,800	5,100	82,900	6.2
2006	82,600	5,400	88,000	6.1
2007	84,000	5,500	89,500	6.1
2008	85,600	5,500	91,100	6.0
2009	86,800	5,600	92,400	6.1

[1]Scenario b. For details see Home Office (2004a)

deterrent or incapacitative effect is considered in Chapter 3 of this volume.

- The rise in the prison population does parallel the changes in sentencing mentioned earlier. This is because, with the exception of early release, the prison service has little ability to influence the numbers it has to deal with.

Sub-groups of the prison population

Changes in the proportions of different subgroups of the population are often higher than for the whole population. This is partly because there is no routine procedure for 'proofing' legislative and sentencing changes against their differential effect on minority groups.

Female prisoners

The proportion of female prisoners has risen from 3.6 per cent in 1980 to 6.2 per cent in 2004. This is partly because the increase has been primarily in women who would previously have been given a community sentence, and the proportion of females given community sentences is more like 12 or 13 per cent. The differences in sentencing for women are covered in more detail in Hedderman (2004) and updated in Home Office (2004c). Broadly speaking:

- The greater use of custody for females is not being driven by an overall increase in the seriousness of offending: e.g. in 2002, 2,740 females out of 8,800 sentenced to immediate custody were sentenced for shoplifting, hardly a very serious offence.
- The custody rate for females sentenced at Crown Court rose from under 30 per cent in 1994 to over 43 per cent in 2002. The custody rate in magistrates' courts for females was three times as high in 2002 as in 1994.
- The average length of sentence for females at the Crown Court rose from just over 18 months in 1994 to 25 months in 2002.

Minority ethnic groups in custody

The percentage of prisoners who are from minority ethnic groups in 2002 was 22 per cent for males and 29 per cent for females, compared with around 7 per cent of the general population of England and Wales. The percentage of prisoners who were foreign nationals was 10 per cent for males and 20 per cent for females. The population of foreign nationals has increased by 120 per cent since 1993 (the first year for which data are available) compared to an increase of 55 per cent in British nationals (see also Chapter 14 by Kemshall *et al.* in this volume).

Prison population on remand

This varied over the last decade from just over 10,000 in the first years of the 1990s to around 12,800 in 2002; this is a slower growth than for the prison population in general. The rise has been much faster for women on remand, where the numbers have risen from 389 in 1991 to 940 in 2002, and women now comprise 7.3 per cent of the remand population. For many people who are eventually sentenced to custody, the time spent on remand is counted as part of their sentence. However, only about 45 per cent of those remanded in custody by the Crown Court are actually sentenced to immediate custody at the end of their remand.

Legislation and policy initiatives affecting the prison population

General initiatives

Routinely published material (see Appendix 1 of Home Office 2002b) acknowledges that the main drivers of prison numbers are legislative and policy initiatives. Politicians tend to be more fatalistic: the present Home Secretary, David Blunkett, has said that prison numbers are a natural consequence of sentences handed down by the courts and if more prisons are needed then they should be built – although some more recent pronouncements, following the Carter Report, imply that the Home Office may have accepted that, given political will, prison numbers could be controlled.

The rise in prison numbers in England and Wales since 1990 has been primarily influenced by the following changes, acting in a cumulative fashion, and influencing sentencers in the way they deal with individual cases before them. Early changes mainly favoured restrictions on custodial sentences:

- The Criminal Justice Act 1988 tightened the restrictions on the use of custody for those under 21, and increased maximum sentences for certain firearms offences and cruelty to children. To balance this in terms of prison numbers, some offences such as criminal damage were made summary below £2000 and there were restrictions on imprisonment for fine default. As a result there are now very few people in prison for fine default, e.g. less than 50 on average during 2001.
- In 1991 and 1992 new offences of aggravated vehicle taking and dangerous driving were created, which led to more prison sentences.
- The Criminal Justice Act 1991 made many changes, with the general rule that custody should be reserved for the most serious offences and punishment should reflect primarily the seriousness of the offence ('proportionality' and 'just deserts'), with previous convictions not being relevant in most cases.

As a result of these changes, the prison population fell to a low level of around 42,000 in January 1993. However, the reduction in the prison population as a result of the 1991 Act was very short-lived and by the end of 1993 the prison population was rising fast. This was primarily due to:

- new Conservative ministers declaring that 'prison works', a rhetoric that had been absent from the Conservative ministers who passed the 1991 Act;
- the Court of Appeal judgment in *Cunningham* (1993) 14 Cr App R (S) 444, which uncoupled the concepts of 'proportionality' and 'just deserts' (see Windlesham 1996, Faulkner 2001, Tonry 2004).

From then on legislation, and ministerial speeches pressing the need for legislation, became progressively more severe, almost certainly convincing sentencers that they too should become more severe in individual cases:

- The Criminal Justice and Public Order Act 1994 gave courts the power to give long sentences to children from the age of 10 to 13 and raised maximum sentence lengths for children aged 15 to 17. It also created Secure Training Centres for juveniles.
- The Offensive Weapons Act 1996 increased sentences for carrying offensive weapons, including knives.
- The Crime (Sentences) Act 1997 introduced 'Plea before Venue' and is estimated to have reduced the prison population by around 500. It also imposed mandatory sentences for repeat offenders: e.g. a life sentence for repeat serious sexual or violent offenders; seven years for repeat offenders convicted of drug trafficking; and three years for repeat burglars. These provisions are still taking effect, but fewer people are being sentenced under these provisions than was originally thought likely.
- The Crime and Disorder Act 1998 replaced the sentence of detention in a Young Offender Institution (YOI) with the Detention and Training Order (DTO), increasing the population by around 200.

There are also other administrative changes that affected the prison population, e.g.:

- From November 1999 measures to reduce delays in court (the 'Narey' measures) were introduced, reducing numbers held on remand by some 1,200.
- From January 1999, Home Detention Curfew (HDC) was introduced for some prisoners coming to the end of their sentence. This has since been extended in various ways, so that now more than 3,000 prisoners at any one time are serving their sentences in the community under HDC, relieving the pressure on the prison estate.
- From April 2001, the introduction of targets to 'close the justice gap' by increasing the number of offenders brought to justice by some 200,000 each year by 2005, has increased the flow of people through the courts, with a consequent effect on prison numbers.

The latest change in legislation, the Criminal Justice Act 2003, attempts to introduce consistency in sentencing, with tougher sentences for serious and persistent offenders and robust innovations in sentencing, especially to short custodial sentences. However, commentators are divided in their analysis of the likely effect of this Act, several complaining that it gives sentencers far too many alternatives for dealing with offenders. The effect on the prison population will be difficult to determine, as it depends on the speed with which the various aspects are implemented. A Home Office statement in November 2003 implied that the tougher sentences would be implemented in 2005, thus increasing numbers, but generic community sentence and other aspects that would reduce prison numbers would not be implemented until later.

Politicians of both parties have defended each of these changes during the last ten years in sentencing terms. However, politicians have never openly discussed the cumulative effect of ten years of punishment initiatives on sentencers, the media and the public; and the resulting increase in prison numbers from 42,000 to 74,000 has been accepted by politicians as no more than a natural consequence of sentencing decisions. This is in contrast, as we shall see below, with some other jurisdictions, in which prison numbers themselves have been the subject of a great deal of public discussion.

Initiatives for the treatment of young people

There have been fundamental changes to the treatment of young people in England and Wales since 1998 and it is useful to look at these.

Scotland has very different arrangements for young offenders from those of England and Wales or Northern Ireland (Bottoms and Dignan 2004). Broadly speaking, the English and Scottish systems pursue their common commitment to utilitarian goals in very different ways. In Scotland, a unified welfare-based system deals with both offenders and those in social need under the age of 16. It separates functions between the courts as arbiters and children's hearings as treatment tribunals. The section below considers the situation in England and Wales, where recent changes have been fundamental.

In England and Wales a correctionalist system committed to preventing offending has evolved since 1998 with a number of institutional changes, overseen by a new body called the Youth Justice Board (YJB) and involving a large number of multi-agency local youth offending teams (YOTs).

A summary of the work of the first five years of this new system was published by the Audit Commission in early 2004 (Audit Commission 2004) and concluded that the new system was a considerable improvement on the old in that young offenders:

- are much more likely to receive an intervention;
- are dealt with more quickly;

Table 2.13 Offenders dealt with in England and Wales under the aegis of the YJB: number of disposals: 2002–3

Type of disposal	Male	Female	Total
Total	135,546	31,379	166,925
Of which			
Pre-Court			
Police reprimand	34,012	13,197	47,209
Final warning alone	5,304	1,563	6,867
Final warning and intervention	15,477	4,189	19,666
First-tier Sentence			
Absolute discharge	3,507	417	3,924
Bind over	1,602	368	1,970
Compensation order	3,112	515	3,627
Conditional discharge	5,883	952	6,835
Fine	9,493	743	10,236
Referral order	22,578	4,778	27,356
Reparation order	3,580	638	4,218
Community Sentence			
Action Plan order	4,554	844	5,398
Attendance Centre order	2,813	238	3,051
Community Punishment and Rehabilitation order	1,546	111	1,657
Community Punishment order	3,069	177	3,246
Community Rehabilitation order	1,856	300	2,156
Curfew order	1,183	110	1,293
Supervision order	9,012	1,682	10,694
Custody			
DTTO (4 months)	2,195	165	2,360
DTTO (4–24 months)	3,817	297	4,114
Section 90–91 (longer custodial sentence)	451	36	487

Source: Youth Justice Board (2004a).

- are more likely to make amends for their wrong-doing;
- (who are on bail) are less likely to offend;
- are likely to be dealt with using more constructive and cheaper options such as the Intensive Supervision and Surveillance Programmes (ISSPs).

Moreover, magistrates in particular are very satisfied with the services they receive from YOTs.

The very wide scope of the work of the Youth Justice Board and the local youth offending teams can be seen from a summary of the actions taken with young people in 2002–3 (see Table 2.13).

A large number of youth interventions occur outside the court situation:

Table 2.14 Sentenced population of young people in prison service custody, England and Wales: 1991–2003

England and Wales	Numbers		
Year	**Males**	**Females**	**Total**
30 June figures			
1991	5,683	110	5,793
1992	5,443	139	5,572
1993	4,925	156	5,081
1994	5,137	139	5,276
1995	5,659	183	5,842
1996	6,363	252	6,615
1997	7,698	251	7,949
1998	8,212	309	8,521
1999	8,025	318	8,343
2000	8,160	377	8,537
2001	8,315	391	8,706
30 November figures			
2002	8,593	486	9079
2003	7,946	384	8330

Source: Home Office (2002b, 2004a).

- Forty-five per cent of interventions are pre-court.
- A further 33 per cent of interventions are first tier, such as referral orders, reparation or compensation orders.
- Also, interventions are tailored to the characteristics of the individual: this can be demonstrated by noting that the proportion of total interventions with females is around 18 per cent, the proportion of first-tier interventions with females is 26 per cent and the proportion of female interventions that end up in custody is 7 per cent.

The net effect of all these changes in England and Wales on the numbers of young people in custody is shown in Table 2.14.

Not all young people in custody end up in prison service custody (Young Offender Institutions); there is a smaller number in local authority secure accommodation or Secure Training Centres. But despite the various new initiatives in youth justice, there has been a gradual rise in the population of young people in prison service custody in England and Wales up to 2002 that parallels the rise in the general prison population. However, around 2003 the position started to change.

The success of YJB policies was shown by figures on prison places published for November 2003, which revealed that the number of young people in custody had fallen by nearly 700 since November 2002. Although detailed statistics have not yet been published by the Home Office, in February 2004 the YJB stated that 'it would reduce the number of places commissioned from the prison service following a decrease of 13% in the numbers of under-18s in custody during 2003 . . . It would reduce the number of places at Castington YOI from 280 to 160 and withdraw all places from Onley YOI.' (Youth Justice Board 2004). Despite this fall, the number of young people in custody is likely to remain very much more than in 1993 for a long time.

Moreover, the recent reduction may be short-lived. The Anti-Social Behaviour Act 2003 was implemented in early 2004 and magistrates were encouraged to make more use of anti-social behaviour orders (ASBOs). Breaching these orders could lead to imprisonment. There were over 1,000 orders made during the first three months of 2004, especially on young people. Although many of these seem to be discouraging criminal behaviour, some are thought to have led to young people being committed to custody earlier than under previous legislation. At the time of writing (May 2004) this seems to be resulting in a reversal in the fall in young people in custody.

Net effect of policy initiatives

The overall position, in March 2004, is thus of a continued increase in total prison numbers from 42,000 in 1993 to over 75,000 in England and Wales by May 2004, with no sign of a reversal in the overall trend.

Comparisons with other jurisdictions

The World Prison Population List (Walmsley 2004) states in its fifth edition that England and Wales in 2002 had a prison population rate of 141 per 100,000 population, the highest in Western Europe. Scotland was not far behind at 129, but by contrast Northern Ireland's rate was only 70.

Such comparisons are based on good statistics with few caveats about data. However, they make no allowance for other factors that influence prison numbers: the crime rate; the extent to which crimes are cleared up; the extent to which accused people are remanded in custody; the length of pre-trial detention; the extent to which courts impose custodial sentences and the length of such sentences; the extent to which sentences are suspended; and the extent to which young offenders in residential establishments are counted as being within the official 'prison population'.

A complete comparison of prison rates would involve building a model that attempted to allow for all these factors. Various authors have tried to allow for some of these: for example, Pease (1994) has related imprisonment rates to police crime rates as well as showing that national prison populations are driven more by sentence lengths than by numbers of those found guilty, confirming the point made earlier. Relating prison numbers to crime rates does not, surprisingly, seem to have gained much favour among analysts, although those arguing for a higher prison population have used it. However, there is value in considering, in Table 2.15, two indicators that compare prison numbers with crime rates: column 6 relates prison numbers to police recorded crime, and column 7 relates prison numbers to the population who have experienced one or more crimes.

Although there are some caveats to these new comparisons,[6] column 6 produces some interesting results in that England and Wales and Scotland no longer have the highest rates in Western Europe. Because of their lower crime rates, countries such as Austria, Greece, Italy, Portugal, Spain and Switzerland are now above them, and Germany, France and the Netherlands are at broadly similar levels. Less can be deduced from column 7, as there are so many missing countries.

The general message is that England and Wales, and Scotland, no longer stand out alone above other European countries, although too much should not be deduced from these figures: for example, for England and Wales it needs to be acknowledged that this is partly because of the change in counting rules for recorded crime, discussed earlier in the chapter, which has recently increased the official crime rate.

Managing prison populations

Whatever comparisons of prison numbers at any one time are used, it is perhaps more important to look at comparisons of trends over time. It is accepted by many commentators that, to quote Tonry (2004), 'a jurisdiction that wants to take control of its prison population and related expenditure can do so.'

Also, Hofer (2003) speaks of prison numbers as being a political construct, in the sense that prison populations are not, as is sometimes stated by politicians, the inevitable consequence of individual sentencing decisions, but are a choice made by politicians, taking into account public acceptability, media comment, resource costs and other social priorities.

Such commentators agree that, as we have shown above, crime rates do not determine prison numbers nor do prison numbers significantly influence crime rates (see Tonry 2004). There are many examples of jurisdictions that have successfully reduced or stabilised prison populations without the crime rate increasing as a result. The implication of the Home Office response to the Carter Report, with its attempt to ensure that the prison population of England and Wales does not rise above 80,000, is that the present UK government would support this capping of the prison population. However, whether this would survive the continuing pressure for greater penal severity stemming from media pressure and increased terrorist activity in Europe remains to be seen.

Table 2.15 Comparisons of prison populations, 2002

Country	Prison population	Recorded crime figures (millions – HOSB 12/03)	Overall prevalence rate of crime (% victimised once or more)	Prison population per 100,000 population	Prison population per 100,000 recorded crimes	Prison population per 100,000 population who were victimised once or more
England and Wales	74,500	5.5	26	141	1,355	542
Scotland	6,600	0.42	23	129	1,571	561
Northern Ireland	1,220	0.14	15	70	871	466
Austria	8,100	0.52	—	100	1,558	—
Denmark	3,400	0.47	23	64	723	278
Finland	3,600	0.36	19	70	1,000	368
France	55,400	4.06	21	93	1,364	443
Germany	81,200	6.36	—	98	1,277	—
Greece	8,500	0.44	—	80	1,932	—
Italy	56,600	2.16	—	100	2,620	—
Netherlands	16,200	1.22	25	100	1,328	400
Norway	2,700	0.32	—	59	844	—
Poland	83,100	1.39	23	218	5,978	948
Portugal	14,300	0.37	15	137	3,865	913
Spain	56,100	1.01	19	138	5,554	726
Sweden	6,500	1.19	25	73	546	292
Switzerland	5,000	0.28	18	68	1,786	378
Australia	22,500	1.47	30	115	1,530	383
Canada	36,000	2.41	24	116	1,494	483
Japan	67,300	2.74	15	53	2,456	347
USA	2,033,300	11.85	21	701	1,716	3,338

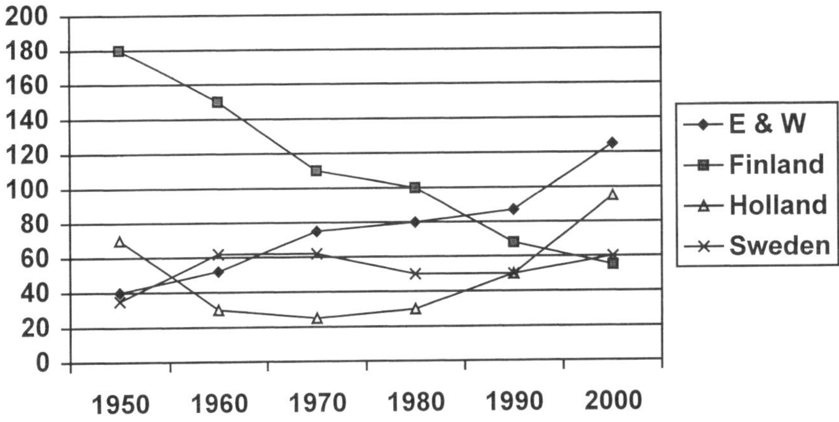

Figure 2.4 Trends in prison populations 1950–2000 in four jurisdictions: England and Wales, Finland, Holland, and Sweden (rates per 100,000 population)

Finally, we can consider trends since 1950 in four comparable jurisdictions – England and Wales, Finland, Sweden and Holland – to show how different politicians have taken different views about prison numbers. These Western European jurisdictions are all members of the EU, with similar democratic institutions. However, their prison populations have shown very different trends in the last half-century.

In England and Wales rates of prison population have increased steadily since the 1950s, although policy interventions reduced the rates between 1991 and 1993 and in 1999 and 2000 (see Tables 2.11, 2.12 and 2.14). During the 1990s there was no corresponding increase in crime (see Table 2.2).

In Finland there has been a steady reduction in prison rates from a very high level, reflecting Finland's previous experience under Russian domination, when high levels of prison numbers were part of the Russian-influenced justice policy. This decrease has been 'The result of a conscious and systematic criminal policy' (Lappi-Seppala 1998) and technically the decrease was brought about by two groups of pressures: de-penalisation, suspended sentences and the use of community service, and the use of shorter prison sentences and more parole.

In Holland there was an anti-penal policy in the 1950s and 1960s, leading to shorter sentences, followed by a period of resource constraints and restrictions on the use of prison. From the mid-1970s there was pressure to expand prison capacity, and rates have increased broadly since then. A leading Dutch criminologist has summarised this:

> . . . the Dutch criminal justice system and the Ministry of Justice have long been operated by a liberal and tolerant elite of experts and

> high-ranking civil servants ... However, this situation has changed dramatically as the numbers of victims of petty offences increased. Moreover crime became a highly topical and marketable subject in the media . . . pressures on the goverment, Parliament and the judiciary for tougher laws and harsher penalties increased. (Junger-Tas 2001: 188)

Swedish prison numbers have been remarkably stable during the last half-century: a rising population during the 1950s was succeeded by a fall in the 1960/70s, as grassroots anti-penal philosophy began to dominate. For some time the population was actually capped by legislation. Since the 1970s there has been a 'successful attempt at keeping prison rates under control in line with ambitions to reduce the negative aspects of sentences' (Hofer 2003). However, the present position is that there are now plans to expand prison capacity to reduce prison overcrowding. Unlike the 1960s in Sweden, the demand for more and longer prison sentences is now an accepted part of public discussion, and the public and politicians are reacting to this.

Conclusions

The main conclusions from the statistics presented in this chapter are:

- Trends in crime, victimisation and punishment are not the inevitable consequences of social and economic forces that cannot be controlled.
- Trends in punishment result from political action (or inaction) manifested in criminal justice structures, resources made available, and government priorities in public expenditure and political judgment about the level of crime acceptable to the general public.
- Governments and justice agencies can control the size of their prison populations if they want to.
- More study should be made of jurisdictions in Europe that have reduced the prison numbers by introducing the concept of administrative crime for minor offences and who give their prosecution service powers to impose financial sanctions for such offences.
- Youth justice policies in England and Wales since 1998 seem to be promising. However, even in this area, the advent of anti-social behaviour orders could adversely affect the useful work being carried out by local YOTs.
- It is important to ensure that new legislation does not have an unfair impact on sub-groups such as women offenders or minority ethnic offenders.

- The public as a whole needs more education in understanding the impact of criminal justice policies and in the measures of crime.

Notes

1 As England and Wales, Scotland and Northern Ireland have very different criminal justice and statistical systems, it is not possible to produce meaningful statistics for the whole of the United Kingdom.

2 In 1980, in England and Wales the only crime statistics published were in the annual *Criminal Statistics*. This represented the national and local totals of crimes recorded by the police. However, the lack of any quality assurance process meant that, despite Home Office counting rules, there was little consistency among police forces. Differences between forces represented local structures for collecting data as much as real differences (Farrington and Dowds 1984), and at that time there were no national victim surveys. Crimes recorded by the police had increased from half a million in 1950 to 2.7 million in 1980, but by current standards there was relatively little public concern about crime levels.

The police now maintain large IT records about crimes committed. These are fed to the Home Office, which produces a large number of statistical volumes and research reports on all aspects of crime and justice. From 1 April 1998, new counting rules for recording crime were introduced and applied on a more consistent basis. A large number of new data sources have also grown up: chief among these are the large-scale victim surveys such as the British Crime Survey in England and Wales; the Scottish Crime Survey and the Northern Ireland Crime Survey. These concentrate on asking members of the public questions such as the extent of victimisation, the reporting of crime and the circumstances of crimes reported.

3 The main limitations of police recorded crime statistics are:

- They are heavily dependent on what kinds of offence it is decided to include: e.g. in the USA no drugs offences are included in the principal 'crime count'.
- Their level is even more dependent on the counting rules applied. In England and Wales, these rules are set down by the Home Office and relate to how many and what types of crime should be counted in certain circumstances.
- They do not include crimes the public do not know about, or decide not to report. So, for example, many small-scale crimes are not reported to the police; especially if no insurance claim is likely to be involved.
- Police officers have a large element of discretion about what they choose to record; especially when they disbelieve the public, consider the event too trivial or not really an offence.
- It is known that some police officers decide not to record certain crimes in order to enhance their own measures of success: e.g. to improve their clear-up (detection) rate.
- They are heavily dependent on public attitudes to reporting crime: e.g. the proportion of rapes reported increased greatly throughout the last 20 years of the twentieth century due to the setting up of rape centres for women.
- They are subject to fluctuation if the police concentrate their efforts on a particular offence type: e.g. street crime, as a response to political pressure in 2002.

- Conversely, police may choose not to notice or count certain offences if there is political discussion about de-criminalisation: e.g. 'indecency between males' in the 1960s or cannabis offences at the start of the twenty-first century.
- In England and Wales, crime statistics do not include crimes recorded by police forces such as the British Transport Police and the Ministry of Defence Police. Neither do they include offences detected by private security agencies, such as store detectives, if these decide not to prosecute.

4 The detailed vision of the Simmons Report required:
- A renewed understanding of the requirements of government statistics in an age of information-based policy;
- A step-change in the use of technology and sharing of information between local and national authorities;
- Revitalising the organisational framework to manage information and make joined-up government a reality;
- Smarter presentation of information to input into strategic prioritisation and performance management;
- Giving the police and the Home Office better analytical tools to deliver improvements in society.

5 The main limitations of crime surveys are:
- As sample surveys they produce only estimates, to a certain degree of confidence, and this means that they cannot always distinguish small rises or falls in crime levels. However, sampling variation can be reduced by increasing the sample size, as with the BCS after 2001.
- The response rate for surveys such as the BCS varies between different subgroups: e.g. by age, gender, household composition. This requires complex adjustments to the results by means of what is called calibration weighting (see Simmons *et al.* 2002: 178).
- Children under sixteen are usually excluded, as is crime experienced by other than households. The latter point can be remedied by conducting surveys of commercial or public businesses (see Mirrlees-Black and Ross 1996).
- Changes in methodology can themselves bring changes in response, independent of real crime changes.
- Not all crime reported to the police can be captured by crime surveys and vice versa. Therefore comparisons can be made only for a subset of all crime.
- Crime surveys usually exclude sexual offences, because of the small number reported to the survey and concerns about the unwillingness of victims to report such offences.
- Surveys are not usually large enough to give good estimates for local areas.

6 Apart from the deficiencies of the statistics mentioned above, which can induce relationships that are statistical artifacts, the prison population in any one year is made up of those committing crimes in many different previous years; people can be sent to prison for other reasons than committing crimes recorded by the police: e.g. by being held on remand awaiting trial even though eventually found to be innocent; for not paying a fine; for committing some non-recordable (e.g. motoring) offences.

References

Allen, J. and Wood, M. (2003) *Crime in England & Wales: Quarterly Update to June 2003*, Home Office Statistical Bulletin 13/03 [www.homeoffice.gsi.gov.uk].

Audit Commission (2004) *Youth Justice 2004. A Review of the Reformed Youth Justice System* (London: Audit Commission).

Barclay, G. and Tavares, C. (2003) *International Comparisons of Criminal Justice Statistics 2001*, Home Office Statistical Bulletin 12/03 [www.homeoffice.gov.uk/rds/pdfs2/hosb1203.pdf].

Bottoms, A. E. and Dignan, J. (2004) 'Youth Justice: in Great Britain', in M. Tonry and A. N. Doob (eds) *Youth Crime and Youth Justice: Comparative and cross-national perspectives* (Chicago: University of Chicago Press), pp. 21–184.

Carter, P. (2003) *Managing Offenders, Reducing Crime: A New Approach* (London: Home Office Strategy Unit).

Carter, P. (2004) *Alternatives to Custody*, see press notices for 7 January 2004, [www.homeoffice.gov.uk].

Councell, R. and Simes, J. (2002) *Projections of Long-term Trends in the Prison Population*, Home Office Statistical Bulletin 14/02 [www.homeoffice.gov.uk/rds/pdfs2/hosb1402.pdf]

Farrington, D. and Dowds, E.-A. (1984) 'Disentangling criminal behaviour and police reaction', in D. P. Farrington and J. Gunn (eds) *Reactions to Crime* (Chichester: John Wiley).

Faulkner, D. (2001) Crime, *State and the Citizen: A field full of folk* (Winchester: Waterside Press).

Flood-Page, C. and Taylor, J. (2003) *Crime in England and Wales 2001/2*, Home Office Statistical Bulletin 01/03 [www.homeoffice.gov.uk/rds/pdfs2/hosb103.pdf]

Hedderman, C. (2004) 'Why are more women being sentenced to custody?', Chapter 4 in G. McIvor (ed.) *Women Who Offend* (London, Jessica Kingsley).

Von Hofer, H. (2003) 'Prison populations as political constructs: the case of Finland, Holland and Sweden', *Journal of Scandinavian Studies in Criminology and Crime Prevention*, July 2003, 4(1), 21–38.

Home Office (2001) *Criminal Statistics, England and Wales, 2000*, Cm. 5312 (London: Home Office).

Home Office (2002a) *Criminal Statistics, England and Wales, 2001*, Cm. 5696 (London: The Stationery Office).

Home Office (2002b) *Prison Statistics, England and Wales, 2001*, Cm. 5743 (London: Home Office).

Home Office (2003b) *Criminal Statistics, England and Wales, 2002*, Cm. 6054 (London: Home Office).

Home Office (2004a) *Prison Population Brief*, November 2003 [www.homeoffice.gov.uk/rds].

Home Office (2004b) *Home Office Reply to the Carter Report* [www.homeoffice.gov.uk].

Home Office (2004c) *Statistics on Women and the Criminal Justice System* [www.homeoffice.gov.uk/rds].

Home Office (2004d) Home Office Counting Rules for Recorded Crime: General rules (London: Home Office) [www.homeoffice.gov.uk/rds/pdfs2/countgeneral04.pdf].

Hough, M. and Mayhew, P. (1983) *The British Crime Survey*, Home Office Research Study 76 (London: Home Office).

Junger-Tas, J. (2001) 'Dutch penal policies changing direction' in M. Tonry (ed.) *Penal Reform in Overcrowded Times* (Oxford/New York: Oxford University Press), pp. 179–189.

Kershaw, C., Chivite-Matthews, N., Thomas, C. and Aust, R. (2001) *The 2001 British Crime Survey*, Home Office Statistical Bulletin 18/01 (London: Home Office) [www.homeoffice.gov.uk/rds/pdfs2/hosb1801.pdf].

van Kesteren, J, Mayhew, P. and Nieuwbeerta, P. (2001) *Criminal Victimisation in Seventeen Industrial Countries: Key findings from the International Crime Victims Surveys* (The Hague: WODC).

Lappi-Seppala, T. (2000) 'The fall in the Finnish prison population', *Journal of Scandinavian Studies in Criminology and Crime Prevention*, 1, 27–40.

Lockhart, B. (1994) *Crime Statistics and Surveys in Northern Ireland*, [www.cain.ulster.ac.uk/othelem/research/escr7.htm].

Maguire, M. (2002) 'Crime statistics' in M. Maguire, R. Morgan and R. Reiner (eds) *The Oxford Handbook of Criminology*, 3rd edition (Oxford: Oxford University Press), pp. 322–375.

Mirrlees-Black, C. and Ross, A. (1996) *Crime against Retail and Manufacturing Premises: Findings of the 1994 Commercial Victimisation Survey*, Home Office Research Study 146 (London: Home Office).

Pease, K. (1994) 'Cross-national imprisonment rates: limitations of method and possible conclusions', *British Journal of Criminology*, 34, 116–130.

Police Service of Northern Ireland (2004) *Recorded Crime in Northern Ireland: 2002/3* [www.psni.gov.uk].

Prison Service (2004) [www.hmprisonservice.gsi.gov.uk].

Scottish Executive (2002) 'The 2000 Scottish Crime Survey: First results', *Crime and Criminal Justice Research Findings* No. 51 (Edinburgh: Scottish Executive Central Research Unit).

Simmons, J. (2000) *Review of Crime Statistics: A discussion document* (London: Home Office).

Simmons, J. and colleagues (2002) *Crime in England and Wales 2001/2*, Home Office Statistical Bulletin 07/02 [www.homeoffice.gov.uk/rds/pdfs2/hosb702.pdf].

Smith, D. J. and Young, P. (1999) *Crime trends in Scotland Since 1950*, Chapter 2 in P. Duff and N. Hutton (eds), *Criminal Justice in Scotland* (Aldershot: Aldgate/Dartmouth).

Tonry, M. (2004) *Punishment and Politics: evidence and emulation in the making of English crime control policy* (Cullompton: Willan).

Walmsley, R. (2003) *World Prison Population List*, 4th edition, Home Office Findings 188 (London: Home Office).

Windlesham, D. (1996) *Responses to Crime*, Vol. 3, *Legislating with the Tide* (Oxford: Clarendon Press).

WODC (2003) *European Sourcebook of Crime and Criminal Justice Statistics*, 2nd edition, Dutch Ministry of Justice Report 212 (The Hague: WODC).

Youth Justice Board (2004), *YJB Annual Statistics 2002–3* [www.youth-justice-board.gov.uk].

Chapter 3

Empirical research relevant to sentencing frameworks

Anthony Bottoms

The choice of a sentencing framework for any given jurisdiction is a complex matter. It will depend in part on the overall constitutional arrangements in that country, and in part on normative choices. (Hence, for example, a strong argument can be mounted on normative grounds for proportionality to be the dominant concept within a sentencing framework: see von Hirsch 1993.) Such issues are of undeniable importance, but they are not the primary focus of this chapter. That is because the questions they raise cannot be settled by empirical research evidence, and this chapter is deliberately restricted to the topic of *empirical research relevant to sentencing frameworks*.

Why, then, this particular focus for this chapter? The main reason derives directly from the so-called 'Report of a Review of the Sentencing Framework for England and Wales', published in 2001 and more commonly known as the 'Halliday Report' after its principal author, John Halliday (Home Office 2001). In the introduction to that report, the review team state:

> The review was born out of a belief that the present sentencing framework suffers from serious deficiencies that reduce its contributions to crime reduction and public confidence. The report finds that belief to be well founded, although the framework also has strengths on which to build . . . (p. 1)

Three years after the publication of the Halliday Report, it seems worth returning to the empirical evidence, to judge whether Halliday's assessments of the potential of sentencing frameworks to contribute to 'crime reduction and public confidence' remain sound. That topic has also recently acquired an additional relevance because the 2004 Civitas Report for the *Rethinking Crime and Punishment* initiative[1] has made a controversial contribution to this debate (Green *et al*. 2004). In the first and longest part of this chapter, therefore, I shall revisit, post-Halliday and post-Civitas, the empirical research evidence on the extent to which criminal justice systems can, through adjustments in their sentencing framework, achieve reductions in crime by means of reform/rehabilitation, deterrence or incapacitation.

Later sections address more briefly two other matters relevant to the general topic of this chapter. The first concerns evidence published by the Home Office (see Jennings 2003) purportedly showing that the altered structural arrangements of the new (post-1998) English youth justice system have substantially reduced reoffending. The second concerns empirical evidence on a topic central to the concerns of the Coulsfield Commission, namely the extent to which sentences specifically designed as 'alternatives to prison' really are applied to persons who would otherwise be sent to prison.

The contribution of sentencing to crime reduction

I shall begin with three propositions that are, I believe, completely uncontroversial, but which are nevertheless worth restating in the present context.

First, crime rates are influenced by many factors other than sentencing. For example, since crime rates are highest among adolescent and young adult males, a demographic 'baby boom' or 'baby slump' can be expected to influence overall crime rates 15 plus years afterwards. Again, most advanced industrial countries experienced a sustained and substantial rise in crime for at least a quarter of a century in the years 1955 and onwards; there is widespread consensus that, in broad terms, a Dutch White Paper was right to attribute that increase to two main factors: first, the considerable increase in the availability of desirable and portable consumer goods during this period, and secondly a decline in the strength of traditional informal social controls in families, schools and local communities, plus an increased use of alcohol and drugs which 'forms part of this pattern of greater individualism' (see Netherlands Ministry of Justice 1985: 10). Turning to more technical matters, there is evidence that various kinds of 'situational crime prevention', such as target hardening and street lighting, can and often do reduce crime (Clarke 1995, Farrington and Welsh 2002); and economic conditions can also often do so, although the evidence on this is quite complex (see e.g. Field 1999, Raphael and Winter-Ebmer 2001, Fajnzylber *et al*. 2002). Given this multiplicity of potential influences on the crime rate, therefore, it is clear that one must be very careful to take such matters into account when assessing, for example, whether a substantially increased use of imprisonment in a given jurisdiction has directly caused a reduction in crime.

Second, it is also worth reflecting on another important limitation on the potential influence of sentencing on crime rates. According to the British Crime Survey, in 2001/2 only 42 per cent of household and personal crimes were reported to the police by the public.[2] Of these, an estimated 60 per cent were recorded by the police (=25 per cent of the original total); and, of the crimes recorded, only 23 per cent were detected (=six per cent of the original total) (Simmons *et al.* 2002: 5, 67). Since the sentencing system can have a direct effect only on those offenders who are detected, some potential limitations are immediately apparent. However, in assessing this matter, one must also bear in mind, first, that many of the undetected or unrecorded crimes might have been committed by some of those who are caught for other offences; and second that there might be a deterrent effect on potential offenders as well as a direct effect on actual offenders. (I return to some of these issues when discussing deterrence and incapacitation below.)

Third, there is no dispute among scholars that the existence of a criminal justice system (and hence of sentencing as part of that system) reduces crime below the levels that it would attain if there were no such system (or only a very poorly functioning system). To take just one example, in September 1944 the occupying Nazi forces in Denmark arrested the entire Danish police force, which for the remainder of the war was replaced by 'an improvised and unarmed watch corps, which was all but ineffectual except when the criminal was caught red-handed'. Robberies and thefts promptly increased dramatically (Andenaes 1974: 16–17).[3] However, in contemporary Western criminal policy debates, no-one is talking about abolishing the police or the criminal justice system. The key issue for present consideration, therefore, is whether specified changes in sentencing frameworks can make a measurable difference to crime rates. Otherwise stated, *to what extent do specific policy changes have marginal crime reductive effects?*

With this much by way of background, we can now turn to the three main mechanisms[4] that the Halliday Report considered as potentially contributing to marginal crime reductive effects arising from a reshaping of the sentencing system. These mechanisms are reform and rehabilitation, deterrence, and incapacitation.[5]

Reform and rehabilitation

In its quest for a way to achieve greater crime reduction through use of the sentencing framework, the Halliday Report placed by far its greatest emphasis on what it called 'reform and rehabilitation'. In contrast to deterrence and incapacitation (see later sub-sections), with regard to reform/rehabilitation Halliday thought that 'the position is a bit clearer, and more positive'. Referring to the so-called 'What Works' developments, and the implementation of associated policies (see Chapter 8 of this volume for details of these developments), the Report commented that 'although the evidence to support them is as yet incomplete, there is a strong enough case to justify looking for a [sentencing] framework that would be more supportive of the attempts being made to reduce reoffending' (Home Office 2001: para 1.69). In an earlier section of the Report which specifically discussed the 'What Works' developments, the following concluding comment was made:

> A reasonable estimate at this stage is that, if the programmes are developed and applied as intended, to the maximum extent possible, reconviction rates might be reduced by 5–15 percentage points (i.e. from the present level of 56% within two years to (perhaps) 40%). In the face of historically unchanging levels of reoffending, that would be a remarkable success. (Home Office 2001: para 1.49; see also Appendix 6 of the same report)

Sadly, three years later this appears to be a most unfortunate, and indeed in some ways a reckless, claim. It is important to spell out with some precision why this is so.

First, and most obviously, recent research evidence on the success of cognitive-behavioural programmes is substantially less promising than the earlier results on smaller-scale, more exploratory programmes.[6] It is very likely, though not yet certain, that these disappointing results are largely attributable precisely to the scale of the operation – that is, for a variety of reasons it is much easier to achieve success with small-scale programmes run by enthusiasts, with tight control over programme integrity, and with well-motivated groups of offenders, than it is when similar programmes are 'rolled out' on a national scale, as has recently been the case in England and Wales.

Second, Halliday's claim was in any case fairly reckless even at the time it was made. The reference, within the paragraph cited above, to *national* reconviction rates appears to suggest that the new 'What Works' programmes might be applied to all offenders in prison and on probation, and that an across-the-board reconviction reduction of up to 15 percentage points could be achieved. The busy policy-maker reading the paragraph was given no hint that, at that date, 'What Works' programmes were actually being applied to only a smallish minority of offenders in prison and on probation.[7] Moreover, it is a cardinal principle of the 'What Works' philosophy that programmes should be carefully targeted, so that they are applied to offenders likely to be suitable for them, and to respond to them, rather than 'across the board' (i.e. 'risk and responsivity': see McGuire and Priestley 1995); and offenders are regularly rejected from programmes for this reason. These simple points should clearly have led to a significantly less ambitious claim than Halliday made.

Third, Halliday's emphasis, within the cited paragraph, is solely on *offending behaviour programmes*, with other possible promising approaches to rehabilitation being left aside in silence. This is extremely unfortunate, since the evidence for the possible success of other approaches is not negligible (see for example Rex 2001, Farrall 2002).[8]

In summary, then, the empirical evidence on reform/rehabilitation is both more promising than Halliday realised (because his attention was virtually confined to offending behaviour programmes), and also less promising than he hypothesised (in relation to programmes). As other chapters in this volume make clear (see especially Chapters 7 and 8), there remains considerable promise in the rehabilitative approach. Whether that promise is sufficient for it to influence the sentencing framework substantially is another question, to which we must return.

Before leaving the topic of reform/rehabilitation, it is worth noting that the naïveté of Halliday's optimistic conclusions on this issue carries its own lessons. He is by no means the first person to have been over-impressed by an apparent 'new utopia' in crime policy; but history teaches that a more sober assessment is normally appropriate when framing policies.

Deterrence

'Deterrence', in a criminal justice context, is avoidance of a potential crime through fear of the consequences. It is customary to divide discussions of deterrence into two types: general and special. 'General deterrence' refers to the impact on *potential offenders* of some aspect of the criminal justice system. For present purposes, I will for obvious reasons focus on whether an enhanced severity of punishment will deter more potential offenders, rather than on the other main topic of general deterrence research, namely whether an enhanced likelihood of detection and conviction will deter more potential offenders. 'Special deterrence', by contrast, refers to the *deterrent impact on the offender being dealt with* by the criminal justice system on a specific occasion. For example, one famous piece of special deterrence research was concerned with whether offenders who were made subject to the 'short sharp shock' detention centre experiment of the early 1980s were more likely to refrain from subsequent offending as a result of going through this intendedly deterrent regime (Thornton *et al.* 1984).[9]

In considering empirical research relevant to sentencing frameworks, general deterrence is more important than special deterrence, because it potentially affects far more people. Moreover, at a commonsense level, it has considerable appeal: it seems to be obvious that if penalties are raised, fewer people will risk those higher penalties by choosing to offend. So, what conclusions can be reached by studying the empirical evidence relating to the possible general deterrent effects of higher sentencing levels?

A research review of precisely this question was funded by the Home Office in the early part of the 1997–2001 Labour government. It was conducted by the Cambridge Institute of Criminology, and I was a member of the research team (see von Hirsch *et al.* 1999).[10] The Halliday Report accurately summarised the main results of the Cambridge review, and adopted them as its own:

> The evidence, though limited in this area, provides no basis for making a causal connection between variations in sentence severity and differences in deterrent effects. The increased likelihood of detection and conviction, however, is statistically associated with declining rates of crime. (Home Office 2001: 129)

Almost as if Halliday did not fully believe this evidence, however, one of his final formal recommendations was that 'The Home Office should consider the scope for further research into ways of increasing current knowledge about the contributions of sentencing to crime reduction through deterrence and incapacitation' (Home Office 2001: 11).

Further research on general deterrence has indeed been published since the Cambridge review of 1999, though very little of it is British, and none is Home Office-funded. Indeed, a particular contribution has come from studies of variations on the 'three strikes and you're out' theme in a number of American states. A careful review of these studies, in the light of earlier research on general deterrence and sentence severity, has recently been published (Doob and Webster 2003). The conclusions of the review are uncompromising:

> Most [previous] reviews conclude that there is little or no consistent evidence that harsher sanctions reduce crime rates in Western populations. Nevertheless, most reviewers have been reluctant to conclude that variation in the severity of sentence does not have differential deterrent impacts. A reasonable assessment of the research to date – with a particular focus on studies conducted in the last decade – is that sentence severity has no effect on the level of crime in society. It is time to accept the null hypothesis. (p. 143)

If past experience is any guide, some might continue to resist this kind of conclusion simply on the grounds that it is counter-intuitive.[11] It may therefore be helpful to rehearse again here one of the key points made in the Cambridge review, which helps to explain the absence of more positive research results on the marginal general deterrent effectiveness of increased sentence severity (von Hirsch *et al.* 1999: 7). For an enhanced penalty level to have a general deterrent effect, it is logically necessary for *all* of five preconditions to be operative. The five preconditions are set out below, with some examples of circumstances in which they might fail to operate:[12]

1. Potential offenders must realise that the average severity of punishment for the offence in question has been raised, because if they do not realise this, deterrence is impossible. (However, offenders are not always well-informed about criminal justice changes.)
2. Potential offenders must take this altered severity into account at the time of the incident, i.e. when deciding whether or not to offend. (However, they might have consumed enough alcohol, or taken enough drugs, not to recall at that moment the enhanced severity; or they might be emotionally aroused by, for example, sexual excitement or the encouragement of their companions, so that the enhanced penalty is forgotten.)
3. Potential offenders must believe that there is a non-negligible likelihood of being caught. (If they really believe/expect/hope that they will not be caught, it does not, of course, matter that sentence levels have been raised; and, as many offenders are well aware, detection levels for many offences, especially property offences, are quite low.)
4. Potential offenders must believe that the enhanced penalty will actually be applied to them if they are caught and sentenced. (This is perhaps the least important of the five pre-conditions.)
5. Even if all the previous pre-conditions have been met (i.e. the potential offenders know about the enhanced penalty, take the enhanced risks into account, think they might get caught and think that if they are caught the higher penalty will be applied to them), for deterrence to be effective potential offenders must still be willing to refrain from offending, in the light of the enhanced penalty. (However, in certain circumstances, potential offenders might decide to take the risk anyway, for example if they are desperate for cash to get their next drug fix, or if they are dependent upon crime for their regular income.)

The conclusions of the Cambridge research review about the limited general deterrent effect of more severe sentences have been generally accepted not only by the Halliday Report but by most criminologists (see for example Doob and Webster 2003). Recently, however, the Civitas Report, mentioned earlier in this chapter, has concluded its review on deterrence and incapacitation in the following way: 'Prison works as a method of protecting the public and deterring criminals, but some commentators are reluctant to accept the truth of this conclusion because they feel that punishment and the rehabilitation of offenders are mutually exclusive alternatives' (Green *et al.* 2004: 33).

At first sight, this appears to challenge the general scholarly view. That perception is reinforced when one considers the only occasion on which the Civitas authors directly quote the Cambridge research; they cite *only* the proposition that von Hirsch *et al.* (1999) 'shared the view of other scholars that criminal punishment has now been shown capable of having deterrent effects' (Green *et al.* 2004: 23). Thus, the Civitas team say nothing about the main conclusion of the Cambridge review, i.e. that, as regards crime reduction, the evidence for the marginal general deterrent effects of greater certainty of apprehension/conviction is substantially more convincing than the evidence for the marginal general deterrent effects of enhanced severity of punishment.

On the other hand, much of the Civitas chapter on deterrence and incapacitation is concerned with comparing crime and punishment trends in the USA and in England and Wales since 1980, using as a main source the work of Langan and Farrington (1998).[13] In a crucial sub-section entitled 'The risk of punishment or the severity of punishment', the Civitas authors conclude that the evidence presented by Langan and Farrington is 'consistent with the theory' that the risk of punishment, rather than the severity of punishment, is 'the most important factor in reducing crime' (Green *et al.* 2004: 28–29). So, despite their rhetoric about 'prison works as a method of . . . deterring criminals' (Green *et al.* 2004: 33), it turns out that the Civitas authors are not, after all, challenging the generally accepted proposition that the marginal general deterrent effects of enhanced severity of punishment are slight, by comparison with enhanced detection/conviction. Perhaps, then, they simply mean that if there were no prisons, crime rates would be higher for reasons of both deterrence and incapacitation; but, if so, they are surely wrong to go on to say that 'some commentators are reluctant to accept the truth of this conclusion', because (see earlier discussion) such a conclusion is in fact totally uncontroversial. The real truth seems to be that the Civitas team, in their discussion of deterrence, have not focused carefully enough on the central issue in this debate, i.e. what are the marginal general deterrent effects of enhanced severity of punishment?

Incapacitation

Under the heading of incapacitation, the Halliday Report considered only evidence from England (Home Office 2001: paras 1.66–1.68, and Appendix 6 paras 25–28). It also considered only what has been described as 'collective incapacitation' (effects on crime rates of the higher use and/or greater length of custodial sentences in general, aimed at incapacitating active offenders of all kinds) rather than 'selective incapacitation' (which entails focusing on selected small groups of offenders believed to be especially dangerous, and giving them very long sentences in order to prevent particularly serious crimes, usually of a sexual or violent kind).

Selective incapacitation is an important topic, but is of little relevance to the 'alternatives to prison' debate, since those possibly targeted for 'dangerousness sentences' will in any event normally be sent to prison. However, the question of collective incapacitation seems clearly to be of interest to the Coulsfield Commission, since if there is evidence that the greater use of custodial sentences would reduce crime, that might constitute a strong political case for not prioritising resources for 'alternatives to prison'.

The Halliday Report's main substantive conclusion on incapacitation was based on modelling work by Home Office researchers. This research, it was reported:

> suggest[s] that the prison population would need to increase by around 15% for a reduction in crime of 1%. If efforts were targeted at particular groups of offenders,[15] for example those with drug problems who commit more offences per year, per offender, a 1% reduction in crime would require a smaller (7%) increase in the prison population. These estimates take no account of the dynamics of crime outside prison . . . (Home Office 2001: para 1.66)

How one assesses the choices posed by this kind of evidence is, in the end, a value judgement, placing the projected crime reduction against the economic and social costs of a larger prison population. The Halliday Report's own conclusion was that at present 'the available evidence does not suggest a case for changing the [sentencing] framework . . . for the sole purpose of increasing an "incapacitation" effect' (para 1.68).

Appendix 6 to the Halliday Report gives more details about the Home Office research referred to. In a survey of self-reported offending among males received into prison in early 2000, the average offending rate per prisoner in the period at liberty before incarceration was 140; and the incapacitation estimate represents 'the avoidance of crimes arising just from imprisoning a person' (p. 130).

Unfortunately, the Halliday Report did not seek to locate this single Home Office study within the extensive US literature on incapacitation. When looked at in that light, the Home Office study can be seen to fall into one of the two main categories of incapacitation research, i.e. the type based on individual offending rates and known as 'simulation studies' (Spelman 2000b). The literature further suggests that there are a number of difficulties with simulation studies which one needs to take into account when interpreting them. In particular, the incapacitation estimates vary widely in different studies depending on (i) differential estimates of average offence and arrest rates per offender; (ii) the extent of co-offending and the assumptions made about it (the worst-case assumption for an incapacitation policy is that all crimes where there are co-offenders would have been committed even if one offender was incarcerated); and (iii) the length of the typical criminal career (a matter of huge importance, because the 'age–crime curve' is a significant problem for any incapacitation strategy).[16]

On the first of these points (average offence rates) Nagin (1998b: 363) notes that the distribution of individual offence rates within a given prison population is often highly skewed, with a small percentage of the population committing crime at extraordinarily high rates. He provides a graph derived from a study of self-reported robberies among Californian prison inmates; in this sample, the mean rate of offending was 43.4 robberies per year at liberty, but the median in the same sample was as low as 3.75. No information is given in the Halliday Report about whether the mean and the median differed in a similar way in the Home Office study, but if they did the implications for the 'alternatives to prison' debate are considerable. We can assume that most detected prolific offenders are already in prison; the case for crime reduction through greater use of imprisonment will therefore depend on the offending rates of those currently receiving the more serious non-custodial penalties. If their offending rates are, as seems quite likely in the light of Nagin's analysis, well below the 140 per annum cited as the mean in the Home Office study, then the incapacitation estimates would obviously reduce. This matter is of some importance, as analysts such as Civitas have already taken Halliday's '140 per annum' figure and applied it in various projections (Green *et al.* 2004: 32).

Linked to this point is the issue of diminishing incapacitative returns when pursuing, in a given jurisdiction, a policy of sustained increases in imprisonment over a long period. In such a scenario, the early increases are very likely to have an incapacitative effect, and they can be expected to 'catch' a reasonable proportion of prolific offenders. However, when further increases in imprisonment are pursued, it is almost certain that more lower-frequency offenders will be caught in the incapacitative net, with diminishing returns for the policy.

I mentioned earlier that there were two main traditions in the US research on incapacitation. One, as we have seen, begins with individual offenders and their self-reported offending. The other tradition is more macro-level, or 'top down', using aggregate 'empirical data on crime rates, prison populations, and other possible causes of crime to link inputs and outputs' (Spelman 2000b: 423). According to Spelman (*ibid.*), this kind of method has the disadvantage that it cannot disentangle incapacitative and deterrent effects, but it is better suited than simulation studies to identify the full empirical effects of the increased use of prison.

And certainly, in the United States there has been plenty of scope for researchers to utilise this kind of research technique, because since 1970 there has been, in effect, 'a nationwide quasi-experiment of unprecedented scale' on the relationship between imprisonment and crime (Spelman 2000b: 419). The rate of *sentenced* prisoners per 100,000 population has risen from 100 in 1970 to 470 in 1999 (Conklin 2003: 81), a growth that has not been principally attributable either to a growth in crime or the number of arrests per crime. Indeed, according to Blumstein and Beck (1999), over the period 1980–1996 the growth in state incarceration for non-drug offences was not in any way attributable to a growth in crimes or arrests, but 42 per cent to an increased tendency to imprison arrested offenders, and 58 per cent to an increase in effective sentence lengths.[17]

So, in the US, a much higher proportion of known offenders now find themselves incarcerated, and for longer, than would have been the case thirty years ago. What effect has this so-called 'experiment in mass incarceration' (or incapacitation) had on crime rates?

The answer is that the 'top-down' researchers are not sure. There are many technical problems inherent in estimating incapacitation rates using this method, especially at a large-area level (see further below), and these problems have resulted in quite widely divergent estimates from different researchers working with much the same sets of statewide data, and using similar statistical techniques. (This divergence has recently reduced, but it remains real enough to demand serious hesitation before placing too much weight on a single study.) These technicalities were reviewed at length in Spelman's (2000b) authoritative *Crime and Justice* paper,[18] which highlighted three studies as reflecting 'a variety of definitions of "best"' (p. 481). The results of these studies was 'remarkably consistent'; namely that 'a one per cent increase in prison population (or, in one case, prison commitment) would reduce the aggregate Index Crime rate by between 0.16 and 0.31 per cent'. Otherwise stated, a ten per cent increase in the prison population would reduce crime by between 1.5 and three per cent, an estimate of incapacitative effect which is greater than that derived by Home Office statisticians for England and Wales using the simulation method (see above). There remains in these US studies, however, a fairly large difference between the upper and lower estimates of effect, and these differences could easily alter one's judgement in a cost-benefit assessment (that is, it is quite plausible that some would be willing to contemplate a ten per cent increase in imprisonment for a three per cent reduction in crime, but not for a 1.5 per cent reduction). Since there seems to be limited technical scope for reducing the scale of this upper/lower estimate difference using large-area data, the large-area level research leaves policy-makers with some very awkward dilemmas (Spelman 2000b).

More recently, Spelman (forthcoming) has become the first researcher in the US to utilise county-level data to study incapacitation. His justification for this innovation is that the relationship between unemployment and crime is significantly greater when analysed at a local rather than national level; that most crime is committed very locally (see Rengert *et al.* 1999, Wiles and Costello 1999); and that the variance in crime rates among the 254 counties in Texas in 1990 and 2000 was more than three times greater than it was among the 50 states in the US, suggesting that 'disaggregation may help us explain both why crime dropped on average and also why it differs so much from one county to the next'.

In his county-level analysis of Texas, Spelman (forthcoming) found that, during the 1990s, the expansion in the use of prisons and jails contributed substantially more than other factors to the drop in violent crime in Texas, and equally with other factors to the drop in property crime. Also, incapacitation was more important in driving crime down in Texas than in the US as a whole (compare Spelman 2000a). This last point reflected the fact that the prison building programme in Texas was much larger, on both a percentage and an absolute basis, than in any other state (the prison and jail populations increased in Texas by as much as 105,000 during the 1990s).

Hence, Texas' prison expansion was exceptionally effective at reducing crime, particularly violent crime, in the 1990s. But the cost implications of this huge prison expansion were of course massive, and Spelman's analyses of prison costs against the value of crime prevented showed a steady decline in the benefit : cost ratio from 1990 to 2000, with the ratio down to 0.4 by 2000. Moreover, as noted above, improvements in the economy and in policing also appeared to account for about half the reduction in property crimes during the 1990s. Hence Spelman (forthcoming) concludes his paper:

> Texas' primary response to the crime problem – massive incarceration – worked. Crime went down and prisons are the biggest reason. But the costs of this apparently successful policy appear to be greater than the benefits. If incarceration were the only means available of reducing crime, Texans would very likely be better off releasing inmates and putting up with a higher crime rate. Fortunately, this is not the only choice available. A growing economy and proactive police officers also appear to have been responsible for reducing Texas crime rates in the 1990s. If crime is to be reduced further in the next decade, it would be wise to turn our attention from prison construction to good jobs and effective policing.

In summary, then, we can conclude from the American experience: first, that prison expansion usually does have an incapacitative effect; second, that the extent of this effect is exceptionally difficult to measure, because of variations and skews in the offence-rate distribution when using simulation studies, and the limitations of large-area data (which most of the existing research has utilised) for macro-level studies; third, that the fact there is an incapacitation effect does not necessarily mean there is a *cost-effective* incapacitative effect; fourth, that after a time of prison expansion (but exactly when is very difficult to judge) diminishing returns from incapacitation set in because the most serious and prolific offenders are already incarcerated; and fifth, that other factors, such as the economy, are also very important in influencing local crime rates (see earlier discussion), and must always be properly taken into account if research estimates of incapacitative effects are to be meaningful.

The analysis of the American experience by the Civitas team does not take full account of these complexities. Their report simply (too simply) concludes that 'Two effects led to the fall in crime in America. First, there was a deterrent effect, and second, an incapacitation effect' (Green *et al.* 2004: 33).[19] On the other hand, Civitas is surely right to say that the very considerable increase in the use of custodial sentences in England and Wales since 1993 (see Chapter 2) will have had some incapacitative effect, since it is 'impossible to argue that incapacitating an additional 20,000 offenders on average a year had no effect at all on crime' (p. 33).

The real issue now, however, is whether further increases in the use of imprisonment in England and Wales would produce substantial further reductions in crime in a cost-effective way. The honest answer to this is that we don't know, because the detailed analyses have not been done. But given the importance of the 'diminishing returns' issue in incapacitation (see above), as well as other matters such as the age–crime curve (see note 16), we certainly do not at present have the data to make a positive case for further incapacitation. The Halliday Report's conclusion therefore still stands: 'the available evidence does not support a case for changing the [sentencing] framework . . . for the sole purpose of increasing an incapacitation effect' (Home Office 2001: para 1.68).

Overall assessment

Overall, then, the conclusion we have reached, on reconsidering Halliday's comments three years later, is that he was right to conclude that there is no strong body of empirical evidence favouring further increases in custody in order to achieve crime reduction through either incapacitation or enhanced general deterrence. Halliday's conclusions on rehabilitation, however, look substantially weaker than they did in 2001, and, sadly, he in any event overstated the case for rehabilitative effects at the time of his report.

Indeed, in the light of the discussions in this chapter, it is prudent to revisit the starting point of the Halliday Report which, as we have already seen, was 'born out of a belief that the present sentencing framework suffers from serious deficiencies that reduce its contributions to crime reduction and public confidence'. At the time of the announcement of the Halliday Report in summer 2000, a number of statements made by the Home Office seemed to suggest, as Andrew Ashworth has rightly put it, that the then government seemed 'determined not to restore and refurbish the 1991 Act [which was based on the principle of desert or proportionality], but rather to move towards a set of components based on individual and general prevention mixed with reparation' (Ashworth

2000: 89; see also the Home Office documents quoted on the same page). The Halliday Report drew back from a thoroughgoing preventive/reparative approach to sentencing, but clearly wanted to move the sentencing framework in a more preventive direction, especially as regards rehabilitation. In the light of the most recent research evidence, and the inherent limitations that any sentencing framework faces in trying to achieve crime reductions (see earlier discussions), it might now be more appropriate to consider retreating from Halliday's arguably over-simplistic conclusion that the pre-2001 sentencing framework 'suffers from serious deficiencies'. In particular, the principle of proportionality might have rather more to offer than the Home Office was willing to recognise when it set up the Halliday Review (see further the discussion in Chapter 16, below; on the Home Office's 2000 view of proportionality, see Ashworth 2000: 89). And if that is so, we might after all find that we can sensibly accommodate the promising approaches to rehabilitation outlined elsewhere in this volume within sentencing frameworks not all that different from those created by the 1991 Criminal Justice Act.

Youth justice[20]

Some might object to the conclusions of the preceding section, in the light of a research analysis that appears to claim very considerable crime-reductive success for the new English youth justice system. If these claims are right, are not the conclusions of the previous section overly modest and pessimistic?

The new English youth justice system was introduced by the Labour government in the Crime and Disorder Act 1998 and, after a period of piloting in selected local areas, it was 'rolled out nationally' in June 2000. The research analysis referred to was carried out by a Home Office researcher (Jennings 2003). It compares the one-year reconviction rates of a general cohort of young offenders dealt with in the first quarter of 2001 (by way of a reprimand, final warning, or court disposal, excluding custody)[21] with an intendedly equivalent 'baseline' sample dealt with in the first half of 1997, before the new youth justice reforms were promulgated.

The research is based on the use of a predictive model that makes use of logistic regression analysis on the 'prechange' group to calculate expected reconviction rates for the 'postchange' group. If expressed in the conventional way, the study then shows a reduction in the expected rate of reoffending in the 2001 sample by 7.7 percentage points,[22] a very large effect. However, the 'headline' claim in Jennings' report is even more dramatic – it argues that there was a 22.5 per cent reduction in reoffending, a figure that has been obtained by expressing the actual reduction in the expected rate as a percentage reduction on the predicted rate.[23]

Moving beyond the headline claim, an appendix table in Jennings' report provides data on the 'percentage improvement over the adjusted predicted rate' for each separate method of dealing with young offenders (pp. 10–11, Table A.1). According to this table, one disposal in particular had an exceptionally high percentage improvement in performance from 1997 to 2001, namely, the reprimand. This finding is not specifically highlighted in Jennings' text,[24] but the result makes the policy analyst immediately wary, for the reprimand is one element of the English youth justice system that changed very little from 1997 to 2001. The implication of the data, if taken at face value, is therefore that a virtually unchanged disposal has contributed particularly greatly to a very significant overall reduction in reoffending rates since the new youth justice system came into effect. Obviously, the validity of such a statement is not transparent, and the analyst necessarily wonders whether other factors might be in play.

Jennings provides data on the numerical distribution of her 1997 and 2001 samples on certain key variables (age, sex, principal current offence, etc.) and, from these data, proportions can easily be calculated. Two points in particular arise from such an analysis. First, the proportion of the 1997 sample who were cautioned was 65 per cent, but in the 2001 sample those 'reprimanded' or 'finally warned' (the post-1997 pre-court disposals, which replaced cautions) constituted 76 per cent of the total. Thus, within the research samples, the 'pre-court disposal rate' rose from 1997 to 2001, which is contrary to the national trend as shown in the published *Criminal Statistics*. Second, for the variable 'current principal offence', the proportion listed as 'other offence' rose from 10.5 per cent in 1997 to 30 per cent in 2001 – a very large increase. Both these reported differences suggest that there might well have been a significant change in the nature of the juvenile cases included within the utilised data samples (cases obtained from the Police National Computer) between 1997 and 2001. The possibility of any such change is not, however, considered in Jennings' report.

What are the implications of these matters for the claimed overall reduction in reoffending from 1997 to 2001? The key questions here seem to be, first, whether or not there has been a significant shift in the composition of the Police National Computer samples from Time 1 to Time 2, and second, whether any such changes are adequately controlled for within the multivariate model utilised in the research study.[25] These issues have been raised with the Home Office, and should become clearer in due course. For the moment, however, it seems most appropriate to remain agnostic on the question of whether Jennings' report provides solid evidence for the overall success of the new youth justice policies in preventing reoffending. That being the case, the Jennings report does not disturb the conclusions reached earlier in this chapter.

The use of sentences as 'alternatives to prison'

There used to be a substantial criminological literature in Britain on the topic of 'alternatives to custody' (see e.g. Bottoms 1987), but this has largely faded from the collective memory since the Criminal Justice Act 1991 set its face against the concept of 'alternatives' (see Chapter 1). In the light of the new climate created by the Criminal Justice Act 2003, the Carter Report and the Coulsfield Commission, it seems worth returning briefly to this topic in a chapter on 'empirical research relevant to sentencing frameworks'.

The prototypical 'alternative to custody' sentence in England and Wales is the suspended sentence, which has, almost from its inception, carried a statutory proviso[26] to the effect that the sentence is to be passed only if, in the absence of any power to suspend, the court would otherwise have passed a sentence of imprisonment. No other sentence has such a proviso.

Early studies of the suspended sentence (Sparks 1971, Bottoms 1981) showed, however, by inference from trends in sentencing data, that courts were tending to pass suspended sentences *not only* in cases where custody would otherwise have been passed, *but also* where another penalty (principally, probation or a fine) would have been passed. This was also shown to be particularly important in cases where a fresh offence was committed during the operational period of the suspended sentence, since such an offender could, on the second court appearance, receive two consecutive sentences of imprisonment where otherwise they might have received none (see the discussion in Chapter 1).

Since the early work of Sparks and Bottoms, two further pieces of evidence that throw light on the use of the suspended sentence in England have arisen, as a result of the following legislation:

(a) The abolition of the suspended sentence for offenders aged 17–21 by the Criminal Justice Act 1982 (which took effect in mid-1983).

(b) The near-abolition of the suspended sentence for offenders aged 21+ by the 'exceptional circumstances' provision of the Criminal Justice Act 1991 (which took effect in autumn 1992).[27]

In both cases, the natural expectation would be that the abolition (or near-abolition) of the power to suspend, coupled with the statutory provision that suspended sentences should be passed only if imprisonment would be imposed if the power to suspend did not exist, would result in an observable increase in the proportionate use of immediate imprisonment. So, other things being equal, if before abolition or near-abolition X per cent received immediate imprisonment and Y per cent a suspended sentence in the age-group in question, then immediately

Table 3.1 Males sentenced for indictable offences by type of sentence or order, 1980–1986 (%)

	Discharge/ fine	Community penalty	Custodial sentence†	Suspended sentence	Other	Total
(a) Age 17 and under 21						
1980	59	18	18	4	1	100
1981	55	21	19	4	1	100
1982	54	22	18	5	1	100
1983	53	24	19	2	1	100
1984	53	25	20	*	1	100
1985	51	27	21	*	1	100
1986	50	27	21	*	1	100
(b) Age 21+						
1980	59	9	17	12	1	100
1981	57	11	18	12	1	100
1982	55	12	19	12	1	100
1983	56	13	19	11	1	100
1984	54	14	20	11	2	100
1985	52	14	21	12	1	100
1986	51	14	21	12	1	100

†Immediate custodial sentence, includes partly suspended sentences from 1983 onwards (for age 21+ only).
*Not available as a sentence in this year.

after abolition the proportion sentenced to immediate custody should be (X+Y) per cent.

Tables 3.1 and 3.2 show what actually happened at the two relevant time periods.[28] In the case of the 1983 abolition for young offenders (see Table 3.1), use of immediate custody increased slightly from 1983 to 1986 for young adults, but it increased to an identical extent also for adult offenders, for whom there was at that time no change to the law relating to the suspended sentence. The figures for immediate plus suspended custody were, for adults: 1982, 31 per cent; 1986, 33 per cent; and for young adults 1982, 23 per cent; 1986, 21 per cent. In other words, custodial sentences as a whole declined for young adults when the suspended sentence was abolished, contrary to the generally upward trend in the use of custody. Most of the previously suspended cases seem therefore to have received non-custodial sentences after the change in the law.

Turning now to the 1992 near-abolition of adult suspended sentences, once again from 1990 to 1995 the immediate imprisonment rate rose to a similar extent for both young adults (for whom there was no change in the law) and for adults. The figures for immediate plus suspended custody were, for young adults: 1990, 15 per cent; 1995, 22 per cent; and for adults: 1990, 27 per cent; 1995, 25 per cent. In other words, custodial

Table 3.2 Males sentenced for indictable offences by type of sentence or order, 1990–1996 (%)

	Discharge/ fine	Community penalty	Custodial sentence†	Suspended sentence	Other	Total
(a) Age 18 and under 21						
1990	55	28	15	*	2	100
1991	52	30	16	*	2	100
1992	52	30	15	*	2	100
1993	51	30	17	*	2	100
1994	47	32	19	*	2	100
1995	45	31	22	*	2	100
1996	43	30	24	*	2	100
(b) Age 21+						
1990	56	15	17	10	2	100
1991	54	16	18	10	2	100
1992	54	18	18	8	3	100
1993	56	23	18	1	3	100
1994	52	25	20	1	2	100
1995	49	24	24	1	2	100
1996	47	24	26	1	3	100

†Immediate custodial sentence, includes partly suspended sentences in years up to 1992.
*Not available as a sentence of the court.

sentences as a whole declined for adults when the suspended sentence was restricted to 'exceptional circumstances' by the 1991 Act, contrary to the upward trend in custody for young adults. Thus, most of the previously suspended cases seem to have received non-custodial sentences after the change in the law. The clear inference, in both this instance and the 1983 change, must be that prior to abolition or near-abolition the suspended sentence was not being used as the legislation prescribed.

The Criminal Justice Act 2003 contains provisions which, when implemented, will abolish the 'exceptional circumstances' restriction on the suspended sentence, and allow that sentence to be imposed with community-penalty style conditions. In the light of the history of the suspended sentence, there is an obvious danger that this new sentence will be used in such a way that it includes not only cases that would previously have received a sentence of imprisonment, but also those that would previously have received a community penalty. Since fresh offences during the operational period of a suspended sentence are more likely to be dealt with custodially than are fresh offences committed during a community penalty, there is the same danger of 'backfiring' that existed in the early years of the suspended sentence, as identified by Sparks and Bottoms.[29]

However, there is other research evidence that, with careful work by the probation service or youth justice teams in their pre-sentence reports, plus good communications with the courts, these kinds of dangers can be successfully avoided when sentence options are specifically designated locally as 'alternatives to custody' (see in particular Raynor's [1998] evidence in the Afan project; and Bottoms [1995] on 'heavy and intermediate treatment' for juveniles in four local areas). It looks as if it might be very timely to return to this evidence, with practical intent.

Notes

1 Civitas, or 'the Institute for the Study of Civil Society', is an independent charity which, in its own words, aims 'to deepen public understanding of the legal, institutional and moral framework that makes a free and democratic society possible' (see the Civitas website [www.civitas.org.uk]). The *Rethinking Crime and Punishment* initiative has been funded by the Esmée Fairbairn Foundation as a 'strategic initiative' during the years 2001–2004 inclusive. The Coulsfield Commission was set up as part of the *Rethinking Crime and Punishment* initiative, but is an independent commission, free to reach its own views.

2 This is within the so-called 'comparable subset' of crimes where British Crime Survey data and police data can be directly compared.

3 It is interesting, and of relevance to this chapter, that this large increase occurred even though 'punishment was greatly increased for criminals who were caught and brought before the court' (Andenaes 1974: 17). This illustrates the point that sentencing policies can easily be of lesser importance, in relation to crime rates, than other social variables.

4 On the importance of the concept of social mechanisms in social science, see Hedström and Swedborg (1996), who argue for 'explanations that systematically seek to explicate the generative mechanisms that produce observed associations between events' (p. 281).

5 In its section on 'improved outcomes', the Halliday Report also briefly considered reparation. Whilst noting 'widespread interest' in restorative justice, however, Halliday concluded: 'Policy and practice in this field is not yet sufficiently developed in England and Wales to justify very specific new elements in the basic framework for sentencing, but the framework should be flexible enough to accommodate future developments of proven value' (Home Office 2001: para 1.70).

6 For probation programmes, see the full discussion in Chapter 8. In prisons, the published evaluations precisely chart the process described in the text. Two cognitive skills programmes ('Reasoning and Rehabilitation' and 'Enhanced Thinking Skills') delivered in prisons in the years 1992–1996 produced better outcomes in the (volunteer) treatment group of adult males serving sentences of two years or more than in a matched comparison group, especially among medium-risk prisoners (Friendship *et al.* 2002). Subsequent evaluations, for prisoners undertaking the same two programmes in later years, showed no

significant differences in outcome between programme starters and comparison groups. The first of these evaluations (Falshaw *et al.* 2003) was conducted with a volunteer treatment group of adult males serving sentences of six months or more, and receiving programmes delivered in 1996–98. The second evaluation, with larger samples (Cann *et al.* 2003) was conducted with both adult males (programmes delivered 1998–2000) and young offenders under 21 (programmes delivered 1995–2000); all participants were serving sentences of six months or more. The Civitas Report (Green *et al.* 2004: 43–4) has attempted to discredit the first of these evaluations (Friendship *et al.* 2002), but the Civitas critique is wholly unconvincing on technical grounds.

7 Numbers of completions for all accredited offending behaviour programmes in prisons (including 'Reasoning and Rehabilitation' and 'Enhanced Thinking Skills': see note 6) have been as follows in recent years: 1998–9, 3129 completions; 1999–2000, 4664; 2000–01, 5986; 2001–02, 6405; 2002–03, 7647 (all data taken from HM Prison Service Annual Reports). This is an impressive rate of increase, but given total prison population figures (see Chapter 2) its is clear that offending behaviour programmes are still being undertaken by only a minority of prisoners.

8 Of special relevance here is the desistance literature (for example Sampson and Laub 1993, Maruna 2001, Farrall 2002, Laub and Sampson 2003). This opens up a whole new agenda on the importance of informal social controls, and of motivation, in relation to the slowing down or termination of criminal careers; and this in turn is congruent with messages from the research on resettlement (Haines 1990). Ironically, the Halliday Report's proposals on the refashioning of short prison sentences are highly congruent with these strands of the research literature, although this research is not referred to in the Report.

9 For the record, in this research no special deterrent effect was discernible.

10 The Cambridge deterrence report is best read alongside another important review of the deterrence literature that appeared at about the same time: see Nagin (1998a).

11 My own view is that the substantive analysis of the review by Doob and Webster is correct, but that it is not necessarily correct to accept the null hypothesis, as they do. The reason for this is that, under the right conditions, there is no reason in principle why more severe sentences could not work as a deterrent. Hence, in certain situations (and/or among some groups of offenders) it is likely that enough of the relevant preconditions could be met for an aggregate deterrent effect to be discernible. To say this is, however, in no way to retreat from the clear message from the existing empirical research, as consistently shown in the reviews by Nagin (1998a), von Hirsch *et al.* (1999) and Doob and Webster (2003).

12 The wording here is not identical to that in the von Hirsch *et al.* review, but the concepts are the same.

13 The Civitas Report focuses only on the USA/England and Wales comparison. It is important to note, therefore, that other cross-national comparisons do not always produce identical results, at any rate using basic data: see for example the discussion in von Hirsch *et al.* (1999: 27–28); also the data for Scandinavia in Lappi-Seppälä (2001: 121), which present a very different pattern to the US/English contrast (imprisonment rates dropped dramatically in Finland from 1950 to 1997, but not in the other Nordic countries; but crime rate trends were similar in all four countries).

14 For fuller discussions of Langan and Farrington's important work, see von Hirsch *et al.* (1999: 25–27) and Doob and Webster (2003: 158–162).

15 This is a strategy normally known as 'categorial incapacitation'. It differs from selective incapacitation in being focused on groups rather than individuals, and it differs from collective incapacitation in being focused on a particular category of offenders, rather than on offenders generally. It can, however, be regarded as a sub-type of collective incapacitation.

16 The age–crime curve shows a peak of offending in the teenage years, and the early twenties as years when there is a particularly rapid decline in recorded involvement in criminal activity. Some of the peak reflects one-off offending, but 'remarkably, the age–crime curve for the general population appears to be replicated . . . for active, serious delinquents' (Laub and Sampson 2003: 91). The importance of this age distribution has repeatedly been stressed by researchers interested in desistance (e.g. Maruna 2001), but arguably its significance is still underrated in crime policy, including in relation to incapacitation (where its implication is that if one is not careful one will be 'incapacitating' some people who would have ceased to offend anyway). A further reinforcement of these issues is found in standard offender risk scores (such as the Offender Group Reconviction Scale [OGRS]), which routinely include age as a predictive variable (the older the offender, the lower the probability of reconviction); any incapacitation policy clearly needs to take this into account.

17 'Effective sentence lengths' means the length of time actually spent in prison, rather than the nominal sentence. If a prisoner is released early on parole, that also reduces his/her effective sentence length; hence, placing restrictions on parole (a commonly applied policy strategy in recent years) will increase average effective sentence lengths. It should be noted that, in the Blumstein and Beck study, the pattern for drugs offences was different from that described in the text; for drugs, the increase in incarceration was driven primarily by a growth in arrest rates and secondarily by an increased tendency to imprison those arrested.

18 As Spelman (2000b, and forthcoming) points out, one main cause of the divergence in estimates concerns whether or not a research study takes account of 'simultaneity', i.e. the fact that the size of prison populations can affect crime rates *and* that the level of the crime rate can affect the use of imprisonment. Studies that take explicit account of simultaneity, and try to disentangle these separate effects, are more likely to be accurate.

19 This claim is made despite the fact that the Civitas team cite without criticism the article by Spelman (2000a) on the 'limited importance of prison expansion'.

20 This section of the chapter is largely derived from a similar previous discussion written jointly by Bottoms and Dignan (2004: 111–114). I am grateful to Jim Dignan for permission to use it here.

21 Convictions resulting in custodial sentences were excluded because of the delaying effect that custody has on the commencement of the period during which the offender is at risk of a further conviction.

22 This is an adjusted figure, to take account of the speeding up of court processing from 1997 to 2000.

23 That is, the (adjusted) expected reconviction rate in 2001 was 34.1 per cent, and the actual rate was 26.4 per cent (7.7 percentage points less). Expressing 7.7 as a percentage of 34.1 yields the figure of 22.5 per cent.

24 As indicated, for the whole 2001 sample the percentage improvement over the adjusted predicted rate was 22.5 per cent. For cases reprimanded, the figure was 47 per cent. The next highest improvement reported, for the final warning, was much lower, at 19.3 per cent. The research report states that the two precourt disposals 'show particularly marked falls in reconviction rates relative to the predicted rates' (Jennings 2003: 7), but it does not draw attention to the large difference between the results for the reprimand and the final warning in this regard.

25 Details of the multivariate controls utilised in the analysis are given in Jennings (2003). The main variables included in the multivariate model were 'the number of offence categories at the current appearance or in the previous criminal career; the length of the criminal career; age of offenders at the current instance; and previous cautions, previous convictions and combinations of the two' (p. 8).

26 The suspended sentence of imprisonment was first introduced into English law by the Criminal Justice Act 1967. The statutory proviso referred to in the text was added by the Criminal Justice Act 1972. See generally Bottoms (1981).

27 Section 5 of the 1991 Act enacted for the first time that 'a court shall not deal with an offender by means of a suspended sentence unless it is of the opinion ... that the exercise of that power can be justified by the exceptional circumstances of the case'. As Table 3.2 shows, this provision hugely reduced the courts' use of the suspended sentence.

28 For simplicity, the analysis is restricted to males, the main recipients of suspended sentences.

29 For a somewhat different analysis of the new suspended sentence, in comparison with Canadian developments, see Roberts (2003).

References

Andenaes, J. (1974) *Punishment and Deterrence* (Ann Arbor: University of Michigan Press).

Ashworth, A. J. (2000) *Sentencing and Criminal Justice*, 3rd edition (London: Butterworths).

Blumstein, A. and Beck, A. J. (1999) 'Population growth in U.S. prisons, 1980–1996', *Crime and Justice: A review of research*, 26: 17–61.

Bottoms, A. E. (1981) 'The suspended sentence in England 1967–1978', *British Journal of Criminology*, 21: 1–26.

Bottoms, A. E. (1987) 'Limiting prison use: experiences in England and Wales', *Howard Journal*, 26: 177–202.

Bottoms, A. E. (1995) *Intensive Community Supervision for Young Offenders: Outcomes, process and cost* (Cambridge: University of Cambridge Institute of Criminology).

Bottoms, A. E. and Dignan, J. (2004) 'Youth justice in Great Britain', *Crime and Justice: A review of research*, 31: 21–183.

Cann, J., Falshaw, L., Nugent, F. and Friendship, C. (2003) *Understanding What Works: Accredited cognitive skills programmes for adult men and young offenders*, Home Office Research Findings 226 (London: Home Office).

Clarke, R. V. G. (1995) 'Situational crime prevention', *Crime and Justice: A review of research*, 19: 91–150.
Conklin, J. E. (2003) *Why Crime Rates Fell* (Boston: Allyn and Bacon).
Doob, A. N. and Webster, C. M. (2003) 'Sentence severity and crime: accepting the null hypothesis', *Crime and Justice: A review of research*, 30: 143–195.
Fajnzylber, P., Lederman, D, and Loayza, N. (2002) 'Inequality and Violent Crime', *Journal of Law and Economics*, 45: 1–41.
Falshaw, L., Friendship, C., Travers, R. and Nugent, F. (2003) *Searching for 'What Works': An evaluation of cognitive skills programmes*, Home Office Research Findings 206 (London: Home Office).
Farrall, S. (2002) *Rethinking What Works with Offenders: Probation, social context and desistance from crime* (Cullompton: Willan Publishing).
Farrington, D. P. and Welsh, B. C. (2002) *Effects of Improved Street Lighting on Crime: A systematic review*, Home Office Research Study 251 (London: Home Office).
Field, S. (1999) *Trends in Crime Revisited*, Home Office Research Study 195 (London: Home Office).
Friendship, C., Blud, L., Erikson, M. and Travers, R. (2002) *An Evaluation of Cognitive Behavioural Treatment for Prisoners*, Home Office Research Findings 161 (London: Home Office).
Green, D. G., Grove, E. and Martin, N. A. (2004) *How Can the Criminal Justice System Reduce the Criminal Activities of Known Offenders?* Final report of Civitas to the Esmée Fairbairn Foundation's *Rethinking Crime and Punishment* Project (unpublished [www.civitas.org.uk/pdf/Civitas RCP Report.pdf]).
Haines, K. (1990) *After-Care Services for Released Prisoners: A review of the literature* (London: Home Office).
Hedström, P. and Swedborg, R. (1996) 'Social mechanisms', *Acta Sociologica*, 39: 281–308.
Home Office (2001) *Making Punishments Work: Report of a review of the sentencing framework for England and Wales* (London: Home Office).
Jennings, D. (2003) *One Year Juvenile Reconviction Rates: First quarter of 2001 cohort*, Home Office Online Report 18/03 (London: Home Research, Development and Statistics Directorate).
Langan, P. A. and Farrington, D. P. (1998) *Crime and Justice in the United States and in England and Wales 1981–1996* (Washington, DC: US Department of Justice).
Lappi-Seppala, T. (2001) 'Sentencing and punishment in Finland', in M. Tonry and R. S. Frase (eds) *Sentencing and Sanctions in Western Countries* (New York: Oxford University Press), pp. 92–150.
Laub, J. H. and Sampson, R. J. (2003) *Shared Beginnings, Divergent Lives: Delinquent boys to age 70* (Cambridge, MA: Harvard University Press).
McGuire, J. and Priestley, P. (1995) 'Reviewing "What Works": past, present and future', in J. McGuire (ed.) *What Works: Reducing reoffending* (Chichester: John Wiley), pp. 1–34.
Maruna, S. (2001) *Making Good: How ex-convicts reform and rebuild their lives* (Washington, DC: American Psychological Association).
Nagin, D. (1998a) 'Criminal deterrence research at the outset of the twenty-first century', *Crime and Justice: A review of research*, 23: 51–91.
Nagin, D. (1998b) 'Deterrence and incapacitation' in M. Tonry (ed.) *The Handbook of Crime and Punishment* (New York: Oxford University Press), pp. 345–368.
Netherlands Ministry of Justice (1985) *Society and Crime: A policy plan for the Netherlands* (The Hague: Ministry of Justice).

Raphael, S. and Winter-Ebmer, R. (2001) 'Identifying the effect of unemployment on crime', *Journal of Law and Economics*, 44: 259–284.

Raynor, P. (1988) *Probation as an Alternative to Custody* (Aldershot: Avebury).

Rengert, G. F., Piquero, A. R. and Jones, P. R. (1999) 'Distance decay re-examined', *Criminology*, 37: 427–445.

Rex, S. A. (2001) 'Beyond cognitive-behaviouralism? Reflections on the effectiveness literature', in A. E. Bottoms, L. Gelsthorpe and S. Rex (eds) *Community Penalties: Change and Challenges* (Cullompton: Willan Publishing), pp. 67–86.

Roberts, J. (2003) 'Evaluating the pluses and minuses of custody: sentencing reform in England and Wales', *Howard Journal*, 42: 229–247.

Sampson, R. J. and Laub, J. (1993) *Crime in the Making: Pathways and turning points through life* (Cambridge, MA: Harvard University Press).

Simmons, J. and colleagues (2002) *Crime in England and Wales 2001/2002*, Home Office Statistical Bulletin 07/02 (London: Home Office).

Sparks, R. F. (1971) 'The use of suspended sentences', *Criminal Law Review*, 384–401.

Spelman, W. (2000a) 'The limited importance of prison expansion', in A. Blumstein and J. Wallman (eds) *The Crime Drop in America* (Cambridge: Cambridge University Press) pp. 97–129.

Spelman, W. (2000b) 'What recent studies do (and don't) tell us about imprisonment and crime', *Crime and Justice: A review of research*, 27: 419–494.

Spelman, W. (forthcoming 2005) 'Jobs or jails?: the crime drop in Texas', *Journal of Policy Analysis and Management*.

Thornton, D., Curran, L., Grayson, D. and Holloway, V. (1984) *Tougher Regimes in Detention Centres* (London: HMSO).

von Hirsch, A. (1993) *Censure and Sanctions* (Oxford: Clarendon Press).

von Hirsch, A., Bottoms, A. E., Burney, E. and Wikström, P.-O. (1999) *Criminal Deterrence and Sentence Severity: An analysis of recent research* (Oxford: Hart Publishing).

Wiles, P. and Costello, A. (2000) *The 'Road to Nowhere': The evidence for travelling criminals*, Home Office Research Study 207 (London: Home Office).

Chapter 4

Public opinion and community penalties

Shadd Maruna and Anna King

In this chapter we will address three main questions:

- What do we know about public opinion and non-custodial penalties?
- What accounts for differences in attitudes between individual members of the public?
- What implications does this research have for efforts to garner public support for non-custodial penalties?

Throughout we will draw on the empirical and theoretical literature on public attitudes toward punishment (especially Roberts and Hough 2002; Roberts *et al.* 2003; Tyler and Boeckmann 1997). Moreover, we will draw on the emerging findings from our own University of Cambridge study of punitive and non-punitive attitudes involving almost 1,000 British adults.

First, though, we will briefly address the issue of why this chapter exists at all – that is, why an understanding of public opinion should even matter in the study of non-custodial penalties. A degree of public acceptance of and confidence in criminal justice practices is clearly necessary for a well-functioning system. Justice systems that are not seen as legitimate by the majority of a population presumably need to resort to brute force and intimidation to enforce the law of the land. Still, these are extreme cases; one can certainly imagine a well-functioning criminal justice system that operates with little or no attention to the minutiae of public concerns. Indeed, according to Ryan (2003) and other criminal justice historians, for much of the last century criminal justice policy in

England and Wales was almost entirely in the hands of a small, male metropolitan elite, and public opinion was taken as something to be managed and circumvented rather than acted upon.

Recent decades, however, have seen a substantial shift away from the expert-driven, bureaucratic model of penal policy to a system driven more explicitly by symbolic and expressive concerns (Garland 2001). There has been a distinct 'emotionalisation of public discourse about crime and law' (Karstedt 2002: 301), and punishment – far from being hidden – has taken on a newly 'emotive and ostentatious' character (Pratt 2000a) with the return of boot camps, chain gangs, capital punishment and the like. In short, with the decline of bureaucratic rationalism in the criminal justice system, public emotions about crime and justice 'may now be translated into action, rather than simply left at the level of "talk"' in a way that would have been hard to imagine 35 years ago (Pratt 2000a). This is nowhere more clear than in the recent Carter Report (Carter 2003) and the Halliday Report (Home Office 2001) which both assign a central role to the improvement of public confidence in criminal justice sentencing.

Nonetheless, the relationship between recent policy developments and public wishes has been anything but direct. A considerable amount of 'populist punitiveness' (Bottoms 1995) – defined as 'allowing the electoral advantage of a policy to take precedence over its penal effectiveness' (Roberts *et al.* 2003: 5) – seems to take place with only a caricatured understanding of the public's real views regarding crime and justice (Roberts *et al.* 2003). Considerable research (see review in Roberts and Stalans 1997) suggests that the public is not nearly as punitive as sentencers, politicians and public officials assume they are. Yet, as Richard Korn (1971) once lamented, the public is one of the 'sacred cows' of criminal justice, often deferred to but never consulted. For instance, Morgan (2002) points out that when US President George W. Bush justified the treatment of prisoners held at Guantanamo Bay by saying they were being treated no better than the American public thought they should be treated, he was hardly basing his assessment on survey data from a representative sample.

As such, systematic reviews of public opinion regarding crime and justice are an important corrective to this 'failure to communicate' between criminal justice and the public (Flanagan and Longmire 1996). As Roberts (1992) eloquently demonstrates in his review, not only is it important to dispel the misperceptions the public holds towards crime, but it is equally urgent to dispel the misperceptions that criminal justice experts and policy-makers have towards the public's opinion on crime and punishment. Dispelling myths about public opinion might be most crucial in the area of non-custodial sentences, as Flanagan (1996) suggests that '*perceived* public opinion' (emphasis added) is the 'greatest obstacle' to the success of community-based penalties. Indeed, in a speech at the annual HM Prison Service Conference in 2002, Lord Chief Justice Woolf lamented the 'regrettable' (but undocumented) 'fact' that 'neither the public nor sentencers have confidence in the community alternative' (cited in Roberts 2002: 34). Likewise, in her keynote address to members of the National Probation Service, Probation Minister Beverley Hughes said, 'Public credibility is crucial to our success. Only if, together, we can convince communities of your role and your reliability will you be able to do your important job effectively' (Home Office 2001). In short, sentencers are reluctant to utilise community penalties, regardless of their levels of effectiveness, if they assume that the public would disapprove of these options.

Public opinion and non-custodial penalties: what do we know?

Fortunately, there has been a flood of recent research and writing about public opinion and criminal justice (e.g. Cullen *et al.* 2000; Roberts and Stalans 1997). In fact – thanks in no small measure to the sponsorship of the Esmée Fairbairn Foundation and its *Rethinking Crime and Punishment Initiative* – much of this research focuses specifically on the British public and has a special focus on attitudes towards incarceration and its alternatives (see e.g. Allen 2002; MORI 2002; Roberts and Hough 2002; Wood and Viki 2004). The present review owes an enormous debt to these works, and was made simultaneously easier and more difficult to write because of their recent publication. Certainly, since there have been numerous state-of-the-art reviews of the research on public opinion (see especially those in Roberts and Hough 2002), there is little need to review this research study-by-study here. Instead, in the short space provided, we will try to make some broad generalisations regarding what the research to date seems to show conclusively on the topic. As will be obvious from the subject headings of these sections, the bottom line is that we do not know a great deal. It is important to recognise that, as (Stalans 2002: 20) and others have argued, researchers have 'barely scratched the surface' of public attitudes regarding punishment. Most often we describe what the public says it wants without providing information about what underlies the preference.

The public is ignorant about criminological research (but so what?)

One of the most frequently repeated findings is that members of the general public generally do not know much about the workings of the criminal justice system, crime rates or the basics of criminology (Roberts 1992; Vandiver and Giacopassi 1997). For instance, in 1998, 59 per cent of the UK public thought that crime rates had increased in the previous two years, and four out of five people continue to overestimate substantially the proportion of crime that is violent (Mattinson and Mirrlees-Black 1998). Likewise, the majority of survey respondents very substantially underestimated the proportion of convicted adult male offenders sent to prison (Hough and Roberts 1998). Only a minority (16 per cent) of respondents correctly identified that most 'known' offenders are adults, not juveniles, and nearly a third thought crime was committed equally by females. Finally, over two-thirds thought that the young were becoming increasingly involved in crime between 1995 and 1997, yet according to official statistics, the number of known juvenile offenders remained constant or fell during this period (Mattinson and Mirrlees-Black 1998).

This 'widespread and systematic public ignorance about crime and justice' (Hough and Parks 2002) has been documented so many times in criminological research (Durham 1993; Morgan and Russell 2000; Tarling and Dowds 1997) that one has the impression it is a source of considerable frustration for those of us who devote our careers to providing a scientific understanding of crime. Yet why should we expect any different? As Indermauer and Hough (2002) point out, the justice system is far from the only aspect of government about which the public are largely misinformed. Surveys of public knowledge of welfare provision or the health service likely show equal confusion.

Moreover, there is no obvious reason why most people should have to be conversant with the details of sentencing procedures, welfare policy or any other public function. Still, as Morgan (2002: 220) argues, 'This is no reason for not consulting them about changes which, ultimately, are likely, in some degree, to affect every household'. Morgan goes on to say that 'To conclude that a degree of public ignorance provides judges and politicians with a free hand to make policies that they deem to be fair and efficient, policies that can then be sold to the public, is to misunderstand what counts as criminal justice' (*ibid.*).

Importantly, academics often decry the 'misunderstanding of the nature of crime and punishment' among the public (Indermaur and Hough 2002), but how settled is the criminologist's understanding of this essential nature? Crime is a social construction, of course, and while we in criminology do our best (considering the circumstances) to measure it with some accuracy, we are all aware of the impossibility of perfect accuracy in this endeavour. Under the circumstances, then, it seems arbitrary if not elitist to devalue the public's construction of crime (seeing as they are the ones who commit, suffer and otherwise experience it) in favour of the Home Office's official construction (Ryan 2003). The *Guardian* crime journalist Nick Davies (2003) captured this well in a recent article entitled 'Exploding the myth of the falling crime rate':

> In the last five years, just about all of [the criminal justice establishment] have thrown their hats and helmets in the air to celebrate a steady fall in crime. The Home Office said it was all down to its crime

> prevention work. The police said it was their new intelligence-led approach. The academics said it was rising consumption, falling inequality, more alarms, fewer adolescent males, a rise in abortions . . . or a fall in unemployment. But what it if it never happened? What if all that research is misleading? What if the truth is that crime didn't fall at all, that it was only the statistics that fell?

Research on public opinion suggests that the public is rather dubious about official crime statistics, whether they are collected by the police or through the British Crime Survey, and to some degree, of course, this scepticism is completely warranted. Still, there is no question that the public, in general, do not approach crime in a scientific manner (and they clearly don't read the journal articles we spend so much time writing). At the same time, there is considerable public interest in all aspects of crime and justice and a seemingly insatiable appetite for often highly distorted tales of 'true crime', 'reality' police dramas and the like. Furthermore, individuals hold very strong beliefs regarding issues of justice and punishment and have no great concern that these beliefs are not founded in criminological science. This seems to be a major annoyance to criminologists, but it is unlikely to change.

Public punitiveness is a myth (but then so is the whole notion of a public opinion)

The public is mad as hell about crime and are not going to take it any more. If the general public had their way, they would string up every paedophile, rapist, burglar, drug dealer and car thief lounging in the luxury holiday camps that claim to be prisons and hang them from the highest tree. At least, according to Cullen *et al.* (2002), that is the basic consensus among politicians and political commentators of both the political left and right. Indeed, this sense that the public harbours increasingly punitive attitudes also extends to numerous criminological theorists (e.g. Pratt 2000b).

Considerable research on public opinion and criminal justice has sought to complicate, if not contradict, this 'myth of the punitive public' (Cullen *et al.* 1997). Certainly, the characterisation of public attitudes as *indiscriminately* punitive is misleading (Innes 1993; Irwin *et al.* 1998; Sprott 1999). Turner *et al.* (1997) argue that the public is better characterised as 'reasonably moderate' rather than punitive. Stalans (2002) decides the public is 'selectively punitive and selectively merciful depending upon the specific conditions' (Stalans 2002: 19), whereas Cullen *et al.* (2000) interpret the public's general view toward the treatment of criminals as simply 'mushy'. Indeed, public opinion research shows rather conclusively that although the general public does largely support harsh punishment for serious offenders, we are also very much in favour of rehabilitation (Cullen *et al.* 1988; McCorkle 1993). Applegate *et al.* (2000) demonstrate that when forgiving attitudes as well as punitive attitudes are measured, forgiving views outnumber punitive.

Importantly, this mushiness may simply be a research artefact. Stalans (2002: 25) writes, 'Public attitudes toward sentencing only appear "mushy" because much research has neglected the critical issue of how people form general attitudes, and how prior attitudes and beliefs about criminals affect sentencing preferences for detailed cases.' First of all, 'punitiveness' as a construct is poorly understood. There is little consensus on how to define this theoretical construct in the literature, making meaningful empirical approximations difficult (Walker *et al.* 1988).

Most often punitiveness seems to be measured by asking respondents what they think the goals of corrections should be. Individuals who favour retribution over rehabilitation are said to be punitive. Yet certainly there are retributivists who support minimal punishment (von Hirsch 1993). Likewise, there are numerous non-retributivist grounds (incapacitation, deterrence) for supporting harsh and severe punishments. Focusing on the public's 'goals' for punishment assumes that punitiveness is goal-driven in an instrumental sense. But research on death penalty attitudes (e.g. Ellsworth and Gross 1994) demonstrates that the rationalisations people give for punitive or non-punitive attitudes carry little actual weight. As psychologists report, 'More often than not . . . behavior is influenced by unconscious processes; that is we act and then, if questioned, make our excuses' (Jacoby *et al.* 1992).

Thus death penalty supporters say they would still support the death penalty even if it were proven that it does not deter crime, and death penalty opponents say they would cling to their opposition even if it were proven that capital punishment did deter crime. Scales asking about the 'goals of punishment' are very useful for teasing apart the various intellectual rationalisations which individuals provide for their beliefs, but they do not gauge levels of emotional intensity regarding preferences in punishment, whatever the supporting or opposing reason may be. As pre-eminent psychologists working on the death penalty Ellsworth and Gross (1994: 32) comment, 'Hardly anyone has asked respondents questions that give them the opportunity to express their emotions directly, and some have intentionally confined their response alternatives to those that are rational.'

Research by Doble (2002) suggests that, unlike criminologists, members of the general public do not see any contradiction in valuing both retribution and rehabilitation. Whereas traditional research designs ask survey respondents to rank in order the 'goals' of corrections (e.g. retribution, rehabilitation, deterrence, etc.) and read much into the findings, Doble's survey design allows respondents to list more than one goal as the most important. He found almost no variation in the designated importance of the goals thought to be in competition (with most respondents favouring punishment, reform and restitution at the same time). He concludes:

> If people simultaneously deem more than one goal to be vital, asking them which goal is 'most important' can be likened to asking someone who is hungry, thirsty, cold and tired, what is most important: food, water, warmth or rest. The answer will be essentially meaningless if the person's real goal is not to have one, but all four of their needs met (Doble 2002: 151).

There are, of course, numerous other limitations to the standard efforts of measuring public beliefs. Flanagan (1996) points out that while the most popular method of researching public opinion is polling, this is limited because: (1) attitudes are dynamic while most surveys are cross-sectional; (2) surveys often ask about very specific attitudes from which it is impossible to generalise;[1] and (3) public opinion is rarely if ever monolithic even when surveys might make it appear so.

This last point is clearly true in the case of punitiveness. Research on death penalty attitudes, for instance, suggests that this issue, like abortion, provokes clear and stark attitudinal differences on surveys – with lots of 'strongly agree'-type responses and few 'undecideds' (Ellsworth and Gross 1994). Moreover, there are some clear and systematic demographic differences in views toward punishment. In the United Kingdom, men, older people, citizens with lower levels of educational attainment, and readers of tabloid newspapers seem to hold significantly more punitive views (Allen 2002; Hough and Roberts 1996). These patterns tend to hold true internationally (see Mayhew and van Kesteren 2002) with stronger gender effects, but a less consistent pattern regarding age and punitive attitudes. Self-identified members of racial minorities in North American samples tend to be much less punitive than non-minorities (Applegate *et al.* 1997). Finally, there are substantial cross-cultural differences in punitive attitudes across place and time. Mayhew and van Kesteren (2002) found in an international comparison that Western European countries rank last in support for imprisonment and first in support for community service. Western European countries also rank lowest in the average length of sentence they recommend for a young recidivist burglar. However, between 1989 and 2000 there was an increase in support for imprisonment in England and Wales of 13 per cent, with the sharpest increase occurring between 1992 and 1996 (6 per cent) (Roberts 2002).

So, is the public punitive? The question might not be worth asking. In his review of the public opinion literature, Warr (1995: 296) concludes, 'Public opinion on crime and punishment encompasses such a wide variety of issues and attitudes that it is pointless to attempt to describe it with any one adjective or phrase'. Simplistic summaries of 'where the public stands' that seek to capture 'the public's true opinion' as if there were such a thing as 'the' public and it had a single 'opinion' about anything, seem largely to be an exercise in futility. As Flanagan (1996) warns, public opinion itself is often created and reified in the process of collecting and reporting the results of public opinion polls (see also Savelsberg 1994).

The public is probably ambivalent toward non-custodial penalties

Where does this leave community penalties in the public's mind? The most common finding in public opinion research regarding non-custodial penalties is that the public is largely unfamiliar with this aspect of the criminal justice system (Hough and Roberts 1998). This is unsurprising as probation officers and community service work are hardly ever featured in the media, at least compared to prisons, policing or the courts. The National Probation Service (2002) recently commissioned a study of the public perceptions of probation in England and Wales involving 1,000 telephone surveys and 665 street surveys with members of ethnic minorities. The findings suggest that 43 per cent of the respondents consider themselves to know only 'a little' about what probation service does; for the minority sample, that number is even less (31 per cent). Only 7 per cent of the public say they know 'a lot' about what the Probation Service does.

Further, from what little the public know, the public is anything but inspired and excited about the potential benefits of non-custodial alternatives. Roberts (2002: 34) writes: 'Most members of the public (and indeed, not a few judges) remain rather sceptical about the utility of [community penalties] for crimes of intermediate seriousness, on the basis that community penalties are not severe enough. This is true around the world.'

This seems to be particularly true of 'traditional' probation work, involving reporting to a probation office for monthly supervisions. Cullen *et al.* (2000) write: 'Citizens appear wary of "regular probation", a sanction that involves minimal contact with the offender.' When members of the public were asked what they thought could help to reduce crime in Britain, the National Probation Service (2002) research found that only 2 per cent spontaneously mention the Probation Service, compared to 77 per cent who cite the police and 13 per cent who mention schools. Moreover, recent polling data in the US suggest that public confidence in the concept and efficacy of probation has declined in recent years (Beto *et al.* 2000).[2]

Indeed, some have suggested that public support for probation in the United States is dangerously low. One of the invited participants at a US conference on 'Rethinking Probation' stated this matter quite bluntly: 'Public regard for probation is dangerously low . . . We have to realise that we don't have broad public legitimacy' (Dickey and Smith 1998: 6). Another participant described the public mood toward community corrections as a 'malaise' (*ibid.*: 5). In recent years, the British probation service has undergone its own period of feeling 'uncomfortable, threatened, unsure of its role, and not at all confident of its social or political credibility' (Garland 1997: 3), although not to the same extent as described in the United States. This period of uncertainty, of course, was one of the factors leading to the 'repositioning' of probation and the formation of the unified National Probation Service with the explicit goal of restoring public acceptance.

However, the idea that the public is strongly opposed to non-custodial sentencing has little support in the research literature. For instance, when asked to rank the crime reduction potential of various parts of the criminal justice system on a scale of 1 to 10, respondents to the National Probation Service research rated probation no worse than the prison system. When asked in an abstract way, 47 per cent of an American sample responded that community sentences are 'evidence of leniency' in the criminal justice system. Yet when asked about individual community corrections programmes, support for each is in the 70 to 80 per cent range (Flanagan 1996). In fact, the majority of studies reviewed find that community penalties are largely supported by the public so long as they are used for non-violent rather than violent offenders (Oregon Crime Analysis Center 1991).

'But why?' What do we know about the origins of these opinions?

Although there has been considerable discussion in criminology about whether or not the 'punitive public' exists, very little research has sought to ask why punitive public attitudes exist.[3] In fact, there is a tendency in some criminal justice research to take the existence of punitive attitudes for granted and assume that public hostility to offenders is natural[4] or innate. In *Punishment and Democracy*, for instance, Zimring *et al.* (2001) argue that public punitiveness has probably been a constant in US history (what changed was the level of victimisation and opportunities for populist political decision-making). Like most other observers, the authors therefore seem to accept popular punitivism 'as a fact of nature' and therefore 'offer no real explanation for it' (Greenberg 2002: 246). Yet comparative and historical research contradicts this image of punitive attitudes as a constant. Sutherland and Cressey (1978) write:

> There has been no constant desire to make all criminals suffer and the system used for inflicting suffering on [criminals] has changed from time to time. The punitive reaction to lawbreaking has not been present in all societies [in fact it] varies from time to time even within a given society. A theory which precisely explains or accounts for all of these variations has not been developed.

Additionally, there seem to be important, individual-level differences in punitive attitudes within a single cultural context. Apparently, the execution of a Death Row inmate can evoke disgust and tears from one person while triggering celebration and cheers from another.[5]

But what accounts for these differences? In their important article '"Three strikes and you're out", but why?', Tyler and Boeckmann (1997) argue that there are two basic theoretical frameworks within which public attitudes toward crime and punishment can be understood: instrumental theories and expressive or symbolic theories (Gabriel and Greve 2003; Girling *et al.* 2002; Tyler and Boeckmann 1997; Tyler and Weber 1982; Wood and Viki 2004). Theoretical discussions of the expressive purposes of punishment have dominated the sociological discussion of punishment from the works of Durkheim and Mead to contemporary work by Garland (1990, 2001) and others. Ironically, empirical public opinion research has been criticised for focusing too much attention on the instrumental, 'capturing only the rational or knowledge-based aspect of opinion and ignoring the emotional side' (Indermaur and Hough 2002: 201).

Instrumental explanations

Instrumental theories (Zimring *et al.* 2001) suggest that punitiveness is motivated largely out of self-interest. Punitive attitudes are likely to result when individuals feel a personal threat to themselves or their communities. People are 'fed up'. Like Charles Bronson in *Death Wish*, they are normal, good-natured individuals who are 'pushed too far' by the crime and disorder around them. Hence, punitive attitudes should be more prevalent in areas of high crime, among individuals who have been victims of crime and who fear repeat victimisation.

A sizeable and consistent body of research fails to support these instrumental hypotheses (Baron and Hartnagel 1996; Cullen *et al.* 1985; Hough and Moxon 1985). For instance, public opinion polling does show a relationship between punitiveness and the fear of crime (Taylor *et al.* 1979), but this seems to be a very modest correlation at best (see Roberts and Stalans 1997) and frequently not replicated (Cullen *et al.* 2000). Additionally, fear of crime does not seem to have a measurable relationship to views on capital punishment (Warr 1995) or support for other specific policies like the 'Three Strikes' legislation (Tyler and Boeckmann 1997). While there has been some support for a link between fear of crime and punitiveness (e.g. Sprott and Doob 1997), a major critique of the research on fear of crime has been its inability to account adequately for such complex relationships (Ditton *et al.* 1999; Hollway and Jefferson 1997).

Moreover, personal victimisation experiences and perceptions of crime salience in one's residential area do not relate consistently to punitive attitudes (Flanagan *et al.* 1985; Langworthy and Whitehead 1986; Quimet and Coyle 1991). In fact, only 9 per cent of the self-reported victims of violent crimes in the 1998 British Crime Survey favoured the incarceration of their offender (Roberts 2002). This research counters intuitive beliefs that victims are most likely to seek retributive or harsh consequences for offenders. Walker and Hough (1988) suggest that one reason for this is that individuals who lack personal experience of victimisation may exaggerate the negative consequences of crime while victims are more pragmatic. Alternatively, it might be that victims underplay the severity of harm done in order to better cope with the experience. Other research such as that of Tufts and Roberts (2002) finds that victimisation is not at all predictive of attitudes. Finally, at the aggregate level, recorded rates of crime do not relate to public demands for punishment in a consistent manner (Mayhew and van Kesteren 2002; Wilkins 1991). Similar conclusions led Tyler and Boeckmann (1997: 252) to comment that 'crime-related concerns are the least important factor' in predicting punitive attitudes and suggest that 'the image of the citizen as supporting punitive public policies because of fear of crime . . . is inaccurate'.

Expressive-emotive explanations

An alternative explanation to the instrumental view is that punitive attitudes serve an *expressive* or symbolic function – which is of course to beg the question 'expressive of what?' (Garland 2001). There is a rich tradition of theoretical work in this area (e.g. Durkheim 1933; Mead 1918) which continues today with work such as Garland's (2001) *The Culture of Control*. The best-known explanations for contemporary punitiveness revolve around 'ontological insecurity' or a widespread sense of anxiety driven by the disembedding processes of modernity that have resulted from the erosion of former social certainties (Bottoms 1995; Ranulf 1938; Vaughan 2002; Young 2003). For instance, Bauman (2000) points to the profound anxiety and insecurity produced by the flexibility of the labour market under the deregulated capitalism favoured by neo-liberal states. Indeed, the relationship between economic insecurity and scapegoating behaviour is well known. For instance, in their now classic study, Hovland and Sears (1940) found that the frequency of lynching in the southern US states was negatively correlated with the price of cotton. When farmers suffered the most frustration, they were most likely to redirect their anger on black men accused of crimes (these findings were confirmed by Hepworth and West's (1988) recent re-examination of these data).

Tyler and Boeckman use the label of 'symbolic theories' to describe a wide variety of accounts that link punitiveness to concerns for moral cohesion and the assertion of community values (these theories are reviewed in considerable detail in Garland 1990). Durkheim (1933) famously argued that punishment served as a ritualistic reaffirmation of community values. Similarly, for Mead (1964: 227), punitiveness offers one of the few occasions when community members can unite around shared interests and an 'emotional solidarity of aggression'. Garland summarises this position as follows: 'Taking part in the emotional defence of "society's interests" against criminal depredations, the individual's aggressions against the "outsider" are aroused and reinforced, as is his or her identification with the in-group' (1990: 64). In their own research, Tyler and Boeckmann find support for such symbolic theories, concluding that two aspects of the social environment are crucial to punitiveness: concerns about the breakdown of family values, and anxiety about population diversity and a lack of community cohesion. They suggest that future research on punitiveness incorporate the findings of research on social identity theory (e.g. Turner *et al.* 1979) regarding the framing of group boundaries.

The suggestion from this literature is that not only are people's attitudes towards crime and punishment emotional rather than rational and utilitarian, but that they are in fact driven by very deep and very personal psychodynamic histories (see Maruna *et al.* 2004). Indeed, Mead also pointed out that punitiveness offers a rare outlet for releasing long-restrained and sublimated hostilities. Finally, Garland (1990) argues that criminals may represent a threat because their behaviours often 'express desires which others have spent much time and energy and undergone much internal conflict in order to renounce' (1990: 239). For this reason, he argues that the public may harbour 'a resentful and hostile reaction out of proportion to the real danger it represents'.

Because of their roots in depth psychology, these symbolic theories are rarely explored 'outside of individual case histories based upon reliable clinical evidence' (Garland 1990: 65). One exception is Gaubatz's (1995) *Crime in the Public Mind*. In an inductive analysis of 24 qualitative interviews with Californians, Gaubatz concludes that punitiveness is a type of 'botheredness' which results from a macro-social displacement effect. Her grounded theory suggests that the pace of social change over the last four decades in the United States exceeded some people's capacity for change. As a result, people's rejection of certain social practices (i.e. interracial marriage, homosexuality) remained intact, but suddenly became unacceptable with changing social mores. She argues that the emotional rejection of certain social practices that could no longer be expressed directly was displaced onto attitudes regarding punishment and crime (criminals being among the last groups of individuals that it was still respectable to hate openly). This research has been widely criticised on methodological grounds. Warr (1995), for instance, questions the small sample size, sample selection procedures and the relation between Gaubatz's conclusions and her actual data. Nonetheless, Gaubatz provides a fascinating attempt at a personological or psychodynamic inquiry into punitive attitudes.

Core beliefs and values

One of the most promising lines of investigation into the psychological formation of attitudes towards criminal sanctioning to date is work in the area of attribution theory. Cullen *et al.* (1985), for instance, look directly to variation in people's attitudes towards punishment, rehabilitation, capital punishment and punishment of white-collar crime, and find that the way people *explain* crime helps explain some of the discrepancies. George Vold (1958: 258) writes: 'There is an obvious and logical interdependence between what is done about crime and what is assumed to be the reason for or explanation of criminality.' Cullen and his colleagues divide attributional beliefs into either 'classical' (dispositional) views that crime is a choice or else lay 'positivist' (situational) views that see crime as a product of circumstances. Numerous previous studies (e.g. Cullen *et al.* 1985; Grasmick and McGill 1994) have found support for the idea that punitive attitudes correlate with classical or dispositional attributions, whereas those who hold more situational attributions tend to be less punitive.[6]

Psychologists are also concerned with another dimension of attributions (stability versus instability) that is often neglected by criminologists, but might be equally important in determining punitive attitudes. That is, regardless of one's beliefs about the origins of criminality, do they believe that people can change? Such a belief in redeemability (or the instability of criminality) may take precedence over attributions in determining punitiveness. Garland (2001: 185) writes, 'Whether the offender's character is the result of bad genes or of being reared in an anti-social culture, the outcome is the same – a person who is beyond the pale, beyond reform, outside the civil community.' A belief in people who are permanently and fundamentally bad almost necessitates their segregation from mainstream society. A belief in redeemability and human malleability, therefore, might be a more robust predictor of punitiveness than the internality/externality (classical/positivist) dimension of attributions.

New research: University of Cambridge Public Opinion Project (UCPOP)

A project designed to build on the above work, incorporating both in-depth interviewing and survey methodology, is currently under way at the University of Cambridge. The first phase of this three-phase project is a postal survey designed to test a variety of theories regarding the correlates of public attitudes, but also to identify two samples: one of British citizens with 'highly punitive' belief scores and a contrasting sample of individuals with strongly non-punitive views. The second phase of the research (currently under way) involves in-depth, exploratory interviews with members of these two groups, in which interviewees talk about their lives: their experiences with being punished, their experiences of punishing others, experiences witnessing punishment, and their general concerns and anxieties. The goal is to find five to ten themes that characterise the world-views or self-identities of each group. The third and final phase of the research will involve bringing large numbers of the initial survey respondents back for a series of experiments designed to see whether raising the salience of various anxieties does consistently lead to increases in punitive responses for randomly selected participants compared to a control group. It is hoped that this triangulation of data will provide more comprehensive information on the psychology of punitive and non-punitive attitudes than has previously been collected.

Below, we briefly discuss the methods of the postal survey and take a look at some early outputs that relate to public attitudes about community penalties.

UCPOP: the postal survey

In June 2003, 3,600 surveys were sent to randomly chosen households in six wards selected for their diversity in income and demographics (as well as their proximity to the investigators). The sampled areas represent both rural and urban areas in the east of England and London, ranging from one of the highest-ranking wards on the 2,000 indices of deprivation (Great Yarmouth) to the lowest (Stapleford). The characteristics of the 941 respondents (see Table 4.1) largely reflected the communities from which they were drawn (see descriptives below).

As with other samples of the British population, the sample is rather neatly divided, with about a third of respondents supporting a greater use of community penalties, another third supporting the more widespread use of imprisonment, and the remaining third largely undecided in the middle.

What does the sample think of alternatives to prison?

Forty-seven per cent agree that if prison has to be used, it should be used sparingly and only as a last option; 31 per cent agree probation or a community sentence (rather than prison) is appropriate for a person

Table 4.1 Some sample characteristics (N = 941)

56% are female.
68% have not completed a university degree.
51% describe themselves as politically conservative.
58% consider themselves religious or spiritual persons.
41% describe the household they were raised in as working class.
72% report their household income as under £40,000.
7% report being convicted of offences more serious than a speeding violation.
47% report knowing someone who has been to prison or who has been on probation.

found guilty of burgary for the second time; 36 per cent would consider volunteering time or donating money to an organisation that supported alternatives to prison; and 36 per cent would consider volunteering for an organisation that supported toughening the sentencing laws in the UK.

Hypotheses and measures

For the purposes of this chapter, we have run some preliminary analyses to see what items included in our survey seem to best predict support for community penalties among our sample. In our analysis, we include the demographic characteristics (age, gender, etc.) thought to be associated with punitive attitudes, and predict that instrumental factors (living in high-crime areas, victimisation experiences) will decrease the likelihood that one will support prison alternatives above and beyond these demographic characteristics. Likewise, we predict that expressive factors (e.g. anxiety about the economy or the state of Britain) will further decrease support for alternatives, controlling even for instrumental concerns.

Finally, we also include a test for the impact of core beliefs about crime[7] on one's support for prison alternatives. In our analysis, we test the effects of these attributions on punitive attitudes while holding other potential correlates of punitiveness constant. In addition, we added our scale on 'belief in redeemability' into the equation. This tests a second, neglected dimension of attribution theory (stability–instability) beyond the internal–external dimension usually tested. The hypothesis here was that individuals who believed deeply in the notion that people can change and that 'even the worst young offenders have the ability to turn their lives around', will be the most likely to support alternatives to prison.

Analyses and findings

To investigate the unique contribution of each set of explanatory variables in predicting attitudes supportive of community sanctions, each model was analysed in four separate steps (see Table 4.2). This technique allows us to assess how each additional model might contribute to the overall variance explained. In the first model, we measure the possible socio-demographic effects on punitiveness. In the second model, measures of victimisation, perceptions of local crime, and fear of crime are added to the equation to test instrumental hypotheses. The third model includes measures which are designed to test expressive hypotheses revolving around social and economic anxieties. Our measures here include: a standard measure of collective efficacy; a measure of anxiety about youth (including items such as 'Young people do not seem to have respect for anything these days'); and an item, global crime salience, measuring whether the person believed crime was increasing or decreasing across the United Kingdom. Finally, in the fourth model we assess the impact of core beliefs on attitudes toward community penalties. Here we would

Table 4.2 Regression models predicting pro-community sanction attitudes

Variable	Model 1	Model 2	Model 3	Model 4
Controls				
Class background	.125**	.123**	.106**	.082*
Gender (male)	−.083*	−.099**	−.097**	−.100**
University	.282***	.251***	.155***	.101**
Income	−.080	−.127**	−.160***	.112**
Race	.064	.080*	.091*	.073*
Age	.080*	.091*	.106**	.142***
Unemployment	.060	.060	.057	.054
Instrumental				
Direct victimisation		.062	.037	.029
Crime salience (local)		.011	.121	.090*
Fear of crime		−.229***	−.120*	−.066
Expressive				
Collective efficacy and trust			.165***	.140***
Anxiety about youth			−.254***	−.176***
Economic pressure			.054	.024
Crime salience (global)			−.176***	−.132**
Core beliefs and values				
Crime is a choice				−.207***
Belief in redeemability				.300***
Adjusted R^2	.102	.133	.290	.403
R^2 change		.035***	.160***	.112***

*p<.05; **p<.01; ***p<.001.

hypothesise, based on previous literature, that those who attribute criminality to the internal disposition of an offender (crime is 'a choice') would be more punitive and therefore less likely to support community penalties. Additionally, however, we hypothesise that those persons who see criminality as a largely unstable trait and believe in offenders' abilities to change their behaviours (reflected in high 'redeemability' scores) will be more supportive of community penalties.

In model 1, university degree, class background, gender and age emerge as significant predictors, suggesting that highly educated, older women of higher social classes are the most likely to support community penalties for offenders. As in previous research, education seems to have the strongest impact. Those with a university education are far more likely to support community sanctions than the less educated, controlling for other demographic factors. Overall, however, these variables explain only about ten percent of the variation in our sample, a result consistent with the 10 per cent usually explained by socio-demographics in similar studies.

In model 2, the socio-demographics act as control variables to test the effects of three main instrumental theory predictors. When socio-demographics are controlled for, fear of crime is the only instrumental variable that is a significant predictor of pro-community sanctions attitudes (.229***). In addition, the effect of personal income was suppressed by the instrumental variables (from –.080 to –.127**). The effects of race and gender are also strengthened when instrumental variables are controlled. Overall, though, the addition of instrumental predictors to the regression only gives the model 4 per cent more predictive power.

In model 3, when expressive variables are added, the R^2 increases 16 per cent.[8] Almost half of the strength of the relationship between fear of crime and pro-community sanctions attitudes, as well as between education and pro-community sanctions attitudes, disappears when expressive variables are factored into the equation (from −.229*** down to −.120* and from .261*** to .155***, respectively).

Finally, model 4 adds scores of dispositional attributions and belief in redeemability to the equation. The addition of these variables helps the model explain 11 per cent more of the variation found in individual differences in pro-community sanctions attitudes in this sample. Several variables decrease very slightly in strength or significance (class, education, income, local crime salience, collective efficacy, anxiety over youth and global crime salience), but overall there are no significant changes to the other variables. Attributions of internality and a belief in redeemability are shown to have significant and unique effects on pro-community sanctions attitudes (−.207*** and .300*** respectively).

In sum, expressive predictors and core beliefs and values have a strong effect on pro-community sanctions attitudes, over and above the effect of both socio-demographics and instrumental factors, as predicted. A belief in redeemability was the strongest predictor of support for pro-community sanctions attitudes. Neither victimisation nor fear of crime contributed significantly to the model once expressive predictors and core beliefs and values were accounted for. While these findings are only preliminary – our research project is not even half done – they do suggest some interesting possibilities for developing a better understanding of public support for community penalties. For instance, the research suggests that the public's lay criminological beliefs and understanding about why people commit crime may play a greater role than actual experiences with victimisation in determining support for community penalties. In other words, there may be a role for public education and working with public views.

Implications for working with public opinion

Academics often seem to wish that public opinion could largely be kept out of the policy-making world. Privately, many of us even long for a system more like the 'cosy, elite policy-making world' described by Ryan

(2003) in his history of criminal justice policy in Britain. Barring such a radical reversal of recent trends, though, numerous observers have suggested strategies for working with public opinion. Roberts *et al.* (2003) outline multiple strategies for mediating and moderating the impact of public opinion on criminal justice policy, including the establishment of institutional layers of protection as buffers between politicians and the judiciary.

Others argue that in order to win public support, community alternatives need an image overhaul. Beto *et al.* (2000: 1) argue, 'Although low ratings [in public opinion polls] obviously are related to poor performance, they also signal a failure on probation's part to convey an image to citizens of a model of practice that embodies widely held values and serves overriding public safety concerns.' Likewise, Maloney *et al.* (2001) argue that the US model of probation has 'gone the way of the Edsel' in terms of performance and reputation, and like the Ford company's infamous failure, probation needs to be retired. Importantly, they not only advocate the end of traditional US probation practice (which they say is based on the 'rather bizarre assumption that surveillance and some guidance can steer the offender straight'), but also dispensing with the 'brand name' of probation in the United States (which they rightly argue is a vague and uninspiring term). They suggest that a more fitting mission and name for probation should be 'community justice'. Indeed, community justice as an ideal has been the subject of considerable excitement and theoretical examination over the past two decades.

Drawing on Anthony Duff's communicative theory of justice, Sue Rex (2002) has argued persuasively that community penalties have the potential to communicate a message to both the public and the offender him or herself. Unfortunately, the potential message to both is often highly diluted and confused because of a lack of consensus regarding the rationale behind these penalties (Kalmthout 2002). Below, we review 'what works' and what probably does not work in terms of changing the public's perception of non-custodial penalties. Some of these conclusions are based on the experiences of campaigning groups (such as the organisation Payback[9]) that have made concerted and substantial efforts to change public opinion on issues of community alternatives (see Bowers 2002).

Appeals to cost-benefits and effectiveness will only go so far

Research conducted by the Centre for Social Marketing at the University of Strathclyde on behalf of the *Rethinking Crime and Punishment Initiative* found that statistical arguments about the effectiveness of non-custodial sentences ultimately had little impact on public views about community penalties (Stead *et al.* 2002: 4): 'Respondents were sensitive to the highly politicised nature of the crime debate, and regarded any use of statistics as spin'. Further, arguments in favour of community alternatives based on the high costs of imprisonment or the growing numbers of citizens incarcerated seemed largely unpersuasive to focus group members. In fact, focusing on the high costs of imprisonment 'simply reinforced the popular view that prisons were full of unnecessary luxuries, and provoked the retort that "they should take away the televisions"' (2002: 3).

If attitudes toward criminal punishment are driven largely by emotive rather than instrumental concerns, as our own research and the wider criminological literature suggest, then rational appeals to the benefits of various justice options will have only limited impact on public views.

Public education will help, but is no panacea

One of the most frequently mentioned strategies for increasing public confidence in community sentences is to provide more and better (i.e. research-driven) information about crime and justice to the public (Gainey and Payne 2003; Roberts and Stalans 1997; Stalans 2002). The research evidence in favour of this strategy, however, is somewhat mixed.

On some levels, it is irrefutable that 'information works'. That is, in almost every survey of the public where such comparisons are made, individuals who are provided with additional information about various sentencing alternatives are less likely to favour these sentences (e.g. by 'sentencing' hypothetical offenders to prison in 'you be the judge'-type exercises) than those who are given no such information (see Roberts 2002). In particular, explaining the variety of restitution and compensation alternatives to respondents who are unfamiliar with community-based penalties has the immediate effect of reducing punitive tendencies in survey respondents (Hough and Roberts 1998). Furthermore, respondents who express punitive views in the abstract often moderate those views when presented with more information about the offenders themselves (e.g. learning that they have suffered abuse in the past, grew up impoverished or are addicted to a drug) (Doob and Roberts 1988).

On the other hand, much of the research demonstrating the impact of education on attitudes shows only very short-term effect.[10] For instance, Gainey and Payne (2003) found that a 35-minute presentation of information about crime and justice can increase support for alternative sanctions, but the duration of this effect is unknown as only an immediate post-test was done. Additionally, much of this research is plagued by what can be interpreted as a 'Hawthorne effect': participants may modify their views on follow-up surveys simply because it is obvious that this is what they are 'supposed to do'. Finally, the practicality of introducing these educational efforts on a large scale is doubtful. Much is made of the impact of 'deliberative polling', whereby attitudes seem to change in light of an educational encounter of sorts (ranging from a lecture to a two- or three-day seminar on issues of crime and justice). Yet considerable research (and personal experience on the part of the authors!) suggest that even an entire academic term spent learning about the ins and outs of criminology and criminal justice has a negligible impact on students' attitudes toward crime (Giacopassi and Blankenship 1991; Jayewardene *et al.* 1977). How much education is really needed to change deep-seated attitudes and how possible would it be to educate the adult population of Britain in this way?

Bowers (2002) argues that attitudes serve four functional purposes: to organise vast amounts of knowledge, to express values, to help defend one's ego and to obtain rewards and avoid punishment. Typically, only the knowledge function is addressed when it comes to strategies for change. Many initiatives or campaigns talk about making messages 'easy to remember and recall', which ignores the possibility that attitudes exist not only to organise information, but also for other reasons. Many attitudes, such as prejudicial ones, are believed to serve purposes that have little if anything to do with knowledge organisation. As such, education may do little to change them: 'As anti-rascist campaigners know only too well, overcoming these rigid stereotypical "schemas" is exceptionally difficult, and generally cannot be achieved with information based initiatives' (Bowers 2002: 25). When attitudes are based on other than informational discrepancies or deficits, they are not easily altered.

Perhaps the most promising findings regarding education, however, are that the active participation of citizens in the criminal justice process increases satisfaction with the service and decreases punitiveness (see Allen 2002). Research suggests that when citizens are actively engaged in criminal justice decision-making – whether it is through serving on a jury (Matthews *et al.* 2003), participating in restorative justice work (Greene and Doble 2000) or even sentencing hypothetical offenders through academic exercises (Roberts and Stalans 1997) – they are less punitive and more likely to support community alternatives. Apparently, easy slogans like 'hang 'em high' or 'lock 'em up' become less tenable when individuals are assigned the responsibility of actually trying to turn such general notions into practice. Yet the average citizen's interaction with the criminal justice system may involve little more than reporting a minor crime to the police. Further, as Morgan (2002: 225) argues, when he or she does report being the victim of crime, 'the likelihood . . . of the crime being cleared up or, even if cleared up, their learning about what happened to "their" offender is low.' Unfortunately, these realities are not likely to change in the foreseeable future.

Schemes to educate and inform the public about the nuances of sentencing, the 'facts' about crime, and so forth are noble, well-meaning efforts, but unlikely to have more than marginal impact on either public understanding of crime issues or punitive, prison-centric attitudes.

The public wants 'affective' as well as 'effective' justice

Indermaur and Hough (2002: 210) argue persuasively that 'Anyone who wants to improve public debate about crime needs to be attuned to [the] emotional dimension [of attitude formation]'. Freiberg (2000) aptly describes this as the difference between 'effective' and 'affective' justice. The punishment of criminal offenders is a deeply emotive issue. Yet saying attitudes are driven by emotion does not make them 'wrong'. Academics tend to favour the rational and logical over the emotive, and dismiss the latter as irrelevant and misguided (Ryan 2003; Tetlock 1994). The public, on the other hand, has little problem with 'gut reactions' and supporting what 'feels right' rather than what they are told is logically correct. If one seeks to sway public opinion, the legitimacy of these other bases for opinion needs to be understood and appreciated. That is, punitive policies and practices have won votes in recent years because they appeal to the emotional needs of late modern voters and tax-payers (Karstedt 2002). Rather than bemoaning this lack of sheer technocratic rationality on the part of citizens, research on punitive attitudes suggests that those in favour of community penalties would do well to make similarly emotive appeals on behalf of non-custodial penalties.

Unfortunately, we know very little about what emotive themes are likely to support community sentences because we know remarkably little about the social psychology of non-punitive attitudes. Whereas the 'authoritarian personality' has generated half a century of research across several academic disciplines, research on the development of liberal, permissive, forgiving or non-punitive outlooks toward punishment is badly lacking (Martin 2001).[11] Indeed, little is known about the existence let alone the origins of public compassion, forgiveness or empathy in regards to criminal offenders. Little in the sociology of punishment (from Durkheim to Garland) could easily account for this sort of empathetic understanding if it exists (and it surely does[12]) outside elite circles suffering from 'liberal guilt'. Reflecting the popular stereotype that 'a liberal is just a conservative who has never been mugged', for instance, Garland (2001: 78) writes: 'The posture of "understanding" the offender (is) more readily attained by liberal elites unaffected by crime or else by professional groups who make their living out of it.' As a result, we can imagine (indeed have seen clearly) how the public's punitive attitudes could be awakened and utilised in support of a repressive criminal justice agenda, but we have little idea how to promote a more tolerant society.

Our own research and that of others suggests that 'redeemability' is a powerful theme for those who support community penalties. Appealing to the public to support community alternatives because 'people can change', and demonstrating this with human interest stories of transformed offenders might have some value. Applegate *et al.* (2000: 742) write, 'Our study shows that the compassionate side of [public attitudes]

– the belief in forgiveness – can also shape how [citizens] "think about crime".'

Some research suggests that the public's hesitations about community corrections can be alleviated by assuring them that the sentence will be 'intensive' (i.e. involving more than just standard probation services). In particular, describing the potential use of electronic monitoring and the like seems to increase public support for non-custodial penalties somewhat (Brown and Elrod 1995; Dowds and Redfern 1994; Gainey and Payne 2003). However, these sorts of 'see how tough we are' arguments can backfire. Essentially, if the public thinks that offenders on community penalties are really so dangerous that they need constant supervision, then why bother with electronic monitoring when prison would do quite nicely? The public holds a 'deeply entrenched view' that 'equates punishment and control with incarceration, and that accepts alternatives as suitable only in cases where neither punishment nor control is thought necessary' (Smith 1984: 171). No matter how tough the restrictions, community penalties simply cannot compete with the iron bars, high walls and razor wire of the prison in the battle for being the 'toughest'.[13]

Far more evidence suggests that the principles of restitution, community service or 'giving something back' appeal strongly to the public (see Gandy 1978; Mattinson and Mirrlees-Black 1998; Shaw 1982). The University of Strathclyde research indicates that arguments about the values and principles underlying non-custodial penalties were far more meaningful to focus-group participants than information regarding the effectiveness or cost-benefits of these sentences (Stead *et al.* 2002). Notions such as 'paying back', 'making good' and 'restorative justice', for instance, were said to 'resonate strongly' with focus-group members (2002: 1). Canadian research by the Angus Reid Group (1997) similarly found the possibility of victim compensation to be a more persuasive argument in favour of community penalties than arguments revolving around the high price tag of imprisonment.

Emotive appeals to the unfortunate circumstances and disadvantaged origins of most criminal offenders seem to carry little weight with the public. Stead *et al.* (2002) report that any argument that appears to be sympathetic to the plight of offenders provoked hostile reactions from their focus groups with British citizens. Yet there was greater success when appeals were based on what Bazemore (1999) calls 'earned redemption', whereby offenders earn their way back into society through structured opportunities to make amends, through positive contributions to their communities. Such demonstrations send a message to the community that the offender is worthy of further support and investment in their reintegration (Bazemore 1999). As one participant in a Rethinking Probation focus group argued: 'Let me put it this way, if the public knew that when you commit some wrongdoing, you're held accountable in constructive ways and you've got to earn your way back through these kinds of good works, . . . [the probation service] wouldn't be in the rut we're in right now with the public' (Dickey and Smith 1998: 6).

By symbolically transforming the probationer into a 'giver rather than a consumer of help', non-custodial penalties might be seen in a more positive light.

Conclusions

Academics are sometimes uncomfortable with the privileging of public opinion (Ryan 2003), and they are even more uncomfortable with the privileging of emotions and the non-rational. Yet supporters of community penalties ignore such things at their own peril. As Garland (1990: 62) argues, reformers' tendency to ignore public punitiveness or dismiss these views as a form of 'false consciousness' is counterproductive: 'If such sentiments do exist, and give support to current penal practices, then penal reformers will have to address themselves directly to popular feelings if they intend to produce real change.'

The public is not nearly as punitive as some politicians seem to think (Roberts 2002), but their public attitudes about justice and punishment are real, not just logical 'mistakes' based on faulty information that can be corrected once more information is provided. Research suggests that the presentation of new information, factual or statistical, and even the open discussion of that new information (as with deliberative polling) can change attitudes, but that change is limited.[14] Hough (1996) discovered this in his focus-group research with members of the British public. Although his research found that educating members of the public about the 'facts' of crime and justice could improve overall levels of confidence in sentencing practices (including the use of non-custodial penalties), Hough concludes that 'It would be a large oversimplification to argue that once people's ignorance about practice has been corrected, opinion and practice fall into line. Our respondents were, in the main, very punitive toward offenders . . . Many of the groups . . . proposed castration – by no means frivolously – as a way of dealing with rapists.'

Understanding the emotive appeal of castration, hanging, and the 'mass imprisonment' of young, minority males (as in the US context, in particular) may require new research methodologies in public opinion research. Working with members of the public who harbour such emotive views will require a new approach to marketing non-custodial penalties. The uncharted territory in the search for knowledge on public opinion is that of emotions. While understanding the relationship of emotions to both punitiveness and forgiveness may be more challenging than mapping a purely cognitive schema, it does not follow that it is beyond our grasp.[15] The exploration of this relationship can only expand our knowledge of attitudes towards offenders. With a better, fuller understanding at hand it is more likely that more effective strategies will not be far behind.

Notes

1. For instance, while one might assume attitudes towards the death penalty might be generalisable to support for longer sentences, this is not the case (see Kury *et al.* 2002).
2. This change in perception may be due to actual changes in practice; where probation 20 years ago may have focused on change and rehabilitation, it may now function solely as an instrument of surveillance.
3. Some notable exceptions include the work of Gaubatz (1995) and Tyler and Boeckmann (1997).
4. Indeed, this argument is made explicit in theoretical work in evolutionary psychology (e.g. Fehr and Gachter 2002), in which support for the punishment of wrongdoers is considered an almost universal human trait, crucial to the evolution of civilisation.
5. Different crimes generally elicit different reactions (Stalans 2002; Altemeyer 1988), but there is very little research about the processes that underlie the ways in which they do. For instance, rehabilitation might be chosen as suitable punishment for a drug offence and 'hard time' for a violent offence. However, this is more easily explained at the surface – one consequence may seem to go 'logically' with the crime. However, why a person is sympathetic towards paedophiles, but then explodes at the mention of white-collar criminals (as in the case of one subject in our interview research), is not as easily explained.
6. Importantly, the way in which one explains crime may come after, not follow, one's preference for punitive policies. It is equally possible that one may believe crime is a choice as a way to justify their deeper needs to be punitive. As such, attributions about the causes of crime may act similarly to deterrent beliefs, 'To the extent that deterrence beliefs are a cognitive justification for an affective value position, those beliefs and the value position they protect will be only minimally responsive to cognitive persuasion' (Tyler and Weber 1982: 242). Such beliefs are thought to be somewhat impenetrable by education because their source is located not in cognitive processes, but in the affective domains that involve social values 'developed during the childhood and adolescent socialisation process' (Tyler and Boeckmann 1997: 254).
7. As discussed briefly above, while individuals may differentiate by crime in their attitudes to punishment, little is known about the ways in which they do. Therefore, we ask about crime in general.
8. Adding variables to an equation will automatically increase variance explained, but there will be differences in that increase depending on how the model is specified.
9. www.payback.org.uk
10. Hough and Park (2002) are a rare exception. They found that long-term attitude change is possible but not very common, and the intervention in question was quite dramatic (a series of lectures from politicians and experts). Additionally, they found long-term attitude change was most likely among more educated individuals.
11. The sociological work of Norbert Elias might be a good starting point for such an analysis.
12. Anecdotal evidence abounds, of course. For instance, the opposition to the tough punishment involved in English detention centres in the 1950s came not from elite penal reformers but 'from the very prison officers expected to

implement these regimes: they found it impossible to do so without suffering severe pangs of conscience', according to Pratt (2000a).

13 At least in the public's mind. Research by Petersilia *et al.* (1986) suggests that many prisoners surveyed would rather spend a short time in jail than very long periods of time on intensive probation.

14 There may be as yet unknown effects of ongoing factual re-education, but research suggests that while repetition may be useful for familiarisation, 'it is unlikely to be instrumental in changing attitudes' (Bowers 2002: 32).

15 While experiments on the willingness to punish have been conducted (i.e. Milgram), we would hope that lines of investigation suggested by this type of review might be undertaken more from a humanistic perspective than a behavioural one. Such research has tended to reduce human experience to stimulus-response sets and in doing so has given us a very clear picture, but of only half of what we need to know.

References

Allen, R. (2002) 'What do the public really feel about non-custodial penalties?', *Rethinking Crime and Punishment* (London: Esmée Fairbairn Foundation), pp. 1–5.

Altemeyer, D. (1988) *Enemies of Freedom: Understanding right-wing authoritarianism* (London/San Francisco: Jossey-Bass Publishers).

Angus Reid Group (1997) *Attitudes to Crime* (Ottawa: Angus Reid Group).

Applegate, B. K., Cullen, F. T. and Fisher, B. S. (1997) 'Public support for correctional treatment: the continuing appeal of the retributive ideal', *The Prison Journal*, 77, 237–258.

Applegate, B. K., Cullen, F. T., Fisher, B. S. and Vanderven, T. M. (2000) 'Forgiveness and fundamentalism: reconsidering the relationship between correctional attitudes and religion', *Criminology*, 38(3), 719–753.

Baron, S. W. and Hartnagel, T. F. (1996) '"Lock 'em up": attitudes toward punishing juvenile offenders', *Canadian Journal of Criminology*, 191–212.

Bauman, Z. (2000) 'Social issues of law and order', *British Journal of Criminology*, 40, 205–221.

Bazemore, G. (1999) 'After shaming, whither reintegration: restorative justice and relational rehabilitation', in G. Bazemore and L. Walgrave (eds) *Restorative Juvenile Justice: Repairing the harm of youth crime* (Monsey, NY: Criminal Justice Press), pp. 155–194.

Beto, D. R., Corbett, R. P. and DiLulio, J. J. (2000) 'Getting serious about probation and the crime problem', *Corrections Management Quarterly*, 4(2), 1–8.

Bottoms, A. (1995) 'The politics of sentencing reform', in C. Clarkson and R. Morgan (eds) *The Philosophy and Politics of Punishment and Sentencing* (Oxford: Oxford University Press), pp. 17–49.

Bowers, L. (2002) *Campaigning with Attitude: Applying social psychology to criminal justice communication* (London: Payback).

Brown, M. P. and Elrod, P. (1995) 'Electronic house arrest: an examination of citizen attitudes', *Crime & Delinquency*, 41(2), 332–346.

Carter, P. (2003) *Managing Offenders, Reducing Crime* [The Carter Report], (London: Home Office).

Cullen, F. T., Clark, G. A., Cullen, J. B. and Mathers, R. A. (1985) 'Attribution, salience, and attitudes toward criminal sanctioning', *Criminal Justice and Behavior*, 12(3), 305–331.

Cullen, F. T., Cullen, J. B. and Wozniak, J. F. (1988) 'Is rehabilitation dead? The myth of the punitive public', *Journal of Criminal Justice*, 16(4), 303–317.

Cullen, F. T., Fisher, B. S. and Applegate, B. K. (2000) 'Public opinion about punishment and corrections' in M. Tonry (ed.) *Crime and Justice: A review of research*, 27 (Chicago: University of Chicago Press).

Cullen, F. T., Pealer, J. A., Fisher, B. S., Applegate, B. K. and Santana, S. (2002) 'Public support for correctional rehabilitation in America: change or consistency?' in J. Roberts and M. Hough (eds) *Changing Attitudes to Punishment: public opinion, crime and justice* (Cullompton: Willan), pp. 128–147.

Davies, N. (2003) 'Exploding the myth of the falling crime rate', *Guardian*, Thursday 10 July.

Dickey, W. J. and Smith, M. E. (1998) *Dangerous Opportunity. Five futures for community corrections: the report from the focus group* (Washington, DC: Department of Justice).

Ditton, J., Bannister, J., Gilchrist, E. and Farrall, S. (1999) 'Afraid or angry? Recalibrating the "fear" of crime', *International Review of Victimology*, 6(2), 83–99.

Doble, J. (2002) 'Attitudes to punishment in the US – punitive and liberal opinions', in J. Roberts and M. Hough (eds), *Changing Attitudes to Punishment: Public opinion, crime and justice* (Cullompton: Willan), pp. 148–162.

Doob, A. N. and Roberts, J. (1983) *Sentencing: An analysis of the public's view of sentencing* (Ottawa: Department of Justice).

Dowds, L. and Redfern, J. (1994) *Drug Education Amongst Teenagers: A 1992 British Crime Survey analysis*, Home Office Research and Planning Unit Paper 86 (London: Home Office).

Durham, A. M. (1993) 'Public opinion regarding sentences for crime: does it exist?', *Journal of Criminal Justice*, 21(1), 1–11.

Durkheim, E. (1933) *The Division of Labor in Society* (New York: The Free Press).

Ellsworth, P. C. and Gross, S. R. (1994) 'Hardening of the attitudes: Americans' views on the death penalty', *Journal of Social Issues*, 50(2),19–52.

Fehr, E. and Gachter, S. (2002) 'Altruistic punishment in humans', *Nature*, 415, 137–140.

Flanagan, T. and Longmire, D. R. (eds) (1996) *Americans View Crime and Justice: A national public opinion survey* (Thousand Oaks, CA: Sage).

Flanagan, T. J. (1996) 'Public opinion on crime and justice: history, development and trends' in T. Flanagan and D. R. Longmire (eds) *Americans View Crime and Justice: A national public opinion survey* (Thousand Oaks, CA: Sage), pp. 1–15.

Flanagan, T. J., McGarrell, E. and Brown, E. J. (1985) 'Public perceptions and criminal courts: the role of demographic and related attitudinal data', *Journal of Research in Crime and Delinquency*, 22(1), 66–82.

Freiberg, A. (1999) 'Affective versus effective justice: instrumentalism and emotionalism in criminal justice', *Punishment & Society*, 3(2), 265–278.

Gabriel, U. and Greve, W. (2003) 'The psychology of fear of crime: conceptual and methodological perspectives', *British Journal of Criminology*, 43, 600–614.

Gainey, R. R. and Payne, B. K. (2003) 'Changing attitudes towards house arrest with electronic monitoring: the impact of a single presentation?', *International Journal of Offender Therapy and Comparative Criminology*, 47(2), 196–209.

Gandy, J. (1978) 'Attitudes toward the use of restitution', in B. Galaway and J.

Hudson (eds) *Offender Restitution in Theory and Action* (Lexington, MA: Lexington Books)
Garland, D. (1990) *Punishment and Modern Society: A study in social theory* (Chicago: University of Chicago Press).
Garland, D. (1997) '"Governmentability" and the problem of crime: Foucault, criminology, sociology', *Theoretical Criminology*, 1(2), 173–214.
Garland, D. (2001) *The Culture of Control: Crime and social order in contemporary society* (Oxford: Oxford University Press).
Gaubatz, K. T. (1995) *Crime in the Public Mind* (Ann Arbor, MI: University of Michigan Press).
Giacopassi, D. J. and Blankenship, M. B. (1991) 'The effects of criminal justice pedagogy on student attitudes', *American Journal of Criminal Justice*, 16, 97–103.
Girling, E., Loader, I. and Sparks, R. (2002) 'Public sensibilities toward crime: anxieties of influence' in A. Boran (ed.) *Crime: fear or fascination?* (Chester, UK: Chester Academic Press), pp. 153–176.
Grasmick, H. G. and McGill, A. L. (1994) 'Religion, attribution style, and punitiveness toward juvenile offenders', *Criminology*, 32(1), 23–47.
Greenberg, D. F. (2002) 'Striking out in democracy', *Punishment & Society*, 4(2), 237–252.
Greene, J. and Doble, J. (2000) *Attitudes towards Crime and Punishment in Vermont: Public opinion about an experiment with restorative justice* (Englewood Cliffs, NJ: John Doble Research Associates).
Hepworth, J. T. and West, S. G. (1988) 'Lynchings and the economy: a time-series reanalysis of Hovland and Sears (1940)', *Journal of Personality and Social Psychology*, 55(2), 239–247.
Hollway, W. and Jefferson, T. (2000) *Doing Qualitative Research Differently: Free association, narrative and the interview method* (London: Sage).
Home Office (2001) 'Beverly Hughes: New era for the National Probation Service', Online newsletter 4 July 2001 (153/2001) [www.gnn.gov.uk/content/detail.asp?ReleaseID=42156&NewsAreaID=2&NavigatedFrom Search=True].
Home Office (2001) *Making Punishments Work. Report of a review of the sentencing framework for England and Wales (July 2001)* [The Halliday Report] (London: Home Office).
Hough, M. (1996) 'People talking about punishment', *The Howard Journal*, 35, 3.
Hough, M. and Moxon, D. (1985) 'Dealing with offenders: popular opinion and the views of victims, findings from the British Crime Survey', *The Howard Journal*, 24(3), 160–175.
Hough, M. and Park, A. (2002) 'How malleable are attitudes to crime and punishment? Findings from a British deliberative poll', in J. Roberts and M. Hough (eds) *Changing Attitudes to Punishment: Public opinion crime and justice* (Cullompton: Willan), pp. 163–183.
Hough, M. and Roberts, J. (eds.) (1998a) *Attitudes to Crime and Punishment: Findings from the 1996 British Crime Survey*, Home Office Research Findings 64 (London: HMSO), pp. 1–4.
Hough, M. and Roberts, J. (eds.) (1998b) *Attitudes to Crime and Punishment: Findings from the British Crime Survey*, Home Office Research Studies 179 (London: HMSO), pp. 1–79.
Hovland, C. I. and Sears, R. (1940) 'Minor studies of aggression: correlation of lynchings with economic indices', *Journal of Psychology*, 9, 301–310.

Indermaur, D. and Hough, M. (2002) 'Strategies for changing public attitudes to punishment', in J. Roberts and M. Hough (eds) *Changing Attitudes to Punishment: Public opinion crime and justice* (Cullompton: Willan), pp. 198–214.

Innes, C. A. (1993) 'Recent public opinion in the United States toward punishment and corrections', *Prison Journal*, 73(2), 220–236.

Irwin, J., Austin, J. and Baird, C. (1998) 'Fanning the flames of fear', *Crime and Delinquency*, 44(1), 32–48.

Jacoby, L. L., Lindsay, D. S. and Toth, J. P. (1992) 'Unconscious influences revealed: attention, awareness, and control', *American Psychologist*, 47(6), 802–809.

Jayewardene, C. H. S., Lang, S. and Gainer, C. (1977) 'Changing attitudes to the criminal justice system through formal education', *Crime and Justice*, 5, 126–130.

Kalmthout, A. (2002) 'From community service to community sanctions: comparative perspectives', in H. Albrecht and A. Kalmthout (eds) *Community Sanctions and Measures in Europe and North America* (Freiburg: Max Planck Institute).

Karstedt, S. (2002) 'Emotions and criminal justice', *Theoretical Criminology*, 6(3), 299–318.

Korn, R. (1971) 'Of crime, criminal justice and corrections', *University of San Francisco Law Review*, 6(1), 27–75.

Kury, H., Obergfell-Fuchs, J. and Smartt, U. (2002) 'The evolution of public attitudes to punishment in Western and Eastern Europe', in J. Roberts and M. Hough (eds) *Changing Attitudes to Punishment: Public opinion crime and justice* (Cullompton: Willan), pp. 93–114.

Langworthy, R. H. and Whitehead, J. T. (1986) 'Liberalism and fear as explanations of punitiveness', *Criminology*, 24, 3(3), 575–591.

Maloney, D., Bazemore, G. and Hudson, J. (2001) 'The end of probation and the beginning of community justice', *Perspectives* 25(3), 24–30.

Martin, J. L. (2001) 'The authoritarian personality, 50 years later: what lessons are there for political psychology?', *Political Psychology*, 22(1), 1–26.

Maruna, S. (2001) *Making Good: How ex-convicts reform and rebuild their lives* (Washington, DC: American Psychological Association).

Maruna, S., Matravers, A. and King, A. (2004) 'Disowning our shadow: a psychoanalytic approach to understanding punitive public attitudes', *Deviant Behavior*, 25, 277–299.

Matthews, R., Hancock, L. and Briggs, D. (2003) *Jurors' Perceptions, Understanding, Confidence and Satisfaction in the Jury System: A study in six courts* (London: Home Office).

Mattinson, J. and Mirrlees-Black, C. (1998) *Attitudes to Crime and Criminal Justice: Findings from the 1998 British Crime Survey*, Home Office Research Findings 111 (London: Home Office).

Mayhew, P. and van Kesteren, J. (2002) 'Cross-national attitudes to punishment', in J. Roberts and M. Hough (eds) *Changing Attitudes to Punishment: Public opinion, crime and justice* (Cullompton: Willan), pp. 63–92.

McCorkle, R. C. (1993) 'Research note: punish and rehabilitate? Public attitudes toward six common crimes', *Crime & Delinquency*, 39(2), 240–252.

Mead, G. H. (1964) *On Social Psychology: Selected papers* (Chicago: University of Chicago Press).

Mead, G. H. T. (1918) 'The psychology of punitive justice', *American Journal of Sociology*, 23, 577–602.

Morgan, R. (2002) 'Privileging public attitudes to sentencing' in J. Roberts and M.

Hough (eds) *Changing Attitudes to Punishment: Public opinion, crime and justice* (Cullompton: Willan) pp. 215–228.

Morgan, R. and Russell, N. (2000) *The Judiciary in the Magistrates' Courts* (London: Home Office).

MORI (2002) 'Policing the possession of cannabis: residents' views on the Lambeth experiment' (London: MORI Social Research Institute).

National Probation Service (2002) *Perceptions of the National Probation Service* (London: National Probation Service).

Oregon Crime Analysis Center (1991) *Intermediate Sanctions* (Salem, OR: Oregon Crime Analysis Center).

Petersilia, J., Turner, S. and Peterson, J. (1986) *Prison Versus Probation in California: Implications for crime and offender recidivism* (Santa Monica, CA: Rand).

Pratt, J. (2000a) 'Civilisation and punishment', *Australian and New Zealand Journal of Criminology*, 33(2), 183–201.

Pratt, J. (2000b) 'Emotive and ostentatious punishment: its decline and resurgence in modern society', *Punishment and Society*, 2(4), 417–439.

Quimet, M. and Coyle, E. J. (1991) 'Fear of crime and sentencing punitiveness: comparing the general public and court practitioners', *Canadian Journal of Criminology*, 33(2), 149–162.

Ranulf, S. (1938/1964). *Moral Indignation and Middle Class Psychology* (New York: Schocken).

Rex, S. and Tonry, M. (eds) (2002) *Reform and Punishment: The future of sentencing* (Cullompton: Willan).

Roberts, J. V. (1992) 'Public opinion, crime, and criminal justice' in M. Tonry (ed.) *Crime and Justice: A review of research*, 16 (Chicago: University of Chicago Press,), pp. 99–180.

Roberts, J. V. (2002) 'Public opinion and the nature of community penalties: international findings', in J. Roberts and M. Hough (eds) *Changing Attitudes to Punishment: Public opinion, crime and justice* (Cullompton: Willan), pp. 33–62.

Roberts, J. V. and Hough, M. (2002) 'Public attitudes to punishment: the context', in J. Roberts and M. Hough (eds) *Changing Attitudes to Punishment: Public opinion, crime and justice* (Cullompton: Willan), pp. 1–14.

Roberts, J. V. and Stalans, L. (eds) (1997) *Public Opinion, Crime and Criminal Justice* (Boulder, CO: Westview Press).

Roberts, J., Stalans, L., Indermaur, D. and Hough, M. (2003) *Penal Populism and Public Opinion: Lessons from five countries* (Oxford/New York: Oxford University Press).

Ryan, M. (2003) 'Populists and publics' in M. Ryan (ed.) *Penal Policy and Political Culture in England and Wales: Four essays on policy and process* (Winchester: Waterside Press), pp. 109–140.

Savelsberg, J. J. (1994) 'Knowledge, domination and criminal punishment', *American Journal of Sociology*, 99(4), 911–943.

Shaw, S. (ed.) (1982) *The People's Justice: A major poll of public attitudes on crime and punishment* (London: Prison Reform Trust).

Simon, R. I. (1999) *Bad Men Do What Good Men Dream: A forensic psychiatrist illuminates the darker side of human behavior* (Washington, DC: American Psychiatric Association).

Smith, M. E. (1984) 'Will the real alternatives please stand up', *New York University Review of Law and Social Change*, 12, 171–197.

Sprott, J. B. (1999) 'Are members of the public tough on crime? The dimensions of public "punitiveness"', *Journal of Criminal Justice*, 27(5), 467–474.

Sprott, J. B. and Doob, A. N. (1997) 'Fear, victimization, and attitudes to sentencing, the courts, and the police', *Canadian Journal of Criminology*, 39(3), 275–291.
Stalans, L. (2002) 'Measuring attitudes to sentencing', in J. Roberts and M. Hough (eds) *Changing Attitudes to Punishment: Public opinion, crime and justice* (Cullompton: Willan), pp. 15–32.
Stead, M., MacFadyen, L. and Hastings, G. (2002) *What Do the Public Really Feel about Non-custodial Penalties?* (London: Esmée Fairbairn Foundation).
Sutherland, E. H. and Cressey, D. R. (1978) *Criminology* (Philadelphia, PA: J. B. Lippincott).
Tarling, R. and Dowds, L. (1997) 'Crime and punishment', in R. Jowell, J. Curtice, A. Park, L. Brook, K. Thomson and C. Bryson (eds) *British Social Attitudes: the 14th Report. The end of conservative values?* (Aldershot: Ashgate Publishing).
Taylor, D. G., Schepple, K. L. and Stinchcombe, A. L. (1979) 'Salience of crime and support for harsher criminal sanctions', *Social Problems*, 26(4), 413–424.
Tufts, J. and Roberts, J. (2002) 'Sentencing juvenile offenders: public preferences and judicial practice', *Criminal Justice Policy Review*, 13, 46–64.
Turner, J. C., Brown, R. J. and Tajfel, H. (1979) 'Social comparison and group interest in ingroup favouritism', *European Journal of Social Psychology*, 9(2), 187–204.
Turner, M. G., Cullen, F. T., Sundt, J. L. and Applegate, B. K. (1997) 'Public tolerance for community based sanctions', *The Prison Journal*, 77(1), 6–26.
Tyler, T. R. and Boeckmann, R. J. (1997) '"Three strikes and you are out", but why? The psychology of public support for punishing rule breakers', *Law & Society Review*, 31(2), 237–265.
Tyler, T. R. and Weber, R. (1982) 'Support for the death penalty; instrumental response to crime, or symbolic attitude?', *Law & Society Review*, 17(1), 21–45.
Vandiver, M. and Giacopassi, D. (1997) 'One million and counting: students' estimates of the annual number of homicides in the U.S.', *Journal of Criminal Justice Education*, 8, 135–143.
Vaughan, B. (2002) 'The punitive consequences of consumer culture', *Punishment and Society*, 4(2), 195–211.
Vold, G. (1958) *Theoretical Criminology* (New York: Oxford University Press).
von Hirsch, A. (1993) *Censure and Sanctions* (New York/Oxford: Oxford University Press).
Walker, N. and Hough, M. (eds) (1988) *Public Attitudes to Sentencing: Surveys from five countries* (Aldershot: Gower).
Walker, N., Hough, M. and Lewis, H. (1988) 'Tolerance of leniency and severity in England and Wales', in N. Walker and M. Hough (eds) *Public Attitudes to Sentencing: Surveys from five countries* (Aldershot: Gower), pp. 178–202.
Warr, M. (1995) 'Public opinion on crime and punishment', *Public Opinion Quarterly*, 59, 296–310.
Wilkins, L. T. (1991) *Punishment, Crime and Market Forces* (Brookfield, VT/Aldershot, UK: Dartmouth Publishing).
Wood, J. and Viki, G. T. (2004) 'Public perceptions of crime and punishment', in J. R. Adler (ed.) *Forensic Psychology* (Cullompton: Willan), pp. 16–36.
Young, J. (2003). 'Merton with energy, Katz with structure: the sociology of vindictiveness and the criminology of transgression', *Theoretical Criminology*, 7, 389–414.
Zimring, F. E., Hawkins, G. and Kamin, S. (2001) *Punishment and Democracy: Three strikes and you're out in California* (New York: Oxford University Press).

Chapter 5

Punishment as communication

Sue Rex

Introduction

The Criminal Justice Act 2003 sets out in legislation for the first time the purposes of sentencing: punishment; reduction of crime (including by deterrence); reform and rehabilitation; protection of the public; and the making of reparation. This makes it pertinent to consider how these purposes – and the normative theories in which they originate – apply to community penalties. Traditionally, debate in penal theory has focused on the competing claims of what are seen as two rival theories: consequentialism and retributivism (or desert). However, most contemporary theorists now favour a 'hybrid' approach combining elements of both (see Bottoms 1995). The difficulty with such a compromise is that it confronts inherent tensions between consequentialism, as an approach that looks forward to reduce future offending, and retributivism, as one that looks backwards to punish the offence.

These tensions have become apparent in the case of community penalties, in relation to which there has been a failure to find a balance between their role as punishments 'deserved' by the offence and their role in crime prevention. One consequence of the various permutations through which community penalties have moved in the successive 'eras' discussed in Chapter 1 has been to create considerable confusion about the purpose of community orders and their place in the sentencing framework. This problem is not confined to England and Wales. Internationally, too, the lack of a clear consensus about the rationales underlying community sanctions has undermined their credibility and application (Roberts 2002, citing Kalmthout 2002).

It was argued in Chapter 1 that the provisions for mixed custody–community disposals in the 2003 Act are likely to reinforce the subordinate role that community penalties play in relation to custody. Certainly, the creation of a 'customised' community sentence will not of itself help to clarify the aims of a community order, nor will simply listing the various purposes of sentencing to which courts are to have regard. To achieve a more rounded understanding of community sanctions, we need to examine their theoretical underpinnings to seek a proper balance between their dual functions of being just punishments and reducing offending. This is not of purely academic concern: a clearer framework would promote the development of community-based sanctions in policy and practice.

Clarifying the framework for community penalties, then, is my aim in this chapter. I draw on theories of punishment in which communication is central, and on views expressed in interviews and questionnaires by people who might be seen to have a particular stake in criminal justice. Before reporting those findings, I start by outlining briefly the various normative theories and their relevance to community penalties.

Applying normative theory to community penalties

Consequentialist penal theory provides the umbrella for the three 'utilitarian' justifications for punishment, all of which are aimed at the 'social good' of reducing crime: deterrence, incapacitation and rehabilitation. All three are among the sentencing purposes listed in the 2003 Act: deterrence and rehabilitation by name, and incapacitation by association with 'protecting the public'. Generally, deterrence and incapacitation, as penal rationales, are seen as operating through the threat or restraint offered by a custodial sentence rather than through community penalties. By contrast, rehabilitation (preventing offending through changing offenders' social circumstances or their attitudes and behaviour) has been the dominant rationale for community penalties, during both the penal welfare 'era' discussed in Chapter 1 and the recent 'What Works' movement (see Chapter 8). In the 'new generation' community penalties that emerged during the 1990s (see Chapter 1), the unifying theme has become one of public protection, a goal that relies on assessing and managing 'risk'. Applied to community penalties, the growing importance of risk can be seen in the development of surveillant or incapacitative measures such as drug testing and tagging as well as in the use of risk assessment to allocate offenders to or exclude them from rehabilitative programmes. In line with that emphasis, the Carter Report (Carter 2003) recommends that the level of intervention within the new generic community sentence should be based on risk assessment and the government agrees (Home Office 2004).

The sentencing trends discussed in Chapters 1 and 2 suggest that a recent focus on crime prevention and risk has eclipsed another function of community penalties: to punish someone who has committed an offence by restricting his or her liberty. This aim was enshrined in the 2003 Act, as in earlier legislation. It stems from retributive penal theory, an approach that looks backwards to the offence for which the punishment exacts retribution (in complete contrast to the forward-looking emphasis in consequentialism). 'Modern' retributivism dates back to the writings of Kant, who objected to utilitarianism on the grounds that human beings – as 'moral agents' – should be used as ends in themselves and not as means to an end (or social good). As we saw in Chapter 1, this approach experienced a strong revival in the 1970s, in the form of the justice model associated with renewed interest in the 'rights' of prisoners as an aspect of human rights (Hudson 1987). According to retributive theory, punishment is justified, not by the benefits it might bring society in preventing crime, but as an intrinsically just response to crime. Although retribution is often equated with a 'punitive' approach to crime, many of its recent proponents, such as von Hirsch (1993), have been motivated by a wish to restrict the power that the state takes over offenders' lives. In short, their position is that the level of punishment should be dictated by the crime committed rather than by an assessment of possible future conduct (or 'risk').

Consequentialist and retributivist rationales both have strong appeal. It is desirable for community penalties to pursue the 'socially useful' goal of reducing crime. It seems no less important for them to act as 'just' responses to crime. The two aims are also interdependent, in the sense that as community orders come to be used for less serious offenders, they will attract people for whom probation resources are not just unnecessary but possibly counter-productive (as argued by Morgan 2003). However, they also act in tension. For it must be tempting to give an offender a condition to attend an accredited programme that might help him or her to move away from offending despite the fact that 'justice' demands a lesser penalty such as a straight community rehabilitation or punishment order. In such circumstances, which should prevail: the need to prevent crime or the requirements of justice?

The final purpose listed in the 2003 Act is the making of reparation to the community or to the victim. This brings us to restorative justice which, as we saw in Chapter 1, has become prominent over the last two decades as a result of a growing concern with the rights of victims (another aspect of the 'rights' movement referred to above). Its current influence arises from dissatisfaction with traditional criminal justice systems as neglecting victims and failing to repair the harms caused by crime. On this point, a number of restorative theorists (but by no means all) draw a sharp distinction between the focus in retributive theory on crimes as 'wrongs' that require 'censure', and the restorative aim of promoting reconciliation through a process involving the victim, offender and the community (Zehr 1990).[1] On the other hand, a number of writers within the 'retributive' paradigm argue that restorative processes already exist within community penalties and could be developed further, pointing to the reparative potential of community service and 'victim empathy' modules within offender programmes (Duff 2001; Raynor 2001; Johnson and Rex 2002).

Punishment as communication

Given the competing attractions of retribution and crime prevention, what is promising about von Hirsch's (1993) desert theory and the communicative penal theory put forward by Duff (2001) is that each has made a serious attempt to reconcile the two aims at the theoretical level. Both writers, unusually, have also devoted some effort to considering how their ideas might apply to community penalties. For von Hirsch they are proportionate punishments that adequately reflect the gravity of many offences, while Duff sees them as intrinsically apt communicative punishments. This provides a further reason to look to their 'hybrid' approaches for a framework for community penalties that are both just (deserved) and socially useful (in preventing crime). However, the two writers differ on certain key questions, as I hope to show in the following discussion.

Von Hirsch (1993) interlocks 'censure' and 'crime prevention' in the general justification for punishment, but does not accord them equal status. He sees conveying censure as the main function of a criminal sanction – as part of a morality that holds people accountable for their actions. For him, the preventive function operates within a censuring framework to supply a prudential incentive – a deterrent – to supplement the normative reason for desisting provided by penal censure. To allow the preventive message to become too prominent would amount to treating offenders, not as moral agents, but as 'tigers in a circus' capable of responding only to threats (von Hirsch 1993: 11). The normative message must be sustained by adhering to the principle of proportionality so that the size of the sanction reflects the comparative blameworthiness (or gravity) of the offence.

For Duff (2001), by contrast, the central aim of punishment is to persuade the offender not to offend again in the future. As 'communication', punishment is both forward-looking to the reform of the offender – his or her repentance through 'moral persuasion' – and backward-looking (retributive) to the offence for which the offender is censured. The latter requires a reasonable relationship between the severity of the punishment and the relative gravity of the offence, providing a range of possible sentences from which to select the one that is substantively apt to 'communicate an appropriate understanding of the particular crime and its implications' (Duff 2001: 143). According to Duff, his view of punishment – not a purely expressive communication but a 'secular penance' – does not require the positive principle of proportionality espoused by von Hirsch (1993).

For his part, von Hirsch doubts whether the state is authorised or equipped to impose the secular penance envisaged by Duff, arguing that efforts at reform are 'additional permissible activities' rather than a fundamental part of the justification for punishment (von Hirsch 1999: 78). For von Hirsch, punishment may not be a 'technique for evoking specified sentiments', yet 'some sort of moral response is expected [from the offender] – an expression of concern, an acknowledgement of wrong-doing, or an effort at better self-restraint. A reaction of indifference would, if the censure is justified, itself be grounds for criticising [the offender]' (von Hirsch 1993: 10).

Their respective theoretical positions mean that von Hirsch shows far less interest in the actual content of different sanctions than Duff, who argues that the material forms that punishment takes should be intrinsically appropriate to achieving the communicative aims outlined above. Here, Duff (2001) believes that sanctions that allow an offender to remain in the community are more fitting as inclusive communicative punishments than imprisonment, which excludes the offender from the normal life of the community for a period. He is also interested in the reparative and restorative possibilities offered by community-based sanctions.

Duff describes the central aims of probation – as understood by many probation officers – as cohering with the communicative aims of transparent persuasion. These are 'to confront offenders with the effects of their offending and thus to help them to face up to the need for changes in their attitudes and behaviour' (Duff 2001: 101). In this account, the requirement for supervision reminds the offender that his/her offence casts doubt on his/her commitment to the community's public values and threatens to undermine the mutual trust on which the community depends. The conditions attached to a probation order aim to bring home to the offender the character and implication of the offences as public wrongs, and to persuade the offender that he or she must (and can) modify his/her future behaviour. According to this logic, offending behaviour programmes should not be seen as therapeutic, but as communicative punishments in which recognition of the wrongfulness of past conduct helps offenders to bring about a change in their behaviour.

Community service, according to Duff (2001), should be seen as a public form of the kind of reparation to which victim–offender mediation can lead, offering rich and substantial censure that aims to bring home to the offender the nature and implications of the offence. Performing work for the community further enables the offender to express his or her understanding of what he or she has done and his or her renewed commitment to the community. It also requires him or her to perform apologetic reparation to the community; even if the offender him or herself does not come to recognise it as such, other citizens should accept that in completing community service the offender has sufficiently apologised for the crime.

The above is quite a restorative account of community service. Indeed, for Duff restoration is not only compatible with retribution but '*requires* retribution, in that the kind of restoration that crime makes necessary can (given certain deep features of our social lives) be brought about only through retributive punishments' (Duff 2003: 44). Arguing that the orthodox punishment paradigm should move towards restoration, Duff foresees that victim–offender mediation could be routinely built into probation orders so that 'the offender communicates to the wider community, as well as to the victim, his apologetic recognition of the wrong he has done' (2001: 104).

Von Hirsch's (1993) main interest in community penalties lies in showing how they might be accommodated within a framework of proportionality to overcome the problems of 'recruitment from the shallow end', 'sanction stacking' and reliance on imprisonment as a breach sanction. In the model developed by Wasik and von Hirsch (1988), sanctions are organised into 'sentencing bands' of roughly equivalent 'penal bite', allowing a choice between two or more equally 'deserved' sanctions on rehabilitative or reparative grounds. This was the kind of compromise adopted in the Criminal Justice Act 1991, which required the sentencer to select the most *suitable* order for the offender that imposed restrictions on liberty *commensurate with* the seriousness of the offence. In the event, the 1991 Act failed to have the desired effect, partly because of a lack of statutory or judicial guidance on 'seriousness'. However, it was also the case that the Act was not really given an opportunity to work, so that reconciliation of proportionality with crime prevention remains worthy of pursuit (Rex 1998; Nellis 2001).

Seeking 'stakeholders'' views

Duff (2001) offers his account as an ideal, and argues that it does not describe or justify criminal justice processes as they operate in practice. Nonetheless, I have conducted empirical research aimed at exploring the possible application of the ideas discussed above to how state punishment is actually delivered, or could be delivered, in the form of community penalties. Through this work, my wish is to promote the closer relationship between high-level normative thinking and ground-level practical decision-making required if we are to start thinking more effectively about punishment (Raynor 1997). I hope that the insights of those making decisions or affected by decision-making in criminal justice might inject some fresh thinking into the normative discussion and suggest ways in which to take forward the questions and debates discussed above.

I would not suggest that the kind of empirical work I have undertaken can 'prove' or disprove theory, or even that normative theory dealing with 'ought' questions is susceptible to 'proof' (Bottoms 2000). However, discordance between penal theory and ground-level thinking, or what

Robinson and Darley (1995) might call 'community standards', seems to me to expose a tension that requires analysis and possibly the penal theorist to change his or her view or to find stronger and more persuasive arguments. At a practical level, too, a penal theorist might be interested in whether his or her theory was likely to 'work': whether certain aspects might require development or adjustment, or whether they could work given certain changes to criminal justice practices.

In the remainder of this chapter I will be discussing the views of lay magistrates, probation staff, offenders and victims collected through interviews and surveys funded by a post-doctoral fellowship with the Economic and Social Research Council. In carrying out the research, I have sought to bring together the insights that might be gained from in-depth qualitative interviews with what can be learnt from quantitative analysis about the relative weight that different groups attributed to various ideas and considerations. There were three stages to my research, starting with detailed exploratory interviews with 63 individuals.[2] I then used the material generated by these to develop a predominantly pre-coded questionnaire, which was piloted before being completed by 771 individuals.[3] Not only did the interviews produce the themes that I drew on in formulating the questionnaire, but they were also the source of a number of phrases used in individual questions as the best way in which to convey particular sentencing purposes or messages in ordinary language. Follow-up interviews with some questionnaire respondents enabled me to discuss specific points raised by the analysis of my initial interviews and the questionnaires, and to investigate apparent tensions revealed by questionnaire responses.[4] Below, I draw on both interview and questionnaire data as appropriate to discuss my findings.

Understandings of penal messages 'on the ground'

What is immediately clear is that a conceptualisation of punishment as communication accorded with the everyday understandings I encountered in interviews and questionnaires. All four groups of respondents saw a court transmitting normative or 'moralising' messages in sentencing an offender. 'Instrumental' messages, too, played a key role in the sense that the experience of being sentenced was clearly intended to elicit a positive response from offenders, usually in the form of making efforts to refrain from offending in the future. Indeed, views supported the kind of 'hybrid' approach envisaged by both von Hirsch (1993) and Duff (2001), according to which punishment looks both backwards to the offence and forwards to the possibility of change. For, although questionnaire respondents clearly prioritised crime prevention as the overriding aim of punishment, they also showed a strong commitment to proportionality in deciding amounts of punishment. Whether they were retributivist or consequentialist in how they prioritised punishment, respondents wanted punishment to be fair as well as socially useful.[5] This and other findings reported below argue against a censuring versus crime-preventive dichotomy as offering a crude characterisation of how people understood the institution of punishment.

Sentencing as moralising

Magistrates, staff and victims, when asked the extent to which they agreed with various statements in the questionnaire summarising the different aims of sentencing, all seemed to place considerable emphasis on the communication of censure. However, Table 5.1 shows that different groups prioritised different aspects of that communication. For magistrates, the main point seemed to be to demonstrate society's disapproval to the offender. Theirs might be interpreted as a somewhat 'symbolic' approach to sentencing in which the offender is dealt with 'externally', reminiscent of von Hirsch's (1993) model as it has been characterised by Bottoms (1998). By contrast, in prioritising the need to make offenders see *why* what they did was wrong, victims and staff seemed to envisage a greater degree of engagement with offenders. This position implies that the offender is a person with a normative outlook capable, as Duff (2001) argues, of seeing his or her crime as wrongful. Consistent with that perspective, both staff and victims put more emphasis than magistrates on showing offenders that they had hurt their victims.

It is interesting that support for retribution was so low – in interview, people expressed some discomfort with 'pure' retributivism (often equated with 'punitiveness'). Another idea with which agreement was low was remorse – these respondents might agree with von Hirsch that 'censure is not a technique for evoking specified sentiments' (1993: 10). Apart from retribution, the statements listed in Table 5.1 found more support among respondents who identified themselves as consequentialists than among retributivists. This was quite possibly because instrumental goals lay behind the normative communication – interviews certainly suggested that the point of conveying a sense of wrongdoing to offenders was to get them to exercise restraint in the future.

Needless to say, offenders are an important audience for what might be described as penal 'moralising'. It is significant therefore that, as a group, participating offenders seemed less convinced by it than other groups (although, when interviewed, other groups too expressed reservations about the value judgements that might be implied). Certainly offenders were less receptive to the expression of disapproval as an aim of sentencing, although more than two-thirds did seem open to persuasion about the wrongfulness of their offences. On both points, the views expressed by probation staff were actually closer to offenders' than to those of their colleagues in community service (CS).

Table 5.1 Moralising aims: percentage agree (and ranking in list of all statements)

Statements	Magistrates % (N=382)	Staff % (N=132)	Offenders % (N=142)	Victims % (N=105)
Disapprove (Show them that society does not like what they did)	81 (1st)	69 (7th)	59 (10th)	76 (5th)
Victim hurt (Show them that they have hurt the victim)	66 (7th)	78 (3rd)	61 (9th)	77 (4th)
Persuade (Make them see why what they did was wrong)	73 (4th)	82 (2nd)	70 (6th)	85 (1st)
Retribution (Make them pay for what they did wrong)	59 (10th)	49 (13th)	40 (13th)	59 (13th)
Reparation (Make them put something back into the community)	66 (6th)	72 (5th)	48 (12th)	77 (4th)
Remorse (Make them feel sorry for hurting someone)	51 (11th)	58 (11th)	54 (11th)	65 (11th)

Note: Thirteen statements in the questionnaire addressed the aims of punishment. See Table 5.3 for statements on crime preventive aims.

A similar picture emerged when respondents were asked about the messages that the court was seeking to convey in sentencing an offender (see Table 5.2). Here, for magistrates as well as staff and victims, the emphasis was on communicating the damage that the offence had caused rather than simply signalling censure for what the offender did. Doubts were expressed, too, in interview about the efficacy of communicating disapproval as such. To reiterate the point made above, it seemed important to persuade offenders *why* what they did was wrong, not just to tell them it *was* wrong. Overall, however, offenders were distinctly less receptive than other groups to these normative messages, and interviewed offenders displayed some resistance to messages that they had committed a wrong.

Sentencing to prevent crime

All groups saw the pursuit of instrumental goals as an important element in sentencing, and this was especially so in the case of offenders. For

Table 5.2 Normative messages: percentage agree (and ranking in list of all statements)

Statements	Magistrates % (N=377)	Staff % (N=131)	Offenders % (N=132)	Victims % (N=106)
Censure (We do not like what you did)	80 (3rd)	75 (3rd)	50 (9th)	75 (5th)
Hurt (What you did hurt someone else)	88 (1st)	88 (1st)	58 (4th)	88 (1st)
Harm (What you did harmed the community)	84 (2nd)	83 (2nd)	44 (10th)	76 (4th)
Boundary (We cannot put up with this kind of behaviour)	72 (5th)	64 (8th)	55 (5th)	77 (3rd)

Note: 10 statements in the questionnaire addressed sentencing messages. See Table 5.4 for statements on crime preventive messages.

offenders, the top five aims of sentencing were all preventive. However, different groups prioritised different aspects of prevention, as can be seen from Table 5.3. Staff rated rehabilitation highest, as did offenders, but it received less support from magistrates or victims. The last placed more emphasis on getting offenders to reform themselves, perhaps influenced by special deterrence and to a slightly lesser extent assisted by encouragement and rehabilitation. As before, there were significant differences between the views of probation and CS staff, with the latter showing far more support than the former for the idea that sentencing should be used to encourage and educate offenders.

Interviews revealed that the messages seen as transmitted in the act of sentencing often implied the expected response (desistance from offending), whether this was couched in the language of threats or in more encouraging terms. That offenders seemed to see sentencing primarily in instrumental terms was once again clear from their ratings of penal messages in the questionnaire (where other groups placed rather less emphasis on instrumental messages than on the normative ones discussed above). Offenders' views, as presented in Table 5.4, painted a picture in which the court was communicating an expectation that they could live lawfully and make something of their lives, backing that up with the threat of dire consequences should they re-appear in court. Conversely, neither magistrates nor staff agreed strongly with the sentence being used to convey a threat; despite the impression gained from interviews that this

Table 5.3 Preventive aims: percentage agree (and ranking in list of all statements)

Statements	Magistrates % (N=382)	Staff % (N=132)	Offenders % (N=142)	Victims % (N=107)
Special deterrence (Show them that crime does not pay)	67 (5th)	64 (9th)	64 (7th)	78 (3rd)
General deterrence (Show other people that they won't get away with crime)	62 (8th)	56 (12th)	61 (8th)	67 (9th)
Incapacitation (Keep them away from offending)	74 (3rd)	73 (4th)	77 (2nd)	65 (10th)
Reform (Get them to change their ways)	79 (2nd)	71 (6th)	70 (5th)	82 (2nd)
Rehabilitation (Help them with the problems behind their offending)	61 (9th)	86 (1st)	79 (1st)	73 (7th)
Encouragement (Get them to do something useful with their lives)	44 (12th)	66 (8th)	72 (4th)	74 (6th)
Education (Teach them how to go on the straight and narrow)	41 (13th)	61 (10th)	73 (3rd)	63 (12th)

was an idea with resonance for magistrates, it received comparatively little support when evaluated against the full range of possibilities. Questionnaire analysis showed that the preference was for expectations to be communicated in more positive terms – that offenders should learn to follow the rules, make amends for their wrongdoing and show that they could live lawfully and even make something of their lives. Generally, the lack of support for amends is surprising, perhaps indicating that community reparation may not be such a popular idea as is commonly supposed.

Responding to penal communication

Given that the messages seen as conveyed in sentencing often implied the expected response, it came as no surprise that questionnaire statements encapsulating how offenders should respond to the experience of being

Table 5.4 Instrumental messages: percentage agree (and ranking in list of all statements)

Statements	Magistrates % (N=377)	Staff % (N=129)	Offenders % (N=134)	Victims % (N=107)
Threat (If we see you here again it will be worse for you)	48 (9th)	46 (10th)	60 (3rd)	66 (6th)
Rules (If you want to live in the community you have to follow the rules)	78 (4th)	69 (5th)	52 (7th)	78 (2nd)
Amends (We expect you to do something to make up for what you did wrong)	61 (7th)	69 (4th)	52 (8th)	63 (7th)
Lawful (We are giving you a chance to show that you can live a lawful life)	61 (6th)	68 (6th)	65 (1st)	59 (8th)
Improve (This is your chance to show you can make something of your life)	56 (8th)	66 (7th)	63 (2nd)	53 (10th)
Learn (This is to help you learn the difference between right and wrong)	40 (10th)	56 (9th)	53 (6th)	59 (9th)

sentenced were generally strongly endorsed (see Table 5.5). Magistrates, staff and victims seemed pretty unanimous that offenders should try to avoid offending in the future; they also agreed that offenders should be willing to change their behaviour. Offenders tended to agree, albeit less enthusiastically than the other groups. Like von Hirsch (1993), respondents seemed to expect a 'moral' response from the offender in terms of an acknowledgement of wrongdoing and an effort at better self-restraint. Indeed, in interview, they seemed highly critical when such a response was not forthcoming, a reaction that does not imply the position argued by von Hirsch (1999) that efforts at reform are peripheral to rather than at the core of sentencing. As well as taking responsibility, offenders were comparatively receptive to the idea that they should show remorse – but not apparently because they had hurt the victim or harmed the community. For offenders to feel ashamed was comparatively unpopular with all groups, mirroring the somewhat negative views expressed in interview about making sentencing a 'shaming' experience.

The picture that emerges from this and the tables presented earlier is of offenders being less keen to identify and receive penal messages than other groups were to transmit them. However, they were reasonably responsive to those messages: their top five options attracted over 70 per cent of agreement, and only one (accept harm) less than 50 per cent. Another finding is the lack of strong support for what might be seen as a reparative – or restorative – model (represented by the last three statements in Table 5.5) beyond 'pay dues' achieving a middle ranking with offenders and 'make up' with victims. This may have been the result of a lack of familiarity with this kind of paradigm, or an inability to associate it with criminal justice.

A possible framework for community penalties

I encountered keen support for community penalties among the people participating in my research. Their confidence arose from the key role that community penalties were seen to play in giving offenders the opportunity, or positively assisting them, to respond appropriately to the expectations placed upon them not to offend in the future. Understood in terms of communicative penal aims, community penalties were seen to have the capacity to combine an appeal to offenders' sense of moral agency (or citizenship) with practical help in overcoming the obstacles to moving away from crime. Comparing how various disposals fared in the questionnaire, probation scored highest according to how people rated its aims as a punishment, whereas community service scored highest in terms of the penal messages that it was seen to communicate. In both analyses, custody was much less popular.

In interview, people often compared community penalties favourably with custody, particularly when it came to encouraging offenders to take responsibility for their offending and for related aspects of their lifestyles. This was not an aim that imprisonment was seen to promote. Indeed, the sentencing aims that questionnaire respondents saw custody delivering – disapproval, retribution and incapacitation – conjure up an image of the offender as someone to whom things are done rather than someone whose active engagement is sought.[6] Variously, according to the people I interviewed, being in prison separated offenders from domestic responsibilities; denied them their capacity to make decisions; relieved them of a sense of further obligation and produced a sense of grievance according to which they were the victims rather than the victimisers. Even so, it was not uncommon for the view to be expressed that, despite its drawbacks, custody was the only way to deal with offenders who persisted in offending despite being given opportunities to desist.

Table 5.5 How offenders should respond to punishment: percentage agree (and ranking in list of 12 statements)

Statements	Magistrates % (N=375)	Staff % (N=128)	Offenders % (N=139)	Victims % (N=108)
Repent (Try to avoid offending in the future)	97 (1st)	95 (1st)	84 (2nd)	98 (1st)
Prepared to change (Be willing to change their behaviour)	88 (5th)	82 (4th)	77 (3rd)	94 (2nd)
Deterred (Want to avoid being punished again)	89 (4th)	80 (5th)	86 (1st)	86 (5th)
Take responsibility (Accept that what they did was wrong)	95 (2nd)	88 (2nd)	74 (4th)	89 (4th)
Show remorse (Show that they are sorry for what they have done)	76 (8th)	65 (10th)	71 (5th)	76 (9th)
Accept hurt (Accept that they hurt the victim)	94 (3rd)	87 (3rd)	58 (9th)	93 (3rd)
Accept harm (Accept that they have harmed the community)	86 (6th)	78 (6th)	48 (12th)	77 (7th)
Feel ashamed (Feel ashamed for what they have done)	67 (12th)	45 (12th)	52 (11th)	73 (10th)
Accept punishment (Accept that it is right for them to do the punishment)	83 (7th)	72 (7th)	65 (6th)	77 (8th)
Pay dues (Be ready to pay their debt to society)	70 (11th)	63 (11th)	63 (7th)	73 (11th)
Make up (Be ready to make up for what they have done wrong)	75 (9th)	70 (9th)	61 (8th)	80 (6th)
Compensate (Try to put right the harm to the victim)	75 (10th)	71 (8th)	54 (10th)	70 (12th)

The centrality of reform in accounts of punishment suggests that my research participants would see this as having a far stronger role than the peripheral one identified by von Hirsch (1999). On this point, my findings were consistent with public opinion research, in which people have been found to place considerable emphasis upon crime preventive and rehabilitative goals and to support community penalties once reminded or made aware of them (Hough and Roberts 2002; Roberts and Stalans 1997; Sanders and Roberts 2000). It also fits with offenders' views and experiences of supervision, which they clearly see as aimed at reducing the likelihood of their future offending (Rex 1999). The desire for punishment to be used in the pursuit of socially useful goals is hard to dismiss, given the regularity with which it is expressed. It seems to go beyond the mere expression of censure – even dialectically defensible censure – as a normative appeal to desist supplemented by the prudential disincentive of hard treatment (von Hirsch 1993, as refined by Bottoms 1998). Indeed, in granting grounds to criticise the offender who reacts with indifference to being punished, von Hirsch (1993) implies that society has a stake in how offenders respond to the experience of being punished. If that is so, it seems to follow that punishment should promote responses that are considered desirable. As Duff (2001) argues, this means that material forms of punishment should cohere with the aims of sentencing, and this is an aspect of punishment in which theorists have a proper interest. In other words, if we want offenders to stop offending, it is not enough to appeal to them to do so and back this up with threats; we should be looking to penal agents to reinforce those messages and assist offenders to meet the implicit expectations. In pursuing these aspirations, community penalties appear to have much to offer.

Looking first at probation, there was a fair degree of consensus among my research participants that this disposal was intended to meet sentencing aims at the core of the whole punishment enterprise. These were making offenders see why what they did was wrong (persuasion) and helping them to tackle the problems behind their offending (rehabilitation). Quite clearly, offenders were not to be let off the hook: the wrongfulness of their behaviour was to be brought to their attention. At the same time, a constructive outcome was to be sought in which offenders were engaged as individuals capable of understanding a moral appeal and worthy of assistance in overcoming what caused them to offend (in the technical language, their 'criminogenic needs'). This is actually very close to the role of 'transparent persuasion' that Duff (2001) attributes to probation, although offenders certainly did not portray probation in Duff's terms as aiming to secure their penitent understanding of their wrongs and therefore their repentance. Nor, incidentally, were probation officers inclined to describe their work in such intimate, almost spiritual terms. That said, offenders could see probation as helping them to develop a better understanding of what caused them to offend, with what consequences and how to avoid the same pitfalls in the future. They could also see the experience as helping them to engage in processes of change: they could learn something and receive encouragement from their probation officer; and they could gain a sense of achievement from engaging in or refraining from certain activities while on probation. Similar accounts have been given in research on offenders' perspectives of probation, where probationers seemed to look for a certain amount of direction and encouragement and were prepared to accept a 'moral appeal' (see Rex 1999 for a summary).

To a large extent, current approaches within probation accord with the picture sketched above, with a focus on confronting offending behaviour and teaching offenders cognitive and problem-solving skills. According to Raynor (2002), there are strong prospects of 'what works' interventions being extended to meet offenders' 'social integration' needs, with pathfinder projects being implemented in basic skills, resettlement and hostel-based work. This prediction may be overoptimistic. True, the Correctional Services Accreditation Panel has widened its remit beyond a focus on programmes to encompass 'integrated systems' such as case management, assessment and resettlement (see Joint Prison/Probation Accreditation Panel 2002; Rex *et al.* 2003). However, it is not clear yet that enough is being done to deal with offenders within their social environments, and to complement work on their thinking and behaviour by attempts to help them with the problems they encounter in the community (Raynor and Vanstone 1997; Rex 2001).

Offenders' reactions to penal messages suggest that a focus on what offenders might be capable of in the future might be more effective than a preoccupation with their past behaviour. As reported above, offenders displayed some resistance to the idea of penal moralising – disapproval of their behaviour and the messages that it harmed the community or hurt the victim. However, 70 per cent of offenders were open to persuasion about why what they did was wrong, and they seemed to accept the expectations that they should live lawfully and make something of their lives. Emerging findings from the desistance literature also favour a future orientation for probation work. Looking at how ex-convicts reform and rebuild their lives, Maruna (2001) identified a process of 'making good' in which the individual selectively and creatively reinterprets past events to suit his or her future aspirations, so justifying one's past while also rationalising the decision to go straight. Dwelling on their past misdeeds may not be the most effective way in which to get offenders to undergo these processes of self-reinvention. This is not to suggest that any discussion of offending is counter-productive, nor that the offence should never be mentioned. Offenders saw themselves as learning from thinking about what caused them to offend and with what consequences. However, Farrall (2002) seems right to argue that the overall context for discussions about offending should be forward-looking, to how offenders might be helped to desist from offending and make something of their lives in the future, rather than caught in a backwards-looking preoccupation with confronting offending behaviour.

Looking at the implications of this for work with offenders, a consideration of why certain kinds of offending are wrong – how other people might be damaged – would provide just the starting point for the intervention, not its main focus. The focus would be on how the individual might be helped to overcome the problems behind his or her offending to live lawfully in the community – whether this meant tackling drugs dependency, a lack of basic skills or access to employment and stable accommodation. The emphasis would be pro-social rather than condemnatory. Maruna (2001) suggests that a psychological turning point for desisting offenders might be provided by 'redemption rituals', in which a penal agent (perhaps a judge or a magistrate) formally certifies the offender as having reformed. Such an approach would be consistent with the use of pro-social modelling to encourage offenders to become active citizens and to learn more socially responsible behaviour, in which rewards are used to reinforce pro-social statements and actions (Trotter 1999). A continuing role for the sentencer would also help to promote a closer integration between the sentence announced in court and the sentence delivered in the community, which a number of research participants recommended as a means to reinforce sentencing messages and clarify what sentences mean.

When it came to community service, the experience of making reparation to the community (in itself not greatly prioritised as a sentencing aim) was seen to have the potential for a positive impact on offenders by encouraging them to live lawful and useful lives. Such a view goes well beyond the image of community service as a classic punishment that can be equated with imposing a 'fine' on the person's time. It even seems to go beyond Duff's (2001) portrayal of the work as enabling an offender to express his or her renewed commitment to the community. Whereas Duff seems to confine himself to what the offender might be expressing in actually undertaking the work, the people I interviewed seemed to be contemplating the impact of that experience on other aspects of offenders' lives. Thus, for example, offenders were seen to gain an insight into what existence was like for particularly vulnerable groups, such as the elderly and disabled. In addition, community service was seen as a motivating, even an educational, experience, which enabled offenders to see that they might have a useful contribution to make to society and to gain 'grounded increments in self-esteem' (Toch 2000).

In these accounts, research participants seemed to be anticipating the rehabilitative and reintegrative aspirations encapsulated by the recent CS pathfinder projects, in which CS supervisors acting as pro-social models used reinforcement and rewards to encourage socially responsible attitudes and behaviour.[7] This approach was implemented on a national scale in October 2003, in the form of the Enhanced Community Punishment scheme, providing an opportunity to see whether those aspirations can be achieved in practice. For the implementation of this approach within CS practice creates significant challenges, not least how to ensure that offenders experience the kind of work placements and supervision that can help them see themselves as capable of making a useful social contribution (see Johnson and Rex 2002; Rex and Gelsthorpe 2004).

The strong endorsement that my research participants gave to proportionality raises the question of whether it is possible to develop community penalties that, while being communicative, retain a sufficient relationship with the gravity of the offence to satisfy the requirements of justice. This question confronts the need to reconcile at a practical level the role of community penalties as punishments 'deserved' by the offence with their role in crime prevention, on which my findings point to a possible way forward. When contemplated by interview participants, departures from proportionality seemed to be downwards. This was because the desirability of taking the opportunity to prevent someone from offending again in the future was seen to override the compulsion to punish him or her. At the same time, what was not contemplated was the imposition of more punishment than was justified by the seriousness of the offence in order to stop that person offending. This does not support the proposal in the Carter Report for levels of intervention to be determined by 'risk', nor the proposition that persistent offenders should be punished progressively more severely (Carter 2003). Within the constraint imposed by the gravity of the offence, however, the approach might be characterised as somewhat 'individualised', taking account of the offender's background and whether the punishment is likely to stop their offending. Views seem consistent with the model around which some consensus appears to be emerging, by which community penalties are ranked in four to six bands and the penalty likely to have the desired impact is selected from the band indicated by the gravity of the offence(s).[8] Such a model would allow the selection of a community penalty that was 'communicatively apt' (Duff 2001), while ensuring that proportionality acted as a real constraint on the amount of punishment that could be imposed. Ranking community penalties into bands of roughly equivalent severity would require comparable punitive values to be attributed to their various dimensions, a task that could be undertaken by the Sentencing Guidelines Council.

Conclusions

Community penalties were clearly seen by research participants to have rich communicative potential. There is a case for giving community-based sanctions a central place in a sentencing framework the focus of which is on persuading offenders of the nature of their offences as public wrongs, encouraging them to take responsibility and assisting them to move forward in a positive, law-abiding way in the future. The views of the people participating in my research point towards certain key principles for the development of communicative community penalties, and I put these forward for discussion. First, censure and consequentialism should be seen as co-equal partners.[9] Second, proportionality should act as a real constraint on the amount of punishment imposed. Third, it is necessary for censure to be 'dialectically defensible' if it is to be acceptable to offenders, taking place within the context of an individualised moral dialogue in which the offender's view is fully considered (Bottoms 1998).[10] Fourth, in understandings of penal messages, neither denunciation nor repentance should be overstated.[11] Fifth, content does matter: society has a stake in how offenders respond to punishment, and therefore punishments should promote desirable responses. Finally, a future orientation towards desistance is more promising than a preoccupation with 'confronting offending behaviour'.

Notes

1 Dignan (2003), for example, sees restorative justice as dealing with wrongs, a position with which Braithwaite (2003) and Walgrave (2003) would strongly disagree.

2 My aim was to interview 60 people, 15 from each of the four groups listed above. In the event, I interviewed 29 women and 34 men – fewer victims than I had hoped (just ten, compared with 22 magistrates). There were 18 probation staff and 13 offenders; perhaps inevitably, the latter had a younger profile than the other groups and only three of them were female (other groups were fairly equally composed of men and women).

3 385 questionnaires were returned by magistrates, 143 by offenders, 132 by probation staff and 111 by victims (the latter were approached through a victims' organisation and therefore unknown to me). Response rates varied widely, but were generally between 30–50 per cent for magistrates and probation staff and as little as 22 per cent for victims. Questionnaires were administered face-to-face to offenders on visits to community service work sites and probation offices, and very few refused. Of the four groups, offenders were more likely to be male (90 per cent) and younger (average age 25), while victims were most likely to be female (60 per cent) and magistrates comprised the oldest group (average age 49).

4 I had hoped to conduct 40 follow-up interviews but delays to this element of the fieldwork meant that it was feasible to complete just 11 interviews.

5 The questionnaire asked whether respondents saw it as more important for the court to make the offender pay for the crime (retributivist) or to stop the offender committing another crime (consequentialist). A clear majority of all groups identified themselves as consequentialist, ranging from 85 per cent of staff to 60 per cent of magistrates. Most also agreed that 'the court should aim

to match the punishment to how serious the crime was', ranging from 97 per cent of magistrates to 65 per cent of offenders. No greater agreement with proportionality was found according to how people prioritised the aims of punishment.

6 The questionnaire asked which of the 13 statements of sentencing aims respondents saw as representing the main purposes of various disposals. Prison was seen primarily in terms of disapproval, retribution and incapacitation; community service as reparation, retribution and encouragement; probation as rehabilitation, persuasion and reform; and tagging as incapacitation, disapproval and retribution.

7 As explained in Rex and Gelsthorpe (2004), the thinking behind the CS projects is that the practical setting in which CS occurs, and the nature of the contacts into which it brings offenders, offer learning experiences at least as powerful as the cognitive–behavioural approach used in general offending programmes. The theory is that the performance of community service may engage offenders in the kind of altruistic activity that produces 'teaching points' similar to those in cognitive skills training, which 'emerge, however, from experience rather than academic training' (Toch 2000: 275). Building on her earlier study of CS schemes in Scotland (McIvor 1992), McIvor (1998) suggests that particularly 'rewarding' community service placements entail some reciprocity and exchange in which the offender both offers service to others and has the opportunity to acquire skills.

8 See Tonry (1998) and Raynor (1997). This is reminiscent of the model originally put forward by Wasik and von Hirsch (1988) and similar to Halliday's outline tariff (Home Office 2001).

9 Crime prevention was prioritised as the overall goal of punishment but was seen as being pursued as much through normative as instrumental means.

10 There were indications that offenders were not entirely receptive to 'penal moralising' because they did not see sentencing as taking sufficient account of their particular circumstances and the impact of the punishment on them. They also seemed to see themselves – and to be depicted by others – as somewhat excluded and alienated from courtroom proceedings in which their future liberty was being determined.

11 Not only was support limited for the idea of prompting remorse as an aim of sentencing or in how particular penalties were portrayed, but interviews indicated some unease with the intimate processes of remorse and apology as played out in the criminal justice setting and with the religious connotations of repentance.

References

Bottoms, A. E. (1995) 'The philosophy and politics of punishment and sentencing', in C. Clarkson and R. Morgan (eds) *The Politics of Sentencing Reform* (Oxford: Clarendon Press).

Bottoms, A. E. (1998) 'Five puzzles in von Hirsch's theory of punishment', in A. Ashworth and M. Wasik (eds) *Fundamentals of Sentencing Theory: Essays in honour of Andrew von Hirsch* (Oxford: Clarendon Press).

Bottoms, A. E. (2000) 'Theory and research in criminology', in R. D. King and E. Wincup (eds) *Doing Research on Crime and Justice* (Oxford: Oxford University Press).
Braithwaite, J. (2003) 'Principles of restorative justice', in A. von Hirsch, J. R. Roberts and A. E. Bottoms (eds) *Restorative Justice and Criminal Justice* (Oxford: Hart).
Carter, P. (2003) *Managing Offenders, Changing Lives: A new approach. Report of the Correctional Services Review* (London: Strategy Unit).
Dignan, J. (2003) 'Towards a systematic model of restorative justice: reflections on the concept, its context and the need for clear constraints', in A. von Hirsch, J. R. Roberts and A. E. Bottoms (eds) *Restorative Justice and Criminal Justice* (Oxford: Hart).
Duff, R. A. (2001) *Punishment, Communication and Community* (Oxford: Oxford University Press).
Duff, R. A. (2003) 'Restoration and retribution', in A. von Hirsch, J. R. Roberts and A. E. Bottoms (eds) *Restorative Justice and Criminal Justice* (Oxford: Hart).
Farrall, S. (2002) *Rethinking What Works with Offenders: Probation, social context and desistance from crime* (Cullompton: Willan).
Home Office (2001) *Making Punishments Work* (London: HMSO).
Home Office (2004) *Reducing Crime – Changing Lives: The government's plans for transforming the management of offenders* (London: Home Office).
Hough, M. and Roberts, J. V. (1998) *Attitudes to Punishment: Findings from the British Crime Survey*, Home Office Research Study No. 179 (London: Home Office).
Hough, M. and Roberts, J. (2002) 'Public knowledge and public opinion of sentencing', in N. Hutton and C. Tata (eds) *Sentencing and Society: International perspectives* (Ashgate: Ashworth).
Hudson, B. (1987) *Justice Through Punishment: A critique of the 'justice' model of corrections* (London: McMillan Education).
Johnson, C. and Rex, S. A. (2002) 'Community service: rediscovering reintegration', in David Ward and John Scott (eds) *Probation – Working for Justice*, 2nd edition (Oxford: Oxford University Press).
Joint Prison/Probation Services Accreditation Panel (2002) *Annual Report 2001/2* [www.homeoffice.gov.uk].
Kalmthout, A. (2002) 'From community service to community sanctions: comparative perspectives', in H. Albrecht and A. Kalmthout (eds) *Community Sanctions and Measures in Europe and North America* (Freiberg: Edition Inscrim).
Maruna, S. (2001) *Making Good: How ex-convicts reform and rebuild their lives* (Washington, DC: American Psychological Association).
McIvor, G. (1992) *Sentenced to Serve* (Aldershot: Avebury).
McIvor, G. (1998) 'Pro-social modelling and legitimacy: lessons from a study of community service', in S. A. Rex and A. Matravers (eds) *Pro-Social Modelling and Legitimacy: The Clarke Hall Day Conference* (Cambridge: Institute of Criminology).
Morgan, R. (2003) 'Correctional services: not waving but drowning', *Prison Service Journal*, 145, 6–8.
Nellis, M. (2001) 'Community penalties in historical perspective', in A. Bottoms, L. Gelsthorpe and S. Rex (eds) *Community Penalties: Change and challenges* (Cullompton: Willan).
Raynor, P. (1997) 'Some observations on rehabilitation and justice', *Howard Journal of Criminal Justice*, 36, 248–262.

Raynor, P. (2001) 'Community penalties and social integration: "community" as solution and as problem', in A. Bottoms, L. Gelsthorpe and S. Rex (eds) *Community Penalties: Change and challenges* (Cullompton: Willan).
Raynor, P. (2002) 'Community penalties: probation, punishment and "what works"', in M. Maguire, R. Morgan and R. Reiner (eds) *The Oxford Handbook of Criminology*, 3rd edition (Oxford: Oxford University Press).
Raynor, P. and Vanstone, M. (1997) *Straight Thinking on Probation (STOP): The mid-Glamorgan experiment*, Probation Studies Unit Report No. 4 (Oxford: University of Oxford Centre for Criminological Research).
Rex, S. A. (1998) 'Applying desert principles to community sentences: lessons from two criminal justice acts', *Criminal Law Review*, 381–391.
Rex, S. A. (1999) 'Desistance from offending: experiences of probation', *The Howard Journal*, 38, 366–383.
Rex, S. A. (2001) 'Beyond cognitive-behaviouralism? Reflections on the effectiveness literature', in A. Bottoms, L. Gelsthorpe and S. Rex (eds) *Community Penalties: Change and challenges* (Cullompton: Willan).
Rex, S. A. and Gelsthorpe, L. R. (2004) 'Using community service to encourage inclusive citizenship', in R. Burnett and C. Roberts (eds) *Evidence-Based Practice in Probation and Youth Justice* (Cullompton: Willan).
Rex, S. A., Lieb, R., Bottoms, A. E. and Goodwin, L. (2003) *JAP Evaluation Final Report*, Home Office Research Study No. 273 (London: Home Office).
Roberts, J .V. (2002) 'Alchemy in sentencing: an analysis of reform proposals in England and Wales', *Punishment and Society*, 4(4), 425–442.
Roberts, J. V. and Stalans, L. J. (1997) *Public Opinion, Crime and Criminal Justice* (Oxford: Westview Press).
Robinson, P. H. and Darley, J. M. (1995) *Justice, Liability and Blame: Community views and the criminal law* (Oxford: Westview Press).
Sanders, T. and Roberts, J. V. (2000) 'Public attitudes towards conditional sentencing: results of a national survey', *Canadian Journal of Behavioural Science*, 32, 199–207.
Toch, H. (2000) 'Altruistic activity as correctional treatment', *International Journal of Offender Therapy and Comparative Criminology*, 44, 270–278.
Tonry, M. (1998) 'Intermediate sanctions in sentencing guidelines', in M. Tonry (ed.) *Crime and Justice: A review of research*, 23 (London: University of Chicago Press).
Trotter, C. (1999) *Working with Involuntary Clients: A guide to practice* (London: Sage).
von Hirsch, A. (1993) *Censure and Sanctions* (Oxford: Clarendon Press).
von Hirsch, A. (1999) 'Punishment, penance and the State', in A. Matravers (ed.) *Punishment and Political Theory* (Oxford: Hart Publishing).
Walgrave, L. (2003) 'Imposing restoration rather than inflicting pain', in A. von Hirsch, J. R. Roberts and A. E. Bottoms (eds) *Restorative Justice and Criminal Justice* (Oxford: Hart).
Wasik, M. and von Hirsch, A. (1988) 'Non-custodial penalties and the principles of desert', *Criminal Law Review*, 555–571.
Zehr, H. (1990) *Changing Lenses: A new focus for crime and justice* (Scottdale, PA: Herald Press).

Chapter 6

Diversionary and non-supervisory approaches to dealing with offenders

George Mair

> The fine is the most commonly used of all penalties available to the criminal courts as a whole and appears to be one of the most effective in relation to offenders of almost all age groups and criminal histories. (ACPS 1970: 5)
>
> We have not investigated the use of fines in detail in this Report as our focus is on alternatives to prison, and it is not often the case that a fine will represent a credible alternative sentence for an offender who would otherwise be imprisoned. (House of Commons 1998: xlvi)

Introduction

A great deal of criminal justice policy and practice over the last 30 years or more has been concerned with the problems caused by what seems to be an ever-expanding prison population. Indeed, a strong case could be made for this as the most significant issue in post-war penal policy. Efforts to combat the rising prison population have included the introduction of new sentences (the suspended sentence, community service orders, probation centres, combination orders); experimental initiatives (intensive probation on at least two occasions – see Folkard *et al.* 1974, 1976; Mair *et al.* 1994); a county-wide experiment in Hampshire in the early 1980s (see Smith *et al.* 1984); new approaches to dealing with defendants (bail information schemes, changes to early release schemes); parole; home detention curfews; and a full-scale reorientation of sentencing philosophy with the 1991 Criminal Justice Act. Yet despite such efforts, the prison population continues to grow, and we now face with some equanimity a prison population that would have been unthinkable 12 years ago.

As might be expected, given its prominence as a policy and practice issue, a considerable amount of academic effort has been devoted to the subject of prison overcrowding and 'alternatives to custody'. For the most part, the research has suffered from two major limitations. First, it has tended to focus on one initiative or approach to the problem at any one time and there has been no incremental development of practice. Second, the problem itself – the size of the prison population – has tended to be viewed in an undifferentiated way. Thus, prison overcrowding may be a result of too many fine defaulters being imprisoned, too many defendants being remanded to custody, too many offenders being sentenced to custody, or to increases in sentence length – and each of these would require different approaches to tackle it. With the Coulsfield Inquiry, a more holistic approach to the topic of alternatives to prison is possible, and in this chapter I will consider the role of so-called 'low-level' approaches to sentencing and the diversion of offenders from court (although it should be noted that such terms as 'low level' or 'shallow end' are part of the problem).

The chapter will focus on fines, conditional discharges and police cautions. The degree of research interest into these three disposals has varied, but they have not been examined as having a serious contribution to make in the debate about alternatives to prison – as the second quote at the head of the chapter suggests. And it is notable that in many of the texts of the 1980s – when the concept of 'alternatives to custody' was an especially significant theme of policy and research – fines, discharges and cautions received relatively little attention (see e.g. Stanley and Baginsky 1984; Pointing 1986; NACRO 1989; Vass 1990). Yet while they might not be considered as offering direct alternatives to custody – at least not in the current punitive climate – they have a key role to play if sentencing as a whole is considered. It is now widely accepted that the community rehabilitation order (CRO), the community punishment order (CPO), and the community punishment and rehabilitation order (CPRO) have in recent years all slipped down-tariff and are dealing with less serious offenders than previously (Mair 1997, 2003; Morgan 2003). If this development is to be countered – and for the credibility of the National Probation Service (NPS) or the planned National Offender Management Service (NOMS) it is essential – then many of those currently receiving community penalties should be fined or even conditionally discharged. Perhaps more important in this context, however, is the need to free up community penalties from 'lightweight' offenders in order for the NPS to be able to accommodate those who are currently being sentenced to short terms of imprisonment. The demands on the NPS have increased dramatically in the past decade, but there has been no commensurate increase in resources so that if the service is to act as a credible alternative to custody it will have to shed its low-risk offenders. This argument has recently been advanced forcefully by Her Majesty's Chief Inspector of Probation, so there is powerful official backing for such a development (HMIP 2003).

Such recalibration (or de-escalation, to use Harris' 1987 term) requires movement on a tariff-wide basis, so that if more offenders are to move from community penalties to fines there will also be a need to make more use of conditional discharges and of cautions, too, so that more offenders are diverted from a court sentence. Cautions also have a positive role to play in so far as they can delay entry to the courts and formal sentencing – and the longer the delay in being dealt with by the courts, the less likely it is that an offender will end up in custody, with all the disadvantages that that entails.

In the remainder of this chapter I will first examine the relevant research; following this, trends in the use of fines, conditional discharges and cautions will be discussed, and any evidence for their effectiveness in terms of reconviction rates. The concluding section will examine the most recent policy developments, and draw together the argument for greater – and more effective – use of these 'low-level' disposals, emphasising their importance in helping to build a coherent, complementary package that can offer a credible, sustained alternative to prison sentences.

The research context

Diversion from court

The caution can play a critical role in helping to avoid prosecution, although it has suffered from not being researched in depth. Studies of cautioning have tended to focus on variations between police force areas in order to point up the inconsistencies involved, and the disparity between Home Office policy and police practice (see e.g. Ditchfield 1976; Laycock and Tarling 1985; Evans and Wilkinson 1990). Recent changes to cautioning policy (the introduction of reprimands and final warnings for offenders under the age of 18) have been aimed at reducing inconsistencies and targeting such disposals at the most appropriate offenders, but while Holdaway (2003) has argued against the negative impact of such changes claimed by some commentators (Muncie 1999; Goldson 2000), research has yet to assess the effect of the changes.

The main impact of cautioning has been on juvenile justice in the 1980s, when a philosophy of 'minimum intervention' associated with Tutt and Giller (1987) argued in favour of cautioning instead of prosecution and advocated a systems approach to effect this. Multi-agency Juvenile Liaison Bureaux were set up in many areas, and the use of cautioning for juveniles increased significantly as a result, without any evidence of 'net-widening' arising from this increase (Bottoms *et al.* 1990). Simultaneously, there was a significant decline in the use of custody (Allen 1991) which is possibly attributable in part to the growth in cautioning, though in hard-nosed research terms this has never been conclusively demonstrated. However, with the hardening of the penal climate in the 1990s the impact of this approach faded. Both the Audit Commission (1996) and New Labour (see Bottoms and Dignan 2004) repudiated the 'minimum intervention' approach, and pre-court diversion was restricted in scope. The introduction of reprimands and final warnings has led to an increase in interventions with young offenders.

The Scottish approach to youth justice has traditionally been more welfare-based and while the use of cautions to divert offenders from prosecution declined in England and Wales from the early 1990s, a diversionary approach has continued in Scotland via the children's hearings system. There are increasing tensions in Scotland between this welfare-based philosophy and more punitive tendencies originating from south of the border, and it will be interesting to see how these play out in the future. But the evidence from England and Wales in the 1980s and from Scotland suggests that diversion from prosecution can work effectively (for a full discussion of the two systems, see Bottoms and Dignan 2004) without serious evidence of net-widening.

It is worth noting one other initiative designed to divert offenders from prosecution – and this one was more focused on adults. The Public Interest Case Assessment (PICA) experiment of the early 1990s targeted defendants recommended for prosecution by the police and referred to the Crown Prosecution Service (CPS). Selected defendants were interviewed by probation staff about their domestic circumstances, health, financial situation and any other matters that might be relevant to 'public interest' considerations. The material collected was passed on to the CPS which, in the light of the added information, was expected to be more likely to discontinue proceedings. An evaluation of the PICA schemes (Crisp *et al.* 1995) found that public-interest discontinuance rates did increase, but the cost of the schemes outweighed any financial savings. As a result of this, as well as the presence of Michael Howard as Home Secretary with an overtly punitive ideology which did not appreciate such ideas as discontinuance or diversion from prosecution, by the time the research report was completed it did not fall on fertile ground and was not developed. If such a scheme were to be revived, it would be in tension with the subsequent so-called Narey reforms (Narey 1997) on the speeding-up of criminal justice, since the collection of additional social information to support public-interest discontinuances is necessarily time-consuming.

Fines and conditional discharges

The conditional discharge can be disposed of relatively simply as there is no research on this court sentence, which is surprising as in 2002 the courts imposed almost 100,000 such sentences – nearly half of them for indictable offences (Home Office 2003). The need for work on this sentence would seem to be important, as while it is a sentence of the court, it also bears similarities with cautions and especially the new conditional caution (see below).

Examined in relation to prison and community penalties, the fine has also roused relatively little academic interest; indeed, it is worth noting that in the *Oxford Handbook of Criminology*, the closest we have to a definitive textbook, only a couple of pages of more than 1,000 are taken up by the fine. Yet the fine remains, as it has been for many years, the most commonly used sentence in England and Wales (with 975,000 imposed in 2002) and its importance is recognised: 'The fine . . . accords with some of the central features of classical jurisprudence, being calculable, unarbitrary and public.' (Bottoms 1983: 186). 'The fine is often presented as the ideal penal measure. It is easily calibrated, so that courts can reflect differing degrees of gravity and culpability. It is non-intrusive, since it does not involve supervision or the loss of one's time. Indeed, it is straightforwardly punitive, "uncontaminated by other values"' (Ashworth 2000: 271–272).

Despite such grandiloquent and positive statements, the literature on fines has concentrated on a handful of closely interrelated themes that have pointed to problems: consistency, assessment and collection/enforcement.[1] These themes were already evident in the Wootton Report, which was responsible for proposing the introduction of community service by offenders; the Committee argued for 'greater consistency' in fining, that fines 'should be assessed according to the offender's ability to pay', suggested that a day fine system was not practicable,[2] and recommended the introduction of an Enforcement Officer to collect overdue fines (ACPS 1970: 5–11). Early work carried out by the Home Office Research Unit examined fine enforcement and found a somewhat bewildering array of practices used to enforce payment, none of which appeared to be especially successful (Softley 1973, 1978), although the later study confirmed earlier claims that that the fine appeared to be 'more effective than other forms of sentence' (Softley 1978: 28) and that employment was a significant factor in the decision to fine. The relationship between employment and fining became more significant in the 1980s due to higher levels of unemployment, and was also noted in two studies by Iain Crow and his colleagues (Crow and Simon 1987; Crow *et al.* 1989) and in relation to the Crown Court by Moxon (1988). Yet another Home Office study noted that:

> In fixing the amounts of fines, courts need to strike a balance between the gravity of the offence and a realistic assessment of what the offender can sensibly pay ... the key to effective enforcement was speed of action, both following default and in following up initial measures where these have failed. Successful enforcement therefore depends on, first, the ability to identify defaulters quickly; second, prompt action against the defaulter once he has been detected; and third, swift follow-up action. (Softley and Moxon 1982: 10)

Enforcement continued to be a topic of interest. Mair and Lloyd examined the use of money payment supervision orders to enforce fines and found a situation of 'considerable confusion' (1989: 28). In an effort to encourage payment of fines by those dependent upon state benefits, a study was carried out to test the feasibility of using deductions from income support for those who were unemployed (Moxon *et al.* 1990a). The results were positive:

> The study suggested that deductions from income support to pay fines would be feasible, and that such a scheme would greatly reduce the number of people imprisoned for default ... in the great majority of cases fines could be paid in this way, even if many of those fined were additionally subject to deductions for the community charge. (Moxon *et al.* 1990a: 12)

Research in Scotland, however, suggested that deductions from benefits were rarely used due to the opposition of sentencers both in principle and as a result of practical, operational problems (Clark 1998).

Day fines may not have been recommended by the Wootton Report, but in its 1977–78 Report *The Reduction of Pressure on the Prison System*, the House of Commons Expenditure Committee recommended that the matter should be looked at again (House of Commons 1978a, b) – a recommendation that was reiterated by various other penal reform organisations throughout the 1980s (see Moxon *et al.* 1990b: 3). The government undertook to 'ensure that the possibility of changing to a day fine system is fully explored' whenever a comprehensive review of financial penalties could be carried out (Home Office 1980: 5), and experiments in what were termed 'unit fines' took place in four courts during 1988–89. The results were unequivocal: 'unit fines are viable, and ... they are likely to achieve savings in enforcement costs relative to sums imposed' (Moxon *et al.* 1990b: 25). As a result, unit fines were a key part of the 1991 Criminal Justice Act, although research carried out to explore practitioners' views of the Act found considerable dissatisfaction with the introduction of the unit fine scheme (Mair and May 1995). In fact, as Cavadino and Dignan (2002) and Brownlee (1998) argue, the principle of unit fines was generally accepted by magistrates and the fines were achieving what they were intended to: 'in the period immediately after implementation the proportionate use of the fine among unemployed offenders rose from 30 to 43 per cent while the average value of the fine imposed on those who were unemployed fell from nearly £90 to under £70' (Brownlee 1998: 145).

While the practical difficulties (for the most part, teething problems) associated with the introduction of unit fines would almost certainly have been overcome, the penal climate was hardening and as a result of this – alongside vociferous opposition by a few magistrates, and media accounts of what appeared to be ludicrously high fines for very minor offences – the unit fine scheme was abolished in the 1993 Criminal Justice Act. Ashworth (2000) also points to the rise in the value of the 'units' between the experiment and the statutory scheme, and an increase in complexity as having caused problems. Unit fines would probably have led to better assessment, reduced inconsistencies, and lower levels of default, but after 1993 the old confusion and wide range of practices returned, as shown by Charman *et al.* (1996) and by Flood-Page and Mackie (1998).

Two publications in 1998 began to argue more positively in favour of the fine, although still noting problems with enforcement. Flood-Page and Mackie (1998: 127), while noting the decline in the use of fines, argued that:

> . . . given that fines yield revenue and are associated with reconviction rates no higher (and if anything slightly lower) than other sentences, there is a strong case for their revival. Put another way, courts used to impose fines in many instances where they would not use them now. There is no evidence that the move away from fines has yielded any benefits in terms of crime reduction.

A comprehensive overview of ways of dealing with offenders repeated these points and added forcefully:

> It is difficult to see much justification for opting for an expensive community penalty if the outcome in terms of future offending is no better than a fine . . . the resources of the Probation Service should not be dissipated on those for whom a fine would serve as well. To do so may have the perverse effect of diluting the impact that the Probation Service can have on those for whom some form of intensive intervention would bear fruit. (Goldblatt and Lewis 1998: 98)

Recent commentators have continued to stress the importance of fines: Morgan (2003) has argued cogently for sentencers to return to the fine, and Hough and his colleagues have spoken of 'Resuscitating fines as a sentencing option' (Hough *et al.* 2003: 62). Such calls are certainly not new: 15 years ago NACRO in a report aimed at displacing custody from its position at the centre of penal policy recommended that 'Urgent attention must be given to strengthening the fine' (NACRO 1989: 56).

The most recent, detailed study of fines reinforces the feeling that nothing much has changed over the last 30 years, as the author's overriding conclusion is that 'policies and practices in enforcement in magistrates' courts are generally in need of a significant overhaul' (Mackie *et al.* 2003: 9).

Compensation orders, introduced in the Criminal Justice Act 1972, sit closely with the fine but while their use has been encouraged, successive research studies have shown problems: difficulties over how to assess and quantify claims, a lack of information about loss or injury, marked differences in successful collection (leading to some victims having to wait for some time for payment), and a lack of awareness that compensation takes precedence over fines or costs (see Newburn 1988; Moxon *et al.* 1992). Despite the interest in restorative justice, which has taken concrete form with the introduction of referral orders and reparation orders for young offenders, there has been no recent research on compensation orders.

Trends in use[3]

In 1980 a total of 220,500 offenders were fined for indictable offences; this figure represented almost half (48 per cent) of all sentences passed by the courts for such offences. By 1986, the total was 150,300 (39 per cent of all sentences) and by 2002 the comparable figure was 78,500 (23 per cent of sentences for indictable offences). Since 1980 there has been a 64 per cent decrease in the use of the fine; a remarkable development that has, for the most part, been only cursorily examined. It tends to be assumed that courts began to use the fine less due to the increase in unemployment in the 1980s, that enforcement became more difficult, and that as the fine lost credibility sentencers looked elsewhere when sentencing offenders found guilty of less serious offences. Unfortunately, looking elsewhere meant moving up-tariff in practice and when this development coincided with the politicisation of law and order that began under the Thatcher governments with its consequences of increased fear of crime and demands for tougher sentencing, what might have begun as 'drift' tended to solidify.

The picture was essentially the same for males and females. Summary offences also saw a decrease in the use of the fine (with regard to summary motoring offences, this was to some extent a result of the increased use of fixed penalties), although the drop was not so dramatic.

Table 6.1 shows sentencing for indictable offences for the years 1981–2002. The steady drop in the use of the fine is clear, as is the increased use of custody and of the probation order (now the community rehabilitation order). The 1991 Criminal Justice Act introduced the combination order (now the community punishment and rehabilitation order) and curtailed the use of the suspended sentence; and in the past few years a number of new sentences have been introduced (the drug treatment and testing order, curfew orders, referral orders, etc.) that have led to the increase in the use of 'Other' sentences. Discharges have begun to drop after a slow increase during the 1980s. Hough and his colleagues have argued, with regard to the increased use of custody, that this is neither a result of an increased number of convictions nor an increase in the seriousness of crime, and these points are just as relevant to trends in sentencing generally (Hough *et al.* 2003). What Table 6.1 does suggest is that key changes took place in the early 1990s around the messy period covering the introduction of the 1991 Criminal Justice Act and its subsequent emasculation by the 1993 Criminal Justice Act. Discharges had been increasing, but after 1993 they began to be used less; the drop in fines seems to have accelerated after 1993; use of the community service order began to drop after a slow rise; and the use of custody, which had been decreasing in the late 1980s, began what has seemed to be an inexorable rise after 1993. In 1991, 54 per cent of sentences for indictable offences consisted of fines and discharges; by 2002 the comparable figure was 38 per cent. During the same period, the use of custody rose by 10 per cent. This is certainly not to argue that those who previously had been fined or discharged were being sentenced to custody, but to demonstrate an upward drift in levels of punishment.

Similar patterns can be seen for particular offences, and burglary has been a key crime in this respect. Table 6.2 shows sentences for burglary between 1981 and 2002 and the trends noted above are more clearly defined. Discharges have decreased from a high of 12 per cent in 1993 to 3 percent in 2002; the use of fines has dropped from 10 per cent in 1993 (21 per cent in 1981) to 2 per cent in 2002; the use of both probation and community service orders has decreased; while custody has risen from 29 per cent in 1993 to 51 per cent in 2002. During the 1993–2002 decade the number of those sentenced to burglary dropped from 40,200 to 26,400 – a decrease of one-third – so it would seem reasonable to conclude that increases in levels of punishment have not been due to the courts having to deal with a rise in the number of offenders convicted of burglary and reacting punitively.

The same trends can be seen for cases of theft/handling where discharges dropped from 27 per cent in 1993 to 20 per cent in 2002; fines dropped from 37 per cent to 19 per cent; community service fell from 10 per cent to 7 per cent; custody rose from 8 per cent to 22 per cent. In the case of violent indictable offences, discharges fell from 25 per cent to 12 per cent; fines from 20 per cent to 11 per cent; and custody rose from 19 per cent to 32 per cent. For both theft/handling and violent offences, the use of probation rose slightly during the period; and in the case of violent

Table 6.1 Sentences passed for indictable offences: 1981–2002 (%)

Year	Dcharg.	Fine	Prob.	CSO	Comb.	Sup.	Susp.	Custody	Other	No.
1981	12	45	7	5		3	7	15	5	464.7
1982	12	44	7	6		3	7	15	5	475.6
1983	13	43	7	7		3	6	16	4	461.8
1984	13	42	8	7		3	6	16	4	449.8
1985	13	40	8	8		3	6	18	4	444.4
1986	14	39	9	8		2	6	18	3	385.0
1987	14	38	9	8		2	7	18	3	386.8
1988	14	39	9	8		2	7	17	4	386.6
1989	16	40	10	7		2	7	16	4	339.0
1990	17	39	10	8		1	6	14	4	341.7
1991	19	35	10	9		1	6	15	4	336.0
1992	21	34	10	10		1	5	15	4	324.6
1993	22	34	10	11	2	2	1	15	4	306.9
1994	20	31	11	10	3	2	1	17	4	313.4
1995	19	30	11	10	3	3	1	20	4	301.9
1996	18	28	11	9	3	3	1	22	4	300.3
1997	18	28	11	9	4	3	1	23	5	318.8
1998	18	28	11	9	4	3	1	23	5	341.1
1999	17	27	11	9	4	3	1	23	5	341.7
2000	16	25	11	9	3	2	1	25	6	326.2
2001	16	24	12	9	2	2	1	25	9	323.2
2002	15	23	12	8	2	3	1	25	11	336.7

offences, community service orders increased. Despite some minor blips, the overall trend is the same: decreased use of fines and discharges, and increased use of custody.

Tables 6.3–6.5 set out sentencing patterns in the magistrates' courts for both indictable and summary offences, and in the Crown Court for indictable offences only. In both Crown Court and the magistrates' courts, there is evidence of a considerable decrease in the use of the fine. In 1991 fines and conditional discharges accounted for 68 per cent of sentences in the magistrates' courts for indictable offences; by 2002 this proportion had dropped to 46 per cent. Over the same period, the use of custody increased three-fold. In the Crown Court a similar picture is found: in 1991, 13 per cent of sentences were fines or conditional discharges, while by 2002 this figure had dropped to 6 per cent. The use of custody increased from 44 per cent to 63 per cent. For summary offences in the magistrates' courts, the fine, although still the predominant sentence by far, has also lost ground.

It is worth noting the increase in the use of 'Other' sentences in Tables 6.3–6.5: in the magistrates' courts for indictable offences their use rose from 2 per cent in 1991 to 12 per cent in 2002; for summary offences there

Table 6.2 Sentences for offences of burglary: 1981–2002 (%)

Year	Dcharg.	Fine	Prob.	CSO	Comb.	Sup.	Susp.	Custody	Other	No.
1981	10	21	7	9		7	8	29	10	72,600
1982	9	19	7	10		6	9	30	10	72,900
1983	9	17	8	11		6	7	33	9	69,700
1984	10	16	9	12		6	6	33	8	70,100
1985	9	15	10	12		6	6	35	8	67,000
1986	9	15	11	13		5	6	35	7	54,200
1987	9	15	12	13		5	7	35	6	54,300
1988	9	14	13	13		4	7	34	5	48,500
1989	10	14	15	13		4	7	32	5	43,300
1990	11	14	16	14		4	7	28	5	43,300
1991	12	12	16	16		3	7	28	5	45,900
1992	12	12	16	17	1	4	6	27	5	44,300
1993	12	10	16	17	4	5	1	29	5	40,200
1994	11	8	17	14	5	6	1	34	5	38,000
1995	10	6	15	13	6	7	0	38	5	35,500
1996	9	6	14	11	6	7	1	41	5	32,400
1997	8	5	13	10	6	7	0	45	5	31,700
1998	8	4	13	9	7	7	1	47	5	31,100
1999	7	4	12	9	6	6	1	49	5	29,300
2000	6	3	11	9	6	6	0	51	7	26,700
2001	4	2	12	8	4	5	0	51	13	24,700
2002	3	2	12	7	4	5	0	51	16	26,400

was an increase from 2 per cent to 6 per cent; and in the Crown Court for indictable offences there was a similar rise from 2 to 6 per cent. This suggests that one possible explanation for the decreasing use of fines and discharges is the existence of more sentences: since the Labour government came to power in 1997 there have been a number of new sentences introduced (e.g. the drug treatment and testing order, the curfew order, the action plan order, the referral order, the reparation order) and within the contemporary punitive climate sentencers may have found it all too easy to subject offenders to a new sentence which claims to be demanding rather than a fine or discharge, with its connotations of a slap on the wrist. Intrusive sentences are being preferred to those which are non-intrusive (fines and discharges).

Examining sentencing trends separately for males and females and for different age groups shows that the patterns discussed above hold true. However, the drop in the use of discharges has been much more pronounced for offenders aged under 17–18 than for their elders, e.g. 52 per cent of males aged 10 to 13 sentenced for indictable offences were discharged in 1992, but only 10 per cent in 2002, while for those aged 18–20 the figure was 17 per cent in 1992 and 14 per cent in 2002. For both

Table 6.3 Sentences in the magistrates' courts for indictable offences: 1986–2002 (%)

Sentence	1986	1991	1996	2001	2002
Absolute discharge	1	1	1	1	1
Conditional discharge	16	23	22	18	17
Fine	48	45	36	30	29
Probation order	9	10	11	12	12
Community service	7	7	9	8	8
Supervision order	3	2	3	3	2
Attendance centre	3	2	2	1	1
Combination order			3	3	2
Suspended sentence	4	3	0	0	0
Custody	8	5	9	14	15
Other	1	2	2	10	12
Total no.	299,500	252,500	229,400	254,400	263,700

Table 6.4 Sentences in the magistrates' courts for summary offences (excluding motoring): 1986–2002 (%)

Sentence	1986	1991	1996	2001	2002
Absolute discharge	1	2	1	1	1
Conditional discharge	4	7	9	10	9
Fine	90	85	83	78	78
Probation order	1	1	2	2	2
Community service		1	2	2	2
Custody		1	1	1	1
Other	4	2	1	7	6
Total no.	443,500	451,200	486,300	439,500	484,600

Table 6.5 Sentences in the Crown Court for indictable offences, 1986–2002 (%)

Sentence	1986	1991	1996	2001	2002
Conditional discharge	5	6	3	3	3
Fine	8	7	4	3	3
Probation order	8	12	10	11	10
Community service	10	13	12	11	11
Combination order			4	2	4
Suspended sentence	14	16	3	2	2
Custody	52	44	61	63	63
Other	1	2	3	5	6
Total no.	85,600	83,500	70,900	68,800	73,000

males and females under the age of 18, the use of discharges has fallen dramatically since 1999 (attendance centre orders too seem to be on the verge of disappearing), while the use of 'Other' sentences has increased substantially. This is to some extent a result of the introduction of new sentences for young offenders (curfew orders, action plan orders, reparation orders, referral orders) and it seems clear that magistrates in the youth courts prefer to sentence offenders to an intrusive sentence where something is done to or with the young offender, than to 'let them off' with a discharge. Bottoms and Dignan (2004) have noted another reason for the drop in the use of conditional discharges:

> . . . this measure [the conditional discharge] was tainted in the eyes of the New Labour government by its association with the so-called excuse culture. Accordingly, the Crime and Disorder Act 1998 provided that, where a young person is sentenced within two years of receiving a final warning, the conditional discharge is not available as a sentence unless there are 'exceptional circumstances' relating either to the offender or the offense. (Bottoms and Dignan 2004: 85)

The increased use of custody is almost ubiquitous across age groups and between genders. It is especially evident in the case of female offenders aged 14–15 to 16–17 (from 1 per cent in 1981 to 8 per cent in 2002), although males in the same age groups have experienced little or no increase. It is also worth noting, for both males and females aged 21+, the near disappearance of the suspended sentence: in 1993, it would appear that the drop in the use of the suspended sentence was taken up by fines, probation, community service and combination orders, but by 1994 the trend changed direction and suspended sentences became absorbed by immediate custody. The significance of the early 1990s for fixing changes in sentencing, especially the increased use of custody, is evident again.

Turning to the use of police cautions (including reprimands and final warnings), Table 6.6 sets out the number of offenders cautioned from 1981, as well as those cautioned as a percentage of all those found guilty or cautioned, for indictable offences. For both males and females, the numbers cautioned and the cautioning rate grew from 1981 to 1993, but since then the figures have decreased steadily; the cautioning rate for males in 2002 was 27 per cent (compared to 37 per cent in 1995) and for females 44 per cent (compared to 61 per cent in 1992). Female offenders are more likely to be cautioned than males, although this overall statistic largely reflects, on average, less serious offences and shorter criminal records among female than among male offenders. Cautioning is a safety-valve which functions to divert offenders from prosecution, and decreases in the cautioning rate would suggest that more offenders are being dealt with in the courts and therefore receiving a sentence of the court, which, as has been shown, is less likely to be a low-level sentence.

Table 6.6 Offenders cautioned for indictable offences (thousands): 1981–2002 (cautioning rate in parentheses)

Year	Males	Females	Total
1981	75.1 (17)	28.8 (31)	103.9 (19)
1982	78.5 (17)	32.9 (34)	111.3 (20)
1983	82.7 (18)	32.2 (34)	114.9 (21)
1984	91.7 (20)	32.4 (35)	124.1 (23)
1985	104.3 (23)	41.1 (41)	145.4 (26)
1986	98.7 (24)	38.2 (44)	136.9 (28)
1987	111.5 (26)	38.3 (45)	149.8 (30)
1988	107.0 (26)	33.7 (43)	140.7 (28)
1989	102.8 (26)	33.2 (44)	136.0 (29)
1990	124.2 (30)	42.1 (49)	166.3 (33)
1991	131.4 (32)	48.5 (54)	179.9 (36)
1992	155.0 (36)	61.1 (61)	216.2 (41)
1993	153.6 (37)	55.9 (60)	209.6 (41)
1994	153.6 (37)	56.2 (59)	209.8 (41)
1995	149.3 (37)	53.3 (59)	202.6 (41)
1996	142.6 (36)	48.2 (56)	190.8 (40)
1997	143.3 (35)	46.0 (52)	189.4 (38)
1998	142.9 (33)	48.8 (51)	191.7 (37)
1999	126.1 (31)	44.5 (48)	170.6 (34)
2000	109.7 (29)	41.2 (47)	150.9 (32)
2001	103.8 (28)	40.1 (46)	143.9 (31)
2002	104.4 (27)	38.5 (44)	142.9 (30)

Tables 6.7 and 6.8 set out the offences for which male and female offenders were cautioned, and once again significant changes are evident. There is a pattern of growth in the number of cautions up to around 1993 and then a decrease. In 1981, offences of theft accounted for 71 per cent of cautions for males; by 2002 this figure had dropped to 29 per cent. In the case of burglary the decrease was from 14 per cent to 5 percent. The effect of policy changes on cautioning can be seen clearly in the use of cautioning for drugs offences; in 1981 such offences accounted for 0.2 per cent of cautions, while by 2002 the figure was 38 per cent. In the case of females, the decrease in the use of cautions has not been so considerable as for males, although the proportionate use has changed – especially in the case of theft, which in 1981 made up 90 per cent of cautions but in 2002 only 61 per cent.

Cautioning rates vary with age. In 2002 the cautioning rate for males aged 10–11 with regard to indictable offences was 83 per cent, while the rate for those aged 21 and over was 19 per cent. In the case of females, the figures were 94 per cent and 32 per cent respectively. Again, however, these figures represent a decrease when compared to 1992, when for males

Table 6.7 Male offenders cautioned by type of offence (indictable) (thousands)

Offence	1981	1985	1989	1993	1997	2001	2002
Violence	4.4	7.1	11.1	18.1	18.4	15.2	17.9
Sex	2.7	2.8	3.4	3.2	1.9	1.2	1.2
Burglary	10.7	13.4	11.1	11.7	8.6	5.7	5.0
Robbery	0.1	0.2	0.3	0.6	0.5	0.5	0.3
Theft	53.3	72.4	56.4	75.7	52.7	36.6	30.7
Fraud	0.9	1.5	2.7	5.3	4.6	3.6	3.3
Criminal damage	1.9	2.9	3.3	3.6	2.4	2.9	2.6
Drugs	0.2	3.1	11.8	31.6	50.0	34.9	39.8
Other	0.9	1.0	2.7	3.8	4.3	3.4	3.6
Total	75.1	104.3	102.8	153.6	143.3	103.8	104.4

Table 6.8 Female offenders cautioned by type of offence (indictable) (thousands)

Offence	1981	1985	1989	1993	1997	2001	2002
Violence	1.2	1.9	3.6	6.0	5.3	4.4	5.7
Sex	0.1	0.1	0.1	0.1	0.0	0.0	0.0
Burglary	0.8	0.9	0.8	1.1	0.8	0.7	0.8
Robbery	0.0	0.0	0.0	0.1	0.1	0.1	0.1
Theft	25.9	36.6	25.5	41.4	30.1	26.9	23.5
Fraud	0.5	0.7	1.4	2.8	2.6	2.2	2.0
Criminal damage	0.2	0.3	0.3	0.5	0.3	0.5	0.5
Drugs	0.1	0.5	1.2	3.5	6.1	4.5	5.1
Other	0.1	0.1	0.2	0.4	0.7	0.8	0.8
Total	28.8	41.1	33.2	55.9	46.0	40.1	38.5

the figures were 96 per cent and 23 per cent, while for females they were 99 per cent and 46 per cent. The decrease in the cautioning rate for those under 18 seems to have been dropping prior to the key year of 1993, when the decrease began for those aged 18 and older.

There are considerable disparities between police forces in cautioning rates, which have a knock-on effect on numbers appearing in court and sentenced. In 2002 nine police force areas had cautioning rates of 40 per cent or more (Dyfed-Powys had a rate of 54 per cent), while 11 had rates of less than 25 per cent (both Cheshire and South Yorkshire had rates of 17 per cent).[4] Disparities in sentencing between courts are, of course, known to exist but these are – at least to some extent – understandable due to local idiosyncracies and cultures, and individuals have been dealt with as a matter of due process. Given governmental policies on cautioning, one would be entitled to expect greater consistency, and the lack of overt due process makes such disparities contribute to inequitable treatment and injustice. With the changes in cautioning leading to greater demands being made on those subject to a caution, it is perhaps worth considering taking all cautioning out of the hands of the police and placing it with the Crown Prosecution Service (CPS); the police could still be involved in the delivery of the caution, but the CPS would take the decision and also be present (the conditional caution will be administered by the CPS but it is planned to leave unconditional cautions in the hands of the police; Home Office 2002: 71).

Despite efforts to expand their use, compensation orders[5] show little evidence of growing in popularity. In the magistrates' courts in 1992, 26 per cent of offenders sentenced for indictable offences were ordered to pay compensation; by 1996 the percentage had dropped to 19 per cent; and in 2002 it was 15 per cent. Comparable figures for the Crown Court were 10 per cent, 8 per cent, and 7 per cent.[6] The average amount awarded in the magistrates' courts for indictable offences increased from £161 in 1992 to £217 in 2002; while in the Crown Court the increase went from £1,147 to £1,486.

Reconviction rates

While other measures may be relevant and reconviction rates do have limitations (see Lloyd *et al.* 1994), reconvictions remain the key measure for assessing the effectiveness of disposals.

Recent reconviction studies have focused on community penalties and prisons, marginalising fines, discharges and cautions (evidence again of our current obsession with 'seriousness'). However, some information is available from official documents. Data from those sentenced in 1993 show that fines had an actual reconviction rate of 43 per cent compared to an expected rate of 44 per cent; and that for conditional discharges the actual rate was 39 per cent compared to an expected rate of 40 per cent (at the same time, the actual rates for probation and community service were higher than expected; House of Commons 1998: 146). A few years later, the Halliday Report noted that '44 per cent of offenders were reconvicted of a standard list offence within 2 years of a conditional discharge in 1995, which was 2 per cent lower than the predicted rate' (Home Office 2001: 43). As Lloyd *et al.* (1994) have argued, reconviction rates are limited as a simple measure of the effectiveness of a sentence, and there tend to be only slight differences between actual and expected rates of reconviction. Taking such strictures on board, fines and conditional discharges cannot be said to demonstrate unfavourable rates of reconviction. Indeed, it is worth noting that fines have consistently been associated with favourable reconviction rates (see Home Office 1964; Softley 1978).

With regard to cautions for those under the age of 18, the Audit Commission (1996: 22) reported that 'cautioning works well for first

Table 6.9 Twelve-month reconviction rates for offenders aged 10–17 by disposal and gender (%)

Disposal	Predicted rate	Actual rate	Male rate	Female rate
Action plan	46.6	51.8	57.1	34.7
Attendance centre	49.0	50.8	53.5	28.6
Community punishment	51.7	47.5	48.3	38.9
Community rehabilitation	52.8	59.3	64.2	35.7
Reparation order	44.9	44.7	48.0	29.5
Supervision order	51.9	60.2	63.6	46.3
Fine	45.7	40.2	41.0	34.6
Conditional discharge	38.9	36.4	38.5	29.2
Caution	23.5	20.7	22.3	16.8
Reprimand	21.0	18.5	21.2	12.4
Final warning	28.2	23.9	25.0	20.0
Other	44.3	49.6	51.9	45.8
All pre-court disposals	23.0	20.0	22.3	14.2
All court disposals	45.4	45.4	47.8	35.7
All disposals	28.6	26.4	29.5	17.6

Source: Jennings (2002). In the case of Attendance centre, Community rehabilitation and Other, the reconviction rates are based on small sample sizes.

offenders and seven out of ten are not known to re-offend within two years'. However, they go on to note that 'the more offences that have been committed, the higher the probability that the offender will be caught re-offending in the future' (*ibid.*) – which is not surprising as one of the key predictors of reconviction is previous criminal record. Hine and Celnick's (2001) study of young offenders who received a final warning found a 12-month reconviction rate of 30 per cent compared to an expected rate of 36 per cent. While possible explanations for this remain tentative (Bottoms and Dignan 2004), the reconviction rate is favourable. Home Office analyses of reconviction rates for those under the age of 18 suggest that reprimands, final warnings, cautions, conditional discharges and fines are performing well in terms of reconviction rates, especially when compared to other court disposals, as Table 6.9 shows (Jennings 2002). And for females they are particularly successful. A further study of a 2001 cohort found even more positive differences between predicted and actual reconviction rates for these disposals (Jennings 2003). While these two studies suggest that in terms of reconviction rates, cautions, reprimands, final warnings, fines and conditional discharges are associated with positive reconviction rates, some methodological issues related to the analyses remain unanswered, so that while the findings are encouraging they should not be treated as definitive (see Bottoms and Dignan 2004: 111–114).

Adults who are cautioned are less likely to be reconvicted than young offenders; in 1991 the reconviction rate for those aged 21 and over after a caution was 11 per cent, while for those aged 18–20 it was 23 per cent (Home Office 1996: 99). So cautions, like fines and conditional discharges, cannot be said to be failing as far as reconviction rates are concerned. In other words, if we measure effectiveness in terms of reconviction rates, these disposals are effective.

Ways forward?

The Halliday Report (Home Office 2001) argued for breaking down the 'serious enough' barrier which divides fines and community penalties,[7] assuming that this might help to dispel the idea that fines should be used only for the least serious cases. The tariff proposed by Halliday suggested three tiers, with fines appearing in each of them. But the options in each tier could be used alone or in combination, and without firm guidelines and rigorous monitoring it would be likely that sentencers would opt for the combinations, so that the effect would be to keep fines as an add-on to other, more intrusive penalties and to increase levels of punishment even more. The government response to Halliday, *Justice for All* (Home Office 2002), does not follow Halliday's proposals for fines. Instead it focuses on fine enforcement: defendants will be obliged to disclose their income before appearing in court, fines officers will be appointed, prompt payment will lead to a discount, while delays will lead to an increase in the amount of the fine (Home Office 2002: 98). The general discourse of *Justice for All* is of seriousness, of high risk, of punishment involving more intrusion; thus the fine is again implicitly relegated to a marginal position.

Conditional cautioning was proposed in the review of the criminal courts carried out by Lord Justice Auld (2001). The government response has been positive; *Justice for All* (Home Office 2002) proposed a formal conditional cautioning scheme and further piloting of deferred cautioning, and the Criminal Justice Act 2003 introduced conditional cautioning. The need for CPS involvement is acknowledged in the case of conditional cautioning, but the deferred caution and the unconditional caution are left in the hands of the police. However, increasing cautioning options with different arrangements for them would not seem to encourage consistency.

The latest proposals for sentencing are contained in the Carter Report (Carter 2003) and the Home Office response to it (Home Office 2004). Carter points to the decrease in the use of fines, claims that fines are effective if used appropriately, and proposes that 'Fines should replace community sentences for low risk offenders' (Carter 2003: 27). He recommends that a day fine system should be introduced and, perhaps most significantly, suggests that fine collection should be one of the responsibilities of the National Offender Management Service (NOMS), which would mean that fines become more closely associated with prison and community penalties. This could have considerable implications for the credibility of fines, but while the government response to the Carter Report was in general positive about rebuilding the fine as a credible punishment, it did 'not accept the recommendation that responsibility for fine enforcement be moved from the Court Service' (Home Office 2004: 12). This would seem to be anomalous if responsibility for the management of other court sentences is to rest with NOMS. Putting aside the many unanswered questions about the organisation and operation of NOMS, why should fines be left to a different agency?

Carter also argues for increased diversion from court, citing the extensive use of cautions, reprimands and final warnings and noting the use in Germany of conditional dismissals as an alternative to prosecution (see Weigend 1995). While the government response is positive about cautions, including building on conditional cautions for adults, it is noticeably silent about the idea of conditional dismissal. One possible problem about developing the conditional caution (introduced in the Criminal Justice Act 2003) is the kind of requirements seen as desirable by the government:

> We intend to develop a similar approach [to reprimands and final warnings] for low risk, low harm adults building on the new conditional cautions in the Criminal Justice Act. This will not be a soft option and our aim will be to link conditional cautions to financial reparation, to the victim, community work, etc. (Home Office 2004: 12)

The additional requirements suggested not only encourage further the idea that more punitive disposals are the answer to offending, but would also seem to risk overlap with community penalties, which would not be a helpful step. There is, in addition, an interesting tension between this proposal and a recommendation made by the Audit Commission in their latest report on youth justice (Audit Commission 2004), where the need for intervention in low-risk final-warning cases is questioned. Indeed, the problem with too many conditions is spelled out in the report: 'care should be taken not to impose excessive conditions on the [community] sentences at an early stage, in order to avoid a rapid escalation towards custody' (Audit Commission 2004: 45). Ironically, the Youth Justice Board has set a target that 80 per cent of final warnings should have an intervention programme by the end of 2004. It may be worth remembering that one of the key 'what works' principles is that low-risk offenders should receive minimal intervention commensurate with their risk level.

The Carter Report offered a coherent approach to sentencing (although not worked out in detail), but the government response has been patchy, agreeing with some recommendations but not with others, thus undermining Carter's overall vision. Such a pick-and-mix approach to sentencing has not been advantageous, and yet it is this approach that has characterised the field (with the honourable exception of the 1991 Criminal Justice Act, and we are all too aware of what happened to that). As noted earlier, a holistic approach to dealing with young offenders was successful during the 1980s. Because the focus was on the system as a whole, diversion and sentencing for minor offenders played a full part; the focus on crime since the 1990s has been on serious, high risk, punishment – terms that do not lead to any interest in lower-level offending or diversion from prosecution. Risk management does not mean dealing only with high risk, yet the way in which risk has been used would suggest that this is indeed the case. By ignoring or marginalising low-risk offenders, we have contributed to the current situation in which high levels of punishment are the norm.

In the end, the exhortations in the Carter Report about rebuilding the fine are simply that: verbal encouragement. The government remains obsessed with improving fine collection; not surprisingly, as the payment rate for 2002, according to a recent Department for Constitutional Affairs Report (2003), was 56 per cent. However, for the first half of 2003, a payment rate of 73 per cent was reached following a concerted effort to concentrate on fine enforcement (Home Office 2004). Whether this figure can be sustained, whether it is cost-effective, and whether such improvement will lead to greater sentencer confidence in the fine remains to be seen, but this is an encouraging development. Perhaps the greatest problem lies in the lack of information available about fines: reading the National Audit Office Report on fine collection (2002), one is struck by the number of times lack of reliable information is mentioned; and reading the evidence given by Sir Hayden Phillips, Permanent Secretary in the Lord Chancellor's Department, to the House of Commons Public Accounts Committee examination into the collection of fines, one feels sorry for the witness as he is forced on numerous occasions to admit that certain relevant statistics are not routinely collected (see, for example, House of Commons 2002: paras 73–82). A thorough analysis of routine data on fines and fine collection would seem to be a vital precursor to any real, sustainable improvements in enforcement.

Two approaches to fines may be worth examining and testing out in practice. The first is the prosecutor fine, which is now well established in Scotland following its introduction on 1 January 1988 (the German conditional dismissal is essentially the same disposal). The procurator fiscal has the power to make a conditional offer to an alleged offender if he/she could be tried in the district court:

> ... if the alleged offender accepts, by paying a specified amount to the clerk of the relevant district court within a certain time (invariably

> 28 days), criminal proceedings shall not be brought . . . [the offender] may opt to pay either in a lump sum or in five instalments . . . In the latter eventuality, payment of the first instalment within the specified period constitutes acceptance of the offer and, thereafter, payments must be made on a fortnightly basis. Outstanding payments may be enforced only through civil debt procedure rather than through the mechanisms used for recovering fines imposed by the criminal courts. In essence, failure to pay the outstanding instalments of a fiscal fine cannot lead to imprisonment. Finally, it is crucial to note that the acceptance of a conditional offer does not amount to a criminal conviction. (Duff 1993: 485)

Duff has argued that the introduction of the prosecutor fine has not led to net-widening in the sense of increased state intervention, and has been successful in terms of diverting thousands of offenders annually from the process of prosecution (1993, 1994). The CPS in England and Wales is to become more heavily involved in the cautioning process (at least as far as conditional cautions are concerned). It is surely worth considering giving them the lead on cautioning generally and, along with this, testing out a form of the prosecution fine. The evidence from Scotland is that it can be used successfully for not just the most minor offences (Duff 1994), and thus can divert offenders away from low-level court sentences. If such developments were to take place, it would also be worth examining if the conditional discharge might be left in the hands of the CPS. Such a move could potentially take thousands of offenders out of the court system, leaving court disposals for more serious offenders.

As a second approach, there is the controversial issue of the unit fine. Recent empirical research by Robin Moore has begun to unpick the attitudes of magistrates, fine defaulters and enforcement officers towards the level of fines imposed; not surprisingly, views varied about whether the amounts imposed were too high. Moore concludes 'that the courts are failing to pay sufficient attention to offenders' financial circumstances' (Moore 2003: 19). As a result, Moore calls for a revised version of the unit fine to be introduced as a two-stage scheme:

> First, a financial penalty could be imposed for a specified number of weeks according to the gravity of the offence. The offence would rightly remain paramount, and fines, like other sentencing disposals, would be imposed for a period of time. Second, the amount to be paid in each week throughout the specified period could be set according to the offender's spare income, subject to a fixed minimum and maximum so as to maintain a level of proportionality with the offence . . . . To explain further how the proposed system would work, one can consider the example of an offender who has committed a standard offence of driving without insurance. The payment time for

> such an offence could be set as 26 weeks, adjustable according to any mitigating or aggravating factors, while the maximum and minimum rates of payment could be set as £50 and £2.75 per week respectively, the latter being the amount that can be deducted directly from benefits. In consequence, if the offender is deemed to have £5 per week spare income, he or she would be required to pay this amount each and every week for a 26 week period. (Moore 2003: 21–22)

As Moore rightly notes, more detailed and accurate information about the offender's financial circumstances would be vital for such a scheme to work. At present, access to information is limited and work will be necessary to break down barriers. Whether or not his proposal is tested out in practice, Moore's point about access to information is pertinent for more effective use of fines in general.

While this chapter has focused on fines, conditional discharges and cautions, the work of the National Probation Service (NPS) cannot be ignored. One of the key tasks of the NPS is risk assessment and risk management, but in practice this means an overriding concern with high-risk offenders (despite this being more at the level of rhetoric than reality) and this in turn means that probation officers who write pre-sentence reports (PSRs) rarely propose fines or conditional discharges. Probation officers have always had an understandable tendency to use the PSR (or its predecessor, the social inquiry report) to market their own disposals, but unless they are prepared to use court reports to propose confidently fines and discharges for low-risk offenders, these sentences will not be used by the courts to the extent they might be. The NPS holds a crucial position in the criminal justice system as a repository of experience for risk assessment and in providing reports for the courts. If risk assessment is to be taken seriously, then it must engage fully with low-risk offenders and propose appropriate disposals. Given the current pressures on the NPS, it may seem counter-productive to suggest greater probation involvement with reports on low-risk offenders, but it should be remembered that only by sloughing off the many low-risk cases that make up their workload can the NPS begin to deal effectively with those more serious cases it sees as its natural constituency.

If the culture of punitiveness that began to emerge in the early 1990s is to be changed, how this should be done in practice? As the Carter Report notes, the role of the Sentencing Guidelines Council will be crucial (Carter 2003), although this will have to be backed by political will. By letting the punitive cat out of the bag with the changes to the 1991 Criminal Justice Act, followed by the 'prison works' era, it is now difficult to see how the new culture of punishment can be reversed. There is much talk of the lack of confidence by sentencers in fines and discharges and a belief in the increasing seriousness of offending, but how deeply rooted are such feelings and what are their origins? A concerted programme of examining sentencers' beliefs and working to change them should surely be possible given the interest of the government about the views of the public. Such an exercise may not be sufficient to overturn punitive culture, but it is necessary to begin the process of change.[8]

All of the evidence demonstrates that fines, conditional discharges and cautions are being used less often; yet the reconviction rates associated with them do not suggest ineffectiveness. Trends in use are not irreversible and with the Carter Report and the government's (slightly lukewarm) response, the time is propitious to make another effort to increase the use of these disposals. Given current levels of employment (higher than they have been for many years) and the consumer culture in which we live, the fine in particular is well placed. Political will is necessary, but with the pressure on the prison system this may be forthcoming.

The three disposals discussed in this chapter could play a significant part in an overall package to provide serious alternatives to custody. There would certainly be tensions involved in putting them into practice: net-widening could be a problem; as could conflicting views about levels of intervention; and speed and due process need to be balanced. But such tensions have always characterised criminal justice initiatives of this kind. As noted at the start of the chapter, we have been down the road of alternatives to custody before and the road is littered with failed initiatives. Examining the problem as a whole and showing how the various aspects connect are necessary in order to break away from earlier initiatives. Criminal justice policy is also moving in the direction of linking the parts of the system rather than seeing them as separate. Fines, conditional discharges and cautions have been marginalised for too long; they need to be reconceptualised as relevant disposals and not as low-level or shallow-end – such terminology does them no favours.

In 1990, Morris and Tonry published *Between Prison and Probation*, which called for effective and principled punishment for offenders using a rational and comprehensive system of sentences. One of their more startling arguments was to 'consider the possibility that the fine might be the punishment of choice for all but a few criminals – the punishment first considered, the punishment to which all the rest are ''alternatives''' (Morris and Tonry 1990: 112). Although Morris and Tonry make a strong case for their proposal, it is unlikely that they ever seriously envisaged it as taking place in the USA where, traditionally, the fine is not commonly used as a sentence of the court. If such a case can be argued for the USA, however, then surely the fine – and the conditional discharge and caution – can regain ground in the UK. If that were to happen, a solid foundation would be in place for the recalibration of sentencing, and effective diversion from custody could take place.[9]

Notes

1 Virtually all of the research into the administrative aspects of fines has been carried out or commissioned by the Home Office, as befits its role as the home of administrative criminology.
2 The day fine, or unit fine as it was named in England and Wales, was developed in an effort to ensure that fines had a more equal impact on offenders regardless of their incomes: 'The essential characteristic of this approach is simply that punishment is expressed in terms of a *number* of units, which is determined according to the seriousness of the offence, having regard to all the facts of the case. The *amount* of each unit is governed by the court's assessment of disposable income, and by that alone' (Moxon *et al.* 1990b :2).
3 All data in this section are taken from the annual Criminal Statistics England and Wales.
4 Leicestershire had a rate of 9 per cent but there was a shortfall in the number of cautions reported.
5 Since the introduction of the compensation order in the Criminal Justice Act 1972, the courts are now required to consider making a compensation order in cases involving death, injury, loss or damage, and to give reasons in open court when an order is not made; see Powers of Criminal Courts (Sentencing) Act 2000.
6 It is possible that this decrease may be related to the increased use of custody, as Court of Appeal guidance is that the compensation order should not be made simultaneously with custody unless the defendant has independent sources of income: *Jorge* [1999] 2 Cr App R (S) 1.
7 The Criminal Justice Act 1991 introduced a threshold between custody and community penalties, so that custody should be used only when the offence is so serious that only custody could be justified; and also between community penalties and fines and other non-custodial sentences: community penalties should be used only where the offence was serious enough to justify such a sentence.
8 The Home Office is currently considering commissioning research intended to update knowledge of sentencing following the Criminal Justice Act 2003.
9 I am grateful to the editors for their constructive comments on early drafts of this chapter.

References

Advisory Council on the Penal System (1970) *Non-Custodial and Semi-Custodial Penalties* (London: HMSO).
Allen, R. (1991) 'Out of jail: the reduction in the use of penal custody for male juveniles 1981–88', *Howard Journal*, 30(1), 30–52.
Ashworth, A. (2000) *Sentencing and Criminal Justice*, 3rd edition (London: Butterworths).
Audit Commission (1996) *Misspent Youth: Young people and crime* (London: Audit Commission).
Audit Commission (2004) *Youth Justice 2004: A review of the reformed youth justice system* (London: Audit Commission).

Auld, Lord Justice (2001) *Review of the Criminal Courts of England and Wales: Report* (London: The Stationery Office).
Bottoms, A. E. (1983) 'Neglected features of contemporary penal systems', in D. Garland and P. Young (eds) *The Power to Punish: Contemporary penality and social analysis* (London: Heinemann), pp. 166–202.
Bottoms, A. E., Brown, P., McWilliams, B., McWilliams, W. and Nellis, M. (1990) *Intermediate Treatment and Juvenile Justice* (London: HMSO).
Bottoms, A. E. and Dignan, J. (2004) 'Youth justice in Great Britain', in M. Tonry and A. N. Doob (eds) *Youth Crime and Youth Justice: Comparative and cross-national perspectives* (Chicago: University of Chicago Press), pp. 21–183.
Brownlee, I. (1998) *Community Punishment: A critical introduction* (London: Longman).
Carter, P. (2003) *Managing Offenders, Reducing Crime* (London: Strategy Unit).
Cavadino, M. and Dignan, J. (2002) *The Penal System: An introduction*, 3rd edition (London: Sage).
Charman, E., Gibson, B., Honess, T. and Morgan, R. (1996) *Fine Impositions and Enforcement Following the Criminal Justice Act 1991*, Research Findings No. 36 (London: Home Office).
Clark, I. (1998) 'The use of direct deductions from benefits in Scottish courts', *Howard Journal*, 37(3), 291–305.
Crisp, D., Whittaker, C. and Harris, J. (1995) *Public Interest Case Assessment Schemes*, Home Office Research Study No. 138 (London: HMSO).
Crow, I., Richardson, P., Riddington, C. and Simon, F. (1989) *Unemployment, Crime and Offenders* (London: Routledge).
Crow, I. and Simon, F. (1987) *Unemployment and Magistrates' Courts* (London: NACRO).
Department for Constitutional Affairs (2003) *Review of Magistrates' Courts Enforcement Strategies – Final Report* (London: Department of Constitutional Affairs).
Ditchfield, J. A. (1976) *Police Cautioning in England and Wales*, Home Office Research Study No. 37 (London: HMSO).
Duff, P. (1993) 'The prosecutor fine and social control: the introduction of the fiscal fine to Scotland', *British Journal of Criminology*, 33(4), 481–503.
Duff, P. (1994) 'The prosecutor fine', *Oxford Journal of Legal Studies*, 14(4), 565–587.
Evans, R. and Wilkinson, C. (1990) 'Variations in police cautioning policy and practice in England and Wales', *Howard Journal*, 29(3), 155–176.
Flood-Page, C. and Mackie, A. (1998) *Sentencing Practice: An examination of decisions in magistrates' courts and the Crown Courts in the mid-1990s*, Home Office Research Study No. 180 (London: Home Office).
Folkard, M. S., Fowles, A. J., McWilliams, B. C., Williams, W., Smith, D. D., Smith, D. E. and Walmsley, G. R. (1974) *IMPACT Intensive Matched Probation and After-Care Treatment: Volume 1 The Design of the Probation Experiment and an Interim Evaluation*, Home Office Research Study No. 24 (London: HMSO).
Folkard, M. S., Smith, D. E. and Smith, D. D. (1976) *IMPACT: Volume 2 The Results of the Experiment*, Home Office Research Study No. 36 (London: HMSO).
Goldblatt, P. and Lewis, C. (1998) *Reducing Offending: An assessment of research evidence on ways of dealing with offending behaviour*, Home Office Research Study No. 187 (London: Home Office).
Goldson, B. (2000) 'Whither diversion? Interventionism and the new youth justice', in B. Goldson (ed.) *The New Youth Justice* (Lyme Regis: Russell House), pp. 35–57.

Harris, M.K. (1987) 'A brief for de-escalating criminal sanctions', in S. D. Gottfredson and S. McConville (eds) *America's Correctional Crisis: Prison populations and public policy* (New York: Greenwood Press), pp. 205–220.
Her Majesty's Inspectorate of Probation (2003) *2002/2003 Annual Report* (London: HMIP).
Hine, J. and Celnick, A. (2001) *A One Year Reconviction Study of Final Warnings* (Sheffield: University of Sheffield).
Holdaway, S. (2003) 'The final warning: appearance and reality', *Criminal Justice*, 3(4), 351–367.
Home Office (1964) *The Sentence of the Court* (London: HMSO).
Home Office (1980) *The Reduction of Pressure on the Prison System: Observations on the fifteenth report from the Expenditure Committee* (London: HMSO).
Home Office (1996) *Criminal Statistics England and Wales 1995*, Cm. 3421 (London: The Stationery Office).
Home Office (2001) *Making Punishments Work: Report of a review of the sentencing framework for England and Wales* [The Halliday Report] (London: Home Office).
Home Office (2002) *Justice for All*, Cm. 556 (London: The Stationery Office).
Home Office (2003) *Criminal Statistics England and Wales 2002*, Cm. 6054 (London: The Stationery Office).
Home Office (2004) *Reducing Crime – Changing Lives: The government's plans for transforming the management of offenders* (London: Home Office).
Hough, M., Jacobson, J. and Millie, A. (2003) *The Decision to Imprison: Sentencing and the prison population* (London: Prison Reform Trust).
House of Commons (1978a) *Fifteenth Report from the Expenditure Committee: The reduction of pressure on the prison system*, Vol. I, *Report* (London: HMSO).
House of Commons (1978b) *Fifteenth Report from the Expenditure Committee: The reduction of pressure on the prison system*, Vol. II, *Minutes of Evidence and Appendices* (London: HMSO).
House of Commons (1998) *Home Affairs Committee Third Report: Alternatives to prison sentences*, Vol. 1 (London: The Stationery Office).
House of Commons (2002) *Committee of Public Accounts – Collection of fines and other financial penalties in the criminal justice system* (London: The Stationery Office).
Jennings, D. (2002) *One Year Juvenile Reconviction Rates: July 2000 cohort* (London: Research Development and Statistics Directorate).
Jennings, D. (2003) *One Year Juvenile Reconviction Rates: first quarter of 2001 cohort*. Home Office Online Report 18/03 [www.homeoffice.gov.uk/rds/pdfs2/rdsolr1803.pdf].
Laycock, G. and Tarling R. (1985) 'Police force cautioning: policy and practice', *Howard Journal*, 24, 81–92.
Lloyd, C., Mair, G. and Hough, M. (1994) *Explaining Reconviction Rates: A critical analysis*, Home Office Research Study No. 136 (London: HMSO).
Mackie, A., Raine, J., Burrows, J., Hopkins, M. and Dunstan, E. (2003) *Clearing the Debts: The enforcement of financial penalties in magistrates' courts*, Home Office Online Report 09/03 [www.homeoffice.gov.uk/rds/onlinepubs1.html]
Mair, G. (1997) 'Community penalties and the Probation Service', in M. Maguire, R. Morgan and R. Reiner (eds) *The Oxford Handbook of Criminology*, 2nd edition (Oxford: Clarendon Press), pp. 1194–1232.
Mair, G. (2003) 'The origins of what works in England and Wales: a house built on sand?', in G. Mair (ed.) *What Matters in Probation* (Cullompton: Willan), pp. 12–33.

Mair, G. and Lloyd, C. (1989) *Money Payment Supervision Orders: Probation policy and practice*, Home Office Research Study No. 114 (London: HMSO).

Mair, G., Lloyd, C., Nee, C. and Sibbitt, R. (1994) *Intensive Probation in England and Wales: An evaluation*, Home Office Research Study No. 133 (London: HMSO).

Mair, G. and May, C. (1995) *Practitioners' Views of the Criminal Justice Act: A survey of criminal justice agencies*, Research and Planning Unit Paper 91 (London: Home Office).

Moore, R. (2003) 'The use of financial penalties and the amounts imposed: the need for a new approach', *Criminal Law Review*, January, 13–27.

Morgan, R. (2003) 'Thinking about the demand for probation services', *Probation Journal*, 50(1), 7–19.

Morris, N. and Tonry, M. (1990) *Between Prison and Probation: Intermediate punishments in a rational sentencing system* (New York: Oxford University Press).

Moxon, D. (1988) *Sentencing Practice in the Crown Court*, Home Office Research Study No. 103 (London: HMSO).

Moxon, D., Corkery, J.M. and Hedderman, C. (1992) *Developments in the Use of Compensation Orders in Magistrates' Courts Since October 1988*, Home Office Research Study No. 126 (London: HMSO).

Moxon, D., Hedderman, C. and Sutton, M. (1990a) *Deductions from Benefit for Fine Default*, Research and Planning Unit Paper 60 (London: Home Office).

Moxon, D., Sutton, M. and Hedderman, C. (1990b) *Unit Fines: Experiments in four courts*, Research and Planning Unit Paper 59 (London: Home Office).

Muncie, J. (1999) *Youth and Crime: A critical introduction* (London: Sage).

NACRO (1989) *The Real Alternative: Strategies to promote community based penalties* (London: NACRO).

Narey, M. (1997) *Review of Delay in the Criminal Justice System* (London: Home Office).

National Audit Office (2002) *Collection of Fines and Other Financial Penalties in the Criminal Justice System* (London: National Audit Office).

Newburn, T. (1988) *The Use and Enforcement of Compensation Orders in Magistrates' Courts*, Home Office Research Study No. 102 (London: HMSO).

Pointing, J. (ed.) (1986) *Alternatives to Custody* (Oxford: Basil Blackwell).

Smith, D., Sheppard, B., Mair, G. and Williams, K. (1984) *Reducing the Prison Population*, Research and Planning Unit Paper 23 (London: Home Office).

Softley, P. (1973) *A Survey of Fine Enforcement*, Home Office Research Study No. 16 (London: HMSO).

Softley, P. (1978) *Fines in Magistrates' Courts*, Home Office Research Study No. 46 (London: HMSO).

Softley, P. and Moxon, D. (1982) *Fine Enforcement: An evaluation of the practices of individual courts*, Research and Planning Unit Paper 12 (London: Home Office).

Stanley, S. and Baginsky, M. (1984) *Alternatives to Prison: An examination of non-custodial sentencing of offenders* (London: Peter Owen).

Tutt, N. and Giller, H. (1987) 'Manifesto for management: the elimination of custody', *Justice of the Peace*, 151, 200–202.

Vass, A.A. (1990) *Alternatives to Prison: Punishment, custody and the community* (London: Sage).

Weigend, T. (1995) 'In Germany, fines often imposed in lieu of prosecution', in M. Tonry and K. Hamilton (eds) *Intermediate Sanctions in Overcrowded Times* (Boston, MA: Northeastern University Press).

Chapter 7

Reparative and restorative approaches

Gill McIvor

Introduction

This chapter focuses on the operation and effectiveness of community disposals that aim to enable offenders to make reparation for their offences, including approaches premised upon restorative justice.[1] The principal focus will be on community service, mediation and reparation and group conferencing, though other less widely used approaches will also be referred to where appropriate.[2] Before discussing the rationale for including in a single chapter what might appear at first sight to represent somewhat disparate penal practices, the origins and key features of these approaches are described.

An overview of reparative and restorative approaches

Community service, which requires that offenders undertake unpaid work for the benefit of the community, was first introduced as a sentencing option in California in the 1960s. During the following two decades it was introduced in most western jurisdictions and throughout the United States and Canada. Community service was first made available in England and Wales in 1973 and in Scotland in 1977, where it proved to be a relatively popular sentencing option with the courts (McIvor 1992).[3] More recently, the term 'community punishment' has replaced community service in England and Wales though, as we shall see, this has also been accompanied by an increased emphasis on 'competency achievement' (Bazemore and Maloney 1994) through the undertaking of unpaid court-ordered work (Rex and Gelsthorpe 2002).

Victim–offender mediation and reparation, on the other hand, which has its origins in Kitchener, Ontario and in the Mennonite movement (e.g. Zehr 1990), aims to involve victims directly in the resolution of their offence. Skilled mediators facilitate an exchange between the victim and offender aimed at providing an explanation for the offence, enabling the offender to appreciate the impact of the offence on the victim and reaching an agreement as to the action to be taken by the offender to repair the harm. Victim–offender mediation and reparation schemes, as Marshall (1999) has indicated, are most typically run semi-independently of criminal justice agencies, though they are often managed by them. Based on the principles of restorative justice (see below), they grew rapidly in number during the 1990s. Bazemore and Umbreit (2001) report that by 1997 there were 320 Victim–Offender Mediation schemes in the United States and Canada and more than 700 in Europe.

Family Group Conferences seek to involve a wider constituency (including 'supporters' of both the victim and the offender) in discussion of the offence and decision-making about the actions to be undertaken by the offender to make amends. The origins of contemporary interest in conferencing lay in dissatisfaction, in New Zealand, with justice processes which offered little victim involvement and which often resulted in discriminatory outcomes for the Maori population. Recognition of these problems brought the legitimacy of traditional justice processes and their outcomes into question. Conferencing was seen as providing a mechanism both for involving victims more directly in the justice process and allowing Maoris to return to their own system of justice. As Maxwell and Morris (1994: 19) explain:

> . . . traditional Maori practice involved the victims, the offender and the families of the victim and the offender, firstly, in acknowledging guilt and expressing remorse and, secondly, in finding ways to restore the social balance so that the victim could be compensated by the group and the offender could be reintegrated into the group.

The objectives of conferencing in New Zealand include: holding the young offender accountable while enhancing their welfare; diversion from court; the use of detention as a last resort; protection of children's rights; participation in decision making by young people and their families; strengthening of family bonds; victim involvement; consensus decision-making; and cultural appropriateness (Maxwell and Morris 1994; Bargen 1996). These objectives are apparent in varying combinations in the different approaches to conferencing, which have subsequently developed in Australia (Alder and Wundersitz 1994) and elsewhere.

The first development of conferencing in Australia was in 1991 in the city of Wagga Wagga in New South Wales (Moore and O'Connell 1994).

The model, which was based on the theory of reintegrative shaming developed by Braithwaite (1989), aimed to shame the young person for their offending behaviour and then reintegrate him/her into the community. Unlike the New Zealand model, there was no explicit objective to repair family bonds by providing young people and their families with access to appropriate resources and services. Since then conferencing has developed across Australia, taking a variety of forms and operating at different points in the criminal justice process (see Daly and Hayes 2001 for a useful overview). It was first introduced in the UK by the Thames Valley Police, using the Wagga Wagga model as adapted by the Australian Federal Police in Canberra in the RISE project (Re-integrative Shaming Experiment) (Sherman *et al.* 1994). Currently, however, the majority of restorative justice schemes in Australia are not police-led.

In Canada the Restorative Justice Options to Parole Suspension project was established in Victoria, British Columbia in 1999. It brings together 'significant others' (including victims' representatives and family members) to identify reparative outcomes and to address the problems experienced by parolees whose risk of re-offending has been assessed as increasing. The aim is to prevent the need for parole to be suspended and the offender returned to prison, by providing opportunities for the offender to be reintegrated into a community of support. A very small-scale evaluation of the initiative (n = 15) suggested that those who participated in it had lower levels of recidivism and spent longer in the community than those who had not (Wilson *et al.* 2002).

Sharing some similarities to Family Group Conferences, *Circle Sentencing* was first developed in the Yukon, Canada in 1991 before being extended to other parts of Canada and the USA. As Bazemore and Umbreit (2001) explain, Circle Sentencing is based upon the traditional sanctioning and community healing processes of First Nation people in Canada and American Indians in the United States. The Circle may include, in addition to the offender and victim, family and friends of both, criminal justice and social services personnel, and interested members of the community. Speaking in turn through a symbolic 'talking piece', members of the Circle seek to gain an understanding of the offence and to identify how all the affected parties can be healed and further crimes prevented (see also Stuart 1996).

Other reparative approaches include *Community Panels* of various types which have been established in a number of jurisdictions. These typically involve trained members of the community deciding on the course of action to be taken by the offender to make reparation for the offence. Initiatives that fall into this category include neighbourhood justice centres, the youth panels in England and Wales and community reparative boards (Dignan 2000).[4] Among the latter, most has been written about the Vermont Reparation Board (the first to be established) which involves meetings between board members and offenders who have been ordered by the court to participate (Bazemore and Umbreit 2001). Reparation Boards typically have not involved victims directly in the process, though increasingly attempts are being made to do this. Only one of the two pilot community panel adult pre-trial diversion schemes in New Zealand involved victims and in that site decisions were made by nominated representatives of the community (Maxwell *et al.* 1999).

Circles of support and accountability were introduced in Canada in 1994 when a group of local people decided to provide assistance to a paedophile who was released back into their community. The model as evolved in Canada involves a professionally supported volunteer framework. High-risk sexual offenders who would not be subject to statutory supervision on release (the 'core members') are provided with support from and held accountable by a small number of volunteers who make contact with them on a daily basis and who hold weekly meetings to address any issues that may arise. Police officers and other professionals may join the circles on every occasion or as required. Wilson *et al.* (2002) report that an initial evaluation of 30 circles in Southern Ontario identified lower than expected levels of recidivism, though this study had no comparison cases against whom the 'circles' cases could be compared. Circles of Support and Accountability have been introduced in the UK through pilots funded by the Home Office and run by the Quakers (in Thames Valley), The Hampton Trust (Hampshire) and the Lucy Faithfull Foundation (various locations). Evaluation of this initiative in the UK is at an early stage (Quaker Peace and Social Witness 2003).

Overview

The term 'restorative justice' is used to denote approaches that aim to hold offenders accountable for their offences while seeking to repair the harm visited upon victims by the commission of the offence. Thus, according to Schiff (1998), restorative justice is about 'healing the harm done to victims and communities as a result of criminal acts, while holding offenders accountable for their actions'. while Marshall (1999: 7) suggests that:

> Restorative justice is centrally about *restoration*: restoration of the victim, restoration of the offender to a law-abiding life, restoration of the damage caused by crime to the community. Restoration is not solely backward-looking: it is equally, if not more, concerned with the construction of a better society in the future.

For justice to be restorative it must, according to Schiff (1998), evidence the consistent involvement of all parties affected by the crime; a focus on the development, implementation and maintenance of healing and reparation rather than retribution and punishment; and satisfaction with the process and the outcome on the part of both the victim and the offender. Similarly, Dignan (2000) has suggested that the key attributes of restorative justice are the principle of 'inclusivity', the balancing of interests, non-coercive practice and a problem-solving orientation.

Reparative approaches and those premised upon restorative justice are not wholly synonymous, but they do overlap: reparation is often a feature of restorative justice, yet reparative objectives and outcomes may be insufficient in themselves to render an intervention 'restorative'. For example, it has long been argued that community service is a reparative disposal (Advisory Council on the Penal System 1970). However, as Immarigeon (1998a) points out, it is rarely victim-driven or victim-focused and the reparation is symbolic in the sense that it is directed towards the community that has been harmed, rather than the individual victims of crime. In this sense community service is reparative but not restorative, unless it can be argued that through the efforts of offenders the community may be 'restored' (Bazemore and Maloney 1994). What characterises each of these approaches, however, is the emphasis placed on reparation or making amends, and where they differ is in the significance placed upon the victim, offender and community[6] in that process. They also differ in terms of their relationships to the formal criminal justice process. In the remainder of this chapter, community service is discussed separately from other 'restorative' approaches which, while differing in focus, objectives and context, share a common concern with the repair of harm caused to the direct (and sometimes indirect) victims of crime.

Relationship to the criminal justice system

The approaches outlined in the previous section have been developed at various points in the criminal justice process. Some have their basis in legislation while others, because they are predicated on principles of voluntarism and non-coercion, operate on a more informal basis.

Community service

In most jurisdictions community service is available as a sanction of the court at first sentence. This is so throughout the UK and in many other Western jurisdictions. In the UK, community service (or community punishment) may be imposed as a 'stand-alone' option or as a condition of a probation order (in Scotland), or in combination with a community rehabilitation order (in England and Wales). In Scotland, attempts have been made to retain community service as a high-tariff sentencing option by requiring through legislation that orders are imposed only if the offender would otherwise be given a prison sentence. Even so, it appeared that the legislation had not been successful in ensuring that all community service orders replaced prison sentences (McIvor and Tulle-Winton 1993).

In some jurisdictions, such as Germany, community service operates as an alternative to imprisonment for fine default. In Scotland, where a high proportion of prison receptions involve fine defaulters, Supervised Attendance Orders (SAOs) were introduced to provide the courts with an alternative to custody for fine default. SAOs involve offenders carrying out between ten and 60 hours of specified activity supervised by the local authority. The specified activity need not involve unpaid work,[7] but in practice this is the model that several schemes have adopted (Levy and McIvor 2000).

Immarigeon (1998b) has observed that very little is known about the operation of community service in the USA, though its use is reported to be widespread. Community service is usually imposed in conjunction with other sanctions and often as part of an intensive supervision package. He suggests that in the USA community service is employed primarily as a punishment, with little attempt to maximise its potential to effect offender change. As Bazemore and Maloney (1994: 25) have observed: 'If the goal is meaningful restoration to the community or offender rehabilitation . . . community service as now practiced in most jurisdictions would be viewed as a failure.' They argue that an increasingly punitive emphasis on community service in the USA appeared to 'remove incentives for creativity in developing either competency building or otherwise meaningful service options for offenders.' (*ibid.*)

Restorative justice

Victim–offender mediation and reparation and family group conferencing may operate at various stages in the criminal justice process. Mediation and reparation has been employed in conjunction with a police warning, with deferred prosecution, in parallel with prosecution, as part of a sentence or following the imposition of a sentence[8] (Marshall 1999). Typically (though not exclusively) these schemes deal with juvenile offenders and with less serious offences though it has been suggested that they might be more effective with offenders convicted of more serious crimes (see e.g. Marshall 1999, Miers *et al.* 2001).

The extent to which mediation and reparation has become a 'mainstream' response to offending differs across jurisdictions. Whilst they typically remain somewhat marginalised in relation to traditional criminal justice processes, in some jurisdictions, such as Austria, they have become more firmly embedded (Kilchling and Loschnig-Gspandl 2000). Similarly, in New Zealand, conferencing has become fully integrated as part of the criminal justice process, with the majority of juvenile justice cases that do not result in a caution being referred to a conference by the police or by the court (Bazemore and Umbreit 2001). In Australia, family group conferencing was introduced on a legislated basis in some states (e.g. South Australia, Western Australia and New South Wales) but not others (Australian Capital Territories and Victoria).

The Crime and Disorder Act (1998) introduced, in England and Wales, a range of initiatives for juvenile offenders that were influenced by restorative justice, including reparation orders and youth panels (Crawford and Newburn 2002, 2003). Referral orders were brought in under the Youth Justice and Criminal Evidence Act 1999 and enable young people pleading guilty to a first conviction to be referred to a youth offending panel who will agree a contract with the young person to be supervised by the Youth Offending Team. The contract is negotiated at a panel meeting – whose participants must include the young person and their parent/carer and can also include the victim and a supporter, along with a supporter for the young person – and is intended to include an element of reparation to the victim or to the wider community. Crawford and Newburn (2003) found that while the introduction of referral orders and youth offending panels in eleven pilot areas had many positive features, the level of victim participation in youth offending panels was low and reparation more commonly took the form of unpaid work for the community rather than direct reparation to the victim of the offence. Dignan (2002) likewise found that the majority (80 per cent) of reparation orders imposed by magistrates involved indirect reparation, with most victims believing that the interests of the offenders had been paramount in the process.

The introduction of family group conferencing in England and Wales has been *ad hoc*, non-statutory and primarily police driven. The first such scheme was established by Thames Valley police and based on the Wagga Wagga model from New South Wales, though some initiatives based on the New Zealand model have also been developed (Dignan and Marsh 2001). Other police-led schemes, focusing upon juvenile offending, were introduced in Humberside and North Nottinghamshire (Dignan 2000). In the Thames Valley programme, restorative cautioning was introduced as an alternative to the traditional cautioning system for juvenile offenders who had committed minor offences. The majority of restorative conferences were not, however, attended by the victim (though the victims' views were otherwise conveyed by the cautioning officers) and most agreed outcomes involved a written or oral apology (rather than financial restitution or unpaid work). Crawford and Newburn (2003) suggest that the approach may be susceptible to 'net-widening' since it represents a change to existing processes rather than an alternative to prosecution.

An evaluation of 46 restorative justice schemes funded by the Youth Justice Board in England and Wales found a tendency to rely too heavily on community reparation and a low level of direct involvement of victims in meeting with their offenders (14 per cent, Wilcox and Hoyle 2004). The pressure to ensure that offenders were 'fast-tracked' was believed to have adversely affected the quality of assessments and preparatory work with victims.

A number of restorative justice initiatives have been established by the Home Office under its Crime Reduction Programme and are subject to ongoing independent evaluation. These schemes – REMEDI, CONNECT and the Justice Research Consortium – operate at various points in the criminal justice system, often with more serious offences and with adults serving prison or community sentences (Shapland *et al.* 2002). Shapland *et al.* (2002) reflect on the difficulties the schemes encountered in attracting sufficient referrals[9] (a problem also identified in the Youth Justice Board projects) and more generally on the challenges faced when introducing restorative justice initiatives into the criminal justice process. An early conclusion from their evaluation was that restorative justice schemes required long lead-in periods before referral mechanisms were operating effectively, suggesting that short-term funding was not an appropriate strategy for initiatives of this kind.

In Scotland, as in many other jurisdictions, restorative justice options have tended to be small in scale and located towards the lower end of the spectrum of offence and offender seriousness. The first pilot schemes were introduced by a voluntary agency as an alternative to prosecution (Warner 1993). Subsequently, additional schemes were introduced under the rubric of pilot central government funding for diversion from prosecution (Barry and McIvor 2000). Restorative justice programmes are now being introduced across Scotland as part of the Scottish Executive's response to 'anti-social behaviour' and youth crime.

The role and relevance of restorative and reparative approaches assume a different dimension in Northern Ireland, where the legitimacy of the criminal justice system has been rejected by sectors of the community (McEvoy and Mika 2002). Here, restorative justice offers some hope for changing attitudes on the part of the police which may help to break down the distrust that has characterised police–public relationships (O'Mahony *et al.* 2002), and for providing an alternative to informalism as manifested in paramilitary punishment violence (McEvoy and Mika 2002). In Northern Ireland, restorative justice initiatives have been introduced by the state as an alternative to prosecution (O'Mahony *et al.* 2002) as well as having been developed at the community level out of the informal tradition (McEvoy and Mika 2002). As McEvoy and Mika (2002: 535) explain:

> These projects were established in large part to facilitate paramilitaries moving away from violent punishment systems developed over the past three decades. Community-based restorative justice projects were designed to allow such paramilitaries to (in their terms) 'disengage responsibility' from such acts, handing dispute resolution back to the local communities from which the conflicts emanate.

McEvoy and Mika (2002) argue for a new informalism based on principles of restorative justice, with local ownership, guidance from locally developed practice standards and a basis in principles of human rights.

Operational issues

The legislative context and the location of these approaches in the criminal justice system will have a bearing on how they operate and upon whom they are targeted. For instance, pre-prosecution programmes tend to focus on relatively minor offenders and offences, though there is some evidence that restorative approaches may be more effective with more serious cases. The perceived limitations of how these approaches have been implemented in practice will also be examined.

Balancing interests of the victim, offender and community

Advocates of restorative justice have argued that one of its strengths is its ability to take into account the interests of victims, offenders and the community. As we have seen, however, the extent to which and the ways in which they are involved vary across models. The question therefore arises as to whose interests should be paramount since this in turn will have implications for the focus and content of programmes and the objectives pursued.

Restorative justice arguably differs from 'traditional' justice insofar as it is 'victim-driven' or 'victim-focused'.[10] In this respect an important objective is to involve victims more directly in the resolution of the offence. However, restorative justice approaches also place varying emphasis upon diversionary goals and upon the reintegration of offenders into their communities.[11] The former, it has been suggested, may result in some innocent defendants pleading guilty to avoid prosecution or agreeing to unnecessarily punitive outcomes. It may encourage offender participation that, if not coerced, could not be described as wholly voluntary and may also result in programmes being developed at points in the criminal justice process at which victims may benefit less (Marshall 1999). It has been argued that voluntary agencies have a key role to play in the development of restorative approaches because statutory organisations such as probation services are identified too closely with the provision of services for offenders (Marshall and Merry 1990, Warner 1993, Faulkner 1996).

Some restorative justice approaches have been criticised for their narrow focus on the resolution of the offence and, concomitantly, their failure to take account of the economic, personal and social context in which the offending occurred. Such criticism has, for example, been directed at police-led conferencing, which has been contrasted with a more holistic approach which is equally concerned with ensuring that offenders have access to necessary resources and supports (Bargen 1996). Other criticisms of police-led conferencing have focused on ethics and rights, or concerns that the police are unlikely to be perceived by offenders as appropriately occupying an 'umpiring' role (Sandor 1994). As Daly (2002) observes, most Australian jurisdictions have moved away from the Wagga Wagga model of conferencing towards one in which greater account is taken of the interests of both victim and offender, though this raises the possibility that the interests of victims might become subjugated to the desire to help the offender to change.

Diversionary conferencing based upon reintegrative shaming is argued to be more effective than traditional juvenile justice processes because, although courts may shame, they also stigmatise since they lack the reintegration ceremonies for which conferences provide (Braithwaite and Mugford 1994, Coumarelos and Weatherburn 1995). However, it has also been argued that conferencing may be as shaming and stigmatising as its alternatives, if not more so. As Polk (1994: 132–133) observes, 'any process . . . which results in the official designation of a person as an offender must, by definition, be seen as organisationally stigmatising'. Marshall (1999: 14) has similarly questioned the effectiveness of shaming in the context of juvenile justice conferencing:

> Braithwaite's theory held that shaming was only positive in its effects if it occurred within and by a community of people that the shamed person respected and was attached to. The artificial imposition of a shaming experience by agents of a statutory power does not seem to accord with that proposition, so it is doubtful whether such a process would be beneficial in its effects on future behaviour.

A relatively high proportion of young people who participated in restorative conferences in Thames Valley (around two-fifths) reported having felt stigmatised by the process (Hoyle *et al.* 2002).

The diversionary conferencing model operates with an admission of guilt prior to an accused being charged. This means that safeguards which would normally accompany an adjudication process are not in place and it is not clear that the safeguards available within conferencing arrangements are always sufficient. Police-led diversionary conferencing, in particular, has been criticised for its failure to pay due attention to the rights of offenders in the conferencing process (e.g. Polk 1994, Sandor 1994, Warner 1994, Bargen 1996, Spencer and McIvor 2000). Criticism of the absence of procedural safeguards in restorative justice practices is also highlighted by Kurki (2003) and Schiff (2003). For example, Kurki (2003) identifies studies of restorative justice in which young people participate unwillingly, are too intimidated to speak and report having little input into decision-making.

The research by O'Mahony *et al.* (2002) and by Warner (1993) has highlighted the potential for more informal criminal justice initiatives to 'widen the net' by drawing in offenders who would otherwise be dealt with by less intrusive means (see also Polk 1994, Sandor 1994). The issue of proportionality has been raised by Spencer and McIvor (2000) who found that most cases eligible for the RISE experiment in Canberra were likely to have received a good behaviour bond, referred to by one of their interviewees as 'a slap on the wrist'. Results from the evaluation of RISE indicated that the average 'fine' (payable to a community charity) in a drink-driving conference was $120 while the average fine imposed by the courts was $414. However, the average number of community service hours imposed on drink drivers in conferences was 26 compared with an average of two hours of community service imposed by the court (Sherman and Strang 1997). One of the advantages of operating conferencing or other forms of restorative justice on a statutory basis is that statutory limits can be placed on the nature and scope of agreements reached (Spencer and McIvor 2000). Even so, as Crawford and Newburn (2003) found in their study of referral orders, the number and nature of elements contained in contracts – and hence their intensity – could vary considerably across orders of similar length.

Access and diversity

Community service orders, certainly as operated in the UK, appear to have been regarded by the courts primarily as a 'young man's punishment', traditionally being used disproportionately with young male offenders (Hine 1993). Concern has been expressed at women's apparent under-representation on orders – possibly because their caring responsibilities towards children and other dependents are perceived as a barrier to the completion of unpaid work (McIvor 2004) – and at the fact that when they are given orders, they receive them at an earlier point in their 'criminal careers' (McIvor 1998a). The comparatively low numbers of women and offenders from ethnic minorities on community service also make it difficult to establish whether features of the disposal that appear to be associated with reduced recidivism among white men apply equally to other groups or whether for these groups other considerations apply (Rex and Gelsthorpe 2002).

Restorative justice has 'inclusivity' as a central principle and there is no suggestion that its use is as gendered as some other approaches (including community service). Strang and Sherman (2003) suggest that as far as victims are concerned, female victims appear to be as positive about participation in conferences as do men. There has been more debate over the experiences of restorative justice of female offenders. On the one hand it has been suggested that conferencing may be a particularly empowering experience for young women through its relative informality[12] and by enabling them to contribute directly to the agreement reached. On the other hand, others have raised concerns about the extent of violent and sexual victimisation among young women and girls who attend conferences (Alder 2000). Given that the likelihood that the perpetrator may be present in the form of a family member, this may render it unlikely that the victimisation is brought to light. On a broader level, the lack of attention in the research literature to the conferencing experiences of young women and girls (as offenders rather than the carers of offenders) means that the nature of any gendered dimension to conferencing remains unexplored (Baines 1996).

Despite its reported origins in indigenous forms of justice (but see Daly 2002), critics of family group conferencing have focused on the under-representation of Maori and aboriginal people in these programmes (e.g. Blagg 1997), with some suggesting that restorative justice practices represent and serve the interests of the white population (Zellerer and Cunneen 2001). Cant *et al.* (1999) report that aboriginal offenders were less likely than non-aboriginals to be referred to the Western Australia Juvenile Justice Teams, attributing this to the fact that their mobile lifestyles made it difficult to arrange family meetings and follow up the action plans that were developed (see also Maxwell 2000). Polk (1994) has argued that while the popularity of conferencing has been derived in large part from its appeal to communitarianism and promise of improved access to justice for minority ethnic groups, it fails to take cognisance of – and therefore have an impact on – wider institutional processes and structures which contribute to marginalisation and exclusion from society. Daly (2000) has likewise suggested that conferencing and other white criminal justice responses may be inappropriate for indigenous youth because they fail to recognise and address structural and political inequalities. She proposes that instead of attempting to assimilate indigenous groups within mainstream criminal justice responses, parallel systems may be required.

There is also a risk that in attempting to achieve simultaneously a range of objectives which may be incompatible, conferencing fails adequately to deliver on any one. As Marshall cautions: 'In its combination of victim restoration, offender reintegration, individual participation and community involvement, conferencing might be seen as Restorative Justice *par excellence*, but it is debatable whether it is either practical or desirable to meet all these ends at one time in the majority of cases.' (1999: 15, original emphasis)

A similar point is made by Whyte (2002: 3) who has suggested that 'anything that unites and is seen to meet the objectives of the political right and left in the UK, USA, Australia and New Zealand has to be treated with some caution and has to be subjected to critical evaluation in its implementation in a Scottish context'.

Enforcement

The options available to deal with non-compliance with reparative or restorative approaches will vary according to the legislative context and the point in the criminal justice process at which they operate. With 'hard end', legislated disposals, failure to comply may ultimately result in revocation of the order and imposition of a custodial sentence. Unless there are adequate checks and balances, 'soft end' programmes may be more difficult to enforce. For example, police-led conferencing in Australia has raised concerns about double jeopardy, which may make it difficult for sanctions to be imposed in the event of an agreement not being fully upheld (Spencer and McIvor 2000). The lack of follow-up and enforceability of restorative justice initiatives has been criticised on the basis that they may undermine their credibility and contribute to the secondary victimisation of victims (e.g. Warner 1993).

Resources

Analysis of the costs of community service in comparison to other disposals are generally favourable. The Scottish Executive (2003), for example, estimated the mean cost of a community service order in 2001 to be £1,823 compared with £15,083 for six months in prison. Taking into account the indirect costs of community service and imprisonment, Knapp *et al.* (1992) concluded that community service was a more cost-effective option, but only if it was being used in a relatively high proportion of cases instead of a custodial sentence.

Although there are little published data on the costs of restorative justice approaches, both Knapp (in Warner 1993) and Dignan (1992) have estimated that the costs of pre-prosecution mediation and reparation compare favourably to prosecution costs, assuming that there is a sufficiently high throughput of cases. However, Miers *et al.* (2001) concluded from their evaluation of seven mediation and reparation schemes in England and Wales that only one – in which many offenders had been convicted of serious offences and/or were serving long prison sentences – appeared to be cost effective.

The model of conferencing adopted in Victoria, Australia has been acknowledged to be very resource-intensive and costly, with cases taking, on average, 38 hours to complete and costing, on average, A$3500[13] (Markiewicz *et al.* 1997). In her critique of juvenile justice group conferencing, Bargen (1996) argued that the Victoria model contained many of the procedural safeguards absent from other models[14] but speculated that its resource-intensiveness could serve as a disincentive to its adoption on a wider basis.

Marshall (1999) has argued that attention must be paid to the resource implications of restorative approaches, especially if the benefits to be gained from the process cannot easily be justified by the resource invested in them. He has, for example, argued that attention should be paid to the use of 'lower-order' restorative justice for minor offences and offenders where there is likely to be less to be gained by victims from the process. In Northern Ireland, O'Mahony *et al.* (2002) estimated that each case referred to the restorative cautioning pilots took between four and five hours of police time, yet the amount of property involved was typically small (less than £15 in value in 80 per cent of cases). Moreover it appeared unlikely that most cases would otherwise have been prosecuted, suggesting that that the process of reparation and accountability was often disproportionate to the harm caused.

Evidence of effectiveness

This section summarises the available international evidence for the effectiveness of reparative and restorative approaches. Whilst some of this analysis will focus on the effectiveness of community service and restorative approaches in comparison with alternative disposals or more 'traditional' responses to offending, particular attention is given to the features of these approaches that appear to be more closely related to success (for example, the quality of the work experience for those given community service and the relative effectiveness of face-to-face and shuttle mediation). In addition to scrutinising evidence of impacts on recidivism, the evidence for other benefits is also examined (for example, victim and offender satisfaction with the process and outcomes of restorative approaches).

The analysis focuses, where possible, upon practice and research in the UK. However, the majority of empirical data for the effectiveness of conferencing derives from New Zealand and Australia and much of the evaluation of victim–offender mediation programmes has been undertaken in North America.[15]

Community service

Community service may, it appears, have a positive impact upon recidivism even though it has not traditionally been regarded as an explicitly rehabilitative disposal (McIvor 2002). Comparisons of recidivism between different sanctions suggest that while prison sentences and community-based disposals have similar reconviction rates (e.g. Barclay and Tavares 1999), offenders on community service often have lower reconviction rates than would be predicted by their criminal history, age and other relevant characteristics (Lloyd *et al.* 1995). For example, May

(1999) found that reconviction rates among offenders given community service were better than predicted even when social factors such as unemployment and drug use were taken into account. In a Swiss study, Killias *et al.* (2000) found lower reconviction rates among offenders sentenced to community service than among those given short prison sentences.

The Scottish Executive has recently published a comparison of reconviction rates following different sentences (Scottish Executive 2001). This analysis suggested that when factors such as sex, age and previous criminal history were controlled for, reconviction rates tended to be similar following prison sentences and a range of non-custodial disposals (such as probation orders, community service and fines). These data suggest that, at the very least, community-based disposals are no less effective than imprisonment. However the custodial sample upon whom the analysis was based included prisoners serving sentences of up to twelve years. If a comparison had been made between offenders given community sentences and those who served shorter prison sentences (for example, up to twelve months) it is likely that community service would have lower reconviction rates than custody. Recent data published by the Scottish Prison Service demonstrate higher return to prison rates for prisoners serving less than six months in prison (Ash and Biggar 2002).

There is some evidence that the quality of the community service experience for offenders may be associated with reductions in recidivism. Killias *et al.* (2000) found a relationship between the perceived fairness of the sentences offenders received and reconviction, leading Rex and Gelsthorpe (2002) to suggest that perceiving a community service sentence as 'fair' makes offenders more receptive to re-integrative opportunities that arise when they undertake court-mandated unpaid work. McIvor (1992) found that reconviction rates were lower among offenders who believed community service to have been worthwhile, with more positive experiences being associated with placements characterised by high levels of contact with the beneficiaries, opportunities to acquire new skills and work that is seen as having some intrinsic value for the recipients.[16] As McIvor (1998b: 55–56) has observed:

> . . . community service placements which were viewed by offenders as most rewarding – and which were associated with reductions in recidivism – might best be characterised as re-integrative and as entailing a degree of reciprocity or exchange. In many instances, it seems, contact with the beneficiaries had given offenders an insight into other people and an increased insight into themselves; the acquisition of skills had instilled in them greater confidence and self-esteem; and the experience of completing their community service orders had placed them in a position where they could enjoy

> reciprocal relationships – gaining the trust, confidence and appreciation of other people and having the opportunity to give something back to them in return.

McIvor (1998b) argued that the effectiveness of community service might be further enhanced if greater emphasis were placed upon the use of pro-social modelling (e.g. Rex 1999; Trotter 1999) and problem solving, with a view to facilitating the reintegration of offenders. As Bazemore and Maloney (1994: 26) observe, '. . . offenders are capable of making positive contributions and, having paid their debt, should be allowed to be accepted back into community life.' They support the development of community service in such a way that it might provide added value to the offender and the community and strengthen the bond between them. Examples of 'service on its highest plane' (1994: 30) include mentoring in intergenerational service; economic development; citizenship and civic participation; helping the disadvantaged; crime prevention projects; and 'giving it back'. This, in turn, would require a redefinition of offenders as resources rather than as 'the problem' (see also Chapter 8, this volume). As they note (1994: 29–30):

> A competency development strategy would require that offenders be placed in positive, productive roles in the community which allow them to experience, practice and demonstrate ability to do something well that others value ... Opportunities of learning and personal development are 'wrapped around' engagement in productive activity rather than being presented as ends in themselves ... Meeting competency development objectives would require that the work be clearly useful for the community, that the offender and his or her labor be viewed as a resource, and that the offender be engaged in such a way that cognitive, social and occupational skill development can occur.

Although the concept of community re-integration is not entirely unproblematic (see, for example, Raynor 2001), in recent years there has been growing interest in the re-integrative potential of community service. In England and Wales this has resulted, in some probation areas, in the accreditation of skills acquired by offenders on community service. Offenders work towards a variety of awards with the assistance of specialist education, training and employment staff (Rex and Gelsthorpe 2002). The aim is to increase the employability of offenders and, consequently, their likelihood of finding work or undertaking further education or training after they have completed their orders.

In April 2001 the Criminal Justice and Court Services Act 2000 came into force, resulting in the community service order in England and Wales being renamed the community punishment order. It is somewhat ironic that legislation enacted to emphasise the punitive nature of community service should be accompanied by a government initiative aimed at enhancing the rehabilitative potential of community punishment orders. Community Punishment Pathfinders were established in 2000 under the Home Office's Crime Reduction Programme. A total of seven pathfinders were set up across ten probation areas and, like the other Home Office Pathfinders, they have been subject to evaluation (Rex and Gelsthorpe 2002). The projects have focused upon the use of pro-social modelling, skills accreditation and addressing the problems underlying offending behaviour in various combinations. In some projects attempts were also made to improve the quality of work placements and hence their perceived value to offenders. One project focused specifically on enhancing the integration of the community service and probation elements of combination orders through improved induction and supervision planning.

Rex and Gelsthorpe found that short-term outcomes were encouraging, with offenders showing reductions in perceived problems and pro-criminal attitudes (as measured by Crime-Pics II, a standardised tool for assessing offenders' problems and their attitudes towards offending). Two-thirds of offenders on orders were viewed by staff as having undergone positive change and as having good prospects of future change while (no doubt because they were relatively low risk in the first place) three-quarters were thought by staff to be unlikely to re-offend. A similar proportion of offenders considered that their experience of community service had made them less likely to re-offend. Importantly, the feature of community service most strongly linked with changes in offenders' attitudes was whether they perceived the work to have been of value to themselves and to the beneficiaries. The next phase of the pathfinder evaluation will examine whether these positive attitudinal changes are translated into reduced rates of reconviction.

Restorative approaches

Proponents of restorative justice argue that it is inappropriate to restrict assessment of its effectiveness to measures of recidivism since they embrace broader aims and give priority to different sanctioning objectives in the response to crime (Bazemore and Umbreit 1995). Indeed, reducing re-offending is perhaps the goal of restorative justice least likely to be achieved because of the limited ability of most approaches to exert an impact on the wider factors that contribute to and sustain offending behaviour (Wundersitz and Hetzel 1996, Ervin and Schneider 1990, Umbreit 1996). Evaluations of restorative justice have therefore also focused on participants' perspectives on the process.

Completion of agreements

Those who have undertaken reviews of evaluations of restorative justice initiatives generally conclude that the majority of mediation sessions or conferences result in an agreement being reached,[17] though the nature of the agreements may vary from a written or verbal apology to financial restitution to unpaid work for the victim or the community. The emphasis placed on different types of agreement likewise varies across programmes (partly reflecting the nature of the offences to which they relate) though Umbreit found that 80 per cent of agreements in mediation and reparation programmes in North America involved restitution.

Completion of agreements reached in restorative justice programmes is also reported to be high, ranging from 70 to 100 per cent in the case of victim–offender mediation (Marshall 1999, Umbreit *et al.* 2002). In the Youth Justice Board restorative justice projects, 83 per cent of offenders completed their order or final warning intervention (Wilcox and Hoyle 2004). Cant *et al.* (1999) found that 95 per cent of conference action plans in Western Australia were completed, while Markiewicz *et al.* (1997) found in Victoria that 90 per cent of conference plans were implemented partially or in full, with those monitored by professionals being more often fulfilled than those monitored by family members. How agreements or plans are monitored and the effect this has on their completion is an interesting question. O'Mahony *et al.* (2002) report that some parents were concerned at the absence of an effective monitoring system to ensure that offenders carried out the agreements reached in the Northern Ireland Restorative Cautioning pilots.

There is also some evidence that restitution agreements are more likely to be fulfilled following mediation or conferencing than in comparison with restitution ordered by a court (Bazemore and Umbreit 2001, Marshall 1999). In the RISE experiment in Canberra, for example, victims were more likely to receive an apology from offenders sent to a conference (74 per cent) than from offenders sent to court (11 per cent). They were also more likely to receive some reparation for the harm caused by the crime (83 per cent) than victims whose cases were dealt with in court (eight per cent) (Strang and Sherman 1997).

Benefits for victims

Research studies have identified a number of benefits that may accrue to victims through participating in restorative justice approaches. Marshall and Merry (1990) found that most victims welcomed the opportunity to meet the offender and valued the benefits of directly exchanging views with the offender, receiving an apology and, in some cases, having the chance potentially to reform the offender and thus prevent future victimisation. In the evaluation of the Youth Justice Board programmes, most victims (and offenders) perceived the process as fair, thought that the intervention had made the offender take responsibility for the offence and thought that the offender better understood the impact of the offending on the victim (Wilcox and Hoyle 2004).

Victims have generally been found to report high levels of satisfaction with the process and outcomes of mediation and reparation, and to be less fearful of further victimisation than if the case went to court (Umbreit *et al.* 2002). Marshall (1999) suggests that victims are likely to gain more if they have an opportunity to meet the offender and have suffered from more serious offences, though in the UK most mediation is indirect[18] and most schemes focus upon relatively minor offences and offenders. Even in North America, only 30 to 40 per cent of cases in four victim–offender mediation programmes resulted in face-to-face mediation between the two parties (Umbreit 1998).

The evaluation of conferencing in Canberra found that victims could benefit from the process of conferencing – which could provide an opportunity for them to voice their experience of the crime and its impact – as well as from its outcomes. Eighty-six per cent of victims invited to conferences actually attended (Sherman and Strang 1997), a participation rate which exceeds that found in New Zealand (Maxwell and Morris 1993) or in most victim–offender mediation programmes.

Family Group Conferencing has also shown relatively high levels of victim satisfaction (e.g. Cant *et al.* 1999; Sherman and Strang 1997, Hoyle *et al.* 2002, Trimboli 2000), though it appears that these are lower, in general, than those obtained in victim–offender mediation programmes, possibly because the views of a wider 'community of interest' (Dignan 2000) have a bearing upon processes and outcomes in the former. Dignan (2000) also suggests that police-led conferencing has tended to produce higher victim satisfaction levels than conferencing facilitated by other agencies within or outside the criminal justice system. This may be because the former place greater emphasis on offender accountability while the latter are also concerned with promoting offender re-integration.

Victim experiences of restorative justice are not, however, uniformly positive. In New Zealand only 51 per cent of victims reported being satisfied with conferencing and 27 per cent reported feeling worse as a result of participating in a conference (Maxwell and Morris 1993). Marshall (1999) suggests that some victims may feel coerced into participating: as Schiff (1998) observes, the amount of coercion associated with restorative interventions is unknown. The risk of secondary victimisation – resulting from the failure of the offender to acknowledge responsibility for the offence, to express remorse or to complete the resultant agreement – has been highlighted by, among others, Warner (1993) and O'Mahony *et al.* (2002).

Daly (2002) has questioned the extent to which conferences are restorative, observing that while victims report a reduced fear of victimisation, they appear equally likely to become more positive and more negative about the offender over time (as do victims who do not attend the conference). The difficulty of achieving truly restorative outcomes may, Daly suggests, be a reflection of the relative fragmentation and anonymity of contemporary societies. A similar view has been expressed by some academics in the UK (e.g. Miers *et al.* 2001; O'Mahony *et al.* 2002) based on the apparent difficulty in achieving processes and outcomes that consistently involve and reflect the interests of victims. This in turn reflects a broader difficulty in defining 'community': as Wilson *et al.* (2002) indicate, the constituency of the 'community' in sentencing circles differs widely between rural and urban areas. Therefore while there is a paucity of data on the operation and outcomes of reparative and restorative approaches in different types of community context, the potential consequences for both victims and offenders of the 'community' in which these approaches operate will require careful attention. For example, Moody (2002) suggests that geographical isolation, difficulties in accessing services and 'cultural differences' can each have an impact on the provision of services to victims in rural areas.

Benefits for offenders

Marshall and Merry (1990) found that many offenders who participated in mediation and reparation were affected by the experience to a greater extent than if they had gone to court. An obvious advantage for offenders – especially those who are diverted from the criminal justice process by participating in a restorative justice programme – is avoidance of a criminal record, court appearance or alternative sanction. Evaluations of mediation and reparation and conferencing have found that most offenders are satisfied with how they have been dealt with and regard both process and outcomes as having been fair (e.g. Sherman and Barnes 1997, Cant *et al.* 1999, Miers *et al.* 2001, Poulson and Elton 2002, Umbreit *et al.* 2002). Similar findings are reported by Crawford and Newburn (2003) in their evaluation of referral orders in England and Wales.

Recidivism[19]

Several studies in the UK and North America have examined recidivism following victim–offender mediation and reparation. The findings have been somewhat mixed, with some showing positive effects, some negative effects and some no effects. For example, Bonta *et al.* (1998), in their meta-analysis of fourteen evaluations, found that restorative justice programmes were associated with an overall reduction in recidivism, though there were wide variations across studies, with some showing increases in offending in relation to comparison cases. Their own study found lower levels of recidivism in comparison with groups of prisoners and probationers, though it is difficult to disentangle the effects of the restorative justice elements of the intervention from those of the other services provided to offenders. Kurki (2003) concludes that individual studies of victim–offender mediation have usually failed to identify statistically significant reductions in recidivism, though combining data from individual studies or by meta-analysis has produced more encouraging results. As she also points out, however, the original studies often have methodological shortcomings relating to selection effects and an absence of sufficient detail as to what actually happened in the context of the intervention.

In North America, Umbreit (1994) reported a 33 per cent reduction in one-year re-offending rates across four programmes: success rates, however, are likely to have been influenced by the quality of individual programmes, and the absence of a control group places limitations on the data (Bazemore and Umbreit 2001). Indeed, one limitation of many evaluations is their lack of adequate comparisons, limited follow-up periods and the relatively small sample sizes involved, the latter reflecting the comparatively informal and often small-scale nature of these programmes. Thus Nugent and Paddock's (1995) finding that young people who participated in a victim–offender mediation programme were less often reconvicted and reconvicted of less serious offence must be interpreted in the light of a limited follow-up and limited controls.

UK evaluations of victim–offender mediation have similarly produced mixed results. Marshall and Merry (1990) found a small effect on recidivism, but only in those cases in which direct mediation had taken place. The police-led Milton Keynes Retail Theft Initiative appeared to have some success with first-time offenders but not with those who had accrued a criminal record (McCulloch 1997). On the other hand, the Leeds Victim Offender Unit – which operates at all stages of the criminal justice process – achieved a 14 per cent reduction in recidivism over two years (Marshall 1999) though it did not have an appropriate control group against which changes in recidivism could be compared.

More recently, Miers *et al.* (2001) found that none of the juvenile schemes in their multi-site evaluation was associated with reduced recidivism. The West Yorkshire scheme was the only one that did appear to affect the frequency and seriousness of recidivism. It was characterised by its focus on offenders convicted of more serious offences and its emphasis on voluntary participation, increasing the likelihood, presumably, that offenders would take part through a genuine wish to make amends rather than as a means of evading a conviction or more severe sanction.

Analysis of self-reported and detected recidivism among young people who participated in the Thames Valley restorative cautioning scheme suggested that one quarter stopped offending or reduced their offending while the likelihood of reconviction within twelve months was halved in comparison with traditional police cautioning practices. However, the numbers involved in the restorative cautioning sample were low (n = 56) (Hoyle *et al.* 2002). The recent evaluation of the 46 Youth Justice Board restorative justice projects provided no evidence of an impact on recidivism against a sample of young offenders sentenced in 2000. Moreover, there was no indication from this study that reconviction rates were lower following more 'restorative' interventions (e.g. meeting the victim rather than engaging in shuttle mediation) (Wilcox and Hoyle 2004).

As Bazemore and Umbreit (2001) acknowledge, there have as yet been few studies of the impact of family group conferences on offender recidivism, making it difficult to gauge their effectiveness in this respect. The RISE evaluation in Canberra found reductions in recidivism among young offenders charged with violent offences who participated in conferences compared to those who were dealt with by the court. No such differences emerged, however, with drink drivers[20] and with young people charged with retail or personal theft (Sherman *et al.* 2000).

Walker (2002) found a reduction in subsequent violent offending among young people who participated in conferences in Hawaii. Together with the RISE findings and the positive outcomes achieved with the use of mediation with more serious offenders in the UK, these data point to restorative approaches possibly having a greater impact upon personal injury than upon property crime. It is also possible that restorative approaches are more effective if they involve an identifiable personal victim as opposed to a 'substitute' victim such as the victim of a previous drink-driving incident or the manager of a chain store (see also Baines 1996).

The initial evaluation of the New Zealand approach also failed to detect any difference in re-offending between conference offenders and a comparison group (Maxwell and Morris 1993, 1994). However a more detailed analysis of the recidivism data revealed a somewhat more complex picture, with offenders who felt involved in a family group conference being less likely to be reconvicted than those who experienced it as negative and shaming (Morris and Maxwell 1998).

As with community service, therefore, the quality of the experience for offenders appears to be crucial. Drawing upon a number of studies, Kurki (2003) concludes that restorative justice practices are more likely to be effective if they are more 'restorative': for example, if they result in the expression of remorse and the reaching of agreements through genuine consensus.[21] Morris and Maxwell (1998) have also suggested that conferences may be more effective if they link offenders into supports and services that can address the wider issues related to their offending, addressing Marshall's (1999) concern that the benefits of restorative justice interventions may be 'undone' when offenders return to their social milieu.

Overall, therefore, the findings in relation to recidivism following restorative justice initiatives (and, more widely, reparative approaches) are somewhat mixed and there appears not to be a straightforward association between these developments and subsequent reductions in officially recorded criminal behaviour. Instead, however, it seems that the effectiveness of community service and restorative justice in this regard may be dependent upon offenders' perceptions that they are being offered the opportunity for meaningful and active participation in a reciprocal exchange. As Kurki (2003: 307) observes, 'it seems more and more important to focus resources and research on the restorative quality of initiatives'.

Conclusions

In the UK there has been growing interest in the potential of restorative justice as evidenced by the recommendation in the Auld Report (2001) that attention should be given by government to the development of approaches of this type, by the subsequent publication by the government of its consultation document on restorative justice (Home Office 2003), by the recommendations of the Carter Report regarding the introduction of statutory conditional cautions (Carter 2003) and by the undertaking of a major inquiry by Justice under the rubric of the Rethinking Criminal Justice Initiative (Tickell and Akester 2004).

That said, the provision of restorative and reparative initiatives is currently uneven and is characterised by the inclusion of a number of fairly disparate initiatives. There is also evidence that, possibly because so many different schemes have been brought under its umbrella, the practice of restorative justice is somewhat removed from its underlying theory (Gavrielides 2003). Finally, as the government has acknowledged, the evidence base for restorative justice is still rather rudimentary (Home Office 2003).

From this brief overview it is possible, however, to conclude that criminal justice responses that are reparative or restorative offer some promise over approaches that are more explicitly concerned with punishment. Whether approaches of this kind are more effective in reducing recidivism has not yet been clearly established, but there is evidence that they often achieve other (and some would argue equally or more important) aims.[22] Furthermore, it appears that how these approaches are implemented is likely to be of critical importance. In particular, how offenders experience restorative or reparative approaches and how well they are able to promote their re-integration in the community seem – on the admittedly as yet rather limited data available – to be related to their success. As Raynor notes elsewhere in this volume, effective rehabilitation is about more than programmes: it also requires attention to the wider social context in which offending occurs. For example, 're-integrative' community service placements appear more likely to encourage desistance than do those that are primarily retributive in content and aim. Similarly, positive offender involvement in conferencing and direct offender–victim mediation have been reported as achieving improved outcomes (*vis-à-vis* recidivism) than those in which offenders feel disengaged or stigmatised or in which shuttle negotiation is used.

This would suggest that there is scope for greater use to be made of reparative and restorative approaches at a more diverse range of points in the criminal justice process than has hitherto been the case, though this should not be to the exclusion of other supports and services for victims (Masters 2002). Even if at worst they appear no less effective than the alternative courses of action that they are intended to replace, options such as community service, mediation and reparation and conferencing have been shown to produce other, less tangible benefits for offenders, for victims and for the community. Moreover, in the UK public support for the use of reparative and restorative approaches has been shown to be high, especially in relation to relatively minor offences and offenders (Dunn *et al.* 2000, Scottish Parliament 2002).[23] This indicates a potential tension between public tolerance and what victims may have to gain.

Arguably scope exists for an expanded role for 'communities' in the development of restorative justice initiatives. The Neighbourhood Renewal Unit's 'New Deal for Communities' programme, which is based in 39 neighbourhoods across England and Wales, aims to make significant and lasting improvements in housing, education, unemployment, crime and health. In its review of the evidence base for neighbourhood renewal, the Unit highlights the potential for local Crime and Disorder Partnerships to develop or support restorative justice initiatives to reduce youth crime while mediation is identified as a potentially effective method for reducing conflicts within communities (Neighbourhood Renewal Unit, undated). Such a development would resonate with Braithwaite's (2002) analysis of the capacity for restorative justice to enable social justice and Kurki's (2003) hypothesis that it may help build social capital among participants and within the wider community.

From a policy perspective, any extension or expansion of the use of reparative and restorative interventions needs to be preceded by considering a number of key questions:

- What are they trying to achieve?
- At whom are they targeted and at which points in the criminal justice process should they be introduced?
- Are they culturally appropriate?
- How are the interests of victim, offender and community represented and balanced and what safeguards are in place?
- How formalised should they be and should they be integrated with or separate from traditional criminal justice processes?

- How might offender integration/rehabilitation be achieved without marginalising victims and placing them at risk of secondary victimisation?
- What systems can be put into place to ensure that completion of agreements can be adequately enforced?
- What resources will be required and how can these be most effectively deployed to maximise their potential benefit?

It is also critically important that much more is learned about the effectiveness of restorative justice, particularly as it operates in a UK context. Some restorative justice initiatives are culturally specific and some communities will present the introduction of approaches of this type with particular challenges. It is therefore crucial that any expanded use of initiatives that have reparation and restoration as a central aim is carefully evaluated to provide a sound basis upon which future policy and practice can be based.

Notes

1 It does not address other victim-related initiatives that have been introduced in recent years which are neither reparative nor restorative. These are discussed in Williams (2002).
2 This chapter does not focus specifically on compensation orders, which are dealt with in Chapter 6; however, reference is made to studies which have compared outcomes of court-ordered compensation and similar agreements reached through restorative approaches.
3 Recent Scottish research also shows high levels of public awareness of and support for community service, which was thought to be used much more commonly than is actually the case (Scottish Parliament 2002).
4 Dignan (2000) also includes the Scottish Children's Hearings within this category. However, although they are aimed at involving the community in responding to the problems experienced by or behaviour of young people, their focus is rarely, if ever, reparative.
5 The question of whether victims should have a greater say in the types of work performed by offenders made subject to community service is an important one. Arguably there should be greater scope for this to occur than exists at present (e.g. Dignan 2003), though the necessary safeguards (for both victim and offender) would need to be applied.
6 But see Schiff (2003) for discussion of the ambiguity of 'community' and Kurki (2000) for a discussion of the differences between 'community justice' and 'restorative justice'.
7 It could, for example, involve educational activities or other activities aimed at 'self improvement'.
8 See, for example, Immarigeon (1996).

9 For example, victim contact work was difficult because effective victim contact procedures had not been developed and implemented by the criminal justice system.
10 Daly (2002), however, has questioned the appropriateness of contrasting restorative justice with retributive justice and rehabilitation since, she argues, restorative approaches can embrace both retributive and rehabilitative elements. The relationship between criminal justice and restorative justice is explored more fully in von Hirsch *et al.* (2003).
11 Though, as Marshall (1999: 28) points out 'neighbourhoods differ in their capacities to support potential offenders in their midst'.
12 Though it is important not to assume that 'informality' is necessarily benign, particularly with respect to women and girls.
13 In the first two years of the pilot the average cost per order – excluding indirect costs – was estimated at approximately A$7500. This sum subsequently reduced as referrals increased, conferences became slightly shorter and convenors spent less time travelling and on case-finding activities.
14 It was operated at the pre-sentence stage by an organisation which was independent of the criminal justice system and included legal representation for young people.
15 Interestingly, given the proliferation of victim–offender mediation in Europe, there are relatively little outcome data available.
16 Offenders least valued work that verged on being demeaning. Requiring offenders to carry out work of this type, isolating them from other volunteers or service users and stigmatising them through requiring that they wear conspicuous uniforms is hardly likely to convey the message that they have something positive to offer society and their local communities. As Ahmed *et al.* (2001) argue, the process of shaming and its outcomes are complex. Effective 'shame management' is required if its restorative or re-integrative potential is to be invoked. This is important in light of the Carter Report's emphasis upon the 'visibility of community punishment' (Carter 2003). Visibility can be achieved in a less stigmatising way than through the wearing of uniforms (for example, through the prominent use of plaques etc. once a project has been completed).
17 For example, Walker (2002) reports that all family group conferences in a programme in Hawaii reached an agreement, while Umbreit (1998) found agreements were reached in 95 per cent of victim–offender mediation sessions across four North American programmes.
18 Dignan (2000) suggests that this may explain why victim satisfaction levels tend to be higher in the USA and Canada than in the UK.
19 A systematic review of restorative justice outcomes being undertaken by Heather Strang and Lawrence Sherman for the Campbell Collaboration has not yet been published. Nor has the Home Office-funded evaluation of restorative justice schemes established as part of the Crime Reduction Programme.
20 In fact, there was some evidence that drink drivers who attended conferences were more likely to commit similar offences in future compared with those who were dealt with through the courts. Sherman *et al.* speculate that this may be because unlike the court cases the conference cases were not disqualified from driving.

21 Simply subsuming practices under the label of 'restorative justice' does not mean that they are necessarily restorative. Kurki (2003) laments the lack of attention to the restorative quality of restorative justice initiatives while Young and Hoyle (2003) discuss the limited restorative focus of police-led cautioning practices in Thames Valley.
22 For example, Wright (2002).
23 But Dunn *et al.* (2000) report that some groups in Northern Ireland (especially those described as 'working class') were unsympathetic towards restorative justice and believed that offenders should be dealt with more harshly.

References

Advisory Council on the Penal System (1970) *Non-custodial and Semi-custodial Penalties* [The Wootton Report] (London: HMSO).

Alder, C. (2000) 'Young women offenders and the challenge for restorative justice', in H. Strang and J. Braithwaite (eds) *Restorative Justice: Philosophy to practice* (Dartmouth: Ashgate).

Alder, C. and Wundersitz, J. (1994) *Family Conferencing in Juvenile Justice: The way forward or misplaced optimism?* (Canberra: Australian Institute of Criminology).

Ahmed, E., Harris, N., Braithwaite, J., and Braithwaite, V. (2001) *Shame Management Through Reintegration* (Cambridge: Cambridge University Press).

Ash, R. and Biggar, H. (2002) *Return to Custody in Scottish Prisons*, SPS Research Bulletin No. 8 (Edinburgh: SPS).

Auld, Lord Justice (2001) *Review of the Criminal Courts of England and Wales* (London: The Stationery Office).

Baines, M. (1996) 'Viewpoints on young women and family group conferences', in C. Alder and M. Baines (eds) *... and When She was Bad? Working with Young Women in Juvenile Justice and Related Areas* (Hobart, Tasmania: National Clearinghouse for Youth Studies).

Barclay, G. C. and Taveres, C. (eds) (1999) *Information on the Criminal Justice System in England and Wales: Digest 4* (London: Home Office Research and Statistics Directorate).

Bargen, J. (1996). 'Kids, cops, courts, conferencing and children's rights: a note on perspectives', *Australian Journal of Human Rights*, 2(2), 209–228.

Barry, M. and McIvor, G. (2000) *Diversion from Prosecution to Social Work and Other Service Agencies* (Edinburgh: Scottish Executive Central Research Unit).

Bazemore, G. and Maloney, D. (1994) 'Rehabilitating community service: toward restorative service sanctions in a balanced justice system', *Federal Probation*, 61(1), 24–35.

Bazemore, G. and Umbreit, M. (1995) 'Rethinking the sanctioning function in juvenile court: Retributive or restorative responses to youth crime', *Crime and Delinquency* 41(3), 296–316.

Bazemore, G. and Umbreit, M. (2001) *A Comparison of Four Restorative Conferencing Models* (Washington, DC: Office of Juvenile Justice and Delinquency Prevention Juvenile Justice Bulletin).

Blagg, H. (1997) A just measure of shame? Aboriginal youth and conferencing in Australia, *British Journal of Criminology*, 37(4), pp. 81–501.

Bonta, J., Wallace-Capretta, S. and Rooney, J. (1998) *Restorative Justice: An evaluation of the Restorative Resolutions Project* (Ottawa: Solicitor General Canada).

Bradshaw, W. and Umbreit, M.S. (2003) 'Assessing satisfaction with victim services: the development and use of the Victim Satisfaction with Offender Dialogue Scale (VSODS)' *International Review of Victimology*, 10(1), 71–83.

Braithwaite, J. (1989) *Crime, Shame and Re-integration* (Cambridge: Cambridge University Press).

Brathwaite, J. (2002) *Restorative Justice and Responsive Regulation* (New York: Oxford University Press).

Braithwaite, J. and Mugford, S. (1994) 'Conditions of successful reintegration ceremonies', *British Journal of Criminology*, 34(2), 139–171.

Cant, R., Downey, R. and Marshall, P. (1999) *Restorative Justice in Western Australia: The operation and evaluation of juvenile justice teams*, Paper presented at the British Criminology Conference, Liverpool.

Carter, P. (2003) *Managing Offenders, Reducing Crime: A new approach* (London: Home Office).

Coumarelos, C. and Weatherburn, D. (1995) 'Targeting intervention strategies to reduce juvenile recidivism', *The Australian and New Zealand Journal of Criminology*, 28, 55–72.

Crawford, A. and Newburn, T. (2002) 'Recent developments in restorative justice for young people in England and Wales: community participation and representation', *British Journal of Criminology*, 42(3), 476–495.

Crawford, A. and Newburn, T. (2003) *Youth Offending and Restorative Justice: Implementing reform in youth justice* (Cullompton: Willan).

Daly, K. (2000) 'Restorative justice in diverse and unequal societies', *Law in Context*, 17, 167–190.

Daly, K. (2002) 'Restorative justice: the real story', *Punishment & Society*, 55–79.

Daly, K. and Hayes, H. (2001) *Restorative Justice and Conferencing in Australia, Trends and Issues in Crime and Criminal Justice No. 186* (Canberra ACT: Australian Institute of Criminology).

Dignan, J. (1992) *Repairing the Damage* (Sheffield: University of Sheffield).

Dignan, J. (with Lowey, K.) (2000) *Restorative Justice Options for Northern Ireland: A comparative review* (Belfast: Northern Ireland Office Criminal Justice Review Group).

Dignan, J. (2002) 'Reparation orders', in B. Williams (ed.) *Reparation and Victim-Focused Social Work: Research highlights in social work*, 42 (London: Jessica Kingsley).

Dignan, J. (2003) *Restorative justice and the law: the case for an integrated, systemic approach*, [www.restorativejustice.org/rj3/RJ_City/Documents/Dignan_paper.htm].

Dignan, J. and Marsh, P. (2001) 'Restorative justice and family group conferences in England', in A. Morris and G. Maxwell (eds) *Restorative Justice for Juveniles* (Oxford: Hart Publishing).

Dunn, S., Morgan, V. and Dawson, H. (2000) *Attitudes to the Criminal Justice System* (Belfast: Northern Ireland Office Criminal Justice Review Group).

Ervin, L. and Schneider, A. (1990) 'Explaining the effects of restitution on offenders: results of a national experiment in juvenile courts', in B. Galaway and J. Hudson (eds) *Criminal Justice, Restitution and Reconciliation* (Monsey, NY: Criminal Justice Press).

Faulkner, D. (1996) *Darkness and Light: Justice, Crime and Management for Today* (London: The Howard League for Penal Reform).

Gavrielides, T. (2003) *Restorative Justice Theory and Practice: Mind the Gap!*, [www.restorativejustice.org/rj3/Feature/2003/December/RJTheory%26 Practice.htm].

Hine, J. (1993) 'Access for women: flexible and friendly?', in D. Whitfield and D. Scott (eds) *Paying Back: Twenty Years of Community Service* (Winchester: Waterside Press).

Home Office (2003) *Restorative Justice: The government's strategy* (London: Home Office).

Hoyle, C., Young, R. and Hill, R. (2002) *Proceed with Caution: An evaluation of the Thames Valley Police Initiative in Restorative Cautioning* (York: Joseph Rowntree Foundation).

Immarigeon, R. (1996) 'Prison-based victim–offender reconciliation program', in B. Galaway and J. Hudson (eds) *Restorative Justice: International Perspectives* (Monsey, NY: Criminal Justice Press).

Immarigeon, R. (1998a) 'Is "community service" restorative justice?', *Community Corrections Report*, 5(4), 49 and 58–59.

Immarigeon, R. (1998b) 'Sentencing offenders to community service: 30 years of practice, promise and pessimism', *Community Corrections Report*, 5(2), 19–20 and 28.

Kilchling, M. and Loschnig-Gspandl, M. (2000) 'Legal and practical perspectives on victim/offender mediation in Austria and Germany', *International Review of Victimology*, 7(4), 305–332.

Killias, M., Aebi, M. and Ribeaud, D. (2000) 'Does community service rehabilitate better than short-term imprisonment? Results of a controlled experiment', *The Howard Journal*, 39(1), 40–57.

Knapp, M., Robertson, E. and McIvor, G. (1992) 'The comparative costs of community service and custody in Scotland', *The Howard Journal*, 31, 8–30.

Kurki, L. (2000) 'Restorative and community justice in the United States', in M. Tonry (ed.) *Crime and Justice: A review of research*, 27 (Chicago, Il.: University of Chicago Press).

Kurki, L. (2003) 'Evaluating restorative justice practices', in A. von Hirsch, J. Roberts, A. E. Bottoms, K. Roach and M. Schiff (eds) *Restorative Justice and Criminal Justice: Competing or reconcilable paradigms?* (Oxford: Hart Publishing).

Levy, L. and McIvor, G. (2001) *National Evaluation of the Operation and Impact of Supervised Attendance Orders* (Edinburgh: Scottish Executive Central Research Unit).

Lloyd, C., Mair, G. and Hough, M. (1995) *Explaining Reconviction Rates: A critical analysis*, Home Office Research Study 136 (London: Home Office). .

Markiewicz, A., Lagay, B., Murray, H. and Campbell, L. (1997) *Juvenile Justice Group Conferencing in Victoria: An evaluation of a pilot program – Phase Two* (Melbourne: University of Melbourne School of Social Work).

Marshall, T. F. (1999) *Restorative Justice: An overview* (London: Home Office Research Development and Statistics Directorate).

Marshall, T. and Merry, S. (1990) *Crime and Accountability* (London: HMSO).

Masters, G. (2002) 'Family group conferencing: a victim perspective', in B. Williams (ed.) *Reparation and Victim-Focused Social Work* (London: Jessica Kingsley).

Maxwell, G. (2000) *Crossing Cultural Boundaries: The experience of family group conferences*, UN Crime Congress Ancillary Meeting, Vienna.

Maxwell, G. and Morris, A. (1993) *Family Participation, Cultural Diversity and Victim Involvement in Youth Justice: A New Zealand experiment* (Wellington, New Zealand: Department of Social Welfare and the Institute of Criminology, Victoria University of Wellington).

Maxwell, G. and Morris, A. (1994) 'The New Zealand model of family group conferences', in C. Alder and J. Wundersitz (eds) *Family Conferencing in Juvenile Justice: The way forward or misplaced optimism?* (Canberra: Australian Institute of Criminology).

Maxwell, G., Morris, A. and Anderson, T. (1999) *Community Panel Adult Pre-trial Diversion: Supplementary evaluation* (Wellington, NZ: Crime Prevention Unit, Department of Prime Minister and Cabinet and Institute of Criminology, Victoria University of Wellington).

May, C. (1999) *Explaining Reconviction Following Community Sentences: The role of social factors*, Home Office Research Study 192 (London: Home Office).

McCulloch, H. (1997) *Shop Theft: Improving the police response,* Police Research Group Paper 76 (London: Home Office).

McEvoy, K. and Mika, H. (2002) 'Restorative justice and the critique of informalism in Northern Ireland', *British Journal of Criminology*, 42(3), 534–562.

McIvor, G. (1992) *Sentenced to Serve: The operation and impact of community service by offenders* (Aldershot: Avebury).

McIvor (1998a) 'Jobs for the boys? Gender differences in referral to community service', *The Howard Journal*, 37(3), 280–291.

McIvor, G. (1998b) 'Prosocial modeling and legitimacy: lessons from a study of community service', in *Prosocial Modeling and Legitimacy: The Clarke Hall Day Conference* (Cambridge: University of Cambridge Institute of Criminology).

McIvor, G. (2002) *What Works in Community Service?: CJSW Briefing Paper 6* (Edinburgh: Criminal Justice Social Work Development Centre for Scotland).

McIvor, G. (2004) 'Service with a smile?: Women and community "punishment" ', in G. McIvor (ed.) *Women who Offend: Research Highlights in Social Work*, 44 (London: Jessica Kingsley).

McIvor, G. and Tulle-Winton, E. (1993) *The Use of Community Service by Scottish Courts* (Stirling: Social Work Research Centre, University of Stirling).

Miers, D. (2001) *An International Review of Restorative Justice*, Crime Reduction Research Series Paper 10 (London: Home Office).

Miers, D., Maguire, M., Goldie, S., Sharpe, K., Hale, C., Netten, A., Uglow, S., Doolin, K., Hallam, A., Enterkin, J. and Newburn, T. (2001) *An Exploratory Evaluation of Restorative Justice Schemes*, Crime Reduction Research Series Paper 9 (London: Home Office).

Moody, S. (2002) 'Responding to victims of crime in rural areas', in B. Williams (ed.) *Reparation and Victim-Focused Social Work* (London: Jessica Kingsley).

Moore, D. and O'Connell, T. (1994) 'Family conferencing in Wagga Wagga: A communitarian model of justice', in C. Alder and J. Wundersitz (eds) *Family Conferencing in Juvenile Justice: The way forward or misplaced optimism?* (Canberra: Australian Institute of Criminology).

Morris, A. and Maxwell, G. (1998) 'Understanding reoffending', *Criminology (New Zealand)*, 10, 10–13.

Neighbourhood Renewal Unit (undated) *What Works? Reviewing the Evidence Base for Neighbourhood Renewal* (London: NRU).
Nugent, W. and Paddock, J. (1995) 'The effect of victim–offender mediation on severity of re-offence', *Mediation Quarterly*, 12(4), 353–367.
O'Mahony, D., Chapman, T. and Doak, J. (2002) *Restorative Cautioning: A study of police based restorative cautioning pilots in Northern Ireland* (Belfast: Northern Ireland Office).
Polk, K. (1994) 'Family conferencing: theoretical and evaluative concerns', in C. Alder and J. Wundersitz (eds) *Family Conferencing in Juvenile Justice: The way forward or misplaced optimism?* (Canberra: Australian Institute of Criminology).
Poulson, B. and Elton, K. (2002) 'Participants' attitudes in the Utah juvenile victim–offender mediation program', *Juvenile and Family Court Journal*, 53(1), 37–45.
Quaker Peace and Social Witness (2003) *Circles of Support and Accountability in the Thames Valley*, [www.quaker.org.uk/peace/qpsdocs/circ.pdf].
Raynor, P. (2001) 'Community penalties and social integration: "Community" as solution and as problem', in A. Bottoms, L. Gelsthorpe and S. Rex (eds) *Community Penalties: change and challenges* (Cullompton: Willan).
Rex, S. (1999) 'Desistance from offending: experiences of probation', *The Howard Journal*, 38(4), 366–383.
Rex, S. and Gelsthorpe, L. (2002) 'The role of community service in reducing offending: evaluating pathfinder projects in the UK', *The Howard Journal*, 41(4), 311–325.
Sandor, D. (1994) 'The thickening blue wedge in juvenile justice', in C. Alder and J. Wundersitz (eds) *Family Conferencing in Juvenile Justice: The way forward or misplaced optimism?* (Canberra: Australian Institute of Criminology).
Schiff, M. (1998) 'Restorative justice interventions for juvenile offenders: a research agenda for the next decade', *Western Criminology Review*, 1(1) [wcr.sonoma.edu/v1n1/schiff.html].
Schiff, M. (2003) 'Models, promises and the promise of restorative justice strategies', in A. von Hirsch, J. Roberts, A. E. Bottoms, K. Roach and M. Schiff (eds) *Restorative Justice and Criminal Justice: Competing or reconcilable paradigms?* (Oxford: Hart Publishing).
Scottish Executive (2001) *Reconvictions of Offenders Discharged from Custody or Given Non-custodial Sentences in 1995, Scotland* (Edinburgh: Scottish Executive Statistical Services).
Scottish Executive (2003) *Costs, Sentencing Profiles and the Scottish Criminal Justice System 2001: Section 306* (Edinburgh: Scottish Executive).
Scottish Parliament (2002) *Public Attitudes Towards Sentencing and Alternatives to Imprisonment* [www.scottish.parliament.uk/S1/official_report/cttee/just1-02/j1r02-pats-01.htm].
Shapland, J., Atkinson, A., Colledge, E., Dignan, J., Howes, M., Johnstone, J., Pennant, R., Robinson, G. and Sorsby, A. (2002) *Evaluating the Fit: Restorative justice and criminal justice*, Paper presented to the Workshop on Restorative Justice, British Criminology Conference, Keele University.
Sherman, L.W. and Barnes, G.C. (1997) *Restorative Justice and Offenders' Respect for the Law*, RISE Working Paper Number 3 [www.aic.gov.au/rjustice/rise/working.html].

Sherman, L., Braithwaite, J. and Strang, H. (1994) *Reintegrative Shaming of Violence, Drink Driving and Property Crime: A randomised controlled trial*, Technical Proposal Appendix for RISE.

Sherman, L. W. and Strang, H. (1997) *The Right Kind of Shame for Crime Prevention*, RISE Working Paper Number 1 [www.aic.gov.au/rjustice/rise/working.html].

Sherman, L.W. and Strang, H. (1997) *Restorative Justice and Deterring Crime*, RISE Working Paper Number 4 [www.aic.gov.au/rjustice/rise/working.html].

Sherman, L. W., Strang, H. and Woods, D.J. (2000) *Recidivism Patterns in the Canberra Reintegrative Shaming Experiment (RISE)* (Canberra: Centre for Restorative Justice, Australian National University).

Spencer, F. and McIvor, G. (2000) 'Conferencing as a response to youth crime', in G. Mair and R. Tarling (eds), *British Criminology Conference: Selected Proceedings. Volume 3* [www.lboro.ac.uk/departments/ss/bsc/bccsp/vol03/spencer.html].

Strang, H. and Sherman, L. W. (1997) *The Victim's Perspective*, RISE Working Papers Number 2 [www.aic.gov.au/rjustice/rise/working.html].

Strang, H. and Sherman, L. W. (2003) 'Repairing the harm: victims and restorative justice', *Utah Law Review*, 15, 15–42.

Stuart, B. (1996) 'Circle sentencing: turning swords into ploughshares', in B. Galaway and J. Hudson (eds) *Restorative Justice: International perspectives* (Amsterdam: Kugler Publications).

Tickell, S. and Akester, K. (2004) *Restorative Justice: The way ahead* (London: Justice).

Trimboli, L. (2000) *An Evaluation of the New South Wales Youth Justice Conferencing Scheme* (Sydney, NSW: NSW Bureau of Crime Statistics and Research).

Trotter, C. (1999) *Working with Involuntary Clients* (London: Sage).

Umbreit, M. (1994) *Victim Meets Offender: The impact of restorative justice in mediation* (Monsey, NY: Criminal Justice Press).

Umbreit, M. (1996) 'Restorative justice through victim–offender mediation: the impact of programs in four Canadian provinces', in B. Galaway and J. Hudson (eds) *Restorative Justice: International Perspectives* (Monsey, NY: Criminal Justice Press).

Umbreit, M. S. (1998) 'Restorative justice through victim–offender mediation: a multi-site assessment', *Western Criminology Review*, 1(1), 1–28.

Umbreit, M. S., Coates, R. B. and Vos, B. (2002) 'Impact of victim–offender mediation; Two decades of research', *Federal Probation*, 65(3), 29–35.

von Hirsch, A., Roberts, J., Bottoms, A. E., Roach, K. and Schiff, M. (eds) (2003) *Restorative Justice and Criminal Justice: Competing or reconcilable paradigms?* (Oxford: Hart Publishing).

Walker, L. (2002) 'Conferencing: a new approach for juvenile justice in Hawaii', *Federal Probation*, 66(1), 38–43.

Warner, K. (1994) 'Family group conferences and the rights of the offender', in C. Alder and J. Wundersitz (eds) *Family Conferencing in Juvenile Justice: The way forward or misplaced optimism?* (Canberra: Australian Institute of Criminology).

Warner, S. (1993) *Making Amends: Justice for victims and offenders* (Aldershot: Avebury).

Whyte, B. (2002) *Crime and Restorative Justice: CJSW Briefing Paper 4* (Edinburgh: Criminal Justice Social Work Development Centre for Scotland).

Wilcox, A. and Hoyle, C. (2004) *The National Evaluation of the Youth Justice Board's Restorative Justice Projects* (London: Youth Justice Board).

Williams, B. (Ed.) *Reparation and Victim-Focused Social Work: Research Highlights in Social Work*, 42 (London: Jessica Kingsley).

Wilson, R.J., Huculak, B. and McWhinnie, A. (2002) 'Restorative justice innovations in Canada', *Behavioral Sciences and the Law*, 20(4), 363–380.

Wright, M. (2002) *An International Approach: What is Restorative justice?*, Paper presented at a seminar in honour of Gunnar Marnell, Stockholm.

Wundersitz, J. and Hetzel, S. (1996) 'Family conferencing for young offenders: the South Australian experience', in J. Hudson, A. Morris, G. Maxwell and B. Galaway (eds) *Family Group Conferences: Perspectives on policy and practice* (Sydney: Federation Press and Criminal Justice Press).

Young, R. and Hoyle, C. (2003) 'New, improved police-led restorative justice?', in A. von Hirsch, J. Roberts, A. E. Bottoms, K. Roach and M. Schiff (eds) *Restorative Justice and Criminal Justice: Competing or reconcilable paradigms?* (Oxford: Hart Publishing).

Zehr, H. (1990) *Changing Lenses: A new focus for criminal justice* (Scottdale, PA: Herald Press).

Zellerer, E. and Cunneen, C. (2001) 'Restorative justice, indigenous justice and human rights', in G. Bazemore and M. Schiff (eds) *Restorative Community Justice: Repairing harm and transforming communities* (Cincinnati, OH: Anderson Publishing).

Chapter 8

Rehabilitative and reintegrative approaches

Peter Raynor

Introduction

The aim of this chapter is to review the contribution of rehabilitative and reintegrative penalties, otherwise known as the stock in trade of probation services and similar agencies which supervise offenders as a court-imposed sanction, or as part of such a sanction. The chapter summarises the major lessons from international research efforts on the effectiveness of penalties and interventions falling under these headings, and reviews what is currently known about their effectiveness in Britain following several years of more or less systematic attempts to apply the lessons of that research. The resulting appraisal of current British efforts is mixed: while final evaluations of many initiatives are still awaited, achievements so far fall short of initial aspirations in several respects. However, because there has been an unprecedented investment in research to accompany the various innovations, a good deal can be learnt. The final section of the chapter outlines some of the reasons for these mixed results and makes some suggestions about future strategies.

First, some clarification is needed about definitions and scope. The term 'rehabilitation' can be used in several senses, all related but not precisely the same. For example, we use it to refer to the process of intervening with offenders to reduce their future offending, and this is the most familiar use in a criminal justice context. However, we also use it to refer to helping medical patients recover some or all of their normal abilities and levels of functioning after surgery or illness. Another use denotes the restoration of a person to his or her former status or group membership after a period of exclusion or censure. Such use is familiar from the practice in totalitarian regimes of declaring that a discarded former leader is, in spite of earlier pronouncements, worthy after all of his or her honoured place in history; but it can also be used of somebody readmitted to a club after a period of disciplinary exclusion, or of a child returned to his or her family after a period in the care of a local authority. All of these familiar meanings hover in the background of a discussion surrounding rehabilitation in penal policy. McWilliams and Pease's influential 1990 paper argued that rehabilitation, in the sense of restoration to the status of a valued member of the community, was actually more relevant and possibly more achievable than the reduction of re-offending. This chapter takes the more conventional view that the main purpose of rehabilitative penalties is to reduce re-offending by those subject to such penalties. However, the relevance of other meanings rests in their implication that the route by which we should do this lies not through incapacitation or simple coercion so much as through helping, encouraging or guiding people to change themselves so that they have less wish, need or disposition to offend.

The notion of 'reintegration' poses similar problems, particularly when it is considered as part of official intervention in the life of an offender following an offence. *Re*-integration implies a return to a former state of social integration that may never have existed for the particular offender, and so may not be available to return to. Conversely, the offender may have formerly been well integrated within a crime-prone environment that would potentially increase the likelihood of future offending on their return. 'Reintegration' also has an established criminological usage based on the work of John Braithwaite (for example, Braithwaite 1989): this envisages reintegration as the process of reinvolving a former offender as a normal citizen in the reciprocal practices of community life, through a form of atonement triggered by effective shaming. This has much in common with that meaning of 'rehabilitation' which draws on notions of restored status and membership, but is usually discussed (as in the preceding chapter) in the context of restorative penalties, which aim explicitly to restore or mend the social bonds and mutual obligations which are understood to have been damaged by the offence.

When used outside the field of restorative justice, 'reintegration' is probably better understood as the attempt to involve former offenders in a network of pro-social opportunities and relationships that will help to maintain a non-offending lifestyle, even if no such network existed before. Haines' (1990) influential review of literature on the after-care of prisoners argued that the most effective after-care services were likely to be those which promoted conditions which Hirschi's (1969) control theory regards as effective in preventing offending, namely the existence of strong social bonds which promote pro-social attachment, commitment, involvement and belief. (Interestingly, Braithwaite has described his reintegration theory as a type of control theory.) Such an understanding therefore helps us to clarify and define the aim of reintegrative approaches as being to establish and/or strengthen social bonds of the kind likely to have a non-criminal, pro-social influence. Reintegration then becomes a means by which the goal of rehabilitation can be pursued. In the areas of correctional practice which are concerned with what happens to prisoners when they come out of prison, this process has been renamed 'resettlement': a government report proposed this term to replace 'throughcare', possibly because of the unfashionable notion of caring implied by the latter (Home Office 1998; see Raynor 2004 for a discussion of the possible meanings of 'resettlement'). In the United States the preferred term for this is 're-entry' into the community (Petersilia 2003), while in the UK the identification of the importance of social bonds and inclusion is evident from the recent interest of the government's Social Exclusion Unit in the problems of ex-prisoners, resulting in a far-reaching report (Social Exclusion Unit 2002).

To sum up then, this chapter is about penalties which aim, in whole or in part, to reduce re-offending by reducing an offender's wish, need and/or disposition to offend, including those which seek to do so by improving pro-social bonds and influences.

The emerging consensus of research

The impact of 'nothing works'

Research on the process and effectiveness of rehabilitation has generally been concentrated on its narrowest meaning, namely the reduction of re-offending. This was a natural consequence of a wish to test the modernist claim that offending could be 'treated' (Garland 1985), but until the late 1980s few convincing successes were recorded. Those that might have attracted attention tended to be overlooked in a policy context which, in many industrial countries, including Britain and the United States, was preoccupied with the containment of public expenditure and consequently encouraged scepticism about the claims of welfare professionals. For example, the wide-ranging American research review (Lipton *et al.* 1975) which produced Martinson's dramatic claim that 'nothing works' (Martinson 1974) actually included a number of studies that showed positive results; however, the negative findings caught public and political attention. A British equivalent concluded that there was no appreciable difference in outcomes between different sentences (Brody 1976), and a rare random allocation study showed no overall significant differences in reconviction between offenders given more probation supervision on lower caseloads compared to those given less supervision on normal caseloads (Folkard *et al.* 1976). This last study effectively closed down government research on the effectiveness of probation for over a decade.

So effectively did 'nothing works' dominate official thinking that the few studies which did show positive results were largely ignored. Two examples particularly relevant to this chapter are worth mentioning. The first was a study that pointed to specific characteristics of probation hostel regimes associated with lower rates of 'failure'; i.e. the early termination of placement due to absconding or a new offence (Sinclair 1971). 'Failure' was in turn highly correlated with reconviction. The second was a study showing lower reconviction rates among released prisoners who had received thorough pre-release preparation (Shaw 1974). Shaw's study echoed the positive findings of an earlier Scandinavian study by Berntsen and Christiansen (1965), but a reason for not acting on its potentially far-reaching implications was found in another Home Office study of pre-release work with prisoners (Fowles 1978), carried out in less favourable circumstances, which did not have a positive result, but was widely and incorrectly presented as a 'replication' of Shaw's study. Both these areas of practice, now renamed 'approved premises' and 'resettlement' respectively, have recently become the subject of 'what works' initiatives, but without perceptible reference to these earlier studies.

The impact in Britain of 'nothing works' on the supervision of adult and juvenile offenders in the community has been fully discussed elsewhere (for example, Raynor and Vanstone 2002). Practice developed, with little evaluation or accumulation of knowledge, while the objectives of community penalties became recast as 'non-treatment' (Bottoms and McWilliams 1979) and as the avoidance of costly custodial punishment or residential care (Thorpe *et al.* 1980). Meanwhile, the research into effective rehabilitation taking place in other countries was largely ignored in Britain, except by a few people (notably Priestley *et al.* 1978; McGuire and Priestley 1985; Thornton 1987). To summarise what is now a familiar story (see particularly Robinson 2001), interest in effective methods of supervision began to re-emerge in Britain in the late 1980s and early 1990s through a series of 'what works' conferences (McGuire 1995), a Scottish research review (McIvor 1990), some promising evaluations of local projects (for example, Raynor 1988; Roberts 1989) and, perhaps most importantly, the results of systematic research reviews using meta-analysis to combine the results of large numbers of studies to reach overall conclusions about what kinds of projects and initiatives had produced promising results. An additional factor may have been a sense that the policy of diversion from custody had limited appeal unless it could be shown that something useful was being done with at least some of the offenders who would otherwise be in prison. The White Paper which preceded the 1991 Criminal Justice Act (Home Office 1990) appeared to assume that community sentences would have a better effect on offenders than custodial sentences, and this helped to challenge the Probation Service to take effectiveness more seriously.

The contribution of systematic research reviews

Initially the most influential of the meta-analytic reviews were those of Andrews and his colleagues in Canada (Andrews *et al.* 1990) and of Lipsey in the United States, which mainly concerned work with young offenders (Lipsey 1992). Some uses of meta-analysis have been subject to criticisms concerning, for example, the risk of subjective judgement in the coding of studies, the small results base for some conclusions, and possible bias resulting from the greater probability of positive findings being accepted for publication (for these and other problems, see Mair 1994). However, the overall conclusions seem sound, particularly considering the large number of studies with contrary findings that would be needed to overturn them. Similar conclusions have been reached by other substantial and rigorous reviews of the crime reduction literature (including Gaes *et al.* 1999; Sherman *et al.* 1998), and the extreme scepticism still shown by some commentators (for example, Mair 2004) can no longer be regarded as realistic.

In meta-analytic reviews, the impact of methods or approaches on offenders is typically expressed as an 'effect size' which indicates the difference in reconviction rates, or sometimes another measure, between those offenders who have experienced particular methods or services and those who have had some other input, or no input at all, depending on the particular study design. 'Effect sizes' can be expressed in a number of ways, including correlation coefficients, odds ratios, 'binomial effect size display' (BESD) or, in the case of outcomes such as change in test scores, the mean change divided by the standard deviation of the initial scores. However, those of most interest for our current purpose concern the reductions in reconviction which are greater than the reductions which would have been produced either by the customary methods or by doing nothing.

A recent comprehensive overview of 30 meta-analytic reviews published between 1985 and 2001 (McGuire 2002: 13) pointed out that 'the impact of "treatment" that can be defined in numerous ways is, on average, positive' but 'the mean effect taken across a broad spectrum of treatment or intervention types is relatively modest'. McGuire summarises that there is a 9 to 10 per cent reduction in reconviction rates in favour of those receiving 'treatment'. Such differences, although 'modest', have considerable policy implications if they can be achieved consistently in an area accustomed to results showing no difference. When types of intervention are restricted to those considered most likely to be useful, effect sizes tend to rise: for example, a meta-analysis of 68 studies looking at the effectiveness of cognitive-behavioural methods with offenders, published at the same time as McGuire's review and therefore not included in it, shows an average effect size approaching 13 per cent (Lipton *et al.* 2002). Using the BESD convention this is approximately equivalent to the difference between a 44 per cent reconviction rate for a 'treatment' group and a 56 per cent reconviction rate in a comparison group. Another review of effective projects in Europe reported a 21 per cent difference in re-offending, measured in various ways, between intervention groups and comparison groups (Redondo *et al*. 2002). Lipsey and Wilson (1998) reported some even larger effect sizes from effective work with young offenders.

Meta-analysis in this field has also been concerned to establish not only whether appropriate work with offenders typically has an impact on future offending but, more ambitiously, to discover what approaches and methods typically produce good results. It is important to recognise that finding an association between particular methods and positive outcomes does not in and of itself demonstrate a causal relationship. Attempts to maximise effects by putting a number of probably effective ingredients together rest at best on a plausible hypothesis which itself requires further evaluation. Nevertheless, throughout the 1990s efforts were made to draw up lists of the characteristics of effective rehabilitative efforts and to use them as a basis for planning services. For example, the Correctional Services Accreditation Panel (CSAP), which approves programmes for implementation with offenders in prisons and within the community in England and Wales, requires applicants to have at least a plausible evidence-based hypothesis and a reasonable plan to test it if they cannot point to positive results already achieved in pilot studies (see Rex *et al*. 2003).

Lists of the characteristics of successful programmes have been produced and updated by a number of commentators, particularly by Andrews and by McGuire, and the latest version points to 18 'principles of effective interventions to reduce recidivism' (McGuire 2002: 24, drawing on Andrews 2001). These can be summarised and in some cases grouped together, hopefully without too much oversimplification, in the following 11 approaches to design and delivery:

- using human service strategies based on 'personality and social learning' theories and on evidence about factors which increase the risk of offending;
- using community-based settings or, if in custody, making services as community-oriented as possible;
- using risk levels and criminogenic needs, assessed by properly validated methods, to inform targeting and allocation to services;
- using multi-modal approaches which match services to learning styles, motivation and aptitude;
- adapting services to difference and diversity, and recognising participants' strengths;

- monitoring continuity of services and care, including relapse prevention;
- giving staff clear guidance on principles and on where they can use discretion;
- monitoring and maintaining programme integrity, i.e. that services are delivered as intended;
- developing staff skills, including the capacity to maintain 'high-quality interpersonal relationships';
- ensuring good knowledgeable management;
- adapting services to local context, client groups and services.

Such lists are, of course, easier to draw up than to embody consistently in service designs. However, it is also striking to see how closely this recent list resembles similar lists drawn up nearly ten years ago (for example, McGuire 1995; Raynor 1996). The message from research has been consistent for some time: the most obvious differences in the new list are a stronger focus on the need for practitioners to use interpersonal skills and exercise some discretion, on the need to take diversity among participants into account, and on the importance of the broader service context in supporting effective intervention.

Interpreting the 'what works' research in practice

At this point it is necessary to record some cautionary notes about how this kind of research is often interpreted. First, it does not offer a guaranteed recipe for success. Lipsey (1999) points to the difference between 'demonstration' and 'practical' interventions. The former are the special pilot projects, which are often the source of the research reviewed, and the latter are the routine implementations that follow organisational decisions to adopt new methods. Better results are more commonly found among the 'demonstration' projects: in Lipsey's study the 196 'practical' programmes reviewed were on average half as effective as the 205 'demonstration' programmes. Even this level of effectiveness depended heavily on a few programmes, as 57 per cent of the 'practical' programmes had no appreciable effect. As Lipsey points out, 'rehabilitative programmes of a practical "real world" sort clearly can be effective; the challenge is to design and implement them so that they are, in fact, effective' (Lipsey 1999: 641). Other researchers have recently drawn attention to the crucial importance of implementation, described as 'the forgotten issue in effective correctional treatment' (Gendreau *et al.* 1999; see also Bernfeld *et al.* 2001). Some studies (for example, Raynor and

Vanstone 2001) have pointed to the particular context of some successful interventions, including enthusiastic practitioners, a culture of curiosity about results and a management style which openly debates principles and methods and encourages staff to own them. Not even the most optimistic senior manager would claim these are always present.

Not only programmes work

Another area of concern about interpretation of the 'what works' literature concerns the concept of a 'programme'. Many attempts to implement the lessons of research have taken the form of structured group programmes, and these are certainly well represented among the interventions that have demonstrated some effectiveness. However, this does not mean that only group programmes work, or that all effective service delivery must take the form of group programmes regardless of context and practicalities. One reason researchers have been particularly interested in these is that they lend themselves much better to systematic research than many other ways of working with offenders. It is a commonplace of human service research that it is very difficult to know what practitioners are really doing, so that even if some good outcomes can be documented, it is impossible to know what produced them. This places enormous difficulties in the way of replication and knowledge accumulation. Structured group programmes, with prescribed content and strategies such as videotaping to confirm delivery as intended, offer a solution to this problem by providing an unusual degree of clarity about what is actually being done with whom, and for how long. The attractions of this for researchers are self-evident. But programmes are not the only form of effective intervention, and even within the programme paradigm groups are not the only delivery option. McGuire defines a programme simply as a 'structured sequence of opportunities for learning and change' (McGuire 2002: 27), while the definition used by the Correctional Services Accreditation Panel for England and Wales is 'a systematic, reproducible set of activities in which offenders can participate' (CSAP 2003: 25).

Over-preoccupation with group programmes also runs the risk of sidelining or neglecting the importance of practitioner skills in the case management and supervision process. There is a substantial research literature concerned with effective practice in psychotherapy and social work, some of which would have been familiar to probation officers trained in England and Wales before the separation of probation officer training from social work training in 1997, and should still be covered in the training of probation and criminal justice staff who gain social work qualifications in other jurisdictions. Particular areas of interest here include core facilitative or therapeutic skills, widely researched in the 1960s (Truax and Carkhuff 1967), which include empathy, positive regard or concern, 'genuineness', and a concrete and specific approach to goals, expectations and processes. Similar issues continue to be identified in more recent research, and are brought together by McGuire (2003) in a recent discussion of the need for a 'working alliance' rather than a coercive or confrontational relationship. These are not woolly aspirations but concrete skills that are strongly supported by evidence and can be enhanced by training (for an example from social work education, see Raynor and Vanstone 1984). There is also a useful body of research on the enhancement of motivation to change (Miller and Rollnick 1992) by using skilled interviewing to increase awareness of a need to change and willingness to do so. Much of the evidence here comes from the field of substance abuse, but there are increasing indications of the relevance of motivational work with offenders (for example, Harper and Hardy 2000).

Other useful components for the development of a 'what works' approach to individual supervision and case management include the practice of 'pro-social modelling', applied to probation practice in Australia by Trotter (1993, 2001) and taken up more recently in a number of British projects (Rex and Matravers 1998). In Trotter's formulation the approach involves both the modelling of prosocial attitudes and behaviour by staff supervising offenders and the acknowledgment and rewarding of such behaviour on the part of offenders themselves. Early research indicated that supervision by officers trained in this approach resulted in lower reconviction rates (Trotter 1993). While official attempts to build on these findings are now beginning in Britain (for example, in the new Enhanced Community Punishment Scheme), other forms of practice which have empirical support are not discussed much, perhaps because they are seen as belonging to the social work tradition rather than the correctional field. These include, for example, 'task-centred casework' (Reid and Epstein 1972), a highly focused approach to identifying problems, reaching agreements about them, sharing responsibility for addressing them and evaluating outcomes. This approach suggests a number of interesting starting-points for thinking about case management, and has even been evaluated in a probation setting with interesting results (Goldberg *et al.* 1985). However, there has been little sign of any recent attempts to build on these.

In a recent article Dowden and Andrews (2004) report on a meta-analysis of the contribution of certain staff skills to the effectiveness of rehabilitative work with offenders. They define these skills as 'core correctional practices' or CCPs, which can be summarised briefly as effective use of authority; appropriate modelling and reinforcement; the use of a problem-solving approach; and the development of relationships characterised by openness, warmth, empathy, enthusiasm, directiveness and structure. The mean effect sizes of programmes were found to be higher when these were present, and significantly higher when other principles of programme effectiveness were also applied: staff skills and programme design complemented each other, rather than one being a substitute for the other. However, the authors point out that 'Clearly these CCPs were rarely used in the human service programs that were surveyed in this meta-analysis . . . These results suggest that the emphasis placed on developing and utilizing appropriate staff techniques has been sorely lacking within correctional treatment programmes' (Dowden and Andrews 2004: 209).

Counter-productive attrition

A third reason for care in drawing practical inferences from the 'what works' research is the problem of those who fail to attend programmes, or who start them but do not complete them. When it is possible to establish what happened to non-completers (which is difficult in some studies), it is not unusual to find that, instead of showing a lower degree of positive programme effects than the completers, they actually show negative effects, faring worse than both the completers and the comparison or control groups. Recent examples of this in British research include the STOP experiment (Raynor and Vanstone 1997) and the evaluation of prison-based cognitive-behavioural programmes (Cann *et al.* 2003). A Canadian example can be found in Robinson (1995). While there may be some selection effects at work here, for example, participants less suitable for the programme or with more problems may be less likely to complete, findings of this kind lead to particular worries about the overall impact of low completion rates. For example, a hypothetical programme which shows offending 10 per cent lower than expected among completers but 10 per cent higher than expected among non-completers will be negative in its overall effect if less than half the participants complete it. It will also be extraordinarily difficult for researchers to determine how far, if at all, any 'programme effect' is present which can be reliably distinguished from a selection effect. Some recent British research reviewed below shows that such an example is not simply fanciful, and this is confirmed by the continuing high rate of attrition reported for current programmes (National Probation Service 2004). However, other recent research suggests that such high attrition is not an inevitable feature of community-based programmes, and that much better completion rates have been achieved in jurisdictions where case management and enforcement are handled differently (see, for example, Heath *et al.* 2002; Miles and Raynor 2004).

The context and aims of early British probation programmes

Finally, there can be aspects of particular studies which research reviews do not easily capture, but which are important when trying to draw practical implications from them. For example, some of the impetus behind the shift towards evidence-based practice in Britain came from early local studies that showed modest positive effects from various forms of special programmes for young adult offenders (Raynor 1988; Roberts 1989). These studies were carried out at a time when young adult offenders were increasingly receiving custodial sentences, after which their reconviction rates were particularly high. The studies were therefore located within the policy context of alternatives to custody, and the special forms of supervision they offered were specifically targeted on young people at significant risk of receiving a custodial sentence and unlikely to be made subject to a standard probation order without special content and requirements. These programmes were therefore a success if they recruited young people who would otherwise receive custodial sentences, and if they achieved better results than the custodial sentences they replaced. One study (Raynor 1988) used similar young people receiving custodial sentences as the comparison group, and also documented local reductions in custodial sentencing during the life of the project. Comparisons with the outcomes of ordinary probation orders were not a major issue because there was plenty of evidence that the project participants would not have received ordinary probation orders. Thus development of such projects made sense as an alternative to custodial sentences, but a different set of questions would have been raised if they had been developed as alternatives to simpler forms of probation order. Also, the very high reconviction rates of young adult offenders following custodial sentences made it easier for non-custodial programmes to out-perform them. It is hazardous to use such studies to promote the advantages of structured and demanding interventions without considering what would otherwise have happened to the offenders concerned.

Some years later, the findings of the STOP experiment (Raynor and Vanstone 1997) were among those that provided support for the feasibility and value of programmes in British probation services (as they were at that time, before the establishment of a single National Probation Service for England and Wales in 2001). However, it is important to recognise that the initial planning of the STOP experiment begun in 1990, in a service still aiming at diversion from custody, and eligibility for the programme was determined in part by an offender's risk of receiving a custodial sentence as well as by a fairly rudimentary assessment of needs. When the courts did not agree with a probation officer's recommendation that a particular offender undertake the programme, the result was almost always a custodial sentence, and actuarial prediction of expected reconviction rates confirmed that programme participants were a high-risk group, comparable to those receiving custodial sentences rather than to those receiving standard probation orders. The beneficial effects of the programme on reconviction were, as usual, fairly modest, and might not have attracted much attention in the 'nothing works' era; however, what is important for current purposes is that those benefits were mainly demonstrated by comparisons with the effects of custodial sentences. The advantages over conventional probation orders were less substantial, but, as in the studies mentioned above, the target group would have been unlikely to receive such orders in any case.

The point of exploring this in some detail is to remind readers that the early evidence of successful programmes for relatively high-risk offenders subject to community sentences in England and Wales was gathered in studies which were looking primarily for appropriate ways to enhance probation orders to make them marketable and effective for those otherwise at risk of custodial sentences. They were not primarily about better ways of supervising people who would receive probation orders anyway; nor were they about substituting programmes for the ordinary processes of supervision by a probation officer. The programmes were an additional element in a probation order, not the whole probation order in themselves. These caveats are particularly important as we turn to considering what has been achieved in Britain so far under the banner of 'what works'.

Implementing 'what works' in Britain

When serious attempts to apply the lessons of the 'what works' literature began in Britain in the late 1990s, different countries and agencies took rather different routes. In Scotland, with different criminal justice legislation, there was a tradition of welfare-centred juvenile justice and a criminal justice social work service provided by local authority social work departments rather than a separate probation service. Consequently, the chosen development strategy emphasised education and incremental development in a context in which implementation was necessarily devolved and localised. For example, the Scottish Office (later, after political devolution, the Scottish Executive) funded a Development Unit and an advanced university course for senior practitioners, and aimed to influence service providers in the right direction by using its powers to set standards and fund services. In England and Wales (the policies come from England, since criminal justice powers are not yet devolved to the Welsh Assembly Government) rather different approaches emerged for young offenders, under the auspices of the Youth Justice Board, and for adult offenders, under the Probation Service. The Prison Service also played a major role, particularly in the early stages, which should not be forgotten, although it is necessarily under-reported here in a chapter concerned mainly with community sentences. The Youth Justice Board, working through Youth Offending Teams (YOTs) in each locality, encouraged experimentation and diversity by funding a wide variety of local schemes. This was probably a good way of engaging the energies and creativity of local agencies and practitioners, but it created problems for research and evaluation, some of which are discussed below.

The Probation Service, by contrast, adopted a highly centralised development strategy accompanied by a systematic programme of research. The combination of setting up a new service while simultaneously transforming its practice has been a huge challenge to staff and managers, leading to many stresses including industrial action, and the achievements of the National Probation Directorate in leading the process of change have been remarkable. The associated research exercise has been very productive, and much of the material in this section is drawn from it. This is not the place to discuss in detail why such a centralised strategy was preferred, but one factor was undoubtedly the national survey undertaken in the mid-1990s (Underdown 1998) which showed that probation services claimed to be operating 267 effective programmes, but only four could actually produce evidence of effectiveness. Another driver was the fact that many of the probation developments were funded through the Crime Reduction Programme, a central government initiative which provided significant treasury funding tied to demanding targets, a requirement to evaluate the effectiveness and even cost-effectiveness of all initiatives, and an expectation, which in retrospect proved to be highly optimistic, that results could be demonstrated within three years.

By the time crime reduction funding became available in 1999, the Probation Service and the Home Office had identified four priority areas for development and research. These were (in no particular order) offending behaviour programmes (involving the delivery of cognitive-behavioural programmes to offenders under supervision); basic skills (using supervision as an opportunity to train educationally disadvantaged offenders in basic literacy and numeracy skills which might help them get jobs); an enhanced version of Community Service (aiming to teach offenders more pro-social attitudes and behaviour as well as useful skills); and resettlement projects for short-term prisoners (often persistent offenders with a high risk of reconviction, but not subject to compulsory post-release supervision and increasingly unlikely to be offered services on a voluntary basis). Each initiative was launched in a number of probation areas and subjected to substantial independent research to evaluate its impact. This was the first concentrated and targeted official research on the effectiveness of the Probation Service's work with offenders since the 1970s, and much the largest body of research on this subject ever undertaken in Britain. All these studies have produced at least interim reports at the time of writing, though information about reconvictions is in most cases not yet available. Space does not allow a full summary here of the findings of each study, but some of the headline results are outlined below.

Some British evaluation results

The studies of offending behaviour programmes are being carried out by Leicester and Liverpool Universities, and interim findings published so far have covered only implementation issues (Hollin *et al.* 2002). However, fuller outcome data are available from a study of one 'pathfinder' cognitive-behavioural programme known as 'Think First', which began to be used in probation settings in 1997, and has been evaluated by the Oxford Probation Studies Unit. This work includes a retrospective study of offenders sentenced to the programme in 1997–8 and a prospective study of offenders sentenced in 2000–1. Although the full report has not been published at the time of writing, some results have appeared in various sources (for example, Ong *et al.* 2003; Roberts 2004). Reconviction rates for programme completers were significantly better than for non-completers, but completion rates were very low at only 28 per cent. Lower-risk offenders were more likely to complete, but their reconviction levels, already low, did not improve. The indications were that better completion rates could be achieved by better targeting, by better case management to motivate offenders, by supporting them through the programme and helping with other problems in their lives, and by better follow-up to encourage use of skills learned on the programme.

Although the retrospective study (Ong *et al.* 2003) found reconviction rates for programme members to be slightly worse than for a custodial comparison group, fully reliable comparisons with the outcomes of other sentences cannot be undertaken until a properly matched comparison group can be created using centrally held data. However, the study already has important implications for targeting. For example, the policy of recruiting as many offenders as possible onto programmes to meet treasury targets has probably tended to undermine the fit between offenders' needs and programmes and contributed to increasing attrition and non-completion, which in turn has reduced the overall impact of the programme if non-completers reconvict more. A difference in reconviction rates in favour of completers is also found in the most recent evaluation of prison-based cognitive skills programmes (Cann *et al.* 2003); in this study, completers also performed better than comparison groups. Of the two earlier evaluations of the prison-based programmes, the first also showed significant positive results (Friendship *et al.* 2002), while the second showed no significant differences, possibly reflecting difficulties in establishing a properly matched comparison group (Falshaw *et al.* 2003). In prison, of course, completion rates are much higher.

The Basic Skills pathfinder was also evaluated by the Probation Studies Unit (McMahon *et al.* 2004). Reported findings include the fact that very few of the many offenders with basic skills needs actually started on projects which were intended to help with basic skills, so that the number of 'completers' was so small that little useful outcome data could be collected. Of 1,003 offenders assessed as having basic skills needs, only 20 remained in the project long enough to be available for interview after training. This study probably needs to be repeated in a context of much better designed service provision: as it stands it tells us more about the extent of implementation problems than about the likely benefit of basic skills inputs.

The Community Punishment pathfinder, evaluated by a team led by the Cambridge Institute of Criminology (Rex and Gelsthorpe 2002; Rex *et al.* 2004), is covered in detail in Chapter 7 but also merits some discussion here, since its aim was to add a rehabilitative component to the existing reparative focus of Community Punishment. The evaluation covered a number of projects that enhanced standard community service provision through pro-social modelling and skills training. Significant gains were seen in crime-prone attitudes, self-reported problems and accredited work-related skills, though some of these were also found in the comparison areas. The reconviction study is still in progress, but few differences in outcome measures are apparent so far between the experimental and comparison areas. The Probation Service is now implementing a related initiative called Enhanced Community Punishment, which was intended to be subject to further evaluation, as required by the Correctional Services Accreditation Panel. At the time of writing, however, the planned evaluation had been cancelled on financial grounds.

The resettlement pathfinders for short-term prisoners (Lewis *et al.* 2003) were evaluated by a team from Bristol, Cardiff and Swansea Universities. This also showed a number of implementation problems: getting off to a slow start and failing to meet target numbers. A second-phase study covering a smaller number of projects is in progress, which aims to apply the lessons of the first evaluation, and a reconviction study is also under way. However, the published study points to some successes: the take-up of post-release assistance was substantially increased by these projects, and participants showed significant positive change in crime-prone attitudes and self-reported problems. What appeared to work best was a combination of facilitating access to resources relevant to prisoners' needs and taking some steps to address their thinking and motivation, particularly through a short cognitive-motivational group programme undertaken before release.

In spite of differences in focus and findings, some themes emerge consistently from these studies. One is implementation: in all cases the experimental projects did not proceed exactly as planned, with subsequent knock-on effects to the research designs. The typical result is not confirmation of 'what works', but rather a better-informed second-phase pilot with a further evaluation. Designs are quasi-experimental with no random allocation, and there are problems in identifying appropriately matched comparison groups, partly due to the fact that, although a nationally standardised system for risk and need assessment is being implemented (OASys Development Team 2001), it was not in place to support the earlier development of 'what works'. Consequently the matching of 'treatment' and comparison groups has tended to be on the basis of criminal history only, and is vulnerable to selection effects arising from differences in need. There are also doubts about whether the quality of reconviction information available from central databases will be good enough to show the fairly modest differences in reconviction rates which might be optimistically expected from these projects (Merrington and Stanley 2000). Nevertheless, the accumulation of a large body of competent research on the current operation and effectiveness of these initiatives is a major step forward in probation research, on which much future work can be built.

The wide range of innovations sponsored by the Youth Justice Board has proved even more difficult to evaluate, largely because many of them looked for local research strategies to be in place before setting up teams of 'national evaluators'. The national evaluators then found little consistency in the scale, methodology, competence, interest in collaboration and, in some cases, even existence of the local evaluation arrangements. These limitations have made it difficult for them to undertake their national task of coordination and collation of findings (Wilcox 2003). Some positive findings have been published, for example in relation to the outcomes of such new practices as final warnings (Hine and Celnick 2001), though without clear evidence that the 'interventions', which accompanied some final warnings, improved their effectiveness. There are also some encouraging studies looking at the implementation of new orders (Holdaway *et al.* 2001; Ghate and Ramella 2002; Newburn *et al.* 2002), but so far there is limited information available concerning the effectiveness of rehabilitative and reintegrative disposals promoted by the Youth Justice Board.

It has proved difficult, for reasons similar to those described by Wilcox (2003), to draw general conclusions from research carried out on rehabilitative efforts such as cognitive-behavioural programmes (Feilzer *et al.* 2004) and substance abuse programmes (Hammersley *et al.* 2004). High attrition and the difficulty of finding appropriate comparison groups have also created problems in assessing the effectiveness of projects, but the reports contain many lessons about implementation. The evaluation of the Intensive Supervision and Surveillance Programme is not published at the time of writing, but few specialists in the field expect it to report a straightforward success. One interesting example of reintegration is the Youth Inclusion Programme, which particularly targets 'at risk' 13- to 16-year-old people in deprived areas (Morgan Harris Burrows 2003). The project aims to involve young people in a range of constructive activities as an early intervention strategy. There are indications of substantial reductions in arrest rates among those involved, but reductions also occur in a comparison group and it is difficult to disentangle selection and maturation effects from programme effects.

Nevertheless, this inclusive approach to work with young people appears promising, not least because it takes a developmental approach and a positive view of their potential. These characteristics are shared with a particularly interesting project in Scotland, the Freagarrach Project (Lobley *et al.* 2001), which works intensively with young people who already have substantial histories of offending, and uses a mixture of activities, programme-like groupwork and mobilisation of assistance from other agencies. The research clearly shows the importance of skilled case management, commitment to the young people and their futures, maintenance of strong and effective working relationships with other agencies, effective engagement of young people in the project and persistence through periods of difficulty – an example of the inclusive approach to young people in trouble which also informs other aspects of the Scottish criminal justice system. The available information on reconvictions looks promising but inconclusive, again because of difficulties in establishing an appropriate comparison group. Some other studies from Scotland also show promising results (for example, the Airborne Initiative, which combined adventurous activity with a short offending behaviour programme; McIvor *et al.* 2000). Overall, however, it is difficult to avoid the conclusion of Merrington and Stanley (2004) that, as far as most of the recent rehabilitative and reintegrative approaches in Britain are concerned, 'it is too early to say what works, what doesn't and what is promising' (Merrington and Stanley 2004: 17–18). In effect, we continue to rely heavily on the international research; however, we can certainly claim to have learned a great deal about difficulties of implementation, which could help to reduce these as the work proceeds.

The 'responsibility model' of rehabilitation

One further area in which suggestive evidence has not so far received much official attention concerns the development of what are increasingly described (for example, by Maruna and LeBel 2003) as 'strengths-based' approaches to rehabilitation and reintegration. Such approaches see offenders not simply as objects of 'treatment' or 'intervention', characterised by needs and deficits and presenting risks, but as active participants in their own rehabilitation, with strengths, skills and potential as contributors to their communities. This has something in common with the meaning of 'rehabilitation' that implies restoration of moral status as a full citizen and a contributing member of society. There is also an evident overlap with the concept of reintegration and with the ideas for constructive handling of crime advanced particularly in America under the label of 'community justice' (Clear and Karp 1999). Space precludes a full discussion of these ideas here, and in some ways they are more familiar as part of the rationale of restorative justice; however, there is a strong case for taking them seriously in discussions of rehabilitation.

For example, the resettlement pathfinder study (Lewis *et al.* 2003) strongly suggested that resettlement services produced better results when substantial attention was paid to issues of thinking and motivation instead of simply to resources necessary to meet welfare needs (Raynor, 2004). Treating offenders as needy and beset by problems perhaps corresponds too closely with some of their own rationales and justifications for offending (Sykes and Matza 1957), while treating them as able to take charge of their lives and overcome obstacles could promote a sense of responsibility and self-efficacy. This could be helpful in preventing recidivism (Zamble and Quinsey 1997) or promoting desistance (Maruna 2004). Other approaches to rehabilitation have explicitly treated ex-offenders as experts, and as people able to put their experience to use in helping others. The New Careers movements of the 1970s and 1980s aimed to retrain former offenders for social work roles, often with other offenders (Seddon 1979). Likewise the involvement of recovered substance misusers in helping others to follow the same path has been a central feature of self-help movements such as Alcoholics Anonymous, where it is seen as part of recovery and of remaining sober. A more recent example is the Lifelines project in Canada, in which the resettlement of released lifers in the community after long periods of imprisonment is assisted by successfully resettled former lifers who act as mentors, supporters and advocates (www.csc-scc.gc.ca/text/prgm/lifeline). This is reminiscent of Braithwaite's (2001) argument that people expect to see offenders taking 'active responsibility' in making positive contributions to the community. Similarly, Hans Toch has recently argued that involvement in altruistic activity itself promotes cognitive change and pro-social learning (Toch 2000), and it has also been suggested that opportunities to contribute to the community should be a normal component of rehabilitative community sentences (Raynor 2001).

The evaluative research literature to support these ideas is not fully developed, and much of what there is concerns restorative justice rather than rehabilitation. These concepts may, however, be more closely related than is generally realised. Researchers are often concerned about how to 'sell' rehabilitation to politicians and the public, and to some extent this reflects concerns about its perceived legitimacy: it is not easy to sell the idea of offenders receiving benefits and services which are denied to similarly needy people who have not offended. This, however, is an image of rehabilitation that flows from the 'deficit model' which sees offenders as characterised primarily by deficiencies to be corrected and needs to be met by others. If instead rehabilitation is seen as work undertaken by offenders to re-fit themselves for participation in the community, then it is a contribution to community well-being; one function of rehabilitative services is to offer opportunities to do this kind of work. Social contract theory suggests that if offenders have had limited opportunities to lead crime-free lives or to learn how this is done, action by the state to improve these opportunities puts them on a more equal basis with other citizens rather than a privileged basis, provided that they are prepared to reciprocate through a serious attempt at self-rehabilitation (see, for example, Hudson 2003, Chapter 4, concerning 'state-obligated rehabilitation'). In this model, rehabilitation is not so much about preventing re-offending as about promoting desistance from offending, and it is something done primarily by the offender rather than to the offender. A programme of research and development along these lines could have much to offer.

The actual and potential contribution of community-based supervision

The many reservations reviewed in the previous section point strongly to the conclusion that evidence-based approaches to rehabilitation and reintegration in Britain have shown some promising signs, but have not yet lived up to the high expectations generated by the international research literature. Although launched and pursued with great ambition and energy, particularly by the new National Probation Service, the evidence-based approaches covered by the shorthand term 'what works' have suffered from problems of uneven implementation and of research which has been, usually for good reasons, less conclusive than policy-makers would have hoped. In addition, the evidence-based approach has been narrowly applied, with a strong emphasis on programmes but less interest in some of the contextual issues which have a direct effect on programme implementation, such as case management, enforcement and the overall sentencing pattern. Some of these limiting contextual factors, such as the non-evidence-based approach to enforcement, may reflect a perception by the Probation Service's leaders that they are not in a strong enough political position to raise these issues; however, this in itself would suggest that the 'what works' initiative has not completely succeeded in one of its early goals, namely to restore political credibility to probation. Overall, in spite of the wide-ranging changes it has brought to both probation and youth justice, the demonstrated impact of evidence-based practice on re-offending in Britain has so far been limited. Attempts to demonstrate general reductions in re-offending following contact with correctional services (Prime 2002) have not sufficiently distinguished between consequences of intervention and consequences of the general fall in reported crime.

The mixed results of the 'what works' experiment also represent a political hazard. The original proponents of 'nothing works' in the 1970s gained currency and attention for their ideas partly because they resonated with the agenda of right-wing politicians opposed to state spending on 'welfare'. The findings were used to support a neo-liberal strategy of economic individualism and 'responsibilisation' (Rose 2000), making citizens responsible for their own welfare in a free market, and relying on deterrence and punishment to maintain social discipline. These ideas still enthuse many on the political right, and there is a risk that a new set of 'nothing works' conclusions will be drawn from the recent British research. Already the right-wing think tank CIVITAS (formerly the 'Health and Welfare Unit' of the Institute of Economic Affairs) has published a somewhat tendentious and selective review of research on the rehabilitation of offenders (Green *et al.* 2004) which presents the rehabilitative agenda as a 'progressive' delusion: in their view, only punishment reinforces the moral accountability of the offender and only increases in imprisonment reduce crime.

There is insufficient space here for a full exploration of these arguments, except to note that they depend fundamentally on a false polarisation between belief in social influences on human action (attributed to 'progressives') and belief in individual freedom and responsibility (attributed to 'realists'). 'Progressives' are supposedly led into overoptimism about rehabilitation and over-indulgence towards offenders by their belief that people are the puppets of social forces, and therefore not culpable; 'realists' supposedly believe that only punishment recognises the person as a free moral agent, capable of choosing to behave wrongly. However, all genuinely realistic accounts of human action move beyond this simple dichotomy to recognise both: choice can be exercised only within social structures which form both the constraints on action and the means of action, and do so in different ways for individuals who are differently placed within them. Thus it makes perfectly good sense both to promote a sense of responsibility for offending and to help offenders to cope with obstacles that might otherwise make them more likely to offend again. Such assumptions lie behind many of the rehabilitative approaches reviewed in this chapter.

To move from these more abstract arguments back to our primary concern with practical consequences, it is clear that the implications of the 'prison works' position are alarming. By way of illustration, CIVITAS has energetically promoted and publicised in Britain the work of the American right-wing social theorist Charles Murray, inventor of the politically convenient theory of the 'underclass' which supposedly perpetuates its own poverty and on which welfare spending is therefore pointless (Murray 1990). From this logically follow Murray's views about penal policy where he has recommended that Britain should aim to have 650,000 people in prison (Murray 2000). Fortunately such extreme notions find few adherents; but many practitioners and managers in the correctional field clearly have a sense that they are engaged in a not particularly successful rearguard action against inevitably rising prison numbers.

This would, however, be an unjustifiably gloomy conclusion to this chapter. Viewed in the context of impending changes in criminal justice, new windows of opportunity will open. Specifically, in England and Wales the new Criminal Justice Act creates both a new single community sentence and new hybrid sentences which combine a real or notional short custodial sentence with a longer period of supervision in the community ('custody-plus' and 'custody-minus'). Both of these offer opportunities to rethink the role of programmes in the overall pattern of supervision, to develop new approaches to case management and to press for a less draconian and more graduated form of enforcement, helping people to complete their programmes rather than preventing them from doing so. Any effective approach to supervision of the offenders who currently receive short prison sentences will require attention to their resources and opportunities in the community as well as to thinking and motivation (Lewis *et al.* 2003; Raynor 2004). Provided that sentencing courts do not overload the new orders with excessive requirements and conditions, the scope for the Probation Service to achieve a better match between services and needs should increase.

Other important changes are likely to follow from the recent Correctional Services Review, which recommends combining the Prison and Probation Services in a new National Offender Management Service (Carter 2003). This presents, at least in theory, an opportunity to manage the 'correctional careers' of persistent offenders in a more planned way, with better use of assessment and intervention and with more control over such important issues as the proportion of an offender's sentence to be spent in custody or in the community. The importance of this last point is emphasised by the projections of prison numbers contained in the Halliday Report, which preceded the 2003 Criminal Justice Act. The principles of Halliday's proposed sentencing framework, in which sentences were to be determined less by strict proportionality ('just deserts') and more by assessments of risk, are beyond the scope of this chapter. However, it is clear that they involve a degree of indeterminacy such that the impact of his proposals on prison numbers was calculated to be anything between a small reduction and an increase of about 6,000 (Halliday 2001). This very indeterminacy points to the need for a strategic approach, overseen by the new offender management service, to ensure that the lower projection applies. Much the same considerations are likely, in due course, to apply in Scotland, where similar problems need to be addressed and where some form of unified correctional system is currently under discussion.

Conclusion: widening the scope of the evidence-based approach

Several aspects of this new context point strongly to the need for a broader approach to evidence-based rehabilitation and reintegration. It needs to be broader in two senses. First, it needs to be concerned with the impact of the whole of an offender's supervision or correctional involvement, not just with 'programmes' as currently understood. There is plenty of evidence, some of which is reviewed above, that proper assessment, preparation, motivation, case-management and reinforcement of learning are essential to support programme effects. Development and evaluation should focus increasingly on this broader concept of human services in rehabilitation, rather than primarily on programmes. Second, the focus needs to expand to consider the operation of the wider criminal justice system within which rehabilitative efforts are located: the impact of the system on the offender, and the capacity of those working with the offender to influence decisions taken about him or her in the system. There is an obvious connection to be made between the attempt to keep an individual offender out of prison and the collective goal of reducing reliance on custodial punishment.

Reference has already been made to the early British studies of effective probation and to their origins in the era of alternatives to custody. It is now clear that there has been a downward drift in the seriousness of the probation order caseload since, for political reasons, reduction in custodial sentencing ceased to be an avowable aim in 1993 (Morgan 2002, 2003). Since then there has been a very substantial investment in documenting and evaluating the effects of programmes on offenders, but an almost complete neglect, at least in the adult jurisdiction, of the impact of new developments on sentencing decisions. Until the collapse and reversal of the core elements of the 1991 Criminal Justice Act, it was not unusual for commentators to describe the Probation Service as capable of having a dual impact, both on the behaviour of individual offenders and on the patterns of decision-making in the criminal justice system, including particularly the level of custodial sentencing (Bottoms and McWilliams 1979; Raynor *et al.* 1994). The main instrument available to influence sentencing patterns was the social inquiry report (now known as the pre-sentence report), which was, at its best, demonstrably effective in this role (Gelsthorpe and Raynor 1995). The absence of any discussion of pre-sentence reports in the Carter Report (Carter 2003) and the lack of attention to system impacts in general in recent British 'what works' research are both regrettable; to continue to ignore these issues in the new policy context would be disastrous.

Among the key practice issues to address in the new context will be:

- Consistent assessment of risks and needs (generally recognised as a necessary underpinning for a range of effective practices [Bonta 1996], but regrettably not yet in general use in Britain [Raynor 2003]).
- Appropriate targeting of the right offenders, including strategies to influence sentencers.
- Programme provision to reflect evidence of needs and likely benefit, rather than pressure to recruit offenders into programmes to meet treasury targets. This could well result in fewer people doing programmes (Clark *et al.* 2002).

- Building positive motivation rather than relying on deterrence.
- Maintaining engagement in change efforts.
- Assisting access to relevant resources and services (e.g. advocacy).
- Maintaining and reinforcing learning.
- Facilitating continued pro-social support.

All of these could be encompassed under the heading of effective correctional case management, and they point to a need for systematic research in this area with a focus both on outcomes, for offenders and for the system, and on a qualitative and appreciative approach to understanding how offenders experience it, how they use it and what they believe they learn. A qualitative study of prison programmes is now planned (see Cann *et al.* 2003). Similar issues arise in relation to staff and sentencers.

Other potential developments are less firmly based in what we already know, but offer the possibility of considerable gains. Such 'promising' areas include greater positive involvement by sentencers in the encouragement and maintenance of change, as pioneered in 'drugs courts' and Drug Treatment and Testing Orders (Turnbull *et al.* 2000). This approach is now being extended in America to 're-entry courts' to oversee the resettlement of high-risk prisoners (Maruna and LeBel 2002, 2003) and is consistent with a developing literature on 'therapeutic jurisprudence' (McGuire 2003) which envisages the court itself as an agent of rehabilitation. Other areas, which have already been mentioned, include mentoring by pro-social volunteers including former offenders, and emphasising the positive contribution of ex-offenders to communities through visible reparation, 'new careers' and other 'strengths-based' approaches which allow offenders to make a valued contribution to communities and allow communities to see offenders making a contribution. Some of these ideas have been explored more fully in the previous chapter on 'Reparative and restorative approaches', but they may also have their place as part of an approach to rehabilitation which could attract significant public support; all the more so if legitimate community representatives could be involved in the choice of reparative work for offenders to undertake (Raynor 2001).

In pursuing such initiatives, a middle way must be found between the centrally directed rapid roll-out of new initiatives which has so far been the preferred approach of the National Probation Service for England and Wales, and the more devolved and piecemeal approach favoured in Scotland and by the Youth Justice Board in England and Wales. This latter approach seems more empowering for practitioners, but places even more obstacles in the path of consistency, quality control and evaluation. If we expect innovations to be firmly grounded in developing knowledge, proper piloting is indispensable, and the rush to 'go to scale' after hasty and incomplete evaluation must be slowed (Merrington and Stanley 2000).

Future pilots should also be designed to be researchable, rather than developed and financed as projects with the evaluation design developed afterwards. Much effort and ingenuity has gone into the design and execution of quasi-experimental evaluation designs simply because no appropriate control group was incorporated from the start, and as we have seen, the results are often open to criticism on the grounds of inadequate matching. Random allocation designs have been little used in British correctional research since the mid-1970s, but the time seems ripe to see what they can offer in a new era of correctional innovation. One promising sign is the use of a random allocation design in a current national evaluation of restorative justice (Shapland *et al.* 2002).

Such a research and development strategy, combined with what has already been learned about 'what works', could help to find and consolidate the appropriate place of community sentences in the range of sentencing options. The aim would be to develop, not only effective rehabilitative penalties, but also an effective strategy for their deployment within the criminal justice system. What such an effective strategy would be is a major issue for the Coulsfield Commission and indeed for all who care about criminal justice.

References

Andrews, D. A. (2001) 'Principles of effective correctional programming', in L. Motiuk and R. Serin (eds) *Compendium 2000 on Effective Correctional Programming* (Ottawa: Correctional Service of Canada), pp. 9–17.

Andrews, D. A., Zinger, I., Hoge, R. D., Bonta, J., Gendreau, P. and Cullen, F. T. (1990) 'Does correctional treatment work? A clinically relevant and psychologically informed meta-analysis', *Criminology* 28, 369–404.

Bernfeld, G., Farrington, D. and Leschied, A. (eds) (2001) *Offender Rehabilitation in Practice* (Chichester: Wiley).

Berntsen, K. and Christiansen, K. (1965) 'A resocialization experiment with short-term offenders', *Scandinavian Studies in Criminology* 1, 35–54.

Bonta, J. (1996) 'Risk-needs assessment and treatment', in A. Harland (ed.) *Choosing Correctional Options that Work* (London: Sage).

Bottoms, A. E. and McWilliams, W. (1979) 'A non-treatment paradigm for probation practice', *British Journal of Social Work*, 9, 159–202.

Braithwaite, J. (1989) *Crime, Shame and Reintegration* (Cambridge: Cambridge University Press).

Braithwaite, J. (2001) 'Intention versus reactive fault', in N. Naffine, R. Owens and J. Williams (eds) *Intention in Law and Philosophy* (Aldershot: Ashgate) pp. 318–357.

Brody, S.R. (1976) *The Effectiveness of Sentencing*, Home Office Research Study 35 (London: HMSO).

Cann, J., Falshaw, L., Nugent, F. and Friendship, C. (2003) *Understanding What Works: Accredited cognitive skills programmes for adult men and young offenders*, Home Office Research Findings 226 (London: Home Office).

Carter, P. (2003) *Managing Offenders, Reducing Crime* (London: Strategy Unit).
Clark, D., Garnham, N. and Howard, P. (2002) *An Evaluation and Validation of the Offender Assessment System (OASys)*, Draft Report to the Home Office (unpublished).
Clear, T. and Karp, D. (1999) *The Community Justice Ideal: Preventing crime and achieving justice* (Boulder, CO: Westview Press).
Correctional Services Accreditation Panel (2003) *Report 2002–2003* (London: CSAP).
Dowden, C. and Andrews, D. (2004) 'The importance of staff practice in delivering effective correctional treatment: a meta-analysis', *International Journal of Offender Therapy and Comparative Criminology*, 48, 203–214.
Falshaw, L., Friendship, C., Travers, R. and Nugent, F. (2003) *Searching for 'What Works': An evaluation of cognitive skills programmes*, Home Office Research Findings 206 (London: Home Office).
Feilzer, M., Appleton, C., Roberts, C. and Hoyle, C. (2004) *Cognitive Behaviour Projects: The national evaluation of the Youth Justice Board's cognitive behaviour projects* (London: Youth Justice Board).
Folkard, M. S., Smith, D. E. and Smith, D. D. (1976) *IMPACT Volume II: The results of the experiment*, Home Office Research Study 36 (London: HMSO).
Fowles, A. J. (1978) *Prison Welfare: An account of an experiment at Liverpool*, Home Office Research Study 45 (London: HMSO).
Friendship, C., Blud, L., Erikson, M. and Travers, R. (2002) *An Evaluation of Cognitive Behavioural Treatment for Prisoners*, Home Office Research Findings 161 (London: Home Office).
Gaes, G., Flanagan, T., Motiuk, L. and Stewart, L. (1999) 'Adult correctional treatment', in M. Tonry and J. Petersilia (eds) *Crime and Justice: A review of research* (Chicago, IL: University of Chicago Press), pp. 361–426.
Garland, D. (1985) *Punishment and Welfare: A history of penal strategies* (Aldershot: Gower).
Gelsthorpe, L. and Raynor, P. (1995) 'Quality and effectiveness in probation officers' reports to sentencers', *British Journal of Criminology*, 35, 188–200.
Gendreau, P., Goggin, C. and Smith, P. (1999) 'The forgotten issue in effective correctional treatment: program implementation', *International Journal of Offender Therapy and Comparative Criminology*, 43, 180–187.
Ghate, D. and Ramella, M. (2002) *Positive Parenting: The national evaluation of the Youth Justice Board's parenting programme* (London: Youth Justice Board).
Goldberg, E. M., Gibbons, J. and Sinclair, I. (1985) *Problems, Tasks and Outcomes* (London: Allen and Unwin).
Green, D. G., Grove, E. and Martin, N.A. (2004) *How Can the Criminal Justice System Reduce the Criminal Activities of Known Offenders?* Civitas Final Report for the Rethinking Crime and Punishment Project [www.civitas.org.uk/pdf/CivitasRCP_Report.pdf].
Haines, K. (1990) *After-Care Services for Released Prisoners* (Cambridge: Institute of Criminology).
Halliday, J. (2001) *Making Punishments Work: Report of a review of the sentencing framework for England and Wales* (London: Home Office).
Hammersley, R., Reid, M., Oliver, A., Genova, A., Raynor, P., Minkes, J. and Morgan, M. (2004) *Drug and Alcohol Projects: The national evaluation of the Youth Justice Board's drug and alcohol projects* (London: Youth Justice Board).

Harper, R. and Hardy, S. (2000) 'An evaluation of motivational interviewing as a method of intervention with clients in a probation setting', *British Journal of Social Work* 30, 393–400.

Heath, B., Raynor, P. and Miles, H. (2002) 'What Works in Jersey: the first ten years', *VISTA*, 7, 202–208.

Hine, J. and Celnick, A. (2001) *A One-year Reconviction Study of Final Warnings* (Sheffield: University of Sheffield).

Hirschi, T. (1969) *Causes of Delinquency* (Berkeley, CA: California University Press).

Holdaway, S., Davidson, N., Dignan, J., Hammersley, R., Hine, J. and Marsh, P. (2001) *New Strategies to Address Youth Offending: The national evaluation of the pilot youth offending teams*, RDS Occasional Paper 69 (London: Home Office).

Hollin, C., McGuire, J., Palmer, E., Bilby, C., Hatcher, R. and Holmes, A. (2002) *Introducing Pathfinder Programmes into the Probation Service: An interim report*, Home Office Research Study 247 (London: Home Office).

Home Office (1990) *Crime, Justice and Protecting the Public*, Cm. 965 (London: HMSO).

Home Office (1998) *Joining Forces to Protect the Public: Prisons-Probation* (London: Home Office).

Hudson, B. (2003) *Understanding Justice*, 2nd edition (Buckingham: Open University Press).

Lewis, S., Vennard, J., Maguire, M., Raynor, P., Vanstone, M., Raybould, S. and Rix, A. (2003) *The Resettlement of Short-term Prisoners: An evaluation of seven pathfinders*, RDS Occasional Paper 83 (London: Home Office).

Lipsey, M. (1992) 'Juvenile delinquency treatment: a meta-analytic enquiry into the variability of effects', in T. Cook, H. Cooper, D. S. Cordray, H. Hartmann, L. V. Hedges, R. L. Light, T. A. Louis and F. Mosteller (eds) *Meta-Analysis for Explanation: A case-book* (New York: Russell Sage), pp. 83-127.

Lipsey, M. (1999) 'Can rehabilitative programs reduce the recidivism of juvenile offenders? An inquiry into the effectiveness of practical programs', *Virginia Journal of Social Policy and the Law*, 6, 611-641.

Lipsey, M. and Wilson, D. (1998) 'Effective intervention for serious juvenile offenders', in R. Loeber and D. Farrington (eds) *Serious and Violent Juvenile Offenders: Risk factors and successful interventions* (Thousand Oaks, CA: Sage), pp. 83-127.

Lipton, D., Martinson, R. and Wilks, J. (1975) *The Effectiveness of Correctional Treatment* (New York: Praeger).

Lipton, D., Pearson, F., Cleland, C. amd Yee, D. (2002) 'The effectiveness of cognitive-behavioural treatment methods on offender recidivism', in J. McGuire (ed.) *Offender Rehabilitation and Treatment* (Chichester: Wiley), pp. 79-112.

Lobley, D., Smith, D. and Stern, C. (2001) *Freagarrach: An evaluation of a project for persistent juvenile offenders* (Edinburgh: Scottish Executive Central Research Unit).

Mair, G. (1994) 'Standing at the crossroads: what works in community penalties?', Paper presented to the National Conference for Probation Committee Members, Scarborough.

Mair, G. (ed.) (2004) *What Matters in Probation* (Cullompton: Willan).

Martinson, J. (1974) 'What works? Questions and answers about prison reform', *The Public Interest*, 35, 22-54.

Maruna, S. (2001) *Making Good: How convicts reform and rebuild their lives* (Washington, DC: American Psychological Association).

Maruna, S. (2004) 'Desistance and explanatory style: a new direction in the psychology of reform', *Journal of Contemporary Criminal Justice*, 20, 184-200.

Maruna, S. and LeBel, T. (2002) 'Revisiting ex-prisoner re-entry: a buzz-word in search of a narrative', in S. Rex and M. Tonry (eds) *Reform and Punishment: The future of sentencing* (Cullompton: Willan), pp. 158-180.

Maruna, S. and LeBel, T. (2003) 'Welcome home? Examining the "re-entry court" concept from a strengths-based perspective', *Western Criminology Review*, 4, 91-107.

McGuire, J. (ed.) (1995) *What Works: Reducing Reoffending* (Chichester: Wiley).

McGuire, J. (2002) 'Integrating findings from research reviews', in J. McGuire (ed.) *Offender Rehabilitation and Treatment* (Chichester: Wiley), pp. 3-38.

McGuire, J. (2003) 'Maintaining change: converging legal and psychological initiatives in a therapeutic jurisprudence framework', *Western Criminology Review*, 4, 108-123.

McGuire, J. and Priestley, P. (1985) *Offending Behaviour: Skills and strategems for going straight* (London: Batsford).

McIvor, G. (1990) *Sanctions for Serious or Persistent Offenders* (Stirling: Social Work Research Centre).

McIvor, G., Jamieson, J., Gayle, V., Moodie, K. and Netten, A. (2000) *Evaluation of the Airborne Initiative (Scotland)* (Edinburgh: Scottish Executive Central Research Unit).

McMahon, G., Hall, A., Hayward, G., Hudson, C. and Roberts, C. (2004) *Basic Skills Programmes in the Probation Service: An evaluation of the Basic Skills Pathfinder*, Home Office Research Findings 203 (London: Home Office).

McWilliams, W. and Pease, K. (1990) 'Probation practice and an end to punishment', *Howard Journal*, 29, 14-24.

Merrington, S. and Stanley, S. (2000) 'Doubts about the what works initiative', *Probation Journal*, 47, 272-275.

Merrington, S. and Stanley, S. (2004) 'What Works? Revisiting the evidence in England and Wales', *Probation Journal*, 51, 7-20.

Miles, H. and Raynor, P. (2004) *Community Sentences in Jersey: Risks, needs and rehabilitation* (St. Helier: Jersey Probation and After-Care Service).

Miller, W. R. and Rollnick, S. (eds) (1992) *Motivational Interviewing: Preparing people to change addictive behavior* (New York: Guilford Press).

Morgan Harris Burrows Consultants (2003) *Evaluation of the Youth Inclusion Programme: End of phase one report* (London: Youth Justice Board).

Morgan, R. (2002) 'Something has got to give', *The Howard League Magazine* 20(4), 7-8.

Morgan, R. (2003) 'Foreword', *Her Majesty's Inspectorate of Probation Annual Report 2002/2003* (London: Home Office).

Murray, C. (1990) *The Emerging British Underclass* (London: IEA Health and Welfare Unit).

Murray, C. (2000) 'Baby beware', *Sunday Times News Review*, 13 February: 1-2.

National Probation Service (2004) *Accredited Programmes Performance Report 2002-3* (London: National Probation Service).

Newburn, T., Crawford, A., Earle, R., Goldie, S., Hale, C., Netten, A., Saunders, R., Hallam, A., Sharpe, K. and Uglow, S. (2002) *The Introduction of Referral Orders into the Youth Justice System*, Research Study 242 (London: Home Office).

OASys Development Team (2001) *Offender Assessment System User Manual* (London, Home Office).

Ong, G., Harsent, L. and Coles, S. (2003) 'Think First Evaluation', Unpublished conference workshop report (London: National Probation Service).

Petersilia, J. (2003) *When Prisoners Come Home: Parole and prisoner reentry* (Oxford: Oxford University Press).

Priestley, P., McGuire, J., Flegg, D., Hemsley, V. and Welham, D. (1978) *Social Skills and Personal Problem Solving: A handbook of methods* (London: Tavistock).

Prime, J. (2002) *Progress Made Against Home Office Public Service Agreement Target 10*, Online Report 16/02 (London: Home Office) [www.homeoffice.gov.uk/rds/onlinepubs1].

Raynor, P. (1988) *Probation as an Alternative to Custody* (Aldershot: Avebury).

Raynor, P. (1996) 'Evaluating probation: the rehabilitation of effectiveness', in T. May and A. Vass (eds) *Working with Offenders* (London: Sage), pp. 242-258.

Raynor, P. (2001) 'Community penalties and social integration: "community" as solution and as problem', in A. Bottoms, L. Gelsthorpe and S. Rex (eds) *Community Penalties: Change and challenges* (Cullompton: Willan), pp. 183-199.

Raynor, P. (2003) 'Evidence-based probation and its critics', *Probation Journal*, 50, 334-45.

Raynor, P. (2004) 'Opportunity, motivation and change: some findings from research on resettlement', in R. Burnett and C. Roberts (eds) *What Works in Probation and Youth Justice* (Cullompton: Willan), pp. 217-233.

Raynor, P. and Vanstone, M. (1984) 'Putting practice into theory – an in-college skills training programme', *Issues in Social Work Education*, 4, 85-93.

Raynor, P. and Vanstone, M. (1997) *Straight Thinking on Probation (STOP): The Mid Glamorgan experiment*, Probation Studies Unit Report No. 4 (Oxford: University of Oxford Centre for Criminological Research).

Raynor, P. and Vanstone, M. (2001) 'Straight thinking on probation: evidence-based practice and the culture of curiosity', in G. Bernfeld, D. Farrington and A. Leschied (eds) *Offender Rehabilitation in Practice* (Chichester: Wiley), pp. 189-204.

Raynor, P. and Vanstone, M. (2002) *Understanding Community Penalties* (Buckingham: Open University Press).

Raynor, P., Smith, D. and Vanstone, M. (1994) *Effective Probation Practice* (Basingstoke: Macmillan).

Redondo, S., Sanchez-Meca J. and Garrido, V. (2002) 'Crime treatment in Europe: a review of outcome studies', in J. McGuire (ed.) *Offender Rehabilitation and Treatment* (Chichester: Wiley), pp. 131-142.

Reid, W. J. and Epstein, L. (1972) *Task Centred Casework* (New York: Columbia University Press).

Rex, S. and Gelsthorpe, L. (2002) 'The role of community service in reducing offending: evaluating pathfinder projects in the UK', *Howard Journal*, 41, 311-325.

Rex, S., Gelsthorpe, L., Roberts, C. and Jordan, P. (2004) *What's Promising in Community Service: Implementation of seven pathfinder projects*, Home Office Research Findings 231 (London: Home Office).

Rex, S. and Matravers, A. (eds) (1998) *Pro-Social Modelling and Legitimacy* (Cambridge: Institute of Criminology).

Rex, S., Lieb, R., Bottoms, A. and Wilson, L. (2003) *Accrediting Offender Programmes: A process-based evaluation of the Joint Prison/Probation Services Accreditation Panel*, Home Office Research Study 273 (London: Home Office).

Roberts, C. (1989) *Hereford and Worcester Probation Service Young Offender Project: First evaluation report* (Oxford: Department of Social and Administrative Studies).

Roberts, C. (2004) 'An early evaluation of a cognitive offending behaviour programme ("Think First") in probation areas', *VISTA*, 8, 137-145.

Robinson, D. (1995) *The Impact of Cognitive Skills Training on Post-release Recidivism among Canadian Federal Offenders*, No. R-41 Research Branch (Ottawa: Correctional Service Canada).

Robinson, G. (2001) 'Power, knowledge and what works in probation', *Howard Journal*, 40, 235-254.

Rose, N. (2000) 'Government and control', *British Journal of Criminology*, 40, 321-339.

Seddon, M. (1979) 'Clients as social workers', in D. Brandon and B. Jordan (eds) *Creative Social Work* (Oxford: Blackwell).

Shapland, J., Atkinson, A., Colledge, E., Dignan, J., Howes, M., Johnstone, J., Pennant, R., Robinson, G. and Sorsby, A. (2002) 'Evaluating the fit: restorative justice and criminal justice', Paper presented to the British Criminology Conference, July, Keele University.

Shaw, M. (1974) *Social Work in Prisons*, Home Office Research Study 22 (London: HMSO).

Sherman, L., Gottfredson, D., MacKenzie, D., Eck, J., Reuter, P. and Bushway, S. (1998) *Preventing Crime: What works, what doesn't, what's promising* (Washington, DC: National Institute of Justice).

Sinclair, I. (1971) *Hostels for Probationers*, Home Office Research Study 6 (London: HMSO).

Social Exclusion Unit (2002) *Reducing Re-offending by Ex-Prisoners* (London: Office of the Deputy Prime Minister).

Sykes, G. and Matza, D. (1957) 'Techniques of neutralization: a theory of delinquency', *American Sociological Review*, 22, 664-670.

Thornton, D. (1987) 'Treatment effects on recidivism: a reappraisal of the nothing works doctrine', in B. McGurk, D. Thornton and M. Williams (eds) *Applying Psychology to Imprisonment: Theory and practice* (London: HMSO), pp. 181-189.

Thorpe, D. H., Smith, D., Green, C. J. and Paley, J. (1980) *Out of Care* (London: Allen & Unwin).

Toch, H. (2000) 'Altruistic activity as correctional treatment', *International Journal of Offender Therapy and Comparative Criminology*, 44, 270-278.

Trotter, C. (1993) *The Supervision of Offenders – What Works? A study undertaken in community based corrections, Victoria* (Melbourne: Social Work Department, Monash University and Victoria Department of Justice).

Trotter, C. (2001) *Focus on People: Effect change* (Dinas Powys: Cognitive Centre Foundation).

Truax, C. and Carkhuff, R. (1967) *Towards Effective Counselling and Psychotherapy* (Chicago: Aldine).

Turnbull, P., McSweeney, T., Webster, R., Edmunds, M. and Hough, M. (2000) *Drug Treatment and Testing Orders: Final evaluation report*, Home Office Research Study 212 (London: Home Office).

Underdown, A. (1998) *Strategies for Effective Supervision: Report of the HMIP What Works project* (London: Home Office).

Wilcox, A. (2003) 'Evidence-based youth justice? Some valuable lessons from an evaluation for the Youth Justice Board', *Youth Justice*, 3, 19-33.

Zamble, E. and Quinsey, V. (1997) *The Criminal Recidivism Process* (Cambridge: Cambridge University Press).

Chapter 9

Electronic monitoring and the community supervision of offenders

Mike Nellis

Introduction

The emergence in the UK of a new, surveillant, modality of control in community supervision is vividly demonstrated by the existence of three private-sector monitoring centres, in Salford, Norwich and Swindon respectively, whose staff know remotely and in real-time whether or not an offender is complying with a curfew, made to a specified location, anywhere in England and Wales. There is a fourth centre in Glasgow, covering the whole of Scotland. These centres receive and record relayed signals from ankle tags worn by offenders, who must remain within close proximity of transmitters attached, for the duration of their court-ordered curfew, to their home telephones. 'Electronic monitoring' (henceforth 'EM') has to date mostly used radio-frequency (r/f) telephony to confirm or deny location, but newer technologies can be encompassed by the term, and are already being experimented with. Voice verification and other biometric forms of identity authentication can be used to monitor presence at several locations, rather than just one. Various global positioning systems (GPS), some using satellites, go beyond specific location monitoring to track offenders' movements and/or deny access to specified exclusion zones. While being mostly concerned with EM-based curfews, this chapter will also allude to these new developments.

The term 'surveillance' – the oversight of people under suspicion[1] – has had a controversial history in the probation and youth justice fields. In policing, by way of contrast, both personal and technological forms of surveillance have been relatively well accepted as necessary means of detecting and preventing crime. Partly because closer links are developing between police, probation and youth offending teams, surveillant practices – specifically, 'dataveillance' (the compiling, aggregating and mining of computerised databases) – are now emerging in community supervision.[2] EM makes use of the same broad developments in information and communication technology to make possible new ways of regulating behaviour and sustaining social order, and it too falls within David Lyon's definition of 'surveillance' as:

> any collection and processing of data, whether identifiable or not, for the purposes of influencing or managing those whose data has been garnered. Notice immediately that I use the words 'personal data'. The surveillance discussed here does not usually involve embodied persons watching each other. Rather it seeks out factual fragments abstracted from individuals. Today, the most important means of surveillance reside in computer power, which allows collected data to be stored, matched, retrieved, processed, marketed and circulated. (Lyon 2001: 2)

Lyon acknowledges that embodied and disembodied contact can be entwined in surveillant practices, and EM is certainly best understood as a socio-technical strategy, not just a technology, which requires human agents (fitting, fixing and removing tags, initiating checkups, processing data) as well as computers to make it work. Nonetheless, playing down co-presence and embodied watching (of real people/'actual selves') and emphasising electronically mediated remote monitoring (of on-screen 'data selves') direct attention to what is truly distinctive and new in community supervision, and sharpen the contrast with the earlier, non-electronic means of monitoring locations and schedules – reporting, tracking and curfews – which cumulatively helped to shape the ethos and purpose of EM.

The precursors of EM

Reporting

Offenders on probation have traditionally been required to report to their supervisor's office, to permit home visits and to keep the supervisor apprised of their address. Apart from residence requirements in homes and hostels, and participation at set times in various community activities, these were the only ways in which an offender's physical location mattered to a probation officer. The traditional (pre-1970s) assumption was that 'reporting' (to the probation office) was a means to an end – the situational context in which therapeutic work was undertaken, or practical arrangements made – rather than an end in itself. In reality, for a range of reasons, reporting – turning up – may well have been accepted in itself as adequate evidence of an offender's compliance, especially in parole supervision, even if, rhetorically, it was disparaged. In the late 1970s, in the aftermath of the 'nothing works' debate, this changed: some commentators argued that the therapeutic potential of probation appointments had been overrated. Bryant (1978: 111), for example, proposed an approach to probation which entailed a probationer 'simply reporting to the reception desk where he would sign a reporting record sheet and would give information about any change of address or employment' – with the option of asking for social work help if s/he wished. In the same year the nascent Chief Probation Officers' Conference envisaged a new purpose for probation as 'the humane surveillance of offenders in the community' (quoted in James 1979: 18). James (*idem*) doubted both the morality and effectiveness of being 'sentenced to surveillance', and even though 'mere reporting' did become a routine feature of some aspects of probation supervision, his derogatory use of the term 'surveillance' expressed the sentiments of most probation officers, at least until the late 1990s.

Tracking

Tracking was a method of intense, individualised supervision of young offenders which emerged in the USA, in 1970, as an alternative to residential and custodial provision, and as a means of phasing release from a secure unit. Regulating an offender's whereabouts and schedules was its distinctive feature. Over a 12-month period, the volunteer sessional workers who undertook tracking were encouraged by their professional supervisors to 'know where the youth is at all times', 'ensure the youth has a highly structured daily schedule' and 'monitor behaviour intensively through frequent, often unannounced visits to home, school, friends' – as well as providing support, counselling, and advocacy (Lyttle 1980: 3). Imported to England in 1980, it chimed with the emerging emphasis – among some but not all social workers – on developing intensified interventions with young people in order to reduce the use of custody. A number of local authority and voluntary-sector schemes were developed in the Probation Service for juveniles, plus one for young adult offenders. Although the latter was opposed by the National Association of Probation Officers (NAPO) for being too intrusive, tracking in many of the other schemes mutated into something with a more supportive, social work ethos (Errington 1985). In a wide-ranging, late-1980s evaluation of intensive work with young offenders, Bottoms and Haines (1993) found no unequivocal evidence that tracking was superior, but were not hostile to the principle (see also Bottoms 1995a). Intensive one-to-one work has survived as 'a key element of effective practice' in Youth Offending Teams (and more haphazardly in the Probation Service) but is more usually called 'mentoring', and is understood as support rather than surveillance (Youth Justice Board 2003). The term 'tracking', however, still denotes the one-to-one element in the multi-modal Intensive Supervision and Surveillance Programme (ISSP) (see below) but the practical difference between 'mentoring' and 'tracking' is fuzzy, possibly varying between projects. (See Nellis (2004a) for a fuller account of tracking.)

Curfews

Curfews – requiring that people remain in their own homes overnight – are not in themselves forms of surveillance, but they do constitute a restriction on location and schedule (Melbin 1987). They became controversial within juvenile justice and probation during the development of intensive day-centre projects (notably the Medway Centre in Kent, which had both juvenile and young adult programmes), as elements of tracking schemes, and in terms of the magistrate-inspired 'night restriction requirement' in supervision orders, enacted in the Criminal Justice Act 1982. Many social work organisations regarded home-based curfews as unwelcome and intrusive, although some parents welcomed them (Riley and Shaw 1980). The fact that their only existing use in a non-residential context – bail curfews, made available in the Criminal Justice Act 1967 and enforced by the police – strengthened social workers' belief that it was a professionally inappropriate measure for them. They argued that enforcing them via late-night spot checks – unless parents were used as proxies – entailed unsocial hours, and, in some urban locations, raised health and safety issues. Two court clerks believed 'unenforceability' was exaggerated by curfew's opponents for strategic reasons: 'this proposition', wrote Tildesley and Bullock (1983: 140), 'gives the impression that successful detection consists solely of an ability to monitor every movement of an offender'. Magistrates nonetheless bowed to probation and social work pressure and made little use of night restriction requirements (Burney 1985).

There is, unsurprisingly, only a limited amount of research on the impact of curfews. Ely *et al.*'s (1987) Home Office-funded evaluation of the Medway Centre's juvenile programme concluded 'that most trainees did observe the curfew restriction', while adding, rather crucially, 'in the strict sense the curfew was not "enforceable"' (1987: 183–184). These authors nonetheless commended 'a surveillance model of supervision' (*idem*: 99) based on their evaluation. They distinguished between contemporaneous, periodic and randomised surveillance, but all three entailed co-presence and entwined social work with surveillance, emphasising the importance of the client–worker relationship. Professional pressure did compel change in the Medway regime, and Mair (1988: 20) later confirmed that curfews, while remaining an option, were no longer standard, and that local magistrates 'rather regretted' this. Nationally curfews, unlike tracking, were not reshaped into something acceptable to field social work and were never used extensively. By 1987 they seemed destined for the penal scrapyard. The advent of an electronic form of enforcement in the Green Paper *Punishment, Custody and the Community* (Home Office 1988) revitalised them, and introduced something wholly new into community supervision.

The development of EM

The electronic monitoring of offenders did not emerge in Britain from social work professionals who were seeking to improve on tracking and curfews, but from outside the conventional channels of penal innovation. *Sunday Times* journalist and prison visitor Tom Stacey founded the Offender's Tag Association (OTA) in 1981 on the basis that most existing alternatives to prison were inadequate (Stacey 1989; McVicar 1989; Nellis 1991). Under pressure to reduce the prison population, the Home Office eventually took Stacey's advice, visited American schemes, and then 'constructed' EM as the logical extension of tracking and curfews. Monitoring an offender's location, especially at night, became a legitimate feature of managing offenders in the community. The 1988 Green Paper launched the Conservative government's 'punishment in the community' strategy, which saw credible and demanding community penalties as the key to reduced prison use, even if it meant challenging the prevalent 'social work' ethos of the Probation Service. It acknowledged that curfews were difficult and expensive to enforce in human terms but argued that:

> electronic monitoring might help to enforce an order which required offenders to stay at home. It is used for this purpose in North America. Less restrictively, it could help in tracking an offender's whereabouts. (Home Office 1988: para 3.2).

The subsequent White Paper, *Crime, Justice and Protecting the Public* (Home Office 1990), committed the government to an electronically monitored curfew order but dropped all mention of tracking (the OTA's preferred approach), possibly because the technology was still too distant. A limited trial of EM curfews with bailees (as an alternative to a custodial remand) was inconclusive in a number of respects (Mair and Nee 1990; Hurd 2003), but the Criminal Justice Act 1991 made the measure available as a sentence (for over-16s, with a six-month maximum period) in its own right. The intensity of Probation Service opposition to tagging had prompted the Home Office to entrust the development of this new penalty to private security organisations.[3] However, trials of EM curfews as a sentence did not begin until 1996, by which time the government's ambition to reduce prison use had been abandoned, and inmate numbers were rising rapidly. Fearing for its future in a new penal climate, and aware that ostensibly liberal countries like Sweden and the Netherlands were becoming positive about EM, the Probation Service reconsidered its position on EM, and some managers became at least cautiously supportive (Whitfield 1997, 2001; Nellis 2000).

Under a modernising New Labour government EM has flourished, with three private companies (Securicor, Premier and Reliance) contracted to share national cover. Home Secretary Jack Straw proclaimed EM 'the future of community punishment' (Home Office 1997) and under him and his successor David Blunkett, eight EM 'programmes' have been phased in since 1999. Curfew orders were rolled out nationally in December 1999, but even before that Home Detention Curfew (HDC), an untrialled, EM-based early release from prison scheme for offenders serving under four years, was launched to help manage the rapidly rising prison population. EM curfews were extended to 10–15 year-olds in February 2001, on the basis of a feasibility study, while a bail scheme, piloted for 12–16 year-olds in April 2002 and extended to 17-year-olds in July 2002 (based on an earlier trial) has also been extended to the whole of England and Wales. An EM early release scheme was introduced for Detention and Training Orders (custodial sentences for under-18s) in May 2002. Intensive Supervision and Surveillance Programmes (ISSPs), multi-component packages which included EM curfews alongside a range of rehabilitative measures targeted on persistent young offenders, were introduced in June 2002. Taking all these developments together, between January 1999 and February 2004, approximately 144,000 offenders had experienced EM (all statistics on annual use from www.probation.homeoffice.gov.uk).

Tagging was piloted later in Scotland than in England, electronically monitored Restriction of Liberty Orders for sentenced offenders being introduced only in August 1998. These encompassed both curfews at a specified place (12 hours per day maximum) and exclusion from a specified place (up to 24 hours per day maximum), for up to 12 months (twice the length of English EM curfew orders). Over the 14 months of the three-site experiment, 152 Orders were made (on 142 offenders), 101 being combined with a concurrent or existing community penalty. Lobley and Smith (2000), the official researchers (see also Smith 2001), calculated that only 40 per cent of the orders were genuinely made as alternatives to custody. They argued that there were no criteria, including cost-effectiveness, on which EM obviously improved on existing community penalties, and discouraged implementation. They emphasised, more than Home Office research had done, that EM sometimes caused increased stress in family relationships. The Scottish Executive (2000) undertook a public consultation on EM and despite its own apparent reservations, let alone the researchers', tagging became available nationally in May 2002, the contract going to Reliance. Smith (2003: 6) concludes that what were 'assumed [by politicians] to be electoral imperatives took precedence over reasoned, empirically-based discussion'. Scotland may yet introduce an equivalent of HDC, although to date there are no plans to use EM in any way in Northern Ireland.

New developments are now occurring in England. All the existing programmes are set to continue, but the EM curfew order becomes one of 12 possible requirements that can be included in the generic community order introduced by the Criminal Justice Act 2003, as well as an ingredient of seamless sentences (mixes of custodial and community measures). The Correctional Services Review (Carter 2003) has announced the imminent introduction of satellite tracking (in part to monitor compliance with exclusion orders) and the Home Office (2004a: 13) response to it states emphatically that 'the use of new technology to provide a means of monitoring the location of offenders under supervision in the community will be an increasing feature of correctional services in the future'. A later strategic plan (Home Office 2004b: 78) indicates that the anticipated tracking pilots are not intended to ascertain whether tracking should be pursued, but simply to test how it works: 'once the technology has been tested we will make tracking much more widely available'. Although tracking technology has been in experimental use in the USA since 1997 (particularly in Florida, Texas, New Jersey and Michigan), there is only limited information about its operation and impact in the public domain.[4] It is used primarily to monitor released prisoners convicted of violent and sexual assault, including juveniles. The technology seems reliable, and even Joan Petersilia (2003: 194), a renowned authority on community supervision, recognises its advantages, while warning that 'correctional technology is developing faster than laws to manage its use'. The Home Office's announcement of a satellite tracking scheme is not 'evidence led' in an academic sense, and suggests that neutral scientific evidence of effectiveness in rehabilitating offenders is becoming less important than political and managerial appraisals of what might be effective in protecting the public (Tonry 2003). The existing EM research is nonetheless worth summarising.

EM research in England

The Home Office's post-1996 research into EM has focused chiefly on the process of implementing EM curfew rather than on the effect of such measures on offender behaviour. Sugg *et al.* (2001) are the exception; they followed up offenders from the second year of the trials over a two-year period, establishing a 73 per cent reconviction rate, mostly for theft and violence, no different from a comparison group. They faintly confirmed the much-quoted Canadian finding that compliance with EM tends to help with compliance with other, more overtly rehabilitative measures (Bonta *et al.* 1999). No Home Office research has attempted to integrate EM with 'what works' initiatives: the emphasis has been on its compliance potential rather than its rehabilitative potential.

EM curfew orders

EM curfew orders were originally trialled in Norfolk, Reading and Greater Manchester. Mortimer and May (1997) examined their use between July 1996 and June 1997. Eighty-three orders were made in the first year, 375 in the second year (after more courts had been brought in to the trial in each area, and as sentencers and agency staff grew more positive about them). Greater Manchester made the most orders, Reading (where probation resistance was strongest) the fewest, although there was noticeable variation between courts in each county. Four out of five orders were imposed by magistrates on adult offenders (only 8 per cent of whom were women). The ages of offenders ranged from 16 to 77, the average age being 26.4. Theft and handling (28 per cent), burglary (19 per cent) and driving while disqualified (13 per cent) were the main offences for which EM curfews were used. Forty-seven per cent of those so sentenced had previous custodial sentences; 75 per cent had had some form of community sentence. Women were less likely to be tagged. Sentencers saw curfew orders as high-tariff penalties and used them instead of custody, community service and combination orders. The average length of curfew order was just over three months. Completion rates (in the second year) averaged 82 per cent, similar to Probation Orders but 10 per cent above Community Service Orders.

Mortimer *et al.* (1999) further explored completion rates, urging caution because of the small numbers involved. The difference between Greater Manchester (at 79 per cent), and Norfolk (at 93 per cent), was explained in terms of more Crown Court orders (generally higher completion rates at 97 per cent) being made in the latter, and more youth court orders (generally lower completion rates at 68 per cent) in the former. There were only 34 women offenders in the two-year sample, but their completion rates (79 per cent) were similar to those for men (82 per cent). There were differences in completion rate by offence type: theft and handling (77 per cent), burglary (74 per cent) and motoring offences (90 per cent overall, though only 74 per cent for TWOC).

Stand-alone orders (45 per cent of the total, 42 per cent in Greater Manchester, 51 per cent in Norfolk and 55 per cent in Reading) had higher completion rates (86 per cent overall) than joint orders (77 per cent for joint probation/curfew orders and 80 per cent with a pre-existing penalty). Stand-alone curfews, it appears, were given for less serious offences. Both probation staff and sentencers were said to favour linked orders, rather than stand-alones, but there were exceptions, and quite large numbers of stand-alones were nonetheless made. Practitioners (in general) thought EM curfews might be helpful in disrupting time-based offence patterns (e.g. daytime shoplifting, late-night violence) or where extra punishment is called for. While sentencers saw merit in subjecting chaotic drug users to the discipline of a curfew, probation officers doubted it. Unanimity was greater regarding the inappropriateness of tagging for persistent (especially domestic) violent offenders, for offenders with physical or mental health problems and where the burden would be too great on family members.

In Greater Manchester and Norfolk, Elliot *et al.* (1999) researched the 'special case' use of EM curfews as alternatives to imprisonment for fine default, along with community service and driving disqualification, introduced by the Crime (Sentences) Act 1997. Community service was used the most (because magistrates believed it gave something back to society), with EM curfews figuring in approximately 13 per cent of cases, on average for 70 days. In the researchers' view, magistrates suffered from 'the misconception that curfews could only be used when they could have a preventive effect' (Elliot *et al.* 1999: 10).

Mortimer and May (1997) estimated the cost of a stand-alone EM curfew as £1,900, and of a joint order £2,700. Equivalent probation and community service order costs were £2,200 and £1,700 respectively. Pointedly, the cost of a joint order was 'similar to the cost of six weeks in local prison or remand centre, or eight weeks in a Category C prison'. On this basis they calculated that if 8,000 probation or CS-linked EM curfew orders were made annually, two-thirds of them displacing three-month custodial sentences, then 1,300 prison places could be saved, with 'potential overall savings [of] several million pounds a year'. This presumably bore on the decision to roll out EM-curfew orders nationally in December 1999. In the event, only 4,000 orders (an average of 350 per month, compared to 4,500 probation orders per month) were made in the first year. Walter *et al.* (2001) researched the orders' implementation in four counties not involved in the original trials, as well as again in Greater Manchester. Previous research was confirmed, but qualified. Although majority opinion was still that an EM-curfew was a high-tariff penalty, all respondents were willing to consider its use lower on the tariff. Sartorial factors possibly impeded the use of tagging with women offenders. Youth Offending Team staff were particularly concerned to tag young offenders only where families were supportive. Bringing breach proceedings (researched here for the first time) was found to be complex, inconsistent and cumbersome. While respondents liked the clear evidence given by EM of compliance and non-compliance, the under-implementation of EM-curfews was significantly explained by magistrates' uncertainty about when to use them, lack of knowledge, lack of confidence and probation officers' limited time to do home visits, leading to a reduced likelihood of their recommending them to court.

Throughout 2003 there was a clear upturn in the use of adult EM-curfew orders: 9,264 compared to 5,628 the previous year. However, using earlier data, James Toon (2003), head of the Home Office Electronic Monitoring Unit, suggests that only 20 per cent of such orders now displace custody. Thirty-two per cent replace other community sentences and (in a massive instance of down-tariffing) 43 per cent replace fines and discharges. This lends inadvertent support to the suggestion by the then Chief Inspector of Probation that stand-alone EM-curfews might be used as a low-tariff alternative to a fine (Morgan 2003), although the National Probation Directorate subsequently discouraged this on cost grounds (letter to Probation Areas from Stephen Murphy, Director of National Probation Service, 31 December 2003).

Home Detention Curfew

The Home Detention Curfew (HDC) (early release) scheme was introduced across the country, without prior trials, in January 1999. 16,000 offenders were released in the first year, after risk assessments had been conducted (Dodgson and Mortimer 2000). This represented 31 per cent of those technically eligible: the Home Office had anticipated 50 per cent, but prison governors, with whom responsibility for release decisions lay, proved cautious. The completion rate was 95 per cent, reflecting the fact that the maximum period of early release at this time was only two months. Of the 5 per cent recalled to prison, 68 per cent failed to comply with the curfew, 25 per cent changed their circumstances such that it was no longer possible to monitor them and 15 per cent were recalled to prison because they were deemed a risk to the public. Release rates varied according to type of penal institution, open prisons (75 per cent) and YOIs (63 per cent) having higher rates than closed training prisons (26 per cent); by offence type and reconviction rate; by gender (40 per cent of women compared to 30 per cent of men); and by ethnicity, with South Asian and Chinese prisoners being released slightly earlier than white and black prisoners, for whom rates were comparable.

A more comprehensive evaluation of HDC was produced after 16 months, by which time 21,400 had been released (Dodgson *et al.* 2001). The release rate remained constant at 30 per cent, and the recall rate at 5 per cent. Recalls were highest for those convicted of burglary, lowest for those convicted of fraud. Thirty-seven per cent of the sample of curfewees interviewed said that the prospect of getting early release on HDC influenced their behaviour in prison, though significant proportions felt ill-informed about it. All felt positive about the experience of being curfewed, as opposed to being in prison, as did their families. Aggressive behaviour towards household members, or monitoring staff, was a reason for recall in a small number of cases. Probation officers developed positive attitudes towards HDC, 76 per cent saying that it helped their work with offenders. A six-month reconviction study was carried out on a sample of offenders released on HDC in May and June 1999, and compared with a control group of those who were refused it. The results were 'broadly neutral', with a 30.5 per cent rate for those on HDC, and 30 per cent for those denied it. All this was sufficient to make HDC credible, but perhaps the most telling figures were those related to cost savings. The average period spent on HDC was 45 days, at a cost of approximately £1,300 per curfew. This reduced the prison population by 1,950 places, saving £63.4 million. Almost 22,000 prisoners had been released on HDC by December 2003, although it has been taken for granted by officials that as the maximum period of early release has increased progressively from 60 to 90 to 135 days (see Chapter 12 for details), the recall rate will have increased from its early high of 5 per cent.

EM bail

The original EM trials in England and Wales in 1989–90 were focused on bail, and while the technology and the principle proved robust enough, low compliance rates meant that bailees were deemed an uncongenial target group (Mair and Nee 1990). Within the post-1996 trials of EM-curfew orders, the Home Office experimented with EM-bail again. Airs *et al.* (2000) examined 9,000 remand decisions made between April 1998 and August 1999: 198 bail curfews were made on 173 individuals, mostly men between the ages of 17 and 35. Very few women were curfewed. This was a lower take-up than expected. Sentencers were not enthusiastic, and few defendants were deemed eligible. Sixty-six per cent of curfewees seriously violated their curfew, 95 per cent having infractions that did not lead to breach. 42 defendants were breached, 24 being remanded in custody; seven re-offended, and eleven absconded. In all, 124 completed their bail curfew, some after breach and continuation. Domestic support was crucial to the success of curfews, with women in the defendant's household sometimes making personal sacrifices to sustain the arrangement. The researchers estimated that only half of the EM-curfews were made on people genuinely at risk of custody and that if this pattern of use could not be improved upon, the cost of a national bail scheme would offset any savings on prison places. EM-bail has thus been used with adults only in special cases since the trials, often with very onerous conditions: most recently with a suspected terrorist released from indefinite detention in HMP Belmarsh on health grounds, at the instigation of an independent panel of judges (*Guardian*, 23 April 2004).

EM with juveniles

EM-curfew orders were extended from over-16s to 10–15 year olds (initially with a three-month rather than a six-month maximum) by the Crime (Sentences) Act 1997, and trialled in two of the three main pilot areas. Elliot *et al.* (2000) examined 155 orders made between March 1998 and February 2000. More orders overall were made in Greater Manchester, but a higher proportion of orders (compared to over-16-year-olds) were made in Norfolk. This was a lower take-up than expected because magistrates felt that few youngsters had the requisite stable home life to make a curfew work, and insisted it was a high-tariff penalty. Most orders were made on over-14-year-olds. Only ten were on girls. Theft and handling offences (36 per cent), burglary (26 per cent) and violence (12 per cent) – a category largely avoided with over-16s – were the most common offences subject to curfews. Twenty-five per cent of youngsters were subject to other orders as well, mostly supervision orders. Over 50 per cent had previous convictions, but only 3 per cent had served a custodial sentence. Four offenders were curfewed for under a month, 38 for between one and two months, 105 for between three and six months, and seven orders exceeded the legal maximum. Sixty-six per cent of the 152 orders on which there were data were completed successfully, a further nine were completed after an initial breach. Only 23 youngsters failed to complete – a better than expected result. Most curfews were made overnight and although they could potentially have been made in school hours, none were. There is no clear evidence that any youngster perceived the tag as a trophy, or felt particularly stigmatised by wearing it, but some families were shamed or embarrassed by it. The researchers estimated that at the same rate of take-up as in the experiment, 1,200 EM curfews per year might be made nationally on 10–15 year olds. Most would replace supervision orders rather than custody, and save £0.03 million. A national scheme for young offenders was rolled out in February 2001, and by December 2003, 2,078 had experienced it. A further 2,078 juveniles experienced EM bail in the April 2002–December 2003 period.

The Intensive Supervision and Surveillance Programme (ISSP) (see also Chapter 11) can be incorporated in a supervision order, bail or a detention and training order. It combines elements of education, reparation, offending behaviour work and EM curfews as well as intelligence-led policing, aiming to reduce both crime and the use of custody. The University of Oxford's interim evaluation of the the first 41 ISSP schemes indicates that tagging was used, in an increasingly standardised way, in 72 per cent of cases, and voice verification – which diminished in use over time – in only 17 per cent of cases (Waters *et al.* 2003). By February 2004 voice verification had been used only 294 times, and may have been discredited for want of proper guidance about its use. A young adult equivalent of ISSP, the Intensive Control and Change Programme (ICCP), is currently available in 11 probation areas, and will be extended to 'more areas and eventually to the whole country' (Narey 2004).

Offender perspectives on EM

One aspect of EM research – the views of offenders subject to it – perhaps deserves special mention, simply because the severity of a penalty is probably best judged by what offenders actually experience, rather than by official declarations of its presumed toughness or public criticisms of its apparent leniency. Home Office research (Mair and Mortimer 1996) has touched on this issue, as has New Zealand research (Gibbs and King 2002) although the most conceptually sophisticated research in the field is American (Payne and Gainey 1998; Gainey and Payne 2000). The data suggest that offenders do experience EM-based curfews as confining and punitive, but, oddly, studies have had little to say about the experience of remote surveillance. Mair and Mortimer (1996: 24) noted some offenders citing 'the feeling of being watched' as a disadvantage of being tagged, while Payne and Gainey (1998) recorded one who said 'Sometimes I get paranoid, but I get over it and get on with it'. Only Richardson (1999, 2002), a British researcher who was tagged as part of her research, goes beyond this, expressing a sense of being 'transparent' to unseen watchers. While she arguably brought a greater degree of reflexivity to the tagging experience than the 'typical' curfewee, she plausibly suggests that the ingredients for interpreting being subject to EM as surveillance do exist.

EM in North America and mainland Europe

EM originated in the USA, and largely through a process of 'policy transfer' (Whitfield 1997; Nellis 2000; Newburn 2002) spread from there to Canada, Singapore, Australia, New Zealand, Europe and latterly South Africa. The emergence of EM house arrest in the USA, from 1982 onwards, is well known, and warrants no repetition here (Nellis 1991; Renzema 1992). What perhaps does matter for present purposes is the state of knowledge in the USA at the point at which it was taken up in England in 1989/90. In 1990 there were an estimated 12,000 American offenders subject to EM, managed by a variety of statutory, private and voluntary agencies, with a diverse range of aims. On the basis of a very limited number of studies the National Institute of Justice (Friel *et al.* 1987) accepted that it could be used as an alternative to custody if properly targeted (although it was often not), but made no claims about its effects on recidivism. They conceded that it made offenders more accountable to their supervisors. Ball *et al.* (1988) adumbrated the policy and practice advantages and disadvantages of home confinement and mapped the ethical, legal and political issues it raised. Schmidt (1991), a Federal Bureau of Prisons researcher, worried that EM was becoming 'equipment in search of a programme' but only a few years later admitted that 'EM has not "taken off" as fast as some had hoped or expected' (Schmidt 1998:

11). USA research has been accessibly summarised by Dick Whitfield (1997, 2001) who, initially as the Association of Chief Officers of Probation (ACOP) lead on EM, has done most to ensure that British practitioners are well informed about its international expansion and the results of available research.

What is the situation now? Mark Renzema, the American psychologist who founded the *Journal of Electronic Monitoring* in 1987 and who is currently undertaking a meta-analysis of EM studies for the Campbell Collaboration, has concluded that after 20 years of electronic monitoring, we do 'not [know] as much as we should'. With a (very roughly) estimated 100,000 Americans daily experiencing EM, and a resurgence of official interest in the technology (Lilly 2003), this is as disappointing as it is alarming. Renzema (2003a: 5) describes his work for the Campbell Collaboration thus:

> As of August 2003, I've looked at around 500 articles from about a dozen countries and found about a quarter of them to be serious attempts at evaluation. Unfortunately, only about 20 are methodologically clean enough for inclusion in my analysis. All that I can see clearly at present is that although EM may be justified on economic and humanitarian grounds, when one applies it in isolation from other services, it has no detectable impact on recidivism. The issue of whether there are synergistic effects when EM is applied in conjunction with focused services in intelligently targeted programs remains open. The aggregating of studies I am currently doing may provide some leads, but is unlikely to provide definitive answers.

Renzema's (2003b) current review of 'electronic monitoring's impact on reoffending' can be found on the Campbell Collaboration website (www.aic.gov.au/campbellcj). It will next be updated in mid-2005. In view of the caution about EM from one of the few internationally recognised experts in the field, it might be thought surprising that EM is growing so rapidly around the world. Policy-makers apply manifestly less exacting standards to evaluative research than the Campbell Collaboration, but it is also reasonable to conclude that the expansion of EM is being driven by factors other than direct effectiveness in reducing crime. Regarding Europe, for example, Renzema (2003a) suggests that all the following purposes are in play, to a greater or lesser degree: reducing correctional costs, reducing the likelihood of stigmatisation (compared to that of a prison sentence); increasing the detectability of non-compliant offenders; reducing social costs by allowing imprisonable offenders to stay in work and support families; and avoiding offender victimisation in prison.

In general, the range, complexity, and legal and administrative idiosyncrasies of mainland European EM programmes (in Sweden, Netherlands,

Belgium, France, Portugal, Catalonia, Germany and Switzerland) defy easy summary, but they warrant some attention because they demonstrate contrasting models of operation from which Britain might learn (Kensey *et al.* 2003; Mayer *et al.* 2003). No other European country (as yet) uses the private sector to deliver EM programmes: in the main it has been integrated into 'public' prison or probation services with greater ease than here, although the German probation service remains ill-disposed towards the experimental schemes running in its country (Haverkamp 2002). Sweden's 'intensive supervision with electronic monitoring' (ISEM) scheme, offered to the majority of offenders who would otherwise serve a three-month custodial sentence, is arguably the most probation-integrated scheme in Europe, and is said to have enabled significant reductions in the use of imprisonment (Carlsson 2003; Olkiewicz 2003). There are no stand-alone curfews in Sweden, but curfew hours are initially much longer than in Britain – on average, in Sweden, there are only 46 hours per week when the offender is not curfewed.

The Conference Permanente Européenne de la Probation (CEP) has recognised the potential significance of EM and has already run three consecutive conferences on it (in 1998, 2001 and 2003, the latter two part-funded by monitoring and security companies). Lilly *et al.* (2003: 10), writing after the 2003 event, suggest that EM 'has become the politically acceptable way of controlling the size of the prison population when it reaches crisis levels' (*idem*: 16). They recognise EM's potential for introducing purely surveillant approaches to offenders but, extrapolating from current mainland European developments so far, they envisage a generally positive, probation-entwined future for it. Their belief that 'EM in Europe has a stronger commercial and practitioner-backed momentum than in the United States' (*idem*) is certainly plausible, but not in itself a guarantee that EM will remain linked or subordinated to rehabilitative goals. In England, EM has not been conceived in these terms.

EM and modes of enforcement

Enforcement is the key to understanding the relationship between EM and traditional community penalties. The Home Office concluded in the late 1990s that existing Probation Service enforcement practices – the strategies by which offenders are encouraged to comply with court-ordered sentences – were inadequate (Hedderman 2003), jeopardising its putative reputation as a 'law enforcement' agency. National standards were already being used to specify both criteria for non-compliance, and timescales for taking breach action. In the new climate of concern these were tightened. Forms of community supervision came to be judged as much by their enforcement potential as by their rehabilitative or crime reduction potential (the more traditional measures), and those whose enforcement was based merely on trusting or incentivising offenders were readily branded 'soft' in comparison to enforcement by real-time surveillance. Compared to human overview, EM reduces many of the uncertainties of community supervision, exerting control at a distance over a sustained period of time, and speeding up informed decision-making (e.g. assessment, review, breach) via the computerised storing of easily retrieved data on patterns of compliance and violation. An emphasis on surveillance 'as the means of obtaining the knowledge that aids risk management' (Lyon 2001: 144) underpinned the Criminal Justice and Court Services Act 2000, which sought to infuse EM (mostly curfews, but also voice verification) across the full range of community penalties, and parole, with a view to making all of them more enforceable (Nellis 2004b). Although Bottomley *et al.* (2004) rightly remind us that there were significant implementation difficulties with some of the new uses of EM proposed by the Act, the scale of the Home Office's ambition regarding EM, demonstrated in this legislation, should not pass unremarked: it even legislated in anticipation of tracking technology becoming available to enforce exclusion orders.

The motive here, in significant part, was political credibility. To be taken seriously as 'law enforcement', community penalties had to become more tangibly enforceable. That some were more promising than others in this regard is made conceptually clear in the following typology:[5]

Typology of enforcement in community supervision

- *Incentive-based enforcement* – offering some desirable state or good at the end of the process, e.g. early revocation, literacy, employment. 'I will give you this'/'you will gain this'.
- *Trust-based enforcement* – creating a sense of normative obligation by seeking the offender's consent; taking the offender at his/her word, accepting their 'promise' to do what is required. 'Be good'/'I believe in you'.
- *Threat-based enforcement* – instilling a fear of future consequences, threatening or administering a sanction at whatever point compliance fails. 'Cooperate or else'.
- *Surveillance-based enforcement* – instilling an awareness of immediate regulation, as a result of being perpetually or intermittently watched; imposing the real-time monitoring of whereabouts and schedules, and storing 'incontrovertible' details on databases. 'I am keeping my eye on you'.
- *Incapacitation-based enforcement* – going beyond the mere restriction to the actual deprivation of an offender's liberty of action, usually, but not

> necessarily, by removing the offender to a place of confinement; *inhibiting*, not just *prohibiting* a particular action. 'I'll stop you in your tracks'.

The concept of 'incapacitation-based enforcement' in community supervision, at least at the present time, may be an oxymoron. Contemporary forms of EM, whether used to confine or locate, are not incapacitative in the way that the locks, bolts and bars of prison are incapacitative. Metaphors like 'electronic ball and chain', 'virtual prison' and 'turning homes into prisons' (see, for example, Gibbs and King 2002) mistakenly imply otherwise. EM, like other community penalties, constrains choice but does not remove it; the curfewees can, if they desire, disregard or remove the tag. Their chances of detection are, of course, heightened, but strictly speaking, this is not the equivalent of being incapacitated – an experience which removes choice, and prevents a particular course of action from being taken regardless of desire. EM is thus confirmed as a surveillant rather than an incapacitative mode of control – it works not by imposing an actual physical restraint on its subjects, but by fostering awareness that they are under constant or intermittent remote 'observation', such that rule-breaking, while still possible, is inadvisable.

Conclusion

With 10,338 people per day electronically monitored in England and Wales, and 393 in Scotland (on 30 June 2004) – and with further expansion likely – it seems indisputable that a new modality of community supervision has emerged. The micro-management of offenders' locations may well have had a previous history in criminal justice – reporting, curfews, tracking – but the addition of various forms of electronic surveillance makes possible an unprecedented degree of pinpointing in real-time. There still remains a discrepancy between government expectations and desires, and the scale of actual use, but this 'implementation gap' may not last. Petersilia's (2003: 91–92) expectation, in respect of the USA, that 'corrections technology will accelerate in coming years and will allow community corrections the option of becoming more surveillance-oriented' is just as plausible here (for indigenous, rather than 'policy transfer' reasons). Following Feeley and Simon (1994), Scheerer (2000), and Fionda (2000), who all envisage a more prominent role for surveillance in the future management of offenders, I have argued elsewhere (Nellis 2003b, 2003c) that a surveillant-managerial paradigm is in the ascendant in British criminal justice, and that on the basis of efficiency and effectiveness criteria set within this paradigm, the more traditional humanistic-rehabilitative paradigm is steadily being found wanting, and waning accordingly. The Probation Service/NOMS transition may, in retrospect, come to be seen in these terms, and certainly the Home Office (2004b: 78) now refers to EM as 'central' to community supervision in a way that it has not done before, without mentioning probation at all. Within a surveillant-managerial milieu – which has been strengthened, culturally and politically, by post 9/11 developments (Ball and Webster 2003; Lyon 2003) – EM as a means of dealing with offenders seems certain to equal in significance educational, behavioural and reparative approaches, and may one day displace them.

The ascendancy of the surveillant-managerial paradigm will be checked periodically (perhaps continuously) by the media-amplified voices of 'populist punitiveness' (Bottoms 1995b), which will claim that surveillant-managerial practices – including EM – are neither retributive, deterrent, incapacitative nor controlling enough, nor adequate to the challenge posed by contemporary criminality. EM-based measures will routinely be likened by 'populist punitivists' in the tabloid press to other community penalties (despite obvious differences) which 'leniently' allow offenders a choice about compliance with their constraints, and be portrayed as something markedly less controlling and painful than prison. The campaign by *The Sun* (7 February 2004) to prevent a young woman prisoner, innocent of, but indelibly associated with, a heinous crime, from being released early on HDC in spring 2004 is emblematic of this particular tendency (see *Guardian* editorial, 14 February 2004).

Debates are likely to continue about the 'proper place' of EM-based penalties on the tariff (see Bagaric 2000 for an Australian commentary on this), but 'populist punitiveness' and practical implementation difficulties notwithstanding, their eventual permeation across the community supervision spectrum is not implausible. EM-curfews may yet be used as a simple stand-alone measure at the lower end (perhaps as an alternative to a fine) and as one component among several at the higher end, in onerous sentencing packages like ISSP and ICCP, and seamless sentences like intermittent custody. In the long run, however, it is traditional humanistic penalties like probation which are most weakened by 'populist punitiveness': EM is undoubtedly vulnerable to populist critique too, but, not being an intrinsically humanistic measure in itself, is better able to withstand it, and more likely to survive. The forms in which it survives are, in principle, open to political and professional argument, but the transformative capacity of the broader technological changes in which it is grounded will continue to stimulate expectations of what is both possible and desirable in crime control.

Notes

1 *The New Shorter Oxford English Dictionary* (1993) makes useful semantic distinctions between 'supervision', 'surveillance' and 'monitoring'. 'Supervision'

means to 'look over' or 'watch over' someone or something, possibly also to give guidance, but without strong connotations of being regulatory. 'Surveillance' does connote regulation, being defined as 'supervision for the purposes of direction or control', or, more strongly still, a 'watch or guard kept over a person or thing, especially one under suspicion'. Etymologically, 'monitoring' shares ancestry with 'admonishing'. A monitor could thus be 'a person who admonishes someone or gives advice or a warning as to conduct'. More aptly still, 'monitor' can be used as a verb to mean 'measure or test at intervals, especially for purposes of regulation or control' and as a noun for 'an instrument or device' for doing this.

2 The growth of dataveillance in community supervision is under-researched, and no clear picture exists of what is happening (see Hebenton and Thomas (1996) and Kemshall and Maguire (2001) for some preliminary observations on offender registration schemes).

3 In Britain, a new occupational group, in the private sector, has already emerged around EM. Compared to the Probation Service and Youth Offending Teams, relatively little is known about the culture and ethos of the monitoring staff in Securicor, Premier and Reliance, or of the technology companies which supply their equipment. Company managers publicly promote their services, and one former field-monitoring officer has described his work (Jones 2003). Ethnographies of these organisations are overdue, although the numbers and identities of the companies involved may change as a result of the official retendering exercise which took place in early 2004, but the results are not yet known.

4 Mark Renzema (1998a, 1998b, 1999, 2000) has paid attention to tracking (and to EM generally) from its onset, and his evidence about its development and impact has been available in the *Journal of Electronic Monitoring*. Whitfield (1997, 2001) was aware of it, and advised caution when Lord Maclean's Committee on the sentencing and treatment of violent and sexual offenders showed interest in it in Scotland (see Scottish Executive 2000: 16). Florida's use of tracking was described by Richard Nimer, formerly of the Florida Department of Corrections, now Business Development Manager of Pro-Tech, a leading EM technology company, at the last of the three Conference Permanente Européenne de la Probation (CEP2003) gatherings. Wallis (2003) made clear on radio that involvement in tracking was the logical next step for probation, given its public protection brief, although the first GPS scheme to be publicly announced in England was for failed asylum seekers awaiting deportation (*Guardian*, 28 November 2003), rather than offenders, but it will also not start until autumn 2004.

5 My typology draws on Bottoms' (2000, 2002) typology of compliance, and refines his concept of 'constraint-based compliance'; enforcement and compliance being, in the context of a community sentence, two halves of the same process. Bottoms' typology relates to the law-abidingness of citizens in general, mine to the specific ways in which offenders can be constrained to comply with a court-ordered sentence. Within the latter framework, even 'incentive-based' and 'trust-based' compliance can be understood and experienced as constraining (and perhaps simultaneously as enabling?), placing commitments and obligations on offenders to which they may not otherwise have directed their energies.

References

Airs, J., Elliot, R. and Conrad, E. (2000) *Electronically Monitored Curfews as a Condition of Bail – report of the pilot* (London: Home Office).

Bagaric, M. (2000) 'Home truths about home detention', *The Journal of Criminal Law*, 66(5), 425–442.

Ball, K. and Webster, F. (2003) 'The intensification of surveillance', in K. Ball and F. Webster (eds) *The Intensification of Surveillance: Crime, terrorism and warfare in the information age* (London: Pluto).

Bonta, J., Rooney, J. and Wallace-Capreta, S. (1999) *Electronic Monitoring in Canada* (Canada: Public Works and Government Services).

Bottomley, K., Hucklesby, A. and Mair, G. (2004) 'The new uses of electronic monitoring: findings from the implementation phase', Unpublished report (Hull: University of Hull Department of Criminology).

Bottoms, A. E. (1995a) *Intensive Community Supervision for Young Offenders: Outcomes, process and cost* (Cambridge: Institute of Criminology).

Bottoms, A. E. (1995b) 'The philosophy and politics of punishment and sentencing', in C. Clarkson and R. Morgan (eds) *The Politics of Sentencing Reform* (Oxford: Clarendon Press).

Bottoms, A. E. (2000) 'Compliance and community penalties' in A. Bottoms, L. Gelsthorpe and S. Rex (eds) *Community Penalties; Change and challenges* (Cullompton: Willan).

Bottoms, A. E. (2002) 'Morality, compliance and public policy', in A. E. Bottoms and M. Tonry (eds) *Ideology, Crime and Criminal Justice: Essays in honour of Leon Radzinowicz* (Cullompton: Willan).

Bottoms, A. E. and Haines, K. (1993) 'Aspects of the delivery on intermediate treatment services', in A. E. Bottoms (ed.) *Community Penalties for Young Offenders: final report to the Department of Health from Phase Two of the Intermediate Treatment Evaluation Project* (Cambridge: Institute of Criminology, unpublished).

Bryant, M. (1978) 'Sentenced to social work?', *Probation Journal*, 25(4), 110–114.

Burney, E. (1985) *Sentencing Young People: What went wrong with the Criminal Justice Act 1982?* (Aldershot: Gower).

Carlsson, K. (2003) 'Intensive supervision with electronic monitoring in Sweden', in M. Mayer, R. Haverkamp and R. Levy (eds) *Will Electronic Monitoring Have a Future in Europe?* (Freiburg: Max Planck Institute).

Carter, P. (2003) *Managing Offenders, Reducing Crime: a new approach* (London: Cabinet Office, The Correctional Services Review).

Conference Permanente Européenne de la Probation (CEP) (2003) 'Electronic monitoring in Europe: report of the CEP workshop', Egmond Aan Zee, Netherlands 8–10 May (Utrecht: Conference Permanente Européenne de la Probation).

Dodgson, K. and Mortimer, K. (2000) *Home Detention Curfew – The first year of operation*, Research Findings 110 (London: Home Office).

Dodgson, *et al.* (2001) *Electronic Monitoring of Released Prisoners: An Evaluation of the Home Detention Curfew Scheme*, Research Study 222 (London: Home Office).

Elliot, R., Airs, J., Easton, C. and Lewis, R. (2000) *Electronically Monitored Curfew for 10 to 15 Year Olds – Report of the pilot* (London: Home Office).

Elliot, R., Airs, J. and Webb, S. (1999) *Community Penalties for Fine Default and Persistent Petty Offending*, Research Findings 98 ((London: Home Office).
Ely, P., Swift, A. and Sutherland, A. (1987) *Control Without Custody? Non-custodial control of juvenile offenders* (Edinburgh: Scottish Academic Press).
Errington, J. (1985) 'In defence of tracking', Letters, *Social Work Today* (21 January 1985), 3.
Feeley, M. and Simon, J. (1994) 'Actuarial justice: the emerging new criminal law', in D. Nelken (ed.) *The Futures of Criminology* (London: Sage).
Fionda, J. (2000) 'New managerialism, credibility and sanitisation of criminal justice', in P. Green and P. Rutherford (eds) *Criminal Policy in Transition* (Oxford: Hart Publishing)
Friel, C. M. Vaughn, J. B. and del Carman, R. (1997) *Electronic Monitoring and Correctional Policy: The technology and its application*, Research Report (Washington, DC: National Institute of Justice).
Gainey, R. R. and Payne, B. K. (2000) 'Understanding the experience of house arrest with electronic monitoring: an analysis of quantitative and qualitative data', *International Journal of Offender Therapy and Comparative Criminology*, 44(1), 84–96.
Gibbs, A. and King, D. (2002) *The Electronic Ball and Chain? The development, operation and impact of home detention in New Zealand* (Dunedin, NZ: University of Otago).
Haverkamp, R. (2002) *Implementing Electronic Monitoring: A comparative study of attitudes towards the measure in Lower Saxony/Germany and Sweden* (Freiburg: Max Planck Institute).
Hebenton, B. and Thomas, T. (1996) 'Tracking sex offenders', *Howard Journal of Criminal Justice*, 35(2), 97–112.
Hedderman, C. (2003) 'Enforcing supervision and encouraging compliance', in W.-H. Chui and M. Nellis (eds) *Moving Probation Forward: Evidence, arguments, practice* (Harlow: Longman).
Home Office (1988) *Punishment, Custody and the Community*, Cm. 424 (London: Home Office).
Home Office (1990) *Crime, Justice and Protecting the Public*, Cm. 965 (London: Home Office).
Home Office (1997) 'Electronic monitoring – the future of community punishment', Press Release, 12 September.
Home Office (2002) *Justice For All*, Cm. 5563 (London: The Stationery Office).
Home Office (2004a) *Reducing Crime, Changing Lives: The government's plans for transforming the management of offenders* (London: Home Office).
Home Office (2004b) *Confident Communities in a Secure Britain: the Home Office Strategic Plan 2004–08*, Cm. 6287 (London: Home Office).
Hurd, D. (2003) *Memoirs* (London: Little Brown).
James, A. (1979) 'Sentenced to surveillance?', *Probation Journal*, 26(1), 15–20.
Jones, A. (2003) 'The Real Tag Team', B.A. Unpublished dissertation (Birmingham: University of Birmingham, Community Justice).
Kemshall, H. and Maguire, H. (2001) 'Public protection, partnership and risk penality: the multi-agency risk management of sexual and violent offenders', *Punishment and Society*, 3(2), 237–264.
Kensey, A., Pitoun, A., Levy, R. and Tournier, P. (2003) *Sous Surveillance Electronique: la mise en place du 'bracelet electronique' en France* (Paris: Direction de

L'adminstration Penitentiare/Centre de Recherches Sociologiques sur la Droit et les Institutions Penales) [the national evaluation of EM, in French only].
Lilly, J. R. (2003) 'From an American point of view: does electronic monitoring have a future in Europe?', in M. Mayer, R. Haverkamp and R. Levy R (eds) *Will Electronic Monitoring Have a Future in Europe?* (Freiburg: Max Planck Institute).
Lilly, J. R., Whitfield, D. and Levy, R. (2003) 'Electronic monitoring in Europe: momentum and caution', *Journal of Offender Monitoring*, 16(2), 10–16.
Lobley, D. and Smith, D. (2000) *Evaluation of Electronically Monitored Restriction of Liberty Orders* (Edinburgh: Scottish Executive Central Research Unit).
Lyon, D. (2001) *Surveillance Society: Monitoring everyday life* (Buckingham: Open University Press).
Lyon, D. (2003) *Surveillance after September 11th 2001* (Cambridge: Polity Press).
Lyttle, W. (1980) 'Discussion of tracking and its background', Unpublished paper presented at meeting of Social Services personnel at Kensington Town Hall, 19 February.
Mair, G. (1988) *Probation Day Centres* (London: Home Office).
Mair, G. and Nee, C. (1990) *Electronic Monitoring: The trials and their results*, Home Office Research Study 120 (London: Home Office).
Mair, G. and Mortimer, E. (1996) *Curfew Orders and Electronic Monitoring*, Home Office Research Study 163 (London: Home Office).
Mayer, M., Haverkamp, R. and Levy, R. (eds) (2003) *Will Electronic Monitoring Have a Future in Europe?* (Freiburg: Max Planck Institute).
McVicar, J. (1989) 'The Damocles detective', *Criminal Justice: the Magazine of the Howard League*, 5(2), 4–5.
Melbin, M. (1987) *Night as Frontier: Colonising the world after dark* (New York: The Free Press).
Morgan, R. (2003) 'Thinking about the demand for probation services', *Probation Journal*, 50(1), 7–19.
Mortimer, E. and May, C. (1997) *Electronic Monitoring in Practice: The second year of the trials of the curfew orders*, Home Office Research Study 177 (London: Home Office).
Mortimer, E., Pereira, E. and Walter, I. (1999) *Making the Tag Fit: Further analysis from the first two years of the trials of curfew orders*, Research Findings 105 (London: Home Office).
Narey, M. (2004) 'My emerging vision for NOMS', Unpublished paper, May 2004 (London: Prison Service).
Nellis, M. (1991) 'The electronic monitoring of offenders in England and Wales: recent developments and future prospects', *British Journal of Criminology*, 31(2), 165–185.
Nellis, M. (2000) 'Law and order: the electronic monitoring of offenders', in D. Dolowitz, Hulme, R., Nellis, M. and O'Neal, F. (eds) *Policy Transfer and British Social Policy: Learning from the USA?* (Buckingham: Open University Press).
Nellis, M. (2003a) 'News media and popular cultural representations of electronic monitoring in England and Wales', *Howard Journal of Criminal Justice*, 42(1), 1–31.
Nellis, M. (2003b) 'Electronic monitoring and the future of the Probation Service', in W.-H. Chui and M. Nellis (eds) *Moving Probation Forward; evidence arguments and practice* (Harlow: Longman).
Nellis, M. (2003c) ' "They don't even know we're there": the electronic monitoring of offenders in England and Wales', in K. Ball and F. Webster (eds) *The*

Intensification of Surveillance: Crime, terrorism and warfare in the information age (London: Pluto).

Nellis, M. (2004a) 'The "tracking" controversy: the roots of mentoring and electronic monitoring', *Youth Justice*, 4(2), forthcoming.

Nellis, M. (2004b) '"I know where you live": electronic monitoring and penal policy in England and Wales 1999–2004', *British Journal of Community Justice*, 2(3), 33–59.

Newburn, T. (2002) 'Atlantic crossing: "policy transfer" and crime control in the USA and Britain', *Punishment and Society*, 4(2), 165–194.

Olkiewicz, E. (2003) 'The evaluation of a three year project on electronic monitoring in Sweden', in M. Mayer, R. Haverkamp and R. Levy R (eds) *Will Electronic Monitoring Have a Future in Europe?* (Freiburg: Max Planck Institute).

Payne, B. K. and Gainey, R. R. (1998) 'A qualitative assessment of the pains experienced on electronic monitoring', *International Journal of Offender Therapy and Comparative Criminology*, 42(2), 149–163.

Petersilia, J. (2003) *When Prisoners Come Home: Parole and prisoner re-entry* (Oxford: Oxford University Press).

Renzema, M. (1992) 'Home confinement programmes: development, implementation and impact', in J. Byrne, A. L. Lurigio and J. Petersilia J (eds) *Smart Sentencing: The emergence of intermediate sanctions* (London: Sage).

Renzema, M. (1998a) 'GPS: is now the time to adopt?', *Journal of Offender Monitoring*, Spring 1998, 5.

Renzema, M. (1998b) 'Satellite monitoring of offenders: a report from the field', *Journal of Offender Monitoring*, Spring 1998, 7–11.

Renzema, M. (1999) 'GPS users report positive experiences', *Journal of Offender Monitoring*, Summer 1999, 5–7.

Renzema, M. (2000) 'Tracking GPS: a third look', *Journal of Offender Monitoring*, Spring 2000, 5–7/27.

Renzema, M. (2003a) 'Where's the research?', *Journal of Offender Monitoring*, 16(2), 6.

Renzema, M. (2003b) 'Electronic monitoring's impact on offending' [www.aic.gov.au/campmbellcj].

Richardson, F. (1999) 'Electronic tagging of offenders: trials in England', *Howard Journal of Criminal Justice*, 38(2), 158–172.

Richardson F. (2002) 'A personal experience of tagging', *Prison Service Journal*, 142, 39–42.

Riley, D. and Shaw, M. (1980) *Parental Supervision and Juvenile Delinquency* (London: Home Office).

Scheerer, S. (2000) 'Three trends into the new millennium: the managerial, the populist and the road towards global justice', in P. Green and P. Rutherford (eds) *Criminal Policy in Transition* (Oxford: Hart Publishing).

Schmidt, A. (1991) 'Electronic monitors – realistically, what can be expected?', *Federal Probation*, June 1991, 47–53.

Schmidt, A. (1998) 'Electronic monitoring: what does the literature tell us?', *Federal Probation*, December 1998, 10–19.

Scottish Executive (2000) *Tagging Offenders: The role of electronic monitoring in the Scottish criminal justice system* (Edinburgh: Scottish Executive).

Smith, D. (2001) 'Electronic monitoring of offenders: the Scottish Experience', *Criminal Justice*, 1(2), 201–214.

Smith, D. (2003) 'Comparative criminal justice: north and south of the border', *Vista: Perspectives on Probation*, 8(1), 2–8.

Stacey, T. (1989) 'Why tagging should be used to reduce incarceration', *Social Work Today*, 20 April 1989, 18–19.

Sugg, D., Moore, L. and Howard, P. (2001) *Electronic Monitoring and Offending Behaviour – Reconviction results for the second year of trials of curfew orders*, Findings 141 (London: Home Office).

Tildesley, W. M. and Bullock, W. F. (1983) 'Curfew orders: the arguments for', *Probation Journal*, 30(4), 139–142.

Tonry, M. (2003) 'Evidence, elections and ideology in the making of criminal justice policy', in M. Tonry (ed.) *Confronting Crime: Crime control policy under New Labour* (Cullompton: Willan).

Toon, J. (2003) 'Electronic monitoring', Paper presented at the British Society of Criminology Conference *Too Many Prisoners*, London, 7 November.

Wallis, E. (2003) interviewed on 'Law in Action' BBC Radio 4, 25 October.

Walter, I. Sugg, D. and Moore, L. (2001) *A Year on the Tag: Interviews with criminal justice practitioners and electronic monitoring staff about curfew orders*, Home Office Research Findings 140 (London: Home Office).

Waters, I., Moore, R., Roberts, C., Merrington, S. and Gray, E. (2003) *Intensive Supervision and Surveillance Programmes for Persistent Young Offenders in England and Wales: Interim national findings* (London: Youth Justice Board/University of Oxford).

Whitfield, D. (1997) *Tackling the Tag: The electronic monitoring of offenders* (Winchester: Waterside Press).

Whitfield, D. (2001) *The Magic Bracelet: Technology and offender supervision* (Winchester: Waterside Press).

Youth Justice Board (2003) *Mentoring: Key elements of effective practice* (London: Youth Justice Board).

Chapter 10

Dealing with substance-misusing offenders in the community

Judith Rumgay

There are three good reasons why an inquiry into alternatives to imprisonment should pay specific attention to the issue of substance misuse. First, the prevalence of alcohol and drug misuse among offenders has been observed in many studies in the UK and elsewhere. Second, the criminal justice system is one of the primary routes of entry into treatment for a substance misuse problem. The combination of these two factors suggests that dealing with substance misuse consumes a very large part of the resources of the criminal justice system and its partners, and commands the attention of practitioners on a daily basis. The third reason refers to the complexity of the social and environmental contexts of offenders' lives, in which sources of personal support are interwoven with relationships that facilitate continuing involvement in crime and drug use. Extrication from the negative influences of this web of conflicting social ties presents a huge challenge to individuals who are all too often poorly equipped, personally and materially, to meet that challenge. These observations will be elaborated on in the following discussion. Together, they warn that to overlook questions of how to provide access to treatment, to enhance treatment effectiveness and to manage a relapsing condition with respect to offenders in community settings, will undermine the potential value of other proposals for strengthening the non-custodial alternatives.

This chapter explores what is known about the links between substance misuse and crime, about patterns of substance misuse and recovery, and about treatment effectiveness. In the light of this understanding of the nature of the problem, it then examines important considerations in the development of community-based programmes for offenders. Thus, the chapter attempts to draw out theoretical issues and policy implications which are of perennial importance in planning community-based interventions, and to examine them within the framework of contemporary policy and practice, rather than to describe the detail of current interventions in a fast-changing environment. In so doing, however, it is inevitably limited by the present heavy emphasis on illicit drug use. While there is a recent resurgence of policy recognition of the significance of alcohol in crime events and criminal lifestyles, this has yet to be translated into a renewal of investment in research (but see Hobbs *et al.* 2003) and practice development. Nevertheless, in many respects, the fundamental issues at stake in this chapter are similar for both alcohol and drug use.

Substance misuse and crime

The prevalence of alcohol misuse among offenders has long been a criminal justice concern. Alcohol consumption prior to offence commission has been associated with many types of crime, including murder (Gillies 1976), rape (Rada 1975; Wright and West 1981), robbery (Walsh 1986), assault (Berkowitz 1986; Mayfield 1976) and burglary (Bennett and Wright 1984). The particular strength of the association between alcohol consumption and violence (Collins 1982) has encouraged research attention on this phenomenon (Miller and Welte 1986; Pernanen 1982), despite the diversity of manifestations of intoxication's relationship to criminal behaviour. Indeed, the notion that the pharmacological properties of alcohol directly influence aggression enjoys unwavering popularity, despite contradictory evidence from both scientific and social research (Rumgay 1998).

The longstanding recognition of an association between alcohol and crime contrasts with the more recent, rapid rise in concern over the prevalence of drug misuse among offenders. The emergence in the mid-1980s of a new generation of youthful heroin users, whose drug involvement coincided with socio-economic disadvantage and distaste for the traditional treatment services, had worrying implications for crime and disorder fuelled by social unrest and a burgeoning illicit drug economy. By the early 1990s, the Advisory Council on the Misuse of Drugs (1991) was warning of substantial involvement of drug abusers in crime and the criminal justice system. The large-scale NEW-ADAM research programme, which studied drug use among arrestees, confirmed the contemporary reality of this prognosis, finding evidence of increasing use of Class A drugs (notably heroin and cocaine or crack cocaine), with particular concentrations of use in certain geographical areas (Bennett 2000). Similarly, a recent survey of prisoners revealed both widespread and frequent heroin, cocaine and crack use among offenders, with 82 per cent of the heroin users reporting daily consumption (Liriano and Ramsey 2003). The costs to the criminal justice system of problem drug use have recently been estimated at £3.5 billion per year, with further 'social' costs to victims, in terms of preventive measures, damage and loss, of up to £12 billion (Godfrey *et al.* 2002).

Preoccupation with illicit drug use has dominated criminal justice policy attention over the past decade, with the result that the implications for social disorder of the steadily growing 'night-time economy' (Hobbs *et al.* 2003) based on conspicuous, yet poorly regulated alcohol consumption, have only recently begun to redress the balance of concern (Cabinet Office 2004). In contrast to alcohol, concerns about the relationship between illicit drug use and crime have conventionally focused on acquisitive crime, based on the assumption (supported by empirical evidence) that the addicted user must fund an expensive habit through crime. Recent estimates of expenditure on drugs suggest that a Class A drug user may spend up to £20,000 per year, a considerable proportion of which is raised through illegal activity (Bennett 2000). It is only comparatively recently that anxiety has begun to attach more strongly to links between drugs and violence. This concern, however, has little to do with a presumed causative connection between the pharmacological properties of drugs and aggression. Rather, it focuses on the potential for violence promoted by turf rivalry between dealers, intimidation of vulnerable people by powerful drug gangs and the exacerbation of problems of urban life in socially disadvantaged areas by the proliferation of drug markets and addict populations. Ethnographic research from the United States has illustrated with depressing clarity the connections between drug misuse, social deprivation, disorder and serious violence (Bourgois 1995; Jacobs 1999, 2000; Venkatesh 2000; Wright and Decker 1997).

Substance-misusing careers

In order to assess the possible impact of treatment interventions on problematic substance use, it is helpful to explore first how individual trajectories of initiation, continuation and desistance from alcohol or drug use develop. Treatment strategies may then be considered within this framework to determine their suitability at different points in a substance-misusing career.

First, it is important to challenge the prevalent assumption that problematic or addictive use of intoxicants, once developed, progresses incrementally, accompanied by steady deterioration in personal and social functioning. Although early drinking problems appear to be associated with later alcoholism, a statistical relationship is revealed only through large-scale demographic studies. At the individual level, drinking patterns fluctuate so considerably over the life course that attempts to predict a particular person's future drinking career based on his/her contemporary status are unreliable (Blane 1979; Collins 1982; Zucker 1979). Indeed, drinking careers are generally marked by a shift from comparatively common problematic drinking in youth towards unproblematic use in maturity (Blane 1979; Collins 1982; Sadava 1987).

Similarly, studies of drug-using careers show that, contrary to popular belief, progression from recreational to problematic use is not inevitable (Wilson 1999; Zinberg 1984), and that even heavy and addicted users are likely ultimately to withdraw (Biernacki 1986; Waldorf *et al.* 1991). The observation that alcohol and drug misusers tend towards sobriety with advancing age parallels the well-established criminological finding that the majority of offenders desist from crime as they mature (Collins 1982; Hirschi and Gottfredson 1983). In both cases, these shifts appear to be associated with changes in perceptions of the attractiveness of the criminal or substance-misusing lifestyle and the acquisition of preferred, pro-social roles that conflict with continuing involvement (Biernacki 1986; Graham and Bowling 1995; Maruna 2001; Shover 1985; Waldorf *et al.* 1991). Consequently, several critiques of contemporary practice in offender rehabilitation have questioned the focus on 'criminogenic needs' and argued instead for a greater concentration on enhancing the factors associated with these processes of natural desistance (Farrall 2002; Maruna 2001). Such a focus would, for example, direct efforts at strengthening pro-social family and community ties, as well as social roles that encourage conformity to conventional moral standards.

There is, however, a potential risk of complacency in the face of these reassuring observations on substance misusing and offending careers. To conclude that sooner or later many offenders will sort their problems out for themselves – even though, crudely, this appears to be the case (Farrall 2002) – encourages a *laissez-faire* approach that overlooks the real hazards associated with their lifestyles until such time as they achieve desistance. The lifestyles, social networks and psychological distress of substance misusers intensify their chances of involvement in crime (Best *et al.* 2003; Grapendaal *et al.* 1995); high-risk sexual activity including prostitution (Baskin and Sommers 1998; Grapendaal *et al.* 1995; Roberts *et al.* 2003; Sánchez-Carbonell and Vilaregut 2001; Taylor 1993); violent victimisation (Baron 1997; Baskin and Sommers 1998); and contraction of serious and communicable diseases including HIV/AIDS, hepatitis and tuberculosis (Bennett 2000; Sánchez-Carbonell and Vilaregut 2001). Moreover, as we have already seen, substantial harms are also inflicted on the victims of their anti-social and high-risk activity, including economic, material, physical and psychological damage.

Within these stressed and hazardous environments, individuals must look for personal support among the same social networks that facilitate their continuing crime (Giordano *et al.* 2002) and drug use (Falkin and Strauss 2003). This point is frequently overlooked in rehabilitative programmes that focus on techniques of avoidance or withdrawal from risky relationships and situations (Falkin and Strauss 2003). Within the addict lifestyle, in which withdrawal or exclusion from pro-social relationships may have featured over extended periods (Grapendaal *et al.* 1995), alternative sources of friendship and support are a scarce commodity that is not regained overnight (Sommers *et al.* 1994). This lack of access to alternative social worlds might be one reason why the use made by alcoholics and addicts of formal agencies of support often appears to serve the purpose of sustaining their continuing lifestyle rather than of attaining radical change (Grapendaal *et al.* 1995; Wiseman 1970). Addicts with extensive prior histories of incarceration and treatment failure seem to hold the greatest pessimism about the likely success of further attempts at reform (Ravenna *et al.* 2001), a finding that may reflect a certain realism about their limited prospects for social advancement (Polich 1980).

A notable feature of studies of associated social and health risks among substance misusers, such as those cited above, is the repeated finding that substance misusers who are also offenders both present the highest risk and are the least likely to access formal support services or to succeed in treatment. For many, it appears that the criminal justice system represents the greatest source of intervention in their lives. There appears to be a 'substantial unmet need for treatment services' among substance-misusing offenders (Bennett 2000: 107). Yet an argument frequently advanced in contemporary rehabilitation discourse is that criminal justice agencies should focus on 'criminogenic need' rather than other types of need commonly regarded as 'welfare' oriented (Andrews and Bonta 1994; see Mair 2004 for a critique of this approach). In practice, there has been a tendency for this position to be reduced to the development of cognitive-behavioural treatment programmes, despite the real complexity and diversity of needs that have been identified as criminogenic in the relevant literature (Rumgay 2004a). Indeed, the evidence reviewed here suggests that, in narrowing rehabilitative effort in this way, a powerful opportunity to influence the level of health and social harm inflicted by addict offenders upon themselves and others may be lost. Thus it is suggested here that an effective strategy for dealing with substance-misusing offenders in the community should provide comprehensively for the range of problems and risks associated with substance misuse.

Theories of substance misuse and addiction

Problems of substance misuse and addiction have attracted considerable theoretical attention, resulting, not in unanimity, but in a diversity of perspectives and, in some cases, strongly held ideologies with respect to their causes and solutions. Each of these theoretical stances has implications for the outcomes that are sought through treatment which, in turn, influence the method and style of treatment delivery. Space prohibits more than a brief explanation of some theoretical approaches that have had a significant impact on the development of treatment alternatives. However, it is important to have some knowledge of the theoretical frameworks within which treatment agencies work in order to assess the prospects for harnessing their contribution to offender rehabilitation in the context of the formal criminal justice system.

The theory that has most widely entered the public consciousness is the disease model, first elaborated by Jellinek (1960) in relation to alcoholism. Jellinek proposed that chronic inebriation results in permanent physiological changes that produce an involuntary reaction of drinking in response to alcohol's presence in the bloodstream. However, it is not Jellinek's theoretical work that has captured public attention so much as the approach of Alcoholics Anonymous to treatment, in which it is assumed that the only recourse of the alcoholic is complete and continuous abstinence to avoid the inevitability of relapse. This approach has spawned a number of formal treatment programmes aimed at achieving total abstinence (most notably, the Twelve-step Programme; see e.g. Nowinski and Baker 1992), as well as a wide range of self-help voluntary groups, based on the original Alcoholics Anonymous model, dealing with a range of addiction problems including drugs, gambling and eating disorders.

In contrast, social learning theory holds that problematic substance use is simply behaviour that has been acquired through learning, both vicariously and in direct experience (Wilson 1987).This theory claims that unwanted learned behaviour may be unlearned, or modified through the learning of alternative techniques of self-management. This perspective has encouraged the development of therapeutic techniques designed to assist the user to reduce the frequency of drinking/drug-using responses in situations identified as high risk for such behaviours. These have included modelling and rehearsing alternative responses to stresses associated with use, development of alternative styles of use that serve to limit consumption, desensitisation to the salience of drinking/drug-using cues and aversion therapy. Complete or permanent abstinence is unnecessary when frequency can be reduced to non-problematic levels and new styles adopted through using these methods. Crucially, therefore, in this perspective, the addict has a choice about treatment outcome in terms of abstinence or continued, but controlled, drinking. Within this approach, relapse into problematic use patterns may be regarded, not as failure, but as a learning opportunity in which the addict may reassess and modify his/her selected strategies and goals.

Contemporarily, one of the most popular theoretical models in the substance misuse field is the 'cycle of change' theory developed by Prochaska and DiClemente (1986, 1994; also Prochaska *et al.* 1992). This theory postulates several stages through which the addict passes on the way towards recovery: pre-contemplation, in which s/he is unconcerned about risks or problems associated with his/her use; contemplation, in which s/he considers the possibility of change; action, in which s/he takes deliberate steps to alter the pattern of use; and maintenance, in which change is sustained through a variety of selected strategies. Relapse is regarded as integral to the process of change, prompting a return to earlier stages in the cycle and a retracing of steps, modifying strategies for achieving change and attempting new ones.

The appearance of the 'cycle of change' theory was particularly timely in the UK, where the discovery of the HIV virus among intravenous drug users in 1985 provoked a major re-evaluation of drug policy and associated interventions (Advisory Council on the Misuse of Drugs 1988). It offered a rationale for attempting to reach the most challenging groups of drug users, invoking strategies aimed at reducing the public health risks associated with their behaviour. Harm-reducing interventions, offered unconditionally upon the user's motivation to seek treatment or to achieve abstinence, were legitimised as constructive strategies for engaging with pre-contemplative users, persisting through relapse and acknowledging the slow pace of change among addicts entrenched in a drug-using lifestyle. The approach was complemented by an emergence of studies emphasising the possibilities for influencing poorly motivated, or pre-contemplative individuals, through techniques designed to elicit self-motivational statements from the user, rather than by imposing the opinion of the therapist (see Miller and Rollnick 1991). These new perspectives have been helpful in extending the interest of substance misuse agencies in reaching out to offenders, who comprise a group characterised by difficulty of engagement as well as high-risk drug-related behaviours.

It is important to note that all of these approaches, despite radical differences in their conceptualisation of the nature of addiction and the goals of change, tend to agree on one particular issue: the *energy* for change lies within the individual; it can be elicited and enhanced, but cannot be imposed externally. Thus, motivation to enter treatment, which may be prompted by external factors including the threat of criminal justice sanctions, is not the same as motivation to change, which can come only from the individual's internal psychological processes (Cahill *et al.* 2003). This point is particularly important for the development of treatment provision within the context of criminal justice sanctions. The deployment of force, which is an available commodity within the penal system, must be calibrated to accommodate this perspective on the significance of personal motivation for two reasons. First, the cooperation of treatment agencies depends upon the sensitivity with which the issue of coercion is managed. Second, the potential for compelling poorly motivated offenders into programmes that set goals beyond their aspirations raises questions about the squandering of expensive resources and the damage to future prospects of positive engagement with users following negative experiences of treatment. These points will be considered in later discussion.

Treatment provision and providers

Over the past decade there has been an expansion in the routes by which offenders may access drug or alcohol treatment through the criminal justice system, reflecting the seriousness with which the problem is viewed at the policy-making level. While this is encouraging in some ways, signalling a greater interest in developing responses that may be moulded to different circumstances, the proliferation also has the potential for confusion between alternatives. Since the Criminal Justice Act 1991, there have been several alternative types of residential and non-residential treatment requirement available for insertion into probation orders, which local probation services have interpreted according to their particular priorities, opportunities and constraints (Rumgay 1994).

Despite this prior growth in alternatives, the government introduced a specific community penalty entitled the Drug Treatment and Testing Order (DTTO) in the Crime and Disorder Act 1998, which, after a pilot stage, was rolled out nationally in 2000. The DTTO contains certain fundamental differences from conventional styles of treatment delivery through requirements in probation orders: a mandate for compulsory drug testing; loss of total confidentiality assurance within the treatment process; relegation of the role of the supervising probation officer to monitoring, enforcement and reporting progress; and inclusion of direct court oversight of the management of orders and progress of individuals.

The DTTO initiative constituted an attempt to introduce the American drug court paradigm, which had become the object of considerable attention and enthusiasm, into the British system. The drug court movement in the United States was spawned from disillusionment with the impact of successive Wars on Drugs that fuelled a massive rise in imprisonment of drug offenders, combined with scant regard to the possibilities for rehabilitation (Goldkamp 2003). The emergent alternative approach welded together the rehabilitative efforts of treatment providers and the legal sanctioning authority of the courts. Within this model, the drug court judge adopted a role in which a keen personal interest in an individual offender's progress in treatment was supported by imposition of sanctions for a poor response and delivery of rewards for positive change. The approach was designed to enhance offenders' access to, and to increase their motivation to engage with, treatment opportunities. Evaluations of these programmes suggest that there are positive outcomes in terms of reduced drug consumption and criminal offences, and that offenders persist in treatment for longer than is typical of interventions that lack the framework of monitoring, encouragement and sanctioning found within the drug court (Belenko 2001).

The distinctive elements of the DTTO render it unique among criminal justice interventions, yet present a paradigm that may be popularly emulated for its promise of an effective marriage between legal sanctioning and rehabilitative treatment agencies (Goldkamp 2003). Evidence is now beginning to emerge as to how local probation and treatment staff have negotiated the ensuing issues of collaboration and implementation at the local level. This is an important area, since the radical innovatory aspects of the DTTO convey a potential for considerable confusion and conflict both within and between agencies. For example, drug treatment agencies have frequently objected to the imposition of urine testing except for clearly defined reasons in pursuit of therapeutic (not punishment) goals; substance misuse agencies have resisted encroachment on the absolute confidentiality with which the clinical relationship is privileged; probation officers' willingness to take literally the limitation of their role as defined in statute is relatively unexplored; and indeed, the interpretation by the courts of their role in direct supervision and sanctioning of individuals raises many questions as to how far sentencers view themselves as willing and competent to act independently of the advice of professionals.

An optimistic view of partnerships between the Probation Service and substance misuse treatment agencies would hope for a collaboration that interprets their respective mandates in ways that derive the maximum treatment opportunities and are acceptable to the professional perspectives of each agency. This feat of inter-agency cooperation is certainly attainable, but not, unfortunately, easily accomplished (Rumgay 2000). A recent evaluation of pilot DTTO programmes revealed many obstacles to effective partnership practice, including the absence of clear role boundaries, poor coordination of professional effort, perceived threats to professional autonomy and conflicting views about treatment and punishment (Turnbull *et al.* 2000; also Rumgay 2000).

The involvement of sentencers in reviews of offenders' progress has also failed to achieve the level of personal continuity that has generally characterised the American experience. While offenders appear to respond positively to a display of personal interest on the part of a sentencer participating in regular review, this impact is lost, and may even be negative, when sentencers are present merely by virtue of their place on the roster of court sittings (National Audit Office 2004; Turnbull *et al.* 2000; Turner 2002). Nevertheless, courts appear to encounter considerable difficulties in overcoming the administrative obstacles to continuity of sentencers at review hearings (National Audit Office 2004; Turnbull *et al.* 2000). American research suggests that disruptions in continuity within the drug court may impede offenders' progress in treatment (Goldkamp 2003).

Local partnership and programme development have been further influenced by the recent drive towards standardisation of practice contained within the effective practice (commonly known as 'what works') initiative (Rumgay 2004b). Programme accreditation by a centralised board has had a strong impact on the diversity of programmes offered at the local level and the autonomy of probation areas to define their own programme menu and partnership arrangements in the light of local needs, opportunities and constraints. For drug and alcohol treatment, it has the potential to restrict the range of options beyond the limits determined by local provision, by focusing the Probation Service's attention and energies on the delivery of specific accredited programmes and by skewing funding towards these (National Audit Office 2004). Accredited programmes for substance misusers – Addressing Substance-related Offending (ASRO) and the Programme for Reducing Individual Substance Misuse (PRISM) – have followed the contemporary preference for cognitive-behavioural treatment of offending behaviour (Hollin *et al.* 2002).

The interim report (Hollin *et al.* 2002) on the implementation of accredited programmes is not encouraging. It illustrates the difficulties of attempting to contain treatment opportunities within a few specific programmes, which inevitably will exclude large numbers of offenders presenting with different or more complex needs from those targeted by the programme available. The lack of flexibility to accommodate the diversity of needs has provoked dissatisfaction among probation staff who have attempted to integrate offenders into programmes for which they are unsuited, resulting in high rates of failure to complete (Hollin *et al.* 2002).

Partnership development has become further complicated by the devolution of responsibility for allocating the funding for treatment provision under the DTTO from the Home Office to the Department of Health (National Audit Office 2004). This will involve the Probation Service in negotiations centrally with the National Treatment Agency, which bears the responsibility for oversight of drug treatment provision in England, and locally with Drug Action Teams, which are charged with the duty of commissioning services at the local level (National Audit Office 2004). Concerns have been expressed that continuing Home Office pressure to expand the numbers of offenders subject to DTTOs will work to the detriment of other local service needs, at a time when Drug Action Teams are also challenged by the National Treatment Agency to increase general access to treatment (National Audit Office 2004). Notwithstanding the issues of equity arising from creating such a contest between offending and non-offending drug misusers (Rumgay 2001), this could ultimately rebound upon provision for offenders themselves by reducing the availability and flexibility of treatment for those who are unsuitable or ineligible for DTTOs (National Audit Office 2004). Moreover, the Criminal Justice Interventions Programme, introduced in 2003 as a joint initiative between the Home Office and the National Treatment Agency in areas of high acquisitive crime, will seek to establish dedicated teams capable of providing integrated drug treatment services across the range of criminal justice settings. The relationship between these initiatives and mainstream local services remains to be clarified through practice development (National Audit Office 2004).

Beyond the existing battery of community penalties, there has been some expansion in access to treatment opportunities on a voluntary basis. The most notable innovation has been arrest-referral schemes, in which substance misuse agency staff visit police stations to offer preliminary introduction, advice and guidance to individuals following arrest. This intervention may be linked to police cautioning as a diversion from prosecution. The need for proactive effort to engage offenders in treatment opportunities is exemplified by the recent finding of poor take-up of services following the limited advice offered to arrestees (Bennett 2000; Matrix, MHA Research and Consultancy 2003). Moreover, the severe reduction in probation service activity with voluntary clients, for example those on release from prison, has created an environment in which introduction to treatment agencies through this route has been curtailed and much is dependent on direct contact between substance-misuse staff and offenders seeking help. Studies repeatedly point to the crucial importance of linking treatment begun in prison to comprehensive after-care services (Bullock 2003; Liriano *et al.* 2003; Matrix, MHA Research and Consultancy 2003).

Both the complex web of statutory and voluntary networks forming the pathways into treatment and the growing diversity of multi-agency arrangements for treatment provision will be affected by the implementation of the Criminal Justice Act 2003, which introduces a single unified Community Order for offenders sentenced to non-custodial supervision. This unified Community Order seeks to merge the provisions that are currently separated by the segregation between the DTTO and the Community Rehabilitation Order (formerly Probation Order) with its available additional requirements for attendance at treatment programmes, including those for substance misuse. At this stage, we can only speculate on the extent to which this will enhance flexibility of treatment provision or, alternatively, compress existing diversity into a narrow band of favoured programmes.

Effectiveness in substance misuse treatment

One of the most thorough evaluations of the effectiveness of drug treatment recently undertaken has been the UK National Treatment Outcome Research Study (NTORS), which followed users for four to five years after their intake into residential and outpatient methadone programmes. A particular feature of the study was its focus on 'conventional' programmes, avoiding the tendency of evaluative research to examine specially constructed experimental projects, which generally enjoy specific funding, training for implementation and high professional motivation deriving from innovation, in contrast to the usual qualities of 'everyday' practice environments. Encouragingly, the study found significant reductions in drug use, the high-risk drug behaviours of injecting and equipment sharing, symptoms of psychological distress and criminal activity one year after intake to treatment. These effects persisted after four or five years (Gossop *et al.* 2003a, 2003b). The substantial decrease in criminal involvement, in terms of self-reported acquisitive crime and drug selling, is of particular interest since, as the authors remark, criminality is not generally regarded as a specific treatment target within the therapeutic drug setting. Nevertheless, desistance from substantial criminal activity occurred, apparently as a consequence of the improvements in problematic drug use and/or psychological health.

This finding of a repercussive impact of drug treatment on associated criminal behaviour, while lacking a specific focus for intervention, suggests that the current interest in developing special, criminal justice system-oriented programmes for offenders, such as the DTTO, may overstate the necessity for such innovations. A more pertinent challenge might be to ensure that offenders have adequate access and encouragement to persist in mainstream treatment opportunities. The characteristics of the population of drug and alcohol-involved offenders, described earlier, suggest that this would be no mean achievement. Yet, substance misuse agencies have demonstrated a willingness to enter into partnerships which expand their own client base as well as provide an essential resource for the Probation Service (Rumgay 2000).

As described earlier, studies of relapse demonstrate the multi-faceted nature of substance misuse problems. For example, while levels of personal confidence and coping are influential on progress, so are social and environmental factors such as leisure-time involvement in substance-misusing social networks, poverty and resource needs (Walton *et al.* 2003). Conversely, depression and social pressure are among the factors contributing to relapse (Cornelius *et al.* 2003).

The importance of generating and sustaining motivation among drug and alcohol involved offenders has been observed. Motivation, as we have seen, is no longer conceptualised as a fixed individual characteristic, impervious to therapist intervention, but as a psychological state open to external influence. Factors that influence perseverance in treatment include the characteristics of the treatment environment and therapists, the availability of social support, external stressors and feelings of personal self-efficacy (Comfort *et al.* 2003; Simoneau and Bergeron 2003). Willingness to engage in treatment may also vary with the type of drug problem: for example, one study found that heroin users were particularly unlikely to enter treatment, an observation that was tentatively attributed to fear of withdrawal (Downey *et al.* 2003). Notably for this discussion of treatment within a penal context, a number of studies have found that while external motivators, such as pressure from probation officers, may facilitate treatment *entry*, they do not appear to improve *maintenance* of recovery (Cahill *et al.* 2003; Simoneau and Bergeron 2003). It has been suggested that 'external motivators may . . . be effective only to the point that they help induce internal motivation' (Cahill *et al.* 2003: 76).

These lessons from the evaluative literature on substance misuse treatment are instructive in so far as they may moderate the invocation of coercion and enforcement. It is very difficult to strike a balance between enforcement and tolerance which respects both realistic treatment goals for a chronically relapsing condition and the need to maintain the credibility of court-ordered sanctions. Thus, while coerced treatment, under the auspices of the DTTO, shows marked reductions in both drug use and criminal activity, this has been at the cost, in England and Wales, of high levels of breach and revocation (Turnbull *et al.* 2000). A recent survey conducted by the National Audit Office (2004) revealed that in 2003 only 28 per cent of DTTOs were completed or terminated early for good progress and that there were 86 breach proceedings initiated for every 100 cases starting on the order. Conversely, while pilot areas in Scotland have enjoyed similarly positive outcomes alongside relatively low breach rates, it has been suspected that this owes much to a level of tolerance that contradicts expectations for rigorous supervision (Eley *et al.* 2002). These findings illustrate the tension between competing needs for flexibility in responding to individual treatment needs and accountability for enforcement within the centrally determined limits contained in national standards for supervision.

Moreover, studies have noted that, even among offenders classified as 'treatment failures' by virtue of their re-offending or non-compliance, some progress towards reduction of consumption has been achieved (Eley *et al.* 2002; Liriano *et al.* 2003; Turnbull *et al.* 2000). Might greater persistence have ultimately yielded positive outcomes in some of these cases? Turnbull *et al.* (2000), reviewing the impact of DTTO programmes, recommend that such orders be exempted from the strict enforcement regulations established in current national standards for supervision in order to legitimise the flexibility and persistence needed for effective practice with a highly vulnerable group of offenders.

The American experience consistently demonstrates that offenders under drug court supervision spend more time in treatment than their counterparts lacking this framework, a gain linked to positive treatment and recidivism outcomes (Gottfredson *et al.* 2003). However, there is also agreement that it remains unclear what precisely the active ingredients in producing this effect are. It is tempting to assume that it is due to the coercive and sanctioning activities of the court, since these characteristics have largely dominated attention. Yet one study has found that raising the perceived level of coercion by increasing the frequency of drug testing appears to promote the likelihood of re-offending, possibly through the negative impact of the supervisory relationship (Haapanen and Britton 2002).

Moreover, the simplistic attribution of the positive impact on retention in treatment to the coercive element of the drug court process overlooks the close interest in and encouragement for treatment progress that is distinctively displayed within this setting, as well as the commitment of treatment providers in this environment to engage with resistant individuals. It is worth noting in this context that drug testing alone has not been found to lead to behavioural changes in consumption or indeed to access to treatment services, resulting in disappointment and disillusionment for those entering programmes of enforced drug abstinence. Notably, these findings held true for offenders undergoing drug testing under a variety of provisions set out in the Criminal Justice and Court Services Act 2000, including arrest, and in compliance with Drug Abstinence Orders, Drug Abstinence Requirements attached to community supervision, and drug testing as a condition of release from prison (Matrix, MHA Research and Consultancy 2003). This suggests that it is the active investment in the *integration* of treatment with surveillance through drug testing that produces the positive effects found for DTTOs.

Issues in community-based treatment for offenders

From the above discussion, it would seem that there are certain crucial issues to be considered when developing treatment provision for substance-misusing offenders. These are suggested as follows:

1. Programmes are generally held accountable, not only for treatment effectiveness, but also to the requirements of the criminal justice system for credibility. Inevitably, compromises must be made between a purely therapeutic ethos and treatment opportunities that will inspire the confidence of the courts. Nevertheless, there appears to be a growing sense, at the policy-making level, that the latter constraint requires programmes to be specially targeted at offenders and delivered within a penal framework. While it seems clear that offenders constitute a group which combines severe drug and/or alcohol problems with poor engagement with treatment services, some of the research mentioned above casts doubt on the wisdom or necessity of confining them entirely within unique and primarily penal programmes. The distinctive framework of the DTTO can encourage the motivation of some offenders, but others fail to thrive in these conditions. Moreover, mainstream treatments have demonstrated a capacity for effective involvement with offenders.

2. The timing of criminal justice system intervention may not coincide with optimum levels of personal motivation for change among offenders. The need to capitalise on the promising results of motivational

work with substance misusers is probably greatest in relation to offenders. This, in turn, suggests that expansions in the accessibility of treatment services, and particularly in forms of outreach, such as arrest-referral schemes and prison after-care, may be particularly important in raising offenders' awareness of and confidence in opportunities for help. Such interventions, however, require sufficient resources to facilitate proactive engagement with offenders.

3. It seems evident that diversity of treatment opportunities is required, including both voluntary and compulsory pathways, rather than constraint within a limited range of specifically accredited programmes. This reflects the diversity of substance misuse and its associated problems. Moreover, treatment provision for offenders might capitalise on the opportunity for reducing social and health risks alongside a focus on offending, particularly given offenders' poor access to mainstream advisory services.

4. A further reason for diversifying treatment opportunities lies in the need for tariff management. While it is tempting to focus on offenders' need for treatment as a justification in itself for intervention, there remains an obligation to ensure, when developing community penalties, that offenders are able to access treatment programmes that reflect the seriousness of their offence.

5. The tension between coercion, enforcement and the pursuit of therapeutic gains requires careful attention. While coercion has a place in the effort to contain offenders entrenched in high-risk lifestyles, over-reliance on enforcement militates against the achievement of lasting therapeutic change (Clear and Hardyman 1990; Petersilia 1999; Petersilia and Turner 1990).

References

Advisory Council on the Misuse of Drugs (1988) *AIDS and Drug Misuse: Part I* (London: HMSO).

Advisory Council on the Misuse of Drugs (1991) *Drug Misusers and the Criminal Justice System. Part I: Community resources and the Probation Service* (London: HMSO).

Andrews, D. and Bonta, J. (1994) *The Psychology of Criminal Conduct* (Cincinnati, OH: Anderson).

Baron, S. W. (1997) 'Risky lifestyles and the link between offending and victimization', *Studies on Crime and Crime Prevention*, 6(1), 53–71.

Baskin, D. and Sommers, I. (1998) *Casualties of Community Disorder: Women's careers in violent crime* (Boulder, CO: Westview Press).

Belenko, S. (2001) *Research on Drug Courts: A critical review. 2001 Update* (New York: The National Center on Addiction and Substance Abuse at Columbia University).

Bennett, T. (2000) *Drugs and Crime: The results of the second developmental stage of the NEW-ADAM programme*, Home Office Research Study 205 (London: Home Office).

Bennett, T. and Wright, R. (1984) 'The relationship between alcohol use and burglary', *British Journal of Addiction*, 79(4), 431–437.

Berkowitz, L. (1986) 'Some varieties of human aggression: criminal violence as coercion, rule-following, impression management and impulsive behaviour', in A. Campbell and J. J. Gibbs (eds) *Violent Transactions: The limits of personality* (Oxford, Blackwell), pp. 87–103.

Best, D., Hernando, R., Gossop, M., Sidwell, C. and Strang, J. (2003) 'Getting by with a little help from your friends: the impact of peer networks on criminality in a cohort of treatment-seeking drug users', *Addictive Behaviors*, 28(3), 597–603.

Biernacki, P. (1986) *Pathways from Heroin Addiction: Recovery without treatment* (Philadelphia, PA: Temple University Press).

Blane, H.T. (1979) 'Middle-aged alcoholics and young drinkers', in H. T. Blane and M. E. Chafetz (eds) *Youth, Alcohol and Social Policy* (New York: Plenum Press), pp. 5–36.

Bourgois, P. (1995) *In Search of Respect: Selling crack in el barrio* (Cambridge: Cambridge University Press).

Bullock, T. (2003) 'Changing levels of drug use before, during and after imprisonment', in M. Ramsey (ed.) *Prisoners' Drug Use and Treatment: Seven research studies*, Home Office Research Study 267 (London: Home Office), pp. 23–48.

Cabinet Office (2004) *Alcohol Harm Reduction Strategy for England* (London: Cabinet Office, Prime Minister's Strategy Unit).

Cahill, M. A., Adinoff, B., Hosig, H., Muller, K. and Pulliam, C. (2003) 'Motivation for treatment preceding and following a substance abuse program', *Addictive Behaviors*, 28(1), 67–79.

Clear, T. R. and Hardyman, P. L. (1990) 'The new intensive supervision movement', *Crime and Delinquency*, 36(1), 42–60.

Collins, J. J. (1982) 'Alcohol careers and criminal careers', in J. J. Collins (ed.) *Drinking and Crime: Perspectives on the relationships between alcohol consumption and criminal behaviour* (London: Tavistock), pp. 152–206.

Comfort, M., Sockloff, A., Loverro, J. and Kaltenbach, K. (2003) 'Multiple predictors of substance-abusing women's treatment and life outcomes: a prospective longitudinal study', *Addictive Behaviors*, 28(2), 199–224.

Cornelius, J. R., Maisto, S. A., Pollock, N. K., Martin, C. S., Salloum, I. M., Lynch, K. G. and Clark, D. B. (2003) 'Rapid relapse generally follows treatment for substance use disorders among adolescents', *Addictive Behaviors*, 28(2), 381–386.

Downey, L., Rosengren, D. B., Jackson, T. R. and Donovan, D. M. (2003) 'Primary heroin users + drug-free treatment: an equation for success?' *Addictive Behaviors*, 28(2), 339–346.

Eley, S., Gallop, K., McIvor, G., Morgan, K. and Yates, R. (2002) *Drug Treatment and Testing Orders: Evaluation of the Scottish pilots* (Edinburgh: Scottish Executive Central Research Unit).

Falkin, G.P. and Strauss, S. M (2003) 'Social supporters and drug use enablers: a dilemma for women in recovery', *Addictive Behaviors*, 28, 141–155.

Farrall, S. (2002) *Rethinking What Works with Offenders: Probation, social context and desistance from crime* (Cullompton: Willan).

Gillies, H. (1976) 'Homicide in the west of Scotland', *British Journal of Psychiatry*, 128, 105–127.

Giordano, P. C., Cernkovich, S. A. and Holland, D. D. (2002) 'Changes in friendship relations over the life course: implications for desistance from crime', Paper presented at the American Society of Criminology Annual Meeting, November, Chicago, Illinois.

Godfrey, C., Eaton, G., McDougall, C. and Culyer, A (2002) *The Economic and Social Costs of Class A Drug Use in England and Wales, 2000*, Home Office Research Study 249 (London: Home Office).

Goldkamp. J.S. (2003) 'The impact of drug courts', *Criminology and Public Policy*, 2(2), 197–206.

Gossop, M., Marsden, J., Stewart, D. and Kidd, T. (2003a) 'Reduction or cessation of injecting risk behaviours? Treatment outcomes at 1-year follow-up', *Addictive Behaviors*, 28(4), 785–793.

Gossop, M., Marsden, J., Stewart, D. and Kidd, T. (2003b) 'The National Treatment Outcome Research Study (NTORS): 4–5 year follow-up results', *Addiction*, 98, 291–303.

Gottfredson, D. C., Najaka, S. S. and Kearley, B. (2003) 'Effectiveness of drug treatment courts: evidence from a randomized trial', *Criminology and Public Policy*, 2(2), 171–196.

Graham, J. and Bowling, B. (1995) *Young People and Crime*, Home Office Research Study 145 (London: Home Office).

Grapendaal, M., Leuw, E. and Nelen, H. (1995) *A World of Opportunities: Life-style and economic behaviour of heroin addicts in Amsterdam* (Albany, NY: State University of New York Press).

Haapanen, R. and Britton, L. (2002) 'Drug testing for youthful offenders on parole: an experimental evaluation', *Criminology and Public Policy*, 1(2), 217–244.

Hirschi, T. and Gottfredson, M. (1983) 'Age and the explanation of crime', *American Journal of Sociology*, 89(2), 552–584.

Hobbs, D., Hadfield, P., Lister, S. and Winlow, S. (2003) *Bouncers: Violence and governance in the night-time economy* (Oxford: Oxford University Press).

Hollin, C., McGuire, J., Palmer, E., Bilby, C., Hatcher, R. and Holmes, A. (2002) *Introducing Pathfinder Programmes into the Probation Service: An interim report*, Home Office Research Study 247 (London: Home Office Research, Development and Statistics Directorate).

Jacobs, B. A. (1999) *Dealing Crack: The social world of streetcorner selling* (Boston, MA: Northeastern University Press).

Jacobs, B. A. (2000) *Robbing Drug Dealers: Violence beyond the law* (New York: Walter De Gruyter).

Jellinek, E.M. (1960) *The Disease Concept of Alcoholism* (New Haven, CT: Hill House Press).

Liriano, S., Martin, C. and Player, E. (2003) 'Results of Evaluations of the RAPt Drug Treatment Programme', in M. Ramsey (ed.) *Prisoners' Drug Use and Treatment: Seven research studies*, Home Office Research Study 267 (London: Home Office), pp. 97–112.

Liriano, S. and Ramsey, M. (2003) 'Prisoners' drug use before prison and the links with crime', in M. Ramsey (ed.) *Prisoners' Drug Use and Treatment: Seven research studies*, Home Office Research Study 267 (London: Home Office), pp. 7–22.

Mair, G. (ed.) (2004) *What Matters in Probation* (Cullompton, Willan).

Maruna, S. (2001) *Making Good: How ex-convicts reform and rebuild their lives* (Washington, DC: American Psychological Association).

Matrix, MHA Research and Consultancy (2003) *Evaluation of Drug Testing in the Criminal Justice System: 3rd Interim Report* (London: NACRO).

Mayfield, D. (1976) 'Alcoholism, alcohol intoxication and assaultive behaviour', *Diseases of the Nervous System*, 37, 228–291.

Miller, B. A. and Welte, J. W. (1986) 'Comparisons of incarcerated offenders according to the use of alcohol and/or drugs prior to offence', *Criminal Justice and Behavior*, 13(4), 336–392.

Miller, W. R. and Rollnick, S. (eds) (1991) *Motivational Interviewing: Preparing people to change addictive behaviors* (New York: Guilford Press).

National Audit Office (2004) *The Drug Treatment and Testing Order: Early lessons* (London: The Stationery Office).

Nowinski, J. and Baker, S. (1992) *The Twelve-step Facilitation Handbook: A systematic approach to early recovery from alcoholism and addiction* (San Francisco, CA: Jossey-Bass).

Pernanen, K. (1982) 'Theoretical aspects of the relationship between alcohol use and crime', in J. J. Collins (ed.) *Drinking and Crime: Perspectives on the relationships between alcohol consumption and criminal behavior* (London: Tavistock), pp. 1–69.

Petersilia, J. (1999) 'Alternative sanctions. Diverting nonviolent prisoners to intermediate sanctions: the impact on prison admissions and corrections costs', in E. L. Rubin (ed.) *Minimizing Harm: A new crime policy for modern America* (Boulder, CO: Westview Press), pp. 115–149.

Petersilia. J. and Turner, S. (1990) 'Comparing intensive and regular supervision for high-risk probationers: early results from an experiment in California', *Crime and Delinquency*, 36(1), 87–111.

Polich, J. M. (1980) 'Patterns of remission in alcoholism', in G. Edwards and M. Grant (eds) *Alcoholism Treatment in Transition* (London: Crook Helm), pp. 95–112.

Prochaska, J. O. and DiClemente, C. C. (1986) 'Toward a comprehensive model of change', in W. R. Miller and N. Heather (eds) *Treating Addictive Behaviors: Processes of change* (London: Plenum Press), pp. 3–27.

Prochaska, J. O. and DiClemente, C. C. (1994) *The Transtheoretical Approach: Crossing traditional boundaries of therapy* (Malabar, FL: Krieger).

Prochaska, J. O., DiClemente, C. C. and Norcross, J. C. (1992) 'In search of how people change: applications to addictive behaviors', *American Psychologist*, 47(9), 1102–1114.

Rada, R. T. (1975) 'Alcoholism and forcible rape', *American Journal of Psychiatry*, 132(4), 444–446.

Ravenna, M., Hölzl, E., Costarelli, S., Kirchler, E. and Palmonari, A. (2001) 'Diary reports on emotional experiences in the onset of a psychosocial transition: becoming drug-free', *Journal of Community and Applied Social Psychology*, 11, 19–35.

Roberts, A. C., Wechsberg, W. M., Zule, W. and Burroughs, A. R. (2003) 'Contextual factors and other correlates of sexual risk of HIV among African-American crack-abusing women', *Addictive Behaviors*, 28(3), 523–536.

Rumgay, J. (1994) 'Drug and alcohol treatment requirements in probation orders: a survey of developments since October 1992', Report to the Home Office Research and Planning Unit (unpublished).

Rumgay, J. (1998) *Crime, Punishment and the Drinking Offender* (Basingstoke: Macmillan).

Rumgay, J. (2000) *The Addicted Offender: Developments in British policy and practice* (Basingstoke: Palgrave).

Rumgay, J. (2001) 'Accountability in the delivery of community penalties: to whom, for what and why?', in A. Bottoms, L. Gelsthorpe and S. Rex (eds) *Community Penalties: Change and challenges* (Cullompton, Willan), pp. 126–145.

Rumgay, J. (2004a) 'Living with paradox: community supervision of women offenders', in G. McIvor (ed.) *Women Who Offend*, Research Highlights in Social Work 44 (London: Jessica Kingsley), pp. 99–125.

Rumgay, J. (2004b) 'The barking dog? Partnership and effective practice', in G. Mair (ed.) *What Matters in Probation* (Cullompton: Willan), pp. 122–145.

Sadava, S. W. (1987) 'Interactional theory', in H. T. Blane and K. E. Leonard (eds) *Psychological Theories of Drinking and Alcoholism* (New York: Guilford Press), pp. 90–130.

Sánchez-Carbonell, X. and Vilaregut, A. (2001) 'A 10-year follow-up study on the health status of heroin addicts based on official registers', *Addiction*, 96, 1777–1786.

Shover, N. (1985) *Aging Criminals* (Beverly Hills, CA: Sage).

Simoneau, H. and Bergeron, J. (2003) 'Factors affecting motivation during the first six weeks of treatment', *Addictive Behaviors*, 28(7), 1219–1241.

Sommers, I., Baskin, D. R. and Fagan, J. (1994) 'Getting out of the life: crime desistance by female street offenders', *Deviant Behavior*, 15, 125–149.

Taylor, A. (1993) *Women Drug Users: An ethnography of a female injecting community* (Oxford: Clarendon Press).

Turnbull, P. J., McSweeney, T., Webster, R., Edmunds, M. and Hough, M. (2000) *Drug Treatment and Testing Orders: Final evaluation report*, Home Office Research Study 212 (London: Home Office).

Turner, R. (2002) *A Qualitative Investigation of Drug Treatment and Testing Orders in the South Yorkshire Probation Area 2001/2* (Leeds: National Probation Service (West Yorkshire)).

Venkatesh, S.A. (2000) *American Project: The rise and fall of a modern ghetto* (Cambridge, MA: Harvard University Press).

Waldorf, D., Reinarman, C. and Murphy, S. (1991) *Cocaine Changes: The experience of using and quitting* (Philadelphia, PA: Temple University Press).

Walsh, D. (1986) *Heavy Business: Commercial burglary and robbery* (London: Routledge and Kegan Paul).

Walton, M. A., Blow, F. C., Bingham, C. R. and Chermack, S. T. (2003) 'Individual and social/environmental predictors of alcohol and drug use 2 years following substance abuse treatment', *Addictive Behaviors*, 28(4), 627–642.

Wilson, A. (1999) 'Urban songlines: subculture and identity on the 1970s northern soul scene and after', unpublished PhD thesis (London: University of London, London School of Economics).

Wilson, G. T. (1987) 'Cognitive processes in addiction', *British Journal of Addiction*, 82(4), 343–353.

Wiseman, J. P. (1970) *Stations of the Lost: The treatment of Skid Row alcoholics* (Englewood Cliffs, NJ: Prentice-Hall).

Wright, R. T. and Decker, S. H. (1997) *Armed Robbers in Action: Stickups and street culture* (Boston, MA: Northeastern University Press).

Wright, R.T. and West, D. J. (1981) 'Rape – a comparison of group offences and lone assaults', *Medicine, Science and the Law*, 21(1), 25–30.

Zinberg, N. E. (1984) *Drug, Set and Setting: The basis for controlled intoxicant use* (New Haven, CT: Yale University Press).

Zucker, R.A. (1979) 'Developmental aspects of drinking through the young adult years', in H. T. Blane and M. E. Chafetz (eds) *Youth, Alcohol and Social Policy*. (New York: Plenum Press), pp. 91–146.

Chapter 11

Intensive projects for prolific/persistent offenders[1]

Anne Worrall and Rob C. Mawby

Home Office research suggests that 10 per cent of offenders (approximately 100,000 people) are committing half of all crime in England and Wales at any point in time (Home Office 2001). It is in this context that we focus in this chapter on intensive projects for prolific/persistent offenders. The Carter Report, published in December 2003, recommended targeted and rigorous sentences, specifying for 'persistent' offenders not only greater control and surveillance, but also help to reduce their offending. This duality has been a feature of recent intensive projects and, given the Labour administration's enthusiastic response to the report (Blunkett 2004), intensive projects for prolific/persistent offenders are likely to maintain their current high profile. Yet these projects in their current incarnation are resource-intensive, potentially expensive and largely unproven. At the same time they represent an imaginative and alternative opportunity for the effective management of this specific group of offenders, whom agencies commonly have difficulties in engaging.

The structure of the chapter is as follows. First, we place intensive supervision projects within their historical context. Second, we identify key common characteristics of intensive supervision projects. Third, we describe the existing provision for adult and young offenders. Fourth, we examine the limited evaluation of the projects, drawing out the main findings, issues and lessons that have arisen to date. Finally, we draw a number of conclusions and make three specific recommendations.

Three generations of intensive supervision

Intensive projects for prolific/persistent offenders can be viewed as both a recent innovation – emerging from the convergence of intelligence-led policing and evidence-based probation, modelled on a European initiative[2] and given impetus by the 1998 Crime and Disorder Act – and as the latest incarnation of a much older penal preoccupation with persistent offending and intensive supervision. To understand the challenges and benefits of the programmes, it is necessary to locate them within both short- and longer-term historical perspectives.

In England and Wales it is possible to identify three 'generations' of intensive supervision initiatives for adult offenders: those which developed in the 1970s, those which were a feature of the 1980s and early 1990s but which continue in various forms to the present time, and those which emerged in the late 1990s and are proliferating in the early years of the twenty-first century. Intensive supervision has been a more integral and continuous part of work with juvenile offenders – for example, Hagell and Newburn's study of persistent young offenders (1994), the 1970s high-intensity alternatives to care or custody for persistent young offenders (Pitts 1990) and the 'tracking' projects which emerged in the early 1980s (see Nellis, this volume). In addition, the Department of Health funded Intermediate Treatment schemes in the 1980s which provided intensive activity-based community supervision projects (see Goldson 2000 for a summary of juvenile justice developments, and Bottoms 1995 for an evaluation of so-called 'heavy-end' intermediate treatment projects for persistent young offenders). By the early 1990s, a more punitive approach was being adopted towards persistent young offenders, and the secure training order was introduced in the 1994 Criminal Justice and Public Order Act (Worrall 1997). The 1998 Crime and Disorder Act established the Youth Justice Board, which resulted in both multi-agency Youth Offending Teams (YOTs) and, more recently, Intensive Supervision and Surveillance Projects (ISSPs) for persistent and serious young offenders.

The 'first generation' of intensive supervision for adults emerged in the 1970s when four probation services participated in the now infamous Intensive Matched Probation and After-Care Treatment (IMPACT) experiment from 1972 to 1974 (Folkard *et al.* 1974, 1976). Based on the traditional 'treatment model' of probation, IMPACT sought to provide 'more social work, more counselling, more help' (Mair 1997: 65) to a small and select caseload of offenders, in the belief that greater frequency of treatment contact would rehabilitate offenders and reduce their criminal activity. The focus was on 'matching' offenders with different personality and social problems to different kinds of probation intervention, and there was virtually no mention within the model of involving any other agencies. The evaluation reports were damning, apparently demonstrating that IMPACT participants were more, rather than less, likely to re-offend than non-participants, and providing evidence in the UK to support Martinson's (1974) claim in the USA (also based on evaluation of similar intensive supervision interventions) that 'nothing works'.[3]

In the 1980s, intensive supervision represented a response to pressures created by a demand for incarceration which exceeded prison capacity and a lack of respect for community penalties. In England and Wales, the government's Green Paper *Punishment, Custody and the Community* (Home Office 1988a) and subsequent Action Plan for dealing with young adult offenders, *Tackling Offending* (Home Office 1988b) led to eight pilot Intensive Probation schemes which ran between 1990 and 1992 and were evaluated by the Home Office (Mair *et al.* 1994; Mair 1997). Unlike the first-generation projects, these projects made many more demands on offenders and included the concept of surveillance. Evaluations of intensive supervision projects were consistently discouraging in terms of their impact on recidivism. Evaluators (Mair *et al.* 1994) also bemoaned the 'lack of innovation' in the schemes. In their favour, it was clear that offenders themselves spoke very positively of the projects, enjoying the additional attention. The projects were also successful in providing greater control or structure for offenders and thus making it more likely that they would persevere with – and possibly benefit from – treatment programmes.

Although intensive supervision projects failed to meet their stated goals, it has been noted that they achieved a 'series of latent goals' (Tonry 1990, cited in Mair 1997: 67): organisational, professional and psycho-political. They enhanced the credibility of probation by appearing to demonstrate a 'change of culture' and a 'reduced tolerance of crime and disorder'. This, in turn, attracted more resources to probation and raised the esteem – and self-esteem – of probation officers. As Clear (1997: 130) succinctly puts it: 'the very fact that intensive supervision projects proliferate is the evidence of their success'.

The current prolific (or persistent) offender projects in England and Wales represent an amalgam of the theoretical underpinnings, policy objectives and multi-agency practices of previous generations of intensive supervision. Combining penal philosophies of deterrence, incapacitation and rehabilitation, these 'third-generation' projects seek to provide a mix of frequent contact, access to treatment (particularly drugs treatment) and community facilities, and constant monitoring. They also seek to demonstrate cost-effectiveness and increased public safety.

The major departure from previous projects, however, is their avoidance of the pitfall of relying on offenders to reduce their own rates of re-offending. This was always the weakest link in the chain and one which consistently undermined claims of success. Instead, it is now accepted that prompt re-arrest (resulting from increased intelligence and monitoring) following re-offending or recall for breach of sentence conditions is also a measure of success. There is, however, a serious flaw in this logic. The possibility that a project could claim success on the basis of arrests and order breaches does seem to be somewhat at odds with the spirit of the exercise, and this conundrum is central to any understanding of the impact and contribution of such projects.

Key characteristics of intensive supervision and monitoring/surveillance projects

Prolific offender projects for adult offenders were originally concerned with the reduction of volume property crime, predominantly theft and burglary, although more recent projects now accept offenders with some form of current or past violence in their records. The central feature of such projects has been the combination of intensive attention from both the police and probation services.

The other characteristics of the projects derive from this central feature. First, the project is staffed by designated police and probation personnel, and located on either police or probation premises (the significance of different locations being as yet unevaluated). Second, participants in the project are required to meet local criteria that categorise them as 'prolific', that is, among the most persistent offenders in the locality.[4] Third, they are subject to formal court orders of supervision or post-custodial licence.[5] Fourth, participants are subject to high levels of police monitoring and programmes of intensive probation supervision which seek to address their offending behaviour (though not normally through groupwork or accredited programmes) and also to assist with other offending-related needs such as housing, substance misuse, leisure, education and employment. Fifth, in order to achieve this, there must be an agreed mechanism of information exchange between participating agencies (not just police and probation). Finally, there is an agreed procedure for swift enforcement in the event of non-compliance or further offending (which requires the cooperation of courts).

Intensive Supervision and Surveillance Programmes (ISSPs) for young offenders share all the key characteristics of projects for adult offenders, although the delivery is by YOTs which are already multi-agency in nature, and there is a greater emphasis on the re-integration of participants into mainstream educational provision. There is also a greater focus on cognitive skills groupwork. The structure of ISSPs is, if anything, even more demanding of participants, with initial requirements of 25 hours' supervision per week and twice-daily surveillance checks, often involving electronic monitoring (see the Audit Commission 2004 report on youth justice, which warns of the potential difficulties arising from multiple requirements within ISSPs that may prove too demanding for some young people). As with adult offenders, young offenders may be selected for participation in ISSPs either as an alternative to custody or as a condition of a Detention and Training Order (DTO) following release from the custodial portion of the order.

The supervision regime

Programmes of intensive supervision are the defining aspect of prolific offender projects. For example, in the Stoke-on-Trent project (which we discuss in more detail below), participants were bound to four weekly appointments that were arranged on an individual basis. Participants risked breach proceedings if they missed these appointments. They included: a weekly office visit, a weekly home visit, consultations with a substance abuse nurse and a doctor, employment/work assessment interviews, and 'healthy lifestyle' sessions. There were also occasional activities and a monthly Multi-Agency Planning and Assessment Meeting (MAPAM).[6] This comprised a formal monthly review of all participants. Chaired by a police chief inspector, the meetings were attended by agencies with an active involvement in the supervision of the participants. These had the purpose of reviewing progress with each participant against formal minuted targets that had been set at the previous meeting. If police intelligence had suggested suspicious sightings or associations, the participant was challenged and required to provide an explanation.

Commonly there were a greater number of contacts than the mandatory four. New participants, for example, required greater supervision initially. In addition, because the participants were, or had been, drugs users, their lifestyles were often chaotic. Consequently there were periods when a participant reached a crisis point and relied on the project team for intensive daily support. This support extended to participants' families, with whom team members worked as one means of attempting to stabilise the participants.

The regime of intensive supervision involved the coordination and cooperation of many organisations, but the contributions of the health representatives were integral to the project. The doctor was a genuine team member and his role became increasingly influential, since all the participants had histories of drug misuse. Taking drugs did not mean that participants automatically breached their conditions for project participation, but it did influence their capacity to participate in activities, their ability to find work, and their relations with family and the project team. Therefore an early step in project participation was fast-tracking an appointment with the doctor, to address the stabilisation of the participant's drugs use. This underpinned everything that followed, though it also raised criticisms of 'less eligibility' and of unfair priority being given to participants.

The supervision regime described aspired to a framework of support that was different to other projects, providing a flexible, responsive service that drew on a range of specialists who would work on a one-to-one basis. Participants considered the project to be unlike their previous experiences of probation and community service. The differences they perceived related to the intensity of contact and the level of support from the project team. The participants were also in agreement that they valued the combination of the project's different elements and activities. They perceived the project to have additional objectives to preventing re-offending, namely assisting reintegration into society and providing support across a range of areas, particularly helping with drugs problems.

In addition to supervising the participants' lifestyles through the regime of appointments, the police would also monitor participants closely. A crime analyst constantly scanned for reported crimes that met the *modus operandi* of participants; incoming intelligence on their movements and associations was constantly reviewed, and the offenders continued to be watched carefully by local policing unit (LPU) officers. The level of monitoring was increased if participants behaved in a manner which suggested they were returning to offending.

Existing provision

There are now at least 40 Intensive Supervision and Monitoring Projects (ISMs) for adult offenders at various stages of development in England and Wales, around 15 of which are currently funded by the Home Office and are being subjected to evaluation. It is apparent that projects are already becoming diverse in terms of their selection of participants, their location, their procedures and their general 'cultures'.

A separate but related development in England and Wales has been that of the Persistent Offender Scheme, which was launched in October 2002 as part of the government's *Narrowing the Justice Gap* strategy. The scheme aims to identify, target and bring to justice adult persistent offenders and then to make provision for their post-sentence rehabilitation (Home Office 2002). Under the National Policing Plan 2003–6, all of the 43 police force areas in England and Wales were required to implement a Persistent Offender Scheme. Following a review of the scheme in autumn 2003, partly to address concerns raised during the early implementation phase, the National Policing Plan 2004–7 confirmed that local policing plans should continue to include clear strategies for the policing (and treatment) of persistent and prolific offenders. A key element of the three-year scheme is the introduction of a web-based IT tool, 'JTrack' which enables persistent offenders to be flagged (by the Police National Computer) and tracked (www.cjsonline.org/njg). This development has the potential to assist in the identification of possible participants for intensive supervision and monitoring projects, though practical experience suggests it has been an expensive and flawed development.

In May 2004, a Joint Inspection Report sought to bring together developments (including ISMs and the Persistent Offender Scheme) relating to persistent and prolific offenders (Criminal Justice Chief Inspectors' Group 2004). It highlighted the continuing problems with definitions and the identification of 'an unmanageable number of offenders not able to be prioritised within existing resources' (2004: 3). Nevertheless, it reinforced the view that there was emerging evidence that intensive interventions can have a positive crime reduction and rehabilitative effect.

The Youth Justice Board introduced ISSPs in 2001, initially funding 41 schemes covering 84 YOTs in England and Wales at an annual cost of £15 million and with a target number of 2,500 starts a year (by December 2003 there had been 7,465 starts). In 2002 the Street Crime Initiative provided a further £6.5 million a year, which allowed the Board to fund a further ten schemes covering 34 additional YOTs (Youth Justice Board 2003). From 2004, they will be available to all sentencers in England and Wales. To support the development of initiatives for tackling crime by persistent young offenders, the Government has also produced an online Crime Reduction Toolkit (www.crimereduction.gov.uk/toolkits/py020403.htm). The ISSP scheme aims to achieve a 5 per cent reduction in frequency and seriousness of offending, and an evaluation is being undertaken by Oxford University that will be completed by Spring 2005 (Merrington and Stanley 2004).[7]

For older (but still young) offenders, the Intensive Change and Control Programme (ICCP) was introduced for 18–20 year-olds in 11 pilot areas during 2003/4. This is a closely monitored community sentence aimed at offenders who are judged to be at either medium or high risk of re-offending. The aim is to reduce reconviction rates by 10 per cent and the use of short custodial sentences by 50 per cent (Merrington and Stanley 2004).

While England and Wales has seen significant changes in the treatment of young offenders, Scotland retains its unique system of Children's Hearings, in which the welfare of the child remains the paramount concern in decisions about children 'in trouble' under the age of 16 years. Nevertheless, in the mid-1990s, two intensive supervision (though, notably, not explicit surveillance) projects were set up by the Scottish Office: Cue Ten and Freagarrach, which we discuss further below. A broader discussion about developments in Scotland concerning persistent young offenders can be found in recent work by McNeill and Batchelor (2002, 2004). They emphasise the dangers of attempting to separate 'analyses of, and responses to, youth crime from analyses of, and responses to, social exclusion' (2002: 40).

The evaluation of prolific and persistent offender projects

Findings

In the above sections we have discussed the context and range of provision. In this section we address the emerging evaluation research studies of prolific and persistent offender projects and then examine emerging lessons and issues regarding implementation and effectiveness. In doing so, we draw on our experiences of recently evaluating two prolific offender projects in Staffordshire.

At the time of writing, the body of evaluation research on prolific offender schemes is neither large nor unequivocal in its findings. The original Dordrecht project that was the inspiration for the UK projects does not appear to have been evaluated formally. Although the Home Office is evaluating the Intensive Supervision and Monitoring projects introduced in 2002, the results of this are not available at the time of writing. A number of these schemes are running independent evaluations in tandem with the Home Office study but, again, published findings have yet to appear.

We are aware, to date, of three independent evaluations that have been completed of existing adult prolific offender projects in the UK. The Burnley/Dordrecht Initiative was evaluated by the University of Huddersfield (Chenery and Pease 2000) and the Newcastle Initiative was evaluated by Keele University (Hope *et al.* 2001). The final reports for these projects were produced in September 2000 and March 2001 respectively. Neither was formally published, although a synopsis of the latter has been published by Staffordshire Probation Area (2001) and also appears on the Home Office Crime Reduction website. Both evaluations were locally funded and were undertaken on very limited budgets; both evaluation teams highlighted the limitations imposed by the resources at their disposal. The evaluation of the Newcastle Project lasted two-and-a-half years and concluded that:

> . . . on the basis of the data available it would seem possible to claim that the project has had a positive effect on the participants (when compared with similar non-participants[8]) that is less than 10% likely to be a matter of chance. In other words, the evaluation team is 90% confident that the project has had an effect in the direction of reducing re-offending rates of participants by over 50% when compared with similar non-participants. It is important that this reduction is not quoted out of context. It does not mean that participants' offending has halved. Rather, it means that, *when compared with similar non-participants,* their rate of offending has fallen from 18% above the non-participants on admission to the project to 35% below the non-participants following the project. (Hope *et al.* 2001)

The evaluation of the Burnley/Dordrecht Initiative was less positive. It concluded that there was no significant difference in the re-offending[9] rates of the participant and comparison groups. Chenery and Pease (2000) compared the 'rate of known offending per month' of each participant with two other matched offenders and found the average number of offences per month was the same for both groups. This suggested that the Burnley project did not have an effect on subsequent rates of offending. However, as the evaluators rightly stressed, the Burnley project increased the possibility of participants' crimes being detected and if the scheme also reduced their number of committed offences, then these two effects would offset each other. They concluded that 'in the real world, reconviction of those who persist in criminality despite help offered constitutes a success, certainly as far as public protection is involved' (2000: 38).

The third evaluation was of the Stoke-on-Trent Prolific Offender Project by a research team from Keele University which included the two authors of this chapter (Worrall *et al.* 2003). We approached this evaluation building on knowledge gained from the evaluation of the Newcastle project. The evaluation had strands that focused on process, outcomes, and cost-effectiveness. In terms of the primary outcome of reducing the offending behaviour of the project participants, the Stoke project was marginally successful. The participant group (of 22 offenders) was matched with a comparison group, and estimation of the effect of the project required an appropriate statistical test of the differences between the two groups in their prior, on-project and post-project convictions. These tests showed that:

- There was no significant difference in pre-project convictions between the participant and comparison groups.
- Participants had a significantly lower number of convictions, on average, while participating on the project compared with the comparison group, who remained at large in the community ($p < .089$). A 10 per cent level of significance was regarded as acceptable given the small sample size.[10]
- There was no significant difference in the average number of convictions between the groups after the participants left the project.

Put another way, the average on-project and post-project offending rate for participants was seven and for comparators was 11. Therefore, during and following project enrolment, participants on average had four fewer subsequent reconvictions than their comparators.

Although the results of the tests tend towards the positive, and enabled the project to be labelled and marketed as 'successful', they are necessarily based on small numbers. We were well aware that these results would not convince sceptics and that, together with the Newcastle and Burnley results, they did not present an overwhelmingly strong case that prolific offender projects are 'what works'.

In addition to these findings concerning reconviction, the cost-effectiveness analysis aspect of the Stoke evaluation led us to conclude that the initiative was highly resource-intensive, indeed some would claim 'expensive'. However, taking into account the reduction in offending of the participants, at least during their period on the project, and the beneficial secondary outcomes to the project (discussed below), it was reasonable to suggest that the project had achieved a satisfactory level of value for money.

With regard to reconviction findings in the evaluation of schemes for persistent young offenders, academics from Lancaster University evaluated the APEX Cue Ten project in Fife, Scotland, and found that project 'completers' went on to offend less seriously and less frequently than 'non-completers' and a comparison group. However, the differences were not statistically significant and 'completers' tended to be those young people with fewest previous charges. Again, similarly to the adult cost-effectiveness study mentioned above, the Cue Ten project was found to be highly resource-intensive, though cost-effective when compared with the costs of supervising the comparison group (Lobley and Smith 1999) (for an executive summary, see www.scotland.gov.uk/cru/kd01/pjo-report-04.htm).

A second Scottish persistent young offender scheme, the Freagarrach Project, was also evaluated by Lancaster University between 1995 and 2000. The evaluation report concluded that Freagarrach reduced the offending rate of 'many of the young people who attended it, at least in the short term' (Lobley *et al.* 2001). The report also concluded that it was 'superficially an expensive project' before the 'total social costs of crime' were taken into account (Lobley *et al.* 2001) (for an executive summary, see www.scotland.gov.uk/cru/kd01/green/freagarrach-04.htm).

The University of Oxford Centre for Criminological Studies' evaluation of ISSP is being conducted over three years. Full findings are not yet in the public domain but initial data suggest that the programmes are targeting persistent young offenders with serious educational and substance-misuse problems.[11] The main challenges appear to be finding suitable accommodation and substance-misuse treatment for the young people on the programmes and securing reintegration into education (Youth Justice Board 2004). A sceptical view of the current state of knowledge about the effectiveness of ISSP is taken by Green *et al.* (2004) on behalf of the Institute for the Study of Civil Society (CIVITAS). They point out that, by early 2004, little evidence had been produced that could validate the impact of ISSP on re-offending. The issue of private agency involvement has also surfaced. PA Consulting were involved in providing a regional and national framework of support for the implementation, and opinions appear divided on how successful this has been.

Thus far, on the basis of reduced offending and cost-effectiveness, we do not appear to have built an overwhelming case for the continued pursuit of these projects. However, taking account of the aforementioned evaluation reports and having spent 18 months observing the operation of the Stoke project on a sometimes daily basis, watching and interviewing practitioners, managers, partners and offenders in different stages of experiencing the project, it is our opinion that projects of this kind have benefits beyond those which can be measured easily by quantitative performance indicators (of conviction rate and cost). In particular, there are perceptible benefits for the project participants and their families. When interviewed, Stoke participants identified a number of positive outcomes including that the project:

- stopped or reduced their offending whilst they were on the project;
- kept them occupied;
- provided them with a sense of purpose;
- helped with their drugs problems;
- built their confidence in doing everyday things, e.g. finding accommodation, dealing with the utility companies, social interaction; and
- helped the rebuilding of relationships with families (partners, children and parents).

These might appear to be the platitudinous comments one might expect from participants on a project that showed interest in them and which they had a vested interest in 'talking-up' (cf. Jones 2002: 193). However, our observation of the project suggested these benefits were genuine. In this respect, the balance of support and surveillance worked in a complementary fashion. In respect of surveillance, one prolific offender talked about how the attention of the police curbed his offending:

> the police seemed to know what I was doing and what I was up to . . . it was getting back to me that they knew what I was doing. People would say you've done this yesterday or that last week and I had done it and the police knew about it – it was uncomfortable.

In respect of support, the project team worked with offenders prior to their participation, helping to prepare them for the rigorous regime. For example, team members visited offenders in prison, and on their release would collect them from the prison gate and transport them to their accommodation, which the team had frequently been instrumental in securing. The following case study from the Stoke project illustrates the level of support that can be provided and what it can achieve.

Case study: Female, aged 19

This participant's parents separated when she was 13 and she subsequently lived in a domestic violence refuge hostel with her mother. By the time she left school she was a regular heroin user and she became involved in prostitution, influenced by older criminals. By the age of 18 she had convictions for burglary, theft from person, assaulting a police officer, handling stolen goods, cocaine possession, and obtaining property by deception.

In October 2001, she was placed on a DTTO but was breached for lack of attendance and in February 2002 received a custodial sentence for burglary. The project team first contacted her in a Young Offenders' Institution and kept in touch when she was moved to an adult women's prison in March 2002.

She was released on licence in May 2002 and worked intensively with the project for her entire three-month licence period. During this period, she maintained the four weekly appointments and engaged with the following agencies:

- the Women's Project (part of a local housing association) which supports the health, educational and social needs of women prostitutes and drug users;
- a local college for basic skills assessments in English and maths and participation in a 'Drop In' course;
- a second local college for constructive leisure classes;
- the Prince's Trust: she took part in and became a team leader involved in a community project at a local day centre;
- Millennium Volunteers;
- the New Vic Theatre *Borderlines* initiative: she participated in the making of the project's video film *Day by Day*.

In addition to linking the participant into these agencies, the project team liaised closely with her family, and worked with the Benefits Agency to relocate her signing office as former associates were intimidating her. The project doctor also conducted consultations with her. Although she left prison drug-free, she relapsed due to peer pressure. The doctor worked closely with her, supervising a subutex treatment programme.

The participant completed her licence period in August 2002. She had complied with all the requirements of her licence and of the project. She had not offended during this period and with the support of the project established a network of supporting organisations. She adhered to her drugs treatment plan and took steps towards making major changes in her life. Although the project team considered that the supervision period was too short, she had progressed significantly over a short period.

Following the expiry of the licence period, she remained in touch with the project on a monthly reviewable basis, though contacts became less frequent. She did not come to police notice again during the course of our evaluation.

Maintenance and secondary benefits

While there were evident benefits for participants and their families, they were not always long-standing. The statistical analysis provided some evidence that the participants reduced their levels of offending while they were actively engaged on the project, but that this progress was not always maintained during the post-project period.[12] This, combined with close observation of the operation of the project and interviews with staff, managers and participants, led us to conclude that the project provided a valuable 'maintenance' function that was effective in the short term and laid foundations for possible longer-term benefits (see also the similar findings in Sinclair 1971, discussed in Bottoms 2001). Once this became clear, it seemed to us that the project should be presented as such in order to manage the expectations of all involved.

Equally it became evident that progress may be interrupted, but not lost. This is a complex picture. Examination of the case file histories confirmed that the prolific offenders accepted by the project were difficult cases with a high risk of re-offending. When the participants were on the project they commonly responded to the interest shown in them, the range of support available and their realisation of the level of monitoring involved. The project team targeted this difficult client group in the knowledge that these people would not necessarily reform their lives as a result of project participation. It was therefore important to accept that for all the progress made, the participants could relapse into offending and return to prison. Yet this was not an end-point; valuable work had been conducted which could be picked up again at an appropriate stage. If a participant returned to the project for a second time, the team practitioners would explore the reason for returning to offending, but at the same time they would use the previous experience and what the individual had learned from it. This was aptly described by the project doctor, who commented that the project had succeeded in engaging people for the first time and could re-engage them. Participants had made progress they had never achieved before, which he believed would have a much more long-standing effect than could be measured in the short term. How and whether a regime of this nature can support desistance from prolific offending are under-researched questions (Farrall *et al.* forthcoming) and there are potential benefits for policy and practice to be gained from engaging with recent studies of desistance (Maruna 2001; Farrall 2002; Maruna and Immarigeon 2004).

In addition to the impact on project participants, a number of wider positive outcomes became evident during our evaluation. These included the benefits of partnership working. The development of constructive relations between agencies, particularly police, probation and health, contributed to the operation of the project. The benefits were tangible at a managerial level in terms of strategic integration and policy-making, and also at the operational level where the different team roles of the police officer, crime analyst and probation officer complemented each other in the intensive supervision and monitoring of the participants. The sharing of information between team members from different agencies worked well and contributed to the ability of the project to monitor and manage offenders.

The project drew on the strengths of the partner agencies and also, through utilising a comprehensive network of other support agencies, it was able to make positive interventions in the lives of the offenders, providing opportunities not previously available to them. These included advice on health and drugs misuse issues, guidance on training and preparing for employment, and the encouragement of constructive recreational activities.

In terms of monitoring and surveillance of the participants, the operation of the project, with a police officer working closely with participants, and with a dedicated crime analyst, improved the amount and flow of intelligence on offenders in Stoke-on-Trent.

We would argue, therefore, that prolific offender projects, if implemented carefully, represent the development of a model of partnership working that balances the care and control of prolific offenders. They have the potential to support offenders, reduce their offending and to bring wider benefits.

Lessons and issues

We have alluded to the complexity of prolific offender projects, and individual projects will not be able to deliver the benefits described above if they are inadequately implemented and managed. In this section, drawing on our evaluation of the Stoke project, we highlight a number of issues and lessons learned that have implications for establishing and delivering a prolific offender project.

Locating and establishing the project

The physical location of a prolific offender project has implications for project culture and processes. The Stoke project had its own police crime analyst and was located in a police station in the office next to the intelligence cell. In contrast, the prolific offender project in neighbouring Newcastle-under-Lyme was situated in probation premises without a bespoke crime analyst. Not surprisingly, the project cultures differed considerably.

At the outset of the Stoke project the choice of a police station location as a project base was problematic. The project, committed to working with offenders, was imposed upon an environment in which the participant offenders were perceived as targets to be locked up as quickly as possible. In this vaguely hostile setting the project continually had to justify its existence to the prevailing police culture. Probation staff felt isolated from their probation colleagues, while police officers involved in the project were regarded with suspicion by police colleagues who saw them as 'supporting' offenders.

Despite the potentially negative aspects of the police station location, this feature, once the project had established a measure of credibility, became one of its strengths, particularly in respect of intelligence links, its access to police intelligence systems and the ease with which it could liaise with the different policing sections. It was also a safe meeting place and secure project base and symbolically the police station location reinforced the crime reduction objective.

True partnership?

Prolific offender projects are based on the premiss that multi-agency cooperation can exist. This is important both at strategic and operational levels. It would be difficult for prolific offender projects to achieve any level of success unless the involved agencies go beyond 'partnership lip service' and genuinely work together. As the evaluators of the Freagarrach Project noted, the success of these types of projects is predicated on (a) embedding projects in a local strategic approach that ensures active and practical inter-agency support and (b) the high-quality work of the implementation team (Lobley *et al.* 2001). These conditions must be created. If we take the Stoke project as an example, this had a multi-agency steering group, probation and police middle managers and a police/probation operational team that successfully coordinated a range of differing agencies, dependent upon project and participant needs. Unless agencies can establish and develop effective inter- or multi-agency frameworks, practices and protocols that allow them to focus on their impact on prolific offenders, such projects have little chance of longevity or, indeed, success.

Team development and project management issues

Prolific offender projects establish multi-disciplinary teams from agencies that have not historically been comfortable bedfellows. In our experience it can be the case that these teams are almost thrown together and are then expected to design their project and individual roles and responsibilities. As the client group can be skilled at playing agencies off against each other, it is important that project personnel work together as a team, build trust in each other and share information. It is also important for team members to adopt a flexible attitude to their roles, while remaining clear about their own purpose and the aims of their home agency in being involved in the project. On a wider level, these projects can raise the question of blurring agency boundaries and the development of 'polibation' (Nash 1999, 2004; Mawby and Worrall 2004).

Working on prolific offender projects can be stressful. It is a relatively new role for both police and probation officers and requires the building and maintaining of relationships with a network of agencies with different objectives and agendas. It involves constant engagement with offenders and their families, whose morale swings from project dependence to detachment. In addition, the supervision of and support for the participants can engender a project culture of working long hours and keeping mobile phones switched on during evenings and weekends. With multi-agency or partnership projects, there are also issues of personnel within teams working under different remuneration and benefits packages. There are inherent difficulties in treating team members equally, when their respective agencies have different policies and regulations concerning hours of work, call-out fees, overtime working, holiday entitlement, and pay and grade structures. These are the messy consequences of partnership working, but they can be addressed through effective project management.

This organisational context is also important in that prolific offender projects thus far have been funded by a mish-mash of short-term funding. This means that they may operate in an atmosphere of uncertainty. For example, while we were evaluating the Stoke project, the project team was frequently required to liaise with funding agencies, visiting inspectors and other projects that were setting up. At the same time the Stoke team members were unsure of their own future with the project, as it existed on successive short-term grants. Beyond the resulting uncertainty, there are wider implications for the sustainability of prolific offender projects and how they should be funded. Innovative projects that are initially financed through specialised and temporary funding streams, if found to be successful, create a dilemma. Should they be mainstreamed and, if they are, will they undermine core services by draining resources (funding and experienced staff)? These are issues that will need to be addressed given the Carter Report's recommendation of 'greater sanctions and help for persistent offenders' (2003: 29).

For the reasons outlined above, effective project management is important to prolific offender projects as the work is innovative, demanding and, possibly, stressful. Teams will need support and guidance from line managers at critical points. Clear line management, clear roles and responsibilities and standard operating procedures are essential. Operating processes that are documented can facilitate the work of remaining and replacement staff in the event of illness and departure. Succession planning also needs to be implemented to minimise the disruption of changing personnel.

Managing the exit

Prolific offender projects provide a framework for intensive supervision and this can engender in participants an over-dependence on the project, resulting in a vacuum in their lives in the post-project period. For the Stoke project, the managers and practitioners were mindful that the project should develop 'moving-on' policies or exit strategies for participants, assisting them in establishing a network of beneficial activities and contacts to support them in the post-project period. In practice during the evaluation period, few participants reached the stage where they were in a position to embark upon a fully independent life. As such the project did not develop tested and proven 'weaning off' and 'moving-on' plans. This is clearly an important consideration given that the statistical analysis suggests that offenders are more likely to be reconvicted during the post-project period than during the on-project period.

Communication needs

It has become commonplace for evaluations to make trite recommendations concerning the development of a communications strategy. Nevertheless, our evaluation of the Stoke project concluded that these projects have specific communications needs. Prolific offender projects require a communications strategy that identifies internal and external stakeholders, determines the level of communication needed with each and how this will be achieved. The communications strategy, at the very least, will need to address:

- Internal team members – to communicate internally between the team members what each person actually does in their own agency and how this transfers to their project role.
- The staff of partner agencies – to inform the different agencies and their sub-units (particularly police units) of the true nature of the project. This can help to alleviate any antagonism which might undermine the positive work of the project. Area probation service staff need to be fully aware of the project so that they can refer appropriate offenders.
- Other linked agencies – to promote the project to magistrates, prisons, partner agencies (for example, housing, education, health).

Conclusions

This chapter has attempted to give an overview of the development and current state of implementation of projects for prolific/persistent adult and young offenders. We can draw the following conclusions:

- Intensive projects for prolific/persistent offenders are not new, though recent projects have innovatory aspects. Hence it is necessary to locate them within both short- and longer-term historical perspectives.
- There exists a range of diverse projects. Although they are not homogeneous, developing differently in their individual contexts and locations, they tend to share a number of key characteristics.
- Although these projects now operate nationally, the local dimension is marked. The two projects we evaluated had very different cultures and ways of working, and anecdotal feedback from a third project in Staffordshire suggests that it is very different again. This has obvious implications for transferability.
- Existing evaluations have not provided overwhelming evidence of reduced offending or cost-effectiveness. However, prolific offender projects are complex in terms of their multi-agency nature and the needs of their clientele. They need to be judged on more than crime rates and cost-effectiveness, though these are of course important. Other criteria which should be taken into account include, on the one hand, health, educational and social benefits for participants and, on the other hand, improved multi-agency working and information exchange between project partners, and improved intelligence on prolific offenders.
- The projects are likely to experience common issues, challenges and potential pitfalls which include:
  - Embedding the project and establishing its credibility;
  - Demonstrating *de facto* effective inter- and multi-agency practices, while recognising the distinctive contributions of each agency and resisting the blurring of agency boundaries;
  - Planning for team development and for human resource contingencies, so that the levels of stress experienced by staff are minimised;
  - Developing a challenging but supportive supervision regime with linked exit strategies, so that participants are not 'set up to fail' by the imposition of unrealistic multiple demands;
  - Identifying and addressing the communications needs specific to the project, so that the aims and objectives of the project are widely understood and criticism about unfair priority and attention being given to 'undeserving' persistent offenders is constructively addressed.

In conclusion, we make the following key recommendations:

1. Projects working intensively with prolific offenders should be regarded as being of a maintenance nature, rather than a short, sharp intervention that acts as a cure-all. Accordingly they should be assessed on how

well they maintain participants during the 'on-project' period. Long-term assessment is a different but related issue and projects also need to be judged on how they affect participants over time – which might involve several relapses and returns to the project.

2. Consideration must be given to creating sustainable funding for these projects so that policy-makers, staff and participants can plan their futures with some degree of financial security.

3. As such projects are implemented more widely, care must be taken that they target offenders who are genuinely high-risk and persistent so that the effect of the project is not diluted, and less persistent or low-risk offenders are not caught inappropriately in the net as it widens.

Notes

1 The Home Office's preferred names for such projects are Intensive Supervision and Monitoring Projects for adult offenders and Intensive Supervision and Surveillance Programmes for young offenders. We continue to use the term 'Prolific Offender Projects' when referring to existing evaluations of projects that were so named.

2 In 1995 a prolific offending project involving both the police and probation services was established in Dordrecht, Holland. It purportedly reduced the number of domestic burglaries (by one-third) and became the inspiration behind a number of UK projects.

3 As Raynor and Vanstone (2002) have since noted, IMPACT did appear to work well with one particular group: those with low criminal tendencies who perceived themselves to have many problems – offenders who might now be described as 'low-risk, high-need'.

4 The official national definition of an adult *persistent* offender is now one who has been convicted of six recordable offences in a 12-month rolling period (which could include six offences on one occasion). The Home Office estimated there to be 33,500 adult persistent offenders in England and Wales in 2003 (Home Office 2003). A *prolific* offender may be so defined on the basis of local intelligence. A *persistent young offender* is a young person aged 10–17 years inclusive who has been sentenced by any criminal court in the UK on three or more separate occasions for one or more recordable offences, and within three years of the last sentencing occasion is subsequently arrested or has information laid against him [*sic*] for a further recordable offence. All these definitions are contested and run the risk of net-widening (see Hagell and Newburn 1994; Soothill *et al.* 2003: 391–393).

5 It should be noted, however, that offenders serving prison sentences may also be included as project 'participants', which raises particular questions. While recognising the wish of workers to have their preparatory work with prisoners acknowledged, it is very difficult to evaluate the impact of the project on offenders whose behaviour and attitudes will be shaped far more by their prison environment.

6 It is important to make the distinction between these project-specific MAPAMs and the different multi-agency public protection arrangements – MAPPAs. The latter arise from the Criminal Justice and Courts Services Act 2000 and are concerned with establishing arrangements (the MAPPAs) to assess and manage the risks posed by sexual and violent offenders.
7 See also Moore (2004) for a discussion of the evidence base in relation to successful intensive projects for young offenders.
8 A comparison group of offenders was formed which matched participants 'like-for-like' with other prolific offenders in order to rule out differences between the groups other than presence on the project.
9 The evaluation considered re-offending in terms of offences 'officially processed or admitted' (Chenery and Pease 2000: 35).
10 The criterion used for judging the strength of these effects (i.e. differences before and after admission) was the t-test statistic, which has attached to it a statement of probability about the result – e.g. a 'p' value. In interpreting these, it may be helpful to say that a difference of $p < .089$ means that the probability of achieving this result by chance is (only) 8.9 in 100.
11 A forerunner of the national ISSP programme based in Kent has been evaluated. Little *et al.* (2004) report that reconviction rates were unaffected by the intervention, but there was a reduction in the volume of crime committed by those participants who re-offended.
12 Earlier research by West (1963) made the similar finding that some 'habitual prisoners' could maintain crime-free gaps that were fuelled by supportive social environments. He termed these 'inadequates', as opposed to the 'aggressives' who were unlikely to respond to external support. More recently Piquero has reviewed the concept of intermittency 'or the observation of temporary suspensions from criminal activity' and its current lack of theoretical explanation (2004: 103).

References

Audit Commission (2004) *Youth Justice: A review of the reformed youth justice system* (www.audit-commission.gov.uk/reports).

Blunkett, D. (2004) *Reducing Crime – Changing Lives: The government's plans for transforming the management of offenders* (London: Home Office).

Bottoms, A. E. (1995) *Intensive Community Supervision for Young Offenders: Outcomes, process and cost* (Cambridge: Institute of Criminology Publications).

Bottoms, A. E. (2001) 'Compliance and community penalties', in A. E. Bottoms, L. Gelsthorpe and S. Rex (eds) *Community Penalties: Change and challenges* (Cullompton: Willan).

Carter, P. (2003) *Managing Offenders, Reducing Crime: A new approach* (London: Home Office).

Chenery, S. and Pease, K. (2000) 'The Burnley/Dordrecht Initiative Final Report' (University of Huddersfield/ Safer Cities Partnership: Burnley, unpublished).

Clear, T. R. (1997) 'Evaluating intensive probation: the American experience', in G. Mair (ed.) *Evaluating the Effectiveness of Community Penalties* (Aldershot: Avebury).

Criminal Justice Chief Inspectors' Group (2004) *Joint Inspection into Persistent and Prolific Offenders* (London: Home Office Communications Directorate).

Farrall, S. (2002) *Rethinking What Works With Offenders* (Cullompton: Willan).

Farrall, S., Mawby, R.C. and Worrall, A. (forthcoming) 'Persistent offenders and desistance', in L. Gelsthorpe and R. Morgan (eds) *Handbook of Probation* (Cullompton: Willan).

Folkard, M. S., Fowles, A. J., McWilliams, B. C., Smith, D. D., Smith, D. E and Walmsley, G. R. (1974) *IMPACT: Intensive Matched Probation and After-Care Treatment*, Home Office Research Study 24 (London: HMSO).

Folkard, M. S., Smith, D. E and Smith, D. D. (1976) *IMPACT: Intensive Matched Probation and After-Care Treatment*, Home Office Research Study 36 (London: HMSO).

Goldson, B. (ed.) (2000) *The New Youth Justice* (Lyme Regis: Russell House Publishing).

Green, D. G., Grove, E. and Martin, N. A. (2004) *How Can the Criminal Justice System Reduce the Criminal Activities of Known Offenders?* (www.civitas.org.uk/pdf/CivitasRCP_Report.pdf).

Hagell, A. and Newburn, T. (1994) *Persistent Young Offenders* (London: Policy Studies Institute).

Home Office (1988a) *Punishment, Custody and the Community*, Cm. 424 (London: HMSO).

Home Office (1988b) *Tackling Offending: An Action Plan* (London: HMSO).

Home Office (2001) *Criminal Justice: The Way Ahead* (London: HMSO).

Home Office (2002) *Narrowing the Justice Gap* (London: HMSO).

Home Office (2003) *Narrowing the Justice Gap and the Persistent Offender Scheme*, National Probation Service Briefing, Issue 14, July 2003 (London: Home Office).

Hope, T., Worrall, A., Dunkerton, L. and Leacock, V. (2001) *The Newcastle Prolific Offenders Project Final Evaluation Report* (Keele University/ Staffordshire Probation Area, unpublished).

Jones, P. (2002) 'The Halliday Report and persistent offenders', in S. Rex and M. Tonry (eds) *Reform and Punishment: The Future of Sentencing* (Cullompton: Willan).

Little, M., Kogan, J., Bullock, R. and van der Laan, P. (2004) 'ISSP: An experiment in multi-systemic responses to persistent young offenders known to children's services', *British Journal of Criminology*, 44(2), 225–240.

Lobley, D. and Smith, D. (1999) *Working with Persistent Juvenile Offenders: An Evaluation of the APEX Cue Ten Project* (Edinburgh: The Scottish Office Central Research Unit).

Lobley, D., Smith, D. and Stern, C. (2001) *Freagarrach: An evaluation of a project for persistent juvenile offenders* (Edinburgh: The Scottish Office Central Research Unit).

Mair, G. (1997) 'Evaluating intensive probation', in G. Mair (ed.) *Evaluating the Effectiveness of Community Penalties* (Aldershot: Avebury), pp. 64–77.

Mair, G., Lloyd, C., Nee, C. and Sibbitt, R. (1994) *Intensive Probation in England and Wales: An evaluation*, Home Office Research Study 133 (London: Home Office).

Martinson, R. (1974) 'What works? Questions and answers about prison reform', *Public Interest*, 35, 22–54.

Maruna, S. (2001) *Making Good: How ex-convicts reform and rebuild their lives* (Washington, DC: American Psychological Association).

Maruna, S and Immarigeon, R. (eds) (2004) *After Crime and Punishment: Pathways to offender integration* (Cullompton: Willan).

Mawby, R. C. and Worrall, A. (2004) '"Polibation" revisited: policing, probation and prolific offender projects', *International Journal of Police Science and Management*, 6(2), 63–73.

McNeill, F. and Batchelor, S. (2002) 'Chaos, containment and change: responding to persistent offending by young people', *Youth Justice*, 2(1), 27–43.

McNeill, F. and Batchelor, S. (2004) *Persistent Offending by Young People: Developing practice*, ICCJ Monograph 3 (London: NAPO).

Merrington, S. and Stanley, S. (2004) 'What works?: revisiting the evidence in England and Wales', *Probation Journal*, 51(1), 7–20.

Moore, R. (2004) 'Intensive supervision and surveillance programmes for young offenders: the evidence base so far', in R. Burnett and C. Roberts (eds) *What Works in Probation and Youth Justice: Developing evidence-based practice* (Cullompton: Willan).

Nash, M. (1999). 'Enter the "polibation officer"', *International Journal of Police Science and Management*, 1(4), 360–368.

Nash, M. (2004) 'Polibation revisited – a reply to Mawby and Worrall', *International Journal of Police Science and Management*, 6(2), 74–76.

Piquero, A. R. (2004) 'Somewhere between persistence and desistance: the intermittency of criminal careers', in S. Maruna and R. Immarigeon (eds) (2004) *After Crime and Punishment: Pathways to offender integration* (Cullompton: Willan), pp. 102–125.

Pitts, J. (1990) *Working with Young Offenders* (London: Macmillan).

Raynor, P. and Vanstone, M. (2002) *Understanding Community Penalties* (Buckingham: Open University Press).

Soothill, K., Ackerley, E. and Francis, B. (2003) 'The persistent offenders debate: a focus on temporal changes', *Criminal Justice*, 3(4), 389–412.

Staffordshire Probation Area (2001) *When the Carrot Meets the Stick* (Stafford: Staffordshire Probation Area).

West, D. (1963) *The Habitual Prisoner* (London: Macmillan).

Worrall, A. (1997) *Punishment in the Community: The future of criminal justice* (Harlow: Longman).

Worrall, A., Mawby, R. C., Heath, G. and Hope, T. (2003) *Intensive Supervision and Monitoring Projects*, Home Office Online Report 42/03 (London: Home Office).

Youth Justice Board (2004) *ISSP: The Initial Report* (London: Youth Justice Board).

Youth Justice Board (2003) *News*, Issue 20, December 2003.

Chapter 12

What guides sentencing decisions?

Martin Wasik

Introduction

In this chapter we examine sentence decision-making, a technically complex area of legal practice. The focus of the Coulsfield Inquiry is on 'Alternatives to Prison', and so the chapter will concentrate on sentencing decisions within and around the custody threshold. Such decisions are the most crucial, and probably the most difficult, which sentencers must make. Our discussion will be informed throughout not only by the legal constraints operational on sentencers, but also by what is known empirically about the process of sentence decision-making, and the impact of various extra-legal influences on sentencers. This chapter is mainly concerned with the position in England and Wales, but with some reference to developments elsewhere as appropriate. This chapter is written at a time when the legislative sentencing framework is in the process of change, as a result of gradual implementation of the Criminal Justice Act 2003, a process which will not be complete until 2007.

A recent report commissioned by the Prison Reform Trust (Hough *et al.* 2003) provides valuable insights in this area. The researchers examined sentencing in 'cusp' (i.e. borderline custody) cases. They found, in the majority of borderline cases which eventually resulted in *custody*, that the decision was driven by: the nature of the offence (i.e. it was so serious that no other sentence was possible), and/or by the offender's past convictions and failure to respond to previous sentences, which effectively ruled out the non-custodial options.

In contrast, in the borderline cases which eventually resulted in a *non-custodial* sentence, a wide range of issues might turn out to be relevant, including:

- the offender's response to prosecution (e.g. evidence of genuine remorse, or a timely guilty plea);
- the personal condition of the offender (e.g. medical or treatable psychiatric problems; a clear motivation to address underlying conditions such as dependency on drugs or drink, or violent tendencies; the offender's youth or old age);
- the personal situation of the offender (e.g. family responsibilities and relationships, employment status and accommodation); and
- the offender's criminal history (e.g. *no* previous convictions, or no *recent* previous convictions, or no *related* previous convictions).

These findings are consistent with the statutory sentencing framework laid down by Parliament in the Criminal Justice Act 1991 (consolidated in the Powers of Criminal Courts (Sentencing) Act 2000), and will remain broadly in line with the new framework introduced in the Criminal Justice Act 2003. The findings also reflect the structured decision-making set out in the sentencing guidelines of magistrates' courts' (Magistrates' Association 2003). These require that magistrates should consider first the seriousness of the offence,[1] second, relevant aggravating and mitigating features of the case, and third, adjustment of the sentence to take account of plea. We have known at least since the decision in *Cox* (1993) that offence seriousness may propel the offender over the threshold for an immediate custodial sentence, while personal mitigation may have the effect of pulling him back, and that principle is now confirmed in statute.[2] In this area of the sentencing hierarchy there are a number of 'alternatives', principally the suspended prison sentence, the community sentence and, perhaps, deferment of sentence. The organisation and content of these sentences are being changed significantly by the 2003 Act, but the threshold criterion of offence seriousness remains.

The context

The legal context for sentencing can be divided into the statutory framework and case law, especially sentencing guidelines. It is not the purpose of this chapter to provide a description of the existing provisions, or to describe their history and development. Such accounts can be found elsewhere (Ashworth 2000; Wasik 2001, 2004b). While sentencers have traditionally enjoyed a large measure of discretion in sentence selection, this has been much reduced in England and Wales (though not to the same extent in Scotland or Northern Ireland) in recent years. In England there has been a great deal of recent legislative intervention in sentencing, and increased formalisation of guidelines for sentencers. Thus far in

Scotland the legislative touch has been lighter, and guidelines are in their infancy.[3] Things may change, however, following the recent establishment of a sentencing commission in Scotland.

At one time the legislative role in sentencing was to prescribe maximum penalties, but otherwise to leave sentencers to get on with the job. Now, however, there is a legislative framework in place within which all sentencing must take place, and a host of detailed procedural and prescriptive rules with which sentencers must comply. Parliament has also required the development of comprehensive and broadly based guidelines for sentencers, first through the creation of the Sentencing Advisory Panel,[4] and now the Sentencing Guidelines Council.[5] A number of specific sentencing rules have been created, some of them highly politicised but poorly thought out. The worst examples have been the mandatory minimum sentences introduced in the Crime (Sentences) Act 1997. They include the 'three strikes rule' for residential burglars[6] and the soon-to-be-repealed 'automatic life for the second serious offence'.[7] The corrosive effects of the latter provision, described by Thomas as 'one of the most disastrous episodes in English penal history' (Thomas 2003), were stemmed only by an inventive interpretation of the section by the Court of Appeal in *Offen (No 2)* (2001), with Lord Woolf CJ calling in aid the European Convention of Human Rights. The relationship between the government and the judiciary over criminal justice matters has deteriorated markedly in recent years, and sentencing has often proved the main battleground. In the Criminal Justice Act 2003 the government has intervened directly again, by prescribing minimum sentences for firearms offences[8] (following media coverage of the shooting of two young women in Birmingham), and it has reacted to the decision of the House of Lords in *Anderson* (2003) that the Home Secretary's power to set tariffs for murderers contravened the fair trial provisions of the European Convention of Human Rights, by prescribing legislative starting points for minimum terms in murder cases.[9]

All these developments have, of course, taken place against the background of a continuing and unprecedented rise in the sentenced custodial population. More people are being sent to prison, and they are being sent to prison for longer periods of time. The use of imprisonment has doubled in the last ten years, despite there being no increase in the numbers of offenders dealt with by the courts over that period. The custody rate has risen from 5 per cent to 15 per cent in the magistrates' courts and from 45 per cent to 63 per cent in the Crown Court. It is important to note, however, that these increases have not been the result of a collapse of sentencer confidence in community sentences. The use of community sentences has also increased, by about 30 per cent over the same period. There has, at the same time, been a very significant decline in the use of the fine, down by about 20 per cent for indictable offences, but the fine remains comfortably the predominant sentencing disposal across the criminal courts.

Judges and magistrates must, of course, bear the prime responsibility for the escalation in the use of custody, but their behaviour cannot be seen in isolation from the political and media contexts, which have been relentlessly punitive. The Carter Report (2003) concluded recently that increased sentencing severity was the result of interaction between legislative and sentencing guideline changes, reduced sentencer confidence in fines, and the relation between public perception, media, politicians and sentencers. Maximum sentences are regularly adjusted by Parliament, almost always in an upward direction. There is an increasing trend for Parliament to legislate for minimum sentences, to prevent judges passing 'lenient' sentences. The legislative starting points for murder in the Criminal Justice Act 2003 are significantly higher than the judicial ones which preceded them. Parliament has signalled that murderers must be sentenced more severely than before, a change which seems to carry inevitable consequences for the sentencing of manslaughter, serious woundings, etc. Some of the sentencers responding in the Hough *et al.* Report (2003) stated that sentencing guidelines inevitably escalate sentencing levels. There is in fact no such inevitable link, but experience shows that there is pressure in this direction, for reasons which have been explored by the present author (Wasik 2004a).

Despite the issuing of a joint statement by the Home Secretary and Lord Chancellor in 2002, which urged the use of imprisonment only for 'violent, sexual and seriously persistent offenders' with greater use of community sentences for the rest, politicians on other occasions fuel public cynicism about community sentences. The furore over the burglary guidelines in *McInerney* (2003), in which the Court of Appeal endorsed the use of community sentences for a significant number of domestic burglary cases, provides a good example. Rather than using that judgment as an opportunity to provide positive endorsement of community sentences, politicians fell over themselves to distance themselves from, and in some cases to pillory, the Lord Chief Justice responsible for issuing the guidelines. The only exception to this was the Lord Chancellor who, on the *Today* programme on Radio 4, backed Lord Woolf's judgment and soon afterwards lost his job. There is now intense media criticism of any sentence popularly regarded as 'soft',[10] or for that matter reform proposals which suggest the use of any sentences other than custodial ones.[11]

Sentencers hear these messages, but they are also aware of the crisis in the prisons, and they receive directives from the Lord Chief Justice saying that they must not ignore the wider picture and should adjust their practices to alleviate overcrowding. It is no surprise that the research evidence shows sentencers to be confused about the changing political and policy scene (Hough *et al.* 2003), and what is required of them. Sentencers read of the apparent public thirst for ever more severe sentencing, but many are also aware of the public attitude studies of Hough and Roberts and others (e.g. Hough and Roberts 2002; Roberts

2002) which show that members of the public, when fully informed of the circumstances of the case, are no more punitive than the courts. Sentencers also see apparent confusion in Court of Appeal pronouncements. Lord Woolf's advocacy of community sentences for domestic burglary has often, in the press, been rather crudely compared with his Lordship's apparent recommendation of at least five years' imprisonment for theft of a mobile phone. This is, of course, a misrepresentation of both the burglary guidelines in *McInerney* and the 'mobile phone judgment' in the street robbery case of *Lobban* (2002).

The government's response to escalating numbers in custody has been, firstly, to build more prisons. Operational capacity of the prisons has been increased by over 50 per cent since 1992, but it still cannot keep up with the growth in the prison population. The second response has been to release many more offenders early. In particular, delegated legislation passed in 2002 (and since extended twice) provides for 'home detention curfew' (HDC) for prisoners serving sentences of between three months and one year, for up to 90 days before the date on which they would have otherwise have been released.[12] This now means that most short-sentence prisoners serve less than half of the sentence announced in court (and many of those nearer to one-quarter of their sentence), a deception of the public which will surely exacerbate the crisis of confidence in the system. Putting it crudely, a sentence of six months often[13] means six weeks served, a sentence of nine months means ten weeks served, and a sentence of 12 months means three months served (Thomas 2003). Release on HDC is at the discretion of the prison governor, the executive thereby undermining sentencing decisions and nullifying differences in sentence length intended by the sentencer to reflect different levels of involvement in the offence. Sentencers are of course aware of the likely impact of HDC, but have been instructed by the Court of Appeal in *Al-Buhairi* (2004) not to try to second-guess whether it will be granted in any particular case. This 'lottery' of short sentences has important implications for the custody threshold.

The elusive custody threshold

At the time of the Criminal Justice Act 1991 there was hope that the Court of Appeal might provide flesh on the bones of the Act's custody threshold criteria. Unfortunately, the Court at that time was more concerned with trying to turn opinion against the Act as a whole, arguing that it was a wholly unnecessary 'straitjacket' on judges, and it failed to seize the opportunity. Initially Lord Justice Lawton had espoused the notorious 'elephant' test for the custody threshold – that 'courts can recognise an elephant when they see one, but may not find it necessary to define it' (see Ashworth and von Hirsch 1997). More generally, according to the Lord

Justice, regard might be had by the sentencer to the views of 'right-thinking members of the public' to determine whether or not a case crossed the threshold (*Bradbourn* (1985), followed in *Cox* (1993)). A later decision, in *Howells* (1999), back-tracked on this earlier approach, and tried to improve upon it. In the end, however, *Howells* simply reiterated a number of well-known and rather general considerations about sentencing that are not specific enough for the purpose. In that case, Lord Bingham CJ declared that there was no 'clear bright line' between 'custody' and 'non-custody'. This is surely right, and it is unrealistic to expect that we could invent a legislative or judicial phrase to capture the equivalent of the 'in/out line' on the American sentencing grids.[14] Even so, progress must be made on this most crucial of all sentencing decisions. Even before the Sentencing Guidelines Council came into being, efforts were being made by the Court of Appeal and the Sentencing Advisory Panel working together to issue guidelines on lower-tariff, either-way offences which raise significant threshold issues and which involve consideration of community sentences. These guidelines include handling stolen goods in *Webbe* (2002), domestic burglary in *McInerney* (2003), child pornography offences in *Oliver* (2003) and offensive weapons offences in *Celaire* (2002). The Magistrates' Courts' Sentencing Guidelines (Magistrates' Association 2003) specify community sentence starting points for a wide range of offences.

A series of well-known Court of Appeal decisions, from *Bibi* (1980) through *Ollerenshaw* (1999) to *Kefford* (2002), contain general policy exhortations to sentencers to restrict their use of custody. While these cases are well known, they appear to have had little or no effect in halting the general sentencing trend in severity. The last-mentioned case, in which Lord Woolf CJ said that the Court's message was 'imprisonment only when necessary and for no longer than necessary' was presided over by three of the most senior judges of the Court of Appeal. It was obviously intended to lay down a marker in the clearest possible terms, and so is worthy of our attention. The offender, while working as a building society cashier, had stolen over £11,000 from customer accounts. The trial judge, following faithfully the guideline case of *Clarke* (1998) on theft in breach of trust, imposed a sentence of 12 months' imprisonment. A significant sum of money had been taken, through repetitive thefts, from customer accounts over a period of years. On considering the defendant's appeal against his sentence, however, the Court of Appeal said that the judge had given insufficient weight to the mitigating factors. The offender had a clean record, he had stopped offending of his own volition, he had pleaded guilty at the first opportunity, and he had repaid all the money. In light of these matters (all of which had been known to the trial judge), the Court of Appeal reduced the sentence to four months. Since the offender had already served three months in custody, this had the happy result of achieving his immediate release. The case was meant to have an impact on sentencing practice, but the Court of Appeal's message is regrettably not as clear as it might be.

The first point is that the guideline case of *Clarke* remains good law, the trial judge in *Kefford* simply having been corrected for giving insufficient weight to the personal mitigation. But in *Clarke* the appellate judges had clearly accepted that cases of theft in breach of trust routinely involve offenders of good character with clean records, which is why such people have been employed in those positions in the first place. The starting points in *Clarke* had already taken those factors into account. How, then, are sentencers meant to interpret *Clarke* in the light of *Kefford*? The second point is that the resulting sentence in *Kefford* was a short period of custody, rather than avoidance of custody altogether. A sentence of four months' imprisonment is just the kind of sentence which Lord Woolf CJ has, on other notable occasions, declared to be undesirable on the ground that such sentences give no chance for constructive work with the offender by the prison authorities. An important example of his Lordship's approach is the guideline case on sentencing for domestic burglary, *McInerney* (2003), which is discussed further below.

An offender like Kefford seems to require little in the way of correctional input. His lapse into dishonesty is unlikely to be repeated, given that he will surely never be re-employed in a position of trust. So, could he not have been dealt with by a top-end community disposal? If the Court of Appeal had taken that line, quashed the prison sentence and substituted, say, a community punishment order of 180 hours, the message to its judicial audience would have been much clearer. Their Lordships may have felt inhibited in doing so for other reasons. The Court is generally very reluctant to say that a sentencer who has sent someone to prison for as long as 12 months has 'erred in principle'[15] in doing so. Such a statement would unfairly undermine the sentencing judge (who, in *Kefford*, had applied the guidelines properly). It might also open up the possibility of the offender applying for compensation from the state for wrongful imprisonment. These seem to be the reasons why a pattern has developed of the Court adjusting sentence in such cases so as to effect the offender's immediate release.[16] A further reason for the Court not going so far is that to have done so would probably have required a full reconsideration of the guideline case of *Clarke*, which could not have been done without first referring the matter to the Sentencing Advisory Panel.[17]

Limiting the use of shorter sentences

In *McInerney* (2003), a sentencing appeal by a defendant convicted of a domestic burglary, the Court of Appeal had opportunity to consider the advice of the Sentencing Advisory Panel. The Panel had proposed four starting points for the offence, when committed by a first-time domestic burglar, and depending on the relative seriousness of the facts: (a) a community sentence for a 'low-level' burglary, (b) nine months' custody for a 'standard' burglary, (c) 12 months' custody for a 'standard burglary with one or more medium relevance aggravating factors', and (d) 18 months' custody for a 'standard burglary with one or more high relevance aggravating factors'. The Panel's adoption of this scale had been heavily influenced by the legislative provision requiring imposition of a sentence of at least three years' imprisonment for the third residential burglary (exceptional circumstances apart). Under the Panel's advice, repetition of burglary would, at each level, have led to a stepped increase in sentence, to three years at level (a) or (b) for the third burglary, 42 months at level (c) and 54 months at level (d). The Court of Appeal, while endorsing much of the Panel's general approach, and all the recommended aggravating and mitigating factors, preferred lower starting points for first-time (and some second-time) burglars. Lord Woolf CJ stated that:

> [T]he Prison Service accepts that there is little it can achieve in the way of turning offenders away from crime during the course of a sentence of up to 12 months . . . We fully accept that there are some cases where the clang of the prison cell door for the first time may have a deterrent effect but the statistics of re-offending suggest that the numbers who will be deterred by their first experience of incarceration are not substantial. If they are not deterred by their first period of incarceration, then it becomes even less likely that a moderately longer sentence (which equally gives no opportunity for tackling re-offending behaviour) will achieve anything. We therefore have reservations about a ladder of increasing seriousness with starting points of nine, 12 and 18 months.

The Court of Appeal agreed with the starting point of a community sentence at level (a), and a starting point of 18 months' custody at level (d), but approved a community sentence starting point at levels (b) and (c).

An important implication of this decision is that, since short sentences are now generally recognised as being largely ineffective, the custody threshold should be raised in an effort to restrict their use. If, for the sake of argument, the imposition of sentences under 12 months are seen generally not to work in deterrent or rehabilitative terms, the custody threshold should in effect be raised to 12 months. This is one area of sentencing policy in which a fair measure of agreement exists between the government and the higher judiciary. The government accepted the same arguments as to the ineffectiveness of short custodial sentences, as presented to them in 2001 in the Halliday Report. Halliday stated that 'one of the most important deficiencies in the present framework is the lack of utility in short prison sentences . . . the sentence is used for large numbers of persistent offenders with multiple problems and high risks of reoffending ... A more effective recipe for failure could hardly be conceived ...' (Halliday 2001, para 3.1). The new design for custodial sentences under 12 months in the Criminal Justice Act 2003 reflects this. Central to the new arrangements (when brought into force in 2005 or 2006) will be a new sentence of 'custody plus', designed to have a short period served in custody and a longer period of structured supervision in the community. This contrasts with the current position in which release from shorter sentences (under 12 months) is automatic at the half-way point (or earlier, on home detention curfew) with little subsequent contact with the offender in the community. Custody plus will have a significant impact on the sentencing powers of adult magistrates' courts. They will be prevented from imposing custody plus for less than 28 weeks at the same time as their current upper limit of six months for a single offence will be doubled to 51 weeks.[18] Custody plus must comprise a *custodial period* (of at least two weeks and not more than 13 weeks) together with a *licence period* of at least 26 weeks. The court may write into the licence period one or more of a wide range of requirements with which the offender must comply. The total term of a custody plus sentence cannot exceed 51 weeks. This means that if the custodial period was set at the minimum of two weeks, the licence period could be set at any period between 26 and 49 weeks. If the custodial period was set at 13 weeks, the licence period could be set at any period between 26 weeks and 38 weeks. It has been said that custody plus will effectively take away the power of magistrates (and, for that matter, the Crown Court) to impose custodial sentences of less than six months (Gibson 2004). What it will clearly do is to take away from the courts the power to pass 'simple' short terms of imprisonment. Under custody plus the courts will still be able to require offenders to serve prison time of between two and 13 weeks, but this will always be associated with lengthy periods of supervision in the community (bringing the total term to at least 26 weeks but not more than 51 weeks), never as a stand-alone punishment. The question for sentencers will then become: given the restrictive and onerous nature of the community requirements of at least 26 weeks which come with a short custodial term, would not a community sentence with appropriate requirements do the job just as well? The issue will be especially acute if the defendant has already spent some time on remand in custody which generally should be deducted[20] for the custodial element of the custody plus sentence.

Custody threshold and the guilty plea

The sentencing conventions related to the discount for guilty plea are in practice the most important sentencing provisions of all. It is well established that a guilty plea has the effect of reducing a custodial sentence by an amount between one-third and one-fifth, depending on the stage at which the plea was tendered (the earlier the better) and the circumstances in which the plea was tendered (a low discount is given if, for example, the offender was caught 'red-handed' and in reality has little option but to plead guilty).[21] Sentencers are required by statute to take these matters into account, and to state in open court that they have taken account of them.[22] Almost all the discussion about the guilty plea discount relates to reduction in length of custodial sentences. It remains unclear how far a timely guilty plea (whether on its own, or in combination with personal mitigation) can rescue an offender from what otherwise would have been a custodial sentence. Common sense would suggest that there must be such cases (perhaps many of them), and the Hough *et al.* (2003) analysis appears to confirm it. There is no clear judicial statement on the point.[23] The Sentencing Advisory Panel (2004b) has recently proposed that the Sentencing Guidelines Council issue guidelines on reduction for guilty plea. It is proposed that sentencers should indicate what the sentence would have been, without reduction for the guilty plea. It is also proposed that a guilty plea should affect the punitive (but not the rehabilitative) requirements in a community sentence as well as the custodial sentences and fines.

The role of the guilty plea in the custody threshold could be extremely important, not least because of the indirectly discriminatory effect of plea. It was shown by Hood in his study of sentencing in West Midlands Crown Courts (Hood 1992) that a significant amount of the differential in sentencing between black and white offenders is due to the greater reluctance of black defendants to plead guilty. This is one of the most important effects of racial discrimination within sentencing. The discount for guilty plea, whatever its considerable system-based advantages in saving time and expense, has an indirectly discriminatory effect on defendants who prefer to have their day in court and take their chances before a jury rather than admitting guilt at the first opportunity.

Custody threshold and criminal record

There is a long-standing controversy over the relevance of criminal record to sentence decision-making (Wasik and von Hirsch 1994; von Hirsch 2002). Sentencers are always required to have regard to the offender's criminal record and his or her 'failures to respond'. Desert theorists have developed the principle of 'progressive loss of mitigation', by which the key driver for sentence is the seriousness of the latest offence, rather than the number of times the offender has been in trouble in the past. Utilitarians, whether for reasons of deterrence, public protection, or simply giving the public a period of respite from persistent lawbreaking, advocate progressively harsher punishment for repeat offenders. Such 'cumulative sentencing' can soon result in a sentence grossly disproportionate to the seriousness of the latest offence, while the desert approach insists on a 'ceiling' based on seriousness of that crime. Halliday took the line that repetition of offending justified progressively harsher punishment, although his rationale is unclear. The Criminal Justice Act 2003 reflects the Halliday approach, although the relevant provision leaves the sentencing courts with room for manoeuvre. Section 143(2) of the 2003 Act, when brought into force, states that:

> In considering the seriousness of an offence ('the current offence') committed by an offender who has one or more previous convictions, the court must treat each previous conviction as an aggravating factor if (in the case of that conviction) the court considers that it can reasonably be so treated having regard, in particular, to:
> (a) the nature of the offence to which the conviction relates and its relevance to the current offence, and
> (b) the time that has elapsed since the conviction.

It is assumed by most commentators that, once this provision is in force, there will be enhanced 'sentencing on the record' and a consequent steep rise in the incarceration rate for persistent offenders. The provision is not due to be brought into force until 2005/6. The prison population is forecast to continue to outstrip available places for some years to come, so there is still time for political pressure to mount, and for the government to have second thoughts. It would not be the first time that a government has produced 'tough' sentencing legislation and then quietly repealed it without ever bringing it into force. If the sub-section does become law, however, much will then depend on the way in which the Sentencing Guidelines Council (advised by the Panel) chooses to interpret it. At one extreme, sentencing guidelines might reflect the differential criminal records of offenders in a clearly stepped manner reminiscent of the American sentencing guideline grids. If so interpreted, it seems obvious that this would involve a further sharp escalation in the use of imprisonment. At the other extreme, the Council may simply take the view that the provision is flexible enough to make little difference to existing sentencing practice.

As with the guilty plea discount, most of the discussion about the relevance of record has been confined to its impact on custodial sentences, and there has been little attention to the relevance of record to community sentences. If we take section 143(2) at face value it is clear that some offenders with records will, simply by virtue of that record, be disqualified from any community sentence. Their persistence alone will take them over the custody threshold. For other offenders, the existence of a record (and hence a history of failure) will further complicate the balance between the 'suitability' and 'proportionality' requirements of the generic community sentence (see later section for details). Take, for example, the use of drug treatment and testing orders. The courts often encounter cases in which the background to the offence is the offender's dependency on drugs. While this will not be regarded as a matter making the offence itself less serious,[24] it may form the basis of an argument that a non-custodial sentence designed to address that underlying condition, such as a drug treatment and testing order, might be preferred. Many sentencers are known to be enthusiastic about the use of drug treatment and testing orders, although evidence of their actual effectiveness is as yet unclear (see Chapter 10, this volume). These orders are designed for use on offenders who are developing, or have developed, a pattern of drug-related offending. Some decisions of the Court of Appeal, therefore, urge sentencers to 'take chances', and to be prepared to try drug treatment and testing orders on offenders with substantial (and quite serious) records of property offending. An example is *Kelly* (2003), in which the Court of Appeal quashed a sentence of 42 months' imprisonment for burglary and other offences of dishonesty on an offender with a large number of similar previous convictions. Field J observed that the sentencing judge's view, that the totality of offending in this case was too great for a drug treatment and testing order, was incorrect. It was often the case that candidates for such a sentence had been guilty of acquisitive offending on a significant scale to fund their addiction. The Court of Appeal substituted a drug treatment and testing order for 12 months.

The most comprehensive guidance on this issue came in December 2003 where, in *Attorney-General's Reference (No 64 of 2003)* (2003), Lord Justice Rose tried to steer a middle course. His Lordship stated that drug treatment and testing orders were 'targeted at persistent offenders of high level criminality . . . the order gave an opportunity to divert offenders from prison and receive appropriate treatment if the sentencer was satisfied of the offender's propensity to misuse drugs'. The drug treatment and testing order was appropriate for an acquisitive offence used to obtain money for drugs, even if a substantial number of offences had been committed by the offender; but it would be rare for an order to be appropriate if there had been an offence involving serious violence. On the facts of the appeal itself, where the offender had pleaded guilty to offences of burglary and aggravated burglary (committed in breach of licence, and involving intimidation of householders at night with the use of a knife), the sentence was unduly lenient. The proper sentence would have been six years' imprisonment.[25] The enormous divergence in sentence between what was thought to be appropriate by the original sentencer, and by the Court of Appeal, is remarkable.

Custody threshold and personal mitigation

Section 166(1) of the Criminal Justice Act 2003 states that nothing shall prevent a court 'from mitigating an offender's sentence by taking into account any such matters as, in the opinion of the court, are relevant in mitigation of sentence'. Personal mitigation may, in an appropriate case, have a powerful effect on sentence, but since such matters fall within the court's discretion, they can be ignored for reasons of public policy. For the most serious offences such as rape,[26] there is little scope for arguments based on personal mitigation. Two of the most important matters of personal mitigation are good character and clean record, but these were said in *Aramah* (1982) to be largely irrelevant when sentencing drug couriers, since it is generally such people who are targeted and recruited to perform that role.

'Good character' basically means an absence of previous convictions, but sometimes sentencers will stretch a point and treat offenders as being of good character if they are only lightly convicted. Mitigation will be stronger, according to Lord Bingham CJ in *Howells* (1999), 'if there is evidence of positive good character (such as a solid employment record or faithful discharge of family duties) as opposed to a mere absence of previous convictions'. In *Clark* (1999), a six-month sentence for a series of frauds was reduced to one week because of the offender's voluntary service to the local community and the fact that she had brought up four motherless nephews and nieces. Personal mitigation of this sort introduces an element of unpredictability into sentencing, and raises the issue of whether success in one's domestic relations is really relevant to the commission of frauds at work. The reverse inference was at work in *Attorney-General's Reference (No 22 of 2002)* (2002), where the trial judge had originally imposed a community rehabilitation order on an offender who had subjected his wife to a violent assault from which she suffered rib fractures and a collapsed lung. The Court of Appeal said that the sentencer had been right to have regard to the man's 'quite outstanding career of public service' and the fact that he had won the George Medal for bravery, but sentence was nonetheless increased to a prison term of six months. Should a defendant's achievements in the public sphere be relevant to offences committed in his domestic life?

Although the Court of Appeal has said that sentencing should be even-handed as between men and women who have committed the same offence,[27] it is well known that the pattern of sentencing disposals of men and women differs markedly. One reason for this is the availability to women of certain matters of personal mitigation which are generally less open to men. In *Mills* (2002), for example, the Court of Appeal observed that when sentencing for an offence of dishonesty a woman of previous good character who was the mother of two young children, the court must bear in mind the consequences to those children if the sole carer was sent to prison. The remarks were made in the context of a crisis of overcrowding in women's prisons, but decisions to the same effect, made at less acute times, can be found.[28] Such cases create a situation of indirect discrimination, since women are more likely to find themselves in the situation of sole carers.[29]

Loss of employment is another factor sometimes urged in mitigation of sentence, particularly as a reason for avoiding a custodial sentence. The argument may be that the offender's good employment record is in itself a reason for passing a more lenient sentence, or it may be that the imprisonment of the owner of a small business would cause other people to lose their jobs.[30] To the extent that unemployment rates are higher among black offenders than white offenders, this sentencing principle inevitably has a indirect discriminatory effect. In *Baldwin* (2002), the offender pleaded guilty to conspiracy to supplying cannabis resin and being involved in the supply of amphetamine sulphate. The Court of Appeal quashed the original sentence of two years' imprisonment, reduced the term so as to allow the offender's immediate release,[31] and added to it a fine of £5,000.[32] The main reason advanced by Lord Woolf CJ for changing the sentence was that, in view of current prison overcrowding, it would be preferable for sentencers to impose a fine rather than imprisonment on an offender who could gain steady employment and live a useful life in the community.

The nature of these issues may change when intermittent custody (another development in the Criminal Justice Act 2003) is brought fully into effect. This is a new form of prison sentence of less than 12 months, to be used for offences which have crossed the custody threshold, as an alternative to full-time custody.[33] The prison sentence is interspersed by periods when the offender is released on temporary licence in the community, and the court may impose additional requirements to be fulfilled during the licence period. The offender must consent to serving the sentence intermittently. At present, intermittent custody is being piloted in a number of court areas. Guidance from the Department of Constitutional Affairs suggests[34] that this form of custody might be especially suitable for the employed (who can serve their sentences at weekends), for carers, or for those in full-time education. In principle, intermittent custody is simply a different way of serving a custodial sentence and will make that custody less disruptive to work, family or educational commitments. The problem, however, is that the new sentence can provide a means of imprisoning offenders who formerly benefited from the personal mitigation described above, and received a community sentence. While this would reduce the element of indirect discrimination, it is presumably not what Parliament intended.

Community sentence

The current legal 'threshold' tests, derived from the Criminal Justice Act 1991, are preserved (with some minor changes of wording) in the Criminal Justice Act 2003. They require the sentencer to ask whether the offence is 'serious enough' to justify a community sentence (Criminal Justice Act 2003, s.140(1)), but not 'so serious' that only custody can be justified (Criminal Justice Act 2003, s.144(2)). If, on application of these tests, a community disposal is found to be the appropriate disposal, the sentencer must ensure that the selected community sentence is 'the most suitable for the offender' but, at the same time, ensure that the restrictions imposed by the order 'are commensurate with the seriousness of the offence' (Criminal Justice Act 2003, s.140(2)). The language of community sentences as 'alternatives' to custody is not, and never has been, reflected in the English sentencing framework. It is certainly possible to accommodate community sentencing within a broad framework of proportionality (see Wasik and von Hirsch 1988), and at least since the 1991 Act community sentences have been regarded as forms of 'punishment in the community', carrying different degrees of restriction on liberty as well as differing utilitarian goals. It should also be noted that the requirement that a defendant should consent to a community disposal, which was once common, has since the Crime (Sentences) Act 1997 been restricted to a small group of orders/requirements.

The next phase in the development of community sentences will be the introduction by the 2003 Act, for offenders aged over 16, of the generic 'community sentence'. When the relevant provisions of the Act are brought into force (now expected to be Spring 2005), a sentencing court imposing a community sentence will include in that sentence one or more requirements taken from a menu set out in section 177 of the Act. These requirements include the performance of unpaid work, curfew, exclusion, drug treatment and testing, etc., which obviously reflect what were formerly the individual orders of community punishment, curfew, exclusion, drug treatment and testing, etc. Under these arrangements the sentencer will pass a 'community sentence', a plainly wrapped parcel which may contain any one or a number of the specified requirements. The background to this development is set out in the Halliday Report (Halliday 2001). Halliday noted that the 'proliferation of new community sentences' had increased sentencing complexity. It is true that the multiplicity of existing community orders has meant that there is much legislative repetition across the various provisions. The creation of the generic order will provide an opportunity to simplify matters. To take just one example, there is a provision to the effect that the offender's sentence in the community must not interfere with the offender's religious observations, or his schooling or work commitments. This currently appears in sentencing legislation in identical wording at least 13 separate times.[35] The creation of the generic sentence will mean that this provision need appear only once.[36]

While there is value in tidying up and simplifying the arrangements for community sentences, the broader policy implications of the generic order are much less clear. Hough *et al.* (2003) found little dissatisfaction among sentencers with the existing range of community sentences. Several respondents said that there had been too many recent changes to community sentencing, and asked for a moratorium on new initiatives. Some of those who thought that there was room for new community alternatives suggested powers which were, in fact, already available to them. The new 'community sentence' is a bland and imprecise description which tells us little. This is a disadvantage since, as Rex (2002) has observed, 'the public, and offenders, seem more likely to understand what an order means when its name describes the activity involved'. Halliday claimed that the proliferation of new community sentences had increased inconsistency of sentencing. That may be true and, on the surface, the generic community sentence will make community sentencing more uniform. But merely to give all community sentences the same *name* of course does not improve consistency since these apparently similar packages will have widely differing contents. Although Halliday stressed that the 'punitive weight' of a given community sentence would require the chosen ingredients to be selected with care, there is an obvious risk that sentencers will over-use their 'shopping list' of requirements in their efforts to find 'suitability' in a community sentence, losing sight of the 'commensurate with seriousness' requirement. There is a further risk with the more uniform 'generic' community sentence. Sentencers may in future tend to use the 'community sentence' only once in an offender's criminal career ('we've tried that already and it failed') rather than, as at present, trying two or three different *forms* of community sentences before deciding that custody has become inevitable.

The White Paper *Justice for All* (Home Office 2002) stated that the new generic community sentence would be 'more demanding' and 'tougher' than community orders have previously been. If this is to be reality rather than just rhetoric, it will probably mean that breach rates will increase, with consequent impact on the prison population. Halliday also proposed that there should be increased use of community sentence and fine in combination. A complex community order, with diverse requirements, and perhaps with additional penalties (not to mention ancillary matters, such as compensation orders) provides opportunities for breach. An often-overlooked provision in the 2000 Act, which is meant to remind the court that when adding sentences together it should not lose sight of the 'totality principle' (the overall severity of the punishment), has been re-enacted in the 2003 Act.[37] The section states that 'nothing prevents' the court from reducing one element in the sentence when adding a second element to it. It is doubtful whether this provides an effective brake on sentencing. There ought to be an obligation on the court to ensure that the total combined sentence is not disproportionate to the offending.

Suspended sentence and deferred sentence

The existing version of the 'suspended sentence' has largely fallen into disuse since the requirement imposed by the Criminal Justice Act 1991 that it be used only in 'exceptional circumstances'. The case law on the meaning of 'exceptional circumstances' in this context is arcane, and the Court of Appeal has been able to offer only a few indications of what would *not* amount to 'exceptional' (*Okinikan* 1993). Practitioners have for years been calling for the reinstatement of the suspended sentence, but there has always been a fundamental problem with it. Although formally categorised as a 'custodial sentence', it imposes no requirements on the offender save that of refraining from re-offending during the operational period of the sentence. Its rationale is that of individual deterrence, since commission of a further offence carries the strong presumption that the full term of the suspended sentence will be activated, to run consecutively to the sentence imposed for the new offence. The suspended sentence is abolished by the Criminal Justice Act 2003. Its replacement, as proposed by Halliday, was to be called 'custody minus' but, under the 2003 Act, this name has been dropped (perhaps it did not sound tough enough) and it simply becomes a new form of 'suspended sentence'.

The sentencing court may pass a sentence of imprisonment for a fixed period (minimum 28 weeks, maximum 51 weeks), and suspend that sentence for the operational period of between six months and two years. The crucial difference with the new suspended sentence is that during the whole (or specified part) of the operational period the court may require that the offender comply with one or more requirements (from a menu in section 190 identical to the requirements which can be included within a community sentence). The new suspended sentence thus has two triggers for breach, rather than one: the commission of a further offence, and the failure to comply with a requirement in the order. The term of imprisonment to be served in consequence of breach is set by the judge when the suspended sentence is passed.

In principle, the new suspended sentence should fit above the custody threshold but just below sentences of immediate imprisonment (and intermittent custody) in the sentencing hierarchy. If the suspended sentence is not deployed very carefully, it can have the effect of increasing the custodial population rather than reducing it. New guidelines must draw upon lessons learned and case-law developed since the 1970s, which has established that a suspended sentence must be passed only when a custodial sentence is otherwise clearly justified, and that the length of the term suspended must be no greater than the length of the immediate term.[38] Guidance from the Sentencing Guidelines Council is required urgently to ensure that all the well-known pitfalls with suspended sentences are avoided this time around (Sparks 1971; Bottoms 1981). Also, some flexibility must be built into the breach provisions, so as to allow the breach court to avoid full activation of the suspended sentence when a new offence committed by the offender is minor, and/or committed near the end of the operational period, or when there has been minor breach of the community requirements. Clearly, the new-style suspended sentence will look much more like the community sentence than it did before. The same community requirements can be written into each, and custody will in each case be a likely sanction for breach.

Deferment of sentence has in the past been a measure used for a specific and narrow purpose. The court has been able to defer passing sentence on an offender for a period of up to six months, to assess the impact on that offender of an impending change of circumstances. Typically, a court might wish to reconsider the matter in light of the offender's voluntary desistance from drugs or drink, or the commencement of employment, or signs of settling down in a new relationship. If the offender responds positively to the opportunity of the deferment, and keeps out of trouble, a lenient disposal is the likely outcome. Deferment has been seen as a useful sentencing option, to be used only occasionally, where circumstances appear promising. Guidance issued by the Court of Appeal in *George* (1984) covers some important procedural safeguards, such as ensuring that the case comes back whenever possible before the same sentencer. The Criminal Justice Act 2003 changes the nature of deferment of sentence, by permitting the court to impose any conditions during the period of deferment that it considers appropriate.[39] These conditions may be the familiar community order requirements adapted for this purpose, or they may be more broadly drawn. Deferment could then function in a manner akin to the community sentence, but with fewer procedural safeguards, and with no real indication of where in the sentencing hierarchy it should come. This measure has the potential to be a loose cannon, and guidelines will be required in advance of implementation to limit the potential scope of deferment. It is suggested that deferment of sentence is appropriate only in a small group of cases, when there is a clear and specific reason for deferral. The offender should, at the time of deferral, know exactly what is being required and, when the matter comes back to court, the same sentencer should whenever possible deal with the matter and have full information on the offender's behaviour to assess compliance.

Conclusion

Unfortunately, now is about the worst time at which to give a balanced and informed assessment of what guides sentencing decisions within and around the custody threshold. The applicable sentencing provisions have been relatively well settled since the 1991 Act, although they have lacked the clarity and precision which would have assisted consistency in outcome. The legislative framework is now undergoing substantial change through the introduction of new custodial sentences, a new structure for community sentences, and some re-shaping of key sentencing principles, such as the relevance of criminal record. The Criminal Justice Act 2003 is being brought into force over a span of several years with (oddly enough) the general sentencing principles being held back until the end. These legislative changes take place against the background of a crisis in the custodial population, which recently hit another all-time high of 75,000 (this figure includes remand as well as sentenced prisoners). It seems that there is little political credit to be gained from trying to tackle this appalling problem. Prison overcrowding is nowhere to be seen in the list of voter concerns approaching an election year. Politically, the issue is best left alone, for fear of appearing 'soft on crime' to political opponents and to the electorate.

Yet there are some real opportunities within the 2003 Act for a de-escalation in the use of custody. There is a legislative squeeze on shorter custodial sentences, and that should translate into greater use of community-based provision, provided that this is funded to the high level which will inevitably be required to accommodate the new sentences under 12 months, especially for 'custody-plus'. The suspended sentence is likely to be popular with sentencers and, provided that it is used in accordance with guidelines, should have a noticeable impact on the use of immediate custody. There may be some scope for reduction in the length of custodial sentences, given that requirements after release will be more onerous and longer-lasting than before, but that argument is weakened by the increased use of home detention curfew. The opportunities exist, but the political messages are, regrettably, mixed. During the passage of the Bill through Parliament, the government played down the community sentence message, and stressed instead minimum custodial sentences for firearms offences and minimum terms for those convicted of murder. Great store has been placed on the Sentencing Guidelines Council to weave a coherent pattern from all of these disparate changes, and to issue coherent and comprehensive guidelines for the criminal courts.[40] The Council has an enormous task ahead of it.

Notes

1 And, in principle, the risk posed by the offender, but that issue is much less important in the magistrates' courts (which are currently limited to a maximum of six months' imprisonment) than in the Crown Court.
2 Criminal Justice Act 2003, s.166(2).
3 See *Du Plooy* (2003), where the High Court of Justiciary issued guidelines on the basis for, and scope of, a reduction in sentence for a guilty plea.
4 Crime and Disorder Act 1998, ss. 80 and 81; Criminal Justice Act 2003, s.169.
5 Criminal Justice Act 2003, s.167.
6 Now in the Powers of Criminal Courts (Sentencing) Act 2000, s.111.
7 *Ibid.*, s.109.
7 Criminal Justice Act 2003, s.287, creating the Firearms Act 1968, s.51A.
9 Criminal Justice Act 2003, s.269 and sched. 21.
10 See, for example, news reports on 24 October 2003, regarding the increasing by the Court of Appeal of a number of sentences for sexual offences. Even *The Times* 'named and shamed', and carried photographs of, 'the judges who even the Court of Appeal thought were too soft'.
11 There was sharp media criticism in May 2004 of the Sentencing Advisory Panel's proposal that the starting point for the least serious category of robbery committed by a juvenile should be a community sentence, despite the fact (as set out in the paper) that currently 40 per cent of juveniles convicted of robbery in the youth court receive non-custodial sentences. See Sentencing Advisory Panel (2004a).
12 Release of Short-term Prisoners on Licence (Amendment of Requisite Period) Order 2002, amending the Criminal Justice Act 1991, s.34A(4).
13 Certain types of offender are excluded from the scheme.
14 Incidentally, it is often forgotten that the figures in the grid below the in–out line refer not to community sentences as such but to 'jail time', and that sentencing schemes in the United States have made little progress in guiding sentencer choice in non-custodial sentencing.
15 The Court of Appeal has declared that it will not interfere with a sentence unless it finds such an error, but the Court often does not follow its own precept. There are numerous examples of the appellate court 'tinkering' with first-instance sentences.
16 Another example is *Baldwin* (2002).
17 Crime and Disorder Act 1998, s. 80; Criminal Justice Act 2003, s.163.
18 Powers of Criminal Courts (Sentencing) Act 2000, s.111.
19 It is worth noting that youth court powers are largely unaffected by the Criminal Justice Act 2003, and that youth court magistrates already have power to pass detention and training orders on a young offender for a period of up to 24 months.
20 See the Criminal Justice Act 2003, s.240 which, when brought into force, will replace the Criminal Justice Act 1967, s.67.
21 *Costen* (1989), *March* (2002)
22 Powers of Criminal Courts (Sentencing) Act 2000, s.152; Criminal Justice Act 2003, s.137. The sentencer is not explicitly required to indicate how much difference the guilty plea has made.

23 In *Howells* (1999), Lord Bingham CJ stated that a guilty plea, especially when coupled with other mitigation, could make the difference between a custodial and a non-custodial sentence.
24 See *Lawrence* (1988).
25 The sentence was actually increased to four years, to allow for the 'double jeopardy' of the offender being sentenced twice. The Court always makes such an allowance when increasing sentence on an Attorney General's Reference.
26 According to Lord Lane CJ in *Billam* (1986): 'Previous good character is of only minor relevance.'
27 e.g. *Okuya* (1984); *Hancock* (1986).
28 *Vaughan* (1982); *Whitehead* (1996).
29 Though not always. *Franklyn* (1981) is an example of sentence being reduced on the ground that the offender was a widower responsible for the care of four children.
30 An example is *Olliver* (1989).
31 The offender had already served the equivalent of a 12-month sentence (i.e. six months in custody).
32 On an appeal to the Court of Appeal by the offender, the appellate court must not substitute a sentence which, taking the case as a whole, is 'more severe' than the original sentence: Criminal Appeal Act 1968, s.11(3).
33 Criminal Justice Act 2003, s.183.
34 'Intermittent custody' 03/2004 DCA.
35 Powers of Criminal Courts (Sentencing) Act 2000, s.37(5), s. 40A(5) [not in force], s.47(2), s.51(4) [by cross-reference], s.60(7), s.70(5), s.74(3), sched. 2, para 2(7), sched. 2, para 3(5), sched. 2, para 7(3), sched. 2, para 8(3), sched. 6, para 2(7) and sched. 6, para 3(6).
36 Criminal Justice Act 2003, s.208. The generic sentence was not needed to bring about this change. It could have been achieved more simply by repealing the 13 provisions and substituting one new section applicable to all the different orders.
37 Powers of Criminal Courts (Sentencing) Act 2000, s.158(2)(a), re-enacted as Criminal Justice Act 2003, s.159(3)(a). The latter states that: 'Nothing ... prevents a court ... from mitigating any penalty in an offender's sentence by taking into account any other penalty included in that sentence ...'.
38 Futher questions arise as to the impact on the length of the term suspended, given that suspension will now carry one or more community requirements.
39 Powers of Criminal Courts Act 2000, s.1(3)(b), as inserted by the Criminal Justice Act 2003, sched. 23.
40 In May and June 2004 the Sentencing Advisory Panel hosted a seies of seminars with representatives from across the criminal justice system. These were designed as the first stage in producing comprehensive guidelines on those measures in the Criminal Justice Act 2003 due for implementation by Spring 2005.

References

Ashworth, A. (2000) *Sentencing and Criminal Justice*, 3rd edition (London: Butterworths).

Ashworth, A. and von Hirsch, A. (1997) 'Recognising elephants: the problem of the custody threshold', *Criminal Law Review*, 187–200.

Bottoms, A. (1981) 'The suspended sentence in England 1967–1978', *British Journal of Criminology*, 21(1), 1–26.

Carter, P. (2003) *Managing Offenders, Reducing Crime (Report of the Correctional Services Review)* (London: Government Strategy Unit).

Department of Constitutional Affairs (2004) 'Intermittent custody', Guidance paper, March 2004.

Gibson, B. (2004) 'The CJA 2003: 'Whither imprisonment in the magistrates' courts?', 168 *Justice of the Peace*, 287–291.

Halliday, J. (2001) *Making Punishments Work: Report of a review of the sentencing framework for England and Wales* (London: Home Office Communication Directorate).

Home Office (2002) *Justice for All* (London: Home Office).

Hood, R. (1992) *Race and Sentencing* (Oxford: Clarendon Press).

Hough, M., Jacobson, J. and Millie, A. (2003) *The Decision to Imprison: Sentencing and the prison population* (London: Prison Reform Trust).

Hough, M. and Roberts, J. (2002) 'Public knowledge and public opinion of sentencing: findings from five jurisdictions', in C. Tata and N. Hutton (eds) *Sentencing and Society: International perspectives* (Aldershot: Ashgate), pp. 157–176.

Magistrates' Association (2003) *The Magistrates' Courts' Sentencing Guidelines* (London: Magistrates' Association).

Rex, S. (2002) 'Reinventing community penalties: the role of communication', in S. Rex and M. Tonry (eds) *Reform and Punishment: The future of sentencing* (Cullompton: Willan), pp. 138–157.

Roberts. J. (2002) 'Public opinion and sentencing policy' in S. Rex and M. Tonry (eds) *Reform and Punishment: The future of sentencing* (Cullompton: Willan), pp. 18–39.

Sentencing Advisory Panel (2004a) *Advice to the Sentencing Guidelines Council 1: Robbery* (London: Sentencing Advisory Panel).

Sentencing Advisory Panel (2004b) *Advice to the Sentencing Guidelines Council 2: Reduction for Guilty Plea* (London: Sentencing Advisory Panel).

Sparks, R. (1971) 'The use of suspended sentences', *Criminal Law Review*, 384–401.

Thomas, D.A. (2003) 'New legislation' 1, *Sentencing News*, 7–9.

von Hirsch, A. (2002) 'Record-enhanced sentencing in England and Wales: reflections on the Halliday Report's proposed treatment of prior convictions', in S. Rex and M. Tonry (eds) *Reform and Punishment: The future of sentencing* (Cullompton: Willan), pp. 197–216.

Wasik, M. (2001) *Emmins on Sentencing*, 4th edition (London: Blackstone).

Wasik, M. (2004a) 'Sentencing guidelines: past, present, and future', in M. Freeman (ed.) *Current Legal Problems 2003* (Oxford: Oxford University Press), pp. 239–264.

Wasik, M. (2004b) 'Principles of sentencing', in D. Feldman (ed.) *English Public Law* (Oxford: Oxford University Press), pp. 1367–1411.

Wasik, M. and von Hirsch, A. (1988) 'Non-custodial penalties and the principles of desert', *Criminal Law Review*, 555–572.

Wasik, M. and von Hirsch, A. (1994) 'Section 29 revised: previous convictions in sentencing', *Criminal Law Review*, 409–419.

Cases

Al-Buhairi [2004] 1 Cr App R (S) 496
Anderson v *Secretary of State for the Home Department* [2003] 1 AC 837
Aramah (1982) 4 Cr App R (S) 407
Attorney-General's References (Nos 4 and 7 of 2002: Lobban) [2002] 2 Cr App R (S) 345
Attorney-General's Reference (No 22 of 2002) [2002] EWCA Crim 1500
Attorney-General's Reference (No 64 of 2003) [2003], *The Times*, December 1, 2003
Baldwin [2002] EWCA Crim 2647
Bibi [1980] 1 WLR 1193
Billam (1986) 8 Cr App R (S) 48
Bradbourn (1985) 7 Cr App R (5) 180
Celaire [2003] 1 Cr App R (5) 116
Clark, The Times, 27 January 1999
Clarke [1998] 2 Cr App R (S) 95
Costen (1989) 11 Cr App R (S) 182
Cox [1993] 1 WLR 188
Du Plooy [2003] SLT 1237
Franklyn (1981) 3 Cr App R (S) 65
George [1984] 1 WLR 1083
Hancock [1986] Crim LR 697
Howells [1999] 1 WLR 307
Ingham (1974) CSP C4.2A01
Kefford [2002] 2 Cr App R (S) 495
Kelly [2003] 1 Cr App R (S) 472
Lawrence (1988) 10 Cr App R (S) 463
Lobban (2002) 2 Cr App R (5) 77
March [2002] 2 Cr App R (S) 448
McInerney [2003] 1 Cr App R 627
Mills [2002] 2 Cr App R (S) 229.
Offen (No2) [2001] 1 WLR 253.
Okinikan (1993) 14 Cr App R (S) 453.
Okuya (1984) 6 Cr App R (S) 632
Oliver [2003] 1 Cr App R 463
Ollerenshaw [1999] 1 Cr App R (S) 65
Olliver (1989) 11 Cr App R (S) 10
Vaughan (1982) 4 Cr App R (S) 83
Webbe [2002] 2 Cr App R (S) 282
Whitehead [1996] 1 Cr App R (S) 111.

Chapter 13

Sentence management

Gwen Robinson and James Dignan

Introduction

'Sentence management' is a relatively new concept, the exact scope and boundaries of which are not clearly defined (cf. Faulkner 2001; Home Office 2001a). While the Halliday Review of the sentencing framework (Home Office 2001a) was largely responsible for the entry of 'sentence management' into criminal justice discourse, the term can more broadly be understood as a testament to the 'managerialisation' of criminal justice which was discussed in Chapter 1. This process has arguably reached its zenith with the publication of the Correctional Services Review (Carter 2003), many aspects of which are relevant to the content of this chapter.

In this chapter we adopt a particular view of sentence management, which we consider most appropriate to the needs of the Coulsfield Commission. We will focus on two main areas, both of which essentially concern the administration or management of community-based sentences, rather than the delivery of specific interventions. The main body of the chapter focuses on the work of the statutory agencies which, along with their various partners, have historically been largely responsible for the implementation of community-based sentences. We pay particular attention to two aspects of the 'case management' process: the assessment of offenders and the enforcement of community orders. We also address separately the management of 'seamless' sentences, which are served partly in custody and partly in the community. In the final part of the chapter we turn our attention to the role of sentencers in the overview and review of community-based penalties – a role which, in England and Wales, is set to intensify in the light of the new sentencing provisions of the Criminal Justice Act 2003. We do not consider sentencing decisions *per se*; these are dealt with in Chapter 12.

Implementing community sentences: introducing 'case management'

Once an offender is made subject to statutory supervision, either on a community order or post-release licence, decisions have to be made about the specific input s/he will receive. Traditionally, such decisions have been informed by an assessment of the offender and the subsequent design of an individually tailored supervision plan, outlining the specific objectives of supervision and the most appropriate methods to achieve them (e.g. Burnett 1996; HMIP 1999). The management and delivery of interventions have tended to be elements of the role of a single supervising officer, often referred to as a 'case worker'.

However, since the 1980s, the increasing use of specialist programmes, inter-sectoral partnerships and multi-component community sentences such as the combination order (now known as the 'community punishment and rehabilitation order') have begun a process of separating the management and delivery of community supervision. Reflecting these developments, the term 'case management' has crept into the discourse concerning community supervision in the last decade or so. However, it is a term which has been the source of some confusion both within and outside the practice context (Oldfield 1998; Holt 2000). Much of the confusion has arisen because while the term 'case manager' may be and often is used to denote the role of a practitioner who manages a caseload, 'case management' more accurately describes a range of activities which may or may not reside with a single individual. In this chapter we use the term 'case management' to refer to 'the responsibilities involved in planning and review, arranging and coordinating each element of supervision, monitoring progress and deciding on required enforcement action' (Underdown 1998: 94). In other words, we define case management as all those aspects of (community) sentence implementation which fall short of the delivery of programmes of intervention.[1]

In the following section we consider in some depth the practice of offender assessment, which is acknowledged as not only the first but also a key part of the case management process.

Assessing offenders

The assessment of offenders has long been appreciated as an essential function for those who work with offenders (Bonta 1996). As Kemshall has pointed out, the assessment of offenders not only frames problems, 'it defines their solutions' (1998: 173). Assessment, then, plays a key role in determining how an offender, or group of offenders, is dealt with or managed in the context of a community sentence. Space precludes a full account of the development of offender assessment methods, so our focus will be the move toward assessment practice that is increasingly structured or standardised, and increasingly oriented toward the prediction of risk.[2]

Bonta (1996) has described three types or 'generations' of offender assessment. The 'first generation' denotes the practitioner's use of experience, interviewing skills and professional judgement to arrive at an assessment of the individual. In contrast to this so-called 'clinical' approach, 'actuarial', or 'second generation' assessment is derived from methods used in the insurance industry, and is based upon statistical calculations of probability. The development of actuarial risk assessment technology can be traced back to the work of Burgess in the 1920s (see also Meehl 1954), but a more contemporary example is the Home Office-developed Offender Group Reconviction Scale (OGRS) (Home Office 1996; Copas and Marshall 1998; Taylor 1999). OGRS was developed on the basis of a national Home Office database consisting of information about the demographic characteristics and offending histories of a large sample of offenders, and was designed for the assessment of offenders aged 17 and over. The instrument provides an estimate of the statistical likelihood of one or more reconvictions within two years of release from custody or from the beginning of a community sentence.[3] The key variables which OGRS considers in calculating the statistical likelihood of reconviction are:

- age;
- sex;
- current offence(s);
- age at first conviction;
- number of previous convictions;
- number of custodial sentences while aged under 21.

The main strength of actuarial methods lies in their reliance on clearly articulated risk factors or indicators which are grounded in empirical data. This means that they can offer high levels of predictive validity or accuracy. However, despite their proven ability to predict risk of reconviction, the utility of actuarial methods is limited in that they are both based on and designed for use with groups or populations of offenders. This means that they cannot provide accurate predictions of risk in respect of individuals.[4] Nor do they assist practitioners in terms of identifying appropriate interventions which might reduce risk.

It is principally in the light of these limitations that researchers began to explore a 'third generation' of assessment methodology, incorporating both static and 'dynamic' factors into the risk prediction process (Bonta 1996). By the mid-1990s, 'what works' research had begun to identify a number of factors pertaining to the lifestyles and attributes of offenders which could be shown to be linked with offending behaviour (e.g. Andrews *et al.* 1990; Andrews and Bonta 1994; Chapter 8, this volume). These factors have come to be known as dynamic risk factors, or criminogenic needs. In terms of assessing offenders, criminogenic needs are a crucial 'discovery' in that they contribute to a more individualised assessment of risk which can usefully point to the areas of the offender's life – such as his or her accommodation or employment situation, drug or alcohol use, or attitudes – which, if subject to intervention and help, are likely to reduce his or her risk of further offending.

Risk/needs assessment instruments

Since the mid-1990s, a number of assessment instruments incorporating dynamic risk factors or criminogenic needs have been available to UK probation areas. Commonly referred to as 'risk/needs' assessment instruments, they have included the ACE system (Roberts *et al.* 1996; Gibbs 1999), and the Level of Service Inventory – Revised (LSI-R) (Andrews and Bonta 1995). By 1998, the majority of area probation services in England and Wales – as well as a number of criminal justice social work departments in Scotland and the Probation Service in Northern Ireland – were using either LSI-R or the ACE system (Raynor *et al.* 2000).

In the light of the popularity of these instruments, and with a view to standardising assessment practice across the 'correctional services', the Home Office announced plans to develop a new 'Offender Assessment System' (OASys) in 1999 (Home Office 1999), which is currently being 'rolled out' (in England and Wales) in both custodial and community contexts.[5] A parallel development, funded by the Youth Justice Board, is the ASSET system for the assessment of young offenders, which is now the standard tool used by all Youth Offending Teams (YOTs) in England and Wales (Baker *et al.* 2002).

Linking research and practice: the potential and problems of risk/need assessment

To date, most of the research on risk/needs assessment instruments has focused on their technical properties and capabilities (e.g. Raynor *et al.* 2000; Baker *et al.* 2002), although a smaller body of research has focused on users' views (e.g. Aye-Maung and Hammond 2000; Robinson 2003). Early research tended to focus on implementation issues, including the ability of practitioners to understand and use such instruments reliably, and their impact on the quality of related areas of practice. Evidence that the use of such instruments had a positive impact on the quality of pre-sentence reports (PSRs) encouraged the use of assessment instruments in conjunction with the preparation of such reports and as a starting point for all subsequent work with offenders (Roberts and Robinson 1998). At the same time, the emergence of a consensus about the 'matching' of offenders to resources on the basis of risk assessment meant that much research attention was devoted to the issue of predictive validity. Confirmation that such instruments were almost as effective as OGRS in predicting risk of reconviction (Raynor *et al.* 2000; Baker *et al.* 2002) facilitated attempts in a number of probation areas to develop allocation policies based on offenders' scores on its chosen instrument (e.g. Robinson 2002). In essence, they have been used as instruments of 'triage': that is, as a means to distinguish offenders with a low risk of reconviction from those posing a higher risk, such that resources can be focused on the latter, on whom they are more likely to make an impact (Andrews *et al.* 1990). More recently this desire to 'rationalise' allocation in line with risk is reflected in the National Probation Service's use of such scores in 'targeting matrices' to determine eligibility for accredited programmes (NPD 2001). Although the Youth Justice Board has not to date issued guidelines regarding the allocation of young offenders to resources in line with ASSET scores, anecdotal evidence indicates that some YOTs may be using such scores to guide allocation decisions.

The fact that areas have been less inclined to exploit some of the other potential applications of risk/needs assessments has largely been due to resource constraints. For example, such instruments can be used to evaluate the effectiveness of interventions. This is achieved by comparing offenders' scores at the start and at the end of a period of supervision (e.g. Raynor *et al.* 2000; Merrington 2001).[6] They can also inform service managers about the spread of criminogenic needs in local offender populations. This information can, in turn, inform spending on specific services to meet those needs (e.g. Merrington and Skinns 2000; Baker *et al.* 2002). However, neither application is feasible on a scale beyond that of individual practice in the absence of effective information systems capable of capturing the data, and of appropriately trained staff to perform data analyses. Few probation areas or YOTs have been able to support adequately resourced research units, although a small number have employed academic researchers to perform such analyses for them.

In the more recent context of OASys and ASSET implementation, the focus is turning toward the potentially key role of such instruments in facilitating an approach to offender management that is at once more consistent, rational and systemic. For example, OASys is seen as crucial both to bringing prisons and probation in line in terms of their approach to risk (Home Office 2001b) and to the 'seamless' management of offenders in, and between, custodial and community settings (e.g. Home Office 1999; NPS 2003; Blair 2000: 73). The Prison Service began using OASys in mid-2003 and the OASys development team recently announced that OASys assessments conducted by probation staff should be following offenders into prisons. It also reported on progress in developing compatible electronic versions of OASys (e-OASys) in prison and probation contexts, offering the possibility of 'area to area data exchange and also data exchange with the Prison Service' (NPS 2003). There are also high hopes for risk/needs assessments in the sentencing context in both the Halliday and Carter reviews. Carter in particular implies a key role for risk/needs assessment in targeting the 'right' offenders for community sentences and reversing the trend of 'down-tariffing' community sentences in the interests of system efficiency and effectiveness (e.g. Raynor 1998; Morgan 2003). However, Carter fails to address the inherent tensions between an approach to sentencing which is dominated by calculations of risk, and one which is concerned with principles of desert and proportionality (e.g. Hudson 2001).

Other problems with the use of risk/needs assessment instruments have also come to light, through the experience of users. First, the integrity of risk/needs assessment cannot be taken for granted. As the Halliday Review recognised, a good assessment is dependent upon good quality information, including accurate criminal history data from the police or CPS, which are not always available when assessments are undertaken. A good assessment is also dependent on practitioners having sufficient time to conduct interviews and other enquiries. Research has shown that the completion of instruments such as ASSET and OASys is a resource-intensive activity. OASys, in particular, has attracted criticism for its length and complexity: its implementation played a role in the industrial action over workloads in many probation areas in 2002–3. In a recent survey conducted by NAPO, over half of the respondents reported that 'manual' OASys completion took over an hour (NAPO 2003). The resource-intensive nature of offender assessment can be particularly problematic at PSR stage when, because of time constraints, completion of a comprehensive instrument such as OASys may not always be feasible or cost-effective.[7]

There is also evidence that, for practitioners, the adoption of risk/needs assessment instruments is costly in other ways. Many practitioners feel ambivalent about the introduction of such instruments, because they are associated with conflicting implications for 'professionalism'. On the one hand, they herald a more standardised approach to assessment, which is associated with enhanced consistency, fairness, accuracy and effectiveness. On the other hand, they tend to de-emphasise the role of professional judgement and consequently generate fears about de-professionalisation (Gibbs 1999; Robinson 2003). In the words of one LSI-R using practitioner, 'I feel it *enhances* [professional credibility], because it's a standardized, verified tool, that you can say you're basing decisions on. But at the same time I think people feel there's a danger that a trained chimp could do it' (quoted in Robinson 2003: 34).

While it is difficult to entirely remove practitioners' fears about increasing standardisation, which of course affects not just assessment but most other areas of practice, it has been argued that greater attention to implementation issues could minimise genuine concerns. If practitioners are to engage positively with instruments like OASys in both the short and longer term, they need to be persuaded that the benefits of such instruments outweigh the costs. Practitioners are likely to be encouraged by tangible evidence that the rich data which such instruments generate are being used to improve the quality of services which offenders receive, and not simply as a means of exerting ever greater control over professional discretion (Robinson 2003).

Managing and delivering community sentences: key issues

Generic vs specialist practice

Until relatively recently, probation supervision tended to be managed and largely (though not exclusively) delivered by the generic case worker or, later, case manager (Burnett 1996). To illustrate this concept, Burnett's study of practice in ten probation areas revealed that offenders tended to be allocated to the probation officer responsible for preparing their pre-sentence report, and to be supervised continuously by the same officer for the duration of their order or licence. Probation officers tended to carry a mixed caseload, and to be responsible not only for case management but also the delivery and/or commissioning of specific interventions. In recent years, however, there has been a trend toward a more specialist model of practice, such that while the generic case manager has by no means disappeared, many probation staff currently fulfil specialist tasks, such as assessment and PSR writing or programme delivery, while others specialise in the supervision of certain categories of offender, such as high-risk (of harm) offenders, often referred to as 'public protection' cases (Robinson 2002). A Home Office study conducted in 2001 revealed that, of 31 probation service areas responding to a survey, 15 had adopted a 'specialist' model of staff allocation (Partridge 2004).[8]

This tendency toward specialisation appears to be attributable to the increasing acceptance of a risk-based system of resource allocation, coupled – at least in England and Wales – with a diminishing pool of professionally qualified practitioners. These twin developments have contributed to a redefinition of 'professional territory', such that the resources of professionally qualified practitioners have come to focus on the management of higher-risk offenders and certain 'key' aspects of the supervision process, while lower-risk offenders and other, lower-profile aspects of case management have increasingly fallen to non-professionally qualified staff[9] (e.g. Partridge 2004; HMIP 2002a).

Research indicates that different models of case management present different benefits – and different costs – for different stakeholders. In a recent Home Office study, Partridge[10] found that the choice of case management model in the areas she visited was largely attributable to senior managers' perceptions of resource efficiency in particular geographical contexts. In 'specialist' areas, senior managers saw specialisation as a means of concentrating scarce professional resources on higher-risk offenders, and specialist models were also associated with 'efficiency gains' by virtue of allowing staff to concentrate on specific tasks. Generic models, on the other hand, were preferred by senior managers in areas characterised by geographical dispersal and/or more limited staff resources, factors which were thought to render a specialist model impracticable.

Among practitioners, however, perceptions of the two models were mixed, particularly in specialist areas. For some practitioners, specialist roles were associated with role clarity and the development of expertise; but others were more likely to experience specialism in negative terms. Indeed, Partridge's research points to the emergence of a 'status differential' among staff carrying out different, specialist roles. Partridge found evidence of an implicit hierarchy whereby specialist staff working with the highest-risk (of harm) offenders were thought to derive the greatest levels of job satisfaction. It was widely believed that these staff were dealing with the most interesting and challenging cases. Meanwhile, staff in other roles felt their job had become more mundane or routine as a result of specialisation. For example, PSR writers felt the specialist model resulted in less varied work for them. Not surprisingly, Partridge observed that staff morale varied across teams.

Although based on relatively small numbers of interviews, these findings do in fact mirror those of an earlier study in two different probation areas (Robinson 2001). In this study, specialist PSR writers were pitied by colleagues in other roles, who viewed report writing as akin to working on a production line and associated it with the lowest levels of job satisfaction. Meanwhile, running accredited programmes and working with 'public protection' cases were viewed as 'elite' roles, carrying more prestige than 'mainstream' roles. These findings are cause for concern, not least because there are ongoing questions about both morale and stress among probation staff which have been consistently ignored by those responsible for the plethora of recent organisational and practice changes (Nellis and Chui 2003; Davies 2004; Farrow 2004).

On a more positive note, Partridge found no evidence of problems with the division of labour between qualified and non-qualified staff, although some arrangements were considered more 'efficient' than others.[11] Partridge's findings add weight to the impression that the sorts of concerns that have been expressed for a number of years about the encroachment of non-qualified staff on professional territory (e.g. Drakeford 1993; NAPO 1998, 1999) have, more recently, tended to be recast as a rational, positive development, wholly in accordance with notions of effectiveness. The work of non-professionally qualified staff is now highly valued, and perceived as 'freeing up' professionally qualified staff to focus their efforts 'where it matters most' (e.g. HMIP 2003; Robinson 2002).

According to Partridge's study, those probation areas which maintained a generic model of practice appeared largely to avoid the problems associated with specialist models. Although less able to foster expertise in particular areas, generic models were valued in that they enabled practitioners to retain a working knowledge of all the various stages of the supervision process, as well as gaining experience of working with a range of offenders. Practitioners in generic contexts were also better able to see the impact of their work on offenders by virtue of their 'end-to-end' involvement in the supervision process. This sense of 'continuity', which many practitioners valued, was also shared by the offenders Partridge interviewed. In specialist models, offenders were more likely to be confused about who was overseeing their order and who to contact in a crisis. Conversely, the less fragmented nature of generic models provided greater continuity of contact, which facilitated not only trust and openness, but also motivation and compliance, particularly at the early stages of supervision.

In the youth justice context, the establishment of YOTs founded on an inter-sectoral partnership model has presented slightly different issues. For example, a tension between generic and specialist models of offender management was evident during the piloting phase of the YOTs, though the evaluators suggested that the multi-agency approach prescribed by the Crime and Disorder Act implied the retention of at least some degree of specialisation on the part of those seconded from the various home agencies (Holdaway *et al.* 2001: 14). The same evaluation found that, while working relationships between staff from different agencies were generally good, there was a degree of tension between 'old' and 'new' staff. Thus, for example, some former youth justice workers – who tended to carry established and heavy caseloads – were resentful of those drawn from newer agencies, whom they perceived to have more scope to undertake more innovative work (Holdaway *et al.* 2001: 8).

Delivery, delivery, delivery

A related issue concerns the relative priority which, in the context of an 'effective practice' agenda, has been afforded to the 'delivery' and 'case management' aspects of offender supervision. In the probation context, it is increasingly being acknowledged that the implementation of centrally defined 'effective practice' has focused too heavily on the development and roll-out of programmes, at the expense of the 'context' in which delivery takes place (e.g. Partridge 2004). Similarly, the dedication of Youth Justice Board funding to specialist projects has been linked with a neglect of the core tasks of case management and 'ordinary' one-to-one work with young offenders. As Burnett and Appleton (2004: 42) have succinctly put it, in youth justice there has been a tendency toward 'more caviar than bread'. In probation it is, ironically, largely in the context of attention to the implementation of accredited programmes in the form of HMIP audits and studies of programme attrition that the neglect of case management has come to light (HMIP 2002b, 2003; Kemshall and Canton 2002). What is increasingly being recognised, then, is that poor case management compromises the effectiveness of programmes (see also Chapter 8, this volume).

This acknowledged neglect of case management is particularly lamentable in the light of the assertions in much of the early 'what works' literature that case management would be crucial to effective supervision (e.g. Underdown 1998; Chapman and Hough 1998). For example, Underdown pointed to the essential role of the case manager as 'change agent' in the context of cognitive-behavioural programmes (Gendreau *et al.* 1999). Underdown argued that by providing preparatory and motivational work prior to programme commencement, supportive work during the programme and rehearsal and/or relapse prevention work following completion, the case manager would be uniquely placed to support the learning processes which cognitive-behavioural programmes promote (see also Holt 2000).

The supervisor/supervisee relationship: a neglected asset?

Within a discourse which emphasises the 'management' of offenders it has become unfashionable to talk about the 'relational basis' of work with offenders (Burnett 2004). But in the face of a trend, identified above, toward specialist practice and the fragmentation of supervision, a growing body of research indicates that both the consistency and quality of offender/supervisor relationships are central to effective practice, in terms of promoting motivation and compliance (in the short term) and desistance (in the longer term) (e.g. Ditton and Ford 1994; Trotter 1996; McIvor and Barry 1998; Rex 1999; Barry 2000; Beaumont *et al.* 2001; Ricketts *et al.* 2002; Hazel *et al.* 2002; Partridge 2004). In short, as Chapman and Hough observed some years ago, case managers ought to 'form the key relationship with the supervised offender [and] represent the probation service to the individual' (1998: 42).

Limitations of space preclude a full overview of the research referred to above, but a small number of examples will illustrate some of the key findings. Rex's (1999) research involved interviews with 21 probation officers and 60 of their probationers. Rex found that those offenders who attributed changes in their behaviour to probation supervision conveyed a sense of being committed to and engaged by their supervising officer. As many as half of the probationers Rex interviewed revealed feelings of personal loyalty and accountability toward their supervisor, and probationers said they were more willing to accept advice or guidance in the context of a genuine, engaging relationship. Rex has subsequently played a key role in promoting supervisory practice along the lines of the 'pro-social modelling' approach developed in Australia by Trotter (1996, 1999), an approach which is founded on the development of constructive relationships between offenders and their supervisors (Rex and Matravers 1998). In another recent study by Beaumont *et al.* (2001), researchers found that in a sample of 105 offenders on community orders, those who reported the most positive experiences had enjoyed a substantial period working with a specific supervisor and described one-to-one contact in positive terms, while those who felt that supervision had been poor pointed to unsatisfactory experiences of one-to-one work (usually too little contact, or contact that was too rushed or superficial). A smaller study of compliance in the context of DTTOs found that, although no single style of intervention suited all probationers, the quality of relationships with staff was critical throughout the order, and 'evidence of personal interest and caring were valued throughout' (Ricketts *et al.* 2002: 38). In Partridge's study, offenders were 'unanimous about the importance of continuity of contact with the same case manager, particularly during the initial stages of their supervision . . . indicating the importance of the case manager as a stable, human link' (2004: 9).

There is a possible parallel here with recent studies of legitimacy in the prison context (e.g. Liebling 2004; Sparks *et al.* 1996), which indicate that the compliance of prisoners with authority is likely to increase if that authority is regarded as legitimate. If, as the studies reviewed above suggest, offenders associate legitimacy with a consistent 'human link', then it is likely that the more fragmented the supervision experience becomes, the less offenders will be inclined to engage meaningfully with the process. With the exception of certain areas of practice,[12] contemporary arrangements appear to be heading further away from the 'ideal' of a consistent, continuous and committed relationship between practitioner (or case manager) and offender (Holt 2000). As Partridge concludes, the different ways in which offenders might respond to complex and highly fragmented arrangements have, to date, tended to be inadequately considered, and models of offender management 'need to acknowledge offenders' experiences and needs' to a much greater degree than they do at present (2004: 5).[13]

It is perhaps ironic that, while the relational or interpersonal dimension of case management is suffering from neglect in the context of probation supervision, the opposite trend is apparent in the context of community punishment, which has enthusiastically taken on board the findings of research on pro-social modelling (Trotter 1999; Rex *et al.* 2003; Gelsthorpe and Rex 2004). The arrival of generic community sentences with 'mix 'n' match' components, and of a variety of new 'seamless sentences' (see further below) present particular challenges in terms of maintaining coherence and continuity in the supervision process. The impact of the new National Offender Management Service (NOMS) is perhaps more difficult to predict. For example, it is not clear how the proposed split between commissioning and delivery will affect case management. Indeed, at the time of writing, the available NOMS literature says nothing concrete about the future of the case management role, which is arguably cause for concern. But what research seems to be telling us is that effective practice demands case managers who are much more than efficient administrators, and that case management requires an investment of resources (including appropriate training) which parallels that which programme deliverers currently receive.

Matching offenders to resources

A final problem with contemporary visions of case management is that they tend to take for granted the availability of appropriate resources to which offenders can be referred. However, in practice, matching offenders to appropriate resources is rather more problematic. For example, while accredited programmes are generally available, they are not always suitable for all, hence the use of 'targeting matrices' based on the risk/needs assessment scores referred to earlier. Even where programmes are deemed suitable, high attrition rates indicate that there are problems in targeting the 'right' offenders (Hollin *et al.* 2002; Kemshall and Canton 2002). Existing research indicates that risk scores on their own are a rather crude rationing device, and that more attention to the specific criminogenic needs of offenders and/or responsivity factors[14] is warranted (Hollin *et al.* 2002; Robinson 2002; Burnett and Appleton 2004; Chapter 14, this volume).

Of course, problems of availability and targeting are not confined to accredited programmes; they also apply to partnership resources. Given a variety of potential local contexts, partnership resources are likely to be more accessible to some case managers (and offenders) than others. Even in areas which support a range of partnership resources, it is not always clear that the available resources are the right ones for local offender populations. To some extent, the latter problem is likely to diminish when aggregate data on the criminogenic needs of local offender populations are extractable from OASys/ASSET databases. However, it is important to recognise that even the most reliable data about offenders' criminogenic needs is only the first step toward developing effective partnerships. As a number of researchers have pointed out, the 'ideal' of effective partnership working is not always easily realised. Among the potential problems associated with contracting for supervision services, Rumgay (2003) includes sustaining accountability for services delivered by partnership organisations, and the need for the 'host' agency to develop management skills to foster and maintain effective partnerships.

In the context of the pilot YOTs, Holdaway *et al.* (2001) distinguished three models of service delivery (including partnership utilisation), which they characterised as 'in-house', 'outsourced' and a hybrid 'mixed economy' model. With the in-house model, responsibility for assessing offenders, consulting with victims and delivering interventions is undertaken by specially trained members of the YOT. With the outsourced model, responsibility for some or all of these tasks is contracted out to one or more non-statutory voluntary-sector organisations. With the mixed economy model, suitably trained or qualified personnel from voluntary sector organisations are contracted by a YOT to work as a member of the team, though this does not preclude the contracting out of particular types of interventions (for example, victim–offender mediation). Although each model was thought to have strengths and weaknesses, a subsequent evaluation focusing on a range of specially funded restorative justice projects reported that those managed in-house were generally more successful than others in contacting victims, obtaining referrals and communicating between agencies.

Enforcement

The enforcement of both community penalties and licences is an integral part of the case management process (Underdown 1998; Holt 2000). For offenders who do not comply with the conditions of their sentence, enforcement action consists of a series of warnings issued by a supervising officer which can culminate in breach proceedings.[15] While 'non-compliance' may be defined in a number of ways, a Home Office study found that the most common reason for non-compliance and initiating breach proceedings was repeated failure to attend scheduled appointments without a reasonable explanation (Ellis *et al.* 1996).[16]

Enforcement policies tend to be justified with reference to the utilitarian purposes of increasing the credibility and/or effectiveness of community supervision (Home Office 2000; Faulkner 2001; Hedderman 2003). With reference to these twin objectives, the enforcement of community sentences is a further area of practice in which professional and local discretion has been reduced, largely through the increasingly strict provisions of National Standards.[17] Following a number of HMIP reports which were critical of areas' performance and resulting legislative changes, National Standards for England and Wales have reduced the number of warnings permitted prior to instituting breach proceedings for offenders on community sentences (though not licences) from two to one in any 12-month period (Home Office 2000), and there has been a corresponding trend toward improvements in enforcement practice.[18]

While there is some evidence that enforcement practice is linked with the credibility of community orders in the eyes of sentencers (Hough *et al.*

2003a; MORI 2003), relationships between enforcement, breach and 'effectiveness' are less clear cut. For example, in respect of prosecuting breaches, significant problems of delay persist. Although the National Probation Service has improved its own performance in terms of reducing delay in initiating breach proceedings,[19] the problem of unexecuted breach warrants has by no means been resolved (Ellis *et al.* 1996; National Association of Probation Officers 2001). Although there is evidence that *some* case managers continue to offer appointments to *some* offenders following the initiation of breach proceedings (see note 20 below), it is nonetheless the case that large numbers of offenders are likely to be falling through the net. Clearly, as more offenders are prosecuted for non-compliance, this problem is likely to be compounded.

In respect of enforcement and effectiveness, two recent Home Office studies do appear to indicate that *appropriate* enforcement action (i.e. issuing warnings or initiating breach proceedings rather than overlooking non-compliance) can be effective in reducing reconviction rates. May and Wadwell (2001) found that where appropriate enforcement action was taken, offenders had a lower than predicted reconviction rate. Hearnden and Millie (2003) subsequently found that those offenders on whom breach proceedings were initiated as a 'final warning'[20] were reconvicted at a lower rate than those on whom breach proceedings were successfully executed (58 per cent as opposed to 77 per cent), although neither group performed as well as those who completed their orders successfully (35 per cent reconvicted) or whose orders were terminated early in the light of good progress (23 per cent reconvicted). Unfortunately, however, this study did not offer risk assessment data for the four groups, which makes it difficult to rule out 'selection effects', i.e. the possibility that the more 'compliant' were in fact lower-risk offenders. Nor is there any useful qualitative research to help us to understand why enforcement practice appears to be related to lower reconviction rates.

The same study also compared the impact of enforcement practice in areas with different enforcement strategies, finding virtually no difference between 'tough' and 'lenient' areas in terms of reconviction rates for offenders against whom breach proceedings were initiated (Hearnden and Millie 2003). While acknowledging some of the methodological limitations of the study, Hedderman and Hough (2004) have argued that it indicates that strictness of enforcement appears to have little impact on the overall reconviction rate, and that offenders appear to be relatively immune to the deterrent threats of probation officers.

It has also been argued that the tightening of national standards around enforcement has not been evidence-based (Hedderman and Hough 2000; Ellis 2000). For Hedderman (2003), mandatory breach after two unacceptable absences can be counter-effective because it reduces the amount of time a supervising officer has to encourage compliance and make the order work. It is also likely, she argues, that those most in need of supervision are those most likely to be breached (and possibly re-sentenced) before they can be transformed into 'compliers'. Given a presumption in favour of custody for adult offenders (in England and Wales) where the court considers the order to be unworkable, this is a serious issue.[21] It is also a particular concern because it has been suggested that there may well be a link between revocation and reconviction rates, although at present research falls short of demonstrating a definite link (Hedderman and Hough 2004).

Encouraging compliance

In recent years, several commentators have argued that instead of asking 'what works?' in enforcement, we ought to be devoting more attention to the question of 'what works?' in encouraging compliance. In other words, what constructive steps can be taken to avoid the resort to breach? This is a valid question because, notwithstanding recent improvements, breach rates continue to underestimate the extent of non-compliance with community sentences and licences. For example, in Farrall's (2002) study of 199 probationers, 40 (20 per cent) did not keep in touch with their supervising officer for extended periods of time. As Hedderman and Hough have argued, 'The "big stick" is neither the only nor the best way of securing offenders' compliance' (2000: 5).

For a number of researchers there is more scope to 'design out' non-attendance (e.g. Bottoms 2001; Ellis *et al.* 1996; Ellis 2000; Faulkner 2001; Farrall 2002; Hedderman and Hough 2000; Hedderman 2003; Hearnden and Millie 2003). To date, the most systematic attempt to develop a theoretical model of compliance is to be found in a recent paper by Bottoms (2001). Bottoms suggests that compliance may come about because of habit, through a calculation of self-interest (including deterrence), because of a sense of moral obligation, or for reasons of situational constraint. Research also supports Bottoms' suggestion that constraint and deterrence – the methods at the heart of national standards – are not the only or indeed the most appropriate strategies. In the most detailed study of enforcement practice in England and Wales to date, Ellis *et al.* (1996) found a variety of examples of practice aimed at sustaining engagement with orders. These included using appointment cards; coordinating appointments with signing-on days for the unemployed; and/or putting the offender on a more (or less) frequent reporting cycle. In one area, following a first failure to attend, probation officers could refer offenders for a visit by a dedicated 'follow-up' officer who tried to trace offenders, initially through a visit to the last known address. Staff in this area considered this to be a more effective method than the 'standard' practice of sending warning letters by post. But as Ellis (2000) has observed, there has been no attempt to commission a more systematic evaluation of their worth.

It has also been argued that there is a case for a system of recognition and reward for compliance, as well as punishment for failure (e.g. Bottoms 2001; Faulkner 2001; Underdown 2001; Hedderman 2003; Hedderman and Hough 2004). At present approximately eight per cent of community rehabilitation orders are terminated early in the light of good progress (Home Office 2004). However, another much-quoted example of building in rewards is the practice in Teesside probation area of providing breakfast to those attending a final programme session. Underdown has further suggested that other incentives might include 'reducing the restrictions or lessening the demands that the overall community penalty imposes' (2001: 120). This, he suggests, might be accomplished by increasing the role of courts in overseeing community orders, an issue to which we return in more detail later in this chapter. Finally, Hedderman and Hough (2004) argue that in addition to rewards for individual offenders, there should be *organisational* rewards for securing compliance. This, they argue, would ensure that areas designed their enforcement strategies to prioritise programme completions rather than commencements, and would hopefully minimise the risk of unnecessary revocations.

Managing 'seamless' sentences

Many of the issues identified above are pertinent to or even magnified in the context of 'seamless sentences'. The term 'seamless sentence' refers to a sentence which is served partly in custody and partly in the community.[22] Although there are principled objections to seamless sentences which we will not review here (see for example Nellis 1999; Faulkner 2001), it is clear that much of the enthusiasm for such sentences stems from a desire to enhance the effectiveness of shorter terms of custody by placing an emphasis on the resettlement needs of prisoners. However, such sentences pose particular challenges from a sentence management perspective. Prominent among these challenges are the requirements of cooperative working between prisons and community-based agencies, as well as between both (statutory) services and the independent sector; the necessity of effective information exchange; and the continuity of interventions and personnel across custodial and community boundaries.

In a recent study of the implementation of the Detention and Training Order for 10–17 year-olds in England and Wales, there was widespread positive feedback about 'co-working' and information sharing between institutions and YOTs during the custody period, and sentence planning seemed to be operating effectively, with 72 per cent of the trainees having the expected number of planning and review meetings (Hazel *et al.* 2002). However, problems ranged from incomplete ASSET forms to mid-placement transfers between institutions, which caused disruption to training plans. Encouragingly, in both institutional and YOT contexts, there was a consensus about the central importance of a key worker with whom the trainee could form a trusting relationship: however, this system of allocating a key worker had not been universally adopted. Some institutions had opted for administrative, office-based 'case workers', reportedly with no dedicated member of staff in day-to-day contact with the trainee.

Managing the transition from the institution to the community was also problematic. Researchers found a lack of preparation for trainees' release and, while YOT staff felt that for the majority of trainees they were able to continue work started in custody, in practice their interventions were limited. Both YOT and institution staff pointed to an imbalance of resources between the two halves of the DTO as a primary obstacle to a 'seamless transition' from custody to community, with local authorities often unable to match the level of services provided by institutions for what the researchers describe as 'this age group of socially disaffected and excluded children' (Hazel *et al.* 2002: 99). There were also problems of inter-agency cooperation in the community context, which resulted in delays in arranging and starting activities such as education and training.

In comparison, 'seamless' provision for adult offenders – which to date refers to the resettlement of offenders in the context of a statutory licence period – has been assessed in a rather less positive light (National Audit Office 2002; Social Exclusion Unit 2001; Home Office 2001b). For example, the report of a recent inspection undertaken jointly by the Prison and Probation Inspectorates found that a number of factors contributed to the severe neglect of prisoners' resettlement needs (Home Office 2001b). These factors included:

- the placing of prisoners far from home;
- ineffective sentence planning and/or execution of sentence plans, largely attributed to: different approaches to and priorities for risk assessment, the absence of a case management approach incorporating relevant staff inside and outside prison, and a lack of monitoring/ accountability;
- a lack of clarification regarding the appropriate role of the home probation officer;
- a lack of particular resources for released prisoners, including accommodation and appropriate services for those with drug and alcohol problems.

The Social Exclusion Unit's (2001) detailed examination of resettlement reached similar conclusions. While noting many examples of positive local initiatives, the report highlighted in particular the absence of a single person responsible for ensuring end-to-end cohesion for individual prisoners. The key recommendations of the Social Exclusion Unit report included, in the context of a national rehabilitation strategy, a 'Going Straight Contract': namely, an enhanced sentence plan, based on a 'comprehensive assessment of need' (presumably enabled by the joint use of OASys) to last from the point of sentence to the end of the sentence in the community. Proposing the delivery of such contracts via a 'seamless case management approach', the Social Exclusion Unit report proposed the piloting of different case management models – initially with 18–20 year olds – all involving joint working between prison and probation services and other statutory and non-statutory organisations (2001: 132–133).

Monitoring and reviewing community sentences: the role of the courts

Another aspect of the seamless sentence involves a radical reconceptualisation first of the role of the sentencer, and second of the sentencer's relationship both with the offender and with those responsible for implementing the sentence. The traditional image of the sentencer was summed up in Zimmerman's reference to the 'dispassionate, disinterested magistrate' (cited in Rottman and Casey 1999: 13), whose responsibility for influencing the offender's behaviour began and ended with the pronouncement of the sentence itself. Sentencers were not expected to interact with defendants, whose own detached and peripheral position during court proceedings was in any case further reinforced by the increasing availability of legal representation. In the event of any subsequent breach proceedings, there was no expectation that the original sentencer would necessarily be responsible for sanctioning an offender.

In recent years this 'culture of compartmentalism' has been in retreat, and the introduction of seamless sentencing is likely to lead to further erosion. Three recent developments are worthy of note. The first relates to a tendency to encourage sentencing courts to assume a 'sentence review' function, which would enable them to monitor the implementation of a penalty and, if felt appropriate, to vary the content of an order in the light of an offender's progress. An early example in England and Wales was the Action Plan Order, introduced by the Crime and Disorder Act 1998. Regular review hearings for those on referral orders were also a feature of the Youth Offender Panel Process, introduced by the Youth Justice and Criminal Evidence Act 1999. More recently, a somewhat similar discretionary review process has been adopted by the Criminal Justice Act 2003 in conjunction with the new version of the suspended sentence order.

The second development also involves the routine use of review hearings, but calls in addition for greater collaboration between sentencers and those responsible for implementing the sentences they pass. Both elements are featured in the Drug Treatment and Testing Order (DTTO), which was also introduced by the Crime and Disorder Act. This order requires offenders – provided they consent – to undergo treatment, and is administered by multi-agency teams, who are expected to provide the court with preliminary information about the suitability of offenders before the order is imposed, and thereafter to furnish it with the results of mandatory drug tests. It also involves regular (usually monthly) review hearings, but instead of being merely permissive, these are intended to operate as an integral part of the order.

Evaluations of the DTTO have produced somewhat mixed findings. An 18-month pilot evaluation reported some implementational problems, including slow initial take-up, but self-report data suggested that offenders had substantially reduced their consumption of drugs and their involvement in acquisitive crime (Turnbull *et al.* 2000a, b).[23] A subsequent two-year reconviction study confirmed that there were statistically significant differences in reconviction rates between those who successfully completed their order (53 per cent), and those whose orders were revoked (91 per cent) (Hough *et al.* 2003b). However, the completion rates for the DTTO were disappointingly low, since only 30 per cent successfully finished the order, while 67 per cent had their orders revoked, and this high attrition rate contributed to an overall reconviction rate for those on DTTOs of 80 per cent. There is some evidence that sentencers approve of the DTTO review process, which may be linked with a desire for greater feedback on cases than they currently receive, but concerns have also been expressed about the relatively high costs and listing difficulties involved in the DTTO review process (Hough *et al.* 2003a).

The third development builds on the previous two by combining the principle of regular review hearings and closer collaboration between sentencer and those responsible for implementing a sentence, with the adoption of a more personalised and participatory form of procedure in which sentencer and offender are also expected to work together towards a successful outcome. This kind of approach is best exemplified by so-called 'drug courts' which were initially established in the USA, but have also been piloted in a number of other jurisdictions including England and Scotland.

Although the DTTO resembles the drug court in many ways, the Glasgow Drug Court has a number of distinctive features that set it apart (Eley *et al.* 2002b).[24] First, the court is staffed (on a part-time basis) by two dedicated sheriffs and a clerk who make up the drug court team. Second, the sheriffs have been trained in dealing with matters of substance abuse, are provided with a comprehensive reference manual and, because of their regular sittings, have become experienced in dealing with drug offenders and are conversant with the problems they face, including the likelihood of occasional relapses. Third, the ethos of the court is described as less punitive and more constructive than the regular Sheriff Courts.

Fourth, the court appears to benefit from more comprehensive information, much of which is provided at pre-court review meetings attended by agency representatives but not by the offender. Fifth, there appears to be a strong emphasis in the review hearings themselves on the value of direct dialogue between sheriff and offender, which appears to account for an appreciable proportion (37 per cent overall) of the total review hearing length. Sixth, the role of the sheriff encompasses the tasks of motivating and encouraging as well sanctioning offenders, and this appears to be reflected in the court's enforcement strategy. Thus, whereas the English DTTO pilots in particular appear to have adopted a rather rigid enforcement strategy involving regular recourse to formal breach procedures, this does not appear to have been the case with either the Scottish DTTO pilots or the Glasgow Drug Court.

It is too early to say how effective the Glasgow Drug Court is, though both local and national evaluations of drug courts in the United States have been broadly encouraging (Belenko 1998, 2001). In the light of the discussion in the previous section, however, one of the most interesting aspects of the drug court approach is that it appears to offer an alternative strategy for securing an offender's compliance rather than relying on the rigid and possibly counter-productive use of automatic breach procedures. The approach also offers an alternative way of resurrecting the relational or interpersonal dimension of case management in the face of the countervailing pressures discussed in the section on managing and delivering community sentences. And finally, the approach also resonates with recent findings that where sentencers are provided with evidence of personal mitigation, including a willingness to address the problems caused by offending behaviour, they may be more likely to avoid the use of custody, particularly in cases that are perceived to be 'on the cusp' of a custodial penalty (Hough *et al.* 2003a).

Summary and conclusion

In this chapter we have examined recent developments relating to the implementation of community-based sentences, with particular emphasis on the processes of offender assessment and community order enforcement. We have also examined the challenge posed by attempts to ensure the 'seamless' management of sentences served partly in custody and partly in the community. And, finally, we have reflected on the changing role of the courts with regard to the monitoring and reviewing of community sentences. Two key themes have been prominent throughout this discussion. The first relates to the continuing importance of relational factors within a sentence management context. The second relates to the growing importance of effective partnership working across a range of hitherto largely discrete criminal justice agencies and groups of personnel.

The two themes are linked, inasmuch as the forging of more collaborative and closely coordinated working partnerships between agencies may help to promote a greater sense of coherence, continuity and 'engagement' in the supervision process itself. The development of effective partnership working is unlikely to happen automatically, however, and poses an immense challenge for all the different agencies involved in the process. Moreover, the scale of the challenge is likely to be increased by the introduction of NOMS, which increases the likelihood of further fragmentation in the range and type of agencies involved in the assessment of offenders, and delivery and enforcement of community interventions. If sentence management at an individual level requires more than simple administrative efficiency, the same is also likely to be true of sentence management at an institutional level, which will require much more than ensuring that community interventions are commissioned on the most cost-effective basis. It is a matter of some concern, therefore, that little thought appears to have been given as yet to the implications of NOMS, specifically within the context of sentence management.

Notes

1 Holt (2000) has usefully described case management as the 'context for supervision'.

2 A thorough risk assessment should consider both the likely *gravity or seriousness* of any future offending behaviour and the *probability or likelihood* of such a behaviour occurring. These two dimensions of risk are commonly referred to as *risk of harm* and *risk of re-offending (or reconviction)* respectively. A further important dimension of risk assessment concerns the likely target(s) or victim(s) of the individual's offending (or other harmful) behaviour (Kemshall 1996). In this section we focus predominantly on prediction of risk of re-offending or reconviction. For a review of the literature on the prediction of risk of harm, see Kemshall (2001).

3 It is understood from the Home Office that there are plans to update the OGRS model using more contemporary (PNC) data rather than data held on the Offender Index.

4 For example, OGRS can do no more than provide an estimate of the probability that *an* offender with a particular set of characteristics will be reconvicted within two years; it does not purport to make an accurate prediction for a specific individual. Thus, if an offender has an OGRS score of 75 per cent, this indicates that three-quarters of offenders of this age and sex and with a comparable criminal record are likely to be reconvicted within two years. The score cannot tell the assessor whether this particular individual will be one of the 75 per cent of offenders with this profile who will be reconvicted, or one of the 25 per cent who will not.

5 OASys was designed to meet a comprehensive specification, such that it includes both an assessment of reconviction (incorporating both static and dynamic factors) and a structured format for the assessment of risk of harm.

OASys also triggers other, more specialist assessments in relevant cases (e.g. basic skills; sexual and violent offender assessments) and provides a system for translating the assessment(s) into a supervision or sentence plan.

6 It should be noted, however, that, in the absence of a control group, the interpretation of changes in scores on such instruments is problematic (Bottoms and Dignan 2004: 102).

7 Research on practitioners' use of ASSET in the context of final warnings for juveniles led to calls for a shorter version of the instrument, which has now been made available (Baker *et al.* 2002).

8 See also Holdaway *et al.* (2001: 40) for similar findings in a youth justice context.

9 The growing diversity of personnel currently involved in the management and delivery of community sentences is arguably the most neglected aspect of recent changes in probation, although a number of commentators have noted the increasingly diverse composition of NPS employees (e.g. Cannings 1996; Statham 1999; Morgan 2003). As Morgan (2003) has noted, currently less than half of NPS staff are qualified probation officers. Probation statistics for 2002 indicate that at the end of 2002, 25 per cent of all maingrade officers were trainees. Meanwhile, in the same year the number of Probation Service Officers (non-professionally qualified probation staff) rose by 14 per cent to 4,100 (Home Office 2004). There are indications in the recent Review of Correctional Services that the growing tendency for lower-risk offenders to receive supervision from non-qualified staff may have been a significant factor behind the renewed emphasis on the fine for such offenders: putting low-risk offenders on probation to receive minimal attention is clearly viewed as wasteful of resources.

10 Partridge interviewed up to 15 staff of various grades and up to ten offenders in each of five case study areas.

11 Partridge found that case management teams which fully utilised PSOs and administrative staff in appropriate roles (e.g. administrative staff monitoring attendance and triggering review; PSOs conducting much of the day-to-day work with lower-risk offenders and commissioning interventions) were beneficial for staff and offenders alike.

12 The importance of the supervisor/supervisee relationship is more frequently recognised in youth justice contexts (e.g. Hazel *et al.* 2002; Burnett and Appleton 2004; Batchelor and McNeill 2004). For example, Burnett and Appleton found that in Oxfordshire's YOT, 'practitioners regarded the casework relationship as the *sine qua non* of working with young people to reduce their offending' (2004: 50). The supervisory relationship is also viewed as crucial to the effective management of offenders assessed as posing a risk of harm to others, albeit the relationship is primarily conceived as a basis for 'intelligence-gathering' rather than therapeutic work (which is not to imply that such work is never therapeutic) (Robinson 2002).

13 It is interesting to note that in a multi-site evaluation of IT for juvenile offenders, Bottoms (1995: 11–21) tentatively suggested that the poorer outcomes (in terms of reconviction rates) for one of the six sites might be attributable to the more fragmented model of delivery adopted there.

14 'Responsivity factors' refer to the learning styles and abilities of offenders, which may differ between individuals (Andrews *et al.* 1990).

15 Section 53 of the Criminal Justice and Court Services Act 2000 imposes a statutory duty on supervising officers to issue a warning to offenders after the *first* unacceptable failure to comply with an order, and to return offenders to court after a second unacceptable failure. The Act also introduces a presumption of imprisonment in such cases, unless the court is of the opinion either that the offender is likely to comply with the order during the remaining period, or that there are exceptional circumstances.

16 This study, which preceded the tightening-up of the enforcement regime referred to above, revealed two main reasons – and two main outcomes – for initiating breach proceedings: when using breach proceedings to ensure compliance ('constructive' breach), supervisors said they recommended that sentencers allowed an order to continue (with a warning about future conduct and/or a small fine); but they tended to recommend revocation and re-sentencing where an order had broken down or where the offender had made no effort to start the order.

17 The supervising officer does however maintain discretion in respect of deciding whether a failure to report or otherwise comply with instructions constitutes 'unacceptable' behaviour, thereby warranting a warning.

18 See Hedderman (2003) for a review of the findings of three independent audits of enforcement practice in respect of orders and licences.

19 A recent NPD publication reports that, by September 2003, 73 per cent of eligible offenders were being breached within ten days, a 20 per cent improvement on performance in the previous year (NPD 2003).

20 Hearnden and Millie found that in some cases breach was initiated to alert offenders to the fact that they were liable to end up at court. Some areas continued to offer appointments in such cases, a process which functioned as 'an extra layer of warning after a final warning, to be applied to relatively motivated offenders whose record of reporting was generally good' (2003: 6).

21 Some of the problems associated with a rigid approach to breach are particularly evident in the context of the more intensive programmes of supervision. The Audit Commission (2004: 43) has recently argued that, in respect of Intensive Supervision and Surveillance Programmes (ISSPs), the response to breach needs to be proportionate to the level of breach, and custody should be used only as a last resort (see also Chapter 11, this volume).

22 Seamless sentences for young offenders ('Secure Training Orders') were first introduced in England and Wales by the Criminal Justice Act 1991, and were extended to adult offenders in the Criminal Justice Act 2003.

23 An evaluation of a number of Scottish pilot DTTO schemes reported similar findings (Eley *et al.* 2002a).

24 The court has the same sentencing powers – including the DTTO, conditional probation orders and deferred sentences – as other Sheriff Courts.

References

Andrews, D. and Bonta, J. (1994) *The Psychology of Criminal Conduct* (Cincinnati, OH: Anderson).

Andrews, D. and Bonta, J. (1995) *The Level of Service Inventory – Revised: Manual* (New York: Multi-Health Systems Inc.).

Andrews, D. A., Bonta, J. and Hoge, R. D. (1990) 'Classification for effective rehabilitation', *Criminal Justice and Behavior*, 17(1), 19–52.

Andrews, D. A., Zinger, I., Hoge, R. D., Bonta, J., Gendreau, P. and Cullen, F. T. (1990) 'Does correctional treatment work? A clinically relevant and psychologically informed meta-analysis', *Criminology*, 28(3), 369–404.

Audit Commission (2004) *Youth Justice 2004: A review of the reformed youth justice system* (London: Audit Commission).

Aye-Maung, N. and Hammond, N. (2000) *Risk of Re-offending and Needs Assessments: The user's perspective*, Home Office Research Study 216 (London: Home Office).

Baker, K., Jones, S., Roberts, C. and Merrington, S. (2002) *Validity and Reliability of ASSET: Final report to the Youth Justice Board* (Oxford: University of Oxford Probation Studies Unit).

Barry. M. (2000) 'The mentor/monitor debate in criminal justice: "what works" for offenders', *British Journal of Social Work*, 30, 575–595.

Batchelor, S. and McNeill, F. (2004, forthcoming) 'The young person-worker relationship' in T. Bateman and J. Pitts (eds) *The Russell House Companion to Youth Justice* (London: Russell House Publishing).

Beaumont, B., Caddick, B. and Hare-Duke, H. (2001) *Meeting Offenders' Needs* (Bristol: University of Bristol School for Policy Studies).

Belenko, S. (1998) *Research on Drug Courts: A critical review* (New York: National Centre on Addiction and Substance Abuse at Columbia University).

Belenko, S. (2001) *Research on Drug Courts: A critical review 2000 update* (New York: National Centre on Addiction and Substance Abuse at Columbia University).

Blair, C. (2000) *Prisons and Probation*, Research Report 6: Criminal Justice Review Group (Belfast: HMSO) [www.nio.gov.uk/pdf/06.pdf].

Bonta, J. (1996) 'Risk-needs assessment and treatment', in A. T. Harland (ed.) *Choosing Correctional Options That Work* (London: Sage).

Bottoms, A. E. (1995) *Intensive Community Supervision for Young Offenders: Outcomes, process and cost* (Cambridge: Institute of Criminology).

Bottoms, A. E. (2001) 'Compliance and community penalties', in A. E. Bottoms, L. Gelsthorpe and S. Rex (eds), *Community Penalties: Change and challenges* (Cullompton: Willan).

Bottoms, A. and Dignan, J. (2004) 'Youth crime and youth justice: comparative and cross-national perspectives', in M. Tonry (ed.) *Crime and Justice: A review of research*, 31, 21–183.

Burnett, R. (1996) *Fitting Supervision to Offenders: Assessment and allocation decisions in the Probation Service*, Home Office Research Study 153 (London: Home Office).

Burnett, R. (2004) 'One-to-one ways of promoting desistance: in search of an evidence-base', in R. Burnett and C. Roberts (eds) *What Works in Probation and Youth Justice* (Cullompton: Willan).

Burnett. R. and Appleton, C. (2004) 'Joined-up services to tackle youth crime: a case study in England', *British Journal of Criminology*, 44(1), 34–54.

Cannings, J. (1996) 'Workforce flexibility', *VISTA*, 2(1), 28–33.

Carter, P. (2003) *Managing Offenders, Reducing Crime: A new approach* (Correctional Services Review) (London: Home Office).

Chapman, T. and Hough, M. (1998) *Evidence Based Practice* (London: Home Office).

Copas, J. and Marshall, P. (1998) 'The offender group reconviction scale: a statistical reconviction score for use by probation officers', *Applied Statistics*, 47, 159–171.

Davies, N. (2004) 'Probation staff use one word to describe the service: "Chaos"', *Guardian*, 14 April 2004.

Ditton, J. and Ford, R. (1994) *The Reality of Probation: A formal ethnography of process and practice* (Aldershot: Avebury).

Drakeford, M. (1993) 'But who will do the work?', *Critical Social Policy*, 13(2), 64–76.

Eley, S., Gallop, K., McIvor, G., Morgan, K. and Yates, R. (2002a) *Drug Treatment and Testing Orders: Evaluation of the Scottish pilots* (Edinburgh: Scottish Executive Social Research).

Eley, S., Malloch, M., McIvor, G., Yates, R, and Brown, A. (2002b) *Glasgow's Pilot Drug Court in Action: The first six months* (Edinburgh: Scottish Executive Social Research).

Ellis, T. (2000) 'Enforcement policy and practice: evidence-based or rhetoric-based?', *Criminal Justice Matters*, 39, 5.

Ellis, T., Hedderman, C. and Mortimer, E. (1996) *Enforcing Community Sentences*, Home Office Research Study 158 (London: Home Office).

Farrall, S. (2002) 'Long-term absences from probation: officers' and probationers' accounts', *Howard Journal of Criminal Justice*, 41(3), 263–278.

Farrow, K. (2004) 'Still committed after all these years? Morale in the modern-day Probation Service', *Probation Journal*, 3: 206–220.

Faulkner, D. (2001) *Crime, State and Citizen: A field full of folk* (Winchester: Waterside Press).

Gelsthorpe, L. and Rex, S. (2004) 'Community service as reintegration: exploring the potential', in G. Mair (ed.) *What Matters in Probation* (Cullompton: Willan).

Gendreau, P., Goggin, C. and Smith, P. (1999) 'The forgotten issue in effective correctional treatment: program implementation', *International Journal of Offender Therapy*, 43(2), 180–187.

Gibbs, A. (1999) 'The assessment, case management and evaluation system', *Probation Journal*, 46(3), 182–186.

Hazel, N., Hagell, A., Liddle, M., Archer, D., Grimshaw, R., and King, J. (2002) *Detention and Training: Assessment of the Detention and Training Order and its impact on the secure estate across England and Wales* (London: Youth Justice Board).

Hearnden, I. and Millie, A. (2003) *Investigating Links between Probation Enforcement and Reconviction*, Home Office Online Report 41/03 (London: Home Office) [www.homeoffice.gov.uk/rds/pdfs2/rdsolr4103.pdf].

Hedderman, C. (2003) 'Enforcing supervision and encouraging compliance', in W.-H. Chui and M. Nellis (eds), *Probation: Theories, practice and research* (Harlow: Pearson Education).

Hedderman, C. and Hough, M. (2000) 'Tightening up probation: a step too far?', *Criminal Justice Matters*, 39, 5.

Hedderman, C. and Hough, M. (2004) 'Getting tough or being effective: what matters?', in G. Mair (ed.) *What Matters in Probation* (Cullompton: Willan).

HM Inspectorate of Probation (1999) *Offender Assessment and Supervision Planning: Helping to achieve effective intervention with offenders*. Report of a developmental thematic inspection (London: Home Office).

HM Inspectorate of Probation (2002a) *Probation Service Workload Prioritisation: Report of an HMIP National Survey* (London: Home Office).

HM Inspectorate of Probation (2002b) *Annual Report 2001/2002* (London: Home Office).

HM Inspectorate of Probation (2003) *Annual Report 2002/2003* (London: Home Office).

Holdaway, S., Davidson, N., Dignan, J., Hammersley, R., Hine, J. and Marsh, P. (2001), *New Strategies to Address Youth Offending: the national evaluation of the pilot youth offending teams*, RDS Occasional Paper No. 69 (London: Home Office).

Hollin, C., McGuire, J., Palmer, E., Bilby, C., Hatcher, R. and Holmes, A. (2002) *Introducing Pathfinder Programmes into the Probation Service: An interim report*, Home Office Research Study 247 (London: Home Office).

Holt, P. (2000) *Case Management: Context for supervision*, Community and Criminal Justice Monograph 2 (Leicester: De Montfort University).

Home Office (1996) *Guidance for the Probation Service on the Offender Group Reconviction Scale (OGRS)*, Probation Circular 63/1996 (London: Home Office).

Home Office (1999) *Effective Practice Initiative: A joint risk/needs assessment system for the Prison and Probation Services*. Probation Circular 16/1999 (London: Home Office).

Home Office (2000) *National Standards for the Supervision of Offenders in the Community* (London: Home Office).

Home Office (2001a) *Making Punishments Work: Report of a review of the sentencing framework for England and Wales* (London: Home Office Communications Directorate).

Home Office (2001b) *Through the Prison Gate: A joint thematic review by HM Inspectorates of Prisons and Probation* (London: Home Office).

Home Office (2004) *Probation Statistics, England and Wales 2002* (London: Home Office).

Hough, M., Jacobson, J. and Millie, A. (2003a) *The Decision to Imprison: Sentencing and the prison population* (London: Prison Reform Trust).

Hough, M., Clancy, A., McSweeney, T. and Turnbull, P.J. (2003b) *The Impact of Drug Treatment and Testing Orders on Offending: Two-year reconviction results*, Home Office Research Findings No. 194 (London: Home Office).

Hudson, B. (2001) 'Human rights, public safety and the probation service: defending justice in the risk society', *Howard Journal*, 40(2), 103–113.

Kemshall, H. (1996) *Reviewing Risk* (London: Home Office).

Kemshall, H. (1998) *Risk in Probation Practice* (Aldershot: Ashgate).

Kemshall, H. (2001) *Risk Assessment and Management of Known Sexual and Violent Offenders: A review of current issues*, Police Research Series Paper 140 (London: Home Office).

Kemshall, H. and Canton, R. (2002) *The Effective Management of Programme Attrition* (London: National Probation Service).

Liebling, A. (2004) *Prisons and their Moral Performance: A study of values, quality and prison life* (Oxford: Oxford University Press).

May, C. and Wadwell, J. (2001) *Enforcing Community Penalties: The relationship between enforcement and reconviction*, Home Office Research Findings 155 (London: Home Office).

McIvor, G. and Barry, M. (1998) *Social Work and Criminal Justice. Volume 6: Probation* (Edinburgh: Scottish Office Central Research Unit).

Meehl, P. E. (1954) *Clinical Versus Statistical Prediction* (Minneapolis, MN: University of Minnesota Press).

Merrington, S. (2001) 'Objectives, intervention and reducing risk', *Probation Studies Unit ACE Practitioner Bulletin No. 3* (Oxford: University of Oxford) [www.crim.ox.ac.uk/publications/psubull3.pdf].

Merrington, S. and Skinns, J. (2000) 'Using ACE to profile criminogenic needs', *Probation Studies Unit ACE Practitioner Bulletin No. 1* (Oxford: University of Oxford) [www.crim.ox.ac.uk/publications/psubull1.pdf].

Morgan, R. (2003) 'Thinking about the demand for probation services', *Probation Journal*, 50(1), 7–19.

MORI (2003) *Magistrates' Perceptions of the Probation Service* [www.probation.homeoffice.gov.uk/files/pdf/Morifinalre port2003.pdf].

National Association of Probation Officers (1998) *NAPO News*, September, Issue 8.

National Association of Probation Officers (1999) *NAPO News*, March, Issue 12.

National Association of Probation Officers (2001) 'Unexecuted Warrants', *NAPO News*, 135, 1.

National Association of Probation Officers (2003) 'OASys and PSR questionnaire – summary', *NAPO News*, 152, 6.

National Audit Office (2002) *Reducing Prisoner Reoffending* (London: HMSO).

National Probation Directorate (2001) *National Management Manual* [www.probation.homeoffice.gov.uk/files/pdf/NationalManag ementManual.pdf].

National Probation Directorate (2003) *Performance Report 10, November 2003* [www.probation.homeoffice.gov.uk/output/page34.asp].

National Probation Service (2003) *What Works News*, Issue 14, August [www.probation.homeoffice.gov.uk/output/Page193.asp].

Nellis, M. (1999) 'Towards "the field of corrections": modernizing the probation service in the late 1990s', *Social Policy and Administration*, 33(3), 302–323.

Nellis, M. and Chui, W.-H. (2003) 'The end of probation?', in W.-H. Chui and M. Nellis (eds), *Probation: Theories, practice and research* (Harlow: Pearson Education).

Oldfield, M. (1998) 'Case management: developing theory and practice', *VISTA: Perspectives on Probation*, 4(1), 21–36.

Partridge, S. (2004) *Examining Case Management Models for Community Sentences*, Home Office Online Report 17/04 (London: Home Office) [www.homeoffice.gov.uk/rds/onlinepubs1.html].

Raynor, P. (1998) 'Reading Probation Statistics: a critical comment', *VISTA: Perspectives on Probation*, 3, 181–185.

Raynor, P., Kynch, J., Roberts, C. and Merrington, S. (2000) *Risk and Need Assessment in Probation Services: An evaluation*, Home Office Research Study 211 (London: Home Office).

Rex, S. (1999) 'Desistance from offending: experiences of probation', *Howard Journal of Criminal Justice*, 38(4), 366–383.

Rex, S., Gelsthorpe, L., Roberts, C. and Jordan, P. (2003) *Crime Reduction Programme: An evaluation of community service pathfinder projects: final report 2002*, RDS Occasional Paper 87 (London: Home Office).

Rex, S. and Matravers, A. (eds) (1998) *Pro-Social Modelling and Legitimacy* (Cambridge: Institute of Criminology).

Ricketts, T., Bliss, P., Murphy, K. and Brooker, C. (2002) *The Life-Course of the DTTO: Engagement with drug treatment and testing orders* (Sheffield: University of Sheffield School of Health and Related Research).

Roberts, C. and Robinson, G. (1998) 'Improving practice through pilot studies: the case of pre-sentence reports', *VISTA: Perspectives on Probation*, 3(3), 186–195.

Roberts, C., Burnett, R., Kirby, A. and Hamill, H. (1996) *A System for Evaluating Probation Practice*, Probation Studies Unit Report No. 1 (Oxford: University of Oxford Centre for Criminological Research).

Robinson, G. (2001) 'Probation, risk and governance', Unpublished PhD thesis (Swansea: University of Wales).

Robinson, G. (2002) 'Exploring risk management in the probation service: contemporary developments in England and Wales', *Punishment and Society*, 4(1), 5–25.

Robinson, G. (2003) 'Implementing OASys: lessons from research into LSI-R and ACE', *Probation Journal*, 50(1), 30–40.

Rottman, D. and Casey, P. (1999) 'Therapeutic jurisprudence and the emergence of problem-solving courts', *National Institution of Justice Journal*, 240, 12–19.

Rumgay, J. (2003) 'Partnerships in the probation service', in W.-H. Chui and M. Nellis (eds), *Probation: Theories, practice and research* (Harlow: Pearson Education).

Social Exclusion Unit (2001) *Reducing Re-Offending by Ex-Prisoners* (London: Office of the Deputy Prime Minister).

Sparks, R., Bottoms, A. and Hay, W. (1996) *Prisons and the Problem of Order* (Oxford: Clarendon Press).

Statham, R. (1999) 'Probation: a life beyond the reviews', *Probation Journal*, 46(1), 26–30.

Taylor, R. (1999) *Predicting Reconvictions for Sexual and Violent Offences Using the Revised Offender Group Reconviction Scale*, Home Office Research Findings 104 (London: Home Office).

Trotter, C. (1996) 'The impact of different supervision practices in community corrections', *Australian and New Zealand Journal of Criminology*, 28(2), 29–46.

Trotter, C. (1999) *Working with Involuntary Clients: A guide to practice* (London: Sage).

Turnbull, P., McSweeney, T. and Hough, M. (2000a) *Drug Treatment and Testing Orders – the 18-month evaluation*, Home Office Research Findings No. 128 (London: Home Office Research and Statistics Directorate).

Turnbull, P., McSweeney, T. and Hough, M. (2000b) *Drug Treatment and Testing Orders Evaluation Report*, Home Office Research Study No. 212 (London: Home Office Research and Statistics Directorate).

Underdown, A. (1998) *Strategies for Effective Offender Supervision: Report of the HMIP What Works Project* (London: Home Office).

Underdown, A. (2001) 'Making "what works" work: challenges in the delivery of community penalties', in A. Bottoms, L. Gelsthorpe and S. Rex (eds), *Community Penalties: Change and challenges* (Cullompton: Willan).

Chapter 14

Dimensions of difference

Hazel Kemshall, Rob Canton and Roy Bailey

Introduction and remit of the chapter

This chapter will consider the provision of non-custodial measures for specific minority offender groups, namely women, ethnic minorities and mentally disordered offenders. Standard non-custodial approaches (such as community punishment or the first tranche of cognitive-behavioural programmes) have often been designed for 'mainstream' white, male and mentally stable offenders, with little attention to minority groups. These programmes have been critiqued on the following grounds: their lack of relevance to the criminogenic needs of minority groups; attrition rates (although the evidence for different attrition rates is not clear: see Kemshall and Canton 2002); lack of use by sentencers; and negative offender views about the appropriateness of supervision programmes. The chapter will consider the extent to which minority offender groups are over-represented in the prison population; the evidence for differential criminogenic needs across these offender groups; and the limited research evidence on both the relevance and effectiveness of non-custodial approaches for these offender groups.

The chapter is based upon a systematic review of the main English-language journal article databases, the Home Office Research, Development and Statistics website, and Home Office publications under section 95 of the Criminal Justice Act 1991.[1] This is necessarily selective and focuses on peer-reviewed material, government-commissioned research and officially produced statistics. Where possible, efforts have been made to supplement this with book material, professional journal articles (often based on small-scale qualitative studies) and local probation area reviews and evaluations of local programmes. The review is therefore illustrative of the main debates rather than exhaustive; due to the diverse nature of the research studies drawn upon, there has been no attempt to meet the standards of meta-analytic inquiry. The chapter is rather a scoping study mapping the key literature and the main arguments in the field. Some caution must also be exercised in the use of official statistics; in particular, concerns have been raised over the completeness of section 95 data (Home Office 2000a). In the case of offenders with a mental disorder or learning disability, reliable statistics have also been difficult to produce.

Differential access to community penalties has raised concerns, not least because it has been implicated in the differential rates of custody across ethnic groups in both the USA and the UK (Garland 2001; Wacquant 2001, 2002) and a disproportionate increase in the numbers of women in the custodial population (Home Office 2002a). At the end of June 2002, 16,170 prisoners in English and Welsh prison service establishments were known to belong to ethnic minority groups (Councell 2003), making up 22 per cent of the male prison population and 29 per cent of the female population. This is a small increase over 2001, when 21 per cent and 26 per cent respectively were from ethnic minority groups. The ethnic minority prison population has increased by 124 per cent since 1992, with the population of 'Chinese and other' prisoners increasing the most over that period (up 183 per cent); white and South Asian prisoners increased the least (46 per cent and 58 per cent respectively). Recent prison service statistics present the prison population by ethnic category (using 2001 census categories), although the caveat is made that a large proportion of ethnic minority prisoners are foreign nationals. Of the British nationals in the male prison population '83% were white, 12% were Black, 3% were South Asian ... and 2% belonged to Chinese or other ethnic minority groups. For female British nationals in the prison population, 83% were white, 13% were Black, 1% were South Asian and 3% belonged to Chinese or other ethnic minority groups.' (Home Office 2003a: 18).[2]

From Home Office statistics on women in the criminal justice system published under section 95 of the Criminal Justice Act 1991, the following key points can be discerned:

- women prisoners make up more than 5 per cent of the prison population;
- there were 3,740 women in prison in 2001;
- between 1993 and 2001 the average population of women in prison rose by 140 per cent as against 46 per cent for men, reflecting sentencing changes at the courts;
- in mid-2001 ethnic minority groups made up 26 per cent of the female population compared to 20 per cent of the male prison population;
- 19 per cent of female prisoners in 2001 were foreign nationals; in June 2001, 92 per cent of sentenced black female foreign nationals were held for drug offences;

- theft and handling remain the most common indictable offence for women, accounting for 60 per cent of female offenders in 2001;
- recent figures suggest that the rise in sentenced prison receptions for women is driven by a more severe response to less serious offences;
- the rate of increase of women being given a custodial sentence at magistrates' court is higher than at Crown Court.

(Home Office 2002a: iii–iv)

Paradoxically, the last two points need to be placed within a broader sentencing context in which:

- women are more likely than men to be discharged or given a community sentence for indictable offences and are less likely to be fined or sentenced to custody;
- women sentenced to custody receive on average shorter sentences than men.

(Home Office 2002a: iii)

The situation for mentally disordered offenders is somewhat more complex. Defining exactly who falls into this group is itself fraught with difficulty (Canton 2002) and may include offenders whose mental health difficulties are significant but not necessarily of a type or severity to bring them within the remit of the Mental Health Act 1983 (NACRO 1998). Thus while some reference point is required for any considered policy discussion, it must be recognised that mental illness encompasses an enormous range of conditions from severe psychosis to mild anxiety and depression, and that 'disorder' can include learning disability as well as personality disorder.

Associated with the definitional problems is the question of prevalence. Although several research studies have been undertaken on the prevalence of mental ill-health among prisoners (for example, Gunn *et al.* 1991; Singleton *et al.* 1998), there are no studies of comparable reliability on the incidence of mental disorder among offenders in the community. However, some inferences can be made from the prison studies. Nadkarni *et al.* (2000) reasonably speculate that the psychiatric profile of residents in a probation hostel is likely to be similar to that of a prison remand population. All prisoners come from – and almost all return to – the community: many will have been in contact with the Probation Service and other agencies before sentence, and most of them will be under supervision after release. Singleton and colleagues (1998) found that 64 per cent of (adult, male, sentenced) prisoners had some form of personality disorder.

Attempts to assess the incidence of mentally disordered offenders on probation and other community agency caseloads have produced widely varying estimates. Vaughan's study identified 7.5 per cent of the probation caseload in the relevant geographical area as mentally disordered (Vaughan *et al.* 2000). By comparison, mentally disordered offenders constituted 7 per cent of those supervised by area mental health teams, 13 per cent of the caseload of the learning disability teams and 3 per cent of those supervised by the drug and alcohol teams. In a recent review (August 2003), teams in nearly half the probation areas in England and Wales participated in a survey that 'found that 27% of offenders on [probation] caseloads were defined by probation staff as having a mental disorder'.[3] The study expresses confidence that this is an underestimate (NAPO 2003). Vaughan *et al.* also found that only about one-fifth of those identified by probation officers as mentally disordered were under formal psychiatric supervision,[4] although much larger numbers will be in contact with psychiatric services at some level.

Despite some caveats, there is significant evidence to show that difference and diversity play a part in differential treatment by the criminal justice system. This is most obviously seen in differing custody rates, but is also evidenced by differing arrest rates and sentencing patterns. The next section will review some of the main reasons for the over-representation of some minority groups in custody and compulsory care.

Are minority groups over-represented in custody and compulsory care?

Since 1992 a series of documents has been published under Criminal Justice Act section 95 covering the prison population, probation caseload, and sentencing practices. By 1999 these publications revealed that African Caribbeans made up approximately 13 percent of the prison population but just under 2 per cent of the general population (Home Office 1999; Matthews 2003). While cross-national comparative studies are still relatively rare, this problem is common to most Anglophone countries (Parenti 1999; Garland 2001) and to other European countries (Tomasevski 1994; Sampson and Lauritsen 1997). A recent study by Hood *et al.* (2003) found that one in five black defendants in the Crown Court and one in ten in the Magistrates' Court believed that they had suffered unfair treatment by receiving a more severe sentence than their white counterparts.

Hedderman (2004a), drawing on Home Office statistics, has demonstrated a dramatic increase in the female prison population between 1992 and 2000, and that, while male receptions rose by 58 per cent in the period, the number of women received tripled from '2200 in 1992 to 7000 in 2000' (2004a: 82). In an in-depth review, Hedderman argues that this change can be explained by the following:

- change in the sentencing patterns for women resulting in a tripling in the use of custody for women (with the use of probation also increasing);
- while the ratio in the use of custody in 1992 between women and men was 1:20, by 2000 it was 1:10;
- there is little evidence of a change in the nature, prevalence or seriousness of female offending, hence sentencers are making greater use of custodial sentences – although the cases coming to court do not reflect a proportionate increase in seriousness.

(Hedderman 2004a; see also Home Office 2001a, 2001b)

Paradoxically, custody and community supervision for women offenders have both risen, and fines have reduced. Rumgay (2004) has argued that this reflects a general 'up-tariffing' of women and a generally harsher sentencing climate. This conclusion is supported by data published under section 95 (Home Office 2002a) in which sentencing patterns in the magistrates' court are seen as particularly problematic. In a large-scale Home Office study Hedderman and Dowds (1997) showed that sentencers were reluctant to impose fines on women largely due to their financial circumstances and child-care responsibilities. The result could either be 'greater leniency' and discharging, or 'greater severity' through the imposition of community supervision. They saw the latter as a significant step on the 'tariff' ladder with the likely imposition of a more severe sentence upon reconviction. Subsequent statistics would indicate that their prediction of higher custodial rates for women has been correct (see also Gelsthorpe and Loucks 1997; Gelsthorpe and Padfield 2003).

The position for mentally disordered offenders is again complex, not least due to the definitional problems discussed above. However, it is clear that the use of treatment orders or conditions under the supervision of the Probation Service has declined. Under the Powers of Criminal Courts (Sentencing) Act 2000 Schedule 2 para 5, the Court can impose a treatment requirement when making a community rehabilitation order. Despite this (and previous legislation of a similar type), the use of such a condition has been in decline since the 1970s (Clark *et al*. 2002). It is now included in less than 2 per cent of all community rehabilitation orders (see Probation Statistics for England and Wales 2002: 30). The Royal College of Psychiatrists (1993) has estimated that at least 3,000 offender-patients would benefit from community supervision, and despite cautious advocacy from Her Majesty's Inspectorate of Probation (1993) for its increased use, its use remains infrequent. The lack of enthusiasm for such community measures in part reflects poor liaison between probation and community psychiatric services,[5] but also a wider context in which penal policy and mental health policy have been meshed with a resulting emphasis upon risk management and public protection rather than care

(Hagell and Dowling 1999). This has been paralleled by a declining confidence in 'care in the community' (Goodwin 1997) and a greater emphasis upon compulsory care based on assessments of risk (Fennell 1999; Laurance 2003). Preoccupations with risk and individual high-profile cases (such as Christopher Clunis) can obscure the general offending profile of mentally disordered offenders. Vaughan *et al.* (2000) examined the offending profile of those offenders identified as mentally disordered and found that, while a significant proportion of those on the probation caseload had committed offences of violence, mentally disordered offenders were also placed on supervision for other offences: theft 24 per cent; burglary 19 per cent; and public disorder offences 14 per cent. The proportion of such offenders placed on community rehabilitation orders for theft was close to the national average (Probation Statistics for England and Wales 2001: 22). However, access to mainstream probation cognitive-behavioural groups remains low (Canton 2002).

The criminal justice route remains a key gateway to mental health provision for many mentally disordered offenders, and is disproportionately used for black mentally disordered offenders (Fernando 1998). A Department of Health report (2003) drew attention to institutional racism within the mental healthcare system and identified an overemphasis upon institutional and coercive treatment for black patients. Bhui *et al.* (2003) also found that in 18 of the 23 studies they reviewed there was a higher compulsory admission rate for black patients, and conversely Asians were referred less often than white patients. The reason for the high rate for black mental healthcare users is not clear, although there is some speculation that this is due to perceptions of higher risk on the part of healthcare workers (Ryan 2003).

Analyses of the reasons for differential sentencing rates are wide-ranging. Wacquant (2001, 2002), for example, locates racially different custodial rates within the shrinkage of welfare and the increased use of the penal system to regulate and control the population (see also Garland 2001), with penal regulation especially targeted at the 'socially excluded' and those perceived to be under-regulated by the labour market (e.g. young black men) (see also Young 1999, 2002; Pitts 2003). Actuarial justice and the rise of a risk-based penality have been implicated by some commentators in the increased use of custody for both ethnic minorities and for women (Hannah-Moffat 1999; Shaw and Hannah-Moffat 2000, 2004; O'Malley 2001; Matthews 2003), and in the increased use of compulsory treatment and care for mentally disordered offenders (Fennell 1999). In brief, actuarial practices are seen to exert a disproportionate impact on marginalised groups (Hudson 2001), and traditional 'needs' are re-inscribed as risks requiring additional surveillance, enforcement, and 'treatment' (O'Malley 2001). This has resulted in a 'new rehabilitationism' (Rotman 1990) with emphasis on 'tough' community penalties, correcting 'cognitive deficits', and re-educating offenders into moral, worthy citizens

(Kemshall 2002a, 2003). The emphasis on 'corrective programmes' as the cornerstone of community rehabilitation orders is seen to have a differential impact upon minority groups, not least in terms of programme content, but also in terms of access: such groups rely on volume, and a steady 'turnover' of offenders and low numbers make groups unviable and provision patchy (Powis and Walmsley 2002). Effective and appropriate targeting remains a significant issue (Powis and Walmsley 2002).

The review of the work of the Joint Accreditation Panel[6] has also addressed the issue of diversity, but found that in the absence of 'evidence relating to diversity ... belief and assertion has tended to acquire the status of "truth" ...' (Rex *et al.* 2003: 31). The review acknowledged ongoing research and that further work was required in this area. The Joint Accreditation Panel has appointed a diversity advisor, and its new terms of reference charge the panel 'with ensuring that diversity issues are taken into account in programme development, accreditation and implementation' (Rex *et al.* 2003: 38; see also Rex and Bottoms 2003). This can include the use of pilot programmes to establish the most effective interventions for minority groups. However, it is too early to evaluate the impact of this change on the work of the panel, or in the accreditation of subsequent programmes.

At the level of practice, individuals within the criminal justice system should make impartial, objective and non-discriminatory decisions. However, there is evidence that such decisions are affected by value judgements, prejudice, vagaries of local practices, institutional culture and institutional discrimination (Hood and Cordovil 1992; Macpherson 1999; HMIP 2000; Gelsthorpe 2001; Raynor and Vanstone 2002; Bowling and Phillips 2003; Gelsthorpe and Padfield 2003; Hood *et al.* 2003; Hedderman 2004a, 2004b; Rumgay 2004). It is also important to recognise that discrimination can take the form of disregarding difference, treating people 'the same' when their circumstances are relevantly different. For this reason, tighter constraints on discretion will not eliminate unfairness (Eadie and Canton 2002)

Literature in this area tends toward either small-scale qualitative studies on the use of discretion in decision-making or inspection and inquiry reports on the activities of criminal justice personnel (e.g. Macpherson 1999; Her Majesty's Inspectorate of Probation 2000). The evidence that such reports result in long-term corrective action is patchy, with some anecdotal evidence that resistance among criminal justice personnel can be increased (see Lea 2003 on policing post-Macpherson). In probation there is Home Office evidence that monitoring under section 95 itself remains incomplete (Home Office 2000a; Her Majesty's Inspectorate of Probation 2000), thus reducing the impact of such material on policy and practice. There is also evidence that assessment practices for access and referral to accredited programmes in probation are differential, particularly between white and ethnic minority offenders, and supervision practice in respect of ethnic minority offenders has raised concerns for the

Inspectorate (HMIP 2000). The follow-up report in 2004 (HMIP 2004) noted improvement, but urged local probation areas to improve the quality of pre-sentence reports (PSRs) on ethnic minority offenders, and to review the outcomes of Specific Sentence Reports in relation to race. Further work on responsivity issues within programmes was also advised.

Evidence for differential 'criminogenic needs'

Criminogenic needs have been defined as those needs 'linked to criminal behaviour' and are seen as key targets for 'correctional intervention' (Bonta 1996: 23, 27). Only those needs linked to recidivism are seen as legitimate for concern and intervention (Gendreau and Andrews 1990; Aubrey and Hough 1997), and the term 'dynamic risk factors' is often substituted for 'criminogenic needs'. While presented within the framework of rehabilitation, the concept belongs very clearly within the post-'nothing works' era (Martinson 1974) and the 'correctional rehabilitation' of the 'New Rehabilitationism' (Rotman 1990). Thus 'needs' are re-inscribed as risks (O'Malley 2001) and interventions are driven by risk classifications (Robinson 1999). The strange linguistic hybrid of criminogenic need seems to function as an ideological hybrid between the world of welfare needs and the world of risk and correction (Kemshall 2003). The term itself is currently subject to debate, with conceptual confusion between 'criminogenic need' and 'human need', and critique of defining such needs as only personal deficit (for the current debate see Andrews and Bonta 2003; Ward and Stewart 2003a, b).

The new rehabilitationism stresses self-management and the inculcation of self-controls (Rose 2000). This individualising discourse has served to restrict interventions to the personal domain of individual change and away from broader issues of social structure (Hannah-Moffat and Shaw 1999). Within probation this is epitomised by cognitive-behavioural programmes that seek to build resilience to criminal behaviour and choices while teaching self-risk management and correcting 'thinking deficits' (Raynor 2002; Kemshall 2003).

There are basically three positions on criminogenic needs and diversity:

- There is little evidence that criminogenic needs are substantially different as between majority and minority groups and there is no reason to change existing provision.
- There is growing evidence that criminogenic needs are substantially different and that therefore changes in existing provision to target such needs are required.
- The third position, which relates solely to ethnic diversity, sees differences in criminogenic needs, but also emphasises that the addi-

tional experience of racism and social exclusion adds a significant extra layer, justifying differential provision such as black empowerment/ development groups.

The first position accepts that mainstream provision is likely to be appropriate with some minor adjustments, focused largely on 'accessibility' issues and making aspects of existing programme content 'culturally sensitive' (e.g. designing more culturally appropriate role-plays, case examples). This is the position taken by the recent Home Office *Diversity Review* on offending behaviour programmes (2002b), and in Powis and Walmsley's (2002) review of programmes for black and Asian offenders carried out for the Home Office. The Probation Service's 'What Works Strategy' (Home Office 2000c) commits the service to ensuring that 'Interventions are designed and delivered in ways which make them accessible and effective for all groups of offenders, including those from ethnic minorities, women and those with disabilities . . .'.

The starting position remains that existing accredited programmes are seen through what Hedderman (2004b) has called the 'prism of white, adult-based provision' (see also NAPO 2002), and other groups remain either invisible or at best marginalised. Attention is then given to improving tutor skills, and in achieving higher levels of responsivity in programme content and delivery while maintaining overall programme integrity (Home Office 2002b; Powis and Walmsley 2002). The invisibility of minority groups in mainstream provision is thus recast as an issue of worker skill and competence, appropriate targeting and assessment, and modification of referral practices and programme content.

The issue is further complicated by the paucity of empirical research, a difficulty acknowledged by the *Diversity Review* and by Powis and Walmsley (2002). The latter were unable to draw any firm conclusions about the extent of difference in criminogenic needs, or about the type of intervention most likely to be successful in reducing offending among black and Asian offenders, although the potential of emerging research to change this position was acknowledged. In addition, Hedderman (2004b), among others, has pointed out the low level of research on women and criminogenic needs: 'Very few studies of women offenders have examined the link between static or dynamic factors and reconviction . . . less than 2 per cent of the 1606 studies indicated in the CDATE meta-analysis database involved women offenders' (2004b: 229).

The second position argues that emerging research indicates significant differences in criminogenic need, particularly between men and women (Gelsthorpe 1999; Howden-Windell and Clark 1999); and between white offenders and ethnic minority offenders (Caddick 1993; Beaumont *et al.* 2001). The research base is limited but growing, and has been largely (although not exclusively) restricted to custodial populations (Clark and Howden-Windell 2000; Knight 2003).

For women offenders, the debate is vigorous and developing (see Hedderman 2004b for a review), and has been assisted by recent section 95 material that has presented a number of key issues for women offenders:

- Over 40 per cent of sentenced women prisoners and over 50 per cent of women on remand have reported being dependent on drugs in the year before coming to prison.
- A recent healthcare assessment of prisoners found that 60 per cent of women rated their health as fair, poor or very poor.
- 15 per cent of sentenced female prisoners had previously been admitted to a mental hospital.
- 37 per cent of women prisoners had previously attempted suicide.
- Educational attainment of women in prison is significantly lower than that of the general population but is slightly higher than that of male prisoners.
- A survey of released female prisoners found that only 25 per cent were in employment when interviewed five to nine months after discharge.

(Home Office 2002a: iv)

In an extensive review of criminogenic factors for female offending, Dowden and Andrews (1999) found similarities with male factors, but also factors specific to the structural position of women in society and differences in motivation to offend.

The Home Office-commissioned report on the criminogenic needs of black and Asian offenders undertaken by Glamorgan and Lancaster Universities is pending publication and should contribute significantly to the criminogenic needs and diversity debate (see also Raynor 2003). In addition, the National Probation Service black and Asian programme pathfinders are subject to evaluation, supported by an extensive collection of offender perception data on programme experiences (Stephens, ongoing[7]). These studies will add to the current low database of offending and criminogenic needs of minority groups, enabling more accurate modelling of offending and profiling of offenders (Lewis 2003), and thereby assisting both policy-makers and practitioners in the current contentious debate about separate or specialist provision for minority offenders (see also Raynor 2003).

Black empowerment models have placed greater emphasis upon difference and diversity (Durrance *et al.* 2001; Durrance and Ablitt 2001; Williams 2001; Durrance and Williams 2003), and the social position of minority groups in society (Bhui 1999). In brief, they argue that minority ethnic groups are differentially affected by social disadvantage and social exclusion, particularly due to their location in 'depressed inner city areas with high levels of unemployment and social conflict' (Bhui 1999: 173). The experience of racism is seen as a significant additional 'layer' with a damaging impact on self-identity. The contention is that this experience is significantly different to that of white offenders, and is significantly linked to offending. However, the supporting evidence is currently low, although this may be rectified by the growing Home Office databases on offending and the collection of offender perceptions of group programmes. It may be that in practical terms the difference in criminogenic needs between white and ethnic minority offenders is slight, but that when taken in conjunction with the effects of negative discrimination, resilience to criminal activity is lessened.

The position on mentally disordered offenders is less straightforward. There is considerable debate about the relationship between mental disorder and offending, particularly violent offending (Prins 1995) and causal connections have been difficult to draw, although there is evidence that 'persons who develop major mental disorders are more likely than persons with no mental disorders to be convicted of criminal offences' (Hodgins 2004: 220) – a situation that Hodgins asserts cannot be explained by discrimination alone. This raises the question of whether mental disorder is itself a criminogenic need or risk factor, or whether mentally disordered offenders simply have more criminogenic needs. Current literature searching would indicate that mentally disordered offenders not only have typically the same criminogenic needs as other offenders, but also that they have more of them. These interact with mental ill health and it is precisely this interaction that exacerbates the distress and the risk.

A particularly complex criminogenic interaction is co-morbidity or dual diagnosis, a combination of a severe mental health problem with problematic substance misuse (Department of Health 2002). This has been recognised as a significant factor in aggression and offending among severely mentally ill people, especially in inner-city areas (Scott *et al.* 1998). A survey in 1999 found that 'Over three-quarters of those prisoners in all sample groups who were drug dependent before prison were assessed as having two or more other mental disorders' (Office of National Statistics 1999), while the Department of Health *Good Practice Guide* suggests that 'Substance misuse is usual rather than exceptional amongst people with severe mental health problems' (Department of Health 2002: 4).

The challenge of providing accessible treatment for people with dual diagnosis is therefore considerable, and generally risk factors may be exacerbated by dropping out of treatment or failure to comply with medication/treatment regimes (Boyd 1996). Other studies have emphasised social deprivation, particularly homelessness (Burney and Pearson 1995; Kennedy *et al.* 1997) and the entry into custody through remands. Social isolation, deprivation and lives of 'spiritual and material' poverty have also been seen as characteristic of the lives of mentally disordered offenders (Keyes 1995).

Literature on differential criminogenic needs argues that the research base, while presently limited, makes an initial case for specific provision targeted at particular criminogenic needs. The literature argues not that criminogenic needs are totally distinctive across diverse groups, but that there are some important differences. While slightly speculative, it is possible to discern already from the research studies that some actuarial factors are likely to be shared, but that dynamic risk factors (or criminogenic needs) are likely to be more differential, especially those related to differences in the context of offending, and the structural position in society of the offender(s).

The relevance and effectiveness of non-custodial approaches for minority offender groups

Non-custodial sentences are wide-ranging, encompassing fines, discharges and community punishment as well as supervisory and rehabilitative options. This section will be restricted to consideration of probation programmes and assertive outreach for mentally disordered offenders as two of the main alternatives to custody and compulsory residential mental health care.

Ethnic minority offenders

While there are more black offenders supervised by the Probation Service than would be expected from their distribution in the general population (Powis and Walmsley 2002), their appropriate targeting and access to cognitive-behavioural groups have been a cause of concern (Home Office 2002b). Conversely, Asian offenders are under-represented on the probation caseload, and small numbers have made access to mainstream provision difficult (Home Office 2002b). The review of the Joint Accreditation Panel has also expressed concern about the ability of currently accredited programmes to meet 'the needs of ethnic minorities, female offenders, and offenders with learning difficulties' (Rex *et al*. 2003: ix).

Powis and Walmsley found that 13 programmes for black and Asian offenders had been developed in ten services, five of which were still running. Of these 13, ten were studied in detail to determine which factors contributed to success or failure, although the latter is defined largely as programme completion and not as impact on recidivism. Only four of the programmes have been formally evaluated, and only two have used any reconviction data. The study is limited as offender perceptions were not collected, and the findings concentrate on the views of staff and not on offenders. The study identified four types of programmes running for black and Asian offenders: black empowerment groups; black empowerment within general offending programmes; black empowerment and reintegration programmes; offence-specific programmes (e.g. drug-impaired drivers). The survey found that:

- there is little separate or specialist provision for black and Asian offenders;
- programmes tend to 'wither away' and are not maintained over the long term;
- staff are committed to providing separate provision, and believe it is effective;
- there is little empirical evidence to support the effectiveness of separate provision.

(Powis and Walmsley 2002)

Evaluations of outcome remain localised to individual programmes and local probation areas (often carried out by local research and information staff; see Dunn 2000; Durrance *et al.* 2001; Williams 2001), and while Powis and Walmsley describe them as encouraging, they remain small-scale and difficult to aggregate into larger data sets as they relate to slightly different group work programmes. There may be potential for further work comparing the outcomes of different provision (see below, National Probation Directorate ongoing research). The evidence that separate provision has any significant impact on attrition rates from programmes is also limited and largely anecdotal (Kemshall and Canton 2002).

In terms of programme success, Powis and Walmsley found that many of the components that made programmes for black and Asian offenders successful were similar to those of mainstream programmes. In brief, these were: commitment, management support, competent supervisors, use of positive role models, focus on offending behaviour as well as black empowerment, active participation and active learning style, effective case management, rigorous targeting criteria, and avoidance of marginalisation of black and Asian participants (2002: 39–44).

The report also recommends further research, particularly on criminogenic needs, and on the evaluation of different programmes for black and Asian offenders. It notes two important studies: a survey of 500 black and Asian men including their perceptions and experiences of probation as well as their criminogenic needs, carried out by Glamorgan and Lancaster Universities (Home Office, pending publication); and a comparison of five programme models to be carried out by the National Probation Directorate due for completion in 2005. The five models are:

- Delivery of a black self-development followed by a general offending behaviour programme for black and Asian offenders.

- Delivery of a black self-development module to black and Asian offenders followed by attendance on a general offending behaviour programme delivered to mixed groups.
- Delivery of a black self-development module plus a reintegration module (e.g. employment).
- Delivery of a mixed general offending programme with mentoring for black and Asian offenders.
- Delivery of Accredited Drink Impaired Drivers programme to Asian offenders.

(Powis and Walmsley 2002: 44)

However, no firm conclusions were offered as to the relative success of these programmes, although the report argues that empowerment programmes alone were likely to be less successful than when attached to offending behaviour programmes. This echoes the work of Durrance and Williams (2003) who, from local, small-scale evaluations, argue that black self-development modules prepare and enable black offenders to make appropriate use of the content of offending behaviour programmes. In practical terms this has resulted not in separate provision *per se*, but in additional provision (often in the form of pre-preparation 'empowerment/development' modules prior to joining mainstream offending behaviour programmes). However, one negative consequence of this approach is that black offenders often attend longer programmes and there is a differential impact in terms of community rehabilitation orders. Whether this results in differential attrition rates from programmes is not yet clear (Kemshall and Canton 2002).

Women offenders

The debate about specific programming for women is vigorous, and takes place against a background of both increasing use of custody for women, and their higher representation on the probation supervision caseload (Rumgay 2004). The reasons for this are not entirely clear, although the general 'up-tariffing' of women, a harsher punitive climate, and the failure of the probation service to remove 'unsuitable women' from its caseload are the most frequently indicted (Worrall 1997, 2002; Rumgay 2004). The case for gender-specific programming is made on the grounds of significant differences in offending profiles and criminogenic needs between men and women, and that the specific needs of women should be addressed (see Rumgay 2004 for a full review). However, the case is made within a difficult context, in particular:

- a low research base to support differing criminogenic needs;

- an emphasis on public protection and dealing with 'risk' rather than 'need';
- correctional programmes based on cognitive behavioural approaches which are perceived as being 'at odds' with some of the key difficulties women offenders are seen to face (e.g. relationships, abuse, emotional issues);
- an emphasis on 'thinking deficits' rather than on structural issues of poverty and oppression;
- difficulties in justifying resources for 'needs' that do not fit the label 'criminogenic' (e.g. abuse);
- an 'ambivalent' government response to female offending, particularly differential criminogenic needs and gender-specific programming (Rumgay 2004; see also Rumgay 1996, 2000; Social Work Services and Prisons Inspectorates for Scotland 1998; McIvor 1999; Chesney-Lind 2000; Home Office 2000b; Chesney-Lind *et al.* 2001; Carlen 2002; Kendall 2002).

The government was concerned enough about the 'increasingly dramatic rise' in the female prison population to initiate a Women's Offending Reduction Programme (WORP) and an action plan was published in March 2004 (Home Office 2004), along with a number of policy considerations in the *Government's Strategy for Women Offenders* (Home Office 2000b). WORP proposes a more 'holistic approach' to women offenders, and to providing more effective community-based interventions 'better tailored to the needs of women offenders' (Home Office 2002b: v). The subsequent action plan provides a comprehensive approach to the reduction of women's offending, including building the evidence base for change and expanding gender-relevant community interventions (Home Office 2004).

This supports Vennard *et al.*'s point that programmes should be appropriately targeted at risk and need (1997; see also Westmarland and McIvor 2002). The case for separate provision for women has, however, been hard to justify, not least on the grounds of low numbers and high cost, although the WORP plan may well change this position. Evaluations have also been limited due to low numbers, and the fact that gender-specific programmes are often hard to sustain (and hence compare) over the long term. Within an official policy context that prioritises cognitive-behavioural approaches to offending behaviour, a 'multi-modal approach' to female offending is advocated (Social Work Services and Prisons Inspectorates for Scotland 1998; Dowden and Andrews 1999; Home Office 2000b), alongside community reintegration and attention to acquisitive crime (often associated with drug use) (see Rumgay 2000; National Probation Service Merseyside 2001, 2002; Clarke 2002).

Mentally disordered offenders

Hodgins (2004) has identified a 'small but burgeoning outcome literature on treatment of offenders with major mental disorders'. She found that effective programmes contained:

- components that have been shown to be effective in the treatment of major mental disorders;
- components that specifically address the co-morbid disorders or problems in autonomous living presented by most offenders with major mental disorders;
- varying levels of supervision for different problems;
- legal obligation for community treatment if compliance is a problem;
- possibility of involuntary hospitalisation for short periods of time;
- adequate social services, income and housing.

Hodgins's second and sixth points reflect the multiple clinical and social problems that characteristically accompany mental disorder among offenders. Her fourth and fifth points raise important issues about care and control (Laing 1999), and the appropriate relationship between voluntary compliance and coercion. Increasingly, government policy on mental health, and particularly mentally disordered offenders, has focused on increasing control and coercion to treatment/medication regimes (Home Office 1999; Jewesbury and McCulloch 2002; Kemshall 2002b; Laurance 2003). This has tended to shift the balance from the diversion of the 'low risk many' to the compulsory management of the 'high risk few' (Davis 1996, Ryan 1999). Assertive outreach (Department of Health 1999; Ryan 1999; Ryan *et al.* 1999), with its emphasis upon intensive and assertive case management of those 'at risk', can be placed within this wider context. In essence it is an intensive case-management system designed to match intensity of resources to patient need and risk, and to coordinate services across a range of agencies. However, Ryan *et al.* concluded that case management was 'only as effective as the supporting services which are available' (1999: 113). It is also difficult to establish how many mentally disordered offenders are diverted into assertive outreach and away from community rehabilitation orders, or who experience assertive outreach as a condition of an order, and how many are within the assertive outreach net rather than in custody.

At the same time, it is essential that all modes of community supervision attend to challenges of securing compliance and engagement rather than placing a self-defeating emphasis on compulsion. Laurance (2003: 82) quotes a psychiatrist:

> . . . you can't eliminate risk in mental health work but you can move towards a system that people feel comfortable with, have trust in and where they feel you are on their side. And if you can make that happen, that is the safest service. You can have a measure with all sorts of restrictions and hurdles and safety measures but if the last person the user wants to see is the psychiatrist that is the least safe option.

Mechanisms of compliance must work together: to the extent that the demands made upon people are seen to be fair and reasonable, compliance is much more likely (Bottoms 2001). Mere compulsion is a weak and temporary control: legitimacy is needed if active compliance is to be secured. For all minority groups, there is a risk that reasonable doubt about the appropriateness of service is interpreted by the service provider as resistance or recalcitrance, to which emphasis on compulsion is mistaken to be the necessary response.

Conclusion

The evidence that difference and diversity have a significant role in the differential experience of minority groups in the criminal justice system is significant. The reasons are complex, often interrelated and are located both at the broad policy level and at the level of individual practices and decisions. The evidence for differing criminogenic needs is in its infancy, but as Lewis (2003) has recently argued, this database will expand with the use of the OASys database and other recently commissioned research. Comparative evaluations of differing programme approaches, of gender-specific programming, and of specialist versus generic provision are also emerging. In practice and policy terms there is enough evidence to indicate that diversity issues should receive greater attention. For example, the following may be a reasonable starting point:

- Alternatives to custody must be subject to a 'diversity test' – not just in terms of programme content and responsivity, but also in terms of differential access, differential impact (e.g. differing attendance demands), and unintended consequences (e.g. 'up-tariffing', or exacerbating the risk of attrition by increasing programme lengths). The Joint Accreditation Panel for cognitive-behavioural programmes has already begun to incorporate parts of this test, but it could be more widely applied (see Rex *et al.* 2003: 32).
- Proposals/alternatives should be robustly examined to ensure that they do not create differential and potentially discriminatory pathways through the criminal justice system.

- Simplistic notions of cost should be replaced with a clearer concept of value for money in which relevance and appropriateness of programmes to the profiles, criminogenic needs and offending patterns of minority groups should be key features. This would turn attention from the supposedly high cost of low-volume specialist groups, to the value for money offered in terms of potentially lower reconviction rates and custody costs. Such an approach would, however, require increased empirical evidence of effectiveness.

- 'What works' has focused almost exclusively on criminogenic needs and 'deficits', in effect the reasons for offending. As Farrall (2002) and Maruna (2002) have recently argued, it may be more productive to understand what contributes to desistance. In this context, it may be helpful to know whether diversity has a role in desistance and, if so, what and how. Is desistance different for different groups? (McNeill 2003).

- 'What works' has also focused attention on risks, and there has been increased research interest in whether risk and diversity are linked (Hannah-Moffat 1999). However, it may be more productive to investigate whether diversity has a significant impact on differing levels of resilience to risk and subsequent pathways out of crime. This in itself may assist policy-makers and practitioners in designing and implementing effective non-custodial disposals.

Finally, section 95 monitoring, and corrective actions arising from it, could be improved. A sufficiently strong case for corrective action cannot always be made, and the imprecision of some section 95 monitoring by key criminal justice agencies is itself an indication of a culture of disinclination and ambivalence. In this climate it is difficult to see corrective action or programme initiatives being sustained over the long term.

Notes

1 This section requires the Secretary of State to publish material that enables those involved in the criminal justice system to meet their duty to avoid discrimination on the grounds of race, sex or any other improper grounds.

2 The estimated general population aged ten and over in England and Wales by ethnic group is: white 91.3 per cent, black 2.8 per cent, South Asian 4.4 per cent, Chinese 0.4 per cent, 'other' 1.2 per cent (Home Office 2003b: Appendix A2).

3 The study explains that probation officers drew on psychiatric assessment to make their judgements here.

4 In the Learning Disability and Drug and Alcohol teams, this proportion is even lower.

5 See for example *Building Bridges* (Department of Health 1995).

6 Now known as the Correctional Services Accreditation Panel (CSAP).

7 Kate Stephens is currently developing a tool for the collection of offender perception data from black and Asian offenders.

References

Andrews, D. and Bonta, J. (2003) 'A commentary on Ward and Stewart's model of human needs', *Psychology, Crime and Law*, 9(3), 215–218.

Aubrey, R. and Hough, M. (1997) *Assessing Offenders' Needs: Assessment scales for the Probation Service*, Home Office Research Study 166 (London: Home Office).

Beaumont, B., Caddick, B. and Hare-Duke, H. (2001) *Meeting Offenders' Needs* (School for Policy Studies: University of Bristol and the National Probation Service, Nottinghamshire).

Bhui, K. (1999) 'Probation-led multi-agency working: a practice model', *Probation Journal*, 46(2), 119–121.

Bhui, K., Stansfeld, S., Hull, S., Priebe, S., Mole, F. and Feder, G. (2003) 'Ethnic variations in pathways used in mental health services in the UK – a systematic review', *British Journal of Psychiatry*, 182, 105–116.

Bonta, J. (1996) 'Risk-needs assessment and treatment', in A. T. Harland (ed.) *Choosing Correctional Options that Work* (Thousand Oaks, CA: Sage), pp. 18–32.

Bottoms, A. (2001) 'Compliance and community penalties', in A. Bottoms, L. Gelsthorpe and S. Rex (eds) *Community Penalties: Change and challenges* (Cullompton: Willan).

Bowling, B. and Phillips, C. (2003) *Racism, Crime and Justice* (Pearson Education: Longman), pp. 87–116.

Boyd 1996; Boyd Report (1996) Report of the Confidential Inquiry into Homicides and Suicides by Mentally Ill People. Steering committee of the Confidential Inquiry. London: Royal College of Psychiatrists.

Burney, E. and Pearson, G. (1995) 'Mentally disordered offenders: finding a focus for diversion', *Howard Journal*, 34(4), 291–313.

Caddick, B. (1993) 'Using groups in working with offenders: a survey of groupwork in the probation services of England and Wales', in A. Brown and B. Caddick (eds) *Groupwork with Offenders* (London: Whiting and Birch), pp. 15–32.

Canton, R. (2002) 'Rights, probation and mentally disturbed offenders', in D. Ward, J. Scott and M. Lacey (eds) *Probation: Working for justice*, 2nd edition (Oxford: Oxford University Press).

Carlen, P. (2002) (ed.) *Women and Punishment – The Struggle for Justice* (Cullompton: Willan).

Chesney-Lind, M. (2000) 'What to do about young girls? Thinking about programs for young women', in M. McMahon (ed.) *Assessment to Assistance: Programs for women in community corrections* (Lanham, MD: American Correctional Association), pp. 139–170.

Chesney-Lind, M., Artz, S. and Nicholson, D. (2001) 'Girls' delinquency and violence: making the case for gender-responsive programming', Paper presented at the American Society of Criminology Annual Meeting, Atlanta, Georgia, 7–10 November 2001.

Clark, D. and Howden-Windell, J. (2000) 'A retrospective study of criminogenic factors in the female prison population', Internal Home Office Report, March.

Clark, T., Kenney-Herbert, J. and Humphreys, M. (2002) 'Community rehabilitation orders with additional requirements of psychiatric treatment', *Advances in Psychiatric Treatment*, 8, 281–290.

Clarke, R. (2002) *Evaluation of the Think First for Women Programme* (Manchester: National Probation Service Greater Manchester, Research and Evaluation Team).

Councell, R. (2003) *The Prison Population in 2002 – A Statistical Review*, Findings No.228 (London: Home Office Research, Development and Statistics Directorate).

Davis, A. (1996) 'Risk work and mental health', in H. Kemshall and J. Pritchard (eds) *Good Practice in Risk Assessment and Risk Management*, Vol. 1 (London: Jessica Kingsley Publishers), pp. 109–120.

Department of Health (1995) *Building Bridges: A guide to arrangements for inter-agency working for the care and protection of severely mentally-ill people* (London: Department of Health).

Department of Health (1999) *Safer Services: National confidential inquiry into suicide and homicide by people with mental illness* (London: The Stationery Office).

Department of Health (2002) *Dual Diagnosis Good Practice Guide*, A Mental Health Policy Implementation Guide (London: Department of Health).

Department of Health (2003) *Inside Outside: Improving mental health services for black and minority ethnic communities in England* (London: Department of Health).

Dowden, C. and Andrews, D. (1999) 'What works for female offenders: a meta-analytic review', *Crime and Delinquency*, 45(4), 438–452.

Dunn, M. (2000) *Recidivism Report of the Black Offender Group Pilots* (West Midlands Probation Service).

Durrance, P. and Ablitt, F. (2001) '"Creative solutions" to women's offending: an evaluation of the Women's Probation Centre', *Probation Journal*, 28(4), 247–259.

Durrance, P., Higgett, C., Merone, L. and Asamoah, A. (2001) *The Greenwich and Lewisham Black and Self-Development and Educational Attainment Group Evaluation Report* (London: Inner London Probation Service).

Durrance, P. and Williams, P. (2003) 'Broadening the agenda around what works for black and Asian offenders', *Probation Journal*, 50(3), 211–224.

Eadie, T. and Canton. R. (2002) 'Practising in a context of ambivalence: the challenge for youth justice workers', *Youth Justice*, 2(1), 14–26.

Farrall, S. (2002) *Rethinking What Works with Offenders: Probation, social control and desistance from crime* (Cullompton: Willan).

Fennell, P. (1999) 'The third way in mental health policy: negative rights, positive rights and the convention', *Journal of Law and Society*, 26(1), 103–127.

Garland, D. (2001) *The Culture of Crime Control: Crime and social order in contemporary society* (Oxford: Oxford University Press).

Gelsthorpe, L. (1999) 'Review of theory in Hereford and Worcester Probation Service, programme for women offenders, Theory Manual', Version 7 (Unpublished).

Gelsthorpe, L. (2001) 'Accountability: difference and diversity in the delivery of community penalties', in A. Bottoms, L. Gelsthorpe and S. Rex (eds) *Community Penalties: Change and challenges* (Cullompton: Willan), pp. 146–167.

Gelsthorpe, L. and Loucks, N. (1997) 'The remanding and sentencing of female offenders in magistrates' courts: views from the bench', *Justice of the Peace and Local Government Law*, Vol. 161, pp. 1132–1134.

Gelsthorpe, L. and Padfield, N. (2003) (eds) *Exercising Discretion: Decision-making in the criminal justice system and beyond* (Cullompton: Willan).

Gendreau, P. and Andrews, D. (1990) 'Tertiary prevention: what the meta-analysis of the offender treatment literature tells us about "what works"', *Canadian Journal of Criminology*, 32, 173–184.

Goodwin, S. (1997) *Comparative Mental Health Policy: From institutional to community care* (London: Sage Publications).

Gunn, J., Maden, A. and Swinton, M. (1991) 'Treatment needs of prisoners with psychiatric disorders', *British Medical Journal*, 303 (10 August), 338–341.

Hagell, A. and Dowling, S. (1999) *Scoping Review of Literature on the Health and Care of Mentally Disordered Offenders*, CRD Report 16 (York: University of York).

Hannah-Moffat, K. (1999) 'Moral agent or actuarial subject: risk and Canadian women's imprisonment', *Theoretical Criminology*, 3(1), 71–95.

Hannah-Moffat, K. and Shaw, M. (1999) 'Women and risk: a genealogy of classification', Paper presented to the British Criminology Conference, Liverpool, July.

Hedderman, C. (2004a) 'Why are more women being sentenced to custody?', in G. McIvor (ed.) *Women Who Offend* (London: Jessica Kingsley), pp. 82–96.

Hedderman, C. (2004b) 'The criminogenic needs of women offenders', in G. McIvor (ed.) *Women Who Offend* (London: Jessica Kingsley), pp. 227–244.

Hedderman, C. and Dowds, L. (1997) *The Sentencing of Women – a section 95 publication*, Research Findings 58 (London: Home Office Research and Statistics Directorate).

Her Majesty's Inspectorate of Probation (HMIP) (1993) *Probation Orders with Requirements for Psychiatric Treatment: Report of a thematic inspection* (London: Home Office).

Her Majesty's Inspectorate of Probation (HMIP) (2000) *Towards Race Equality: Thematic inspection summary report* (London: HMIP).

Her Majesty's Inspectorate of Probation (HMIP) (2004) *Towards Race Equality. Follow-up inspection report* (London: HMIP).

Hodgins, S. (2004) 'Offenders with major mental disorders', in C. Hollin (ed.) *The Essential Handbook of Offender Assessment and Treatment* (Chichester: Wiley).

Home Office (1999) *Managing People with Dangerous Severe Personality Disorder: Proposals for policy development* (London: Home Office).

Home Office (2000a) *Statistics on Race and the Criminal Justice System* (London: Home Office, Research, Development and Statistics Directorate, National Statistics).

Home Office (2000b) *The Government's Strategy for Women Offenders* (London: Home Office).

Home Office (2000c) 'What works strategy for the Probation Service', *Probation Circular 60* (London: Home Office).

Home Office (2001a) *Statistics on Women and the Criminal Justice System: A Home Office publication under Section 95 of the Criminal Justice Act 1991* (London: Home Office).

Home Office (2001b) *Criminal Statistics, England and Wales, 2000* (London: Home Office).

Home Office (2002a) *Statistics on Women and the Criminal Justice System. A Home Office publication under section 95 of the Criminal Justice Act 1991* (London: Home Office).

Home Office (2002b) *Offending Behaviour Programmes: Diversity review report on cognitive skills programmes* (London: Home Office).

Home Office (2003a) *Prison Population Brief, England and Wales*, October 2003 [www.homeoffice.gov.uk/rds/whatsnew1.html].

Home Office (2003b) *Statistics on Race and the Criminal Justice System. A Home Office publication under section 95 of the Criminal Justice Act 1991* [www.homeoffice.gov.uk/rds/pdfs04/s95race2003.pdf].

Home Office (2004) *Women's Offending Reduction Programme*, Action Plan (London: Home Office).

Hood, R. and Cordovil, G. (1992) *Race and Sentencing – A Study in the Crown Court* (Oxford: Clarendon Press).

Hood, R., Shute, S. and Seemungal, F. (2003) *Ethnic Minorities in the Criminal Courts: Perceptions of fairness and equality of treatment* [www.dea.gov.reseasrch/2003/2-03es.htm].

Howden-Windell, J. and Clarke, D. (1999) 'The criminogenic needs of female offenders: a literature review' (London: HM Prison Service, Unpublished).

Hudson, B. (2001) 'Crime, risk and justice', in K. Stenson and R. Sullivan (eds) *Crime, Risk and Justice: The politics of crime control in liberal democracies* (Cullompton: Willan), pp. 144–172.

Jewesbury, I. and McCulloch, A. (2002) 'Public policy and mentally disordered offenders in the UK', in A. Buchanan (ed.) *Care of the Mentally Disordered Offender in the Community* (Oxford: Oxford University Press), pp. 46–64.

Kemshall, H. (2002a) 'Effective probation practice: an example of "advanced liberal" responsibilisation', *Howard Journal of Criminal Justice*, 41(1), 41–58.

Kemshall, H. (2002b) *Risk, Social Policy and Welfare* (Buckingham: Open University Press).

Kemshall, H. (2003) *Understanding Risk in Criminal Justice* (Buckingham: Open University Press).

Kemshall, H. and Canton, R. (2002) *The Effective Management of Programme Attrition*, A report for the National Probation Service (commissioned by the Welsh region) (Leicester: De Montfort University).

Kendall, K. (2002) 'Time to think again about cognitive behavioural programmes', in P. Carlen (ed.) *Women and Punishment: The struggle for justice* (Cullompton: Willan), pp. 182–198.

Kennedy, M., Truman, C., Keyes, S. and Cameron, A. (1997) 'Supported bail for mentally vulnerable defendants', *Howard Journal*, 36(2), 158–169.

Keyes, S. (1995) 'Revolving doors: eggs, empathy, and Erewhon', *Criminal Justice Matters*, 21, 3–4.

Knight, V. (2003) *An Investigation into Minority Ethnic Prisoners' Knowledge and perceptions of the Probation and Prison Service in the east of England* (Leicester: De Montfort University).

Laing, J. (1999) *Care or Custody: Mentally disordered offenders and the criminal justice system* (Oxford: Oxford University Press).

Laurance, J. (2003) *Pure Madness: How fear drives the mental health system* (London: Routledge).

Lea, J. (2003) 'Institutional racism in policing', in R. Mathews and J. Young (eds) *The New Politics of Crime and Punishment* (Cullompton: Willan), pp. 48–70.

Lewis, C. (2003) *Modelling Crime and Offending – Recent Developments in England and Wales*, Occasional Paper No. 80 (London: Home Office, Research Directorate and Statistics).

Macpherson, Lord (1999) *The Stephen Lawrence Inquiry*, Cm. 4262-I (London: Stationery Office).

Martinson, R. (1974) 'What works? Questions and answers about prison reform', *The Public Interest*, 10, 22–54.

Maruna, S. (2002) 'Desistance from crime and offender rehabilitation: a tale of two research literatures', *Offender Programs Report* 4 (1), 1–13.

Matthews, R. (2003) 'Rethinking penal policy: towards a systems approach', in R. Matthews and J. Young (eds) *The New Politics of Crime and Punishment* (Cullompton: Willan), pp. 223–249.

McIvor, G. (1999) 'Women, crime and criminal justice in Scotland', *Scottish Journal of Criminal Justice Studies*, 5(1), 67–74.

McNeill, F. (2003) 'Desistance-focused probation practice', in W.-H. Chui and M. Nellis (eds) *Moving Probation Forward: Evidence, arguments and practice* (Harlow: Pearson Education), pp. 146–162.

NACRO (1998) *Risks and Rights: Mentally disturbed offenders and public protection*, A Report by NACRO's Mental Health Advisory Committee (London: NACRO).

Nadkarni, R., Chipchase, B. and Fraser, K. (2000) 'Partnership with probation hostels: a step forward in community forensic psychiatry', *Psychiatry Bulletin*, 24, 222–224.

NAPO (2002) *Accredited Programmes Policy* (London: NAPO).

NAPO (2003) *Mentally Disordered Offenders: A briefing* (London: National Association of Probation Officers).

National Probation Service Merseyside (2001) *Policy and Practice in Relation to Women Offenders SDPP* (Liverpool: National Probation Service Merseyside).

National Probation Service Merseyside (2002) *Strategy for Reintegration of Women Offenders* (Liverpool: National Probation Service Merseyside).

Office of National Statistics (1999) *Substance Misuse Among Prisoners in England and Wales* (London: Office of National Statistics) [www.statistics.gov.uk/pdfdir/drugs0799.pdf].

O'Malley. P. (2001) 'Risk, crime and prudentialism revisited', in K. Stenson and R. Sullivan (eds) *Crime, Risk and Justice: The politics of crime control in liberal democracies* (Cullompton: Willan).

Parenti, C. (1999) *Lockdown America: Police and Prisons in the Age of Crisis* (London: Verso).

Pitts, J. (2003) 'New Labour and the racialisation of youth crime', in J. Hagedorn (ed.) *Gangs in the Global City: The limitations of criminology* (Champaign, IL: University of Illinois Press).

Powis, B. and Walmsley, R. K. (2002) *Programmes for Black and Asian Offenders on Probation: Lessons for developing practice*, Home Office Research Study 250 (London: Home Office, Offenders and Corrections Unit).

Prins, H. (1995) *Offenders, Deviants or Patients?*, 2nd edition (London: Routledge).

Raynor, P. (2002) 'Community penalties: probation, punishment and "what works"', in M. Maguire, R. Morgan and R. Reiner (eds) *The Oxford Handbook of Criminology*, 3rd edition (Oxford: Oxford University Press), pp. 1168–1205.

Raynor, P. (2003) 'Evidence-based probation and its critics', *Probation Journal*, 50(4), 334–345.

Raynor, P. and Vanstone, M. (2002) *Understanding Community Penalties* (Buckingham: Open University Press).

Rex, S. and Bottoms, A. (2003) 'Evaluating the evaluators: researching the accreditation of offender programmes', *Probation Journal*, 50(4), 359–368.

Rex, S., Lieb, R., Bottoms, A. and Wilson, L. (2003) *Accrediting Offender Programmes: A process-based evaluation of the Joint Prison/Probation Services Accreditation Panel*,

Home Office Research Study 273 (London: Home Office Research, Development and Statistics Directorate).

Roberts, J. (2000) 'Women-centred: the West Mercia community based programmes for women offenders', in P. Carlen (ed.) *Women and Punishment: The struggle for justice* (Cullompton: Willan), pp. 110–124.

Robinson, G. (1999) 'Risk management and rehabilitation in the probation service: collision and collusion', *Howard Journal of Criminal Justice*, 38(4), 421–433.

Rose, N. (2000) 'Government and social control', *British Journal of Criminology*, 40, 321–339.

Rotman, E. (1990) *Beyond Punishment: A new view on the rehabilitation of criminal offenders* (Westport, CT: Greenwood Press).

Royal College of Psychiatrists (1996) *Report of the Confidential Inquiry into Homicides and Suicides by Mentally Ill People*, Steering Committee of the Confidential Inquiry (London: Royal College of Psychiatrists).

Royal College of Psychiatrists (2003) *Press Release* (London).

Rumgay, J. (1996) 'Women offenders: towards needs-based policy', *VISTA*, 2(2), 104–115.

Rumgay, J. (2000) 'Policies of neglect: female offenders and the probation service', in H. Kemshall and R. Littlechild (eds) *User Involvement and Participation in Social Care* (London: Jessica Kingsley), pp. 193–213.

Rumgay, J. (2004) 'Living with paradox: community supervision of women offenders', in G. McIvor (ed.) *Women Who Offend* (London: Jessica Kingsley), pp. 99–125.

Ryan, P. (1999) 'Assertive outreach in mental health', *Nursing Times Clinical Monographs*, 35 (London: Nursing Times Monograph).

Ryan, P. (2003) 'Mental health (review)', *Research Matters, Community Care*, October 2003, pp. 37–42.

Ryan, P., Ford, R., Beardsmore, A. and Muijen, M. (1999) 'The enduring relevance of case management', *British Journal of Social Work*, 29, 97–125.

Sampson, R. and Lauritsen, J. (1997) 'Racial and ethnic disparities in crime and criminal justice in the United States', in M. Tonry (ed.) *Ethnicity, Crime and Immigration* (Chicago: University of Chicago Press), pp. 311–374.

Scott, H., Johnson, S., Menezes, P., Thornicroft, G., Marshall, J., Bindman, J., Bebbington, P. and Kuipers, E. (1998) 'Substance misuse and risk of aggression and offending among the severely mentally ill', *British Journal of Psychiatry*, 172, 345–350.

Shaw, M. and Hannah-Moffat, K. (2000) 'Gender, diversity and risk assessment in Canadian Corrections', *Probation Journal*, 47(3), 163–172.

Shaw, M. and Hannah-Moffat, K. (2004) 'How cognitive skills forgot about gender and diversity', in G. Mair (ed.) *What Matters in Probation* (Cullompton: Willan), pp. 90–121.

Singleton, N., Meltzer, H., Gatward, R., Coid, J. and Deasy D. (1998) *Psychiatric Morbidity among Prisoners: Summary report* (London: Government Statistical Service).

Social Work Services and Prisons Inspectorate for Scotland (1998) *Women Offenders – A Safer Way. A review of community disposals and the use of custody for women offenders* (Edinburgh: Stationery Office).

Tomasevski, K. (1994) *Foreigners in Prison* (Helsinki: European Institute for Crime Prevention and Control).

Vaughan, P., Pullen, N. and Kelly, M. (2000) 'Services for mentally disordered offenders in community psychiatric teams', *The Journal of Forensic Psychiatry*, 11(3), 571–586.

Vennard, J., Sugg, D. and Hedderman, C. (1997) *Changing Offenders' Attitudes and Behaviour: What works?* (London: Home Office).

Wacquant, L. (2001) 'Deadly symbiosis: when ghetto and prison meet and merge', *Punishment and Society*, 3(1), 95–113.

Wacquant, L. (2002) 'From slavery to mass incarceration', *New Left Review*, January/February, 41–60.

Ward, T. and Stewart, C. (2003a) 'Criminogenic needs and human needs – a theoretical model', *Psychology, Crime and Law*, 9(2), 125–143.

Ward, T. and Stewart, C. (2003b) 'The relationship between human needs and criminogenic needs', *Psychology, Crime and Law*, 9(3), 219–224.

Westmarland, N. and McIvor, G. (2002) 'What works with women on probation? Key findings from research with women in Scotland', Paper presented at the British Criminology Conference, Keele, 17–20 July.

Williams, P. (2001) *Evaluation of the Black Offender Groupwork Programme* (Greater Manchester Probation Service).

Worrall, A. (1997) *Punishment in the Community: The future of criminal justice* (London: Longman).

Worrall, A. (2002) 'Missed opportunities? The Probation Service and women offenders', in D. Ward, J. Scott and M. Lacey (eds) *Probation Working for Justice*, 2nd edition (Oxford: Oxford University Press), pp. 134–148.

Young, J. (1999) *The Exclusive Society* (London: Sage).

Young, J. (2002) 'Crime and social exclusion', in M. Maguire, R. Morgan and R. Reiner (eds) *The Oxford Handbook of Criminology*, 3rd edition (Oxford: Oxford University Press), pp. 457–490.

Chapter 15

Attitudes to punishment in two high-crime communities

Anthony Bottoms and Andrew Wilson

This chapter differs in scope from the other main chapters in this volume. Other chapters are principally literature reviews, but in this chapter we present some key results from a fresh piece of empirical research, specially commissioned by the Coulsfield Committee (see Preface).

The starting-point for this research was the well-known criminological finding that, in residential areas, generally speaking communities with high crime rates are also areas where many known offenders live (Bottoms and Wiles 2002). One main reason for this empirical connection is that offenders commit many of their crimes close to their homes, or to other places that they know well (Wiles and Costello 2000). Given that this is the case, however, we know surprisingly little about how residents of high crime communities view the offenders who live in their midst. It is well established that such residents strongly dislike the crimes and disorder that can at times make their areas a misery to live in. But do they take a punitive stance towards the offenders, or – given that many of the offenders are the sons, brothers or friends of community members – are they inclined to a more compassionate approach?

To explore these issues, two areas of Sheffield were chosen for study, both of which are high-crime, high-offender rate communities. Both are also areas of high social deprivation. At the outset, there was no particular reason to believe that the residents of these areas would have different views as to how offenders should be dealt with. However, as it turned out, the two areas present markedly different profiles in this respect, and a main purpose of this chapter is to explore these differences.

To consider the questions we were interested in, a twofold methodological approach was adopted, within the limits of the restricted timescale and budget available for the research. First, a formal survey was conducted of a small sample of the general adult population in each area, to ascertain in a structured way their opinions on appropriate punishments, and other issues. By deliberate design, this survey included many questions identical to those being used by Shadd Maruna and Anna King in their work on public opinion and punitiveness (see Chapter 4 of this volume), so that cross-area comparisons could be made with areas in the south of England.[1] Secondly, Andrew Wilson also carried out many hours of informal observation in the two areas, as well as semi-structured interviews with a range of persons concerned with keeping order in the two communities; these persons included the police, community wardens, anti-social behaviour personnel, housing tenancy enforcement officers, members of the local crime and disorder partnership, and community workers.

In this chapter, we present primarily the main results from the formal survey. Thus, the chapter should be read in many ways as a community-orientated complement to Chapter 4, though one that is focused exclusively on high-crime neighbourhoods.[2] However, the marked differences between the two areas also present challenging problems of explanation which require us to consider in some fresh ways what community residents mean when they demand 'tough action' against offenders in their areas; and to explore these issues we touch briefly on some non-survey-based observational and interview findings. (We have, however, reserved for a later publication the full discussion of those parts of our data which derive from non-survey sources.) At the end of the chapter, we consider the implications of our findings for the 'alternatives to prison' debate. Given the small scale of the study, it must be regarded as primarily exploratory; nevertheless, we think that some potentially important issues are raised by the findings.

The structure of the remainder of this chapter is, therefore, as follows. The first section describes the areas (including sub-area differences within them). Next, we provide details of the official crime patterns in the areas, and the offender rates. The survey methodology is then outlined, following which the main results of the survey are presented and discussed. Finally, hypotheses relating to the explanation of these results are discussed, and the implications of the findings are considered.

The areas and sub-areas

This section presents a description of the two areas, referred to for simplicity as area A and area B. The descriptions move from a general outline of the areas as a whole to consideration of some key differences within the areas. For analytical purposes, area A and area B have both been sub-divided into three sub-areas, each of which has some special features, though as we shall see these sub-area differences proved ultimately to be of limited significance in relation to the cross-area difference in punitiveness.

Area A – pen portrait

Area A is situated just over a mile from the city centre. The Index of Multiple Deprivation (IMD) score for the area is 71.5, which places area A in the most deprived 10 per cent of wards in England. In the 2001 Census, the total population of area A was 6300 (see Table 15.1 for relevant census data).

The area is ethnically diverse, with a large and mixed ethnic minority population, mostly African-Caribbean and Pakistani. There are significant Somali and Yemeni communities, and there has recently been a large number of asylum seekers moving into the area. At the time of the 2001 Census, just under half the residents described themselves as 'white British' (Table 15.1), and the 2002 General Household Survey indicated that 12 per cent of respondents had applied for refugee status.

At the time of the 2001 Census, just under half of all households in the area were in the social housing sector (local authority or housing association; see Table 15.1) although in the year before our survey there had been significant demolition of some local authority housing. The private sector housing in the area is rather variable, with some quite large and good properties, but others in a poor state of repair. There have been some changes in the local housing market, however, and a rising demand for housing as prices elsewhere in the city have escalated.

The commercial heart of the area is a small location which is popular with some groups as a meeting place. However, it is an environmentally poor area, with shop fronts in need of upgrading, a number of derelict properties, and a need for additional facilities in the area. Nevertheless the 2002 Household Survey found that 65 per cent of residents were happy with the area, and 44 per cent felt part of the community. This might be connected with the fact that the area has been the target for a number of special initiatives, which are described later.

Sub-area A1 is the least deprived of the three sub-areas within area A, with about two-thirds of the houses in owner-occupation, and higher employment rates and car ownership rates than the other sub-areas (Table 15.1). The housing stock in this sub-area is mostly nineteenth century, with some large family houses. There is some social housing, including a small council estate consisting of four medium-rise blocks, but for topographical reasons this is fairly isolated from the rest of the sub-area. Sub-area A3 is predominantly an area of social housing (70 per cent of households). This sub-area has a significant refugee population, and ethnically has fewer British Asian residents, and more black residents, than the other sub-areas. Sub-area A2, at the time of the 2001 Census, had

Table 15.1 Demographics – Area A and its three sub-areas

	Area A1	Area A2	Area A3	Whole Area A
Total population (N)	**2,180**	**1,790**	**2,379**	**6,349**
Sex (%)				
Male	48.7	53.4	49.2	50.2
Female	51.3	46.6	50.8	49.8
Ethnicity (%)				
White British	48.8	47.2	44.6	46.8
Mixed White and Black Caribbean	1.6	4.3	4.0	3.2
Black or Black British Caribbean	6.0	9.5	10.0	8.5
Black or Black British African	3.2	3.6	15.8	8.0
Asian or Asian British Pakistani	28.8	22.2	9.4	19.7
Other ethnic groups	11.6	13.2	16.2	13.8
Total	100	100	100	100
Age (%)				
0–15	28.0	22.3	27.6	26.1
16–19	6. 9	7.4	6.8	7.0
20–29	12.2	15.1	15.8	14.4
30–44	22. 1	21.1	19.6	20.9
45–59	14.7	13.7	12.6	13.6
60+	15.6	20.4	17.1	17.5
Total	100	100	100	100
Economic activity *(Persons aged 16–74) (%)				
People in full time employment	29.0	23.2	20.0	24.0
People in part time employment	10.6	7.2	9.0	9.0
Self-employed	5.5	4.3	2.7	4.1
Economically active students	2.8	2.9	3.7	3.2
People in employment (total)	**47.4**	**36.9**	**34.0**	**39.4**
Other economic categories (Inactivity) (%)				
Unemployed 16–74	7.6	11.5	11.1	10.1
Retired 16–74	9.3	13.0	11.7	11.3
Permanently sick or disabled 16–74	9.5	9.0	11.4	10.1
Economically inactive student	9.1	10.3	10.2	9.9
Looking after home/family	9.2	9.5	11.0	10.0
Economically inactive. Other	6.8	8.6	8.7	8.1
People economically inactive (total)	**51.5**	**61.9**	**64.1**	**59.4**
+Household tenure (%)				
Owner-occupied households	63.0	36.5	15.9	35.9
Rented from local authority	8.3	25.8	58.2	33.8
Rented from housing association	5.1	15.2	11.5	13.7
Rented from a private landlord	10.6	16.5	10.1	12.2
Other demographic features				
Lone parent family (dependent child)	9.1	9.9	13.3	11.0
At a different address in previous 12 months	15.5	16.2	17.1	16.3
Households without a car	42.7	62.7	66.6	58.4
People with no qualifications	37.6	45.8	46.8	43.4
**Persons Aged 16–74 (N)*	**1,417**	**1,258**	**1,581**	**4,256**
+Number of households (N)	**742**	**757**	**1,015**	**2,514**

Source: 2001 Census

intermediate population characteristics as between the other sub-areas, with a very mixed housing tenure between social housing, owner-occupier and private rented. However, it is in this sub-area that demolitions of council-owned properties have recently taken place, so that 2001 Census data are no longer at all reliable.[3]

All three sub-areas have high mobility rates. At the time of the 2001 Census, about one household in six throughout area A had lived at a different address twelve months previously. The age-structure of all three sub-areas was also similar, with about a quarter of the population aged under 16, a fifth aged 16–29, and 30 per cent aged 45 or over (Table 15.1).

Area B – pen portrait

Area B is situated just over three miles from the city centre, two miles further out than area A on the same side of the city. The majority of the area consists of two sub-areas that were originally 100 per cent council estates. In the post-war period, these two council estates diverged markedly in reputation, one becoming notorious as one of the most criminal areas in the city, while the other retained its traditional reputation as a desirable estate (for a full discussion of these areas as they were in the 1970s, see Bottoms *et al.* 1989). More recently, these sub-areas have become more similar again, partly because of significant demolition on the more criminal estate, and partly because of a decline in the reputation of the other estate. Adjacent to these two council estates are a number of small areas of predominantly owner-occupied housing, two of which fall within area B's boundaries; these we have grouped together as a third sub-area (though geographically they are not contiguous). Thus, the three sub-areas that we identified in area B were the traditionally criminal council area (B1), the traditionally desirable council area (B2) and the adjacent owner-occupied areas (B3). The total population of the whole area, at the time of the 2001 Census, was 6600 (see Table 15.2 for relevant census data).

By 2001, as a result of changes in the housing market (principally the right-to-buy legislation), only about half the households in sub-areas B1 and B2 were renting from the local authority, with about a third owner-occupied. In B3, by contrast, about 90 per cent of households were in owner-occupation. Not surprisingly, area B3 was the least deprived of the three sub-areas. The other two sub-areas do not fall within a clearly defined IMD group, but they are within the top ten deprived areas (out of one hundred) within Sheffield, according to data published by the local health authority and based on benefit claims. Since Sheffield itself has higher-than-average scores on the IMD, area B is clearly a deprived area.

In marked contrast to area A, area B is very predominantly (about 90 per cent) an ethnically white area, and this is the case in all three sub-areas. The area also has a lower mobility rate than area A (10 per cent

Table 15.2 Demographics: Area B and its three sub-areas

	Area B1	Area B2	Area B3	Whole Area B
Total Population (N)	**2,283**	**2,352**	**1,941**	**6,576**
Sex (%)				
Male	45.3	48.4	51.2	48.1
Female	54.7	51.6	48.8	51.9
Ethnicity (%)				
White British	89.7	86.5	92.1	89.3
Mixed White and Black Caribbean	1.4	2.0	0.9	1.5
Black or Black British Caribbean	1.2	1.9	0.8	1.3
Black or Black British African	0.5	0.9	0.0	0.5
Asian or Asian British Pakistani	2.7	2.8	2.1	2.5
Other Ethnic Groups	4.5	5.9	4.1	4.9
Total	100	100	100	100
Age				
0–15	24.7	25.8	22.5	24.4
16–19	6.1	5.8	4.4	5.5
20–29	9.6	9.7	11.2	10.2
30–44	21.2	20.9	24.8	22.1
45–59	17.6	14.0	20.4	17.1
60+	20.4	23.5	16.4	20.3
Total	100	100	100	100
Economic activity *(Persons aged 16–74) (%)				
People in full time employment	31.3	28.8	43.8	34.4
People in part time employment	12.8	10.4	17.3	13.4
Self-employed	3.9	3.2	6.1	4.4
Economically active students	1.3	2.5	2.4	2.1
People in employment (total)	**49.3**	**44.9**	**69.6**	**54.0**
Other economic categories (Inactive) (%)				
Unemployed 16–74	6.5	5.5	3.4	5.2
Retired 16–74	11.9	15.6	12.0	13.2
Permanently sick or disabled 16–74	12.6	11.3	4.8	9.9
Economically inactive students	4.2	5.0	2.5	4.0
Looking after home/family	9.0	10.4	4.4	8.0
Economically inactive other	5.9	6.2	2.7	5.0
People economically inactive (total)	**50.1**	**54.0**	**29.8**	**44.9**
+Household tenure (%)				
Owner-occupied households	34.0	27.6	88.4	47.2
Rented from local authority	48.5	53.5	4.9	38.2
Rented from housing association	10.2	11.5	0.9	8.1
Rented from a private landlord	3.1	3.3	4.2	3.5
Other demographic features				
Lone parent family (dependent (child)	12.2	13.5	4.8	10.6
People at a different address in previous year	12.6	10.2	6.0	9.8
Households without a car	50.5	55.7	21.7	44.4
People with no qualifications	49.5	53.0	35.7	45.5
**Persons Aged 16–74 (N)*	**1,523**	**1,517**	**1,412**	**4,452**
+Number of households (N)	**908**	**983**	**733**	**2,624**

Source: 2001 Census

versus 16 per cent in the year before the 2001 Census). Car ownership rates in sub-area B3 are the highest for any of the six sub-areas, and sub-areas B1 and B2 have a slightly higher car-ownership rate than sub-areas A2 and A3. Employment rates in sub-areas B1 and B2 were at about the same level as sub-area A1, and higher than A2 and A3, at the time of the 2001 Census. As in area A, the age-structure of the sub-area populations within Area B did not differ greatly, but at the time of the 2001 Census, area B as a whole had a somewhat lower proportion than area A of people in the most crime-prone ages (16–29: area A, 21 per cent; area B, 16 per cent), and a correspondingly higher proportion of people aged 45+ (area A, 31 per cent; area B, 37 per cent) (Tables 15.1 and 15.2).

Recorded crime in the two areas[4]

Both areas have high recorded crime rates – among the highest in Sheffield residential areas. Table 15.3 shows rates of recorded crime per 1,000 resident population (as measured by the 2001 Census) by area and sub-area. As may be seen, both areas had very similar rates in 2002/3, and area B's crime rate was stable from 2002/3 to 2003/4. In 2003/4, however, area A's crime rate apparently declined. Closer inspection shows that the overwhelming bulk of this reduction occurred in sub-area A2, and this appears to be strongly related to the demolitions in that sub-area (see note 3 above).[5] These demolitions rendered highly problematic, from 2003 onwards, the use of 2001 Census data as a denominator in calculating the crime rate in this area; for this reason, when considering recorded crime in this chapter, we focus primarily on area comparisons for 2002/3.[6]

Although the two areas had, overall, similar recorded crime rates in 2002/3, there were some significant differences in the rates for the sub-areas within each area. The sub-areas with the highest recorded crime rates were the traditionally criminal council estate in area B, and the sub-area within area A where the demolitions subsequently took place. The lowest overall crime rate was found in sub-area B3, the owner-occupied sub-area within area B (Table 15.3).

Turning to types of recorded crime in 2002/3, relevant data are given in Tables 15.4 and 15.5, on a percentage basis within each area or sub-area. Looking first at area differences, area A had a markedly higher proportion of drug offences, and a higher proportion of violent offences, than area B. This accords with a standard perception in the city of area A as a drug-dealing area, and one where offences involving weapons (firearms or knives) are not infrequently reported. By contrast, in area B the two kinds of crime which featured more prominently in the proportionate distribution of recorded crime were vehicle crime and criminal damage.

There are also some sub-area differences as regards type of crime. These are, however, confined to area B, where criminal damage featured much

Table 15.3 Recorded crime rates per 1000 population (based on 2001 Census), by area and sub-area, 2002/3 and 2003/4

	2002/3	2003/4
Area A		
A1	153	159
A2	285	(175)*
A3	119	92
Whole area	174	(138)*
Area B		
B1	249	255
B2	193	172
B3	76	83
Whole area	178	175

*Population base known to be seriously inaccurate owing to demolitions and rehousing (see text).

Table 15.4 Area A – types of recorded crime (%), 2002–3

	Sub-area A1	Sub-area A2	Sub-area A3	Whole area
Violence	15.6	16.5	15.8	16.1
Vehicle crime (including damage to vehicles)	23.7	23.9	27.5	24.8
Burglary	19.8	18.2	25.4	20.5
Theft/fraud/handling	15.9	12.7	6.0	11.9
Criminal damage	12.9	15.9	13.7	14.5
Shoplifting	1.5	0.2	—	0.5
Drugs	7.2	7.5	9.9	8.0
Other	3.3	5.1	1.8	3.7
Total	100.0	100.0	100.0	100.0
Total recorded crimes	333	490	284	1,107
Crimes per 1000 population (2001 Census)	153	274	119	174

more prominently in B1 and B2 than in B3, whereas burglary accounted for a higher proportion of crimes in B3 than in the other two sub-areas. Within area A, there was basically a similar proportionate distribution of recorded crimes across the three sub-areas.

We turn finally to the official offender rates for the areas. Here data are available solely on a whole-area basis, with no sub-area breakdowns.

The dataset we used contains details of all offenders resident in and offending in South Yorkshire for 47 months from April 1998. Many of

Table 15.5 Area B – types of recorded crime (%), 2002–3

	Sub-area B1	Sub-area B2	Sub-area B3	Whole area
Violence	9.3	10.1	6.1	9.2
Vehicle crime (including damage to vehicles)	37.3	27.5	43.0	34.2
Burglary	16.0	16.7	29.5	18.0
Theft/fraud/handling	10.7	13.6	10.1	11.8
Criminal damage	24.1	23.1	6.7	21.5
Shoplifting	0.7	6.2	2.7	3.1
Drugs	1.2	1.8	2.0	1.5
Other	0.5	0.9	—	0.6
Total	100.0	100.0	100.0	100.0
Total recorded crimes	568	454	149	1,171
Crimes per 1000 population (2001 Census)	249	193	76	178

these offenders had multiple addresses during this period, so assessing area offender rates is difficult. An initial calculation was made counting one offender at every address at which, during the 47 months, he/she is known to have lived; on this basis, area A had 656 'offender addresses' and area B had 353. However, as there are a number of criminal justice-linked hostels etc. in area A, but fewer in area B, and as such accommodation (e.g. a bail hostel) is often only a temporary address, this method of calculation might weight the scales unfairly against area A. An alternative, *offence-based* measure was therefore also calculated; this counted the total number of detected offences attributable to offenders while they had an address in the stated area. On this basis, the count for area A was 1,792, while that for area B was 1,036. On either method of calculation, therefore, it would seem from official data (at least up to 2002, which is the latest data we have) that area A has a more significant resident offender group than has area B. That, plus its offence profile focused around drugs and violence (see above), no doubt accounts for the fact that, among criminal justice professionals, area A is usually perceived as more of a 'criminal area' than area B, notwithstanding their overall similarity in 2002/3 in recorded offence rates, and area A's decline in rate in the following year.

The survey

The survey of residents was constructed in a way that would allow us to gain insights into the specific community influences on punitiveness in

Table 15.6 Survey response by area and sub-area

	A1	A2	A3	Total A	B1	B2	B3	Total B	All cases
Total N issued to interviewers	88	71	35	194	65	84	41	190	385
Interview completed	*39*	*28*	*11*	*78*	*24*	*37*	*17*	*78*	*156*
Interview refused	10	10	1	21	16	10	6	32	53
Unable to participate – language	1	5	1	7	1	0	0	1	8
Unable to participate – other	13	5	1	19	9	6	2	17	36
Unable to contact	16	11	4	31	9	22	13	44	75
Electoral Register out of date/invalid	9	12	17	38	7	9	3	19	57
Response rate (%)*	49	48	61	50	41	49	45	46	48

*The percentage of valid cases with completed interviews. (Valid cases are those issued to interviewers, less those where the Electoral Register was invalid or out of date.)

areas A and B, while at the same time replicating some of the Maruna–King questions on punitiveness to allow for comparison with their results.

The survey was a random survey conducted on a personal interview basis, with a prior letter informing the addressee that it was proposed to call. (Names and addresses were taken from the Electoral Register.) Budget restrictions meant that we could not employ a market research company to conduct the fieldwork, so the survey was small-scale, with all interviews carried out by Andrew Wilson and one assistant (Arabella Smallman). In each area, the eventual number of completed interviews was 78 (total N = 156), and the response rate in both areas was also similar (area A, 50 per cent; area B, 46 per cent: for full details see Table 15.6). Direct refusals were somewhat higher in area B than in area A (32 as against 21).

We would have preferred a higher overall response rate than 48 per cent, but socially deprived areas of this kind tend to have low survey response rates, and we were additionally hampered by the time of year at which the survey was conducted (December 2003/January 2004).[7] As we achieved similar response rates in both areas, and as a main feature of the survey is comparison between the areas, we are reasonably satisfied that reliance can be placed on the results. That is especially the case because our exploration of response bias (see below) found no systematic response differences between areas A and B.

The question of potential survey response bias was considered for five main variables:

1. *Sub-area* Response rates did not differ significantly by sub-area; and with two exceptions all sub-areas had response rates between 45 per cent and 49 per cent (Table 15.6). The exceptions were sub-area B1, with a response rate of 41 per cent, and a high number of direct refusals; and area A3, which had technically a high response rate, although its total number of interviewees was very small (11).[8]

2. *Gender* There was no overall gender bias in the sample in area A (53 per cent male). However, in the small subsample in sub-area A3 there was an over-representation of males (7 males, 4 females). A reverse issue arose in area B, where the interviewed group was 62 per cent female, against an Electoral Register sampling frame distribution of 56 per cent female; however this difference was not statistically significant. Gender was in any case not significantly related to punitiveness (see later discussion), so area gender differences would be of little serious consequence for our main analyses.

3. *Age* According to the 2001 Census, among persons aged 20 and over in the two areas, a minority (47 per cent) in area A, and a small majority (54 per cent) in area B were aged 45 or over (see Tables 15.1 and 15.2). In our interviewed samples, however, higher proportions in both areas were in this older age bracket (60 per cent in area A, 65 per cent in area B). There was, therefore, in the sample as a whole an over-representation of older people ($P<0.5$).

4. *Length of residence* High proportions of respondents in all areas had lived in the area for twelve years or more. (In area B, the figure was 82 per cent, with little variation between sub-areas; in area A the figure was lower, but still high at 63 per cent.) We have no direct data comparisons for this variable, but given the census data on mobility (see Tables 15.1 and 15.2) it seems highly probable that we have a response bias towards longer-stay residents in both main areas (related, of course, to the age issue noted above). From our point of view, this may be no bad thing, for the net result is that we have particularly sampled the views on punitiveness of those who are most familiar with the areas in question.

5. *Housing tenure* Tenure data for both areas in 2001 are given in Tables 15.1 and 15.2. Confining ourselves to a simple owned/rented division, in area B the housing tenure of interviewed residents roughly corresponded to the census distributions (with all B3 respondents being owner-occupiers). That was also true for sub-areas A1 and A3, but in sub-area A2 (where – see above – much local authority housing had recently been demolished), by the date of our survey 64 per cent of the research respondents were owner-occupiers.

In general, therefore, our samples probably over-represent long-stay and older residents. There is also a slight differential gender response in the two main areas, though gender is not related to punitiveness. These features of the achieved sample, especially long-stay residence, should be borne in mind in considering the survey results.

Survey results: perceptions of areas and victimisation

We begin our reporting of the survey results with some responses on residents' perceptions of the areas, including area crime.

One of the survey questions asked whether respondents felt at home in the area, and the great majority answered affirmatively (88 per cent in both areas). Thus, although these were high-crime, high-deprivation areas, the great majority of residents did not feel alienated living in them.

An important question asked respondents who had lived in the area for over three years whether, in their opinion, the area had recently gone up, gone down or stayed the same. In area A, overall feelings on this question were fairly equally divided between the three possible responses, with slightly more feeling the area had improved rather than gone down. In area B, by contrast, many more respondents felt that the area had stayed the same; of those thinking otherwise, slightly more felt it was deteriorating rather than improving. Thus, overall, a significantly higher proportion of respondents in area A thought the area was improving (36 per cent) than in area B (twelve per cent) ($P < .001$).

Turning to crime, respondents were asked to agree or disagree with the statement 'Crime is a serious problem where I live'. Results are shown in Table 15.7.

Four points are notable in these results. First, in all sub-areas except A1, a majority of respondents view crime as a serious problem locally. Second,

Table 15.7 Responses to the statement 'Crime is a serious problem where I live', by area and sub-area

	% agreeing
Area A	58
Sub-area A1	39
Sub-area A2	79
Sub-area A3	73
Area B	73
Sub-area B1	92
Sub-area B2	67
Sub-area B3	65

there is a remarkably low percentage of respondents in sub-area A1 who view local crime as a problem, despite a not insignificant level of recorded crime (see Table 15.3). Third, within area B the residents of B1 are most likely to perceive local crime as a serious problem, just as they have the highest sub-area recorded crime rate (Table 15.3). Finally, taking the results as a whole, there are significantly more residents who perceive crime as a serious problem in area B than in area A ($P < .05$), notwithstanding broadly similar official crime rates (though with a recent decline in area A), higher offender rates in area A, and the city-wide reputation of area A for violence and drug dealing.

Within the framework of a shortish interview, we judged it impracticable to ask a full set of crime victimisation questions, along the lines of the British Crime Survey. We did, however, use a basic set of such questions,[9] and the main results are summarised in Table 15.8.[10]

As can be seen, the proportion of respondents in areas A and B who were victims of any crime or abuse in the last twelve months ('prevalence') was identical in the two areas at 49 per cent. However, there were slightly more multiple victims in area B, leading to a slightly higher incidence or 'victimisation score' for that area. In comparing this result with the recorded crime figures reported earlier, however, it is important to recognise that victimisation surveys by their nature exclude victimless crimes, and that includes drugs offences. In the present instance, it is clear from many sources (see Tables 15.4 and 15.5, plus other sources to be mentioned later) that area A has more drugs crime than area B; and if that is taken into account, then the message of Table 15.8, plus the evidence relating to drugs, is that the two areas had broadly similar crime rates at the time of our survey. The rate of reporting of crimes to the police was also similar (Table 15.8).

Turning to types of victimisation, the most striking result was the markedly higher reported rate of victimisation for criminal damage in area B than in area A (with sub-area B2 featuring most prominently for this within area B). Again, this result is congruent with those for recorded crime (Tables 15.4 and 15.5). Results for car crime and personal crime were, however, less congruent with the official crime data.[11]

In the final and more general part of the survey, respondents were asked for their general perceptions of the kinds of crime committed in their area. The results are shown in Table 15.9, and as will be seen they again mirror in some ways the police-recorded crime data for the areas. Thus, mentions of burglary were similar in the two areas, but drug crime was considered to be more prevalent in area A, as was theft from cars. By contrast, both joyriding and damage were more frequently mentioned in area B, just as they were in the official crime data (Tables 15.4 and 15.5).

Table 15.8 Residents' reports of crime and disorder victimisation in last year (% figures unless otherwise stated)

	Area A	Area B
Frequency of victimisation		
None	51	51
Once	32	24
Twice	6	6
3+	10	18
*Victimisation score**	76	91
*Reported to police?***		
Yes	50	39
Some not all	26	37
No	24	24
% of all respondents mentioning victimisation for:		
Burglary/theft in dwelling†	21	17
Car crime††	12	8
Criminal damage	—	18
Personal crime†††	15	24

*For this score, a respondent who reported one victimisation in the last year was counted as one; two victimisations scored two; and three or more victimisations scored three. The total for the area was then divided by the number of respondents, and multiplied by 100.
**These percentages use a base of victimised respondents only.
†Includes burglaries of sheds and garages.
††Includes theft of and from vehicles, and taking without consent.
†††Includes assault, theft from the person and abuse in a public place (not necessarily as a criminal offence).

Table 15.9 Survey respondents' perceptions of 'the regular crimes committed in this neighbourhood' (%)

Crime type	Area A	Area B
Burglary	40	42
Drug crime (including dealing)	22	13
Theft from car	14	9
Joyriding	6	15
Damage	3	9
Other	6	5
Don't know	8	6

Survey results: punitiveness

Using Maruna and King's questions, we constructed a punitiveness scale consisting of a summation of the responses to seven agree/disagree statements:[12]

1. With most offenders, we need to 'condemn more and understand less'.
2. Opportunities for rehabilitation should always be available no matter how serious a crime someone has committed.
3. My general view towards offenders is that they should be treated harshly.
4. If prison has to be used, it should be used sparingly and only as a last option.
5. We should bring back the death penalty for serious crimes.
6. Prisoners should have access to televisions or gym facilities.
7. Probation or a community sentence (rather than prison) is appropriate for a person found guilty of a burglary for the second time

For each question, a simple numerical scale was used, with '6' representing the most punitive response and '1' the least punitive. Hence, overall, the scale ran from a minimum of 7 to a maximum of 42 points, with a mid-point of 24/25. The mean scores on this index for respondents in our areas and sub-areas are shown in Table 15.10.

All the sub-areas in area B have mean scores above the mid-point in the scale; by contrast, the total score for area A, and the scores for two of the

Table 15.10 Punitiveness and redeemability scales: mean scores by areas and sub-areas

		Punitiveness		**Redeemability**	
	N.	**Mean**	**Standard deviation**	**Mean**	**Standard deviation**
Area					
A1	39	21.4	7.46	13.2	2.93
A2	28	23.1	8.35	12.2	3.68
A3	11	28.0	7.66	12.1	2.95
Total area A	78	23.0	8.02	12.7	3.22
Sub-area comparison	—	P<.10	—	NS	—
Area					
B1	24	27.9	5.93	12.3	3.40
B2	37	28.7	6.48	12.1	2.81
B3	17	28.5	6.74	12.6	2.09
Total area B	78	28.4	6.30	12.2	2.85
Sub-area comparison	—	NS	—	NS	—
Overall Total	156	25.7	7.69	12.5	3.04
Comparing area A/B	—	P<.001	—	NS	—

three sub-areas, are below the mid-point. The overall difference in mean scores between areas A and B (23.0 versus 28.4) is statistically highly significant ($P < .001$). This was an unexpected finding, but of course it could be explicable by various social differences between the two areas (such as differences in age or educational qualifications) and we return to this later. For the moment, it is also important to note that when the punitiveness scores for the Sheffield areas were compared with those in the Maruna–King study, the differences were all the more striking: area B returned a higher punitiveness score than any of Maruna and King's areas, while area A was less punitive than any of those areas.[13]

Following Maruna and King, we also constructed a 'redeemability' score, which in our study consisted of three statements:[14]

1. Most offenders can go on to lead productive lives with help and hard work.
2. Even the worst young offenders can grow out of criminal behaviour.
3. After an offender has done his/her time, the slate should be wiped clean and they should be allowed to move on in society without obstacles.

Although, on an individual respondent basis, the 'punitiveness' and 'redeemability' scores were inversely correlated ($r = -.514$, $P < .01$), nevertheless there were no statistically significant *area* or *sub-area* differences in the mean scores for redeemability (see Table 15.10). The scale for this construct ran from a minimum of 3 to a maximum of 18, with a mid-point of 10/11. The mean for the whole sample was 12.5, i.e. above the mid-point of the scale, indicating generally positive responses. Although not reported in their chapter in this volume, in Maruna and King's study there was a very similar result on the area point: i.e. redeemability was significantly correlated with punitiveness on an individual basis, but there were no area differences in mean scores for redeemability.[15] Taken together, these results seem to have a policy significance, namely that there is reasonable public support for the idea that offenders should be allowed opportunities to redeem themselves, and this is true in areas with high punitiveness scores as much as in other areas.

Explaining the area difference in punitiveness – a multivariate approach

Obviously, the apparent difference in punitiveness levels between area A and area B presented us with an important problem for explanation. However, as discussed above, there could have been some relatively straightforward factors that would account for the area difference: for example if older people hold markedly more punitive views, and area B had many more older people in the sample, this might in itself explain the difference.

To explore these matters, we conducted a regression analysis (similar to those reported by Maruna and King in Chapter 4), with the punitiveness scale as the dependent variable (i.e. the data item whose variance among sample members we were attempting statistically to explain).[16] The final regression model was developed only after much preliminary exploration of the data, which it is not practicable to discuss here.[17] We can, however, note that the final model has a very respectable adjusted R^2 of 0.57;[18] and when considered in detail the model has a number of points of interest, which we will now discuss.[19]

We begin with the variables which were, within the model, statistically significantly related (at the five per cent level of significance) to punitiveness scores. These variables are set out in Table 15.11; here, we consider them in a more narrative style under a number of convenient subheadings:

1. *Redeemability* The redeemability scale was highly related to punitiveness – if a respondent thinks that offenders are redeemable, his/her overall attitudes are less likely to be punitive. However, as discussed above, this item does not help to explain the area difference in punitiveness, because areas A and B did not differ significantly in their mean scores on redeemability (Table 15.10).

2. *Ethnicity-related variables* Two ethnicity-related variables appear in the model. First, the small number of Pakistani-origin respondents were particularly punitive, possibly because of their acceptance of Islamic law ('Sharia') principles. Second, and on a more community-focused basis, respondents who mentioned something positive about multiculturalism were less likely to be punitive.[20] Both these variables were much more commonly found among respondents in area A than in area B.

3. *Age-related variables* There were also two age-related variables. One of these was only indirectly connected with age: those respondents with more negative attitudes to 'the youth of today' were more likely to be punitive,[21] and such attitudes were significantly more likely to be expressed in area B ($P < .001$).[22] The other age variable was 'being over 55 and not retired'; such respondents were significantly less punitive either than retired persons or younger persons, though the reasons underlying this unusual finding would require further exploration.[23]

4. *Ties to the area* We constructed a scale based on three questions assessing area 'rootedness'; these related to how long the respondent had lived in the area; whether other family members also lived locally;

Table 15.11 Multiple regression model with punitiveness scale as the dependent variable

Model	Beta	t	Sig
(Constant)		10.826	.000
Redeem scale	−.443	−8.092	.000
Qualified to HND or above level*	−.209	−3.461	.001
Attitudes towards youth scale	.189	3.068	.003
55 or over and not retired*	−.140	−2.641	.009
Ties in the area scale	.161	2.633	.009
Mentioned something positive about multiculturalism in the area*	−.140	−2.303	.023
Ethnicity Pakistani*	.126	2.248	.026
Area A resident*	−.127	−2.014	.046

Adjusted $R^2 = 0.57$.
*Indicates 'dummy variables', that is, 'devices which make it possible to manipulate nominal scale data almost as if they were interval scale data. Each category on a nominal scale may be assigned a dummy variable which can take only two values. For instance if one was considering Protestants, Catholics, and others, a dummy variable assigned to the category Protestant could be coded 1 for all Protestants and 0 for everyone else . . . Each of the dummy variables thus created may be assumed to be measured on an interval scale and manipulated accordingly, e.g. multiple regression may be performed' (Miller and Wilson 1983: 34).

and whether the respondent had attended school in the area. A high score on this scale was associated with more punitive attitudes; and the mean score for respondents in area B was significantly higher than for those in area A ($P < .001$).[24]

5. *Higher qualifications* As Maruna and King had also found (see Chapter 4), persons with higher educational qualifications (in this survey, measured as HND and above) were less likely to have punitive attitudes; and there were significantly more such people in area A ($P < .005$).

6. *Area effect* Finally, even when all the above matters had been controlled for in the multivariate model, a statistically significant area effect remained. That is to say, area A was still significantly less punitive than area B ($P < .05$), even when account had been taken of differences in higher qualifications, area rootedness, attitudes towards youth, a positive attitude towards multiculturalism, and so on.[25]

It is obviously important to discuss the area effect more fully, but before doing that two other important matters should be briefly considered. The first of these is whether any *sub-area effects* (as opposed to area effects) could be discerned. Since Table 15.11 contains no sub-area variables, this required fresh analyses, which were of three main types.[26] Assessing the results of these analyses, the following conclusions could be drawn. Within area A, sub-area A3 appeared to be clearly more punitive than the other two sub-areas;[27] however, it would be unwise to over-interpret this finding since the sample in sub-area A3 consisted of only eleven cases (see earlier discussions). Within area B, there was some tentative evidence that sub-area B1 was less punitive than the other two sub-areas;[28] however, it would be unwise to over-interpret this finding since the results *are* tentative, and moreover B1 was the sub-area with the lowest survey response rate and the highest direct refusal rate (see Table 15.6). Given the above results, the main focus of the ensuing discussion must obviously be on the main area A/area B contrast, which is statistically robust. However, in passing it is worth commenting briefly on the B1 result, because this sub-area had the highest recorded crime rate within area B, and also the highest proportion of respondents saying that crime was a serious problem in the area (see Table 15.7). Clearly, then, there is no simple correlation between believing that crime is a serious local problem and that offenders should be dealt with harshly.

Our final comment in this section concerns those variables which do not appear in Table 15.11. It is not appropriate to discuss these at length, but two are worth a brief mention. One of these is gender, which often appears as a significant variable in surveys of punitive attitudes (including in the work by Maruna and King reported in Chapter 4), but does not do so here, and was indeed not statistically significant on a simple comparison of means.[29] A clue to a possible reason for this finding is that these were both high deprivation neighbourhoods, and previous analyses of British Crime Survey data on 'fear of crime' have shown that 'gender disparities in the experience of feeling unsafe are greater within rich households than they are in poor households ... which suggests that one of the effects of poverty is to partially obscure gender differences' (Pantazis 2000, p.422). It may perhaps be the case that this is true of punitiveness as well as the experience of feeling unsafe.

The other type of variable that does not appear in Table 15.11, possibly to the surprise of some readers, is any kind of measurement of social capital. We did in fact use scales measuring both 'area cohesion' and 'area collective efficacy',[30] and a combined score aggregating these two. All of these scales were inversely related to punitiveness scores at the ten per cent significance level on a simple bivariate correlational basis,[31] but none was sufficiently robust to appear in the final model reported in Table 15.11. A possible reason for this result was that the least economically deprived sub-areas within areas A and B (A1 and B3 respectively) were the top two sub-areas for both 'area cohesion' and 'area collective efficacy', but as regards punitiveness, one (A1) was liberal while the other (B3) was not.

Explaining the area difference in punitiveness: three hypotheses

As we have seen, the significant difference in punitiveness levels between areas A and B remained robust even after controlling for many other relevant variables in a multivariate model. It is worth pausing to emphasise how surprising this is, particularly as the less punitive area (area A), while by late 2003 it had a slightly lower recorded crime rate, nevertheless had similar victimisation prevalence (Table 15.8), a higher offender rate and more drug dealing than area B. How then can we explain this striking contrast in punitiveness scores, which (see earlier discussion) also placed areas A and B at the extreme ends of the continuum of areas considered by Maruna and King?

We developed three hypotheses as possible explanations, and we will consider each separately, although as will be seen two of them are interconnected.

Hypothesis 1: ethnic mix

As we have seen, positive views about multiculturalism were, in the final multivariate model, associated with lower punitiveness. Such views were expressed only in area A, no doubt because of its obvious multi-ethnic, cosmopolitan character as an area. 'Negative views about multiculturalism' was another dummy variable that was included in the multivariate analyses, and it was positively associated with punitiveness, though not quite strongly enough to appear in the final model.[32] However, such views were expressed *both* in area B *and* in area A, and there was no statistically significant area difference in the frequency with which respondents offered negative views of this kind.

Early in our analysis, it was suggested by some who learned of our area-difference results on punitiveness that the difference could be attributable to the differential ethnic mix of the two areas. It was noted that in the social psychological literature, it has been found that 'a lack of positive previous experiences with out-group members creates negative expectations about interracial interactions, which result in inter-ethnic-group anxiety' (Plant and Devine 2003). It was hypothesised, therefore, that the lower proportion of ethnic minority residents in area B would lead to greater inter-group anxiety among white residents in area B than in area A, which, it was further suggested, could lead to greater punitiveness, especially where offenders were from a minority ethnic group. However, as noted above, this hypothesis has received only limited support from the empirical analysis. 'Negative attitudes to multiculturalism' are indeed associated with punitiveness, but they are not differentially clustered by area. 'Positive attitudes to multiculturalism' are associated with non-punitiveness and *are* clustered in one area (area A); however, this variable is already controlled for in the multivariate model, and the area difference in punitiveness remains significant even after such controls.[33] Overall, therefore, this hypothesis is not strongly supported, and we need to look elsewhere for a more adequate explanation.

Hypothesis 2: signal disorders

In an important recent paper, Martin Innes and Nigel Fielding (2002), both of the University of Surrey, have put forward the concept of 'signal crimes' and 'signal disorders'. Their paper starts with the observation that 'police forces throughout Britain are currently grappling with a new problem' (para 1.1), namely the paradox that overall crime levels have been falling since the mid-1990s, but public anxiety remains high (on this, see Lewis's discussion in Chapter 2 of this volume). It is then argued that different crimes and disorders might have differential effects in what they signify to a wider audience in terms of fear (or, more technically, there are 'social semiotic processes by which particular types of criminal and disorderly conduct [can] have a disproportionate effect upon fear of crime': Abstract). For example, three spouse murders in a smallish town in a year would be unusual, but would not necessarily create widespread fear in the community at large, because they would be seen as 'private matters'; but the abduction and murder of a local schoolgirl on her way to school would almost certainly generate a much more powerful signal of fear throughout the community. Following this general logic, the key question in considering the apparently persisting sense of public anxiety (see above) becomes: 'what is sending signals fuelling the high public anxiety about crime in Britain today?'

These basic ideas have more recently been developed by Martin Innes into some formal definitions, in which the concept of 'risk' has replaced the concept of 'fear of crime'. This change has occurred because Innes's more recent work focuses particularly upon the general public's *perception of neighbourhood safety*, and 'risk' is therefore understood as a perceived potential threat to neighbourhood safety. The key formal definitions are:[34]

(i) A *signal crime* is a criminal incident that acts as a warning signal to people about the presence of risk.
(ii) A *signal disorder* is a form of disorderly conduct that indicates to people the presence of risk. Signal disorders are either 'physical', involving degradation to the environment; or 'social', involving behaviour.
(iii) A *control signal* is an act of social control that communicates an attempt to regulate disorderly and deviant behaviour. Control signals can be positive or negative.

This set of concepts is now being utilised in a major operational way, in England and Wales, in the National Reassurance Policing Project (NRPP),

Signal	Ward					
	A	B	C	D	E	F
1	Drugs	Youths	Youths	Youths	Youths	Drugs
2	Youths	Litter	Graffiti, litter and public urination	Vandalism and Damage	Drugs	Youths
3	Assault	Damage	Damage	Public violence and drinking	Damage and graffiti	Public drinking
4	Burglary	Public drinking	Public violence and mugging	Racing vehicles and skateboarding	Abandoned/ racing vehicles	Anti-social neighbours
5	Mugging	Public violence and speeding	Drugs	Murder	Burglary	Damage
6	Public drinking	Verbal abuse	Burglary	Verbal abuse	Gangs	

Figure 15.1 National Reassurance Policing Project: top 'signals' across trial wards
Source: University of Surrey

but space constraints forbid any discussion of that project here.[35] As part of the NRPP, detailed qualitative interviews are being conducted by the University of Surrey in 16 areas across Britain, asking representative respondents in each area questions about what, in their particular neighbourhood, they would identify as the key potential 'risks', as defined above. The early results from six wards are shown in Figure 15.1.[36]

A number of things are striking about the information in this figure. First, there is some significant variation by area in the details of the responses. Second, however, there are some common themes that clearly emerge as the first three perceived 'signals' of lack of neighbourhood safety in the six wards; namely youths, drugs, litter/graffiti, damage and public drinking. Third, it is extremely interesting that burglary does not appear in the 'top three' in any of the six areas, and only features at all in three areas.[37]

What explains the second and third points above? We will have to await the more detailed results of the University of Surrey's work before a definitive answer can be given, but provisionally it would seem that the answer lies in the fact that the commonly identified signals (youths,

Table 15.12 Percentage mentions of selected 'undesirable features of areas', and 'suggestions for improvement' (from qualitative analysis of interview comments)

N	A1 (39)	A2 (28)	A3 (11)	Area A (78)	B1 (24)	B2 (37)	B3 (17)	Area B (78)
Youths (as problem in the area)	36	42	27	33	63	68	71	67
Drug dealing/drug users	69	82	45	71	50	62	24	50
Poor street lighting	31	21	27	24	42	49	47	46
Problem families	0	7	9	4	25	32	18	27
Vandalism	8	11	0	8	29	30	29	29
Intimidation, fear of reprisals	0	4	0	3	8	14	6	10
Litter and dumping rubbish	15	21	36	21	17	24	24	22
Youth facilities needed in the area	38	29	9	31	33	35	18	31
More police (on the beat) needed	31	46	18	35	42	70	53	58

damage, drugs, etc) all focus on what are perceived as *disorderly events occurring in public space*. Thus, perhaps, they send a powerful message to residents (in a way that residential burglaries do not) that 'my area is out of control'.[38]

How is all this relevant to areas A and B? We have already noted in earlier sections that 'criminal damage' featured proportionately more prominently in area B than in area A in the recorded crime figures, the victimisation data, and the perception of regular crimes committed in the neighbourhood. Table 15.12, based on responses to open-ended questions in the survey (on perceptions of undesirable features of the area, and suggestions for improvement) supplements those data. Responses relating to 'youths as a problem' and to vandalism were markedly more common in area B, as were complaints about 'problem families' (a group that can also send disturbing 'signals', in the language of Innes and Fielding).[39] Poor street lighting and an absence of adequate policing were also more commonly perceived in area B, a point on which we comment more fully below. By contrast, drug problems were, not unexpectedly, more commonly mentioned in area A (though the rate of mentions in area A was perhaps higher than expected).

In general, and leaving aside for the moment the important question of drugs, these data suggest that 'signal disorders' (as defined by Innes and Fielding) were more commonly perceived to be present in their area by the residents of area B. It is also reasonable to suppose – although it would need further research to test the matter definitively – that the presence of 'signal disorders', and therefore of perceived insecurity in public places in the neighbourhood, can promote more punitive attitudes.

We now need to confront an important issue. The 'signal crimes and disorders' perspective is to a large extent about perceptions; so, *must the perceptions have some basis in reality for a 'signal disorder' to be perceived?* This question is given added point by the earlier research of Girling, Loader and Sparks (2000) in Macclesfield (which they accurately describe as a town epitomising 'Middle England'). The authors are clear that 'people from many diverse parts of Macclesfield face problems (of low-level disorder and petty crime) caused by groups of teenagers hanging around', albeit differentially so in different areas. But, significantly, they continue:

> Yet it is also evident from our research that residents interpret the presence and behaviour of these teenagers in contrasting ways and invest it with varying degrees of significance; *and these interpretations cannot simply be read off from actual levels of disorderly or criminal activity.* They also appear to depend on which of Macclesfield's composite areas one is talking about (their respective histories, demographies, internal relations, trajectories and so on), and on the biographical relationship its inhabitants have to the place they reside in – how it fits into their past, present and possible futures. (p. 82, emphasis added)

The authors thus do not suggest that residents' perceptions of disorder have no basis in reality, but they do suggest that reports of disorder, and the significance that is attached to them by local residents, need to be understood and interpreted in a contextual way. On the basis of our research, we concur with this view. In area B, our research observer was sometimes initially puzzled when he went up to the estate of an evening and found very little happening in the public spaces of the area.[40] Yet there was no doubt that incidents which disturbed residents considerably did sometimes occur, as some of our survey respondents made clear:

> There's a lack of things to do [for young people], so they hang around, drinking under age, smash bottles in the middle of the road. [Points at three white youths.] They are the main problem around here. One of them lives a couple of doors down so *we* don't get aggro – they don't mess on their own doorstep.
>
> I was never a racist but now I'm like that . . . [gestures with his hand to show he's on the balance]. The problem here is kids in groups, with coloured lads leading, you can't ask them anything. I asked them to keep the noise down but one just told me to get back in the house, saying 'I know my rights'. Kids have took over . . .
>
> There's a lot of vandalism. I don't feel as safe as I used to. You can't complain, because of worry about repercussions. I was waiting at the bus stop, I got abuse off people sitting on the hedge when I asked them to get off.
>
> I've told you about them Asian lads coming back into this area looking for them [local youths] and they are running down the backstreets, down people's gardens, they were shouting 'fetch the police, there are some Asians after us'. You know what makes me sick

> is everyone accuses everyone of being an informer but surprise surprise this lot were screaming for the police.

Such incidents (bottles smashed in the road; abuse in response to polite requests; inter-group conflict involving running into people's gardens) do not have to happen often for them to be perceived as 'signal disorders', exemplifying a more general sense of threat.[41] Moreover, in interpreting (or not) a particular incident as a 'signal disorder', it is not at all surprising if residents take into account their more general understanding of the area, its strengths and its weaknesses. Indeed, Martin Innes reports (in a personal communication) that the perception of 'an area going downhill' is one of the most potent factors associated with a strong sense of 'signal disorders' in a given neighbourhood. While respondents in area B mostly did not believe that their area was going downhill, they were significantly less likely than residents of area A to consider that it was improving (see earlier discussion). It is also highly relevant to recall that, in the studied areas, strong ties to the area predicted punitiveness, and that such ties were more often present among respondents in area B. Thus, in area B we found a combination of (i) strong 'area rootedness', (ii) the presence of 'signal disorders' *and* (iii) a lack of optimism about the future of the neighbourhood while, for example, policing and street lighting remained unattended to (Table 15.12). This seems to be a powerful set of contextual circumstances which could explain the higher punitiveness level of this area compared to that of area A.

We are left, however, with the drugs issue. Although drugs were perceived by residents of area B as quite problematic (Table 15.12), on every indicator available to us in this research, drugs were seen as a greater problem in area A (see e.g., Tables 15.4, 15.5 and 15.12). Moreover, drugs were one of the principal 'signal disorders' identified in Martin Innes's ongoing research (Figure 15.1). Yet area A is not only significantly less punitive than area B, it is also, at least on raw data, less punitive than any of the areas studied in Maruna and King's research (see previous discussion). Do these points count as evidence against the validity of Hypothesis 2 as an explanation of differential area punitiveness? This is an important question, which we will postpone until Hypothesis 3 has also been considered.

Hypothesis 3: social control

In an important piece of research on neighbourhood change in residential areas of Chicago, Richard Taub, Garth Taylor and Jan Durham (1984) showed that crime levels are an issue for residents and potential residents in judging the quality of life in an area. However, these judgments were, in this study, found to be comparative rather than absolute (e.g. 'is this area better than an area that I might consider moving to?'); moreover, crime levels were only one among a number of factors that might influence people in assessing the quality of an area. In particular, an expressed intention to move out of the area was statistically more closely related to a perceived general lack of safety in the area than to actual levels of criminal victimisation.

Taub *et al.* (1984: 18–25) strategically selected for special study eight Chicago communities with systematically differing values on three dichotomised variables (since $2 \times 2 \times 2 = 8$). The three key variables were: were crime rates high or low; was the area racially stable, or was there an influx of new black residents; and were property values appreciating rapidly or only slowly? Of special interest for present purposes are the two neighbourhoods that combined high crime and rapidly appreciating property values, a combination which shows that high crime can accompany perceived social desirability. Crucially, in both these areas both perceived and actual risk of crime was high, but so was residents' satisfaction with safety levels. Also, 'in each neighborhood, there [were] highly visible signs of extra community resources being used to deal with the crime problem' (Taub *et al.* 1984: 171–172). This evidence therefore suggests that, if the authorities can create a general sense of social control and safety in an area, people will be less socially anxious despite actual high crime levels; and, of course, if they are less socially anxious then it is reasonable to postulate that they might also be less punitive. Evidence of reduced social anxiety being generated in this way was particularly strong in one Chicago neighbourhood, which witnessed strongly purposeful action, and a significant injection of resources, from powerful agencies.[42] In Innes and Fielding's terms, action of this type could therefore generate a *powerful positive control signal* (see earlier discussion).

These considerations have some direct relevance to experience in area A. In 2001, this neighbourhood received a large grant from central government, since when considerable amounts of money have been spent on improving the appearance and the security of the area. This has included building projects, improved street lighting, clearing up litter and fly-tipping, and the creation of a dedicated community police unit; also, after the date of our survey (but known to be imminent then), community wardens and a dedicated anti-social behaviour team were introduced. The previously-mentioned demolitions in sub-area A2, although not related to the central government grant, had the further effect of removing many void properties and some of the least desirable housing in the area.

There have also been two large city- and county-wide police operations against drugs and street crime, both strongly associated with area A. The first, in 2002, saw 70 additional police officers, some drafted in from Doncaster and Barnsley, to cut street crime in Sheffield as a whole. The second, in July 2003, was aimed at key parts of the South Yorkshire drug market, and in area A this resulted in a number of arrests of alleged drug dealers. This, together with the additional police presence from the new community-based officers (see above), plus the installation of CCTV, has significantly reduced the level of visible drug dealing in the area and, it is claimed, has displaced the drug market to the fringes of area A. All this seems to help to explain why, although drugs featured strongly in comments from survey respondents about the undesirable features of area A (see Table 15.12), this problem was not perceived as getting out of control, and indeed (see earlier discussion) 36 per cent of surveyed residents thought the area was improving.

Further assistance in understanding this last point can be derived from comparing the findings of our research in area A with those of John Graham (2000) following fieldwork in a part of the same area some three years earlier. Graham reported that the local drug-user population was not particularly extensive, but users came to 'East Rise' (his pseudonym for one part of area A) from many towns within a 50-mile radius, 'so it is very much the dealing and the influx of people from outside the area that impacts on the community'. That impact, as Graham described it, was one of significant fear, intimidation, and the feeling that nobody in power would listen to the residents.[43] By late 2003, such feelings still existed among some residents, but were substantially reduced: the various initiatives described above had, it seems, sent powerful 'control signals' so that the area no longer felt alien to its own residents. Drug dealing still existed, and so did violence (sometimes involving weapons) arising from such dealing, but despite these activities, the area itself – analogously to Hyde Park-Kenwood (see n. 42) – felt much safer than it had done before the control measures were taken.

In area A, then, authorities of various kinds had recently paid much attention to the area; and this seems to have led to at least a small reduction in recorded crime levels (see earlier discussion), and a greatly improved sense of social control among the residents. Area B, by contrast, was – in the period before our survey – relatively neglected by the authorities. In particular, as both our research observer and our survey results attest, its street lighting was noticeably worse than that of most of area A,[44] and policing levels were also lower (see Table 15.12). Indeed, research observation suggested a notable lack of active police presence in area B (though patrol cars often passed through). On the few occasions the police were observed in the sub-areas, they appeared to be responding to a specific situation. All of these sightings were in sub-area B1; our observer did not encounter any similar situation in sub-areas B2 or B3. These observations are, of course, supported by residents' responses in Table 15.12, where complaints about the absence of policing featured much more prominently for area B than for area A. Overall, therefore, it would be reasonable to conclude, in support of this third hypothesis, that 'control signals' were definitely more evident to the residents of area A than to those of area B, and that this could well have contributed to area A's lower punitiveness levels.[45]

Assessing the hypotheses

At the outset of this chapter, we indicated that this is a small, exploratory study. This is an appropriate point to repeat that message, and to emphasise that not too much should be read into our results. That is particularly the case with our discussion of the hypotheses, since these were developed *post hoc* in an attempt to explain some totally unexpected findings.

Nevertheless, we think we can plausibly say that both Hypothesis 2 (on 'signal disorders') and Hypothesis 3 (on 'social control') seem to have some potential validity in explaining the differential punitiveness of areas A and B. Indeed, Hypotheses 2 and 3 are themselves clearly inversely linked, because 'signal disorders' normally indicate to the public a worrying *lack* of adequate social control, whereas successful community action, such as that taken in Hyde Park-Kenwood (see n. 42), sends a powerful 'control signal'.

In concluding our discussion of these hypotheses, it is, we think, appropriate to return to the work of Girling *et al.* (2000) in Macclesfield. On the basis of their empirical research, these authors concluded that:

> . . . people's worries and talk about crime are rarely *merely* a reflection of behavioural change and 'objective' risk (though they represent lay attempts to make sense of such changes and risks), but are also 'bound up in a context of meaning and significance, involving the use of metaphors and narratives about social change' (Sparks 1992: 131). We have sought . . . to demonstrate this by providing a grounded sociological account of how crime works in everyday life as a cultural theme and token of political exchange; of how it serves to condense, and make intelligible, a variety of more difficult-to-grasp troubles and insecurities – something that tends to blur the boundary between worries about crime and other kinds of anxiety and concern. We have attempted to show that in speaking of crime people routinely register its entanglement with other aspects of economic, social and moral life; attribute responsibility and blame; demand accountability and justice, and draw lines of affiliation and distance between 'us' and various categories of 'them'. (p. 170, emphasis added).

One of the categories of 'them' to which residents may refer in this way is, of course, the category of 'offenders'. Hence, if Girling *et al.* are right (and we think they are), attitudes to the punishment of local offenders are (at least in part) a way of drawing 'lines of affiliation between "us" and . . . "them" '. It is not at all surprising if the drawing of such lines is deeply contextually embedded in the overall culture, social life and politics of local residential communities.

McInerney and redeemability

We turn finally to a different set of issues, triggered by the answers to a rather lengthy question that we placed at the end of our interview schedule. This referred to a guideline sentencing judgment of the Court of Appeal that was delivered in December 2002 by Lord Woolf (Lord Chief Justice) in the case of *McInerney*.[46] Our question asked:

> In a recent major case in the Appeal Court, the Lord Chief Justice dealt with cases of house burglary involving theft of items like TV, a video and some jewellery by a burglar. He said first- or second-time burglars like this should usually receive a community sentence, but such sentences should be subject to conditions that made sure that the sentence was an effective punishment, and that it tried to tackle underlying problems such as drug-related offending. The Lord Chief Justice also said that this would provide greater public protection than a short prison sentence, because a high proportion of people released from prison committed further crimes soon after release.
>
> Do you agree or disagree with the view of the Lord Chief Justice?

We were able to compare respondents' answers to this question with those given to an earlier question on the appropriate sentence for a second-time burglar (see item 7 on the punitiveness scale, as specified earlier in this chapter). Taking the two questions together, we classified the answers into three main groups:[47]

- 'Liberals', i.e. those favouring a community sentence on punitiveness question 7, and also agreeing with the judgment in *McInerney*.
- 'Persuaded', i.e. those favouring a prison sentence on punitiveness question 7, but agreeing with the judgment in *McInerney*, and who therefore by implication were apparently persuaded by the reasoning in that judgment.[48]
- 'Unpersuaded', i.e. those favouring a prison sentence on punitiveness question 7, and maintaining that stance by disagreeing with the judgment in *McInerney*.

Overall, this analysis produced 43 'liberals', 65 'persuaded' and 42 'unpersuaded'. Arguably, the Lord Chief Justice could be pleased with the results, on two grounds. First, about 70 per cent of all respondents (i.e., 'liberals' plus the 'persuaded') agreed with his reasoning when it was put to them; and secondly, of those who favoured prison in response to question 7 on the punitiveness scale, 61 per cent (65 out of 107) were

Table 15.13 Responses to the Court of Appeal's reasoning in *R. v. McInerney*

	'Liberals'	'Persuaded'	'Unpersuaded'
N.	43	65	42
Total (%)	29	43	28
Area A (%)	39	38	23
Area B (%)	18	49	33
*Punitiveness (mean)	17.7	27.0	31.4
	(SD 6.16)	(SD 5.76)	(SD 5.06)
†Redeemability (mean)	14.0	12.5	10.9
	(SD 2.24)	(SD 3.01)	(SD 2.89)

*t-tests for these differences show both the liberals/persuaded and the persuaded/unpersuaded comparisons to be significant at P<.001.
†t-tests for these differences show both the liberals/persuaded and the persuaded/unpersuaded comparisons to be significant at P<.01.

apparently persuaded by Lord Woolf's arguments. Interestingly, this last proportion did not vary by area. However, and not surprisingly in the light of the results reported earlier in this chapter, area A had a higher initial proportion of 'liberals' (see Table 15.13).

It could be (and indeed has been) objected that our *McInerney* question is too much of a leading question, expecting the answer 'yes'. However, detailed consideration of the data in Table 15.13 suggests that a face-value interpretation of the responses might not be inappropriate. On mean punitiveness scores, for example, while the three main groups have very significantly different scores, the average of the eventually 'persuaded' group is much closer to the more punitive than to the more liberal extreme.[49] On the other hand, mean redeemability scores for the 'persuaded' are mid-way between the 'liberals' and the 'unpersuaded', and therefore not as close to the 'hard-line' group as in the case of the punitiveness score.[50] Thus, the 'persuaded' group were *both* relatively punitive (though not quite as punitive as the unpersuaded group) *and* also relatively strong in their endorsement of redeemability. Such results seem entirely consistent with a face-value interpretation of the *McInerney* question; on this view, the 'persuaded' are in the 'firm but fair' category, that is, they want justice to be firmly administered, but in a way that allows offenders the opportunity to change.[51] And if this question can be treated at face value, then its implications for the 'alternatives to imprisonment' debate are encouraging, because they suggest first, a high degree of potential support for community penalties, even in a high punitiveness area such as area B; and second, a significant linkage between that support and support for the concept of 'redeemability' (as was also suggested by the regression analysis – see Table 15.11).

Implications for community penalties

In one sense, it could be said that our empirical research in two high-crime areas of Sheffield did not yield the dividends that we originally thought likely. That is to say (see the introduction to this chapter), since those who commit crimes in high-crime areas are very often residents of those areas, it seemed possible that we might obtain some interesting specific comments from respondents on how such offenders should be dealt with. We did ask some open-ended questions of this kind in our community survey, but most respondents had relatively little to say about such matters, and very few had much specific knowledge of community penalties.

But while that aspect of the survey was disappointing, the main results obtained have been both unexpected and challenging. Having now set out these results in detail, what implications can we draw from them, in policy terms, for the future of community penalties?

We will approach this issue in a rather tangential way, by discussing a recent joint project of the Magistrates' Association and the Probation Boards Association, known as LCCS (or 'Local Crime: Community Sentence'). The mission statement of the project is: 'magistrates and probation working together with [the] community to improve public confidence in sentencing and raise awareness of the effectiveness of community penalties'. In the pilot phase of this project, three areas were selected (Hampshire and the Isle of Wight; Lancashire; and Northumbria) and, in each area, a series of public presentations was made by a magistrate and a probation staff member working together. Audiences were a matter for local choice, but included groups such as residents' associations, neighbourhood watch groups, community wardens, rotary clubs, student groups, Citizens' Advice Bureaux, 'friends and families of lesbians and gays', etc. An evaluation of the project by King's College, London (King and Grimshaw 2003) reported that a starting-point for the presentations made was some prior research evidence on public attitudes to sentencing:

> Hough and Roberts (1998) found that the majority of a large British sample thought that judges were too lenient, but when presented with a burglary case made decisions that were close to current sentencing practice. In particular it was shown that lack of knowledge about community sentencing alternatives was associated with punitive choices. Information about alternatives to custody increases preferences for alternatives to custody (Hough and Roberts 1999).

The evaluation of LCCS showed that the presentations made by this project had similar effects to those reported by Hough and Roberts; that is to say, people given a sample case were more punitive before the presentation than afterwards, and in general 'the presentations succeeded in their aims of getting members of the public to think about community sentences as a serious sentencing option' (King and Grimshaw 2003: 20). In the light of this success in the pilot areas, LCCS is now being extended to many more areas.

On the basis of this evidence, there is clearly promise in the LCCS approach. That promise is further supported (although on a more microcosmic scale) by the results from the *McInerney* question in our own survey. In that question, the reasoning of the Lord Chief Justice in favour of community penalties was briefly explained to respondents; and this had the effect of producing a more sympathetic approach to the possibility of community penalties for some residential burglars than had previously been the case. Crucial to this change of heart was the widespread, and encouraging, reserve of public opinion in favour of the concept of 'redeemability' (see earlier discussions).

And yet . . . Despite the clear promise of the LCCS approach, one aspect of it makes us rather uneasy. The implicit model of the LCCS seems to be that of a teacher–pupil relationship; that is to say, the magistrate/probation presenters explain the system and its constructive options, and the community groups improve their knowledge and (tend to) change their attitudes. What seems to be structurally rather suppressed by this approach is the possibility that magistrates and probation staff might themselves have something to learn from the community groups, if they want to enhance the case for community penalties.

Our research results suggest that LCCS – and the probation service more generally – might usefully consider a more dialectical, two-way approach of this kind. If we are right in our interpretation of the results, especially through Hypotheses 2 and 3, then 'signal disorders' in an area tend to promote punitiveness, whereas positive 'control signals' tend to dampen such attitudes, and to make it more likely that respondents would support community penalties as an alternative to imprisonment in appropriate cases. If that is the case, then those who wish to promote 'alternatives to prison' should not only provide more information about such penalties to community groups (as LCCS seeks, quite sensibly, to do), but also try to be very sensitive to local conditions of disorder, lack of control, etc, which might very easily erode the social confidence of local people and make them much less willing to support 'alternatives to prison'.

At present, an approach of this latter kind is hindered by the fact that correctional agencies, especially the probation service, have to a large extent retreated from community involvement in favour of the delivery of 'programmes' and the like in city centre offices. Thus, in Areas A and B, our research observer reported that the probation service was completely invisible in a ground-level community context, and the youth offending team largely so. Moreover, qualitative interview evidence suggested that, even among residents who support in principle the idea of 'alternatives to imprisonment', there was often scepticism – especially of course in area B – that the offenders, insisting on their 'rights' as they do, and not infrequently abusing those who seek to intervene to moderate their behaviour (see earlier quotations), would actually comply in anything other than a nominal sense with the requirements of community orders. The policy logic arising from these considerations seems to be that correctional agencies working with offenders in high-crime communities need – in conjunction of course with other partners such as the police – to send some more obvious and more positive 'control signals' to the residents of such areas, indicating that the area's offenders are being dealt with constructively, and on a basis of an adequate understanding of the fears and hurts of other residents living in the area. Such an approach seems all the more appropriate because residents' support for the principle of redeemability remains high, even in a high-crime area with a high punitiveness score such as area B (see earlier discussion).

We do not seek here to say more about how such an approach might be developed in detail;[52] our aim has been simply to raise an important issue for debate, based on the results of our research.[53]

Notes

1 We are most grateful to Shadd Maruna and Anna King for permission to utilise their questions in this way.

2 Because the chapter is in an important sense complementary to Chapter 4, we have not thought it necessary to reference here the general research literature on public attitudes to punishment; readers are referred to the list of references for Chapter 4.

3 According to a source at Sheffield Housing Department, from 2001 to the beginning of 2004 a total of 398 council properties were demolished in area A, almost all in sub-area A2. However, many of these properties were voids before demolition. The council rehoused occupants of 146 of the properties, and a few other families may have made their own arrangements. If we conservatively assume that 150 households were displaced by the demolitions, this was nevertheless a very large-scale population change in sub-area A2, which at the time of the 2001 Census had 757 households (see Table 15.1).

4 We are most grateful to our colleague Dr. Andrew Costello, who supplied all the data used in this subsection. These data are derived from Costello's longstanding and ongoing collaborative research programme with South Yorkshire Police.

5 A key factor here is of course the population reduction created by the demolitions. However, also relevant is the fact that many void properties, which had acted to an extent as crime-attracting, were also knocked down.

6 Nevertheless, it should be noted that not all of the reduction in recorded crime in area A in 2003/4 can be directly attributed to the demolitions. It is quite

likely that a further contributing factor to the decline was an enhanced sense of social control in the area, related to a major government-financed initiative; we discuss this towards the end of this chapter.

7 We were obliged, by the timetable of the Coulsfield Commission, to conduct the survey in these months. There is no doubt, however, that the dark nights dissuaded some residents from wanting to invite our interviewers into their homes.

8 This low N occurred despite a largish total census population (see Table 15.1). The apparent discrepancy appears to be attributable principally to (i) low electoral registration in a sub-area with many refugees, and (ii) rapid turnover leading to a high number of electoral register invalidities relative to the addresses issued to interviewees (see the penultimate row of Table 15.6).

9 Interviewers initially said: 'Now I'm going to ask you to tell me about any crimes or incidents (such as abuse or disorder) that have happened to you since last Christmas.' A set of offence categories was then read out (burglary of your home; burglary of shed or garage; theft in the dwelling; joyriding; theft from a car; theft from your person; criminal damage; fraud; abuse in a public place; and other). For each category, respondents were asked to state how many times victimisation of this type had occurred, and whether the last offence in each category had been reported to the police.

10 We have restricted this analysis to area differences, rather than showing sub-areas, because – as is common with victimisation surveys, even in high crime areas – a high proportion of respondents have no victimisations to report, so sub-area analysis quickly leads to very small numbers.

11 In the case of personal crime, reasons for this include: (i) the item includes abuse as well as assault, and (ii) our survey respondents mostly did not include persons involved in the drug trade, and their disputes constituted a significant proportion of the assaults in area A.

12 Maruna and King had ten items in their punitiveness scale, but we omitted three of these for a mixture of statistical and conceptual reasons. Statistically, in the Sheffield responses, the inter-item correlations of these variables with the main punitiveness variables were not strong. Two of the omitted items related to 'volunteering my time or donating money' to organisations (respectively, one supporting 'tougher sentencing laws in England' and one supporting 'alternatives to prison'), and it was found in interviews that issues such as whether the respondent had the time or inclination to join organisations were sometimes more important in framing responses than the punitive/non-punitive dimension of the questions. (Indeed, nearly half the whole sample either disagreed or agreed with *both* these questions simultaneously). The final omitted item was: 'After an offender has done his/her time, the slate should be wiped clean and they should be allowed to move on in society without obstacles.' This item was found to correlate better with other 'redeemability' items (see below) than with the main punitive items, and conceptually it also seemed to fit better with the redeemability scale, so it was transferred to that scale.

13 These comparisons were made using Maruna and King's ten-item punitiveness score (see note 12 above).

14 As with the punitiveness scale (see note 12) this is a change from Maruna and King, who used a four-item scale for redeemability. The change was, as before,

made for a mixture of statistical and conceptual reasons, and as noted above (n. 12) it involved the transfer of one item from the punitiveness to the redeemability scale.

15 This is using Maruna and King's four-item scale for redeemability (see n. 14 above).

16 The regression analysis was carried out for us by Tessa Peasgood of the University of Sheffield School of Health and Related Research (ScHARR), to whom we wish to express our deepest thanks.

17 The predictors (independent variables) used in the model were determined primarily by an understanding of what might theoretically be expected to predict punitive views, plus findings from past research. Predictors which were insignificant at the five per cent level were subsequently removed from the model. This approach is comparable to a backward elimination method in which all possible predictors are entered into the model. The predictor with the smallest partial correlation with the outcome (or dependent) variable is first considered for removal. The significance is compared to a removal criterion (the probability of the F statistic not being significant at five per cent), which if it is met (i.e. the predictor is not making a statistically significant contribution to how well the model predicts the outcome), the variable is removed.

18 R^2 is a statistic that measures the total amount of variance that is statistically explained by the regression model, in this case 57 per cent.

19 The use of an OLS regression model ideally requires that the residual (error term) be normally distributed. In this model, one statistical test (Kolmogorov-Smirnov) suggested that the residual was not significantly different from a normal distribution, but another test (Shapiro-Wilk) showed that it was ($P < .03$). Thus, the residual is close to, but not actually, a normal distribution. The principal reason for the abnormality was two cases in area B with an unusual combination of scores ('outliers'); when these cases were removed from the model, the residual was not significantly different from a normal distribution, whether measured by the Kolmogorov-Smirnov or Shapiro-Wilk test. Nevertheless, it did not seem appropriate to exclude the two outliers from the substantive analysis, not least because they were both area B cases with low punitiveness scores. Further testing showed that, if the regression model was restricted to variables with at least a five per cent level of significance (as opposed to the ten per cent that we initially adopted), the inclusion or exclusion of the outliers made no difference to the final list of variables included (although, of course, the betas and t values for each variable were different). We concluded that it was appropriate to use the final model as presented here.

20 There was no item on the interview schedule directly tapping views about multiculturalism. This item has therefore been derived from qualitative analysis of interviewees' responses to general open-ended questions (such as the advantages and disadvantages of living in the area).

21 This scale was a composite of two questions: (i) 'Young people don't seem to have any respect for anything any more;' and (ii) 'The behaviour of adolescents today is worse than it was in the past.'

22 The mean score on this scale in area A was 9.67 (SD 2.48) and in area B 10.86 (SD 1.35). These are high average scores, as the scale had a minimum of 2 and a maximum of 12. The difference in scores between areas cannot be attributed to a higher proportion of youth in the population in area B, because the areas were

similar in this respect (area A, age 0–15 26 per cent; age 16–19, seven per cent; area B, age 0–15 24 per cent, age 16–19 six per cent: see Tables 15.1 and 15.2).

23 The finding is, nevertheless, a robust one. We identified it only because early regression runs identified both 'retired' and 'age 55+' as significantly related to punitiveness within a multivariate model, but with different signs ('retired', +; age 55+, −). This was obviously potentially confusing, so we replaced these variables with the dummy variable as described.

24 The mean score in area A was 1.27 (SD 0.96) and in area B 2.08 (SD 0.88).

25 It is worth noting that in the regression model with the two outliers excluded (see note 19 above) the significance level of the area effect was enhanced ($P<.002$ rather than $P<.05$).

26 In *Method I*, we re-ran the main model shown in Table 15.11, but replacing the 'area A dummy variable' with a series of sub-area dummy variables. This was done using both a 'liberal' sub-area (A1) and a 'punitive' sub-area (B3) as a base. In *Method II*, we replicated the procedure for Method I, except that the analyses were carried out separately for two subsamples, i.e. area A and area B cases were treated in separate regression analyses. In *Method III*, we retained the procedure of using separate area subsamples, but carried out a full backwards elimination procedure (see n. 17) for each area.

27 A3 was clearly distinguishable from A1 and A2 using Methods I, II and III (see n. 26 above).

28 Using Method I (see n. 26 above) with A1 (a liberal sub-area) as a base, dummy variables for B2 and B3, but not B1, were significant in the model. Using Method II, there were no significant sub-area variables in the model. Using Method III, a B1 sub-area dummy appeared as significant at the ten per cent level, with a negative relationship to the dependent variable (punitiveness).

29 Mean punitiveness scores by gender were: females 26.3 (SD 7.06), males 25.0 (SD 8.38), $P>.1$.

30 The area cohesion questions asked respondents to agree or disagree with the following statements: (1) 'I could rely on my neighbours to help in times of trouble'; (2) 'This part of the area is a close-knit neighbourhood'; (3) 'People in this part of the area generally don't get along with each other'; and (4) 'Generally speaking, people around here can be trusted'. The area collective efficacy questions were adapted from Sampson *et al.* (1997), and asked respondents to state how likely it was that their neighbours would intervene personally in the following situations: (1) 'Suppose some teenage children were truanting from school and hanging around on a street corner in school time'; (2) 'Suppose a fight broke out between three 11-year-olds on a pavement in front of some houses'; (3) 'Suppose some teenagers were being rude to an old person in the street, calling her names and being disrespectful to her'; and (4) 'Suppose a group of teenagers was spraying some graffiti on a local building'.

31 Correlations with the punitive scale were: area coherence −.229 ($P<.004$); collective efficacy −.148 ($P<.065$); 'social capital' (combined area coherence and collective efficacy) −.240 ($P<.003$).

32 It should be made clear that both 'positive' and 'negative' views were expressed only by a minority of respondents, so there was a large middle group. As previously noted (n. 20), no direct question on this issue was asked in the interview.

33 Although it is true that this might not be a full control because no direct question on multiculturalism was asked (see n. 20), hence there could be some

residual effects of this variable among respondents who made no explicit comment on the matter.

34 Derived from literature distributed by the National Reassurance Policing Project.

35 For details of the NRPP, see its website [http://www.reassurancepolicing.co.uk].

36 Figure 15.1 is derived from a presentation made by Martin Innes at the University of Cambridge in April 2004, and is used with permission.

37 For a very interesting precursor to these results, see the similar findings in Shapland and Vagg (1988), Ch. 4.

38 It is relevant here to note that Wikström and Dolmén (2001), in a large survey study in Sweden, found that minor social disorder played a key role in generating fear of crime (pp. 132–133). See also Pantazis (2000).

39 Some respondents in area A commented that, as a result of the demolitions and rehousing in sub-area A2 (see earlier discussion) there were now fewer problem families in the area.

40 Of course, this might have been partly a function of the time of year at which most of the observational work was done (February to May). But again, the finding has precedents in the literature: 'While people were uneasy about – for example – youths on street corners, the "street corner youth count" was very low' (Shapland and Vagg 1988: 64).

41 On the potential role of feelings of general-societal threat in generating punitive attitudes, see Rucker *et al.* (2004).

42 This was the Hyde Park-Kenwood area, where the University of Chicago is situated (see Taub *et al.* 1984: 96–102). Following major white out-migration from the area in the 1950s, and the in-migration of new (mostly black) residents with substantially lower income levels, there were widespread fears that the area would suffer urban blight and community disintegration. The consensus was that an urban renewal programme was needed, to rid the area of its most deteriorated housing. The University spent large sums from its endowment fund for this purpose, and was also instrumental in obtaining federal funds and encouraging private investment in the area. The University and/or local citizen groups also: '(i) pressurized the city authorities to enforce regulations against the multi-occupation of certain dwellings, (ii) provided low-cost second mortgages to encourage university staff to live in the area, (iii) assembled a large private security force with a radio link to the Chicago Police Department, and (iv) created a fleet of buses, and installed emergency telephones at key points, to enhance feelings of personal safety' (Bottoms 1994: 644–645). The net result was the creation of a racially-mixed (60 per cent white) but residentially stable area (no further 'white flight'), rapidly appreciating property values, and widespread feelings of safety, despite continuing high crime rates.

43 Representative quotations from residents included the following: 'a lot are too frightened to complain or come forward'; 'we daren't walk to the Recreational Centre whilst it's dark'; 'I've walked past them, sat there on the road, wrapping stuff up'; 'there are needles in the garden at top of close'; and 'if [the] authorities would just listen to us' (all from Graham 2000).

44 For a systematic review of research on the effects of improved street lighting on crime, see Farrington and Welsh (2002). This review suggested that improved lighting did reduce crime, but, as the reduction was as much in

daytime as in night-time crime, an explanation 'focussing on [lighting's] role in increasing community pride and informal social control may be more plausible than a theory focussing on increased surveillance and increased deterrence' (p. vi). In other words, improved street lighting seems to send a powerful 'positive control signal' which improves residents' confidence in the area by day as well as by night.

45 We indicated earlier that there is some tentative evidence that B1 is the least punitive sub-area within area B, despite having the highest recorded crime rate and the highest proportion of residents believing that 'crime is a serious problem where I live' (Tables 15.5, 15.7). A possible reason for this tentative finding is evidence consistent with the 'positive control signals' hypothesis developed above. In particular, for approximately two years prior to our survey, sub-area B1 (but not B2 or B3) had been patrolled by 'community wardens' employed by the local authority Housing Department. Amongst other things, these wardens receive from residents reports about graffiti, fly-tipping, abandoned properties and abandoned vehicles, and they also challenge youths behaving in an antisocial way. It is reported that the wardens' work has, over time, gradually gained wide acceptance among adults in the sub-area, and it is notable that respondents in the sub-area, despite the high crime rate, were less likely than respondents in B2 and B3 to say that more police patrols were needed (Table 15.12). Indeed, though the differences were often very small, it was striking that on every single item in Table 15.12, the ratings for sub-area B1 were less unfavourable than those for B2, despite higher crime in B1. The odds of such a result occurring by chance are very small.

46 *R v McInerney, R v Keating* [2002] EWCA Crim 3003.

47 This excludes four cases with missing values, and two who (confusedly) did not favour a prison sentence on punitiveness question 7, but disagreed with the judgment in *McInerney*.

48 Question 7 on the punitiveness scale refers to a second-time burglar, while the *McInerney* judgment refers to first- or second-time residential burglary. Thus, the issues raised are not identical, but we regarded them as sufficiently close to justify the classification shown in the text.

49 It should be noted that there is a small element of duplication here, since punitiveness question 7 is involved in constructing the liberal/persuaded/unpersuaded categorisation, and it is also of course one of the seven items that go to make up the punitiveness scale.

50 In interpreting these results, it is important to bear in mind that, in the interview situation, all items on the punitiveness and redeemability scales had already been answered before the *McInerney* question was posed.

51 Our interviewers were also inclined to support a face-value interpretation of the results of the *McInerney* question, reporting that many respondents gave it very careful consideration.

52 Matters are however taken forward a little more specifically in the Editors' Chapter 16. It is also relevant to report that quite a few survey respondents mentioned community work by offenders within their community as a possible way of offenders making reparation to ordinary residents. It ought to be possible to develop this kind of approach without incurring the obvious dangers of stigmatisation and exclusion in such situations (see Chapter 7).

53 We would like to express our thanks to several people whose comments have helped us to refine the argument in this chapter: participants at a Centre for Criminological Research seminar at Sheffield University; Barrie Irving of the Police Foundation; and – especially – Gerry Rose. All remaining errors, omissions and infelicities are, of course, our responsibility.

References

Bottoms, A. E. (1994) 'Environmental criminology', in M. Maguire, R. Morgan and R. Reiner (eds) *The Oxford Handbook of Criminology* (Oxford: Oxford University Press), pp. 585–656.

Bottoms, A. E. and Wiles, P. (2002) 'Environmental criminology', in M. Maguire, R. Morgan and R. Reiner (eds) *The Oxford Handbook of Criminology*, 3rd edition (Oxford: Oxford University Press), pp. 620–656.

Bottoms, A. E., Mawby, R. I. and Xanthos, P. (1989), 'A tale of two estates', in D. Downes (ed.) *Crime and the City* (London: Macmillan), pp. 36–87.

Farrington, D. P. and Welsh, B. C. (2002 *Effects of Improved Street Lighting on Crime: A systematic review*, Home Office Research Study 251 (London: Home Office).

Girling, E., Loader, I. and Sparks, R. (2000) *Crime and Social Change in Middle England: Questions of order in an English town* (London: Routledge).

Graham, J. (2000), 'Drug markets and neighbourhood regeneration' (Unpublished report available from the Centre for Analysis of Social Exclusion, London School of Economics and Political Science).

Hough, M. and Roberts, J. (1998) *Attitudes to Punishment: Findings from the British Crime Survey*, Home Office Research Study 179 (London: Home Office).

Hough, M. and Roberts, J. (1999) 'Sentencing trends in Britain: public knowledge and public opinion', *Punishment and Society*, 1: 11–26.

Innes, M. and Fielding, N. (2002) 'From community to communicative policing: "signal crimes" and the problem of public reassurance', *Sociological Research Online*, 7(2) [www.socresonline.org.uk/7/2/innes.html]

King, J. and Grimshaw, R. (2003) 'Evaluation of the "Local Crime: Community Sentence" project pilot, final summary report', in Magistrates' Association and Probation Boards Association, *LCCS Evaluation Report*, June (London: Magistrates' Association and Probation Boards Association).

Miller, P. McC. and Wilson, M. J. (1983) *A Dictionary of Social Science Methods* (Chichester: John Wiley & Sons).

Pantazis, C. (2000) '"Fear of crime", vulnerability and poverty: evidence from the British Crime Survey', *British Journal of Criminology*, 40: 414–436.

Plant, E. A. and Devine, P. G. (2003) 'The antecedents and implications of interracial anxiety', *Personality and Social Psychology Bulletin*, 29: 790–801.

Rucker, D. D., Polifroni, M., Tetlock, P. E. and Scott, A. L. (2004) 'On the assignment of punishment: the impact of general-societal threat and the moderating role of severity', *Personality and Social Psychology Bulletin*, 30: 673–684.

Sampson, R. J., Raudenbush, S. W. and Earls, F. (1997), 'Neighborhoods and violent crime: a multi-level study of collective efficacy', *Science*, 227: 918–924.

Shapland, J. and Vagg, J. (1988) *Policing by the Public* (London: Routledge).

Sparks, R. (1992) 'Reason and unreason in left realism: some problems in the constitution of fear of crime', in R. Matthews and J. Young (eds) *Issues in Realist Criminology* (London: Sage), pp. 119–135.

Taub, R. P., Taylor, D. G. and Dunham, J. D. (1984) *Paths of Neighborhood Change: Race and crime in urban America* (Chicago, IL: University of Chicago Press).

Wikström, P.-O. H. and Dolmén, L. (2001) 'Urbanisation, neighbourhood social integration, informal social control, minor social disorder, victimisation and fear of crime', *International Review of Victimology*, 8: 121–140.

Wiles, P. and Costello, A. (2000), *The 'Road to Nowhere': The evidence for travelling criminals*, Home Office Research Study 207 (London: Home Office).

Chapter 16

Pulling some threads together

The editors

In this concluding chapter, as commissioning editors we have taken it upon ourselves to provide some overall reflections on the chapters in this volume. Necessarily, this takes us at times into the realm of future policy. We emphasise, however (see Preface), that the chapters were commissioned primarily to assist the Coulsfield Committee, which has (gratifyingly) taken them very seriously in developing its own conclusions and policy proposals. This chapter is in no sense a substitute for the Coulsfield Committee report, which we would urge all our readers to study closely. Rather, we have tried to write a 'stand-alone' chapter that, as our title suggests, seeks to pull together some of the threads of the preceding chapters, to provide a fitting conclusion to this book.

This final chapter, however, is written by the same three hands responsible for Chapter 1, so it will come as no surprise that there are some important points of continuity with that chapter. In particular, Chapter 1 identified seven features of a new 'era of community penalties' that had emerged in the years since 1990, and argued that these features were 'explicable largely in terms of the apparently increasing development of a form of "late modern society"'. (The seven identified features were punishment; technology; managerialism; partnership; effectiveness and risk management; 'creative mixing'; and reparation.) Many aspects of this major change in the field of community penalties cannot, we would argue, be easily or sensibly reversed; this includes, for example, both the advent of electronic monitoring and the development of an enhanced managerialism. Chapter 1 ended, however, by suggesting that 'alternatives to prison' is not a static concept, 'and there is scope for innovation and creativity as we look towards the future'. This concluding chapter tries to reflect both of these features – that is, accepting that some things have changed irrevocably, but looking to the future with hope and creativity.

The prison population – trends and prospects

It is clear from Chapter 2 that there has been a steep rise in the prison population in England and Wales over the last decade, which is projected to continue over the next five years. Such population growth can be seen as an integral feature of the 'late modern' penal scene in many countries (Garland 2001), though not all (Zedner 2002). The recent surge in the English prison population has not, however, been necessitated by a rise in the crime rate since, whether measured by official statistics or victimisation surveys, this has fallen since 1995.[1] Yet public perceptions of crime are significantly different from what official or survey data tell us,[2] and it is hard to understand fully what feeds this enduring belief in inexorably rising crime. Partly, it would seem, attitudes have been set by forty years of rising crime before the mid-1990s; partly, views of national crime rates are formed by media reports that emphasise any increases in crime figures and highlight negative crime stories;[3] partly, the wider insecurities of late modern societies may find concrete focus in beliefs and anxieties about crime.[4] Whatever the truth of such matters, the public is at any rate correct to believe that crime in Britain is still high compared with most other European countries (Chapter 2). Indeed, when prison numbers are related to crime rates, England and Wales and Scotland no longer stand out as the most punitive jurisdictions in Europe.[5]

Against this background, it is pertinent to ask whether the Government should be trying to reduce or restrain the prison population at all.[6] Certainly, the Carter Report (Carter 2003) and the Home Office response to it (Home Office 2004a) imply a target for prison numbers well below the official projections, so it is reasonable to assume that the official aim is restraint. But why? One explanation lies in the economic and social costs – both for the individual and for the community at large – of providing prison places, of supporting the dependents of incarcerated adults, of dealing with the consequent loss of accommodation and employment. Another is the limited efficacy of further prison expansion, in terms either of incapacitation or deterrence, as reviewed in Chapter 3.

On the other hand, in Chapter 3 it was suggested that it is unwise to expect sentencing to make a major difference to crime rates as a whole – factors such as the age profile of the general population, economic and social conditions, and detection rates are more important. Moreover, as discussed in Chapter 4, arguments about limiting prison use based on cost and effectiveness cut little ice with the public. So perhaps one should not be too utilitarian or consequentialist in matters of justice and sentencing. From a normative perspective, one can turn the question on its head to ask *why* prison, rather than *why not* prison? What justifies the complete deprivation of liberty entailed in a prison sentence? As revealed in Chapter 4, the idea that the public is strongly opposed to non-custodial sentencing is not upheld by public opinion research, which has generally found the public to be supportive of the idea of the redeemability of many offenders, and hence willing to consider community penalties for most non-violent offenders (in other words, the vast majority of offenders). Moreover, there are striking differences in punitiveness in different high-crime communities (Chapter 15).

Using non-custodial penalties

Coupled with the changes in the prison population over the last decade, there have been important changes in the populations receiving community penalties, fines and discharges. These are reviewed in Chapters 2 and 6. There has been a sharp decline in the use of the fine since 1980 (from 45 per cent of sentences for indictable offences to 23 per cent), and a drop in the use of discharges (which rose during the 1980s) since 1993 (from 22 per cent to 15 per cent). This raises the question: if these disposals were once seen as adequate for just over half the offenders convicted of indictable offences, why is that no longer the case? In relation to the fine, the problem appears to lie in doubts about its use for low-income offenders, and its enforceability: both are deficiencies that could be addressed, given the will and sustained effort.[7] The discharge appears simply not to be regarded as sufficiently interventionist.[8] The same is true of the caution (and its juvenile equivalent), which has also experienced a steady decline from 1993.[9] The Government's solution in the case of the adult caution is to introduce conditional cautions (in the Criminal Justice Act 2003), and then to try to ensure that the conditions do not amount to a 'soft option' (Home Office 2004a). However, there is a significant difficulty here, since if the conditions attached to 'conditional cautions' are not 'soft', then obviously the content of the lower reaches of community penalties set by the courts should be even less 'soft', and so on.[10] Moreover, reviewing experience in the field of youth justice, the Audit Commission (2004) – the original critics of a system in which 'nothing happens' – now questions the wisdom of intervening in low-risk final warning cases, and sees imposing excessive conditions at an early stage as potentially likely to propel people towards eventual custody.

The corollary of the decline of fines and discharges has been an increased use of community penalties, but these are often now imposed on offenders at a low tariff point. For half the offenders who now receive a community punishment order, it is upon their first conviction, and nearly half have been convicted of a summary offence.[11] In the case of theft/handling (a broad indictable offence category that includes many minor cases), a higher proportion of offenders convicted in 2002 actually received a custodial sentence (22 per cent) than a fine (19 per cent), with 37 per cent receiving community penalties. In 1993, the respective proportions were eight per cent, 37 per cent and 25 per cent, a dramatic illustration of the extent to which sentencing has changed in less than ten years. One consequence of these trends is for the National Probation Service to have become overwhelmed by lower-risk offenders, on whom its expertise is arguably wasteful. Another consequence is a loss of proportionality – the link between offence seriousness and sentence severity enshrined in the Criminal Justice Act 1991. As Wasik points out in Chapter 12, the Criminal Justice Act 2003 appears to have retreated from the principle of proportionality to provide a list of purposes for sentencing, amongst which no priorities are indicated. The Sentencing Guidelines Council will have the onerous task of providing guidance on which purpose should be prioritised in which circumstances, and to make sense of the multiplicity of changes in the 2003 Act. We will have to wait and see how much weight is accorded to proportionality in the Council's guidance.

Immediate prospects for 'alternatives to custody'

At the time of writing, we face major impending reforms in the areas of sentencing and sentence management. In addition to the 2003 Act, there is the Carter Report on Correctional Services leading to the creation of the National Offender Management Service (NOMS) (see Preface and Chapter 1). It is at present very difficult to foresee what impact these reforms will have in terms of promoting custodial sentences or the use of alternatives. However, there are at least some grounds for suspecting that their effect on the prison population could be inflationary rather than diversionary.

Looking first at the 2003 Act, courts will no longer be able to pass 'simple' short terms of imprisonment, but will have to combine a custodial term of between two and thirteen weeks with a licence period of between 26 and 49 weeks (the whole 'package' not to exceed 51 weeks for a single offence). In Chapter 12, Wasik envisaged that these provisions might discourage the use of short sentences of imprisonment in favour of a community sentence. However, it is also conceivable that sentencers (especially magistrates) will be attracted by what they see as the deterrent impact of a very short custodial term, followed by the positive help afforded by a period of post-release supervision. So we could see greater, not less, use of short custodial sentences in the future. Much will depend on how the Sentencing Guidelines Council delineates the threshold between the community sentence and custodial provision, and whether the Council encourages sentencers to use community supervision without a custodial component. Much will also depend on how much attention courts pay to the Council's guidance.[12]

Wasik suggests that the creation of a single generic community sentence might discourage sentencers from their present practice of using a number of different *forms* of community sentence (community punishment, community rehabilitation, etc.) for the same offender before concluding that custody has become inevitable. Sentencers might also be inclined to include more rather than fewer requirements in the new generic community sentence, both in search of 'suitable' requirements and to demonstrate that the sentence is sufficiently tough and demanding. If this occurs, it will have obvious implications for breach rates and ultimately the prison population, both because some defaulters will be sentenced to prison for breach, and because some will be seen as unsuitable for a community sentence on the next occasion, having failed to respond on this one.

Another area in which the prospects for custodial (and non-custodial) sentencing are unclear relates to persistence, where there is at least a possibility that the current raft of initiatives will result ultimately in greater use of custody. As discussed by Wasik in Chapter 12, section 143 of the 2003 Act (by which previous convictions are to be treated as aggravating) may well lead to enhanced 'sentencing on record'. This could increase the use of custody for persistent offenders, in cases where the offence triggering the current conviction might not in itself be of a seriousness to justify a custodial sentence. Again, much will depend on how the Sentencing Guidelines Council interprets the provision.

The Carter Report (Carter 2003) and the Home Office response (Home Office 2004a) certainly both visualise greater sanctions, and ultimately custody, for persistent offenders. Carter also envisages 'greater help' for persistent offenders, and the Government refers to 'a range of new disposals, short of a full-time prison sentence, to enable [sentencers] to impose tough and flexible sentences on persistent offenders' (Home Office 2004a: 13). Presumably, what is envisaged here are the various forms of intensive community programmes recently developed for persistent offenders, as well as semi-custodial arrangements such as intermittent custody and the new suspended sentence (both also provided for in the 2003 Act). Reviewing in Chapter 11 experience with intensive projects for prolific and persistent offenders, Worrall and Mawby refer to the varied and contested definitions of 'persistent' and 'prolific'. These create clear risks of net-widening; as the earlier experience discussed in Chapters 1 and 3 showed, it is very difficult to ensure that an 'alternative' is used for an offender who would otherwise have received a custodial sentence, rather than one who would have received a less intrusive non-custodial penalty. Indeed, those risks were exposed in the recent report of the Joint Inspection into Persistent and Prolific Offenders (HMCIC *et al.* 2004), which showed that the then official definition of a 'persistent offender' (since modified) produced a large number of offenders the majority of whom had been convicted of offences towards the lower end of the scale of seriousness (36 per cent convicted of shoplifting). On this point, the Government's thinking appears confused, as it was capable of stating within the same paragraph both that Intensive Supervision and Monitoring Programmes (ISMs) should be used for the highest-risk offenders, and that they should eventually replace prison sentences for the increasing number of relatively low-risk and first-time offenders given a prison sentence in recent years (Home Office 2004a: 13).

A major change on the horizon is the establishment of the National Offender Management Service (NOMS), which will seek eventually to introduce a thoroughgoing purchaser–provider split in the arrangements for managing sentenced offenders.[13] This will separate functions that are both currently undertaken by the Probation Service, so that the organisation commissioning interventions for offenders (and working with courts) will be entirely separate from the people (in the public, private or voluntary sector) delivering interventions. In effect, the Probation Service as we know it will be abolished, with part of its functions being taken over by 'Public Sector Interventions' and part by NOMS. Clearly, if and when it is implemented, this reform will fundamentally alter the landscape within which 'alternatives to custody' are now delivered, with potentially unpredictable consequences.

At present we know little about the eventual practical implications of NOMS in terms of how, and by whom, individual offenders will be managed. In Chapter 13, Robinson and Dignan consider a range of case management models, and conclude that the current trend toward specialisation by task, and the fragmentation of provision for offenders, is not necessarily the best way to ensure either compliance or longer-term behavioural change. It is hoped that, in working toward the implementation of NOMS, the lessons of recent research on offenders' experiences of different models of case management will be heeded.[14] It is also hoped that in the new NOMS structure there will be a recognition of case management as a skilled role which can be pivotal to effective supervision. News that work is under way in two 'pathfinder regions' to develop a case management approach for NOMS is a welcome sign that the case management role is indeed being taken seriously (Home Office 2004b).

Likely futures for community penalties

The chapters within this volume present a myriad of fascinating possibilities for non-custodial penalties, which reflect the major changes in this field in the last decade or so (see the introduction to this chapter). In general, we would advocate a spirit of cautious optimism in taking these developments forward, in order to learn from experience and research, and to preserve the proverbial baby when throwing out the bathwater (although, certainly, some of the bathwater does need to be disposed of!). Below, we review some of the more significant initiatives discussed in the previous chapters, and their implications for the future shape of non-custodial sanctions. All offer some cause for hope, though caveats must be made about the provisional nature of many of the findings emerging so far from research, particularly on the crucial issue of effectiveness in reducing offending.

One very important development has been the 'What Works' movement and the associated research, discussed by Raynor in Chapter 8. This development retains much promise, though initial expectations were at times overstated (see also Chapter 3). (Moreover, the first major published evaluation of a probation pathfinder offending behaviour project ['Think First'] has shown disappointingly low completion rates: Stewart-Ong *et al.* 2004.) What lessons should we draw from this experience? One possible policy response might be to abandon accredited programmes, or at least to put much less emphasis on (or resources into) this kind of work with offenders. However, another possible response – which we would advocate – is to review how such programmes are delivered and to whom, and to support the implementation strategies and the social contexts likely to maximise their effectiveness. Such an approach would take seriously the positive research evidence that undoubtedly exists (see Chapter 8), but would deliberately jettison what we regard as the unfortunate tendency in recent years to view offending behaviour programmes as, more or less, 'magic bullets'.[15] It would also be helpful to slow down the pace of implementation to allow the properly evaluated piloting of new approaches.

Above all, the lesson of the recent past is that a degree of care is required about the way in which promising new developments are implemented. Sadly, in the first flush of enthusiasm for offending behaviour programmes, there was a tendency to make inflated claims about their likelihood of reducing reconviction rates, and then to recruit to them as many offenders as possible in order to meet ambitious, managerially-set policy targets for 'programme completions'. Almost inevitably, such strategies erode the effectiveness of programmes as unsuitable offenders are selected, and then fail to complete the programme, or fail to benefit from it. To reiterate a point we made at the start of this chapter, it is probably unrealistic to expect programmes or other sentencing initiatives, at least in the short term, to reduce overall crime rates in other than small ways. This does not, however, invalidate rehabilitation as a proper sentencing goal, in order to prevent reoffending among as many offenders as possible, as well as to restore offenders as full citizens and contributing members of society (on which we say more below).

Another 'growth' area for non-custodial sanctions has been in the intensive projects for persistent offenders discussed in Chapter 11, with ISMs for adults, the ISSP for young offenders, and the ICCP for young adults. Despite the popularity of such projects, there is as yet limited evidence of their effectiveness. However, Worrall and Mawby point to other benefits identified by project participants such as keeping offenders occupied, helping them build up their confidence, and improving family relationships. Superficially, the attention and resources being directed at such projects represent a success story for community-based sanctions and perhaps a genuine attempt to provide sanctions that will replace custody for a significant number of offenders. However, as discussed above, they create a real risk of net-widening, whereby they might draw in offenders who otherwise would have received a non-custodial sanction rather than a custodial sentence. This raises the question of how to ensure that persistent offender projects are directed at offenders truly at the cusp of a custodial sentence. To the more limited definition of persistence recommended by the Joint Inspection team (see above), we would add that project criteria should incorporate some notion of offence seriousness to ensure that participants have been convicted of sufficiently serious offences to warrant the level of intervention into their lives (and the resources devoted to them). This would help to reinstate proportionality in sentencing, on which we say more below.

Substance-misusing offenders – many of whom are also prolific offenders – are another group on whom the attention of policy makers has come to concentrate in recent years, and for whom new types of specialist provision have been developed. In Chapter 10, Rumgay reviewed the emergence of the Drug Treatment and Testing Order (DTTO), a new community penalty for drug-using offenders which constitutes an attempt to combine the rehabilitative work of treatment providers with the legal sanctioning authority of the courts. As Rumgay explains, evaluative research on the DTTO has, to date, yielded mixed results, with some marked reductions in drug use and criminal activity among DTTO completers, but at the cost of high levels of breach and revocation. In many ways Rumgay's observations about the difficulties of balancing realistic goals and a tolerant approach toward enforcement against the need to maintain the credibility of a court-ordered sanction parallel some of the dilemmas which face those charged with managing projects for persistent and/or prolific offenders, as discussed in Chapter 11. In her chapter, Rumgay also alerts us to the potential danger of eschewing proportionality in favour of the pursuit of therapeutic gains in the context of sanctions such as the DTTO.

It is a measure of the degree of change in community penalties in the last decade that the developments we have so far discussed (offending behaviour programmes, intensive programmes for persistent offenders, and DTTOs) do not by any means exhaust the list of innovations in this field. One very important addition to the range of available interventions has been electronic monitoring, which Nellis in Chapter 9 makes clear is now a well-established sanction. Indeed, this kind of surveillance looks likely soon to extend beyond curfews into other forms of surveillance such as satellite tracking, and to permeate the entire spectrum of community-based sanctions. (One significant development in this regard has been the regular inclusion of electronic monitoring in intensive projects such as ISSPs, in combination with rehabilitative measures). In describing these developments, Nellis argues that they have arisen as much as a consequence of a preoccupation with protecting the public as of the result of scientific research evidence about the efficacy of this kind of surveillance. Indeed, the attraction of the curfew backed by electronic monitoring lies precisely in its ability to bring together substantial restrictions on offenders' liberty in the form of home confinement (i.e. true punishment) and reassurance that the public is safe from offenders whose whereabouts can be verified through technology (see Chapter 1). Intensive programmes can then add rehabilitation to the mix (it having been argued that electronic monitoring by itself is not very effective in bringing about enduring reductions in offending). This kind of 'creative mixing' – of punishment, surveillance and rehabilitation – has become a feature of what we described in Chapter 1 as a new generation of community orders, evident in DTTOs (see above) as well as intensive projects for persistent offenders. With the impending introduction of the customised Community Order (see Chapter 1), it seems that the days of the single-component community sentence (such as probation supervision or unpaid work) might well be numbered. It is indisputable that creativity and commitment have been devoted to multi-component initiatives, which can claim considerable achievements in harnessing offenders' motivation. However, we have already alluded to the danger that enthusiasm for these new approaches will override the crucial link between the gravity of the offence and the severity of the sentence. As multi-component community sentences become more common, it could become more difficult to sustain a reasonable relationship between offence and sentence, and there is a real danger that the trends identified in Chapters 2 and 6 will intensify unless there is a concerted attempt to arrest them. At worst, this could lead to increasingly intensive orders absorbing ever less serious and low-risk offenders and offering no real alternative to prison at all. Later in this chapter, we put forward some suggestions that we believe may help to establish a more central role for non-custodial sanctions in the sentencing framework and begin to reverse these trends.

A further set of fresh initiatives that have gained popularity in recent years, and that seem very apposite in the non-custodial (or community) setting, can be placed beneath the broad umbrella of restorative justice, discussed by McIvor in Chapter 7. Once again, these initiatives have been embraced enthusiastically, particularly in relation to young offenders, where restorative justice has shaped some major reforms in Northern Ireland, and also (though to a more limited extent) in England and Wales (reparation orders, and referral orders to the new Youth Offender Panels). However, the evidence that such approaches are effective in reducing recidivism is at present patchy, although they appear to offer other benefits to victims and offenders that are of some importance (such as a greater sense of participation and resolution for victims, and enhanced opportunities for reintegration for offenders). Additionally, it seems that a high level of agreements are completed and fulfilled and that victims are far more likely to receive restitution following mediation or a conference than following court proceedings. Nonetheless, a degree of circumspection is again required before extending such approaches too hastily to adult offenders, since McIvor, in Chapter 7, makes clear that they present a number of challenges in relation to which further careful evaluation is required. These include ensuring meaningful victim participation, ensuring access for offenders across gender and ethnicity, and preserving appropriate safeguards for offenders in conferencing arrangements and the size of sanctions imposed as a result. McIvor ends her chapter by distilling experience of restorative justice schemes from around the world into a number of highly pertinent questions. If these considerations are overlooked or ignored, there is a potential danger that restorative justice schemes may become discredited as quickly as they have been taken up in the UK.

One final question which requires some attention in this section on 'likely futures for community penalties', and which is perhaps given special pertinence by the growth of restorative justice approaches, is: 'what should be the role of the community in community penalties?' One of us recently asked a group of experienced probation officers, in a classroom context, to consider two questions: (i) *does* 'the community' currently play a significant role in the delivery of community penalties?, and (ii) *should* it? Very interestingly, the majority responses were, respectively, 'no' and 'yes', a disjunction which is perhaps in itself a matter for concern. The fresh research from Sheffield reported in Chapter 15 would support the view that it is a serious mistake to ignore local communities in delivering community penalties, because some such communities (like Area B in the Sheffield research) are experiencing significant local disorder, and feeling themselves under-policed, to an extent which makes residents very unlikely to be supportive of community penalties unless some ameliorative action is taken to improve general social control in the area. On the other hand, even in such an area, underlying support for the principle of the 'redeemability' of offenders remains high. Obviously, general neighbourhood social control is primarily a matter for agencies such as the police and the local authority, rather than the probation service or youth offending teams. Nevertheless, in considering the future of community penalties, correctional agencies such as the Probation Service probably need to pay significantly more attention than they do at present to the local community context in which offenders live, and where they often commit their offences. In England and Wales, potentially important links between local neighbourhoods and community penalties already exist through community punishment orders and the Youth Offender Panels,[16] while in Northern Ireland the Probation

Service has deliberately maintained its community links to a greater extent than its English counterpart (see Chapter 1). It would not take much imagination to build on such examples, and to link them with more general local social control initiatives in high-crime areas, as developed by the police and the local authority. This could fruitfully extend the range of police–probation joint working (already greatly advanced in recent years as a result of persistent offender projects and Multi-Agency Public Protection Arrangements), and it could also help to reduce significantly the real social anxieties of some high-crime communities.[17] It must be said, however, that such agendas have not so far appeared to rank high in the priorities of NOMS, nor do they fit very comfortably with NOMS's ultimate aspirations for a thoroughgoing purchaser–provider split managed by only twelve Regional Offender Managers in England and Wales. There are important and difficult issues here which require further attention.

Some suggestions for future directions

In this final substantive section, while continuing to draw out themes from chapters, our voice becomes more personal and prescriptive. We repeat, however (see the introduction to this chapter) that our primary purpose remains that of providing an informed overview rather than writing a set of policy proposals.

Role clarity and public support

One urgent requirement is to clarify the role of community-based sanctions and the circumstances in which (and the offenders for whom) they are likely to gain public support. The points were made in Chapters 4 and 5 that in England and Wales – and internationally – the credibility and use of community sanctions has been undermined by a lack of clarity about their rationale and place in the sentencing framework, especially given the rapid social and penal changes of the last thirty years (see Chapter 1). Certainly, non-custodial sanctions have a low profile with the general public, which is largely unfamiliar with – and possibly uninspired by – the details of non-custodial alternatives. However, in Chapter 4 it was suggested that there is a great deal of untapped public support for community sanctions for non-violent offenders, with most people polled supporting individual community corrections programmes when these programmes are explained. Whilst arguments about cost-effectiveness and efficacy may be counter-productive or viewed with suspicion, it seems that the more emotive aspects of crime and criminal justice may provide the key to why ordinary people might be prepared to support non-custodial measures. Maruna and King suggested that the idea of redeemability might be a powerful means of generating interest in community penalties, on the basis that 'people can change', and building on the appeal of notions such as 'paying back' and 'making good'. This is further supported in the new Sheffield study (Chapter 15), although – picking up the emotive theme – that was only fully the case where people felt that their local neighbourhood had an adequate degree of basic social control.

The discussion in Chapter 4 suggested that the communicative themes explored in Chapter 5 may well resonate with general members of the public as with the groups interviewed and surveyed by Rex. On the premise that providing a single catch-all community sentence and listing the various purposes of sentencing in the Criminal Justice Act 2003 will not provide a clear rationale for non-custodial measures, Chapter 5 investigated the possible application of a theory in which communication is central. It suggested that community-based sanctions may be more fitting as inclusive communicative punishments than prison, and that they offer important reparative and restorative possibilities that chime with the restorative justice themes discussed in Chapter 7. Reform was accorded a central role in the accounts of punishment given by the people participating in Rex's research, and strong support was expressed for community-based sanctions – findings in keeping with the public opinion research summarised in Chapter 4. In terms of communicative penal aims, community penalties were seen as having the capacity to combine an appeal to offenders' sense of moral agency (their citizenship) with practical help in overcoming the obstacles to their moving away from crime. Non-custodial sanctions were compared favourably with custody when it came to encouraging offenders to take responsibility for their offending and related aspects of their lifestyle. These findings present a strong case for according a central role to community-based sanctions in a sentencing framework, the focus of which is on persuading offenders of the nature of their offences as public wrongs, encouraging them to take responsibility and assisting them to move towards positive law-abiding behaviour. This is not to suggest, however, that it should be a goal of sentencing to reduce overall levels of crime. Reducing crime is a different and more aggregative aim from the impact that we might seek to have on the individual offender who is going through the sentencing and punishment process, and in our view the second is the more appropriate goal.

Engaging offenders in processes of change

An important point to emerge from the findings presented in Chapter 5 is that it might be more promising to adopt a forward-looking orientation towards desistance rather than a backward-looking pre-occupation with 'confronting offending behaviour', as has tended to be the case recently with the vogue for offending behaviour programmes (see also Farrall

2003). What this would mean is that a consideration of why the offending was wrong would provide the starting point for interventions in which there was a pro-social focus on what the offender might be capable of in the future, rather than a simple condemnatory focus on his or her past behaviour. This idea in fact forms quite an important theme in a number of other chapters in this volume, starting with the notion of 'redeemability' discussed by Maruna and King in Chapter 4 and also utilised by Bottoms and Wilson in Chapter 15. It is certainly implicit in the reparative and restorative approaches reviewed by McIvor in Chapter 7, where the offender's future reintegration is a key feature, alongside his offering restitution to the victim and undertaking reparation for the victim or the community. Furthermore, in Chapter 8, Raynor discusses a 'responsibility' model of rehabilitation in which offenders are seen not simply as 'objects of intervention', but as active participants in their own rehabilitation and potential contributors to their communities. Robinson and Dignan also consider in Chapter 13 what a number of studies have found about the 'neglected asset' of the supervisory relationship, and its importance in motivating offenders to engage in the process of changing their behaviour.

Developing the point a little further, Chapters 10, 11 and 13 all contain instances of what can be achieved when rehabilitation and surveillance are combined imaginatively with a keen personal interest in offenders' progress towards crime-free (and drug-free) lives, whether through Drug Courts, DTTOs or intensive persistent offender projects. The Glasgow Drug Court described in Chapter 13 seems to have been successful in adopting a model developed in the US in which the sentencer plays an active role in motivating offenders and reviewing their progress within the context of a more informal participatory procedure. Although this kind of model inspired DTTOs with their provision for regular court reviews of sentence, their implementation appears to have been hampered by a somewhat rigid approach to enforcement and difficulties in ensuring that the original sentencers conducted subsequent reviews. Some provision for court review has been made in the Criminal Justice Act 2003 in relation to the new suspended sentence, and it will be interesting to see how the role of the sentencer is developed in this context.

Related to these points is the strong case made by Kemshall, Canton and Bailey in Chapter 14 for the need to address diversity in developing alternatives to prison. This is a point that it is only too easy to neglect in a rush to embrace exciting new initiatives, as experience with developing accredited programmes on the basis of 'What Works' principles demonstrated (though there have been recent efforts to redress this deficiency in the accreditation process: see Rex *et al.* 2003). One suggestion was to subject 'alternatives' to a diversity test to examine issues of differential access, impact and unintended consequences. The authors also helpfully propose that a focus on desistance rather than on needs and deficits should itself be examined from the perspective of diversity to see whether desistance, resilience to risk and pathways out of crime are different for different groups.

Resurrecting proportionality

In our view it has become urgent to reintroduce the topic of proportionality into discussions on alternatives to prison. In relation to non-custodial sanctions, proportionality seems to have been overlooked lately, given the overwhelming late-modern emphasis on risk, and/or the eagerness to embrace new approaches to divert offenders from a custodial sentence (the latest example being persistent and prolific offender projects). We admit to finding it surprising that the notion that the sentence should bear a reasonable relationship to the gravity of the current offence should currently have so little political appeal, given the interest in human rights and justice alluded to in Chapter 1. Within a decade, proportionality has moved from a central role in the sentencing framework in the Criminal Justice Act 1991 to a position where it warrants barely a mention in policy documents such as the Carter Report (2003). That report, although it gestured at proportionality in stating that sentences need to reflect the seriousness of the offence, when it came to the substance of its proposals was overwhelmingly more interested in persistence and risk. Thus, 'risk' was the principle according to which it was recommended that offenders should be categorised into those suitable for diversion for fines, 'more demanding' community sentences, or custody, with persistent offenders receiving greater control and surveillance and help to reduce their offending. Carter also proposed that the three levels within the new generic community sentence should be based on a risk assessment of offenders, an approach with which the Home Office agreed (Home Office 2004a). No mention was made of the Halliday Report's earlier suggested outline tariff for the single community sentence based on the 'punitive weight' of the ingredients (Home Office 2001).

Although it has preserved most of the 'commensurability' language of the 1991 legislation,[18] the Criminal Justice Act 2003 has retreated from desert as the organising principle for sentencing by creating a fresh context with *first*, a list of purposes of sentencing which has no overall priorities, and *second*, an emphasis on persistence as meriting enhanced punishment.[19] Unless proportionality is accorded a significant role in sentencing, there is a real danger that non-custodial sentences will slip still further down tariff than they already have, and increasingly complex and intensive orders will be imposed on offenders who have been convicted of relatively minor offences. It ought to be possible to balance proportionality with 'risk' in a properly tiered approach to community penalties, along the lines proposed by Halliday (Home Office 2001) as well as other commentators.[20] A starting point might be the suggestion by Wasik in

Chapter 12 for an obligation on courts to ensure that the total combined sentence is not disproportionate to the offending. It seems that we will now be looking to the Sentencing Guidelines Council to provide this kind of guidance to the courts.

Reinstating non-intrusive measures

In Chapter 6 Mair made the important point that ensuring that alternatives to prison have a proper place on the tariff involves paying attention to disposals at the lower end of the tariff, as well as considering more intrusive measures. Unless we strengthen disposals such as the fine, the long-term decline in their use seems likely to continue, and offenders for whom a fine should be perfectly adequate will be subjected to measures that require intervention from a penal agent. The decline has arisen from the severe neglect that the fine has suffered recently both in policy and research terms, despite the considerable practical advantages discussed in Chapter 6. One obvious step on which work has already commenced is to improve the collection of fines (see n. 7 above). Quite clearly, however, fines will become easier to enforce if more realistic fines are imposed so that unemployed or low-waged offenders do not accumulate multiple fines running into many hundreds of pounds that they have no serious expectation of paying (as one often sees now). Carter (2003) in effect recommended re-introducing unit fines in the form of day fines, but a certain amount of resistance by courts to varying the size of a fine according to means would need to be overcome if this kind of approach is to succeed. More detailed and accurate information about the offender's financial circumstances would also be required, and steps taken to avoid the disproportionately high fines that caused the downfall of the unit fines scheme after the Criminal Justice Act 2001. More adventurously, Mair raised in Chapter 6 the possibility of introducing a prosecutor fine (as in Scotland), as part of a more developed package of measures directed at diverting minor offenders from court.

This raises the question of why English courts should be dealing with the least serious and lowest-risk offenders at all. One option explored in Chapter 6 was to develop the prosecutor's role, building on Scottish and European experience, a radical step in the English jurisdiction (where diversionary measures have traditionally been the preserve of the police rather than the relatively recently established Crown Prosecution Service). However, the Crown Prosecution Service is already mandated to take over the new conditional cautions (see above), and Mair's proposal that they should have responsibility for all cautions has logical appeal. One consideration that would need to be borne in mind is the very different profile prosecutors and police officers have with offenders in England and Wales (where Crown Prosecutors can hardly be said to carry the same authority as Procurators Fiscal in Scotland). Mair suggested that a police officer could still be involved in delivering a caution, and this would ensure that it carried sufficient weight with the recipient – at least until English prosecutors had developed the authority commensurate with their expanded role.

Conclusion

As this book goes to press, the English penal system stands at a significant point in its history. The Criminal Justice Act 2003 is on the statute book, but most of its provisions have yet to be brought into force. The NOMS has been born, but plans for the rapid and total implementation of the Carter Report have been put on temporary hold (see Preface) in the hope of providing better long-term solutions than would probably have emerged from the timetable of change initially proposed. Much, therefore, will become clearer, in policy terms, in the next year or two.

In the late-modern world, research has become integral to at least some aspects of penal policy, as the rush to expand offending behaviour programmes and the current doubts about that rush both clearly attest. This book has been written by researchers, and within its chapters much relevant research has been ably summarised, we hope in an accessible manner. By its nature the volume cannot, nor does it pretend to, offer instant solutions to current policy issues. But it does, we hope, provide essential information, and highlight a number of key issues, that should be pondered by anyone, in any jurisdiction, interested in the provision of effective 'alternatives to prison' in a contemporary context. Within the United Kingdom, resolving these issues necessarily involves the appointed leaders of NOMS and the Youth Justice Board, and their Scottish and Northern Irish counterparts; but it is also a matter for politicians and, ultimately, the general public, who are on the front line in bearing the anxieties and insecurities of twenty-first century British society. For this reason we have paid more attention to 'public opinion' (see Chapters 4 and 15) than has been customary in books on alternatives to prison, and for this reason also we have emphasised the theme of 'late modernity' in Chapter 1, and to an extent in this chapter. Policy questions in the field of 'alternatives to prison' rightly raise many technical questions, but a number of recent developments (increased use of technology, managerialism and 'populist punitiveness' to name only a few) are essentially the product of more general social change, as we have tried to highlight. Both technical research results *and* a nuanced understanding of the nature of contemporary late modern societies are, we would argue, essential background ingredients for those who wish to develop optimal policies and practice in the field of alternatives to prison.

Notes

1 That is, with the exception of recorded violent crime, where much of the apparent increase has been due to changes in recording procedures.

2 The British Crime Survey asks respondents whether, in their perception, crime has increased or decreased nationally in the last two years. The latest data show that two-thirds (65 per cent) thought that crime had increased during this period, and nearly half of these (31 per cent) thought it had increased 'a lot'. See Dodd *et al.* (2004: 17).

3 The influence of the media in this matter can be inferred from the British Crime Survey data about perceptions of crime in the last two years (see n. 2 above). As well as asking about national trends, the survey also asks about local trends. It has been consistently the case that respondents perceive lower increases in local crime rates than in the national rates (in 2003, 53 per cent thought local crime had increased, and 20 per cent thought it had increased a lot – cf. the figures in n. 2). For local crime rates, citizens have sources of information additional to the mass media; for national crime rates, they usually do not.

4 On this theme, see for example Girling, Loader and Sparks' (2000) study of Macclesfield, discussed briefly in Chapter 15 above.

5 However, caution is required in interpreting such figures, since an official encouragement to record more crimes on ethical grounds (as has occurred in recent years in England and Wales: see Chapter 2) can lead to an apparent, but actually illusory, reduction in the rate of 'prison population per 1,000 crimes'.

6 At least one pressure group (CIVITAS) now takes the view that this is not an appropriate policy goal. For a discussion of aspects of its case, see Chapter 3.

7 On unit fines, see the final subsection of this chapter. On enforcement, some areas have already begun imaginative schemes to bring collection offices closer to residential communities, i.e. adopting a facilitative rather than a merely punitive approach. The Courts Act 2003, Schedule 5, also incorporates a range of measures designed to improve collection: these include greater use of private contractors and incentives for early payment.

8 It is for this reason that s. 66(4) of the Crime and Disorder Act 1998 forbids (save in exceptional circumstances) youth courts from passing conditional discharges within two years of a 'final warning'.

9 It is important to emphasise that 'interventionist' does not necessarily mean 'punitive', although sometimes (see ensuing discussion) the language of 'avoiding a soft option' is indeed adopted. A motive for intervention might be crime reduction rather than simple 'punitive weight', and this has been the case with the so-called 'change packages' attached to final warnings in the English youth justice system since 1998 (though whether they actually do reduce crime is so far unproven: see the review by Bottoms and Dignan 2004).

10 An example of this difficulty is seen in the Carter Report (2003), which recommends (p. 27) that 'fines should replace community sentences for low-risk offenders' who go to court. Immediately before this (pp. 26–27), the Report similarly argues that 'there is considerable scope for low-risk, low-harm adult offenders who plead guilty to be diverted from the formal court process', but then goes on to suggest that they could receive conditional cautions which would be linked with 'financial reparation to the victim, *restorative work,*

victim–offender mediation or *community work*' (emphasis added). There is an obvious inconsistency here with the recommendation for fines to replace community work for low-risk offenders who go to court, but this inconsistency is not recognised in the text.

11 It is salutary to compare these figures with the brave words in the 1970s about the then community service order being primarily an 'alternative to custody': see Chapter 1.

12 For those who think this might be an unduly cynical remark, the history of the suspended sentence is salutary. Since 1972, there has been explicit statutory guidance stating that this sentence should not be imposed unless, in the absence of the power to suspend, the court would have passed a custodial sentence; but it is clear from statistical evidence that this is not how courts have used this sentence (see Chapter 3).

13 See, however, our comment in the Preface about the recent slowdown in the implementation of this vision.

14 A particular danger of managerially-led systems is fragmentation, since from the point of view of the manager one can break down the overall task into many discrete sub-tasks, and then think about achieving efficiency savings in respect of each sub-task. Such an approach can easily overlook the fact that the recipient sees and evaluates all the sub-services as part of the overall service. If they are not properly connected, he/she is sure to notice, and overall effectiveness may be impaired.

15 On this theme, see the essay by Rex (2001), written before the most recent research results on offending behaviour were available. Rex concluded:

> programmatic work must not eclipse the social environments in which offenders are placed, which play a crucial role in their ability to make – and to sustain – decisions not to offend. Nor should opportunities be lost for practitioners to promote, and build upon, the normative development that seems to help motivate people to move away from crime (p. 80).

16 Youth Offender Panels include 'lay' or 'community' panel members. In their report on the pilot period of this new set of procedures, Crawford and Newburn (2003) report that 'a significant body of community panel members was recruited in all the pilot areas', although there were difficulties in achieving true community representativeness (p. 90). Additionally, 'in a relatively short space of time, panel members appear to have become effective chairs of panels and facilitators of inclusive deliberations' (p. 132).

17 This could be linked with the agenda of the National Reassurance Policing Project, discussed briefly in Chapter 15.

18 For example in s. 152 on the 'custody threshold', and in s. 148 on the requirements relating to the Community Order.

19 Thus, for example, the custody threshold requires that a court must be satisfied that the current offence(s) is/are 'so serious that neither a fine alone nor a community sentence can be justified for the offence', but s. 143(2) now freshly provides that in assessing the seriousness of an offence, except in specified circumstances 'the court must treat each previous conviction as an aggravating factor'.

20 For example, Tonry (1998) suggests that the most promising approach might be to introduce four to six 'zones of discretion' with provision for roughly equivalent community (or intermediate) sanctions to be interchanged. This proposal seems to be bear some resemblance to the model developed by Wasik

and von Hirsch (1988) on which the Criminal Justice Act 1991 was based. Raynor (1997) also suggested that it is possible to rank community sanctions in broadly comparable levels of seriousness, citing the five bands introduced by some probation services under the 1991 Act.

References

Audit Commission (2004) *Youth Justice 2004: A review of the reformed youth justice system* (London: Home Office).

Bottoms, A. E. and Dignan, J. (2004) 'Youth justice in Great Britain', *Crime and Justice: A Review of Research*, 31: 21–183.

Carter, P. (2003) *Managing Offenders, Changing Lives: A new approach. Report of the Correctional Services Review* (London: Strategy Unit).

Crawford, A. and Newburn, T. (2003) *Youth Offending and Restorative Justice* (Cullompton: Willan).

Dodd, T., Nicolas, S., Povey, D. and Walker, A (2004) *Crime in England and Wales 2003/2004*, Home Office Statistical Bulletin 10/04 (London: Home Office).

Farrall, S. (2002) *Rethinking What Works with Offenders: Probation, social context and desistance from crime* (Cullompton: Willan Publishing).

Garland, D (2001) *The Culture of Control* (Oxford: Oxford University Press).

Girling, E., Loader, I. and Sparks, R. (2000) *Crime and Social Change in Middle England* (London: Routledge).

HM Chief Inspector of Constabulary, HM Chief Inspector of Probation, HM Chief Inspector of the Crown Prosecution Service, HM Chief Inspector of the Magistrates' Courts Service and HM Chief Inspector of Prisons (2004) *Joint Inspection Report into Persistent and Prolific Offenders* (London: Home Office).

Home Office (2001) *Making Punishments Work* (London: HMSO).

Home Office (2004a) *Reducing Crime – Changing Lives: The Government's plans for transforming the management of offenders* (London: Home Office).

Home Office (2004b) *Reducing Re-offending: National Action Plan* (London: Home Office).

Raynor, P. (1997) 'Some observations on rehabilitation and justice', *Howard Journal of Criminal Justice*, 36: 248–262.

Rex, S. A. (2001) 'Beyond cognitive-behaviouralism? Reflections on the effectiveness literature', in A. E. Bottoms, L. Gelsthorpe and S. Rex (eds) *Community Penalties: Change and Challenges* (Cullompton: Willan).

Rex, S. A., Lieb, R., Bottoms, A. E. and Wilson, L. (2003) *Accrediting Offender Programmes: A process-based evaluation of the joint Prison/Probation Services Accreditation Panel*, Home Office Research Study No. 273 (London: Home Office).

Stewart-Ong, G., Harsent, L., Roberts, C., Burnett, R. and Al-Attar, Z. (2004) *Think First Prospective Research Study: Effectiveness and reducing attrition* (National Probation Directorate).

Tonry, M. (1998) 'Intermediate sanctions in sentencing guidelines', *Crime and Justice: A Review of Research*, 23: 199–253.

Wasik, M. and von Hirsch, A. (1988) 'Non-custodial penalties and the principles of desert', *Criminal Law Review*, 555–571.

Zedner, L. (2002) Dangers of dystopias in penal theory', *Oxford Journal of Legal Studies*, 22: 341–366.

Index